D0762968

Elementary Modern Standard Arabic

Part 1

Arabic Pronunciation and Writing;
Arabic Grammar and Vocabulary, Lessons 1–30

edited by
Peter F. Abboud
PROFESSOR OF ARABIC, UNIVERSITY OF TEXAS, AUSTIN

Ernest N. McCarus
PROFESSOR OF ARABIC, UNIVERSITY OF MICHIGAN

CONTRIBUTORS
Peter F. Abboud
Zaki N. Abdel-Malek
Najm A. Bezirgan
Wallace M. Erwin
Mounah A. Khouri
Ernest N. McCarus
Raji M. Rammuny
George N. Saad

The right of the
University of Cambridge
to print and sell
all manner of books
was granted by
Henry VIII in 1534.
The University has printed
and published continuously
since 1584.

Cambridge University Press
Cambridge
New York New Rochelle
Melbourne Sydney

Published by the Press Syndicate of the University of Cambridge
The Pitt Building, Trumpington Street, Cambridge CB2 1RP
32 East 57th Street, New York, NY 10022, USA
10 Stamford Road, Oakleigh, Melbourne 3166, Australia

First published by Department of Near Eastern Studies, University of Michigan, as *Introduction to Modern Standard Arabic: Pronunciation and Writing and Elementary Modern Standard Arabic,* Part One, 1983
Reprinted 1983, 1984 (twice), 1985 (twice), 1986, 1987

Library of Congress catalogue card number: 82-22021

British Library Cataloguing in Publication Data

Elementary modern standard Arabic.—2nd ed.
Vol. 1
1. Arabic language—Grammar
I. Abboud, Peter F. II. McCarus, Ernest N.
492'.782421 PJ6075
ISBN 0 521 27295 5 Part 1
ISBN 0 521 27296 3 Part 2

Tapes to accompany this volume can be purchased from:
Media Resources Center, Tape Duplication Services,
416 S. Fourth Street, Ann Arbor, MI 48109, USA

PREFACE

This book is the outcome of discussions and exchanges of opinions that took place at the Arabic Teachers' Workshops that were held during the summers of 1965, 1966 and 1967. At the first workshop held in Ann Arbor, Michigan in June 1965 and directed by Charles Ferguson, but more specifically at the second workshop held at Columbia University in New York City in June 1966 and directed by Peter Abboud, it was the opinion of the participants that there was need for an elementary textbook which (1) was expressly designed for the undergraduate student at universities in the U.S. and Canada, (2) was written by a team of Arabic language teachers consisting of native and non-native speakers, linguists and people whose primary interest was literature and the social sciences, (3) implemented the principles of the audio-lingual approach to language teaching, and (4) presented in a culturally meaningful context the elements of Modern Standard Arabic. Subsequently, in June 1967, Peter Abboud directed a third workshop at Princeton University, in Princeton, N.J., consisting of five members and chaired by Ernest McCarus, the purpose of which was to determine the principles on which such a book should be based, to discuss its content and methodology, and to prepare a few sample lessons. The document that this committee prepared was made available on request to all teachers of Arabic in the United States and Canada during the academic year 1967-68, and a detailed questionnaire was prepared and sent to some twenty Arabists in the U.S. and abroad eliciting comments on various parts of the document. The team, consisting of Peter F. Abboud, Najm A. Bezirgan, Wallace M. Erwin, Mounah A. Khouri, Ernest N. McCarus and Raji M. Rammuny, met for a preliminary session in April 1968 at Ann Arbor to plan for the work of the summer. Actual work on the book started the first week in June and went on until mid August. The various responsibilities were divided as follows. The four native speakers composed and/or selected and adapted from literature the basic texts and wrote the greater part of the drills. The two non-native speakers were responsible for writing the grammatical notes, which describe such items and structures as occurred in the basic texts, and the section on the phonology and script (with supplementary writing drills written by Raji Rammuny). Peter Abboud coordinated the activities of both groups. Throughout the summer each group studied and commented on the work of the other, revisions were made, and the final draft was approved by the whole team.

The book, with the exception of the introductory ten lessons on pronunciation and writing, was revised in the summer of 1975 by Peter F. Abboud, Zaki N. Abdel-Malek, Wallace M. Erwin, Ernest N. McCarus and George N. Saad in the light of considerable experience with it in the classroom. The basic texts were enlarged and expanded but the same vocabulary was retained in the book overall, with a few additions. The grammar notes were completely rewritten, with a number of changes in the order of presentation of grammatical features. The drills were also completely rewritten, with the addition of several new types such as recognition and translation drills. A new feature was the section of written and aural comprehension passages for further reading and listening practice. Part Two saw a formal change, the use of Prepatory Sentences to provide for the introduction in context of the new vocabulary items.

It is our pleasant duty to express our thanks to the many organizations, groups and individuals who contributed to the production of this book. Funding support was received from the quondam Interuniversity Program for Near Eastern Languages then chaired by the late T. Cuyler Young of Princeton University and from the U.S. Office of Education of the Department of Health, Education and Welfare; thanks are also given to the Department of Near Eastern Studies of the University of Michigan, with special acknowledgement for the support of the late George G. Cameron, then chairman. Valuable input was received from the members of the Arabic Teachers Workshops and from our consultants Frederic J. Cadora and Carolyn G. Killean. We also benefitted from the experience and insights of our graduate assistants Nora Kalliel, Amy Van Voorhis, and Eleanor Rhinelander Young. The tape recordings were done by Ernest T. Abdel-Massih, Ernest N. McCarus, Raji M. Rammuny and Magda M. Taher. Ernest N. McCarus was in charge of the initial production of the book and subsequent distribution and management of the sale of the books.

Finally, we would like to express our gratitude to the many colleagues both in this country and abroad who have used Elementary Modern Standard Arabic over the years and have helped it achieve whatever success it has had.

Peter F. Abboud
Ernest N. McCarus

INTRODUCTION

This book presents the basic structures of Modern Standard Arabic (MSA), that formal Arabic which is written and spoken in the contemporary Arab World. In its written form it is used almost exclusively in any printed publication anywhere in the world today; as such it is the direct descendent of the Arabic of the Koran, the poetry of Pre-Islamic Arabia, and the classical literature of the Golden Age, the major differences being in lexicon and style. It is also an oral medium of expression used in formal situations ranging from a radio newscast to a lecture or other formal address to an international conference. Used orally it may be modified in varying degrees, depending on such factors as the nature of the occasion, the makeup of the audience, the speaker's control of MSA, etc. MSA is a universal form of Arabic learned in schools across the Arab world; it is opposed to dialectal or colloquial Arabic, of which there is a particular variety for each community and differs according to region and such social factors as religion, socio-economic status, etc. The dialects are used for all non-formal situations--at home, at work, social occasions, etc.--all the usual day-to-day activities.

The Arab does not keep MSA and his own dialect separate, but mixes them according to the degree of technical complexity of his subject, the degree of formality of the occasion, etc. When speaking his dialect he will bring in MSA in varying degree, and when speaking MSA he may introduce colloquialisms into it if it does not impair understanding on the part of the listener.

For a non-Arab to be said to "know Arabic" he or she must master both MSA and any colloquial dialect.

The goal of this course is to train the learner to read MSA and to respond to it orally. Writing in Arabic is also drilled both as a skill in its own right and to aid in the mastery of reading and speaking MSA. It covers the writing system, phonology, a basic vocabulary of approximately one thousand words, the morphology, and the basic syntactic structures of the language.

It is articulated with Modern Standard Arabic. Intermediate Level by Peter Abboud, Ernest Abdel-Massih, Salih Altoma, Wallace Erwin, Ernest McCarus and Raji Rammuny, which concentrates on vocabulary, expression and advanced syntax and takes the learner to the advanced stage.

Part One of this book contains a ten-lesson introduction to the pronunciation and writing system of Modern Standard Arabic and Lessons 1-30, followed by an Arabic-English Glossary and a grammatical Subject Index. Part Two completes the course with Lessons 31-45. It includes appendices providing verb tables (conjugation paradigms of the various forms of the verb and of the various root types), names of days and months and of the Arab states, and lists of all the adjectives by lesson, particles by subclass, and verbs by lesson and type occurring in both parts; cumulative English-Arabic and Arabic-English Glossaries; and a grammatical subject index covering the entire book.

In addition to the book there are tapes which contain recordings of the pronunciation, reading and dictation drills of the ten-lesson introduction of Part One, and of the Basic Texts and drills that are designated as being "(on tape)" or "(also on tape)" in Lessons 1-45. Since the drills tagged "(on tape)" are not found in the book, there is available a pamphlet for teacher's use called Recorded Drills to Accompany Elementary Modern Standard Arabic containing them and the drills marked "(also on tape)". The tapes and/or the pamphlet may be purchased from:

Media Resources Center
Tape Duplication Services
University of Michigan
416 S. Fourth Street
Ann Arbor, Michigan 48109
U.S.A.
Telephone: (313) 764-5360.

Structure of Lessons 1-45

Lessons 1-5 contain three parts: Basic Text, Vocabulary, and Grammar and Drills. Lessons 6-30 have in addition to these, two other parts: Comprehension Passages and General Drills. Lessons 31-44 have five parts also, but in each of these lessons, instead of the Vocabulary part that follows the Basic Text, there are Preparatory Sentences preceding it. The last lesson, Lesson 45, consists of verses from the Holy Qur'ān, a few ḥadīths, and a short poem by Mikhā'īl Nu^c^ayma.

The purpose and content of each part is described below.

(1) Basic Text. The purpose of the Basic Text is to present new lexical and grammatical materials in a context that is meaningful and suitable for intensive oral work. The Basic Text occupies a central role in each lesson; the student should make every attempt to familiarize himself or herself thoroughly with it up to the point of memorizing it.

Two approaches have been used in the composition of these texts: a grammar-based approach, in which every lesson is built around certain grammatical structures which are presented in a predetermined order, and a topic-based approach, used in the later lessons, in which a topic of interest is chosen and whatever vocabulary and grammatical structures are necessary to deal with it meaningfully are used, subject to the constraints necessary in a beginning textbook. The earlier texts are functional in nature and deal with introductions, greetings, dialogues, etc. Later texts are narrative or expository and deal with the culture, society, history, geography, economics and politics of the Arab World; they also include literary selections such as short stories, a play, a poem, etc. The subjects are basically non-controversial; needless to say, however, they do not necessarily represent the personal opinions of the authors.

The Basic Text is unvoweled, in order to prepare the student to handle materials actually printed in Arabic today, which are unvoweled. Passive words, which are words that are needed in a particular context but which the student is not responsible for, either because of their highly specialized meaning or because of their low frequency of use, are voweled and glossed in the margin.

Wherever appropriate, the Basic Text is followed by questions which will serve as the basis for discussion in class.

Each Basic Text through Lesson 40 is followed by an English translation which reflects the structure of the Arabic text, while at the same time attempting to render the passage into as good idiomatic English as possible. The Basic Texts of Lessons 41-44 are not translated. Translations are provided for the selections in Lesson 45.

(2) Vocabulary. In Lessons 1-30, all new words and phrases occurring in the Basic Text are listed in their order of occurrence and are fully voweled. From Lesson 31 on, the new words of the Basic Text are introduced in Preparatory Sentences; following the preparatory sentence in which it occurs, each new word is also listed and voweled. In either case, whether in a vocabulary list or after a preparatory sentence, the following information is given with a new word: (a) the plurals of nouns and adjectives, preceded by a dash (following the lesson that introduces plural formation); (b) the imperfect stem vowel of Form I verbs (following the lesson where imperfect stems are discussed); (c) the verbal noun of all verbs, simple or derived, preceded by a comma (following the lesson where the verbal nouns are treated); (d) any preposition required for particular meanings of the verb, in parentheses if its omission does not change the meaning of the verb; and (e) the basic meaning of the word in English; the contextual meaning for that lesson, if different from its basic meaning,is also given after the basic meaning.

The Preparatory Sentences in most lessons center around a common theme in order to help the student better to retain the vocabulary; in a couple of lessons, the new words are given in miscellaneous, unrelated sentences, in the order in which they occur in the Basic Text.

Vocabulary is strictly controlled. The number of new words per lesson is limited to between 15 and 20 words, not counting proper names (e.g., Beirut), and loan words (e.g., film, cinema). Once a word is introduced, every effort is made to use it in the following lesson; in any case, it is invariably used at least once in the next four lessons for at least 20 subsequent lessons. This constant reinsertion of words into the lessons helps the student learn and retain active vocabulary, which is a major source of difficulty in learning Arabic.

(3) Grammar and Drills. The grammar notes explain the structures that have appeared in the Basic Text, though in a few cases, in the

interest of presenting an overview of a particular grammatical feature, structures presented in more detail in later lessons are anticipated. Thus, when the nominative case first comes up for discussion, the student is told there are two other cases in Arabic to be discussed later. An average of four to five new grammar points, major or minor, are introduced in each lesson. The structure is explained with examples and, where appropriate, it is compared to or contrasted with a related English structure; a rule is then stated; and, if needed, further examples are given. Each note is immediately followed by one or more exercises designed specifically to drill the point in question. This provides immediate reinforcement of the rule and confirmation of the student's comprehension of it.

A number of points related to the grammar notes should be emphasized: (1) The notes cover only the structures of this book; since it is an elementary level text, features appropriate to a more advanced level have been excluded. (2) For the sake of having complete coverage, we have included some grammatical structures which some teachers might feel are too complicated and too advanced for beginning students, such as the extensive discussion of the numeral system, etc. They should feel free to postpone or to ignore such structures. (3) The grammatical presentation is pedagogically oriented and has been written with the needs of the average, linguistically unsophisticated student in mind. No attempt is made here to present the "neatest" or theoretically most defensible linguistic analysis; an easily understandable, simply written presentation, yet one that is thorough (incorporating the latest findings of research on Arabic) and consistent has been given. (4) In the grammatical analysis we present here, we are well aware of the fact that we depart at several points from the well established norms of traditional Arabic grammars; again, we have consciously opted for what we believe to be an analysis which best meets the needs of English-speaking learners of Arabic.

(4) Comprehension Passages. Starting with Lesson 6, every lesson contains one or more reading passage, and every third lesson, beginning with Lesson 15, a listening passage recorded on tape. The selections contain only familiar vocabulary and grammatical structures; vocabulary that is essential to a selection but which the students have not had is glossed in the margin. The purpose of these passages is to give students the opportunity to use what they have learned in reading for pleasure and practice in reading and aural comprehension. Every passage is followed by a drill or more to test their general understanding of it.

(5) General Drills. These differ from the grammar drills in that the latter concentrate on and highlight a specific grammatical point, whereas the general drills review the content of the lesson as a whole and vocabulary or grammatical structures from previous lessons. The General Drills also provide a systematic and regular review of basic grammatical structures.

A few points pertaining to all the drills in this course are in order. (1) Drills are marked as either (a) On Tape, which indicates that the drill is to be done in the language lab; the items of the drill are not provided in the book; and printed texts are given in the teacher's Pamphlet; or (b) Also on Tape, which indicates that the drill is to be done orally in class, but the student can also find it recorded on tape for further reinforcement; or (c) Written, which indicates that the nature and content of the drill require that it be done as a written assignment. If not marked as (a), (b), or (c) above, the drill is designed for oral work in the class. (2) Each drill is also identified as to type, i.e., as to whether it is a substitution, transformation, completion, expansion, translation, etc. drill. In a transformation drill, an arrow usually shows what is being transformed into what. An illustrative example in Arabic is usually provided and is translated into English. (3) The teacher should feel free to skip some of the General Drills when and if he or she thinks the students do not need the review the drill provides.

This course was designed on the principle that the most effective language learning is based on the four skills of listening, speaking, reading, and writing. All four of these areas are well represented in the drills of this book. While the various parts of a given lesson are thoroughly integrated with each other, they are organized in such a way that the teacher can start with the Basic Text, Vocabulary or Grammar Section as preferred. The final goal of each lesson should be thorough mastery of the Basic Text.

Special attention should be paid to the following points:

(1) Grammar and Drills. The grammar notes are complete and intended to enable the student to learn the new structures at home without a teacher. The student should be required to study the grammar outside of class and to prepare the written drills as homework to be handed in and the oral drills as the basis for oral drill in the classroom. Only when students find difficulty with a particular point should it be gone over in class. This frees the class hour for maximum oral practice and exposure to the language.

(2) Comprehension Passages. The main objective of these passages is general comprehension; they are not meant to be translated or read aloud. These passages and their drills are best assigned as homework.

(3) General Drills. These are meant for review purposes. The teacher should feel free to select only those drills which the class needs.

Classroom Expressions

In order to create an atmosphere conducive to the learning of Arabic--as well as to provide additional drill in the language--it is recommended that the class be conducted as far as possible in Arabic. The following expressions are suggested; they should be used at first only by the teacher, with the class simply responding to them with appropriate action. Eventually after the sounds have been covered in the phonology sections, the class may be permitted or requested to use them actively.

plural	fem. sing.	masc. sing.	
أَعيدوا	أَعيدي	أَعِدْ	'repeat!'
مِنْ فَضْلِكُمْ	مِنْ فَضْلِكِ	مِنْ فَضْلِكَ	'please!'
اِقْرَأُوا	اِقْرَئي	اِقْرَأْ	'read!'
أَجيبوا عَلى السُّؤالِ	أَجيبي عَلى السُّؤالِ	أَجِبْ عَلى السُّؤالِ	'answer the question!'
اِسْأَلوا	اِسْأَلي	اِسْأَلْ	'ask!'
أُكْتُبوا	أُكْتُبي	أُكْتُبْ	'write!'
أُكْتُبوا عَلى اللَّوْحِ	أُكْتُبي عَلى اللَّوْحِ	أُكْتُبْ عَلى اللَّوْحِ	'write on the board!'
تَرْجِموا	تَرْجِمي	تَرْجِمْ	'translate!'
قوموا	قومي	قُمْ	'stand up!'
اِذْهَبوا الى اللَّوْحِ	اِذْهَبي إِلى اللَّوْحِ	اِذْهَبْ إِلى اللَّوْحِ	'go to the board!'
قولوا	قولي	قُلْ	'say...!'
هَلْ فَهِمْتُمْ ؟	هَلْ فَهِمْتِ ؟	هَلْ فَهِمْتَ ؟	'do you understand?'

نَعَمْ ، فَهِمْتُ	'Yes, I understand.'
لا ، لَمْ أَفْهَمْ	'No, I don't understand.'
ما مَعْنى هٰذِهِ الْكَلِمَةِ ؟	'What does this word mean?'
ما مَعْنى هٰذِهِ الْجُمْلَةِ ؟	'What does this sentence mean?'
أَعيدوا مَعًا ، مِنْ فَضْلِكُمْ	'Repeat all together, please.'

Abbreviations and Symbols

AP	active participle
acc.	accusative
adj.	adjective
C	any consonant
coll.	collective
conj.	conjunction
d., du., D	dual
DD	identical second and third radicals
e.g.	for example
ex., Ex.	for example
f., F.	feminine; female
F	first radical in a root
foll.	following; followed
gen.	genitive
imperf.	imperfect
indic.	indicative
juss.	jussive
L	last radical in a root
lit.	literally
m., M.	masculine; male
M	second of three radicals in a root
n	noun
neg.	negative
nom.	nominative
obj.	object
p., pl., P.	plural
prep.	preposition
pron.	pronoun
Q.A.	questions and answers
s., S.	singular
S	second of four radicals
S_1	the first student
S_2	the second student
s.o.	someone
s.th.	something
suff.	suffix
T	third of four radicals
T	teacher
v	any vowel
VN	verbal noun
1	first person
2	second person
3	third person
-	a prefix or suffix must be added here
→	is to be changed to
↔	change drill item given to other form

ط ١	اَلطّالِبُ الأَوَّلُ
ط ٢	اَلطّالِبُ الثّاني

TABLE OF CONTENTS

SECTION 1. ARABIC PRONUNCIATION AND WRITING

Lesson One الدرس الاول

Consonants

د d as in deed

و w as in way

ب b as in boy

ن n as in now

Vowels

ا aa as in Dad

َ a (no English equivalent)

Stress

Sukuun ْ

Voicing

Punctuation Marks

A. Pronunciation

The phonological system of Modern Standard Arabic is made up of 28 consonants and 6 vowels. Fifteen of the consonants are very much like English sounds and will present no difficulty. These are:

د	d as in day
و	w as in wake
ب	b as in bake
ن	n as in none
ذ	th as in this
ت	t as in take
ف	f as in face
ى	y as in yell
م	m as in make
ث	th as in thin
س	s as in sake
ز	z as in zeal
ش	sh as in shake
ك	k as in kind
ج	j as in joke

The first four of these consonants will be taken up in this lesson: د d, و w, ب b and ن n.

The six vowels fall into two groups, three short and three long, as follows:

Short		Long	
َ	a	ا	aa
ُ	u	و	uu
ِ	i	ى	ii

Short َ a and long ا aa are dealt with in this lesson.

There are no exact correspondences between English and Arabic vowels; they may differ in quality, and they may behave differently under certain circumstances. Accordingly, any comparisons between English and Arabic vowels are at best rough approximations and intended only as general guides to pronunciation. Your best guide to proper pronunciation is your teacher (or tape) whom you should listen to as carefully as possible and imitate as faithfully as possible.

Arabic aa ا is a long vowel--that is, sustained in pronunciation, as a rule twice as long as a short vowel. In quality, it is pronounced roughly like a in English "had" or "tab." Short a َ is not only shorter in duration but also it differs in quality from aa: it is less like the a of "had" but ranges more between the e of "bet" and the u of "but"; imitation of your teacher is necessary here, because not only does َ a not exist in English, it also varies somewhat from speaker to speaker over the Arab world. The following drill contrasts long aa ا and short a َ :

Drill 1. On tape. Listen to the following contrastive pairs, then repeat on signal:

بَنْ — بانْ

دَنْ — دانْ

نَنْ — نانْ

وَنْ — وانْ

In careful speech long aa ا is held twice as long as short a in any given utterance. Often, however, especially in rapid speech, long vowels are shortened, so that the difference in vowel quality becomes an important clue in distinguishing between the two vowels. Listen for and produce this difference in quality as well as the difference in length.

B. Reading

There are several ways in which the Arabic writing system differs from that used in English. First, Arabic is written from right to left. Second, Arabic letters have no special forms used, like the capitals of the Latin alphabet, at the beginning of sentences and proper nouns. Third, on the other hand, many Arabic letters have several different forms, the use of which depends on whether the letter is connected to a preceding or a following letter, or to both, or to neither. Fourth, in Arabic the short vowels are normally not represented at all, although they may be indicated by small marks placed above and below the consonant letters. An Arabic text in which these marks are written is said to be vowelled. Most written Arabic, however--books, newspapers, magazines, signs, personal letters--is entirely or mainly unvowelled, and consequently an important part of the student's task is to become accustomed to reading material of this sort. Finally, the difference between printed and handwritten Arabic is not so great as in English. In both printing and handwriting, many of the letters in a word are connected, and with a few exceptions the shape of the letters is basically the same in both styles. Nevertheless, Arabic handwriting does have its own conventions, and the development of skill in its use is an important goal of this course.

The long vowel aa (as in English Dad) is represented by the following letter:

ا

The Arabic name of this letter is ألف ʔalif. The consonant d as in deed is represented by the letter

د

The Arabic name of this letter is دال daal. These letters can be used to spell the following combinations:

دا	daa
داد	daad
دادا	daadaa

Drill 2. Read the following:

دا ، دادا ، دا ، داد ، دادا

C. Writing

Writing, in Arabic, is more than just a means of communication; it is a major art form. Where one might find pictures and sculpture in the West, in the Arab world there are friezes and decorative designs composed of letters, words, and sentences in intricate and attractive patterns. Many of these designs embody verses from the Qur'an and thus take on religious as well as artistic significance. Particular respect, therefore, is accorded to those who write with great style and beauty. More generally, good handwriting is considered one of the essential marks of any educated person, and from that point of view is a worthy goal of all students of the language.

The acquisition of an easy, legible handwriting, particularly in a completely unfamiliar alphabet like the Arabic, demands a great deal of patient, repetitive effort, and the drills in these first units are designed to provide guidelines for efficient practice of this sort. If the student learns and practices correct handwriting techniques from the beginning, he will form habits which in later stages will allow him to perform rapidly and effortlessly the mechanical processes of handwriting, and free his conscious attention for matters of grammar and content.

As was mentioned in the preceding section, certain combinations of Arabic letters in either a printed or a handwritten word are--indeed must be--connected, that is, written with a continuous uninterrupted line. In this respect, there are two major categories of letters: a non-connector is a letter which is never connected to a following letter (though a preceding letter may be connected to it). A connector is a letter which is always connected to a following letter. There are six non-connectors among the twenty-eight letters of the alphabet; the rest are all connectors.

Another important feature of Arabic letters is the use of dots above or below the letter to distinguish letters from each other; some letters have no dots and some have one, while others have two or three. For example, و w has no dots; ب b has one dot below while ت t is exactly like ب except that it has two dots above.

The writing of the letters ا and د will now be taken up. The explanations are included in the book, and the exercises are to be done on the work sheets supplied with this textbook.

1. The letter ا alif aa:

Printed	ا
Written	ا

is a single horizontal stroke written from top to bottom; it rests on the line. It is a non-connector (never connected to a following letter). Drill 3. In writing supplement.

2. The letter daal d:

Printed	د
Written	د

is a non-connector written with a single stroke; it rests on the line. Drill 4. In writing supplement.

3. The letter that represents the consonant w (as in way) is

و

Its Arabic name is واو waaw. Examples:

وا	waa
واو	waaw

Drill 5. Read the following words:*

واو	داد
واد	واد
داو	واو
داد	واد

The letter waaw w:

Printed	و
Written	و

is a non-connector written in one stroke; the circle is above the line, while the tail is below the line. Drill 6. In writing supplement.

4. Short a is written by means of the diacritic sign

َ a

Its Arabic name is فتحة fatha; it is written over consonant letters, as, for example

دَدَ	dada	دَ	da
وَدَ	wada	وَ	wa

---

* In the early lessons made-up words are used in order to permit full drill; real words will be used increasingly as more letters are learned

The vowel sign <u>fatha</u> <u>a</u> is a short stroke written above a consonant letter.

<u>Drill 7</u>. In writing supplement.

5. <u>Stress</u>: If the Arabic word has a long vowel followed by a consonant, that vowel is <u>stressed</u> (that is, pronounced louder than the other vowels); otherwise, the first vowel of the word is stressed

<u>Drill 8</u>. Read the following:

CáCaa	CaáCa	CáCa
وَدا	دادَ	دَدَ
دَوا	وادَ	وَدَ
دَدا	واوَ	وَوَ
	داوَ	دَوَ
	دادَ	دَدَ

<u>Drill 9</u>. Read the following:

وادَ ، دادَ ، دَدَ ، دَوَ ، وَدَ ، داوَ ، واوَ ، وَدا ، وادَ ، دَوَ

6. <u>Sukuun</u>. There is a special symbol ° (سُكون <u>sukuun</u>) written over a letter to indicate the absence of any vowel after that consonant, as

دادْ	<u>daad</u>
دَدْوَ	<u>dadwa</u>
دَوْدادْ	<u>dawdaad</u>

7. <u>Stress</u>. A short vowel followed by two consonants receives the stress; read:

CáCCaCa	CáCCa	CaaC
دَوْدَوَ	دَدْوَ	داد
وَدْوَدَ	دَوْدَ	داو
	وَوْدَ	واو
	وَدْوَ	واد
	دَدْوَ	داد

If a word contains both a long vowel followed by a consonant and a short vowel followed by two consonants, the one nearest the end of the word is stressed; read:

CaCCaáCa
وَدْوادَ

Drill 10. Read the following: دَوْدادَ

دَدْوَ ، داوْدَ ، وَدادْ ، وَدادَ ، داوادْ ، وَدْوَدَ ، دَوْدَوَ ، داوَ

واوْ ، واوا ، داوَ ، وادْ

8. The letter that represents the consonant b is ب

داب daaba

Its Arabic name is باء baa?.

The letter ب differs from the preceding three letters in an important way:

ا,د and و are non-connectors: letters that cannot be connected in writing with the following letter. ب , on the other hand, can be joined to a following letter, in which case it takes a special shape بـ :

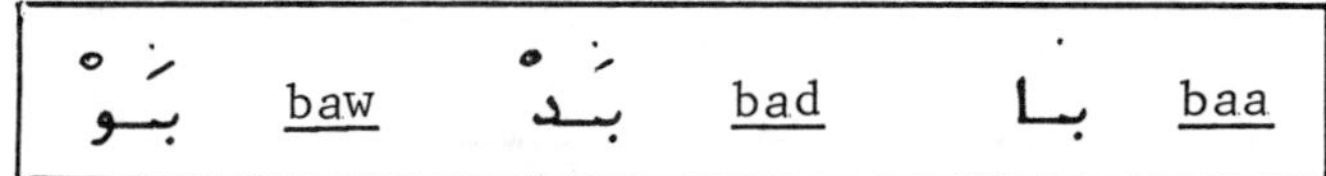

When ب is joined to both the preceding and the following letter it is written thus:

بَبا	babaa

Finally, when ب is joined only to the preceding letter, it takes the shape ـب

بَبَ	baba

The form occurring as the last letter of the word and after a non-connector is the independent or full form; the joined forms of letters consist of only the distinctive part of the letter--a certain shape, and its dot, if any. Thus, the characteristic part of ب , namely بـ , is common to all of its shapes.

The following chart summarizes the various shapes of ب :

	Shape	Example	
a. Independent (not joined on either side)	ب	دابَ	daaba
b. Joined to preceding letter only	ـب	بَبَ	baba
c. Joined to following letter only: at beginning of word after non-connector	بـ	بابَ دَبابَ	baaba dabaaba
d. Joined on both sides	ـبـ	بَبا	babaa

Drill 11. Read the following:

بابَ ، بَدَوَ ، دَبَبَ ، باوَدَ ، وَبَدَ ، بَوابَ ، دَوْبَ ، دَوْباد

The shapes of baa? b are

	Printed	Written
a.	ب	ب
b.	ـب	ـب
c.	بـ	بـ
d.	ـبـ	ـبـ

All four shapes are written on the line. Drill 12. In writing supplement.

9. The letter that represents the consonant n as in now is

ن

Its name in Arabic is نون nuun. It has the following shapes; note that the shapes in c. and d. are identical to the corresponding forms of ب except that they have a dot above rather than below the letter.

	Shape	Example	
a. Independent	ن	دانَ	daana
b. Joined to preceding letter only	ـن	بَنْ	ban
c. Joined to following letter only	نـ	نابَ وَنابَ	naaba wanaaba
d. Joined on both sides	ـنـ	بَنَوا	banawaa

Drill 13. Read the following:

بانَ ، بَنا ، دَنَبَ ، دَوابَ ، دانَ ، نابَ ، نَبْنَبَ

نَبْنابْ ، نَدَوْ ، بَنَوا

7

The shapes of nuun n are

	Printed	Written	Variant
a.	ن	ن	~
b.	ـن	ـن	~
c.	نـ	نـ	
d.	ـنـ	ـنـ	

All four shapes are written on the line; note that shape b. is joined at the top rather than at its base ـبـن ban, while ب is jointed at the base ـبب bab. Shapes a. and b. have two common written variants, ن and ~. Drill 14. In writing supplement. Drill 15. On tape. Dictation. (Each of ten items will be read twice; write down in Arabic script and hand in to your teacher.)

10. Summary. Stress rules. Word stress falls on that long vowel followed by a consonant (VVC) or that short vowel followed by two consonants (VCC) which is nearest the end of the word.

Drill 16. Read the following with proper stress:

بَنْدَنَ ، باوَبَ ، دَوابَ ، نَبْنَبَ ، داوانْ ، بَدْوانَ ،

بَدْوَ ، دَبْدابْ ، بَدْوَنَ

If neither of these combinations (VVC or VCC) occurs, then the first vowel of the word is stressed (except that the stress does not go back beyond the third last syllable).

Drill 17. Read the following:

بَدَنَ ، بَدَنا ، نَوَدَ ، نَوَدَنا ، بَنا ، نَدَبَ

نَدَبْنا ، وَنَدَبَ ، وَنَدَبْنا ، دَوَدانَ

11. Voicing. It is useful to describe consonants in terms of voicing--the vocal tone produced by the vibration of the vocal cords. We speak by exhaling air from the lungs through the windpipe and the throat and then out the mouth or the nasal passage. At some point along the way the stream of air is modified in various ways producing various sounds. The air stream can be stopped completely and then released, producing a slight explosion of air. This is called a stop consonant, or, simply, a stop; English p, for example, is a stop: say "papaw" and listen for the explosion with the p. Another kind of consonant is the fricative, produced by only partially blocking off the air stream, so that some air does pass through, but with friction. An example of this is English th as in think, where the tongue channels the air through a narrow passage at the upper teeth.

Now to return to the windpipe: at the opening at the top are two muscles called the vocal cords. These vocal cords can also modify the air stream. They can either be relaxed, as in pronouncing s (as in sun), or vibrate, giving off a vocal resonance--a kind of humming noise--as in z (as in blizzard). Hold your hand on your head and say ssss; now do the same with zzzz; you can actually feel the vibration that accompanies the z. This vibration effect is called voicing, and z is called voiced while s is unvoiced. Other voiceless-voiced pairs of fricatives in English are f-v; th (as in thin) - th (as in this); and sh-z (as in azure).

The easiest way to tell whether a stop is voiced or not is by seeing whether you can pronounce it before s or z. For example, you can say ats but not atz; since s is unvoiced, so is t. On the other hand, you can say ads only with difficulty, but you can easily say adz; thus, d is voiced. The other voiceless-voiced pairs of consonants in English are p-b, t-d, k-g, and ch-j (as in judge). All other English consonants except h and all vowels are voiced.

Arabic also has, of course, voiced-voiceless pairs of consonants, and you will find it useful in mastering some of the less familiar sounds if you have some understanding of the feature of voicing.

12. Punctuation Marks

Arabic punctuation marks are like those of European languages, a few showing reversal of direction. They are:

Symbol		Arabic Name	English Equivalent
.	النُّقْطة	ʔannuqṭa	. (period)
،	الفاصِلة	ʔalfaaṣila	, (comma)
؛	الفاصلة المَنْقوطة	ʔalfaaṣilatul-manquuṭa	; (semicolon)
:	النُّقطتان	ʔannuqṭataan	: (colon)
؟	عَلامة الاسْتِفْهام	ʕalaamatu-listifhaam	? (question mark)
!	علامة التَعَجُّب	ʕalaamatut-taʕajjub	! (exclamation mark)
" "	المُزْدَوِجان	ʔalmuzdawijaan	" (quotation mark)
...	علامة الحَذْف	ʕalaamatul-ḥaðf	...(suspension points)
—	الشَّحْطة	ʔaššaḥṭa	- (dash)
/	الخَطّ المائل	ʔalxaṭṭul-maaʔil	/ (slash, slant line)
( )	القَوْسان	ʔalqawsaan	( ) (parentheses)
[ ]	القَوْسانِ الكَبيران	ʔalqawsaanil-kabiiraan	[ ](brackets)

Lesson Two الـدرس الثانى

Consonants:

1. ذ ð th as in English this

2. ت t as in English take

3. ف f as in English fat

4. ي y as in English yell

5. م m as in English make

Vowels:

6. ُ u as in English put

7. و uu as in English boon

8. Double consonants: shadda ّ

1. ذ ð

a. Pronunciation

This consonant is the same as the English sound spelled th in this, either, soothe. It is a voiced sound, and quite different from the voiceless sound, also spelled th, that is found in thin, ether, tooth. Although these are distinct sounds--compare "either" and "ether", "bath" and "bathe"--English spells them both with the th. Arabic on the other hand, has a separate letter for each. We accordingly use two separate symbols to distinguish the two, ð being used to represent voiced th.

b. Reading

The letter which represents the sound ð (as in this) is

ذ

This letter is called ذ ðaal. It is a non-connector, and is exactly like د d in its various shapes except that it has a dot over it. Its two shapes are:

Position	Shape	Examples
a. Independent	ذ	ذا ðaa نوذ nawða
b. Joined to preceding letter only	ـذ	بذان baðaan ونذ wanaða

Drill 1. The following items all begin with ذ . Read.

ذانْ   ذانَ   ذوابْ   ذَنَبَ

ذابْ   ذابَ   ذنابْ   ذَبَنَ

ذاوْ   ذاوَ   ذنانْ   ذَنَدَ

ذادْ   ذادَ   ذوانْ   ذَبَدَ

Drill 2. Some of the following items begin with ذ , some with د . Read.

ذانْ   داوَ   دَوانْ   ذَنَدَ

دانْ   ذابَ   دبابْ   دَنَبَ

دابْ   ذانَ   ذبانْ   دَبَدَ

ذادْ   ذادَ   دوابْ   ذَبَنَ

Drill 3. The following items have ذ in various positions. Read.

نَذَبَ ، ذَوْ ، ذابَ ، نذود ، نبذ ، ذات ، ذان ، نذوب ، نوذ

بذ ، ذوبان ، ذد ، نذب ، ذنون ، ذدا

c. Writing

Printed	ذ
Written	ذ

ذ is exactly like د with the addition of a dot. Drill 4. In writing supplement.

2. ت t

a. Pronunciation

Arabic ت t is like English t in take.

b. Reading

The letter that represents the sound t (as in take) is

ت

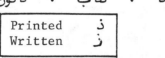

This letter is called تاء taaʔ. It is exactly like ب in all its shapes except that it has two dots above instead of one below. The shapes are:

Position	Shape	Examples	
a. Independent	ت	بَناتْ	banaat
b. Joined to preceding letter only	ـت	بَنَتْ	banat
c. Joined to following letter only	تـ	تابَ	taaba
		باتا	baataa
d. Joined on both sides	ـتـ	بَنَتا	banataa

Drill 5. The following items have ت t in various positions. Read:

تَبِنْ ، دَنَتْ ، نَتَنْ ، وَتَبْ ، مَوْت ، فات ، تَبَتْ ، بَنَتْ ، نَبْتَتان ، نَبات ، ذات

c. Writing

Printed	ت
Written	ت

ت is exactly like ب except that it has two dots above rather than one below. Note that two dots are printed ¨ and written ـ . Drill 6. In writing supplement.

3. ف f

a. Pronunciation

Arabic ف f is exactly like English f in face.

b. Reading

The letter that represents the sound f (as in face) is

ف

This letter is called فاء Faaʔ. Its shapes are:

	Position	Shape	Examples	
a.	Independent	ف	نذف	nadafa
b.	Joined to preceding letter only	ـف	نتف	natafa
c.	Joined to following letter only	فـ	فات	faata
			دفن	dafana
d.	Joined on both sides	ـفـ	تفات	tafaata

Drill 7. Each of the first four columns below illustrates one of the shapes of ف ; Column e includes them all. Read:

e	d	c	b	a
فانْ	بَفَتْ	فانَ	نَتَفْ	وَدَفْ
دَفَنَ	تَفْتَ	فَتَنَ	تَفْتَفَ	نَفافْ
فَنَّ	نَفا	فاتَ	وَنَفَ	دافَ

c. Writing

	Printed	Written
a.	ف	ف
b.	ـف	ـف
c.	فـ	فـ
d.	ـفـ	ـفـ

Written on the line. Drill 8. In writing supplement.

4. ي y

a. Pronunciation

Arabic ي y is exactly like English y in yell.

b. Reading

The Arabic letter that represents the sound y (as in yell) is

ي

It is called ياء yaa', and has the following shapes:

Position	Shape	Examples	
a. Independent	ي	نايْ	naay
b. Joined to preceding letter only	ي	بَنْيَ	banya
c. Joined to following letter only	يـ	يَدٌ	yad
		دايَنَ	daayana
d. Joined on both sides	ـيـ	بَيانْ	bayaan

Note: The last two shapes of ي are exactly like those of ب and ت except for the number or position of dots.

In some Arabic publications, e.g., those of Egypt, shapes a. (independent) and b. (joined to preceding letter only) are written without the two dots, thus:

ناي
نای } naay

Drill 9. The following items have ي in various positions. Read.

ذَين ، مَداي ، يَدان ، فَنْيَ ، بَيات ، بَناي ، بَيان ، داي

c. Writing

	Printed	Written
a.	ى	ي
b.	ي	ي
c.	يـ	يـ
d.	ـيـ	ـيـ

Shapes a. and b. are written below the line, while c. and d. are on the line, like the corresponding shapes of ت and ن . Drill 10. In writing supplement.

5. م m

a. Pronunciation

The consonant م m is pronounced exactly like English m in make.

b. Reading

The letter that represents the sound m (as in make) is

م

Its name is ميم miim and its shapes are as follows:

Position	Shape	Examples	
a. Independent	م	دام	daama
b. Joined to preceding letter only	ـم	يتم	yatama
c. Joined to following letter only	مـ	ماذا	maaðaa
		دامت	daamat
d. Joined on both sides	ـمـ	نمت	namat

Drill 11. Each of the first four columns below illustrates one of the shapes of م ; Column e. includes them all. Read:

e	d	c	b	a
تَمام	نَمَت	مَدام	تَم	دام
دَمْدَمَ	تَمام	مَدَد	دَنَم	تام
دَوام	فَمَن	مَن	تَنَم	يَوم
مَمات	تَمَن	مَدْفَن	وَيَم	نَدَم
نَمَت	يَمَن	ماذا	يَيْتَم	يَنام

c. Writing

	Printed	Written
a.	م	م
b.	ـم	ـم
c.	مـ	مـ
d.	ـمـ	ـمـ

Note that the shapes joined to preceding letter are joined from above, thus: بم bam, بتم بما. Drill 12. In writing supplement.

6. ُ u and 7 و uu

a. Pronunciation

The short vowel ُ u is pronounced roughly like the vowel of put, and the long vowel uu like the vowel of moon. As in the case of َ a and ا aa, the long vowel is about twice as long in duration as the short. In the following drill, note particularly that stress falls on the syllable containing a long vowel.

Drill 13. On tape. Repetition. Contrast between u and uu.

بُ   بو   دُبُرْ   دُبور

مُنْ   مونْ   سُرُر   سُرور

تُنْ   تونْ   يُمُت   يَموت

مُتْ   موتْ   دُب   د وب

ذُبْ   ذ وبْ   دُفُن   دُفون

At the end of a word, the short vowel u and the long vowel uu are not distinguished in pronunciation, except in extremely precise speech: They are both pronounced with the vowel of moon, but shorter.

Drill 14. On tape. Listening. Contrast final u/uu.

ذُدُ   ذُدو

يَموتُ   يَموتو

ذادُ   ذادو

نارُ   نارو

نادُ   نادو

بابُ   بابو

دابُ   دابو

نُبُ   نُبو

يَذوبُ   يَذوبو

6.b. Reading

The short vowel u (as in put) is represented by the sign ُ written above the consonant letter, as in

دُمْتُ	dumtu

The Arabic name for this sign is ضَمّة damma.

Drill 15. Read:

دُنْيا ، يَذُمْ ، ذُبابُ ، مُنْذُ ، دُمْتُمْ ، يَمْدُدْ ، مُدامُ ، نُباتُ

بُدْ ، يَدُمْ ، يُذابُ ، دُب ، مُنْيا ، مُفْتا بُنْيانُ

c. Writing

Printed	بُ
Written	بُ

Drill 16. In writing supplement.

7.b. Reading

The long vowel uu (as in moon) is represented by the letter

و

This is the same letter that represents the consonant w (see previous lesson). If و follows ُ , it represents uu, as in

دُود	duud

Otherwise, it represents w, as in

دَوْد	dawd
نَدْوَ	nadwa
واو	waaw

In voweled texts, it is customary to omit the ْ before و uu, thus:

دود	duud
دَوْد	dawd

Drill 17. Read the following:

a. و = uu   يَدومُ ، مُنْبوذ ، فوتو ، توما ن ، مَمْنونُ ، نوران ، توت ، يانوت

b. و = uu or w   نَوْمُ ، يَذوبُ ، مَوْتُ ، ذَوَبانُ ، مُنونُ ، يَوْمُ ، تَوْمانُ ، نون ، فَتْوَ

8. Double Consonants: shadda ّ

a. Pronunciation

Double consonants. Any Arabic consonant can be doubled, that is, prolonged in its pronunciation. For example:

دَنَتْ	danat	'it approached'
دَنَّتْ	dannat	'it buzzed'

English has double consonants (we are speaking here of sounds, not letters) only in two-word combinations, in some compound words, and in some words with certain prefixes, for example:

hot time (contrast with "high time")
book-case (contrast with "bookish)
unnatural (contrast with "a natural")

Arabic, on the other hand, has double consonants in a very great number of words of all types. In many cases, as in the Arabic example shown above, it is only the single versus the double consonant which distinguishes two words of quite different meaning; therefore it is very important to learn to recognize and pronounce double consonants correctly.

Drill 18. On tape. Repetition. Contrast C/CC

فَنّان	فَنان	مَنَّتْ	مَنَتْ
مَدّاد	مَداد	نَمَّتْ	نَمَتْ
تَنّين	تَنين	نَتَّفَ	نَتَفَ
بَدَّد	بَدَد	فَتَّنَ	فَتَنَ
		بَيَّمْ	نَيَمْ

b. Reading

A double consonant is indicated by the sign ّ, written above the consonant letter, for example:

وّد	<u>wadda</u>
فنّان	<u>fannaan</u>

The Arabic name of this sign is شَدّة <u>shadda</u>. Note that the vowel signs <u>َ a</u> and <u>ُ u</u> are written over the sign <u>ّ</u>, as in

يَمُدَّ	<u>yamudda</u>
يَمُدُّ	<u>yamuddu</u>

<u>Drill 19</u>. Read.

وَدَّ ، دَبَّ ، تَمَّ ، مَوَّنَ ، نَتَّفَ ، فَنّانْ ، تامَّ ، ذمَّ

تَتَمَّ ، نَمَتَ ، بَذَّ ، نَيَّمَ ، وَفَّتَ ، بَوّابُ ، تَيّانُ

c. <u>Writing</u>

Printed	ودّ
Written	ودّ

<u>Drill 20</u>. In writing supplement

<u>Drill 21</u>. On tape. Dictation.

Lesson Three

الدرس الثالث

Consonants

1. ث th as in English thin

2. ر r as in Spanish pero

3. س s as in sad

4. ص ṣ (no English equivalent)

Vowels

5. ِ i as in pit

6. ي ii as in machine

1. ث θ

a. Pronunciation

ث is pronounced exactly like th in English three, thin, think, ether, path, etc. It is a consonant entirely distinct from ð ذ (th in this) presented in Lesson Two. Compare

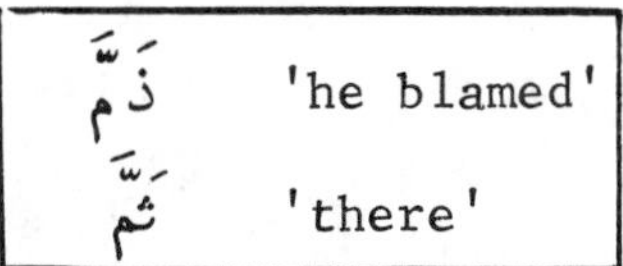

ذَمَّ	'he blamed'
ثَمَّ	'there'

Drill 1. On tape. Repetition. Contrast ث / ذ

ث : ثان ↓ ثَوْب ↓ باثا ↓ بَثاث ↓ فَثَّ ↓

ذ : ذان ذَوْب باذا بَذاذ فَذَّ

b. Reading

The letter that represents the sound th as in thin is

ث

The phonetic symbol used to transcribe it in this book is θ (Greek theta). The Arabic name of the letter is ثاء θaaʔ. It has the following shapes:

Position	Shape	Examples	
a. Independent	ث	باث	baaθ
b. Joined to preceding letter only	ـث	بَثَّ	baθθa
c. Joined to following letter only	ثـ	وَثَبَ	waθaba
d. Joined on both sides	ـثـ	فَثَبَتَ	faθabata

The shapes are identical to those of ب and ت except that it has three dots above.

Drill 2. The first four columns below correspond to the various shapes in the chart above; Column e. combines all shapes. Read the following:

e	d	c	b	a
بَثُوثْ	بَثَتَ	ثان	بَثّ	ماث
نَمَثْ	تَثَبُ	ثَبَتَ	مَثّ	واث
ثَمودَ	بُثَنْ	ثَمَنَ	نَمَثّ	بَدَثْ
بَثَيْثَ	تَثاوَبَ	ثَوْم	فَثّ	دوث
باث	نَثوبُ	وَثَنْ	تُثّ	رَوْث
مَبْثوث	مَثْدَ	ثُمّ	مَبَثّ	فَدَثْ

c. Writing

Printed	ث
Written	ث

Exactly like ب except that it has three dots above. Note that the three dots printed are ∴ while they are written ^ . Drill 3. In writing supplement.

2. ر r

a. Pronunciation

ر r is quite unlike English r, which is more vowel than consonant. English r is the vowel u in but pronounced with the tip of the tongue turned back and with rounded lips as in red rat. Some children fail to turn their tongue tip back, producing w instead of r: wed wat. Arabic ر r, on the other hand, is a consonant: It is a tongue-flap like r in Spanish or Italian caro 'dear'. Arabic ر r is produced by tapping the tip of the tongue once quickly behind the upper teeth. While English r is not a flapped consonant, this sound is found in English: English t between vowels, as in waiting, bottom, Betty, later, etc., is normally pronounced as a tongue flap rather than a stop consonant (the way it is pronounced in tea or eat). Practice Arabic, by first practicing t (or tt) in English ought'a go, lotta water, I gotta go, etc., and then use that pronunciation of t for Arabic ر.

Drill 4. On tape. Imitation: ر r

Arabic رّ rr is a trill: a rapid succession of many flaps. This does not exist in English at all, but is best compared with Spanish rr as in carro 'cart', perro 'dog'. After you have mastered the flap, practice making a number of them in quick succession, until you get a "feel" for the trill; then, hopefully, the trill will come with additional practice.

Drill 5. On tape. A. Repetition B. Imitation. Contrast ر / رّ

B.	A.		
مَرَّ	دَرَّبَ	—	دَرَبَ
بَرَّ	بَرَّدَ	—	بَرَدَ
فَرَّ	وَرَّمَ	—	وَرَمَ
وَرَّ	مَرَّنَ	—	مَرَنَ
ذَرَّ	فَرَّدَ	—	فَرَدَ

b. Reading

The letter that represents Arabic r is ر

The Arabic name is راء raa? . It has the following shapes:

Position	Shape	Examples
a. Independent	ر	ثارَ θaara
b. Joined to preceding letter only	ـر	بَرْدَ barda

Drill 6. The first two columns below correspond to the shapes in the chart above, while Column c. contains both shapes. Read the following:

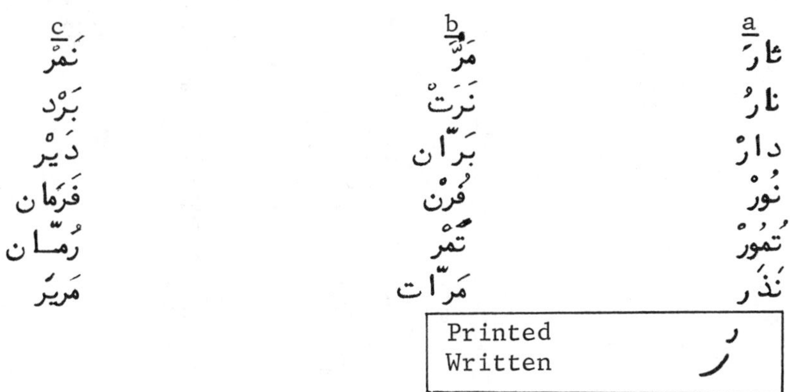

c. Writing

Note that ر begins above the line and extends below the line. Drill 7. In writing supplement.

3. س s

a. Pronunciation

Arabic س s corresponds to English s as in sad, sack, see. (Arabic س is dental--pronounced with the tongue tip at the upper teeth--, while English s is alveolar--pronounced slightly behind the teeth--giving a slightly lower-pitched s.)

Drill 8. On tape. Repetition. Contrast سّ / س

a.	b.
بَسَتَ	بَسَّتَ
ماسَ	ماسَّ
نَسَمَ	نَسَّمَ
نَسَبَ	نَسَّبَ
مَساس	مَسّاس

3.b. Reading

The letter that represents the s as in see is

س

The Arabic name is سين siin. It has the following shapes:

Position	Shape	Examples
a. Independent	س	باسَ baasa
b. Joined to preceding letter only	ـس	مَسَّ massa
c. Joined to following letter only	سـ	سَمَنَ samana
d. Joined on both sides	ـسـ	بَسَمَ basama

Drill 9. Read:

e	d	c	b	a
سَبَّ	بَسَمَ	سادَ	مَسَّ	باس
سام	يَسُود	سُبَّر	بَسُّ	راس
روس	فَسْرَ	سُفُن	يَمَسُّ	ناس
نَبَسَ	فَساد	سُرور	تَبَسُّ	فَرَس
فَرَسَ	تَسَمَّرَ	سافَرَ	نَبُسُّ	دَرْس
سَفَرَ	بَسّام	سَيّار	يَنْمَسّ	مُدَرِّس
نافَسَ	مَسْوَدّ	سَدَّ	نَسَّ	دُروس

c. Writing

	Printed	Written
a.	س	س
b.	ـس	ـس
c.	سـ	سـ
d.	ـسـ	ـسـ

Note that shapes a. and b. are joined above the line, while c. and d. are joined on the line: بَسْ bas but بَسَرَ basara. Drill 10. In writing supplement.

4. ص ṣ

a. Pronunciation

Arabic ص ṣ is a velarized alveolar s. It is alveolar, which means that it is produced not at the teeth, like س, but further back in the mouth. It is velarized, which means that the back part of the tongue is made tense (with some raising up toward the soft palate or velum), giving the s-sound a velar effect. Thus, ص sounds quite different from س.

Drill 11. Identification drill. Teacher says ssss and ṣṣṣṣ a couple of times while class listens. Then he produces one of them, and the class identifies it as Column A or Column B.

A	B
سّ sss	صّ ṣṣṣ

Drill 12. Production drill: ص/س in isolation. (Class as whole, then individual students pronounce س and ص in isolation.)

The different effect of plain consonants, e.g., س ,and velarized consonants, e.g., ص, is quite striking. Notice how the quality of the long vowel ا aa changes in a word with ص .

Drill 13. On tape. Repetition. Contrast س / ص

A	B
سام	صام
ساد	صاد
سان	صان
ساس	صاص
ساب	صاب
ساذ	صاذ
سار	صار
ساث	صاث

Note that the vowel ا aa has two pronunciations: like the vowel a in English sad, sand, sag after س and, after ص, like the vowel o in English sod, sob or the aw in saw. The a of sad is produced further front in the mouth as compared to the o of sod, just as س is produced further front in the mouth than ص . The American hears the s in sass and the s in sauce as the same, but hears the vowels in those two words as completely different. The Arab, on the contrary, hears the vowels in those two words as variations of a single vowel, namely ا aa, but hears the two s's as completely different. He would write the English word sass as ساس and the word sauce as صاص .

Velarized consonants (of which there are four: ص ṣ ض ḍ ط ṭ ظ ẓ) affect all vowels in this way, causing them to be pronounced more back in the mouth. The vowel َ a when next to velarized consonants is pronounced like o in English hot, cot, but is always short in duration.

Drill 14. On tape. Repetition. Contrast س / ص

B.	A.
صَبَرَ	سَبَرَ
صَمَنَ	سَمَنَ
صَذَمَ	سَذَمَ
مَرَصَ	مَرَسَ
نَصَّ	نَسَّ
بَرَصَ	بَرَسَ

سَيْد	صَيْد
سَيْف	صَيْف
سَوْن	صَوْن
مَسّ	مَصّ

The vowels و uu and ُ u, being already back, are not made any backer by velarized consonants. However, the quality of tenseness that is found in velarized consonants is also evident in the vowels.

Drill 15. On tape. Repetition. Contrast س / ص

A.	B.
سُور	صور
سون	صون
سود	صود
سوب	صوب
سوم	صوم
سين	صين
سير	صير
سيس	صيص
سيف	صيف
سيد	صيد

Thus, there are two important points about س and ص : (1) They are pronounced differently and (2) they markedly affect the quality of adjacent vowels. You must master the pronunciation of the two s's; but, at least as important, you must produce the proper vowels when you speak and react to the vowels when you listen. In all likelihood, the Arab will be at least as much influenced by your vowels as he will be by your consonants.

b. Reading

The letter that represents Arabic ṣ is

ص

The Arabic name is صاد ṣaad. It has the following shapes:

Position	Shape	Examples	
a. Independent	ص	بَرَص	baraṣ
b. Joined to preceding letter only	ـص	نَصُّ	naṣṣu
c. Joined to following letter only	صـ	صاد	ṣaad
d. Joined on both sides	ـصـ	بَصَر	baṣar

Drill 16.

e	d	c	b	a
نُصوص	مَصَرَ	صَفَّ	نَصَّ	بَرَص
مَصُون	بَصَم	صُفوف	يَنُصُّ	باص
صُفْر	نُصُب	صارَ	رَبَص	ماصّ
وَصْوَص	نَصَف	صَبَر	بَصَّ	بوص
صَنَم	تَصُبُّ	صَدْر	نَمُصُّ	نوص
صَوْت	مُصَوَّر	صادر	فَصَّ	فُرَص
صَرَف	فَصَم	صَوْت	مَصَّ	باصّ
باصات	مَصْدور	صَمَد	نَبَص	مَرْص

c. Writing

	Printed	Written
a.	ص	ص
b.	ـص	ـص
c.	صـ	صـ
d.	ـصـ	ـصـ

When joined to following letter (c. and d.) ص has a little kink in the line before the following letter is begun; it is joined to a preceding letter by a line coming from under it. Drill 17. In writing supplement.

5. ـِ i

a. Pronunciation

The vowel ـِ i corresponds to the vowel i in English bit; it is always short in duration. Arabic i, unlike English i, never becomes like u in but. English i, when unstressed, tends to be pronounced like u in but. For example, i in deistic, where is is stressed, is pronounced like i in mist, while i in deist, where de is stressed, is pronounced like u in bust. If this habit is carried over into Arabic confusion may result. For example, the following two words are differentiated only by the final vowel:

مُدَرِّس mudárris 'teacher'

مُدَرَّس mudárras 'taught'

The American student must be on his guard not to substitute a for unstressed i, lest he be misunderstood. Arabic ـِ i when adjacent to a velarized consonant is also backed in pronunciation, sounding something like the e in English nurses.

Drill 18. On tape. Repetition. Contrast س / ص

6. Arabic ي ii corresponds to the i in English machine or the ea in bead; it is twice as long as ـِ i in duration. Following a velarized consonant there is a short transition vowel (like u in but) between the consonant and the vowel.

Drill 19. On tape. Repetition. Contrast س / ص

B.	A.
سينْ	سِنْ
صين	صِنْ
تين	تِنْ
مين	مِنْ
دين	دِنْ
فين	فِنْ

Long يِii and short ـِ i are both pronounced alike as the last sound of a word: the vowel quality of ee in beet, but short.

Drill 20. On tape. Listening. Final i and ii.

دَرْبي /دَرْبِ ، سيرى/سيرِ ، بَيْتي/ بَيْتِ ، بابي/بابِ ، مُرِّى/مُرِّ ، فَمي/فَمِ ، بَدَني/بَدَنِ ، نَصّي/نَصِّ

b. Reading

The short vowel i is represented in the Arabic writing system by a special sign, placed under a consonant letter as in

مِنْ	min

The Arabic name of this sign is كسرة kasra. If the consonant letter has shadda ـّ, kasra may be written either under the letter or under kasra:

دَرِّسْ ، دَرِّسْ darris

In this book kasra is written under shadda.

Drill 21. Read:

مِنْ ، مَرِّسَ ، ذَنَبِ ، سَيِّد ، سَمِنَ ، نَفِسَ ، بارِد ، سِرْ ، صِر
فَسِّرْ ، مُدَرِّس ، بِنْتُ ، ثابِتُ ، بَدَوِيّ ، دَسِمَ ، نَتِنَ ، نادِر ، نُصِّبَ ، نِمْرُ

The long vowel ii is represented in the Arabic writing system by kasra followed by the letter ي :

فِي	fii
سِين	siin

The writing of kasra before and sukuun over ي when it has this value of ii is usually omitted: سِيْن or سين siin.

Drill 22. Read: سين ، سَمين ، بَريد ، بيبان ، رَصِدَ ، مَديد ، فَريد
تِنّين ، تَمْرين ، مَدين ، مُدير ، سَرير ، نَديم ، بَدين ، رَبيب ، تَدْبير ،
صين ، رَنين ، تين ، سَمير

c. Writing

Printed	ب
Written	ب

Drill 23. In writing supplement.
Drill 24. On tape. Dictation.

Lesson Four — الدرس الرابع

Consonants

1. ز z as in zeal

2. ش š as in shake

3. ل l as in leaf

4. ط ṭ (no English equivalent)

5. Nunation: ٌ -un

   ٍ -in

   ً -an

1. ز z

a. Pronunciation

The consonant ز z is a voiced sibilant. It is pronounced like the z in English zeal, gazelle, Liz.

b. Reading

The letter which represents the sound z (as in zeal) is

ز

This letter is called زاى zaay. It is a non-connector, and is exactly like ر r except that it has a dot over it. Its shapes are as follows:

Position	Shape	Examples
a. Independent	ز	زادَ zaada وَزَنَ wazana
b. Joined to preceding letter only	ـز	بَزَرَ bazara فَزَّ fazza

Drill 1. Columns a and b below illustrate each of the two shapes; Column c includes both. Read:

c	b	a
زَيْت	يَزورُ	زادَ
مَــزَّ	نَزيدُ	زارَ
بَزّون	مَــزَّ	وَزير
وَزَرَ	رَمْــز	فَوْزٌ
نِزار	فَزّان	فازَ

c. Writing

Printed Written	ز

ز z is written exactly like ر r (see 3.2) with the addition of the dot. Both are non-connectors.

Drill 2. In writing supplement.

2. ش š

a. Pronunciation

The consonant ش š is pronounced like the sh in English shape, bishop, rush.

b. Reading

The letter which represents the sound š (as in shake) is

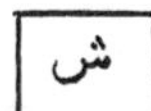

The Arabic name of this letter is شين šiin. It has the following shapes:

Position	Shape	Examples	
a. Independent	ش	ناوَش	naawaša
b. Joined to preceding letter only	ـش	دَبَش	dabaš
c. Joined to following letter only	شـ	شَباب	šabaab
d. Joined on both sides	ـشـ	نَشَرَ	našara

Drill 3. Columns a to d below illustrate the four shapes shown above; Column e includes them all. Read:

e	d	c	b	a
شاويش	بَشير	شاى	دَبَش	ناوَش
بَشَّر	بَشَّر	رَشيد	شاويش	فاش
رَشّ	نَشَرَ	شَباب	رَمَش	فَرَش
رَفَش	يَشْرَب	شَرِب	ريش	فِراش
بَشَّر	فَشَر	شَريف	نابِش	راشّ

c. Writing

		Variant
Printed Written	ش	

ش š is written like س s (see 3.3), with the addition of the three dots, which are written in a single movement as a small curved tent-like figure: ش . This figure is added only after the completion of the word, or of the next non-connector, if any.

Variant Shapes. The full shapes (a. and b.) may also be written without the three dots ^ but with a downward slanting stroke at the end instead:

Drill 4. In writing supplement.

3. ل l

a. Pronunciation

The Arabic sound ل l is like the English l, but there is an important difference. Most speakers of American English pronounce their l's with the back of the tongue raised somewhat toward the velum--resulting in a velarized l, very much in the same way as Arabic ص s is a velarized s. This velarized quality of the English l is especially noticeable at the end of a word, for example in feel or bell; it is less noticeable, though still present in varying degrees, at the beginning of a word, for example in leaf. In Arabic the velarized l is found in the word for "God" أَللّٰهُ ʔallaah and a few others. Elsewhere, however, the Arabic l has a non-velarized or "clear" sound. The clear l results when the back of the tongue is relaxed and not raised. In the following drill you will hear a series of English words containing l, each followed by a similar Arabic word or syllable with the Arabic clear l. Listen to the difference in quality in the two types of l.

Drill 5. Contrast between English and Arabic l. Listen.

فيل	feel
ديل	deal
ميل	meal
بَل	bell
تَل	tell
سَل	Sal
بَلِي	belly
نلي	Nelly
مَلَن	melon
فَلَن	felon
لِيف	leaf
لِين	lean
لَف	laugh
لِفْت	lift
لَمْ	lamb

Drill 6. On tape. Imitation. Arabic words with ل

لَفَتَ   بَلَهْ   يُفْلِسُ   يَلْبَسُ   دَلَّ   فيلْ

لِيبِيا   سَليم   مُسْلِمْ   يَلْبَثُ   سَلَّالْ   نالْ

لامَ   سَلام   يُفْلِتُ   يَلْزَمُ   فُلّ   مالْ

مِيلْ	ذَلَّ	فَلْفَلَ	يَتْلُونَ	بِلادْ	لَبِسَ
رَسولْ	مَلَّ	زَلْزَلَ	يَتْلو	وَلَدْ	لَكِنَّ
دُوَلْ					

b. Reading

The letter which represents the sound l is

ل

The Arabic name of this letter is لام laam. It has the following shapes:

Position	Shape	Examples
a. Independent	ل	مال maal
b. Joined to preceding letter only	ـل	فَتيل fatiil
c. Joined to following letter only	لـ	لَبِسَ labisa دَلَّسَ dallasa
d. Joined on both sides	ـلـ	بَلَد balad

Note that ل followed by ا takes the special shape لا . When joined to a preceding letter, it is connected by a vertical line rising from the line, e.g., بِلا bilaa.

Drill 7. Columns a to d below illustrate the four shapes shown in a to d above; Column e includes them all.

e	d	c	b	a
دَلال	بَلَد	لَن	ميل	مال
مُسْلِم	بلاد	لَذيذ	فيل	دُوَل
ليبيا	سَلام	لُبنان	نيل	نالَ
بَرميل	سَليم	لولو	رُسُل	فول
فِلْفِل	فِلْم	وَلَد	نِلْنَ	رَسول

c. Writing

Printed	ل
Written	ل

(1) Independent form. The bottom curve is rounded and may extend somewhat below the line.

(2) Joined to preceding letter only. The preceding letter is joined to ل just above the curve; the pen moves upward and then retraces its path downward and into the curve.

(3) Joined to following letter only. The pen starts at the top and moves downward.

(4) <u>Joined on both sides</u>. The pen moves from the preceding letter upward, and then retraces its path downward and into the following letter.

<u>Drill 8</u>. In writing supplement.

4. ط ṭ

a. <u>Pronunciation</u>

The consonant ط ṭ is a voiceless alveolar stop. Like ص ṣ, it is a velarized sound, and it differs from the plain ت t in several important ways: (1) For ت t (a dental stop) the tip of the tongue touches the back of the upper teeth; while for ط ṭ (an alveolar stop) a larger area of the front upper surface of the tongue makes contact with the alveolar region (the gum ridge behind the upper teeth). (2) The ت t, like English t, is often aspirated (that is, it is produced with a slight puff of breath); while ط ṭ is not aspirated. (3) Finally, ت t is a plain (non-velarized) sound, the back of the tongue remaining relaxed and low in the mouth; while ط ṭ is velarized: the tongue is tense, and the back part is raised toward the velum. Like all velarized consonants, ط ṭ affects the quality of adjacent vowels (see 3.4). In the following drill you will hear an Arabic word containing ت t, and then a similar word containing ط ṭ. Listen carefully, and repeat each word, imitating as closely as you can both the different consonants and the vowel qualities accompanying each.

<u>Drill 9</u>. On tape. Repetition. Contrast ت / ط

تاب	طاب
بَتَرْ	بَطَرْ
رَبَتَ	رَبَطَ
تَلَّ	طَلَّ
بَتَّ	بَطَّ

<u>Drill 10</u>. On tape. Imitation. Additional examples of ṭ

طالِب	طَبيب	وَطَنْ	رَبَطَ
قَطّ	بَطَرْ	طَمَسَ	طَويل
رَطْل	تَسَلَّطَ	وَسَطْ	طَنْطا

b. <u>Reading</u>

The letter which represents the sound ṭ is

ط

The Arabic name of this letter is طاء ṭaaʔ. It has basically the same shapes in all positions:

Position	Shape	Examples	
a. Independent	ط	شُباط	ṣubaaṭ
b. Joined to preceding letter only	ـط	نَفْط	nafṭ

Position	Shape	Examples
c. Joined to following letter only	ط	طالِب ṭaalib وَطَن waṭan
d. Joined on both sides	ـطـ	يَطِيرُ yaṭiiru

Drill 11. Each of the columns a to d below illustrates one of the four shapes shown in a to d above; Column e includes them all.

e	d	c	b	a
طَمَر	يَطِيرُ	طالِب	نَفْط	شُباط
ناطَ	قَطَن	طَبيب	رَبَطَ	بَلاط
قَطَف	مَطَر	طَمَسَ	بَطّ	سَوط
نَمَط	سُلْطان	رَطْل	بَطْ	قَناط
طين	لَطَمَ	رَطَن	مَلَطَ	سِراط

c. Writing

Printed:	ط
Written:	

(1) Independent form. Begin the loop at the lower left, move up and to the right, then down and back around to the left. Next, add the vertical stroke, beginning at the top; the bottom of this stroke should not quite touch the loop.

(2) Joined to preceding letter only. Move into the loop from the preceding letter and then move up and to the right as in (1) above; in moving down and back keep the body of the loop above the original connecting line. Then add the vertical stroke, as above.

(3) Joined to following letter only. Printed: طـ Written:
Make the loop as in (1) above, but continue immediately into the following letter. Add the vertical stroke only after completing the word, or after the next non-connector, if any.

(4) Joined on both sides. Printed: ـطـ Written:
Move into the loop from the preceding letter as in (2) above, but continue immediately into the following letter. Add the vertical stroke only after completing the word, or after the next non-connector, if any.

Drill 12. In writing supplement

5. Nunation

Many Arabic nouns and adjectives have inflectional endings -un, -in, and -an, in which the three different vowels indicate different cases, and the -n indicates indefiniteness (usually indicated in English by the indefinite article "a, an"). For example:

Nominative case:	darsun	'a lesson'
Genitive case:	darsin	
Accusative case:	darsan	

The use of -n as an ending indicating indefiniteness is called nunation. The -n of nunation is written in a special way: by writing the preceding vowel sign twice. Following are details for each of the three vowels:

a. The ending -un may be written with two ḍamma signs over the preceding consonant (see 2.7), one of them usually in a reversed position: ـُوٌ. More commonly, however, the doubling is represented by a single ḍamma with an additional short downward stroke: ـٌ. Examples:

دَرْسٌ	darsun
طالِبٌ	ṭaalibun
وَلَدٌ	waladun

b. The ending -in is written with two kasra signs (3.5) under the preceding consonant: ـٍ. Examples:

دَرْسٍ	darsin
طالِبٍ	ṭaalibin
وَلَدٍ	waladin

c. The ending -an is written with two fatḥa signs over the preceding consonant (see 1.6); and the two fatḥas are regularly followed by an ʔalif ا , written as the last letter of the word. This ʔalif is a spelling convention associated specifically with the ending -an, and does not indicate a long vowel. The preceding letter is joined to it or not, according to the usual rules. Examples:

دَرْسًا	darsan
طالِبًا	ṭaaliban
وَلَدًا	waladan

In unvowelled text the nunation signs, like the short vowel signs, are usually not written; but the ʔalif which accompanies the ending -an remains:

درس	darsun
درس	darsin
درسا	darsan

Drill 13. Read.

شَمْسٌ ، زَيْتٌ ، بَدَوِيًّا ، طَوِيلٍ ، مَكْتَبٍ ، صَفًّا ، شامِلٌ ، بَلَدًا

وادٍ ، فِلْمًا ، سَفَرٌ ، ثانٍ ، مُراسِلًا

Drill 14. On tape. Dictation.

Consonants

1. ك k as in kind

2. ق q (no English equivalent)

3. ج j as in judge

4. خ x like ch in German Nacht

5. أ ʔ (glottal stop: see below)

6. Pause

1. ك k

a. Pronunciation

Arabic ك k is like English k in kind, key, cook.

Drill 1. Production

شِلَكٌ	مَكَّثَ	مَكَثَ
شِكَاكٌ	سَكَّرَ	سَكْرَانٌ
رَكِيكٌ	سُكَّرٌ	كَرِيمٌ
شِيَكٌ	سِكِّيرٌ	كَمَا
مَلَاكٌ	شُكِلَ	كَامِلٌ
سُلُوكٌ	فَكَّرَ	مَكْرَمٌ

b. Reading

The letter that represents the consonant k as in kind is

ك

The Arabic name of this letter is كاف kaaf; it has the following shapes:

Position	Shape	Examples
a. Independent	ك	يَدُكَ yaduka
b. Joined to preceding letter only	ـك	مَلِكٌ malikun
c. Joined to following letter only	كـ	كَرِيمٌ kariimun ماكِنٌ maakinun
d. Joined on both sides	ـكـ	سِكَكٌ sikakun

ك has a special shape when joined to a following ل , or another ك :

كُل	kul
كا	kaa
كِك	kik

Note that ک joins ا and ك at the line, كا, كك, but joins ل above the line. كل

Drill 2. Read:

كانَتْ وَتَكونُ ، كُنَّ ، ساكِمٌ ، مَمْلوكٌ ، كَنَدا ، أُمْريكا ، مَكْتَبٌ ، كِتابٌ ، كَتَبَ ، سُكّان

c. Writing

Printed	ك
Written	ك

(1) Independent form:
ك rests on the line, with the horizontal base line fairly flat.

(2) Joined to preceding letter:
The preceding letter is joined to ك at its base.

(3) Joined to following letter:
This is like the corresponding form of ل with the addition of the stroke at top, which is added after the following connected letters are completed.

(4) Joined on both sides:
Same as (3) above, but joined at base to preceding letter. If the following letter is ر it is joined as follows: شكر ، بكر

Drill 3. In writing supplement.

2. ق q

a. Pronunciation

ق is a voiceless uvular stop; it is produced by making contact between the back of the tongue and the uvula (the tip of the soft palate, projecting into the pharynx). It differs from ك in the following ways: (1) ك , like English k, is aspirated, while ق is not. (Aspiration is a puff of air given off with the t in take, p in pay, and c in cool.) (2) ك and English k are pronounced further forward in the mouth after front vowels (e.g., ee in keep, a in candy) and further back after back vowels (e.g., au in caught, oo in cook). ق , on the other hand, is always uvular. (3) ق , like the velarized consonants, goes with the back pronunciation of vowels, while ك goes with the front ones: كاد is pronounced with the vowel of cad while قاد is pronounced with the vowel of cod. In practicing the pronunciation of ق , say, for example, caught, cod, called but using the deepest part of the tongue you can in pronouncing the k sound.

Drill 4. On tape. Repetition. Contrast ك / ق

b.	a.
قاد	كاد
قاق	كاف
قاس	كاس
قيس	كيس
يَقْبُرُ	يَكْبُرُ

b.	a.
تَقْرير	تَكْرير
مَساق	مَساك
سَلَق	سَلَك
شَقّ	شَكّ
دَقّ	دَكّ

b. Reading

The letter that represents the sound q is

ق

The Arabic name of the letter is قاف qaaf. It has the following shapes:

	Position	Shape	Examples	
a.	Independent	ق	شَرْق	šarq
b.	Joined to preceding letter only	ـق	صَديق	ṣadiiq
c.	Joined to following letter only	قـ	قاف	qaaf
			فُنْدُق	funduq
d.	Joined on both sides	ـقـ	تَقَدُّم	taqaddum

Drill 5. Read:

قاف ، شَرْق ، صَديق ، فُنْدُق ، تَقَدُّم ، قادِر ، قادَت ، دَقيق ، قَصْر ، قُصور

c. Writing

Printed	ق
Written	ق

Independent shape. ق differs from ف in shape in that it is more rounded, while ف is flatter.
Variant Shape. The first two shapes are often written without the two dots but with a tail added to compensate for their absence: ـق ، ق

Drill 6. In writing supplement.

3. ج

a. Pronunciation

The letter ج represents a variety of pronunciations over the Arab world, all of which are found in English. In Cairo and Alexandria it is pronounced like g in gold (sometimes like j in judge); in North Africa and the Levant it is pronounced like s in English pleasure; and in the rest of the Arab world, like j in English judge. Your choice of pronunciation should depend upon the pronunciation of your teacher. The choice is not crucial to anything, since it is always easy to change if you decide to do so.

In this book we assume the pronunciation of ج as j in judge.

b. Reading

The Arabic name of the letter

ج

is جيم jiim; ج has the following shapes:

Position	Shape	Examples
a. Independent	ج	تاج taaj
b. Joined to preceding letter only	ـج	ناتج naatij
c. Joined to following letter only	جـ	جميل jamiil دجاج dajaaj
d. Joined on both sides	ـجـ	نجيب najiib

Drill 7. Read:

تاجٌ ، جَميلٌ ، نَجيبٍ ، جُمَلٌ ، جِدًّا ، وَجَدَ ، جَمالُ ، راجٍ ، جَديدٌ ، تَجْديدٍ

c. Writing

Printed	ج
Written	ج

(1) Independent shape.
The characteristic part جـ is written above the line, while the "tail" is below.

(2) Joined to preceding letter only.
The characteristic part is open rather than a closed circle. The preceding letter is joined from above rather than at the line: مج mj, لج lj, كج kj, etc. Letters of the ب class have these special shapes before ج or ج for example, بج or نج ، يج or تج ، ثج or بج.

(3) Joined to following letter only. جـ The letter characteristic is joined to the following letter, e.g., جا jaa.

(4) Joined on both sides. ـجـ Note that this shape is open on both sides. Preceding letter is joined from above, e.g., بجا bajaa.

Drill 8. In writing supplement.

4. خ x

a. Pronunciation

خ x is not a modern English sound. It does occur in many other languages, such as ch in German Nacht, x in Russian xorošó, etc. It is a voiceless velar fricative: It is produced by narrowing the passageway between the back of the tongue and the velum, so creating friction as the air passes through; the vocal cords are at rest. Try to produce خx using the very back of the tongue to partially cut off the air stream as you exhale. خx differs from ك x in that the latter completely stops the air stream in its passage from lungs to mouth, then releases it. خ x almost blocks it off, but not quite, giving its fricative effect. Practice by saying aka, ak-ka, ax-xa--that is, make the complete closure for ك k after the vowel a, then relax the tongue enough to let air through; خx should result.

Drill 9. On tape. Repetition. Contrast ك / خ

خ x	ك k
خال	كال
خَدّ	كَدّ
خاف	كاف
بَخا	بَكا
بَخَرَ	بَكَرَ
بَخَّرَ	بَكَّرَ
بَخَّلَ	نَكَّلَ
مُبَخِّر	مُبَكِّر
شاخ	شاك
شيخ	شيك

b. Reading

The letter that represents the sound x is

خ

The Arabic name of the letter is خاء xaa?. It is exactly like the letter ح in all its shapes, except that it is characterized by one dot above rather than one dot below. It has the following shapes:

Position	Shape	Examples	
a. Independent	خ	مَناخ	manaax
b. Joined to preceding letter only	ـخ	تاريخ	taariix
c. Joined to following letter only	خـ	خامِس	xaamis
		فاخِر	faaxir
d. Joined on both sides	ـخـ	بِخَيْرٍ	bixayrin

Drill 10. Columns a, b, c, d, below correspond to a, b, c, d, in the chart above; e combines all four. Read the following:

e	d	c	b	a
راسِخ	فاخِر	خامِس	تاريخ	مَناخ
خادِم	ساخِر	خال	وَسَخ	صُراخ
باخ	رَخيم	خَرَجَ	مَلَخ	شَرْخ
ماخِر	زاخِر	خام	لَطَخ	فَرْخ

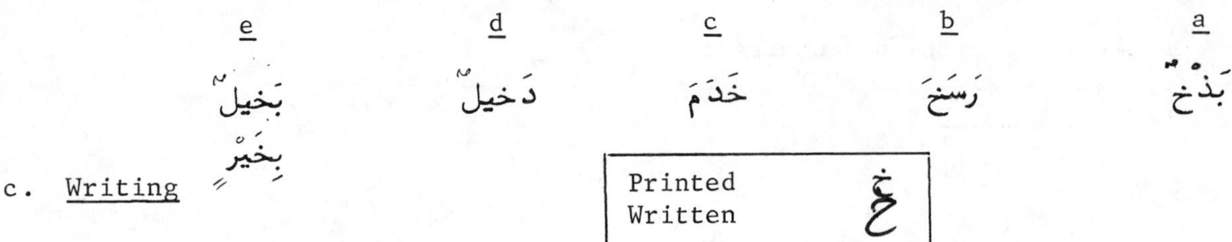

c. Writing

Printed	غ
Written	غ

The letter غ has the same shapes as ع , with the difference in the dots.

Drill 11. In writing supplement.

5. ا ʔ

Glottal stop ʔ is a consonant sound heard in English, German and other European languages, but not represented in the spelling. It is produced by blocking off the air stream at the top of the windpipe, and then releasing it. This is what happens when you take a deep breath, hold it, and then release it. It occurs as the "catch in the throat" in English expressions such as "uh-oh!" It is also used in English to clarify syllable division, as in "I didn't say 'some mice' I said ' some ice'," where ice is preceded by glottal stop. It is also used this way in German, as in vereinigte, where glottal stop separate ver- and -ei-, as opposed to verein, where the syllables are ve and rein. Practice glottal stop by saying a series of vowels, e.g. ah, with a clear break between them; there should be a glottal stop at each break.

English words beginning with vowels are often pronounced with glottal stop, but we are conditioned to it and do not hear it. In Arabic, every word beginning with a vowel is pronounced with initial glottal stop. As a matter of fact, no syllable in Arabic can begin with a vowel; every syllable begins with some consonant or other, including glottal stop. In the following drill, listen for the glottal stops at the beginning of each word.

Drill 12. On tape. Imitation. أ

أَنا ، أَنْتَ ، أَنْتِ ، أَيْنَ ، أَساسِيّ ، أَلْخامِس ، أَوَّل ، أُسْتاذ ، أَمْريكا

أَجْنَبِيّ ، أُمّ ، أُخْرى ، أَكْمِل

b. Reading

Glottal stop is not represented by a letter, but by the sign

ء

The Arabic name of this sign is هَمْزَة hamza. Hamza is sometimes written over or under certain letters, called "seats", or else aloof. In this lesson we take up the writing of hamza as the first sound of the word, and in the following lesson we deal with it in the other parts of the word.

At the beginning of the word, hamza is always written with ا as its seat; if the following vowel is ِ i, hamza is written under ا , thus: إ ʔi. Otherwise, hamza is written over its chair, thus: أَ ʔa and أُ ʔu.

أَ ʔa as in أَنْتَ ʔanta

أُ ʔu as in أُسْتاذ ʔustaað

إِ ʔi as in إِمْشِ ʔimshi

Drill 13. Read the following:

أَنا ، أَنْتَ ، أَنْتِ ، أَمْسِ ، أَخٌ ، أَيْنَ ، أُسْتاذٌ ، أَسْلَمُ ، أُخْتٌ ، أُدْرُسْ

أُرْسِلُ ، أُدْرِكُ ، إِلْزَمْ ، إِسْمٌ ، إِسْلامٌ ، إِنَّ ، إِنْتَخَبَ ، إِنْتاجٌ

c. Writing

Printed	ء
Written	ء

Hamza written aloof is ء . Hamza with ا as seat: أ and إ .

أَنا ، أُسْتاذٌ ، إِذْهَبْ ، أَنْتَ ، أُسِرَ ، أَبٌ ، أُخْتٌ ، أُديرُ ، بَدَأَ

أَدَبٌ ، أُسْتاذٌ ، أَخْبارُ

Drill 14. In writing supplement.

6. Pause

Arabic words can be pronounced in either of two ways: in their full form or in their pausal form. In the full pronunciation the word is pronounced in its entirety; for example, the full pronunciation of أَنتَ (or أَنتَ) is ʔanta. The pausal form is a shortened one, where a word-final short vowel is not pronounced; thus, the pausal form of أنتَ ʔanta is ʔant, and the pausal form of أَيْنَ ʔayna is ʔayn. If the vowel has nunation, that n is not pronounced either; for example, the pausal form of طالبٌ taalibun is taalib and the pausal form of طالبٍ taalibin is taalib. In case of accusative nunation, e.g. طالبًا taaliban, the pause form is spelled ا and has the value aa, e.g. طالبًا taalibaa.

The full form is used when the word in question is followed without interruption by another word, for example, أَنتَ in أَنتَ سامي 'you are Sami.' (ʔanta) The pausal form on the other hand is used when there is any kind of interruption or pause after the word in question; this of course includes full stop at the end of a sentence. Thus, أَنتَ is pronounced in its pausal form in the following sentences, where a dash -- is used to indicate an interruption in speech:

مَنْ أَنْتَ ؟ (ʔant) 'Who are you?'

أَنْتَ — سامي (ʔant) 'you--are Sami.'

Pronouns and verbs are marked for gender in Arabic; for example, أَنْتَ is 'you' speaking to a male while أَنتِ is the form used in speaking to a female. The pausal form of both of these is, technically speaking, ʔant. However, to avoid confusion, verbs and pronouns in the second person feminine singular always retain the final i in pause as well as in the full pronunciation. Thus, the pause and full forms of أَنْتِ are ʔanti 'you' (feminine singular).

Drill 15. Read the following sentences, paying careful attention to the pause and full pronunciation of أَنْتَ 'you'.

أَنْتَ سامي 'You are Sami.'

مَنْ أَنْتَ ؟ 'Who are you?'

أَنْتَ فريد 'You are Farid.'

مَنْ أَنْتَ ؟ 'Who are you?'

أَنْتَ سَليم	'You are Salim.'
مَنْ أَنْتَ ؟	'Who are you?'
أَنْتَ أَمين	'You are Amin.'
مَنْ أَنْتَ ؟	'Who are you?'
أَنْتِ نانسى	'You are Nancy.'
مَنْ أَنْتِ ؟	'Who are you?'

<u>Drill 16</u>. Read each of the following sentences twice: first, with no pauses or inter-interruptions, and secondly, with pauses at every dash. Use the pause and full forms as appropriate.

Example: أَنْتَ-سامى 'You are Sami.'

أَنْتَ — سامى <u>ʔ anta</u> <u>saamii</u>; <u>ʔant</u>--<u>saamii</u>

أَنْتَ — سَليم	'You are Salim.'
أَنْتَ — فَريد	'You are Farid.'
أَنْتَ — رَشيد	'You are Rashid.'
أَنْتَ — أَمين	'You are Amin.'
أَنْتَ — كَريم	'You are Karim.'
مِنْ أَيْنَ — أَنْتَ ؟	'Where are you from?' (speaking to a boy)
مِنْ أَيْنَ — أَنْتِ ؟	'Where are you from?' (speaking to a girl)
انا طالِبٌ — مِنْ بَيْروت	'I am a student from Beirut.'
انا طالِبٌ — مِنْ تُونِس	'I am a student from Tunisia.'
انا طالِبٌ — مِنْ فَرَنْسا	'I am a student from France.'
انا طالِبٌ — مِنْ لَنْدَن	'I am a student from London.'

<u>Drill 17</u>. On tape. Dictation.

Lesson Six — الدرس السادس

Consonants
1. ه h as in hat

2. ح ḥ (no English equivalent)

3. ء ʔ glottal stop in middle and end of word

4. Voweled and unvoweled texts

5. Writing of foreign words in Arabic script

1. ه h

a. Pronunciation

Arabic ه h is like English h in hot, hat, heat; it is a voiceless glottal fricative. Arabic ه h differs from English h in the following ways: (1) it is pronounced with more force than is English h; (2) it can be pronounced at the end of a syllable or word, while English h is pronounced only at the beginning of a syllable; and it may be doubled (held twice as long). Listen to the pronunciation of ه in the following drill, repeating each item.

Drill 1. On tape. Imitation.

c.	b.	a.
تَمَهَّل	نَسْهَر	هٰذا
بَهّار	شَهْر	هُنا
يُشَهِّى	شُهْرَة	هِىَ
جَهَّز	يَهْتَمّ	هُم
جَهِّز	كِتابُهُ	مَشْهور
	مُديرُه	أَلأَزْهَر
	أَيوه	شَهيد
		هَيْكَل
		مَناهِج

b. Reading

The letter that represents the consonant h as in hat is

ه

The Arabic name is هاء haaʔ; it has the following shapes:

Position	Shape	Examples
a. Independent	ه	أَبوهُ ʔabuuhu
b. Joined to preceding letter only	ـه	دَرْسُهُ darsuhu
c. Joined to following letter only	هـ	هُنا hunaa أَلأَزْهَر ʔalʔazhar
d. Joined on both sides	ـهـ	نَهْر nahr

Drill 2. Read:

هُنا ، هُناك ، هُوَ ، هِيَ ، نَهار ، مُديرُه ، مَشْهور ، مَشاهير ، تَمَهَّل ،
كِتابُه ، شَهْر ، نَهْر ، أَهْلاً ، شَهادَتُه ، مَكْتَبة ، هامّ ، فيه ، هُم
سَهْل ، لَه

c. Writing

Printed	ه
Written	ه

(1) Independent shape : ه

(2) Joined to preceding letter only: ـه Variant: ـہ

(3) Joined to following letter only: هـ

(4) Joined on both sides: ـهـ

Drill 3. In writing supplement.

2. ح ḥ

a. Pronunciation

ح ḥ does not exist in English; it is a voiceless pharyngeal fricative. It is produced with the base of the tongue near the back of the pharynx (throat) and the pharynx walls strongly constricted. Like ه h it can occur in any position of the word and can be pronounced doubled. It differs from ه h in that it is articulated with greater force. The tongue is relatively relaxed for ه but strongly tensed for ح One suggestion for mastering ح is to whisper "Hey you!" as loud as you can, trying to get the h as deep in the throat as possible.

Drill 4. On tape. Repetition. Contrast ح / ه

ح	ه
حاء	هاء
حال	هال
حَوْل	هَوْل
بَحّار	بَهّار

ح	ه
مَحَلّ	مَهَلّ
فَحْم	فَهْم
مَشْحور	مَشْهور
فاح	فاه
شاح	شاه
مَشْبوح	مَشْبوه

ح ḥ differs from خ x in that there is no contact whatsoever between the base of the tongue and the velum for ح as there is for خ (see 5.4). When you are pronouncing ح be sure to keep the back of the tongue low so that it cannot come close to the velum and so produce خ . They are quite distinct in sound, the ح being a "pure" sound while خ has a kind of scraping effect. The following drill contrasts these two sounds.

Drill 5. On tape. Repetition. Contrast ح / خ

ح	خ ←
حال	خال
حام	خام
حَليل	خَليل
حَلّ	خَلّ
سَحَّر	سَخَّر
رَحيم	رَخيم
أَحْبار	أَخْبار
باح	باخ
ساح	ساخ
نَفَح	نَفَخ

b. Reading

The letter that represents the consonant sound ḥ is

ح

Its Arabic name is حاء ḥaa? ; it has the following shapes:

Position	Shape	Examples
a. Independent	ح	صَباحٌ ṣabaaḥun
b. Joined to preceding letter only	ـح	فَتَحَ fataḥa

c. Joined to following letter only	حـ	حالٌ haalun واحِدٌ waahidun
d. Joined on both sides	ـحـ	مَتْحَفٌ mathafun

It is exactly like ج and خ except that it has no dots.

Drill 6. Read:

صَباحٌ ، حالٌ ، حَمْد ، اَلْحَمْدُ ، مَرْحَباً ، فَتَحَ ، سَحْل ، حَديثٌ ،
أَلْحُصول ، سَماحٌ ، حَضَرَ ، بَحْث ، صَحيحٌ ، مَرَحْ ، مَتْحَفٌ ، سَمَحَ ،
حَمَلَ ، قَبيحٌ

c. Writing

Printed	ح
Written	ح

Same as ج , but without the dot.

Drill 7. In writing supplement.

3. ء ʔ

In Lesson Five the writing of hamza as the first sound of the word was dealt with; this lesson deals with hamza in the other positions (1) at the end of the word and (2) in the middle of the word.

a. Pronunciation

Glottal stop is a full-fledged consonant and, like any other consonant, can be pronounced in syllable-final or word-final position and can be doubled.

Drill 8. On tape. Repetition.

a. -aʔa-/ -aa-

سال — سَأَل

سال — ساءَل

داب — دَأَب

ناب — نَأَب

b. VʔC/VVC

بوس — بُؤْس

راس — رَأْس

روس — رُؤْس

بيس — بِئْس

c. -VV/ -Vʔ

مَلا — مَلاَ
بَدا — بَدَأْ
شاطى — شاطِئْ
هُدوّ — هُدوءْ

d. ءّ

سُؤال — سأَّال
رَأْس — تَرآّسَ

b. Reading

There is one cardinal rule in the reading of hamza: if there is a seat, ignore it. The seats are ى , e.g. ئ or ئـ ; و , e.g. ؤ ; and ا , e.g. أ . The seat is not pronounced, but is only an orthographic convention in the spelling of words with hamza.

Drill 9. Read:

أَمين ، إِسْم ، أُكْتُبْ ، مَبْدَأْ ، جُزْءّ ، بَدَأَ ، هادِئ ، سَأَلَ ، سُئِلَ ، فُؤاد ، رَأْس ، مَلأْ ، مَبْدَأْ ، تَرَأَسَ ، لُؤْلُؤْ ، سُؤْدُدٌ ، بِئْرٌ ، رَئيسٌ .

While hamza's seat is not pronounced, it does indicate the nature of adjacent vowels, as will be seen in the following section.

c. Writing

Hamza is written either with a seat or aloof (without a seat). We shall deal with it first aloof, then with a seat.

Hamza is aloof in the following cases:

(1) At the end of a word, when it follows a consonant or long vowel (that is, when it follows sukuun ْ). Examples:

سوءٌ ، بُطيءٌ ، ماءٌ ، مَجيءٌ ، فاءٌ ، بَذيءٌ ، باءٌ ، داءٌ ، مَساءٌ ، بَدْءٌ ، جُزْءٌ ، رُزْءٌ ، فَيْءٌ ، شَيْءٌ ، نَوْءٌ ، فَيْءٌ ، عِبْءٌ .

(2) In the middle of a word, after و whether representing a long vowel, e.g. مُروءات or a consonant, e.g. مَوْءودات or between the two alifs, e.g. إجراءات
Examples:

ضوءُهُ ، مَوْءودات ، مُروءَتُهُ ، يَسوءون ، إجراءات
إِخْصاءات ، مُروءات ، نُبوءات ، تَوْءَمان .

Hamza is written with any of three seats: ا (أ or إ), و (ؤ), or ي (ئ , ئـ). The choice of seat is determined as follows:

(1) At end of word.
The preceding vowel determines the seat, which is homogeneous with the vowel: ِ requires ى , as in شاطِئ ; ُ requires و , as in تَواطُؤ ; and َ requires ا , as in مَبْدَأ . Examples:

تُوبُؤٌ ، بَدَأَ ، مُبْتَدِئ ، نَبَأٌ ، لُؤْلُؤٌ ، بادِئ ، قَرَأَ
تَواطُؤ ، طارِئٌ ، مَلَأَ .

Drill 10. In writing supplement.

(2) In the middle of the word.
In this position the vowels on both sides of hamza are considered, and the chair is chosen according to the following priorities: i - u - a. That is, if there is ِ i on either side of hamza, the seat is ى : ئـ . Examples:

رَئِيس ، رِئاسَةٌ ، سُئِلَ ، سُوَيْئِل ، مُتَفائِلٌ ، بِئْرٌ .

If there is no ِ i but there is ُ u on either side, the seat is و : ؤ . Examples:

فُؤادٌ ، سُؤْدُدٌ ، مَسْؤُول ، تَساؤُلٌ ، بُؤْسٌ ، سُؤالٌ ، لُؤْلُؤٌ .

Otherwise, the seat is ا : أ . Examples: سَأَلَ ، رَأْسٌ ، تَرَأَّسَ ، رَأَتْ ، رَأَيْتُ .

Nunation after ء . Two alifs do not normally occur in succession. Therefore, if a word with word-final hamza on or after alif receives accusative nunation, then accusative nunation is written without alif, as in : قَمِيءٌ — قَمِيئاً ; إِجْراءٌ — إِجْراءً ; مَبْدَأٌ — مَبْدَأً ; نَبَأٌ — نَبَأً ; مَلَأٌ — مَلَأً ; إِبْتِداءٌ — إِبْتِداءً ; بادِئٌ — بادِئاً .

Otherwise, the usual rules apply, for example: جُزْءٌ ، جُزْءٍ ، جُزْءاً ؛ رُزْءٌ ، رُزْءٍ ، رُزْءاً .

Drill 11. On tape. Dictation.

Note: The choice of seat for hamza is determined by adjacent vowels; thus, in unvoweled texts the seats of hamza are important clues to the voweling. For example, سأل cannot have ِ or ُ next to ء , and must be read either سَأَلَ , which means 'he asked' or سَأْلَ , which has no meaning.

4. Voweled and Unvoweled Texts

Thus far we have encountered only voweled script--written with short vowels, shadda, etc., e.g. مَكْتَبٌ maktabun. Texts may also be unvoweled-- written with letters only, and no auxiliary signs, e.g. مكتب maktabun. (Hamza, however, is always written.) For anyone who knows Arabic, the lack of voweling poses no serious problem, because in any given context there is usually only one possible reading. To give an example from English, anyone who knows English should be able to read the following sentence:

Ths wrtng sstm 'mts shrt vwls.

This system works well for Arabic, because every syllable begins with a consonant, and only short vowels are omitted. It would not work for English because English does have syllables beginning with vowels, and even has words consisting entirely of vowels, e.g. "a". In the previous example, we were obliged to indicate the initial vowel of "omits" with an apostrophe.

Arabic publications are normally unvoweled, with only an occasional vowel sign written to avoid ambiguity. As a rule, only scriptures, such as The Koran and the Bible, and elementary readers are fully voweled. In this text we will follow custom and leave our texts unvoweled. In the vocabulary sections words are fully voweled; in grammar notes, words may be fully or partially voweled to clarify or highlight certain points of grammar. Unvoweled texts should not constitute a problem, since the words therein will be either familiar, so that voweling is superfluous, or listed fully voweled in the vocabulary section.

5. Writing of foreign words in Arabic script

In writing foreign words in Arabic script, certain special conventions are observed in the rendering of consonants and vowels that are not found in Modern Standard Arabic.

Vowels. There are two points to be made here. First, since the short vowel points are generally omitted (see previous section), the letters ا, و and ي are used to indicate vowel quality rather than quantity. Thus, both short a and long aa are represented by ا ; u and uu by و, and i and ii by ي . Examples are نانسي naansii which is pronounced nansii 'Nancy'; سميث 'Smith'; فيلم (also فِلم)'film'.

The second point concerns vowels that do not exist in MSA. The vowel ee (like a in English date, or e in they) is represented in Arabic script by ي , e.g. سِكرتير sikriteer 'secretary'. The vowels o in English wrote and o in hot are both represented by و , e.g. أوتيل ʔoteel 'hotel'; بوب boob 'Bob'.

Consonants. Arabic lacks a p (as in pipe), and generally spells it with ب b, or occasionally with a special symbol پ p, as in بيانو or پيانو 'piano'. The consonant v is likewise generally spelled with ف f but sometimes with the special symbol ڤ v, as in فرساي or ڤرساي virsaay 'Versailles'. The consonant g is spelled with ج in Egypt, where this letter represents g; elsewhere, g is represented by ك k or غ , e.g. إنجليزي or إنكليزي ʔingliiziyy 'English'; كونغرس koongris 'Congress'.

Lesson Seven

الدرس السابع

Consonants

1. ع (no English equivalent)

Symbols

2. Madda: ـٓ

3. Dagger ʔalif: ٰ

4. taaʔ marbuuṭa: ة

1. ع ʕ

a. Pronunciation

The Arabic consonant ع has no English equivalent. It is a voiced pharyngeal fricative, and is thus the voiced counterpart of the voiceless pharyngeal fricative ح ḥ (see 6.2). In making this sound, the muscles of the pharynx are tightened, causing the throat passage to be quite constricted, and resulting in a "squeezed" sound. This constriction of the pharynx is the same as that found in ح ḥ, but with ع there is not so much friction noise, and voicing (vocal cord vibration) continues throughout. In the first drills below you will hear the ع contrasted with other Arabic sounds. Listen carefully.

Drill 1. On tape. Repetition. Contrast between a long vowel and a long vowel plus ع . Listen and repeat.

ما	ماع
لا	لاع
با	باع
بي	بيع
ني	نيع
شي	شيع
ذو	ذوع
كو	كوع
بو	بوع

Drill 2. On tape. Repetition. Contrast between ء ʔ and ع ʕ. Listen and repeat.

أَن	عَن	سَأَل	سَعَل	باء	باع
أَب	عَب	سائِل	ساعِل	ماء	ماع
أَوْ	عَو	وأْد	وَعْد	بَدَأ	بَدَع
أَم	عَم	بائِد	باعِد	نَبَأ	نَبَع

Drill 3. On tape. Repetition. Contrast between ح ḥ and ع . Listen and repeat.

حال	عال	بَحَث	بَعَث	روح	روع
حام	عام	سَحَل	سَعَل	راح	راع
حاد	عاد	ساحِل	ساعِل	نَفْح	نَفْع
حَبَر	عَبَر	لَحَّن	لَعَّن	نَبَح	نَبَع
حَمَل	عَمَل	بَحَّر	بَعَّر	لَحْلَح	لَعْلَع

Drill 4. On tape. Imitation. Additional examples of ع in various positions. Listen and repeat.

عال	نَعْل	لَعَّب	شَعْب	يَلْعَب	إِجْتِماع
عام	تَعلَّم	صَعَّب	أَعْجَب	إِنْعَقَد	تابِع
عالَم	مُسْتَعِدّ	بَعَّد	بَعْد	موعِد	مَع
عِلْم	مُعَلِّم	فَعَّل	فَعْص	يَنْعَم	إِسْتَمَع
عَرَب	لَعَّن	سَعَّر	تَعليم	يُرْعِب	رَجَع

b. Reading

The letter which represents the sound ʕ is

ع

The Arabic name of this letter is عَين ʕayn. It has the following shapes:

Position	Shape	Examples	
a. Independent	ع	باعَ	baaʕa
b. Joined to preceding letter only	ع	يَبيعُ	yabiiʕu
c. Joined to following letter only	عـ	عالَمٌ	ʕaalamun
		ساعاتٌ	saaʕaatun
d. Joined on both sides	ـعـ	بَعَثَ	baʕaθa

Drill 5. Each of the columns a to d below illustrates one of the four shapes shown above; Column e includes them all. Read:

a	b	c	d	e
باعَ	يَبيعُ	عالَمٌ	بَعَثَ	عَرَفَ
إِجْتِماعٌ	مَعَ	ساعاتٌ	صَعْبٌ	مَعروفٌ
راعَ	مُجْتَمَعٌ	عَن	بَعْدٌ	مَوْعِدٍ
رَوْعٌ	جَمَعَ	عَلَّمَ	تَعْليمٌ	باعٌ
ساعٍ	سَمِعَ	عَقَدَ	بَعْلٌ	إِجْتَمَعَ

c. Writing

(1) Independent shape.

Printed	ع
Written	ع

Begin at the top right.

(2) Joined to preceding letter only.

Printed	ـع
Written	ـع

Move from the preceding letter leftward, then up and around to the right, then down and leftward again, crossing the original line, and finally rightward for the bottom loop. The small top loop should be somewhat flat on top; the large bottom loop extends below the line.

(3) Joined to following letter only.

Printed	عـ
Written	عـ

Begin as for (1), but omit the bottom loop and move directly to the following letter.

(4) Joined on both sides.

Printed	ـعـ
Written	ـعـ

The loop should be flat on top, as in (2).

Drill 6. In writing supplement.

2. The sign madda ~

In most positions in a word, the sequence ʔaa is represented by the sign ~ (called madda) written over an alif. Examples:

آثارٌ ʔaaθaarun

أَلْقُرْآنُ ʔalqurʔaanu

تَآمَنَ taʔaamana

Drill 7. Read:

آلافٌ ، آثارٌ ، قَرَآ ، تَآمَنَ ، أَلْقُرْآنُ

However, after u, i, or ii, this sequence is written in accordance with the usual rules for hamza given in 6.3:

سُؤالٌ suʔaalun

رِئاسَتُهُ riʔaasatuhu

بَرِيئانِ bariiʔaani

Drill 8. In writing supplement.

3. Dagger ʔalif

In a few very common words, the long vowel aa is represented not with the letter ʔalif after the consonant but with the sign ' written over the consonant. This sign is a short vertical stroke with the appearance of a small ʔalif, and is called "dagger ʔalif". Examples:

هٰذا haaðaa 'this'

ذٰلِكَ	ðaalika	'that'
أَللّٰهُ	ʔaḷḷaahu	'God'
لِلّٰهِ	lillaahi	'for God'

This dagger ʔalif is omitted in unvowelled text:

ذلك	ðaalika

Drill 9. In writing supplement.

4. The taaʔ marbuuṭa ة

a. Pronunciation and general remarks

The letter ة (in Arabic called تاء مربوطة taaʔ marbuuṭa 'tied t') serves a double function. Phonologically, it represents the sound t (exactly the same sound as the one represented by ت ; see 2.2). Examples:

مَلِكَةٌ	malikatun	'queen'
طالِبَةٌ	ṭaalibatun	'female student'
فَتاةٌ	fataatun	'girl'

Grammatically, it indicates feminine gender in the noun or adjective in which it appears, as illustrated by the three examples above.

Three are four additional points to be noted about the taaʔ marbuuṭa:

(1) It occurs only as the last consonant of a word. If a suffix involving additional letters is added to such a word, the ة is changed to ت . Contrast:

مَلِكَةٌ	malikatun	'queen'
مَلِكَتُهُمْ	malikatuhum	'their queen'

(2) It is always preceded by either the short vowel َ a or, in a much smaller number of words, by the long vowel ا aa, as illustrated earlier.

(3) The ʔalif which is normally written with the accusative nunation (see 4.5) is not written after ة :

مَلِكَةً malikatan

(4) The pausal form of ة in all cases (-atun, -atin, -atan) is a:

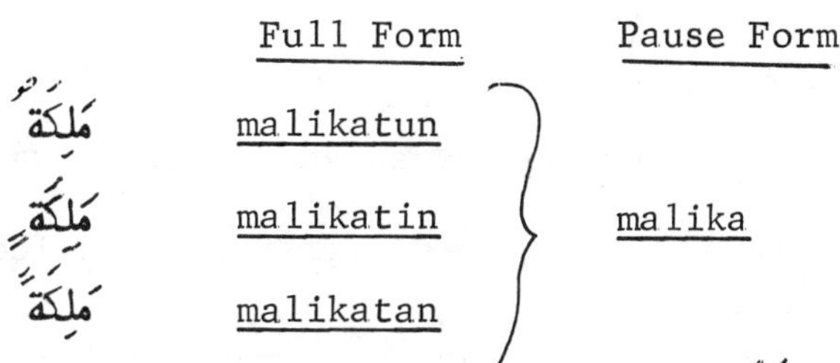

	Full Form	Pause Form
مَلِكَةٌ	malikatun	malika
مَلِكَةٍ	malikatin	
مَلِكَةً	malikatan	

Note the change in stress between the full form of مَلِكَةٌ malíkatun and its pause form málika.

Drill 10. Read the following words first in the full form and then in the pause form:

مَلِكَةٌ ، مَدْرَسةٌ ، مَكْتَبَةٍ ، مُدَرِّسَةٍ ، طالِبَةٌ ، كُلِّيَّةٌ ، مُديرَةٌ ، جُمْلَةٍ ،
كَلِمَةً ، فَتاةٍ .

b. Reading

The letter

ة

represents the sound t. It occurs only as the final letter in a word, and has the following shapes, which are identical, except for the two dots, to the corresponding shapes of ه h (see 6.1):

Position	Shape	Examples
a. Independent	ة	مُدَّةٌ muddatun
b. Joined to preceding letter only	ـة	جُمْلَةٌ jumlatun

Drill 11. Read in full form:

Ending in ـة	Examples ending in ة
جُمْلَةٍ	مُدَّةٌ
طالِبَةٌ	مُديرَةٌ
مُعَلِّمَةٌ	سِكْرتيرَةً
آنِسَةٍ	سَيِّدَةٍ
مَكْتَبَةً	قَريبَةٌ
جامِعَةٍ	مَشْهورَةٍ
زائِرَةٌ	فَتاةً

Words ending in ة have pausal forms (see 5.6) in which the t sound and any following sounds are dropped, for example:

	Full form	Pausal form
مُدَّةٌ	muddatun	
مُدَّةٍ	muddatin	mudda
مُدَّةً	muddatan	

In formal or precise speech an h sound is added in the pausal form: muddah.

Drill 12. Read each of the following items first in full form and then in pause form:

طَبيبَةٌ ، مُدَّةٍ ، أُسْتاذَةً ، صَعْبَةٍ ، سَيّارَةٌ ، شَرِكَةٌ ، ساعَةٌ ، مُراسِلَةً ،
شَهادَةٍ ، صَديقَةٌ ، طائِرَةٌ ، مُعادَةً ، تَرْبِيَةٍ .

Words ending in ة have pausal forms in which the t sound is replaced by h:

	Full form	Pausal form
فَتَاةٌ	fataatun	
فَتَاةٍ	fataatin	fataah
فَتَاةً	fataatan	

Drill 13. Read each of the following items first in full form and then in pausal form:

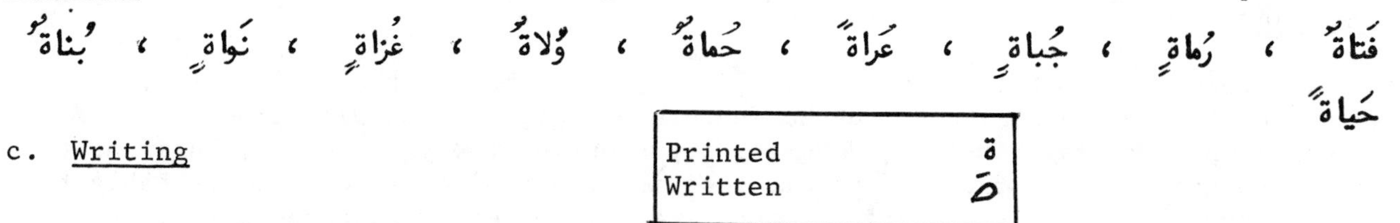

فَتَاةٌ ، رُمَاةٍ ، جُبَاةٍ ، عُرَاةً ، حُمَاةٌ ، وُلَاةٌ ، غُزَاةٍ ، نَوَاةٍ ، بُنَاةٌ
حَيَاةً

c. Writing

Printed	ة
Written	ـَ (written form)

The written forms of ة are the same as the corresponding forms of ه h, with the addition of the two dots (written as a short horizontal stroke).

Drill 14. In writing supplement.

Drill 15. On tape. Dictation.

Lesson Eight الدرس الثامن

Consonants

1. غ ɣ (no English equivalent)

2. Wasla: ٱ

3. Numbers 1 - 10

1. غ ɣ

a. Pronunciation

غ is a voiced velar fricative. It is like خ with the addition of voicing. If you can produce خ and then simply add the feature of voicing, you will produce غ . Another approach is to say "ah-gah", "ahg-gah", prolonging the g , then withdrawing the back of the tongue slightly from the velum, creating the desired friction. Probably the simplest way to achieve غ is to gargle without water; indeed, the Arabic for "to gargle" is ɣarɣara غَرْغَرَ

Drill 1. On tape. Repetition. Contrast غ / خ

غ	خ
غال	خال
غِلاف	خِلاف
غَيْر	خَيْر
رَغْو	رَخْو
غَرْغَرَ	خَرْخَرَ
تَغَيَّر	تَخَيَّر
شَغَرَ	شَخَرَ
تَفْريغ	تَفْريخ
ساغ	ساخ

b. Reading

The letter that represents the consonant ɣ is

غ

Its Arabic name is غين ɣayn, and it has the following shapes:

Position	Shape	Examples
a. Independent	غ	فارِغٌ faariɣun

b. Joined to preceding letter only	ـغ	صائغ	saaʔiɣun
c. Joined to following letter only	غـ	غال ألأغاني	ɣaalin ʔalʔaɣaanii
d. Joined on both sides	ـغـ	بَغْداد	baɣdaad

غ is exactly like ع in all its shapes, except that it has one dot above.

Drill 2. Read:

غال ، لُغَةٌ ، بَغْداد ، فارِغٌ ، صائِغٌ ، أَلْمُغَنّى ، غِناءٌ ، غَدًا ،
أَلْمَغْنى ، غالِبٌ ، غَداءٌ ، تَغَيَّرَ ، غَرْبٌ ، بَلَغَ ، غالِبٌ ، غَيْر

c. Writing

Printed	غ
Written	غ

غ is written like ع in all shapes, with the addition of a dot above.

Drill 3. In writing supplement.

2. ٱ ألْوَصْلَة

The word اِسْمٌ meaning 'name' is unusual in that it is pronounced اِسْمٌ only when it is the first word after pause. If it follows any other word or prefix the initial glottal stop and vowel (اِ) are elided (not pronounced). For example:

اِسْمٌ	'a name'	(ʔismun)
هٰذا اسْمٌ	'This is a name.'	(haaðaasmun)

Note that while the pronunciation changes, the letter spelling does not: اسم retains its alif in both cases. However, there is a sign indicating elision of initial glottal stop and its vowel that is used when texts are fully voweled: ٱ as in

اِسْمٌ	ʔismun
هٰذا ٱسْمٌ	haaðaasmun

The Arabic name for ٱ is وَصْلَة waṣla, which means "connecting, joining"; that is, the two words are joined together in pronunciation as if one.

Two other common nouns that begin with elidable hamza are اِبْنٌ 'son' and اِثْنانِ 'two', for example

هٰذا ٱبْنُهُ	'This is his son.'	haaðaabnuhu

Also, elidable hamza is found in (a) all imperative verbs that begin with أُ or اِ, (b) all perfect tense verbs that begin with اِ, and (c) verbal nouns of Forms VII-X. Illustrations:

a.	أُكْتُبْ	ʔuktub	'Write!'
	وَٱكْتُبْ	waktub	'And write!'

إِسْتَمِعْ ʔistámiʕ 'Listen!'

قالَ ٱسْتَمِع qaalastámiʕ "He said, 'Listen!'"

b. اِسْتَمَرَّ وٱسْتَمَرَّ ʔistamarra wastamarra 'He continued and continued'.

c. إِنْتِخابٌ بَعْدَ ٱنْتِخابٍ ʔintixaabun baʕdantixaabin 'Election after election'

Finally, waṣla is with the definite article, for example,

أَلْمَكْتَبُ ʔalmaktabu 'The office'

في ٱلْمَكْتَبِ filmaktabi 'in the office'

See Grammar Section C, Note 1, of this lesson for the definite article.

If waṣla follows a consonant, a helping vowel, generally, i, is added to that consonant. Thus إِسْتَقْبَلَتْ 'she received' and أَلْمُدير 'the director' go together to form the sentence

إِسْتَقْبَلَتِ ٱلْمُديرَ 'She received the director.' (ʔistaqbálatilmudiira)

Other examples are:

عَنِ ٱلْمُدير 'concerning the director' (عَنْ = 'concerning')

في أَيِّ مَكْتَبِ ٱلْمُدير ؟ fii ʔayyi maktabinilmudiir ? 'What office is the director in?'

Note: In this book the following convention will be used to denote an elidable glottal stop: the word is written without initial hamza but with a vowel sign. Thus,

اِسْمُهُ 'his name'

is pronounced ʔismuhu after pause but -smuhu after another word, as in

ما ٱسْمُهُ ؟ 'What is his name?' maasmuhu?

This convention will be used in the vocabulary sections of these lessons and in the Glossary of the book; elidable hamza will be referred to as "waṣla". Further examples:

إِبْنٌ 'son' ʔibnun

أَلاِبْنُ 'the son' ʔalibnu

3. Numbers 1 - 10

Following are the numerals in Arabic from one to ten:

	Printed	Written
1	١	١
2	٢	٢
3	٣	٣
4	٤	٤

	Printed	Written
5	٥	٥
6	٦	٦
7	٧	٧
8	٨	٨
9	٩	٩
10	١٠	١٠

The Arabic for 'zero' is صِفْرٌ : ٠ ٠

<u>Lesson Nine</u> <u>الدرس التاسع</u>

1. Consonant ض ḍ (no English equivalent)

2. <u>^{c}alif</u> <u>maqṣuura</u> ى <u>aa</u>

3. Numbers 11 - 19

1.ض ḍ

a. <u>Pronunciation</u>

The Arabic sound ض ḍ has no English equivalent. It is a velarized voiced alveolar stop, and is pronounced like ط ṭ (see 4.4) with the addition of voicing. From another viewpoint, it is like د d, with the addition of velarization. Remember, when making this or any velarized sound, to keep your tongue tense, with the back part raised high in the mouth. In the drills that follow, note also the effect which ض ḍ, like other velarized consonants, has on the quality of adjacent vowels.

<u>Drill 1</u>. On tape. Repetition. Contrast between د d/ض ḍ. Listen and repeat.

(Final)	(Medial)	(Initial)
باد باض	بدْعة بضْعة	دام ضام
عَدّ عَضّ	يَدوم يَضوم	دالّ ضالّ
بَيْد بَيْض	يُدير يُضير	دام ضام
عَوَّد عَوَّض	أَرْدَت أَرْضَت	دار ضار
فاد فاض	رِداء رِضاء	دَرْب ضَرْب

<u>Drill 2</u>. On tape. Repetition. Contrast between ط ṭ and ض ḍ

غَطّ غَضّ	خَطَر خَضَر	طَلّ ضَلّ
فَرَط فَرَض	تَوَطَّأ تَوَضَّأ	طَمَر ضَمَر
خَطّ خَضّ	نَطَح نَضَح	طَمّ ضَمّ
رَبَط رَبَض	خَطيب خَضيب	طائِر ضائِر
خاط خاض	أَخْطَر أَخْضَر	طاء ضاء

<u>Drill 3</u>. On tape. Imitation. Further examples of ض ḍ. Listen and repeat.

حَضَرَ ، ضَحِكَ ، مَوْضوعٌ ، قاضٍ ، ضَخْمٌ ، باضَ ، وَضَعَ ، أَرْضٍ ،

حَضَّرَ ، أَيْضاً ، ضاعَفَ ، فاضَ ، واضِحٌ ، ضاعَ ، عَضَّ ، فَضْلٌ ،

ضَلَّ ، إِنْضَمَّ ، فِضَّة ، ضَمَرَ .

b. Reading

The letter which represents the sound ḍ is

The Arabic name of this letter is ضاد ḍaad. It shapes are exactly like those of ص ṣ, with the addition of the dot:

Position	Shape	Examples	
a. Independent	ض	مَرَضٌ	maraḍun
b. Joined to preceding letter only	ـض	مَرِيضٌ	mariiḍun
c. Joined to following letter only	ضـ	ضَمَّةٌ	ḍammatun
		رَضِيتُ	raḍiitu
d. Joined on both sides	ـضـ	بَيْضَاتٌ	bayḍaatun

Drill 4. Each of the columns a to d below illustrates one of the form shapes listed above. Column e includes them all. Read:

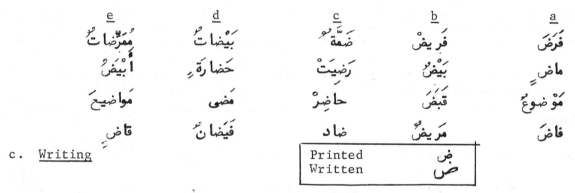

e	d	c	b	a
مُمَرِّضَاتٌ	بَيْضَاتٌ	ضَمَّةٌ	فَرِيضْ	فَرَضَ
أَبْيَضُ	حَضَارَةٍ	رَضِيتْ	بَيْضُ	مَاضٍ
مَوَاضِيعَ	مَضَى	حَاضِرْ	قَبَضَ	مَوْضُوعٌ
قَاضٍ	فَيَضَانٌ	ضَاد	مَرِيضٌ	فَاضَ

c. Writing

Printed	ض
Written	ض

The written forms of ض ḍ are the same in all positions as for ص ṣ, with the addition of the dot.

Variant shape. The independent shape and the shape joined to preceding letter only may alternatively be written with a short downward slanting stroke at the end instead of the dot. For example:

مَرَضٌ	maraḍun
مَرِيضٌ	mariiḍun

Drill 5. In writing supplement

2. The ʔalif maqṣuura ى

a. Pronunciation and general remarks

In a considerable number of Arabic words, a final long vowel aa is represented not by the usual ʔalif but by a special letter ى called أَلِفٌ مَقْصُورَة ʔalif maqṣuura 'shortened alif'. For example:

بَرى	baraa
بَنى	banaa

Two points may be particularly noted about ى :

(1) The long aa sound represented by ى is exactly the same sound as that represented by the regular ʼalif; thus no new pronunciation feature is involved.

(2) The ى occurs only as the last letter of a word; if a suffix is added to such a word, the ى is changed to ا. Contrast:

بَنى	banaa	'he built'
بَناهُ	banaahu	'he built it'

b. Reading

The letter

represents the long vowel aa. It occurs only finally. Its shapes are identical to the corresponding shapes ي y except that they have no dots:

Position	Shape	Examples
a. Independent	ى	نادى naadaa
b. Joined to preceding letter only	ـى	رَمى ramaa

Drill 6. Read:

مَتى ، رأى ، عَلى ، مَقْهو ، إشْتَرى ، قَضى ، رَوى ، موسى ،

لَيْلى ، قُرى ، سَحى ، نَدى ، رَمى ، إنْبَرى ، إسْتَولى

c. Writing

The written shapes of ى are exactly like the corresponding shapes of ي y (see 2.4), without the dots.

Drill 7. In writing supplement

Drill 8. On tape. Dictation.

3. Numbers 11 - 19

Following are the numerals from 11 through 19:

	Printed	Written
11	١١	١١
12	١٢	١٢
13	١٣	١٣

	Printed	Written
14	١٤	١٤
15	١٥	١٥
16	١٦	١٦
17	١٧	١٧
18	١٨	١٨
19	١٩	١٩

Lesson Ten الدرس العاشر

1. Consonants ظ (no English equivalent)

2. The Alphabet

3. Numbers 20 - 1,000,000

1. ظ

a. Pronunciation

ظ is a velarized voiced interdental fricative; it is like ذ with the addition of velarization (the tensing up of the base of the tongue; see Lesson 3.4). It consequently goes with the back varieties of the vowels. In the following drill, note the difference in quality between ظ and ذ as well as the different effect they have on adjacent vowels.

Drill 1. On tape. Repetition. Contrast ظ / ذ

ظ	ذ
ظالّ	ذالّ
ظَرْف	ذَرْف
ظَميم	ذَميم
نَظَرَ	نَذَرَ
ناظِر	ناذِر
مَظَلَّة	مَذَلَّة
بَظَرَ	بَذَرَ
بَظَّ	بَذَّ
فَظّ	فَذّ
أَفْظاظ	أَفْذاذ

b. Reading

The letter that represents the consonant ʒ̣ is

ظ

Its Arabic name is ظاء ʒ̣aaʔ , and it has the following shapes

Position	Shape	Examples
a. Independent	ظ	أَفْظاظٌ ʔafʒ̣aaʒ̣un

b. Joined to preceding letter only	ـظ	مُحافِظٌ muhaafiẓun
c. Joined to following letter only	ظـ	ظاءٌ ẓaaʔun مُوَظَّفٌ muwaẓẓafun
d. Joined on both sides	ـظـ	نِظامٌ niẓaamun

Its shapes are identical with those of ط with the addition of a dot.

Drill 2. Read:

مُعْظَم ، ناظِرٌ ، نَظَرَ ، فَظٌّ ، عُكاظ ، مَظْهَرٌ ، ظَهْر ، أَفْظاظٌ ، مَحْظوظ
حَظٌّ ، مُحافَظَة ، ناظِرٌ ، ظَلَّ ، نِظامٌ ، مُنَظَّمَة .

c. Writing

Printed	ظ
Written	ظ

Like ط with a dot.

Drill 3. In writing supplement.

Drill 4. On tape. Dictation

2. The Alphabet

The order of letters in the Arabic alphabet (حُروفُ ٱلْهِجاءِ) is as follows:

ا ب ت ث ج ح خ د ذ ر ز س ش ص ض ط ظ ع غ ف ق ك ل م ن ه و ى

Note that أَلِفٌ مَقْصورة (ى), هَمْزة (ء) and تاءٌ مَرْبوطة (ة) are not included as letters of the alphabet.

When the alphabet is used in outlines, the following order is used, usually recited as words, as follows:

أَبْجَد هَوَّز حُطِّي كَلَمُن سَعْفَص قُرِشَت ثَخَذٌ ضَظَغ

The handwritten form of the first three letters, when used in enumerating items, is ا (= a.), ب (= b.) and ج (= c.).

3. Numbers 20 - 1,000,000

Following are the numerals over 19:

		Printed	Written
20	عِشْرونَ	٢٠	٢٠
25	خَمْسَةٌ وَ عِشْرونَ	٢٥	٢٥
30	ثَلاثـونَ	٣٠	٣٠
40	أَرْبَعـونَ	٤٠	٤٠
50	خَمْسونَ	٥٠	٥٠

		Printed	Written
60	سِتّونَ	٦٠	٦٠
70	سَبْعونَ	٧٠	٧٠
80	ثَمانونَ	٨٠	٨٠
90	تِسْعونَ	٩٠	٩٠
100	مِئَةٌ (also مِائَةٌ)	١٠٠	١٠٠
1,000	أَلْفٌ	١٠٠٠	١٠٠٠
1,000,000	مِلْيونٌ	١٠٠٠ ٠٠٠	١٠٠٠,٠٠٠

WRITING DRILLS

Drill 3

Drill 4

Drill 6

Drill 7

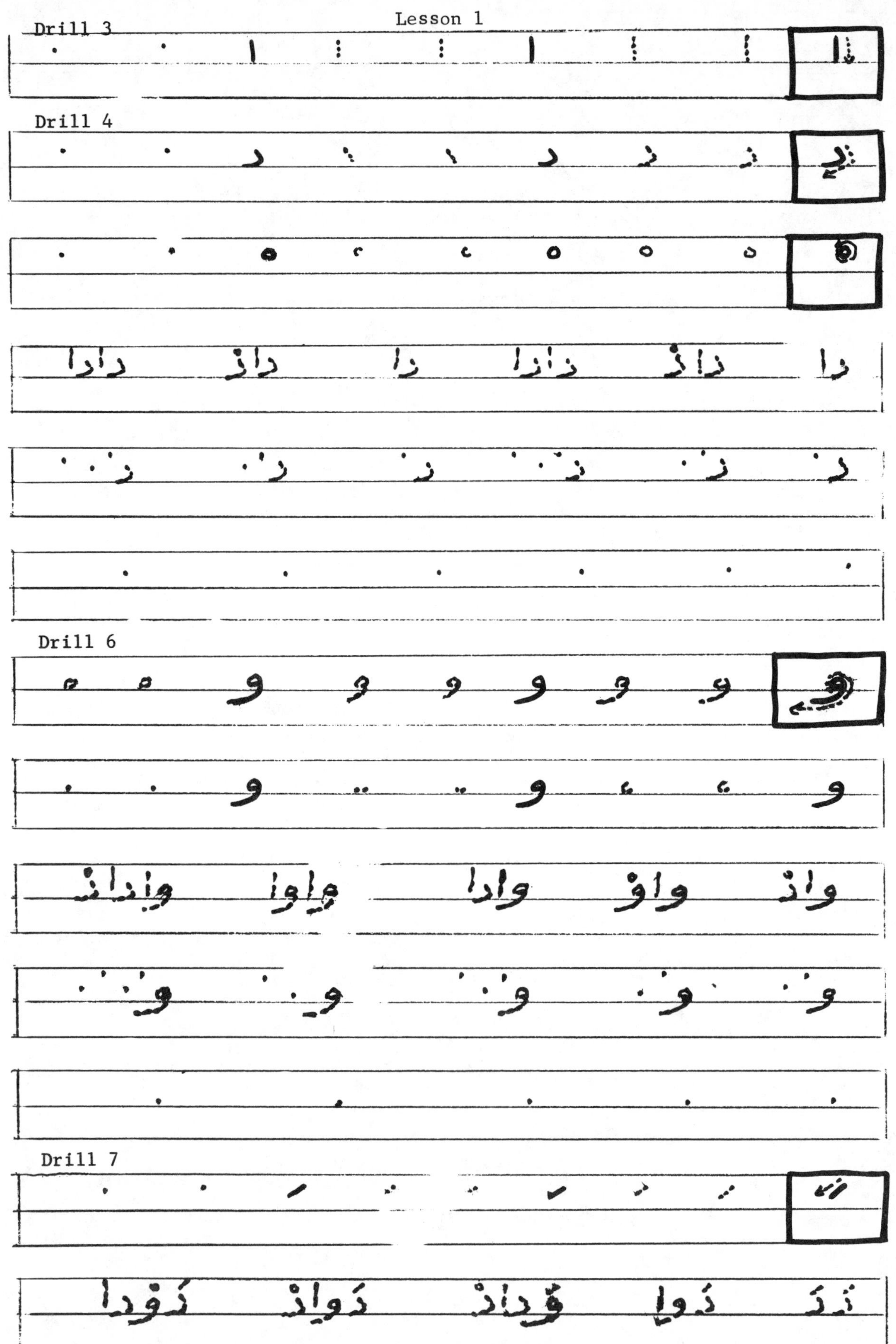

Drill 12

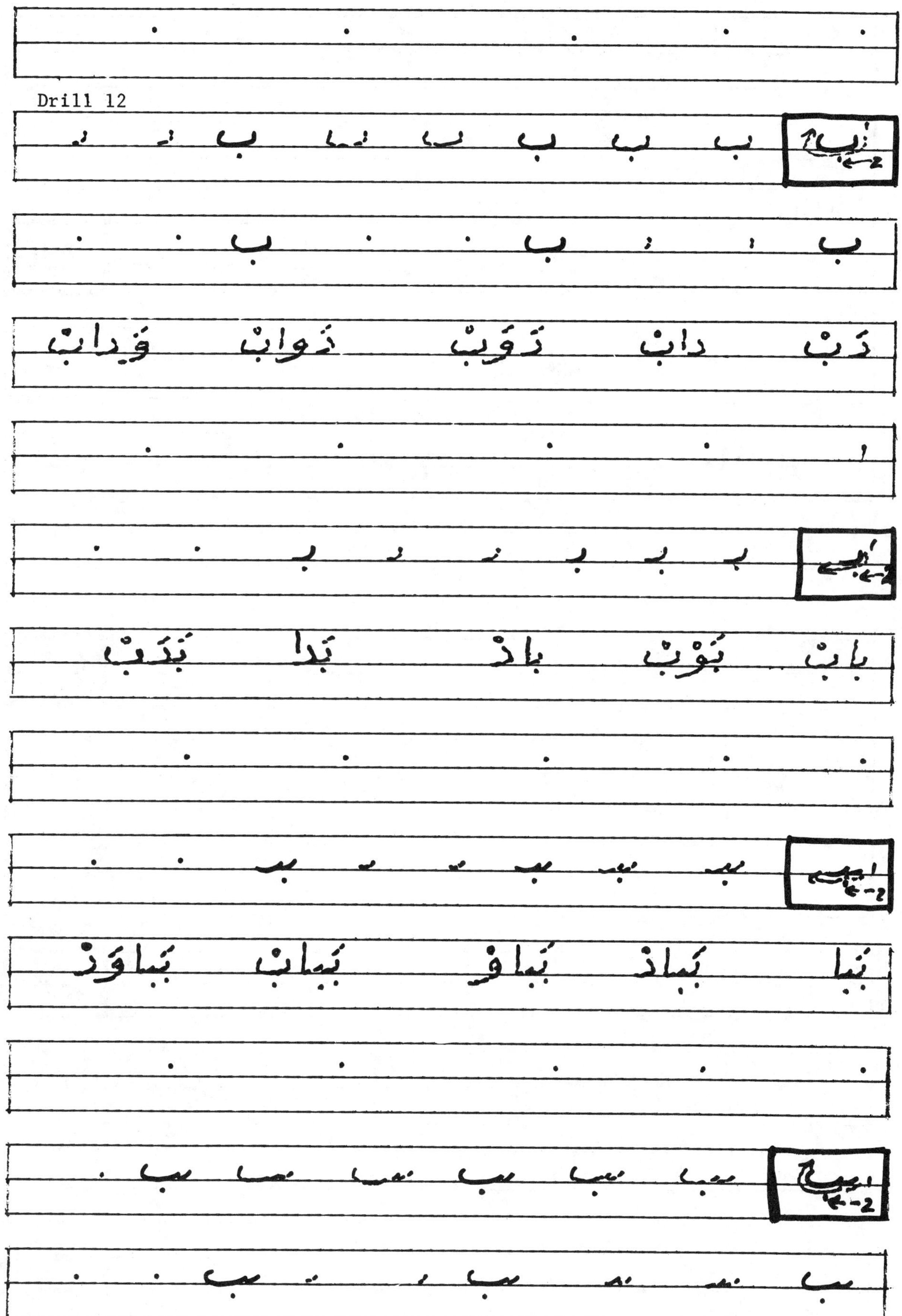

Drill 14

بَنا بَنَو بَنان بَند وَبَنان

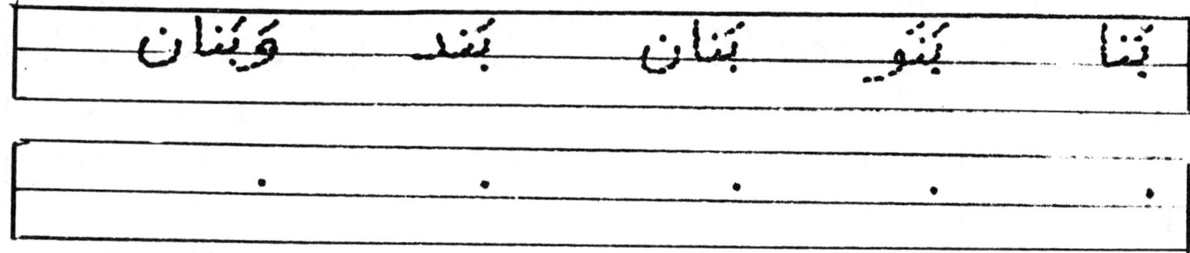

Lesson 2

Drill 4

ز ز ز ز ز ز

زاب زان زار زَنَب زُواب

Drill 6

ت ت ت ت ت ت

زات بات نَبات زَوَت زُوات

ـتـ ـتـ ـتـ ـتـ ـتـ ـتـ

زَنَت نَبَت زابَت بانَت بَنَت

تـ تـ تـ تـ تـ تـ

تابَت بائَت تَبَن تَداوُت تَوائِت

ـبـ ـتـ ـبـ ـبـ ـتـ

بَتات نَتَن بُنَتا بَنتوين نُبْتَتان

Drill 8

ف ف ف و ف و ف

نَدَف داف وَزَف نُواف ثُتاف

ـف ـف ـف ـب ـب ـف

وَنَف زَنَف بَتَف وَنَف نَثَف

فـ فـ فـ ه ه فـ

فات فَن فَتَن نَفَن وَفاد

ـفـ ـفـ ـفـ ـبـ ـبـ ـفـ

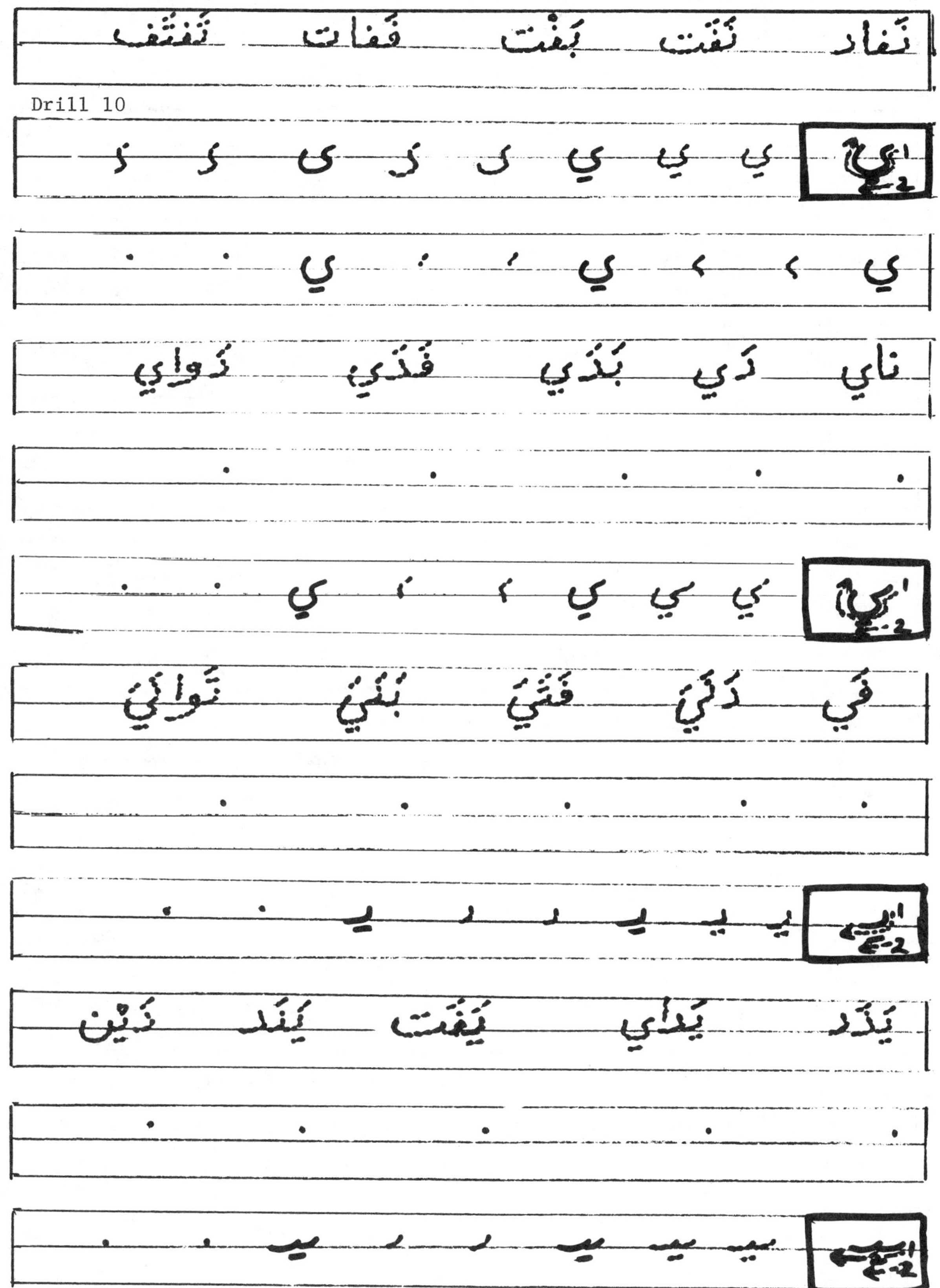

Drill 10

Drill 12

نحن نحت ممات تمام نمتم

Drill 16

دُبّ ذُباب مُنْذُ دُفْتُم بُنْيان

Drill 20

تَمَّ وَدَّ فَنَّان بَوَّاب تَيَمَّم

Lesson 3

Drill 3

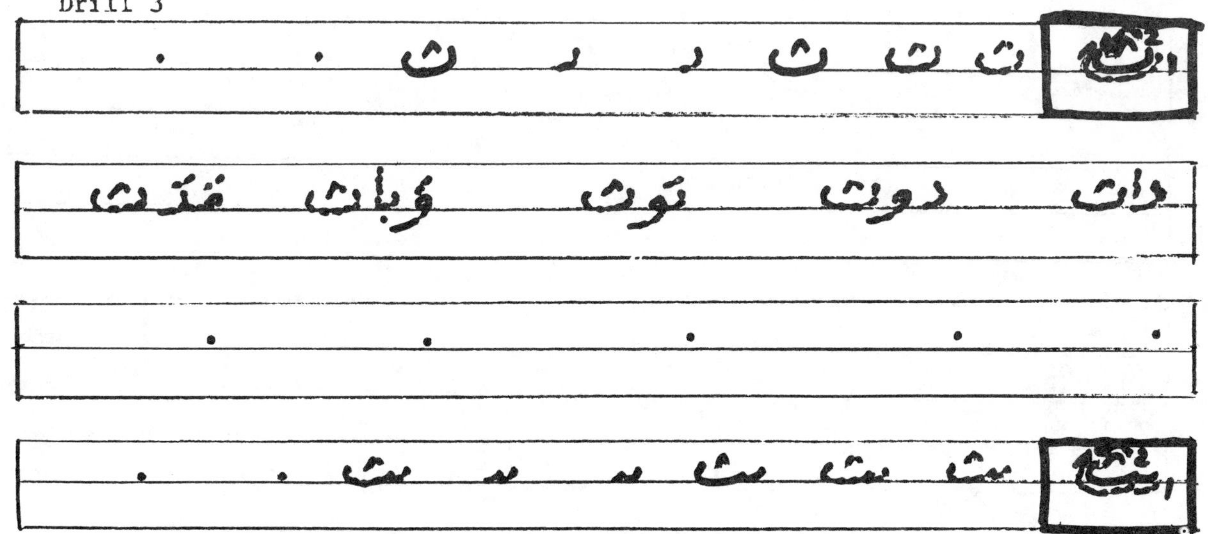

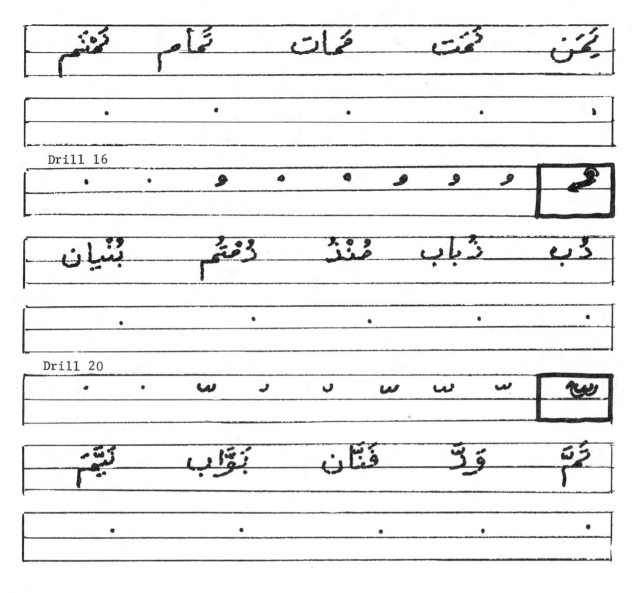

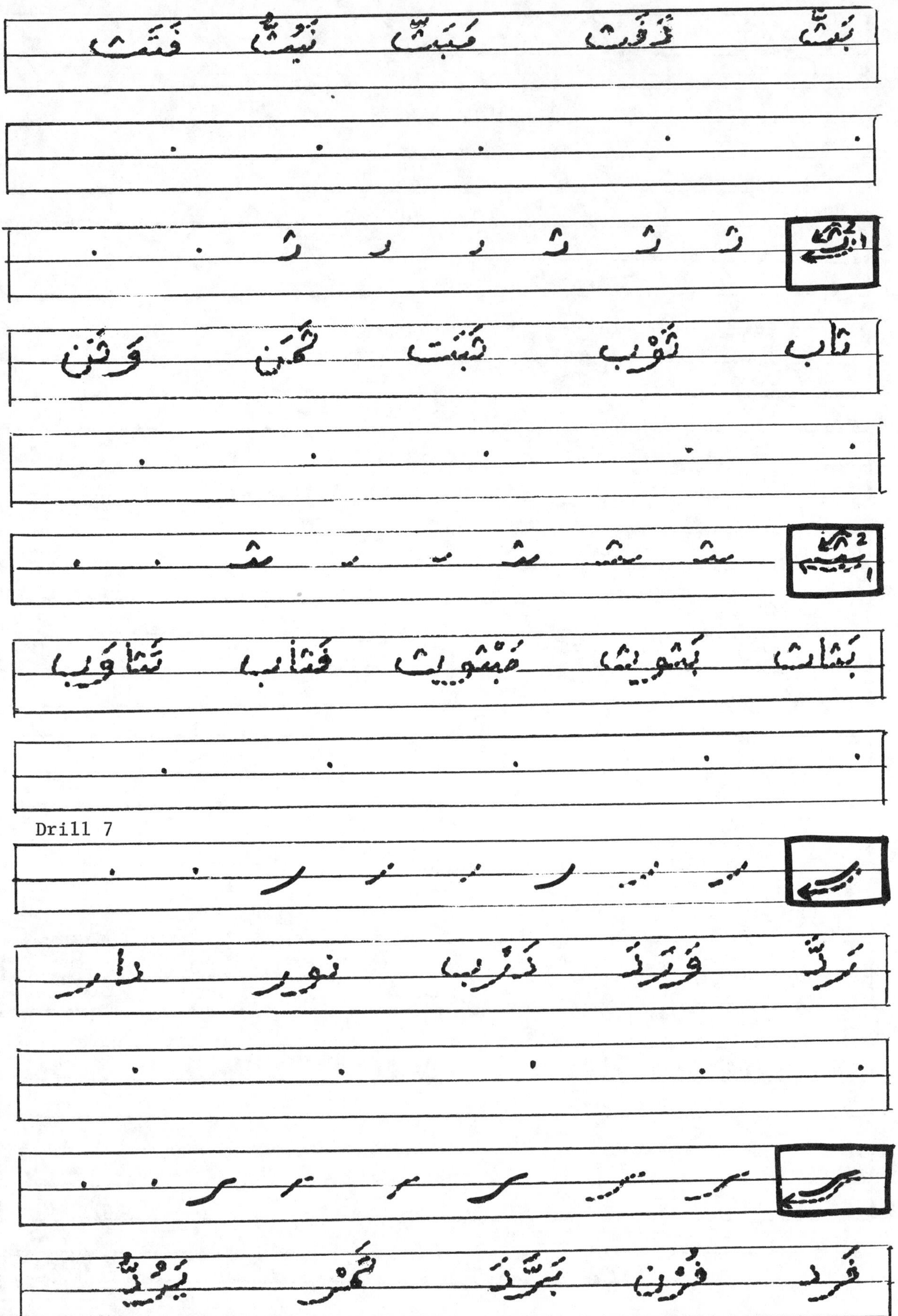

Drill 7

Drill 10

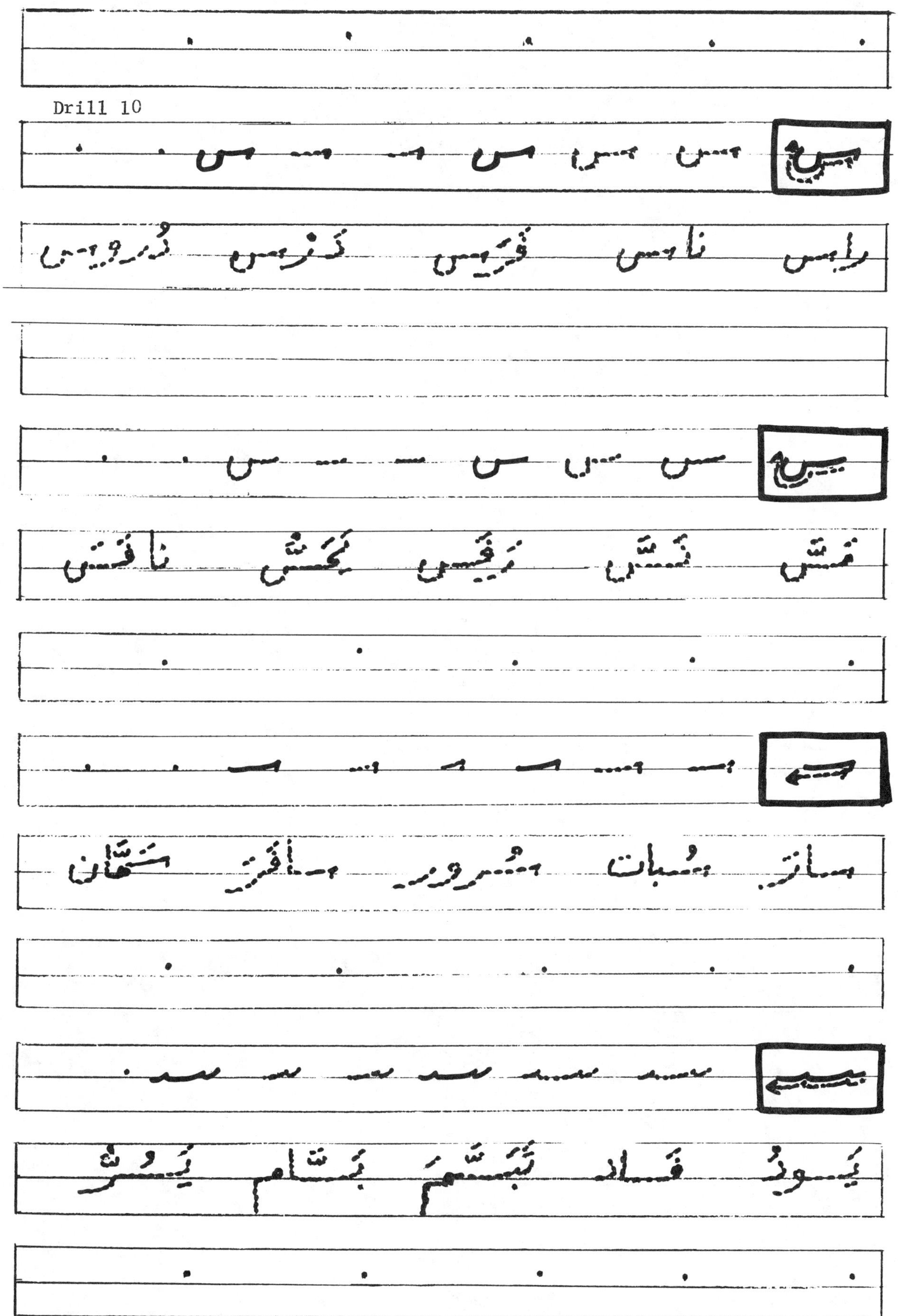

Drill 17

ص ص ص ص ص ص ص

رَصَّ بَرَصَ قُرْص باصّ بوص

ص ص ص ص ص ص ص

نَصَّ مَصَّ تَرَبَّص تَمَصَّص يَتَمَصَّص

ص ص ص ص ص ص

صام صَبَر صَوْت صَنَف صَكَر

ص ص ص ص ص ص ص

نَصَب قَصَم مُصَوَّر مَصْدُور نُصُوص

Drill 23

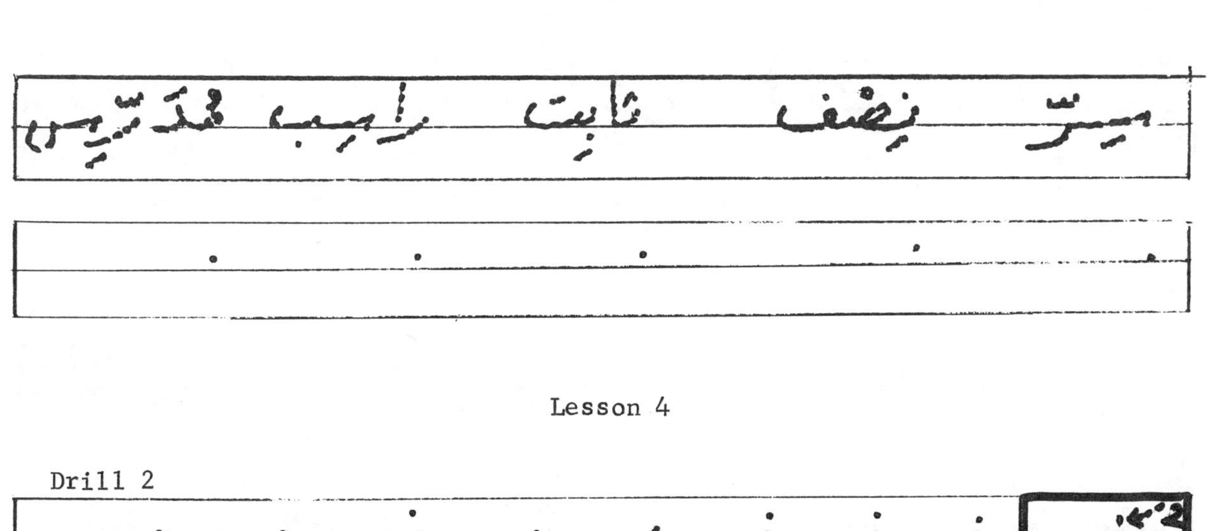

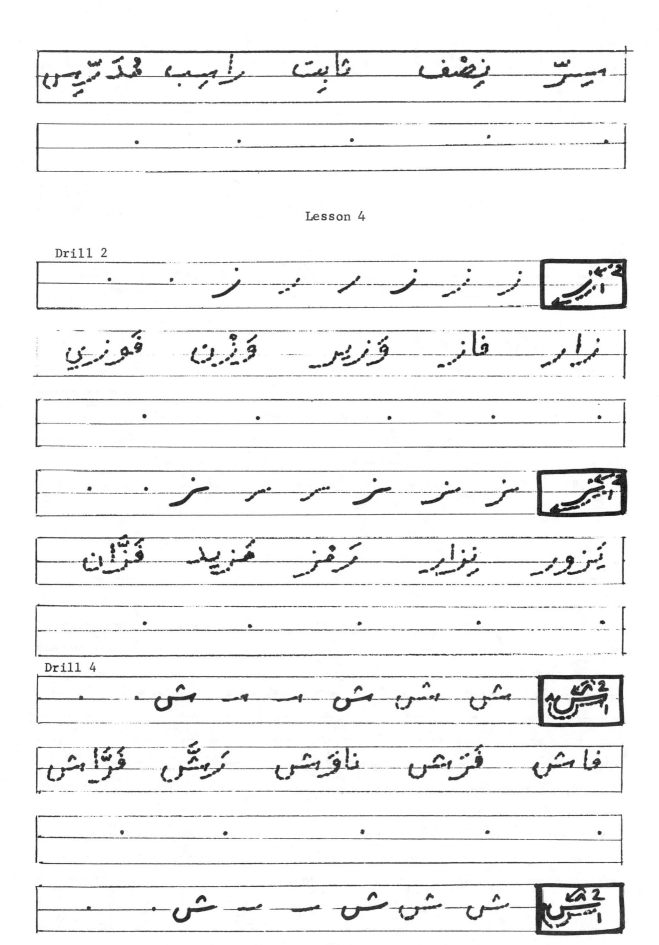

Lesson 4

Drill 2

Drill 4

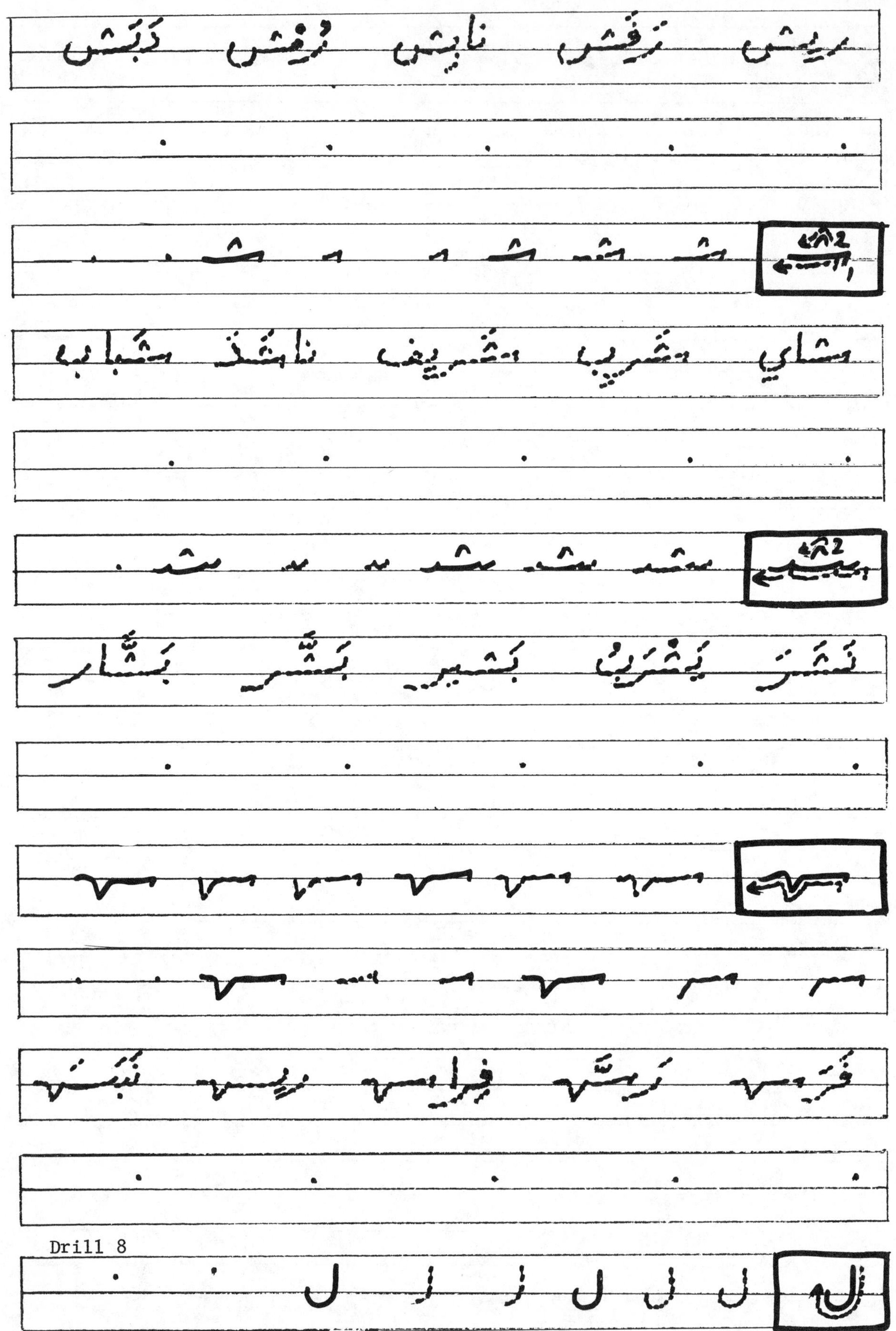
Drill 8

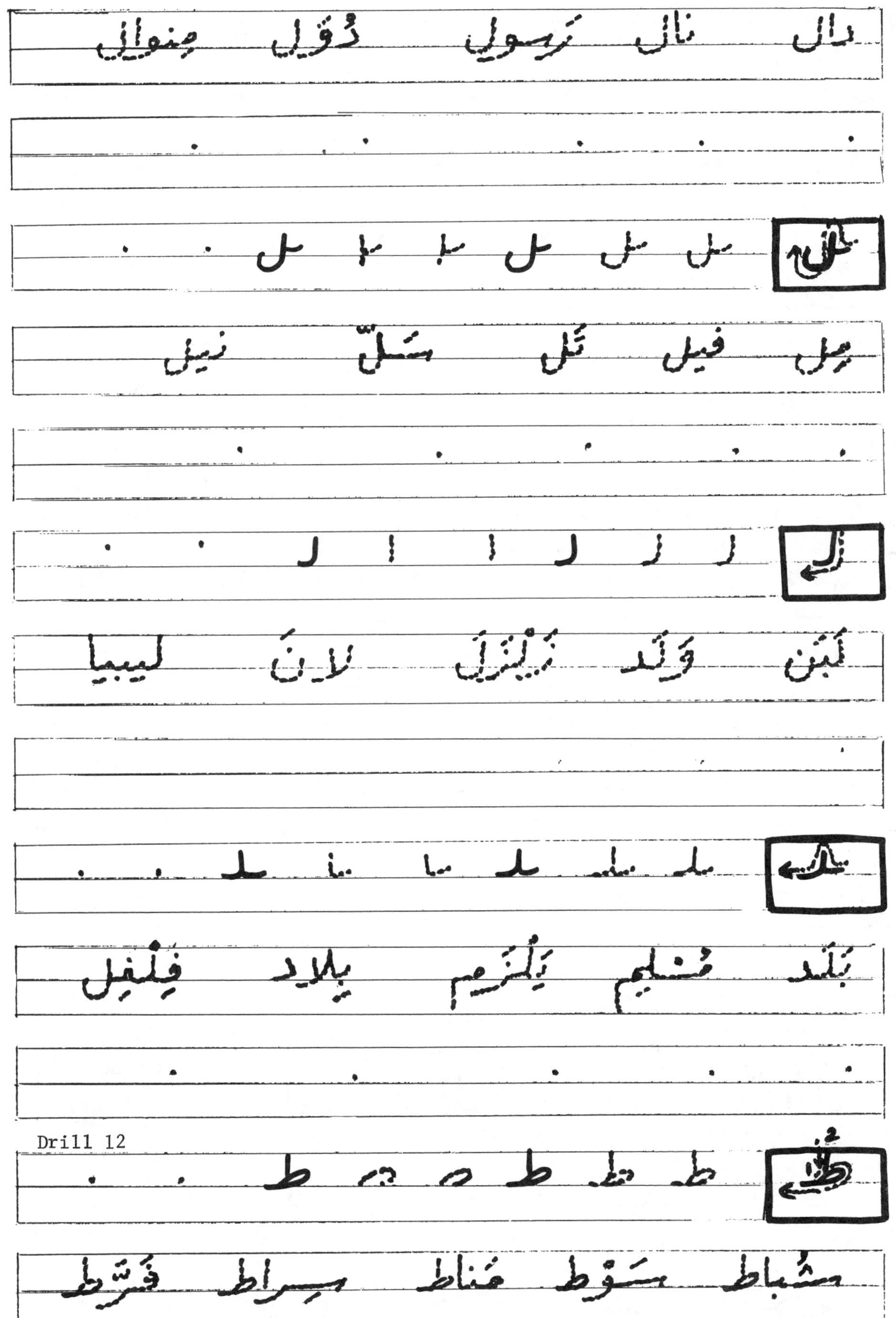

Drill 12

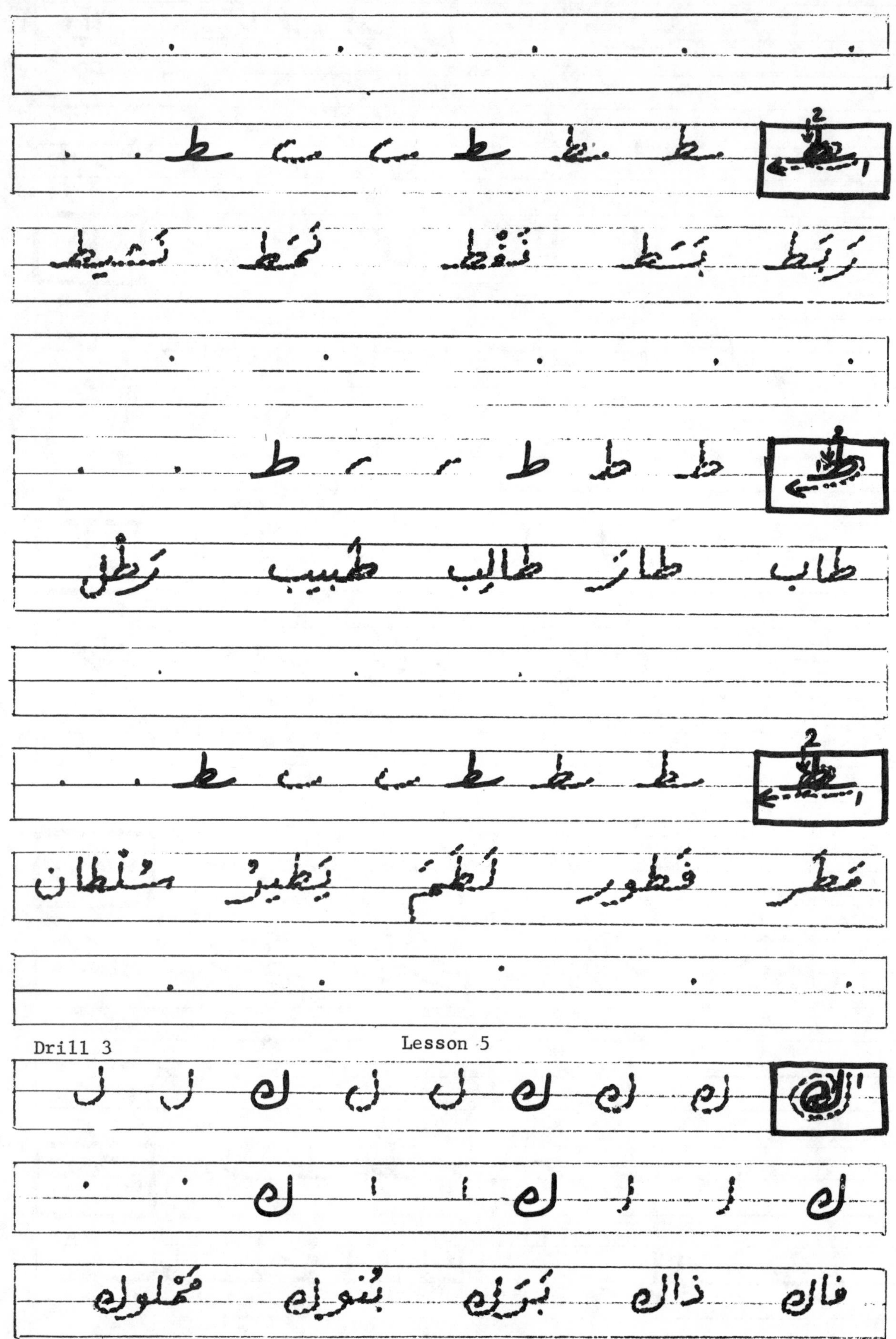
ربط بسط فقط نمط نشيط
طاب طار طالب طبيب رطل
مطر فطور لطم يطير سلطان
Drill 3
Lesson 5
فال ذال برك بنوك مملوك

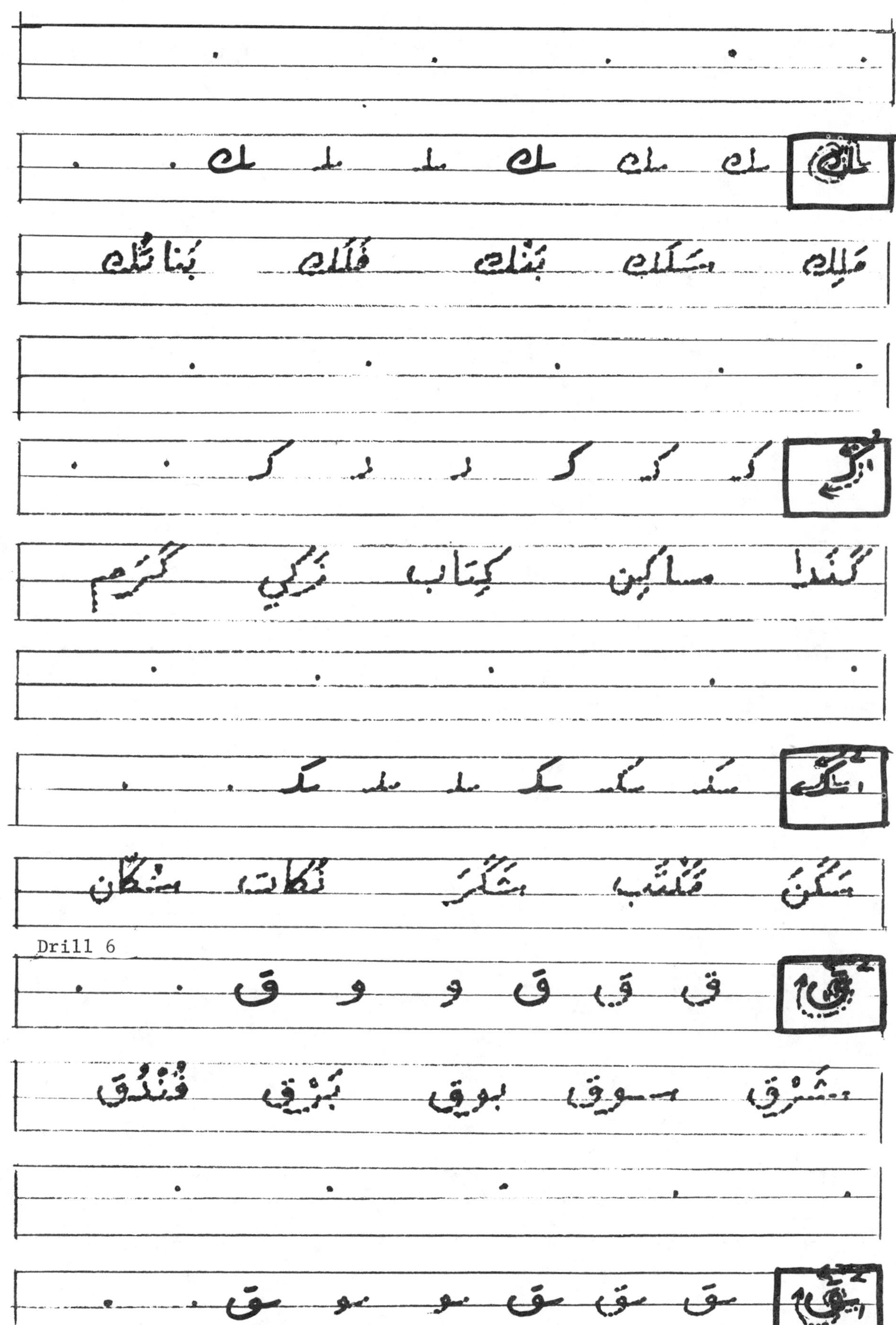

Drill 6

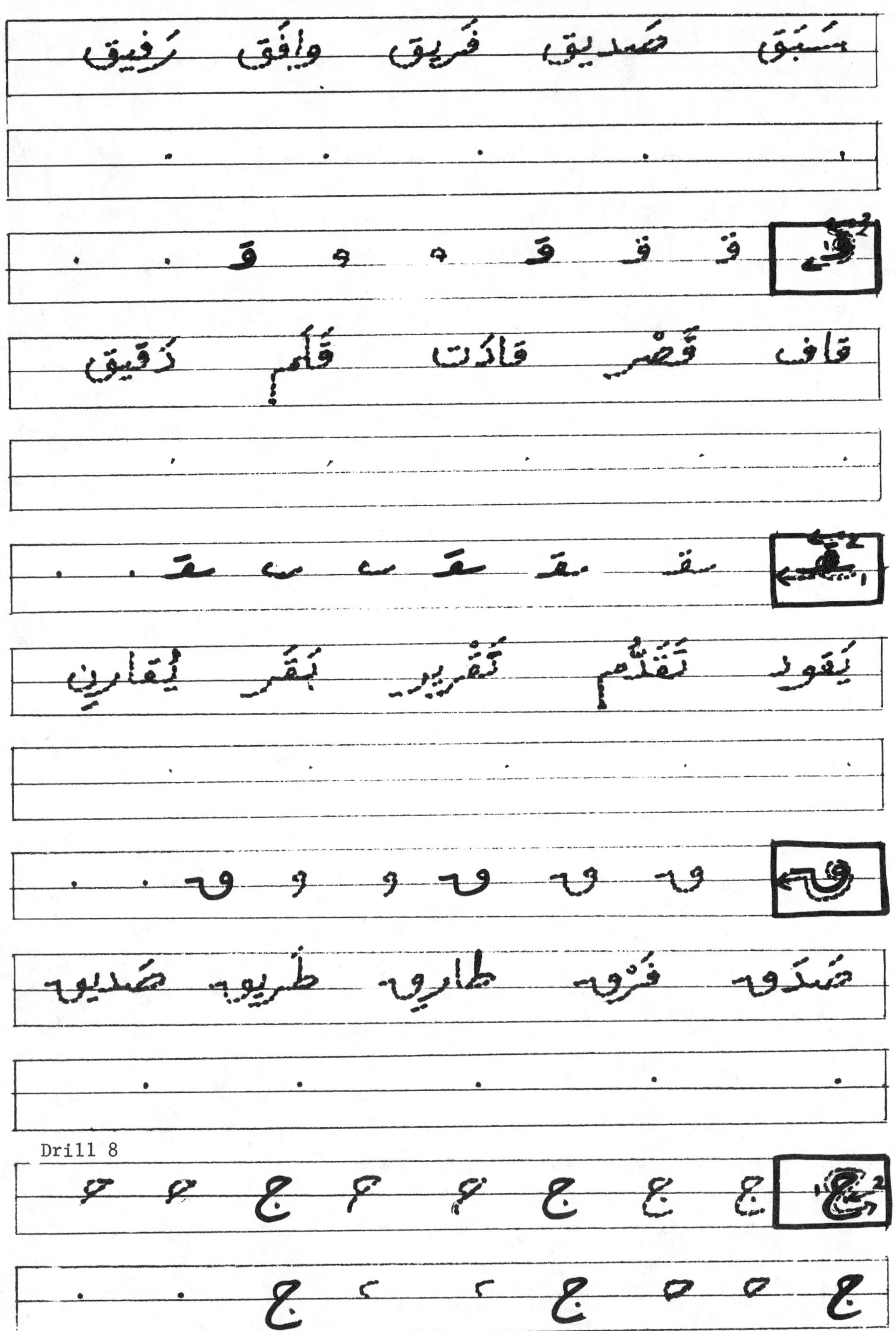
سبق صديق فريق وافق رفيق
قاف قصر قائد قلم
يقود تقدم تقرير بقر يقارن
صندوق فرق طارق طريق صديق
Drill 8

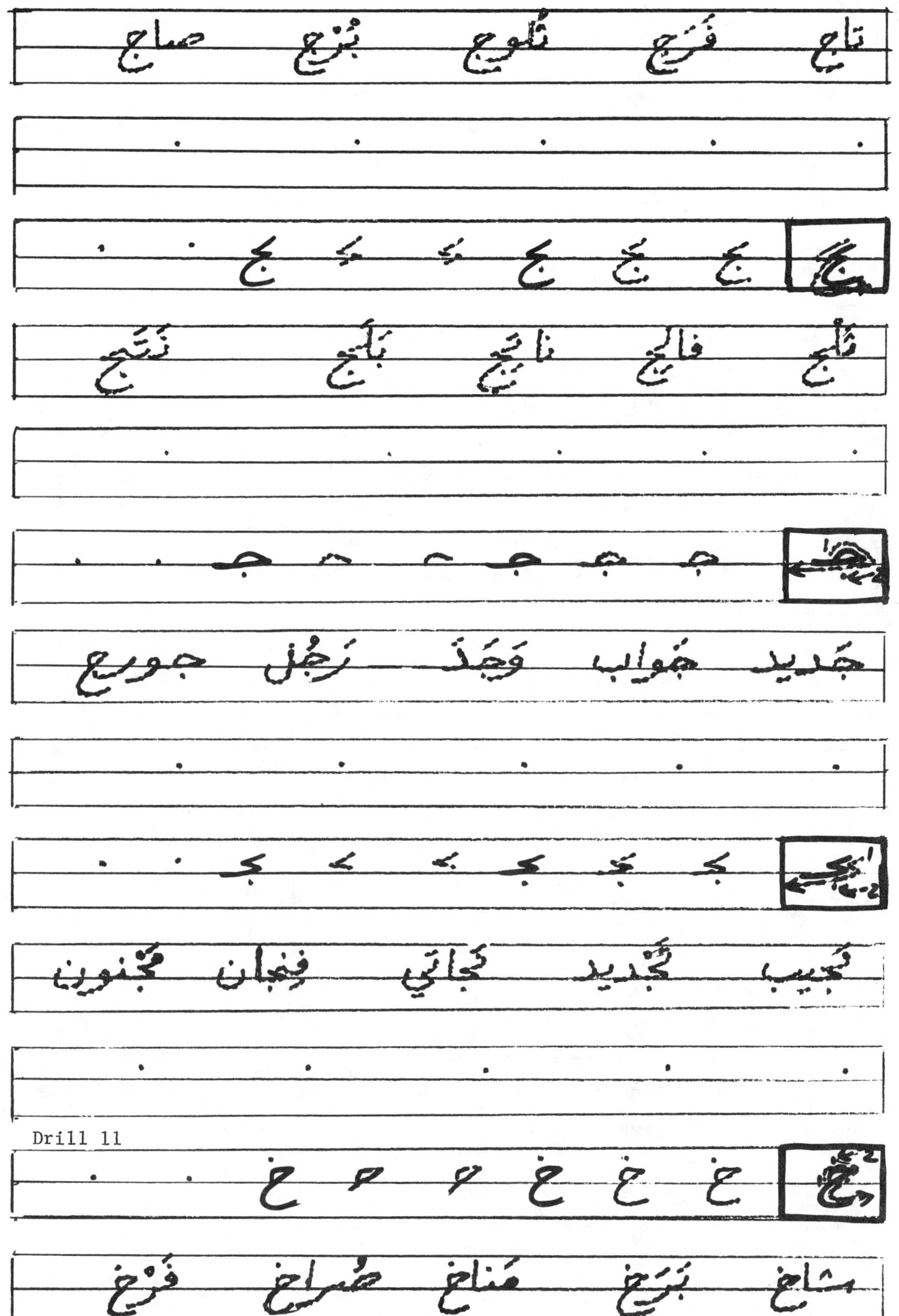

تاج   فَرَج   تَلوج   يُنتِج   صاج

ج   جَ   جِ   جَ   جَ   ج

ثَلج   فالِج   نائِج   بَلج   نَنتِج

ج   ج   ج   ج   ج

جَديد   جَواب   وَجَد   رَجُل   جورج

ج   جَ   جَ   جَ   جَ

جَبيب   جَديد   جَائي   فنجان   مجنون

Drill 11

خ   خ   خ   خ   خ

مشاخ   بَرَخ   مَناخ   صُراخ   فَرَخ

85

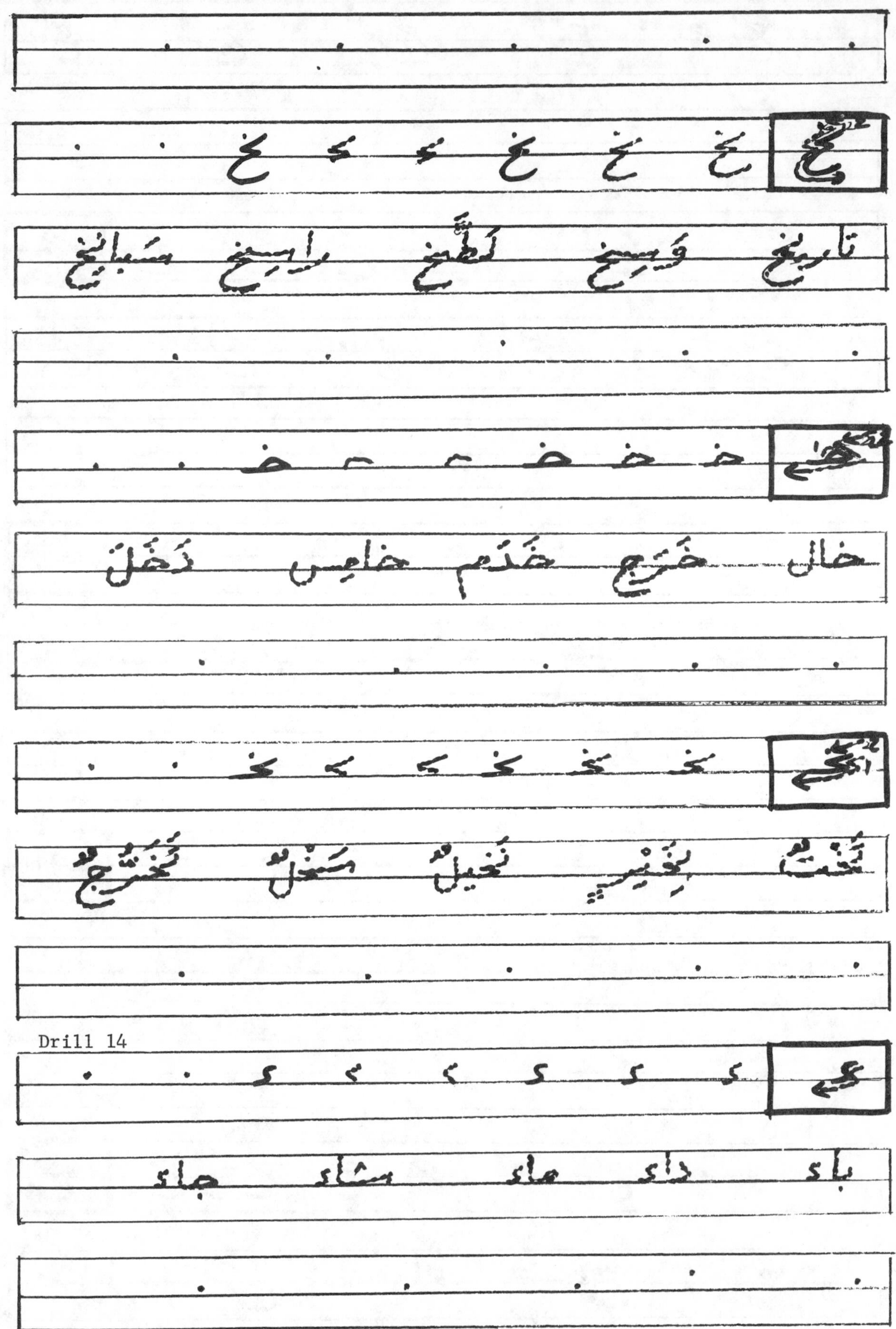

Drill 14

Lesson 6

Drill 3

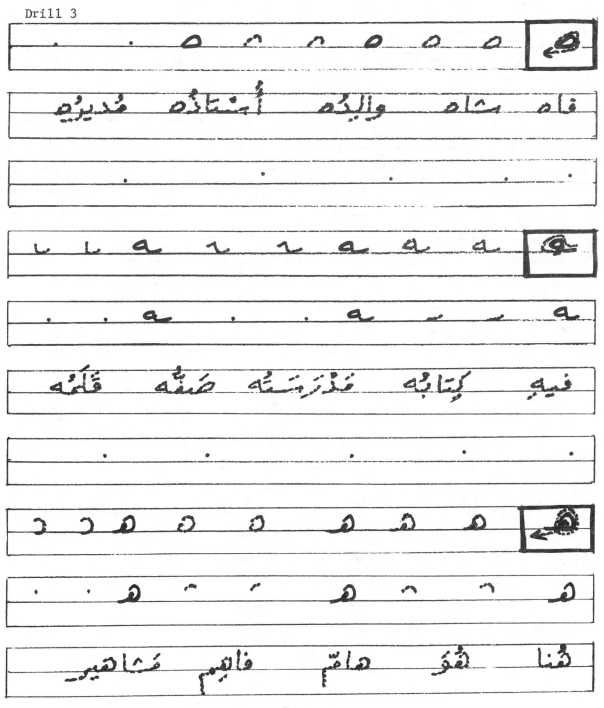

ه

فاه شاه والِدُه أُستاذُه مُديرُه

ه

فيهِ كِتابُه مَدْرَسَتُه صَفُّه قَلَمُه

ه

هُنا هُوَ هاشِم فاهِم مَشاهير

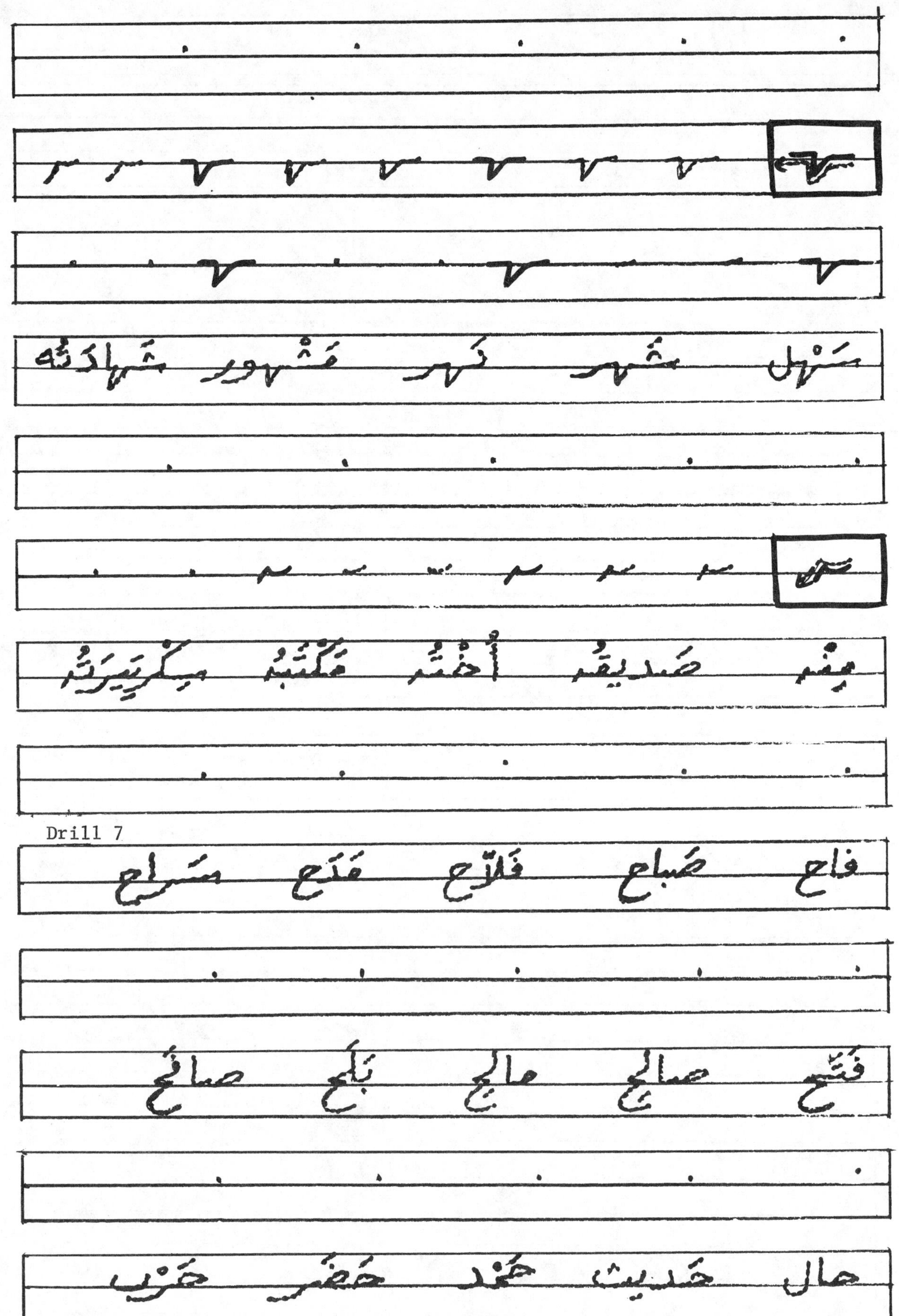
سهل شهر نهر مشهور مشاهدة
فيه صديقه أخته مكتبه سكرتيرته
Drill 7
فاح صباح فلّاح قدح مسراح
فتح صالح مالح بلح صافح
حال حديث حمد حضر حرب

مُتْحَف مَحَلّ مَحْمود مُحامي تَشْجيع

Drill 10

سوء بَدْء ماء جُزْء ضوء

بَطِيء مَجِيء شَيْء قَيْء هادِئ

مُرُوءات إحصاءات بُؤْبُؤ لُؤْلُؤ نُبُوءة

رَئِيس مُسْئِل مُتَفائِل بِئْر قائِد

فُؤاد سُؤْدُد تَساؤُل بُؤْس لُؤْلُؤ

سَأَلَ رَأْس فَأْر رَأَت رَأَيْتُ

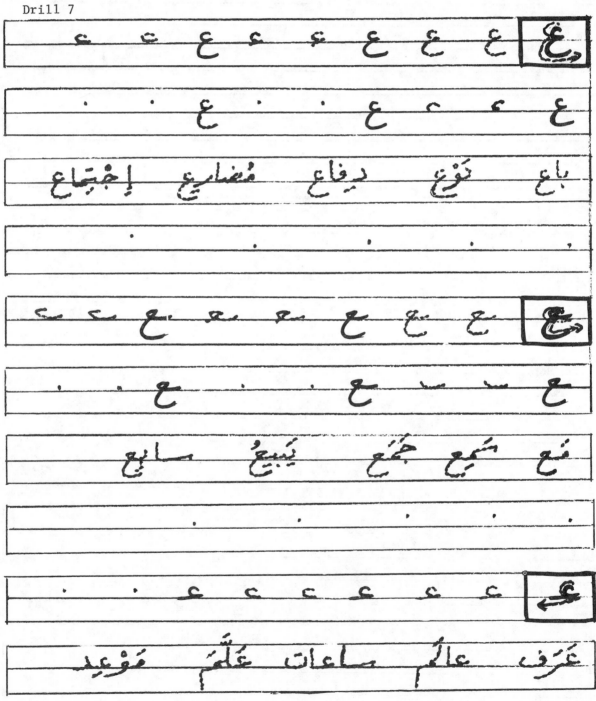

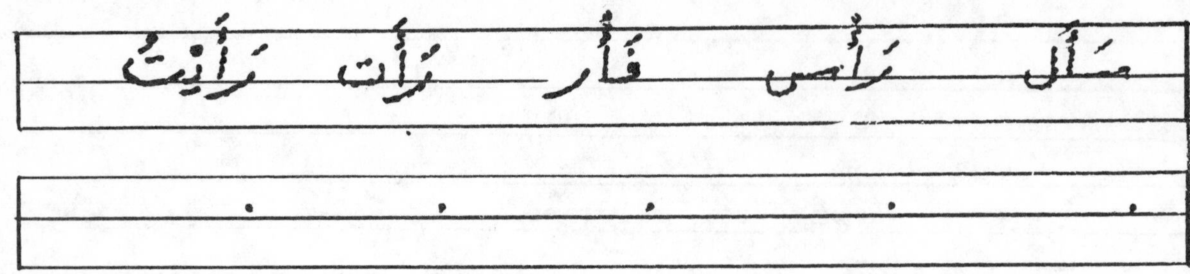

Lesson 7

Drill 7

ع ع ع ع ع ع ع ع ع ع

ع ع ع ع

باع نَوْع دِفاع مُضارِع إِجْتِماع

ـعـ ـعـ ـعـ ـعـ ـعـ ـعـ ـعـ ـعـ ـعـ

ـعـ ـعـ ـعـ

مَع سَمِيع جَمَع يَبِيعُ سابِع

عـ عـ عـ عـ عـ عـ عـ

عَرَف عالِم ساعات عَلَّمَ مَوْعِد

نَعَم صَعْبٌ بَعْض تَعْلِيم مَعْرُوف

Drill 8

آب آخَر آثار آداب قُرْآن

Drill 9

هٰذا هٰذِهِ ذٰلِك الله هٰؤُلاء

Drill 14

سَيّارَةٌ مُديرَةٌ طائِرَةٌ كَبيرَةٌ جَديدَةٍ

مَدْرَسَةٌ جامِعَةٌ مَكْتَبَةٌ جَميلَةٌ قَديمَةٍ

لَيْلَةٌ ثَلاثَةٌ ساعَةٌ مَدِينَةٌ قِصَّةٌ

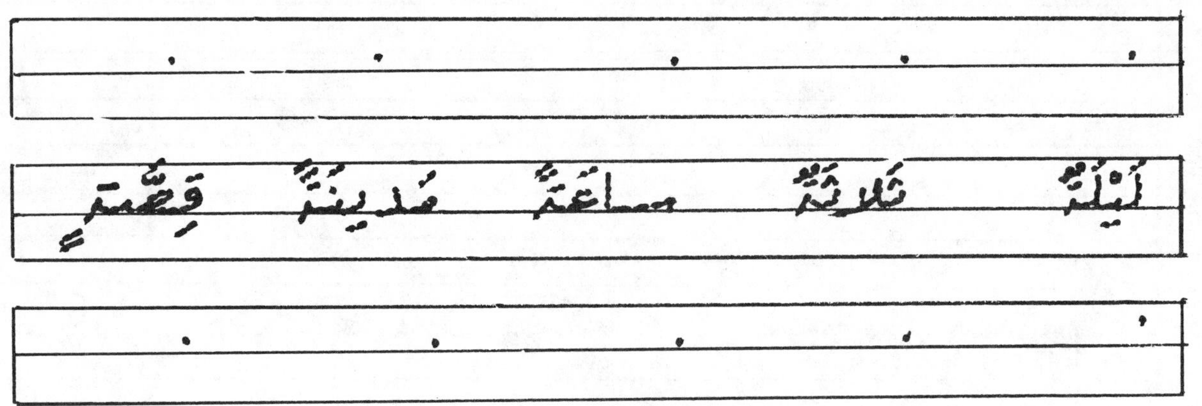

Lesson 8

Drill 3

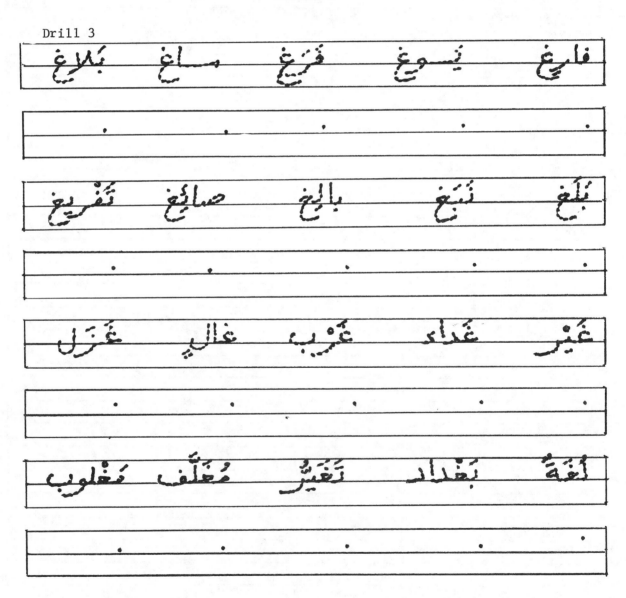

فارِغ يَسوغ فَرَّغ ساغ بَلاغ

بَلَغ نَبَغ بالِغ صائِغ تَفْريغ

غَيْر غَداء غَرْب غالي غَزَل

لُغَةٌ بَغْداد تَغَيُّر مُغَلَّف مَغْلوب

Drill 5

مَرَض قاضٍ فاض رِياض عَرْض
مَريض قَبَض رابِض حامِض أَبْيَض
ضَحِك وَضْع ضَمّة مَوْضوع مُحاضِرة
حَضَر أَيْضاً مُمَرِّضة إِنْضَمّ حَضارة
رِياص فاص مَريص أَبْيَص حامِص
Drill 7
رَأى إِشْتَرى نادى ذَرى قُرى

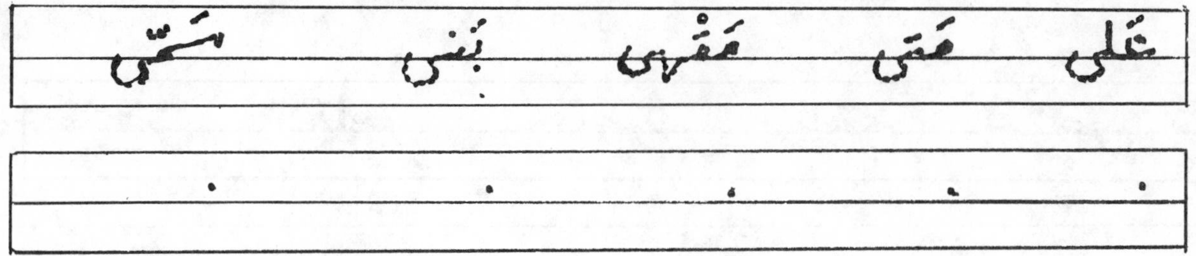

Lesson 10

Drill 3

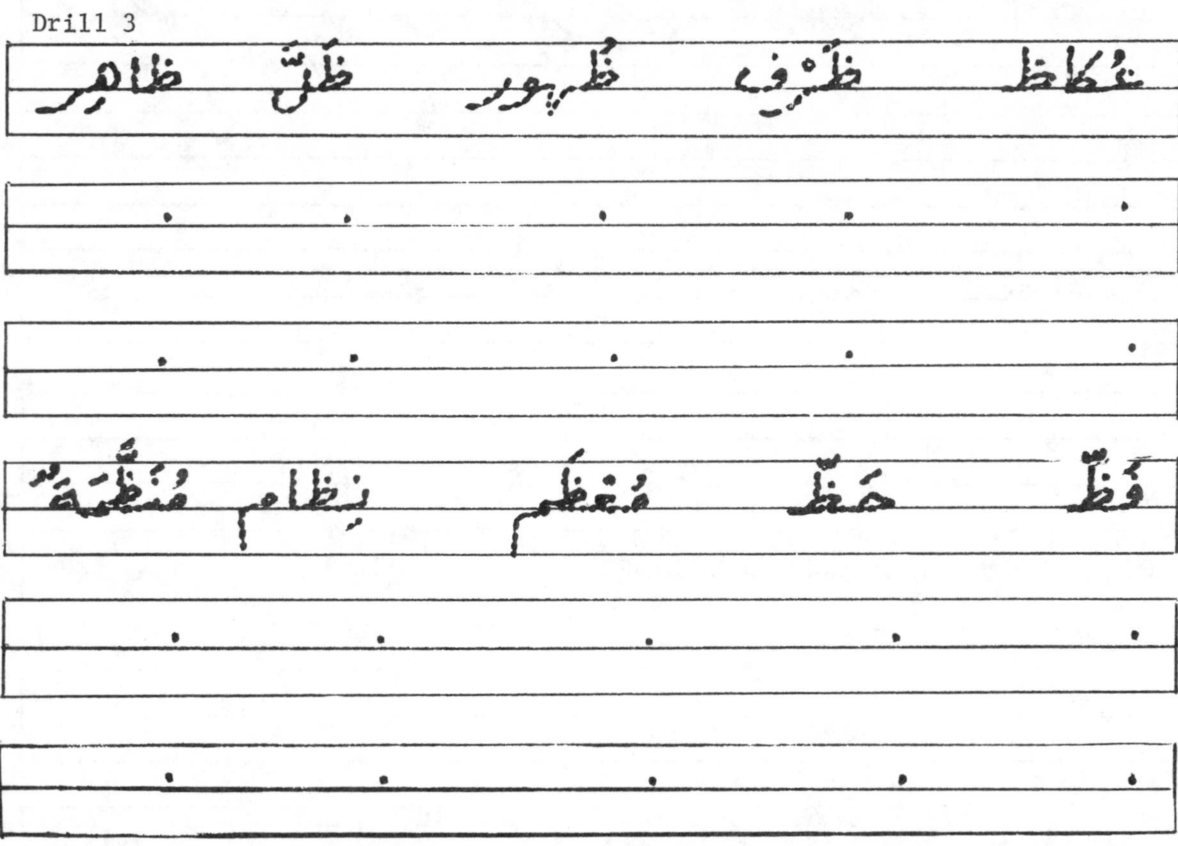

Phrases and Sentences

مع السلامة ، صباح الخير ، كتاب الأستاذ

الجامعة الأمريكية ، الموظف لبناني ، هذه مديرة

سليم من الأردن ، بغداد في العراق ، المكتبة قريبة جداً

المدرّسة الجديدة مصريّة ، مريم موجودة في الصف

Copy the following Arabic expressions:

الْعِلْمُ نورٌ.	Knowledge is light.
الْعِلْمُ	(the) knowledge
نورٌ	light
الصَّبْرُ مِفْتاحُ الفَرَجِ.	Patience is the key to a happy ending.
الصَّبْرُ	(the) patience
مِفْتاحُ	key
الفَرَجِ	freedom from grief or sorrow
رَأْسُ الحِكْمَةِ مَخافَةُ اللّٰهِ.	The beginning of wisdom is the fear of God.
رَأْسُ	head
الحِكْمَةِ	(the) wisdom
مَخافَةُ	fear
اللّٰهِ	God
طوبى لِصانِعي السَّلامِ.	Blessed are the peace-makers.
طوبى	blessedness
لِصانِعي	to the makers of
السَّلامِ	(the) peace

SECTION 2. ARABIC GRAMMAR AND VOCABULARY

Lesson One

أَلدَّرْسُ ٱلأَوَّلُ

A. Basic Text — أ ـ النص الاساسيّ

You and I — انا وانت

١ . ـ انا سليم . من انت ؟	I'm Salim. Who are you?
٢ . ـ انا سمير .	I'm Samir.
٣ . ـ ومن أنت ؟	And who are you?
٤ . ـ انا مريم .	I'm Maryam.
٥ . ـ من هذا يا مريم ؟	Who's this, Maryam?
٦ . ـ هذا سامي .	This is Sami.
٧ . ـ ومن هذه يا سامي ؟	And who is this, Sami?
٨ . ـ هذه وداد .	This is Widad.
٩ . ـ هل انت فريد ؟	Are you Farid?
١٠ . ـ نعم . انا فريد .	Yes, I'm Farid.
١١ . ـ هل انت وداد ؟	Are you Widad?
١٢ . ـ لا . انا مريم .	No, I'm Maryam.

B. Vocabulary — ب ـ أَلْمُفْرَدَاتُ

دَرْسٌ	lesson
أَلأَوَّلُ	the first
نَصٌّ	text
أَساسِيٌّ	basic
أَنَا	I
وَ	and

أَنْتَ	(m.s.) you
سَليم	Salim (m. name)
مَنْ	who?
سَمير	Samir (m. name)
أَنْتِ	(f.s.) you
مَرْيَم	Maryam, Miriam, Mary (f. name)
هٰذا	(m.s.) this, that
يا	(vocative particle: see C.4 below)
سامي	Sami (m. name)
هٰذِهِ	(f.s.) this, that
وِداد	Widad (f. name)
هَلْ	(interrogative particle)
فَريد	Farid (m. name)
نَعَمْ	yes
لا	no

C. Grammar and drills — ج – أَلْقَواعِدُ وَالتَّمارينُ

1. Equational sentences
2. Gender in pronouns
3. Interrogatives
4. Vocative: يا
5. Word order: Pronouns

1. Equational sentences

Arabic sentences are of two types, those with verbs, called verbal sentences, and those not containing verbs, called equational sentences. Verbal sentences will be introduced in Lesson 6.

The equational sentence consists of two parts, a subject and a predicate. As in English, the subject may be any kind of noun or pronoun, while the predicate may be either of these, as well as adjectives, adverbs, or prepositional phrases. The following diagram illustrates the structure of the equational sentence (read from right to left):

Predicate	Subject	
سَليم	أنا	'I am Salim.'
مَرْيَم	أَنْتِ	'You are Maryam.'
فَريد	هٰذا	'This is Farid.'

Arabic equational sentences generally correspond to English sentences in which the verb is "am", "is" or "are"--that is, a present-tense form of "to be". As in English, the Arabic predicate may identify the subject, as in "I am Salim", or describe it, as in "Salim is from Syria" or "Salim is Syrian."

2. Gender in pronouns

The English pronouns "he" and "she" show a difference in gender: "he" is masculine, while "she" is feminine. Arabic has not only this distinction between "he" and "she", it also has pronouns for "you" which show a difference in gender: أَنْتَ 'you' is masculine singular, used only in speaking to a male person, while the feminine أَنْتِ 'you' is used only in speaking to a female:

هَلْ أَنْتَ سَليم ؟	'Are you Salim?'
هَلْ أَنْتِ مَرْيَم ؟	'Are you Maryam?'

At the end of a sentence, or elsewhere when a pause follows, the pause form of the masculine pronoun is أَنْتَ ?ant. The feminine form, however, is أَنْتِ ?anti in all positions. Examples:

مَنْ أَنْتَ ؟	'Who are you?' (to a male) = ?ant
مَنْ أَنْتِ ؟	'Who are you?' (to a female) = ?anti

The Arabic demonstrative pronoun likewise shows a distinction in gender: هٰذا is masculine singular and هٰذِهِ is feminine singular. The proper choice must be made, depending on whether the pronoun refers to a male or a female, as in

هٰذا سَليم وَهٰذا فَريد وَهٰذِهِ وِداد	'This is Salim, this is Farid, and this is Widad.'

هٰذا and هٰذِهِ refer not only to things near the speaker but to things near the person addressed as well; they may accordingly be translated by "that" as well as by "this".

Arabic has only two genders, while English has three--masculine ("he"), feminine ("she"), and neuter ("it"). When it is a matter of natural gender--humans, animals, etc.--Arabic هُوَ 'he' and هِيَ 'she' and English he and she correspond to each other nicely. Inanimates, however, are all referred to as it in English, while they must be masculine or feminine in Arabic. In these instances, Arabic هُوَ and هِيَ are translated by English "it". Thus, هُوَ referring to فَريد is "he", but referring to الدَّرْس is "it".

Drill 1. Recognition of masculine and feminine.

Teacher supplies the cue, student supplies a male or female name. (Suggestion: Write a list of Arabic names on the board, in separate columns for m. and f.)

T(eacher)	:	أنا سليم • أنتِ
S(tudent)	:	أنتِ وداد
	أنتَ	أنا
	هذا	أنتِ
	هذه	هذا

3. <u>Interrogatives</u>

If an Arabic sentence contains an interrogative word, such as 'who?', that word is first in the sentence:

مَنْ أَنْتْ ؟	'Who are you?'

Now do Drill 2.

If the sentence is a question which may be answered by "yes" or "no", the interrogative particle هَلْ is used to introduce it. In other words, a statement may be changed into a yes-or-no question simply by beginning with هَلْ. (There are also particular intonation patterns associated with questions; since these vary from one region to another, the student is best advised to imitate his native-speaker model.). This particle has no equivalent in English, where questions have a different word order from statements. Here are examples:

Statement	هٰذا سَمير	'This is Samir.'
Question	هَلْ هٰذا سَمير ؟	'Is this Samir?'
Statement	أَنْتِ وِداد	'You are Widad.'
Question	هَلْ أَنْتِ وِداد ؟	'Are you Widad?'

Now do Drills 3 and 4.

Drill 2. Chain drill.

Teacher introduces himself; asks first student من أنت ؟ . S_1 replies, then asks next student (S_2) من أنت ؟ , continuing around the class.

T : أنا (سليم) . من أنتَ ؟

S_1 : أنا (روبرت) . من أنتِ ؟

S_2 : أنا (نانسى) ...

Drill 3. Question/answer with هَلْ .

Teacher asks each student هل أنت ___؟, using names of class members.

T : هل أنت (روبرت) ؟

S_1 : نعم . أنا (روبرت) .

T : هل أنت (نانسي) ؟

S_2 : لا . أنا (سالي) .

Drill 4. (Also on tape) Question formation with هَلْ .

Teacher supplies statement, student forms question using هَلْ . Ex.

T : هذا سمير .

S : هل هذا سمير ؟

هذه مريم .　　هذا سامي .

هذا سليم .　　هذه نانسي .

هذه وِداد .　　هذا فريد .

4. Vocative: يا

In Arabic, when someone is directly addressed by name or title, the particle يا is used just before the name or title, for example:

مَنْ هٰذا يا سَليم ؟ 'Who is this, Salim?'
يا وِداد ! 'Widad!'

This is called a vocative particle. It corresponds to the old English word 'O', as in 'O King!', but in modern English it is usually left untranslated.

Drill 5. (Chain drill) من هذا ؟ with vocative.

Teacher asks S_1 about S_2, S_1 asks S_2 about S_3, and so on around the class. If, for example, S_1 doesn't know S_2's name, he asks him first, then continues with the drill.

T to S_1	:	من هذه يا (روبرت) ؟
S_1	:	من أنتِ ؟
S_2	:	أنا (نانسي) .
S_1 to T	:	هذه (نانسي) .
S_1 to S_2	:	من هذا ، يا (نانسي) ؟

5. Word order: Pronouns

In the title of the Basic Text above, note that the first-person pronoun comes first:

أنا وَأنْتَ	'I and you.'

This is of course the reverse of the usual English order 'you and I'. When there is a series of pronouns, or pronouns and nouns, the regular order in Arabic is: first person, second person, third person, noun. Other examples:

أنا وَسَمير	'Samir and I'
أَنْتَ وَوِداد	'You and Widad'

Drill 6. (On tape) Dictation.

Lesson Two

أَلدَّرْسُ الثّانِي

أ ـ النص الاساسيّ

A. Basic Text

استاذ وطالب

Professor and Student

١ ـ ما هذا يا فريد ؟	What's this, Farid?
٢ ـ هذا كتاب .	This is a book.
٣ ـ وما هذه ؟	And what's this?
٤ ـ هذه ورقة .	This is a sheet of paper.
٥ ـ هل هذا باب ؟	Is that a door?
٦ ـ لا . هذا شبّاك .	No, that's a window.
٧ ـ وهذه ؟	And this?
٨ ـ هذه طاولة .	This is a table.

من أين أنت ؟

Where Are You From?

٩ ـ سليم ـ أنا سليم . وهذا سامي.	I'm Salim. And this is Sami.
١٠ـ روبرت ـ أنا روبرت . وهذه نانسي.	I'm Robert. And this is Nancy.
من أين أنت يا سليم ؟	Where are you from, Salim?
١١ـ سليم ـ أنا من بيروت .	I'm from Beirut.
١٢ـ روبرت ـ أنا من آن آربر .	I'm from Ann Arbor.
١٣ـ سليم ـ أين آن آربر ؟	Where's Ann Arbor?
١٤ـ روبرت ـ آن آربر في ميشيغان.	Ann Arbor is in Michigan.
١٥ـ سليم ـ هل أنت طالب ؟	Are you a student?
١٦ـ روبرت ـ نعم ، أنا طالب .	Yes, I'm a student.
١٧ـ سليم ـ ونانسي ؟	And Nancy?
١٨ـ روبرت ـ هي طالبة من آن اربر كذلك .	She's a student from Ann Arbor, too.
هل سامي طالب ؟	Is Sami a student?
١٩ـ سليم ـ نعم ، هو طالب من دمشق .	Yes, he's a student from Damascus.

B. Vocabulary — ب ـ أَلْمُفْرَداتُ

آلثّانِي	the second	نانسي	Nancy
أُسْتاذٌ	professor	بَيْروتُ	Beirut
ما	what?	آن آرْبَر	Ann Arbor
كِتابٌ	book	في	in
وَرَقَةٌ	sheet of paper, piece of paper	ميشِغان	Michigan
بابٌ	door	طالِبٌ	student
شُبّاكٌ	window	طالِبَةٌ	(f.) student
طاوِلَةٌ	table	كَذٰلِكَ	likewise, too
مِنْ	from	هِيَ	she
أَيْنَ	where?	هُوَ	he
روبِرْت	Robert	دِمَشْقُ	Damascus

Additional vocabulary

قَلَمٌ	pen, pencil	لُبْنانُ	(m.) Lebanon
لَوْحٌ	blackboard	سورِيّا	(f.) Syria
كُرْسِيٌّ	chair	أَمْرِيكا	(f.) America

C. Grammar and drills — ج ـ أَلْقَواعِدُ وَالتَّمارِينُ

1. Interrogative in phrase
2. Nunation in nouns
3. Case: General
4. Nominative case
5. Gender in nouns

1. Interrogative in phrase

As was shown in the last lesson (1.C.3) an interrogative word comes first in the sentence. Sometimes, however, the interrogative word is part of a phrase (functioning as the object of a preposition) as in مِنْ أَيْنَ 'from where?'. In such cases the entire phrase is the first element of the sentence, as in the second sentence below:

أَيْنَ سَلِيمٌ ؟	'Where is Salim?'
مِنْ أَيْنَ سَلِيمٌ ؟	'Where is Salim from?'

Notice that in English a phrase like 'from where?' may be separated, with 'from' coming at the end. Example: 'Where are you from?' This cannot be done in Arabic, where the interrogative phrase is always an undivided unit at the beginning of the sentence.

Drill 1. Chain drill.

S_1: I am from _____. أنا من ______ .

Where are you from? من أين أنت ؟

S_2: I am from _____. أنا من ______ .

Where are you from? من أين انت ؟

Drill 2. (Also on tape) Question formation.

Form a question from the following sentences using من أين ؟ .

Sami is from Lebanon. → Where is Sami from? سامى من لبنان ← من أين سامي؟

١ ـ هي من سوريا ٤ ـ هو من دمشق

٢ ـ وداد من بيروت ٥ ـ سمير من لبنان

٣ ـ انتَ من امريكا ٦ ـ انتِ من ميشغان

2. Nunation in nouns

The final n in forms such as طالِبٌ is known as nunation (in Arabic تَنْوِين). It is a mark of indefiniteness, corresponding in general to the

English indefinite article "a, an", as in "a student", or to the absence of any article in words like "bread", "milk", or "students". An Arabic noun normally has nunation unless it is made definite; thus for example, when the definite article اَلْ is added to a word the n of nunation is dropped.

Definite		Indefinite	
'the student' (m.)	اَلطّالِبُ	طالِبٌ	'a student' (m.)
'the student' (f.)	اَلطّالِبَةُ	طالِبَةٌ	'a student' (f.)

Names of cities, countries, and female persons do not take nunation; examples are بَيْروتُ Beirut', لُبْنانُ 'Lebanon', and مَرْيَمُ 'Maryam'.

3. Case: General

In English the function of words in a sentence is indicated to a large extent by word order. Note the following sentences:

The student invited the teacher.

The teacher invited the student.

In the first sentence, we know that it was the student who issued the invitation and the teacher who was invited, because the word student precedes the verb invited and the word teacher follows it. In the second sentence the roles of student and teacher with respect to the act of inviting are reversed, and again it is the word order which tells us who does what. In the case of pronouns, the word order gives the same kind of information, and also the form of the pronouns is different:

He invited her.

She invited him.

In Arabic word order is important too, though not always the same as in English. However, the Arabic noun (like an English pronoun) has different forms depending on what function it has in a particular sentence. These forms are called case forms. Arabic nouns have three case forms, called nominative, genitive, and accusative. Here, for example, are the three case forms for the noun 'a student':

	Masculine		Feminine
Nominative	طالِبٌ		طالِبَةٌ
Genitive	طالِبٍ	'a student'	طالِبَةٍ
Accusative	طالِبًا		طالِبَةً

As the table shows, the difference between one case and another lies in the vowel endings of the noun--here -u for the nominative, -i for the genitive, and -a for the accusative.

Each case is used for several different sentence functions, and these will be described as they occur. This lesson illustrates four functions of the nominative case, as described in 4 below.

Personal and place names from foreign languages, such as روبِرْت 'Robert' and ميشِغان 'Michigan' do not receive these case endings.

Drill 3. Written. Recognition: Case marker in indefinite nouns and adjectives.

Write the vowel which marks the case in each of the following words: Ex.

u طالِبٌ

طالبةٌ	شبّاكاً	أستاذٌ	لوحٍ
باباً	درسٌ	طاولةٍ	ورقةٌ
نصٍّ	اساسيٌّ	سليمٍ	كتاباً

4. Nominative case

a. Nouns occurring in titles or headings (like the headings of the parts of this lesson), or occurring in lists, or mentioned in grammar notes or drills, etc. are in the nominative case. Such instances of the use of nouns in the nominative are referred to as citation forms. Examples:

هَلْ هٰذِهِ " بابٌ " ؟	'Is this (word) "door"?'
أَلنَّصُّ الأساسيُّ : " أُسْتاذٌ وَطالِبٌ ".	'Basic Text: "Professor and Student"'

b. A noun functioning as the subject or as the predicate of an equational sentence is in the nominative case; this noun may have one or more modifiers:

سَليمٌ طالِبٌ .	'Salim is a student.'
وِدادُ طالِبَةٌ مِنْ بَيْروت .	'Widad is a student from Beirut.'

In these sentences سَليمٌ and وِدادُ are subjects, and طالِبٌ and طالِبَةٌ are predicates; they are, accordingly, in the nominative case, as is shown by the vowel u. (In the ending -un the -n is nunation: see 2 above.)

(We shall see later that there is a situation where the subject of an equational sentence is in the accusative case, and that the predicates of verbs are also in the accusative case.)

Now do Drill 4.

c. A noun after the vocative particle يا is in the nominative case and without nunation:

يا سَليمُ !	'Salim!'
يا أُسْتاذُ !	'Professor!'

Drill 4. (On tape) Substitution.

5. Gender in nouns

Arabic nouns have either of two genders: masculine or feminine. If the noun refers to an animate being, then its gender agrees with the natural gender of the referent. Thus the following nouns are masculine:

سَليمٌ	'Salim'	أُسْتاذٌ	'professor'
روبرت	'Robert'	طالِبٌ	'student' (male)
سَميرٌ	'Samir'		

and the following are feminine:

وِدادُ	'Widad'	طالِبَةٌ	'student' (female)
مَرْيَمُ	'Maryam'	سامِيَةُ	'Samiya'

The gender of names of cities and countries is almost entirely predictable. All names of cities are feminine, such as

بَيْروتُ 'Beirut' and واشِنْطُن 'Washington'.

Names of countries are also feminine, the common exceptions being

لُبْنانُ 'Lebanon', العِراقُ 'Iraq', الأُرْدُنُّ 'Jordan', السّودانُ 'The Sudan' and المَغْرِبُ 'Morocco'. Other exceptions to this rule will be so marked in the vocabulary lists.

The gender of almost all other nouns depends on the form of the word itself. The suffix ـَةٌ -a(t)- indicates feminine gender; a noun without a feminine suffix is masculine. Thus, وَرَقَةٌ 'a sheet of paper' and طاوِلَةٌ 'table' are feminine, while كِتابٌ 'book', بابٌ 'door', شُبّاكٌ 'window', قَلَمٌ 'pencil', لَوْحٌ 'blackboard', كُرْسِيٌّ 'chair' and نَصٌّ 'text' are masculine. The few exceptions to this rule will also be noted as they occur.

The feminine suffix ـَةٌ is also used to derive a feminine noun from a masculine one, as in طالِبٌ – طالِبَةٌ ; pairs of this type are exceedingly common. It is a general rule that whatever comes in male-female pairs in the real world, like kings and queens, poets and poetesses, male students and female students, etc., are expressed in Arabic by pairs of words such as طالِبٌ — طالِبَةٌ , where ـَةٌ — designates the female member of the pair. Thus, سَيِّدٌ is 'Mister' and سَيِّدَةٌ is 'Mrs.', أُسْتاذٌ is a male professor and أُسْتاذَةٌ is a female professor; مُدَرِّسٌ is a male instructor while مُدَرِّسَةٌ is a female one. There are several pairs, however, where the two words are completely different, like أَبٌ 'father' and أُمٌّ 'mother'. There are also instances where a feminine noun has no masculine counterpart, such as آنِسَةٌ 'Miss', or a masculine noun has no feminine counterpart, such as إِمامٌ 'Imam'. Henceforth in this book, when a masculine noun with animate referent is listed, it is to be assumed that the feminine counterpart may be automatically formed by adding ـَةٌ ; thus, مُراسِلٌ 'reporter' (m.) implies مُراسِلَةٌ 'reporter' (f.), and مُراسِلَةٌ will be listed under مُراسِلٌ . If the feminine form is different, as in أَبٌ 'father' and أُمٌّ 'mother', both forms will be given. If no masculine or feminine counterpart exists, that fact will be noted. <u>The same arrangement will hold for adjectives as well.</u>

Gender not only identifies the sex of the referent (for animate beings), it also serves an important grammatical function. Masculine nouns are replaced by masculine pronouns and, as we will see, are modified by masculine adjectives; feminine nouns require feminine pronouns and adjectives. This feature of agreement in gender is a great aid in helping identify the referent of a pronoun or the noun modified by a particular adjective.

<u>Drill 5</u>. Written. Recognition drill: Gender.

Place M after the masculine nouns and F after the feminine nouns in the following listing:

مكتب	'office'	مُدير	'director'
آنسة	'Miss'	القاهِرة	'Cairo'
سيّد	'Mister'	العراق	'Iraq'
جامِعة	'university'	استاذة	'professor'

حَمْد	'praise'	مـتْحف	'museum'
سيّارة	'automobile'	موظّف	'employee'
بغداد	'Bagdad'	أمّ	'mother'
تاريخ	'history'	مَساء	'evening'

Drill 6. Written. m. → f. with ة .

Change the following nouns from masculine to feminine by adding ـة :

زائر	'visitor'	كَريم	'Karim'
صَديق	'friend'	سامي	'Sami'
عربيّ	'Arab'	مُوَظّف	'employee'
مُدرِّس	'teacher'	أَجْنَبيّ	'foreign'
مُدير	'director'	جَديد	'new'

Drill 7. Written.

Turn the statements below into questions, using مَنْ or ما as appropriate.

'This is Samir. → Who is this?' هذا سمير ← من هذا ؟

'This is a sheet of paper. → What is this?' هذه ورقة ← ما هذه ؟

هذا درس	هذا لوح
هذه طاولة	هذا سليم
هذا سامي	هذا كتاب
هذه وداد	هذا شبّاك
هذا نصّ	هذه وداد

Drill 8. (Oral or written) Conjunction with وَ .

Two sentences will be given. Make one sentence with the subjects joined with وَ . Ex.

'I am from Lebanon.' 'Farid is from Lebanon.'	→ ←	انا من لبنان فريد من لبنان

'I and Farid are from Lebanon.' انا وفريد من لبنان .

انتِ من بيروت سامي من بيروت	هو من مشغان نانسي من مشغان
هي من دمشق وداد من دمشق	انا من سوريا انتَ من سوريا

Drill 9. Variable substitution.

Substitute the following words for the underlined words, making the appropriate changes.

انا طالب من لبنان

٥ - انتَ ـــــ ـــ ـــ	١ - انتِ ـــــ ـــ ـــ
٦ - هذه ـــــ ـــ ـــ	٢ - هو ـــــ ـــ ـــ
٧ - ـــــ طاولة ـــ ـــ	٣ - نانسي ـــــ ـــ ـــ
	٤ - ـــــ استاذ ـــ ـــ

Drill 10. (On tape) Written. Dictation.

Lesson Three

أَلدَّرْسُ ٱلثّالِثُ

A. Basic Text — أ ــ النص الاساسيّ

In the Office — في المكتب

١ . الاستاذ فريد ــ صباح الخير .	Good morning.
٢ . الآنسة هند ــ صباح النور .	Good morning.
٣ . الاستاذفريد ــ من السكرتيرة في هذا المكتب ؟	Who's the secretary in this office?
٤ . الآنسة هند ــ أنا .	I am.
٥ . الاستاذفريد ــ من المدير ؟	Who's the director?
٦ . الآنسة هند ــ السيد سليم .	Mr. Salim.
٧ . الاستاذفريد ــ هو عربيّ ، أليس كذلك ؟	He's an Arab, isn't he?
٨ . الآنسة هند ــ نعم ، هو من القاهرة	Yes, he's from Cairo.
هل انت مدرّس ؟	Are you a teacher?
٩ . الاستاذ فريد ــ نعم ، أنا مدرّس .	Yes, I'm a teacher.
١٠. الآنسة هند ــ هل أنت جديد هنا ؟	Are you new here?
١١. الاستاذ فريد ــ نعم .	Yes.

B. Vocabulary — ب ــ أَلْمُفْرَداتُ

الثّالِثُ	the third
مَكْتَبٌ	office (place)
الأُسْتاذُ	the professor; sir, Mr. (see Note 1 below)
صَباحَ الخَيْرِ	Good morning
آنِسَةٌ	Miss; young lady
صَباحَ النّورِ	Good morning (response)
سِكْرِتيرٌ	secretary (pron. sikriteer)

هِنْدٌ	Hind (f. name)
مُدِيرٌ	director
السَّيِّدُ	Mr.
عَرَبِيٌّ	Arabic, Arab; an Arab
أَلَيْسَ كَذٰلِكَ ؟	Isn't that so?
القَاهِرَةُ	Cairo
مُدَرِّسٌ	teacher
جَدِيدٌ	new
هُنَا	here

Additional Vocabulary

الخَرْطُومُ	Khartoum
السُّودَانُ	(m.) Sudan
الرِّيَاضُ	Riyadh
السَّعُودِيَّةُ	Saudi Arabia
الكُوَيْتُ	(m.) Kuwait
العِرَاقُ	(m.) Iraq

Note 1.

The Arabic equivalent of the English title "professor" is أُسْتَاذٌ (أُسْتَاذَةٌ), but the use of the term differs somewhat from English. In Arab countries, not only a professor at a university is called أُسْتَاذٌ (أُسْتَاذَةٌ) but in general any person in a learned field, such as lawyers, literary persons, and teachers in a secondary school. In addition, the term أُسْتَاذٌ (but not أُسْتَاذَةٌ) is used to address any man--whether an acquaintance or a stranger on the street--to whom it is appropriate to show courtesy or respect. For a lady in these circumstances one uses the title آنِسَةٌ "miss" or سَيِّدَةٌ "madam".

Note 2.

In Arabic the first name rather than the family name is commonly used with titles such as أُسْتَاذٌ, آنِسَةٌ, سَيِّدٌ , etc.

C. Grammar and drills 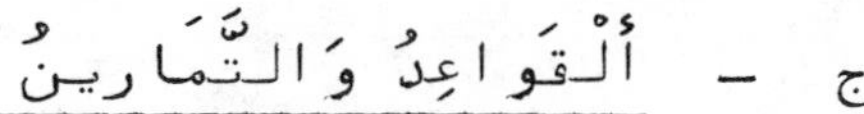 ج –

1. The genitive case: Object of preposition
2. Helping vowels
3. The definite article
4. Demonstrative phrases
5. Agreement of predicate adjective
6. Numerals 1-5

1. The genitive case: Object of preposition

The object of a preposition is in the genitive case. For the great majority of nouns, the genitive case ending is -i (see 2.C.3); illustrations:

في المَكْتَبِ	'in the office'	مِنَ القاهِرَةِ	'from Cairo'
فى الخَرْطومِ	'in Khartoum'	مِنَ اللَّوْحِ	'from the blackboard'
فى الشُّبّاكِ	'in the window'	مِنْ فَريدٍ	'from Farid'
في الكِتابِ	'in the book'	مِنَ الكِتابِ	'from the book'
فى النَّصِّ	'in the text'	مِنَ السّودانِ	'from the Sudan'

For those words which do not take nunation (see 2.C.2), the genitive case ending is -a , as for example:

في بَيْروتَ	'in Beirut'	مِنْ دِمَشْقَ	'from Damascus'
في لُبْنانَ	'in Lebanon'	مِنْ مَرْيَمَ	'from Maryam'

(If, however, such words are made definite they then take the regular genitive case ending in -i , e.g.

في هٰذا اللُّبْنانِ .	'in this Lebanon'

)

<u>Drill 1</u>. Written. Recognition drill: Case.

In the following words or phrases, circle the vowel (or vowel plus nunation) marking case; then write N (Nom.) or G (Gen.). <u>Ex</u>.

N اَلطّالِبُ

١ - اَلْقَلَمُ
٢ - مِنْ مُدِيرٍ
٣ - فِي الْمَكْتَبِ
٤ - وَرَقَةٌ
٥ - مِنَ الْكِتابِ
٦ - فِي بَيْرُوتَ
٧ - بَيْرُوتُ

2. <u>Helping vowels</u>

In English, groups of consonants--three, four, or even more--may occur all in a row with no vowels in between, for example <u>-bstr-</u> in <u>abstract</u> or <u>st pr</u> in <u>best price</u>. In Arabic, however, it is a general rule that <u>no more than two consonants can occur together</u>, no matter whether within a single word or at the end of one word and the beginning of the next. Thus, within a single word there may be groups of two consonants together, such as <u>-kt-</u> in مَكْتَبٌ 'office' or <u>-nt-</u> in أَنْتَ 'you', but never more than two. And, within a sentence, a word may end in one consonant and the following word begin with one consonant (a total of two consonants in a row), for example <u>-n h-</u> in مَنْ هٰذا ؟ 'Who's this?', or <u>-n b-</u> مِنْ بَيْرُوتَ 'from Beirut', but there can never be more than two consonants in this situation. Often there is no problem, since no Arabic word in isolation ends or begins with more than one consonant. In some words beginning with a <u>hamza</u>, however, this <u>hamza</u> and the following vowel are dropped (elided) when the word is not first in the sentence. The most common of such words are those with the definite article أَلْ 'the'. Thus 'the director' is أَلْمُدِيرُ /ʔalmudiir/ (beginning with one consonant) if it is the first word in the sentence, but

اَلْمُدِيرُ /-lmudiir/ if any other word precedes it. Now, in effect, the word begins with two consonants, -lm-. If the preceding word ends in a vowel, as in أَنْتَ ٱلْمُدِيرُ (ʔanta lmudiir) 'You are the director', there is still no problem. But if the preceding word ends in a consonant, for example مَنْ 'who?', there would theoretically be three consonants in a row: man lmudiir. Since, by the rule cited above, this is an impossible combination, a vowel is inserted after the first consonant in order to break up the sequence of three--

مَنِ ٱلْمُدِيرُ؟	(mani lmudiir)	'Who is the director?'

and the whole sequence is pronounced as one uninterrupted unit: /manilmudiir/. The inserted vowel is called a helping vowel. In the great majority of cases the helping vowel is i, as above. In one case only it is a: when the preceding word is مِنْ , 'from' and the following word begins with the definite article:

مِنَ ٱلْمُدِيرِ	(mina lmudiir)	'from the director'

In a few cases the helping vowel is u; these will be pointed out as they occur.

Note that the rule forbidding three consonants in a row applies also when two of these consonants are identical--that is, a double consonant written in Arabic with a shadda. Thus, when first in the sentence, 'the student' is أَلطَّالِبُ (ʔaṭṭaalib), and when preceded by another word it is ٱلطَّالِبُ (-ṭṭaalib). If the preceding word ends in a consonant, the appropriate helping vowel is inserted:

مَنِ الطَّالِبُ ؟	(mani ṭṭaalib)	'Who's the student?'
مِنَ الطَّالِبِ	(mina ṭṭaalib)	'from the student'

3. <u>The definite article</u>

a. The definite article in Arabic is أَلْ , and basically means the same as English "the". It has two pronunciations, depending on whether or not it follows immediately after pause (any interruption in speaking or reading). The form after pause is أَلْ , written as part of the following word: أَلْمُدِيرُ 'the director'.

Now do Drill 2.

If أل does not follow a pause, e.g.:

فِي ٱلْمَكْتَبِ	(filmaktab)	'in the office'
أَيْنَ ٱلْمَكْتَبُ؟	(?aynalmaktab)	'Where is the office?'

it is pronounced as part of the preceding word, with ?a- elided; ال is then written with waṣla: فِي ٱلْمَكْتَبِ. Note that before ال , فِي fii is pronounced fi-. In the examples above, the words preceding ال end in vowels. If, on the other hand, the preceding word ends in a consonant, a helping vowel i is suffixed to it; for example:

(manilmudiir)	مَنْ + أَلْمُدِيرُ ⟵ مَنِ ٱلْمُدِيرُ

The preposition مِنْ has the special form مِنَ (with the helping vowel a) before the article, e.g. مِنَ ٱلْقَاهِرَةِ (see 2 above).

Note the pronunciation of أل in the following words:

أَلدَّرْسُ ، أَلسِّكْرِتِيرَةُ ، أَلنَّصُّ ، أَلسَّيِّدُ

In these words, the ل of the article is not pronounced, but the following consonant is doubled instead. This doubling of the following consonant occurs whenever أل precedes a consonant which is pronounced in roughly the same area as ل itself--at or behind the upper teeth. On the other hand, if the following consonant is pronounced at the lips, as م in مَكْتَبٌ, or in the back part of the mouth, as خ in خَرْطُومٌ، ل is pronounced as ل .

The words أَلْقَمَرُ 'the moon' and أَلشَّمْسُ 'the sun' illustrate this dichotomy, and are conventionally used to label the two groups of consonants. Thus, م is قَمَرِيَّةٌ 'lunar', a "moon-letter", and د is شَمْسِيَّةٌ 'solar', a "sun-letter". The sun-letters are all dental or palatal:

ت ث د ذ ر ز س ش ص ض ط ظ ل ن

The remaining are moon-letters. Note that ج and ي are exceptions to the rule: they are moon-letters even though they are palatal.

In the writing system اَلْ is always spelled with ل regardless of how it is pronounced; however, it is voweled to reflect actual pronunciation: اَلْ before moon-letters, e.g. اَلْمُدِيرُ, but ال before sun-letters, with ـّ over the following consonant: اَلسَّيِّدُ ، اَلدَّرْسُ . Hamza is usually omitted. Now do Drill 3.

b. Use of the definite article in place names. Arabic often uses the definite article in place names, as in أَلْقَاهِرَةُ 'Cairo', أَلْخَرْطُومُ 'Khartoum'. This is true of English as well, for example "The Netherlands", "The Sudan". Of course, Arabic and English do not necessarily use the definite article on the same names, so each place name must be learned carefully with or without the article, as the case may be.

c. Use of the article in titles. In English, the article "the" is not usually used with titles followed by names (Mr. Jones, Miss Smith). In Arabic, however, the article is used with such titles in referring to the person concerned, but not in addressing him directly, for example أَيْنَ السَّيِّدُ سميث 'Where is Mr. Smith?' but صَباحَ الخَيْرِ يا سَيِّدُ سميث 'Good morning, Mr. Smith.'

Now do Drills 4, 5, 6 and 7.

Drill 2. (Also on tape) Transformation: Indefinite ⟶ definite.

Teacher supplies indefinite noun and adjective; student adds the definite article, to make a sentence. Ex.

T: 'a book' - 'new'	الاستاذ : كِتابٌ - جديدٌ
S: 'The book is new.'	الطالب : الكتابُ جديدٌ.

Repeat with:

١ – مدير – جديد	٥ – مدرّس – جديد
٢ – قلم جديد	٦ – كرسيّ جديد
٣ – استاذ جديد	٧ – باب جديد
٤ – مكتب جديد	٨ – كتاب جديد

Drill 3. (Also on tape) Transformation: Indefinite → definite.

Teacher supplies indefinite noun and predicate; student adds the definite article to make a sentence. Ex.

'a student' - 'new'	الاستاذ : طالب – جديد
'The student is new.'	الطالب : الطالب جديد.

Repeat with:

نص – جديد	شبّاك – جديد
لوح – جديد	طالب – جديد
سكرتير – جديد	درس – جديد

Drill 4. (On tape) Written. Recognition: Definite/indefinite.

Drill 5. (On tape) Substitution.

Drill 6. Question formation: مَنْ with definite article.

Teacher provides noun or noun phrase, first student makes a question with مَنْ, second student substitutes appropriate pronoun for the noun. Ex.

T: 'The director'	الاستاذ : المدير
S_1: 'Who is the director?'	الطالب الاول : من المدير ؟
S_2: 'Who is he?'	الطالب الثاني: من هو ؟

Repeat with:

٥ ـ الطالب
٦ ـ المديرة
٧ ـ المدير

١ ـ السيّد سليم
٢ ـ الاستاذ
٣ ـ السكرتيرة
٤ ـ الآنسة وداد

Drill 7. Question/answer with مِنْ أَيْنَ ; مِنْ with definite article.

Teacher provides name and place name. First student makes question with مِنْ أَيْنَ, second student answers. Ex.

T: 'Farid' - 'Cairo'	الاستاذ :	فريد ـ القاهرة
S_1: 'Where is Farid from?'	الطالب الاول ط١ :	من اين فريد ؟
S_2: 'From Cairo.'	الطالب الثاني ط٢:	من القاهرة .

Repeat with:

١ ـ سامي ـ الرياض
٢ ـ وداد ـ العراق
٣ ـ سليم ـ الكويت

٤ ـ هند ـ السعودية
٥ ـ سمير ـ السودان
٦ ـ فريد ـ القاهرة

4. Demonstrative phrases

In the phrase فِي هٰذا الْمَكْتَبِ 'in this office' the words هٰذا الْمَكْتَبِ are translated "this office". A construction of this type, consisting of a demonstrative pronoun followed by a noun with the definite article, is a demonstrative phrase. Further examples follow:

هٰذا الدَّرْسُ	'this lesson'	هٰذِهِ الآنِسَةُ	'this young lady'
هٰذا الطَّالِبُ	'this student'	هٰذِهِ الوَرَقَةُ	'this piece of paper'
هٰذا الكُرْسِيُّ	'this chair'	هٰذِهِ الطَّاوِلَةُ	'this table'
هٰذا المُدَرِّسُ	'this instructor'		

The demonstrative pronoun is the same gender as the noun that forms a phrase with it. The definite article plays a very special role in demonstrative phrases: it binds the demonstrative and the noun into a single unit, a phrase that can function like a single word. For example, in فِي هٰذَا الْمَكْتَبِ 'in this office' cited above, هٰذا المَكْتَبِ is the object of the preposition فِي . On the other hand, it is the subject in the sentence

هٰذا المَكْتَبُ جَدِيدٌ. 'This office is new.'

The definite article in demonstrative phrases is not translated into English; it serves merely to join the two words into a single unit. If the article is omitted, the result is two separate units--specifically, subject and predicate. Contrast the following sentences:

Predicate	Subject		
جَدِيدٌ	هٰذا الكِتابُ	'This book	is new.'
جَدِيدَةٌ	هٰذِهِ المُدَرِّسَةُ	'This instructor	is new.'
مُدَرِّسَةٌ	هٰذِهِ	'This	is an instructor.'
وَرَقَةٌ	هٰذِهِ	'This	is a piece of paper.'
هٰذا الطّالِبُ	مَنْ	'Who	is this student?'

Drill 8. (On tape) Written. Recognition: Demonstrative phrase.

Drill 9. (Also on tape) Question formation: Demonstrative phrase.

Teacher provides a sentence, student makes a question with a demonstrative phrase. Ex.

T: 'This is a director.' — الاستاذ : هذا مدير .

S: 'Who is this director?' — الطالب : من هذا المدير ؟

Repeat with:

١ ـ هذه مدرّسة .
٢ ـ هذا طالب .
٣ ـ هذا سكرتير .
٤ ـ هذه مديرة .
٥ ـ هذا مدرّس .
٦ ـ هذه طالبة .
٧ ـ هذه سكرتيرة .
٨ ـ هذا مدير .

5. Agreement of predicate adjective

An adjective functioning as the predicate of an equational sentence is called a predicate adjective, for example جَدِيدٌ in

هَلْ أَنْتَ جَدِيدٌ هُنا ؟ 'Are you new here?'

Adjectives in general have varying forms indicating case, definiteness, gender, and number. A predicate adjective is nominative in case, and indefinite (i.e., has nunation if it is the kind of word which takes nunation). It varies in gender and number, however, depending on the subject of the sentence. If the subject is masculine singular the predicate adjective is also masculine singular, and if the subject is feminine singular the predicate adjective is also feminine singular. Examples:

هَلْ أَنْتَ جَدِيدٌ هُنا ؟	'Are you (m.) new here?'
هَلْ أَنْتِ جَدِيدَةٌ هُنا ؟	'Are you (f.) new here?'

Examples in which the subject is plural will be given later.

Drill 10. (Also on tape) Substitution: Predicate adjective agreement.

Substitute the words given for the underlined word in the model sentence, making the appropriate changes.

'Sami is an Arab.' سامي عربيّ.

السيّد سمير	هو	هي
الآنسة وداد	هذا	انتِ
انتَ	هذه	سامي

Drill 11. Written. Completion and translation.

Complete the following with an appropriate word or phrase, then translate the resulting sentences.

'This book'→'This book is new.'   هذا الكتاب ← هذا الكتاب جديد.

١ ـ هذه المديرة ________ .

٢ ـ السيّد سمير ________ .

٣ ـ هذا ________ .

٤ ـ انا ________ .

٥ ـ الاستاذ فريد ________ .

6. Numerals 1-5 (On tape)

The following forms of the numerals are used in counting:

1	one	وَاحِدٌ	١ ـ
2	two	إِثْنَانِ	٢ ـ
3	three	ثَلَاثَةٌ	٣ ـ
4	four	أَرْبَعَةٌ	٤ ـ
5	five	خَمْسَةٌ	٥ ـ

Lesson Four

أَلدَّرْسُ الرَّابِعُ

أ ـ أَلنَّصُّ الأَساسيُّ　　A. Basic Text

في الجامعة　　At the University

١ ـ نجيب : مرحبا	Hello.
٢ ـ الاستاذة : مرحبا	Hello.
٣ ـ نجيب : كيف الحال ؟	How are you?
٤ ـ الاستاذة : بخير الحمدلله .	Fine, thank you.
٥ ـ نجيب : هل أنت السكرتيرة ؟	Are you the secretary?
٦ ـ الاستاذة : لا . لست سكرتيرة ـ انا استاذة .	No, I'm not a secretary; I'm a professor.
٧ ـ نجيب : اليس الاستاذ فريد موجودا هنا ؟	Isn't Professor Farid here?
٨ ـ الاستاذة : هو في المكتبة .	He's in the library.
٩ ـ نجيب : هل المكتبة بعيدة ؟	Is the library far?
١٠ ـ الاستاذة : لا . ليست بعيدة جدا .	No, it's not very far.
١١ ـ نجيب : شكرا يا أستاذة .	Thank you, professor.
١٢ ـ الاستاذة : عفوًا .	You're welcome.

B. Vocabulary　　ب ـ أَلْمُفْرَداتُ

أَلرَّابِعُ	the fourth	بِخَيْرٍ	(I'm) fine.
جامِعَةٌ	university	أَلْحَمْدُ لِلّٰهِ	Praise be to God.
نَجيبٌ	Najib (m. name)	لَسْتُ	I am not
مَرْحَبًا	hello	أَ	(interrogative particle; see C.2 below)
كَيْفَ الْحالُ ؟	How are you?		

لَيْسَ	he/it is not
مَوْجُودٌ	present (adj.)
مَكْتَبَةٌ	library
بَعِيدٌ (مِنْ)	far (from)
لَيْسَتْ	she/it is not
جِدّاً	very
شُكْراً	Thank you!
عَفْواً	You're welcome (response)

Additional vocabulary

لَسْتِ	you (f.) are not
لَسْتَ	you (m.) are not
مِصْرُ	Egypt
المَغْرِبُ	(m.) Morocco
الرِّباطُ	Rabat (capital of Morocco)
تونِسُ	Tunis; Tunisia
الأُرْدُنُّ	(m.) Jordan
كَلِمَةٌ	word
جُمْلَةٌ	sentence

Note on greetings

1. مَرْحَباً (pronounced marḥaban or marḥaba) is a friendly, somewhat informal greeting. The response is the same.

2. كَيْفَ ٱلْحالُ means literally "How is the condition?" It is a polite enquiry about health. The response, بِخَيْرٍ , means literally "in (a state of) well-being, or prosperity".

3. أَلْحَمْدُ لِلّٰهِ means literally "Praise belongs to God, Praise is God's" and is often used as a response to the question "How are you?" The impli-

cation is, of course, that all is well (thanks to God), and so أَلْحَمْدُ لِلّٰهِ itself may serve as the entire answer. The phrase is also commonly used on other occasions as well, to express happiness--or resignation--over what has happened.

C. Grammar and drills   ج – أَلْقَواعِدُ وَالتَّمارينُ

1. Negative of equational sentences: لَيْسَ
2. Interrogative أَ
3. Word order: جِدًّا
4. Numerals 6-10

1. Negative of equational sentences: لَيْسَ

As we have seen before (1.C.2), equational sentences have no verb. They are made negative, however, by use of the verb لَيْسَ which means 'is not', 'are not', or 'am not' and has different forms depending on the subject. Here are examples showing equational sentences and the corresponding negatives:

Affirmative:	سَليمٌ مِنْ بَيْروتَ .	'Salim is from Beirut.'
Negative:	لَيْسَ سَليمٌ مِنْ بَيْروتَ .	'Salim is not from Beirut.'
Affirmative:	مَرْيَمُ هُنا .	'Maryam's here.'
Negative:	لَيْسَتْ مَرْيَمُ هُنا .	'Maryam isn't here.'

Some points should be noted here. First, the usual word order in these negative sentences is (لَيْسَ[1] - subject[2] - predicate[3]). (Here, and elsewhere, we use the form لَيْسَ as a cover-term, meaning "any form of" that verb.) Second, the form لَيْسَ is used when the subject is masculine singular (like سَليم) and the form لَيْسَتْ is used when the subject is feminine singular (like مَرْيَم). Third, the subject of لَيْسَ is in the nominative case.

The following are examples of equational sentences in which the subject is a personal pronoun, and their corresponding negatives:

Affirmative:	هُوَ في القاهِرةِ.	'He's in Cairo.'
Negative:	لَيْسَ في القاهِرةِ.	'He's not in Cairo.'
Affirmative:	هِيَ هُنا.	'She's here.'
Negative:	لَيْسَتْ هُنا.	'She's not here.'
Affirmative:	أَنْتَ مِنَ الخَرْطومِ.	'You're from Khartoum.'
Negative:	لَسْتَ مِنَ الخَرْطومِ.	'You're not from Khartoum.'

The point to note here is that when لَيْسَ is used, it is not necessary to have a separate pronoun subject, since the form of the verb itself clearly indicates whether the subject is 'he', 'she', 'you (masculine)', and so on. Here are all the singular forms of the negative verb لَيْسَ :

3 MS	لَيْسَ	'(he, it (m.)) is not'
FS	لَيْسَتْ	'(she, it (f.)) is not'
2 MS	لَسْتَ	'you (m.) are not'
FS	لَسْتِ	'you (f.) are not'
1 S	لَسْتُ	'I am not'

The pronoun subject <u>may</u> be used if special emphasis is called for:

لَسْتَ أَنْتَ المُديرَ هُنا . أَنا المُديرُ.	'<u>You</u>'re not the director here; <u>I'm</u> the director!'

Finally, <u>the predicate of a sentence made negative by لَيْسَ is in the accusative case:</u> ـَ. (This rule applies only to nouns and adjectives, and not to prepositional phrases and adverbs, as only the former have varying case endings.) Here are examples:

لَيْسَ فريدٌ المُديرَ.	'Farid isn't the director.'
لَيْسَتْ سِكْرِتيرةً .	'She's not a secretary.'
لَسْتَ جَديداً هُنا .	'You're not new here.'
لَسْتِ عَرَبِيَّةً .	'You're not an Arab.'
لَسْتُ طالِباً .	'I'm not a student.'

Drill 1. (Also on tape) Recognition: Subject of لَيْسَ .

Give the independent pronoun corresponding to each of the following forms of لَيْسَ . Ex.

'He is not from Beirut' ليس من بيروت ــ هو

١ ــ لستِ من بيروت . ٤ ــ لستَ من بيروت .

٢ ــ لستُ من بيروت . ٥ ــ ليسَ من بيروت.

٣ ــ ليستْ من بيروت. ٦ ــ لستِ من بيروت .

Drill 2. (Also on tape) Negation.

Negate the following sentences using the appropriate form of لَيْسَ . Ex.

'She's a new student.' هي طالبةٌ جديدةٌ .

'She's not a new student.' لَيْسَتْ طالبةً جَديدةً .

١ ــ هو طالب . ٤ ــ هي عربيّة من لبنان .

٢ ــ انتِ جديدة هنا. ٥ ــ انا من الاردنّ .

٣ ــ انتَ المدير هنا. ٦ ــ انتَ في المكتبة .

Drill 3. Written. Negation.

Negate the following sentences using the appropriate form of لَيْسَ ; be sure to write the vowel sign for the case of the predicate. Ex.

'Samir is a professor.'⟶ سَميرٌ أُستاذٌ .

'Samir is not a professor.' لَيْسَ سميرٌ استاذاً .

١ ـ نانسي مدرّسة .　　　　٥ ـ سليم من المغرب .

٢ ـ فريد موجود في المكتب .　　　　٦ ـ المدير عربيّ .

٣ ـ الجامعة بعيدة .　　　　٧ ـ نجيب في الجامعة .

٤ ـ سامي في المكتبة .　　　　٨ ـ الشباك جديد .

2. Interrogative أَ

In addition to هَلْ (see 1.C.3) there is another interrogative particle with the same general function: to introduce a question which may be answered "Yes" or "No". This particle is أَ , and since it consists of only one letter it is written as part of the following word. In some contexts either هَلْ or أَ may be used, for example:

هَلْ هٰذا كِتابٌ ؟ أَهٰذا كِتابٌ ؟	'Is this a book?'
هَلْ هُوَ مِنْ بَيْروتَ ؟ أَهُوَ مِنْ بَيْروتَ ؟	'Is he from Beirut?'

There are some contexts, however, in which هَلْ is preferred, for example, before words beginning with wasla, such as those with the definite article:

هَلِ الْمُديرُ في الْمَكْتَبِ ؟	'Is the director in the office?'

And there are other contexts in which أ is the usual choice, for example before a negative:

أَلَيْسَ الْمُديرُ في الْمُكْتَبِ ؟ أَلَيْسَ كَذٰلِكَ ؟	'Isn't the director in the office?' 'Isn't it so?'

Drill 4. Question formation. هَلْ / أَ

Form questions from the following statements, using أَ or هَلْ as appropriate. Ex.

'This is a door.' ← هذا باب

'Is this a door?' هل هذا باب ؟ ← أهذا باب

'The word is new.' ← الكلمة جديدة

'Is the word new?' هل الكلمة جديدة ؟

'The library is not far away.' ← ليست المكتبة بعيدة

'Isn't the library far away?' أليست المكتبة بعيدة ؟

١ — المدير موجود هنا.	٤ — هذه الجامعة جديدة.
٢ — هذه الطالبة عربية.	٥ — ليست الجملة عربية.
٣ — لستَ من تونس.	٦ — الاستاذ فريد من الرباط.

Drill 5. (Also on tape) Question formation: أليس Ex.

'Salim is a student.' سليم طالب .

'Isn't Salim a student?' أليس سليم طالباً ؟

١ — الاستاذ من القاهرة.	٥ — هذا الكتاب جديد.
٢ — هو من بيروت.	٦ — هي طالبة من لبنان.
٣ — المديرة موجودة هنا.	٧ — انا عربيّ.
٤ — المكتب بعيد من الجامعة.	٨ — انتِ من السودان.

3. Word order: جِدّاً

The adverb جِدّاً 'very' follows the adjective it modifies, instead of preceding it as in English:

اَلْمَكْتَبَةُ بَعِيدَةٌ جدّاً.	'The library is very far away.'
لَيْسَ هٰذا الكُرْسِيُّ جَدِيداً جِدّاً.	'This chair is not very new.'

Drill 6. (On tape) Sentence addition: جدّاً

Drill 7. Written. Question formation

Form questions from the following statements, choosing from these question words the one which questions the underlined word(s).

مَنْ ، ما ، أين ، هل ، أ ، أليس ، من اين

١ ـ هذا الاستاذ من مصر.

٢ ـ الآنسة هند موجودة في المكتبة.

٣ ـ هذا المدرّس سامي.

٤ ـ هذا الكتاب جديد.

٥ ـ الطالب من المغرب.

٦ ـ الجامعة بعيدة من هنا.

٧ ـ ليس هذا الاستاذ من الرباط.

٨ ـ الاستاذ فى بيروت.

4. Numerals 6-10

The following forms of these numerals are used in counting:

6	six	سِتَّةٌ	٦ ـ
7	seven	سَبْعَةٌ	٧ ـ
8	eight	ثَمانِيَةٌ	٨ ـ
9	nine	تِسْعَةٌ	٩ ـ
10	ten	عَشَرَةٌ	١٠ ـ

Drill 8. (On tape) Substitution.

Lesson Five

أَلدَّرْسُ الْخامِسُ

أ - النص الاساسيّ

A. Basic Text

امام المتحف الوطني

In Front of the National Museum

١ - الزائر- أهذا هو المتحف الوطني القديم أم الحديث ؟	Is this the old national museum or the new one?
٢ - الموظف: هذا هو المتحف الحديث . المتحف القديم بناء بعيد من هنا .	This is the new museum. The old museum is a building far from here.
٣ - الزائر: هل أنت موظّف هنا ؟	Are you an employee here?
٤ - الموظف: نعم .	Yes.
٥ - الزائر: من المدير ؟	Who is the director?
٦ - الموظف: الدكتور براون ، هو رجل اجنبيٌّ مشهور .	Dr. Brown. He is a famous foreigner.
٧ - الزائر: من اين هو ؟	Where is he from?
٨ - الموظف: هو من امريكا . هل أنت امريكيٌّ؟	He's from America. Are you American?
٩ - الزائر: لا . أنا فرنسي ، هل المدير موجود في المتحف؟	No, I'm French. Is the director in the museum?
١٠- الموظف: نعم . هو في مكتبه .	Yes, he's in his office.
١١- الزائر: أين مكتبه ؟	Where is his office?
١٢- الموظف: مكتبه هو المكتب الكبير القريب من الباب .	His office is the large one near the door.
١٣- الزائر: واين مكتبك ؟	And where is your office?
١٤- الموظف: مكتبي امام مكتبه .	My office is across from his.

B. Vocabulary ب ـ أَلْمُفْرَداتُ

أَلْخامِسُ	the fifth	براون	Brown (name)
أَمامَ	in front of, across from	أَمْريكِيٌّ	American
مَتْحَفٌ	museum	رَجُلٌ	man
وَطَنِيٌّ	national; nationalist(ic)	أَجْنَبِيٌّ	foreign; foreigner
زائِرٌ	visitor (n.); visiting (adj.)	مَشْهورٌ (بِ)	famous (for)
قَديمٌ	old, ancient	فَرَنْسِيٌّ	French; Frenchman
أَمْ	or	مَكْتَبُهُ	his office
حَديثٌ	modern, new	كَبيرٌ	big, large; important; senior
مُوَظَّفٌ	employee, official	قَريبٌ (مِنْ)	near (to)
بِناءٌ	a building	مَكْتَبُكَ	your (m.s.) office
دُكْتورٌ	doctor; Ph.D. (pron. duktoor)	مَكْتَبي	my office

Additional vocabulary

فَرَنْسا	France
صَفٌّ	class; classroom

C. Grammar and drills ج ـ أَلْقَواعِدُ وَالتَّمارينُ

1. Noun-adjective phrases
2. Pronoun of separation
3. Nisba: The relative adjective
4. وَهْوَ and وَهْيَ
5. Pronoun suffixes with nouns

1. Noun-adjective phrases

Note the underlined phrase in the sentence below:

هٰذا هُوَ الْمَتْحَفُ الْحَديثُ.	'This is the new museum.'

In this phrase the noun الْمَتْحَفُ 'the museum' is modified by the adjective الحَديثُ 'new, modern'. Such a construction is a noun-adjective phrase, and there are two points to be noted about it. First, the adjective follows the noun it modifies, instead of preceding it as in English. Second, the adjective agrees with its noun in several ways: (a) in gender: if the noun is masculine, the adjective has its masculine form, and if the noun is feminine, the adjective has its feminine form:

الرَّجُلُ الْمَشْهورُ	'the famous man'
الجامِعَةُ الْمَشْهورةُ	'the famous university'

(b) in case: the adjective is in the same case as the noun:

هذا هو الدرسُ الثالثُ.	'This is the third lesson.'
في الدرسِ الثالثِ	'in the third lesson'

(c) in definiteness: if the noun is definite, the adjective has the definite article. A noun is definite not only when it has the definite article itself, but also when it has an attached pronoun suffix (see 5 below), or when it is a proper name. If the noun is indefinite, the adjective is also indefinite. Examples with definite nouns:

المكتبُ الجديدُ	'the new office'
مَكتبُهُ الجديدُ	'his new office'
مصرُ القديمةُ	'ancient Egypt'
جورج الثالِثُ	'George the Third'

Examples with indefinite nouns:

> بِنَاءٌ بَعِيدٌ   'a distant building'
>
> فِي جَامِعَةٍ مَشْهُورَةٍ   'in a famous university'

Now do Drill 1.

The noun-adjective phrase functions as a single unit in a sentence, the whole phrase serving as subject, predicate, object of a preposition, after هٰذَا in a demonstrative phrase, and so on.

Note carefully the distinction between constructions like the two following:

> المَتْحَفُ مَشْهُورٌ.   'The museum is famous.'
>
> المتحفُ المشهورُ   'the famous museum'

The first is a complete sentence, consisting of a subject and a predicate; as a predicate the adjective agrees with the noun subject in gender but not in definiteness. As for case, in sentences like the one above both subject and predicate are nominative, as we have already seen (see 2.C.4.) (The predicate is usually indefinite, but may rarely be definite if the meaning requires.)

The second example above is not a sentence but only a noun-adjective phrase; here an adjective agrees with its noun in gender, definiteness, and case.

The adjective in a noun-adjective phrase may itself be modified, usually by a simple adverb or by a prepositional phrase. The noun and the adjective with its modifiers are all part of the noun-adjective phrase:

> بِنَاءٌ بَعِيدٌ جِدّاً   'a very distant building'
>
> بِنَاءٌ بَعِيدٌ من هنا   'a building far from here'

(Note that, in English, an adjective which has modifiers sometimes must follow the noun, as in the second example above.)

Finally, the noun-adjective phrase may consist of a noun and two or more adjectives in a string, each one following the rules of agreement mentioned above. Only the last of two or more adjectives may have a modifier. Examples:

أَلْمَتْحَفُ الْوَطَنِيُّ الْقَدِيمُ	'the old national museum'
في جامِعَةٍ عَرَبِيَّةٍ مَشْهورَةٍ جِدًّا	'in a very famous Arab university'

Now do Drills 2, 3 and 4.

<u>Drill 1</u>. Written. Recognition drill: Agreement.

Identify the features (gender, case, definiteness) shared by the members of each noun-adjective phrase below. <u>Ex</u>.

'The new student' الطالبُ الجديد

Definite, masculine singular, nominative case

١ — في المتحف الوطنيّ	٤ — امام الرجل الامريكيّ
٢ — زائر اجنبيّ	٥ — من مكتب كبير
٣ — المكتبة الحديثة	٦ — الدرس الاوّل

<u>Drill 2</u>. (Also on tape) Substitution: Noun-adjective phrases.

Substitute the listed indefinite adjectives for the underlined definite adjective in the model sentence, making the adjective definite.

a. Masculine:

'The new professor is from Khartoum.' الاستاذ <u>الجديد</u> من الخرطوم.

مشهور

قديم

موجود هنا

اجنبيّ

عربيّ

b. Feminine:

'The new professor (f.) is from Khartoum.' الاستاذة الجديدة من الخرطوم.

Repeat, using same adjectives as above.

Drill 3. Written or oral. Word combination.

Combine the following words into meaningful sentences, as shown, making any necessary changes. Ex.

واشنطن	اجنبي	استاذ
'Washington'	'foreign'	'professor'

'The foreign professor is from Washington.' الاستاذ الاجنبي من واشنطن

١ ـ مدير ـ سودانيّ ـ الخرطوم

٢ ـ مدرّسة ـ عربيّ ـ العراق

٣ ـ طالب ـ سعوديّ ـ الرياض

٤ ـ استاذة ـ مصريّ ـ القاهرة

٥ ـ موظّف ـ جديد ـ تونس

Drill 4. (On tape) Written. Recognition: Noun-adjective phrase.

2. Pronoun of separation (ضَميرُ الْفَصْلِ)

We have seen that هٰذا مُتْحَفٌ is an equational sentence meaning 'This is a museum', and that هٰذا ٱلْمتحفُ is a demonstrative phrase (not a complete sentence) meaning 'this museum'. How then does one say in Arabic 'This is the museum'? The answer is: هٰذا هُوَ ٱلْمُتْحَفُ. In such a construction هُوَ is called a pronoun of separation, serving to separate the demonstrative and the definite noun and thus to distinguish the whole construction from هٰذا ٱلْمُتْحَفُ 'this museum'. The pronoun of separation agrees with the subject in gender and number. Thus, if the subject is masculine singular, the pronoun is هُوَ as above; if the subject is feminine singular, the pronoun is هِيَ . Other examples:

Phrase	هٰذا الْبِناءُ	'this building'
Sentence	هٰذا هُوَ الْبِناءُ.	'This is the building.'
Phrase	هٰذِهِ الْجامِعَةُ	'this university'
Sentence	هٰذه هي الْجامِعةُ.	'This is the university.'
Phrase	هٰذا الرَّجُلُ الْمَشْهورُ	'this famous man'
Sentence	هٰذا هُوَ الرَّجُلُ الْمشهورُ.	'This is the famous man.'

The pronoun of separation is normally used also after any subject, demonstrative or not, when that subject is long or complex, or when the predicate begins with the definite article or is otherwise definite, as in:

هٰذا هُوَ الْقَديمُ.	'This is the old one.'
أَلأُسْتاذُ هُوَ فَريدٌ.	'The professor is Farid.'
سَليمٌ هُوَ الأسْتاذُ.	'Salim is the professor.'

Contrast the last sentence with سَليمٌ آلأُسْتاذُ , which would normally be understood to mean "Salim, the professor".

Drill 5. Transformation: Demonstrative phrase ⟶ sentence with definite and indefinite predicate:

T : 'this large building' الاستاذ: هذا البناءُ الكبيرُ

S_1: 'This is the large building.' الطالب الاول : هذا هو البناء الكبير.

S_2: 'This is a large building.' الطالب الثاني: هذا بناء كبير.

Repeat with:

١ ـ هذا المتحف القديم

٢ ـ هذه الموظّفة الاجنبيّة

٣ ـ هذا الرجل المشهور

٤ ـ هذه المكتبة الحديثة

٥ ـ هذا البناء الكبير

٦ ـ هذا الموظّف المشهور

3. Nisba: The relative adjective

English has various devices for making adjectives from nouns, as illustrated by these examples:

Noun	Relative Adjective
America	Americ<u>an</u>
Rome	Rom<u>an</u>
Finn	Finn<u>ish</u>
element	element<u>al</u>
base	bas<u>ic</u>

In Arabic, the main device for making such adjectives from nouns is the suffix ـِيّ -iyy- (feminine ـِيَّة -iyya(t)-) added to the noun in place of any case ending it might have. Appropriate case endings are then added after this suffix.

Noun		Adjective		
		m.	f.	
لُبْنانُ	'Lebanon'	لُبْنانِيٌّ	لُبْنانِيَّةٌ	'Lebanese'
مِصْرُ	'Egypt'	مِصْرِيٌّ	مِصْرِيَّةٌ	'Egyptian'
وَطَنٌ	'fatherland, nation'	وَطَنِيٌّ	وَطَنِيَّةٌ	'national'
أَساسٌ	'base'	أَساسِيٌّ	أَساسِيَّةٌ	'basic'

Adjectives formed with this nisba suffix (Arabic نِسْبَةٌ 'relationship') are called "nisba" or "relative" adjectives; they follow the same rules of agreement as any other adjective. The nisba suffix has been borrowed into English on such words as Iraqi, Kuwaiti, Baghdadi, etc.

In forming a relative adjective from a noun the nisba suffix is added to the noun stem, that is, the original noun stripped of any of the following that it might have:

(a) the definite article: أَلْعِراقُ 'Iraq'-- عِراقِيٌّ 'Iraqi'

(b) feminine suffix: أَلْقاهِرَةُ 'Cairo'-- قاهِرِيٌّ 'Cairene'

(c) these vowels or combinations:

-aa	أَمْريكا	'America'	أَمْريكيّ	'American'
	فَرَنْسا	'France'	فَرَنْسيّ	'French'
-iyaa	ليبيا	'Libya	ليبيّ	'Libyan'
	سوريا	'Syria'	سوريّ	'Syrian'

Very often, in practice, يّ -iyyun is pronounced ي -ii in its pausal form.

Nisba adjectives which are not formed according to the rules above or which have special meanings will be listed in the coming vocabularies; you will be expected to recognize or to form all other (regular) ones.

Drill 6. (Also on tape) Transformation: Prepositional phrase → nisba.

a. 'The professor is from Lebanon.' → ← الاستاذ من لبنان

'The professor is Lebanese.' الاستاذ لبنانيّ .

١ ـ الاستاذ من مصر

٢ ـ الاستاذ من القاهرة

٣ ـ الاستاذ من امريكا

٤ ـ الاستاذ من الرباط

٥ ـ الاستاذ من العراق

٦ ـ الاستاذ من تونس

٧ ـ الاستاذ من لبنان

٨ ـ الاستاذ من الاردنّ

b. 'The library is in America.' → ← المكتبة في امريكا

'The library is American. المكتبة امريكية

١ ـ فى تونس

٢ ـ فى فرنسا

٣ ـ في السودان

٤ ـ في المغرب

٥ ـ في الجامعة

٦ ـ في السعوديّة

Drill 7. Substitution: Nisba with أَمْ .

'Is the director from Lebanon or Iraq?' الاستاذ : هل المدير من لبنان أم العراق ؟

'Is the director Lebanese or Iraqi? الطالب : هل المدير لبنانيّ ام عراقيّ؟

Repeat with the following:

١ ـ من امريكا ام فرنسا ؟

٢ ـ من تونس ام المغرب ؟

٣ ـ من بيروت ام دمشق ؟

٤ ـ من الرياض ام الرباط ؟

٥ ـ من مصر ام سوريا ؟

٦ ـ من الاردن ام الكويت ؟

Drill 8. Written. Transformation: Feminine → masculine.

Rewrite the following sentences, changing all <u>feminine</u> forms to <u>masculine</u>. <u>Ex.</u>

'The new student (f.) is Lebanese.' ←	الطالبة الجديدة لبنانية.
'The new student (m.) is Lebanese.'	الطالب الجديد لبنانيّ.

١ ــ الزائرة الاجنبية اردنيّة.

٢ ــ الموظّفة الجديدة عربيّة .

٣ ــ المديرة الموجودة هنا سودانيّة .

٤ ــ الاستاذة الجامعيّة مشهورة .

٥ ــ المدرّسة المصريّة قاهريّة.

4. <u>وَهْوَ and وَهْيَ</u>

The particle وَ 'and' is one of those Arabic particles that are spelled with one letter, written as part of the following word, and unstressed. Before the words هُوَ 'he' and هِيَ 'she', however, وَ is preferably stressed and the two pronouns lose their first vowel, thus:

وَهْوَ	'and he'	(wáhwa)
وَهْيَ	'and she'	(wáhya)

Drill 9. Transformation: Conjunction with وَهْوَ .

Combine the two sentences provided into one sentence, using وَهْوَ or وَهْيَ .

<u>Ex.</u>

'The student's in the library.'	الطالب فى المكتبة .
'The student's Lebanese.' ←	الطالب لبنانيّ.
'The student's in the library and he's Lebanese.'	الطالب في المكتبة وهو لبنانيّ .

١ ــ { المدير موجود هنا. / المدير قاهري . }

٢ ــ { المتحف قديم. / المتحف كبير جدّا. }

٣ – المكتبة في القاهرة.
المكتبة حديثة.

٦ – الكلمة موجودة في الكتاب.
الكلمة عربيّة.

٤ – الجملة في الدرس.
الجملة اساسيّة.

٧ – الطالب في الصف.
الطالب اجنبي.

٥ – الكرسي في المكتب.
الكرسي كبير.

5. Pronoun suffixes with nouns

In addition to independent pronouns, such as أَنا 'I', أَنْتَ 'you' and هُوَ 'he', Arabic has pronoun suffixes--short forms added to the end of words. These suffixes may be added to most parts of speech, with different meanings resulting in each case. Pronoun suffixes added to nouns express possession. For example, the suffix ـهُ 'him' may be attached to the noun مَكْتَبٌ 'office' to give مَكْتَبُهُ 'his office'. There is a pronoun suffix corresponding to each of the independent pronouns. The singular forms are as follows:

	Independent	Suffix	Example	
3 MS	هُوَ	ـهُ	مَكْتَبُهُ	'his office'
3 FS	هِيَ	ـها	مكتبُها	'her office'
2 MS	أَنْتَ	ـكَ	مكتبُكَ	'your office'
2 FS	أَنْتِ	ـكِ	مكتبُكِ	'your office'
1 S	أَنا	ي	مكتبِي	'my office'

Three points may be noted about these constructions:

(1) When a pronoun suffix is added to a noun, the noun thereby becomes definite, and thus never has nunation or the definite article:

مَكْتَبٌ	'an office'	مَكْتَبُهُ	'his office'
اَلْمَكْتَبُ	'the office'		

In a noun-adjective phrase, the noun with pronoun suffix must therefore take a definite adjective:

مَكْتَبُهُ الْجَدِيدُ	'his new office'
جامِعَتُكَ الْكَبِيرَةُ	'your large university'

(2) Pronoun suffixes are added to the noun after the case ending:

Nom.	مَكْتَبُكَ	'your office'
Gen.	مكتبِكَ	
Acc.	مكتبَكَ	

The first person singular suffix ي 'my', however, is added directly to the stem of the noun without the case ending:

Nom./Gen./Acc.	مكتَبي	'my office'

(3) When ـهُ 'his' is added to a word ending in ـِ <u>i</u>, ي <u>ii</u> or ـَيْ <u>ay</u>, its vowel is changed to ـهِ <u>-hi</u>. Contrast the shape of ـه in the genitive as opposed to the other two cases.

Nom.	مَكْتَبُهُ	'his office'
Gen.	مكتبِهِ	
Acc.	مكتبَهُ	

This is strictly a matter of pronunciation; it happens after all parts of speech and is automatic after <u>i</u>, <u>ii</u>, or <u>y</u>.

<u>Drill 10</u>. (Also on tape) Substitution/transformation: Independent pronoun or noun → pronoun suffix. <u>Ex</u>.

كِتابُهُ ← هُوَ - كِتابٌ

'his book' 'he' - 'book'

كِتابُها ← مَرْيَمُ - كِتابٌ

'her book' 'Maryam' 'book'

Repeat with:

أنا	المدرّس
أنتِ	الاستاذة
هي	أنتَ
مريم	هو
سامي	المدرّسة

Drill 11. Written. Recognition: Possessive pronoun.

The following nouns have attached pronoun suffixes. Write the independent pronoun (أَنا ، هُوَ ,etc.) which corresponds to each suffix. Ex.

كِتابُهُ هُوَ

'his book' 'he'

درسكَ	استاذها
قلمها	مديركَ
مكتبي	كتابكِ
مدرّسكِ	مكتبتي
ورقته	جامعته

Drill 12. (On tape) Written. Recognition: Pronoun suffixes.

Lesson Six الدرس السادِسُ

أ - النص الاساسيّ

الدراسة في امريكـــا

حضر كريم الى امريكا مِن لبنان ودرس في جامعة جورجتاون ・وبعد الحصول على شهادة في اللغة الانكليزية رجع الى بيروت ودرّس في مدرســـة ثانويّة ・

وداد صديقة كريم ・ درست اللغة العربيّة في الجامعة الامريكيّـــة في بيروت ، وبعد سنة انتقلت الى جامعة تكساس في أوستن ・ بعـــــد الاِنْتِهاءِ من الدراسة ، رجعت الى الشرق الاوسط ودرّست في جامعة بغداد・ completing

A. Basic Text

Studying in America

Karim came to America from Lebanon and studied at Georgetown University. After obtaining a degree in the English language, he returned to Beirut and taught in a secondary school.

Widad is Karim's friend. She studied the Arabic language at the American University in Beirut, and after a year she transferred to the University of Texas at Austin. After completing her studies she returned to the Middle East and taught at the University of Baghdad.

B. Vocabulary ب - المفردات

أَلسّادِسُ	the sixth
دِراسَةٌ	study, studying (n.)
حَضَرَ الى ، مِن	he came to, from
كَريمٌ	Karim (m. name)

إِلى	to
دَرَسَ	he studied
جورجْتاون ، جورج تاون	Georgetown
بَعْدَ	after (prep.)
أَلْحُصُولُ عَلى	obtaining (n.)
شَهادَةٌ	diploma, degree
لُغَةٌ	language
لُغَوِيٌّ	(nisba of لُغَةٌ) linguistic, language-(adj.); linguist, grammarian
إِنْكِليزِيٌّ ، إِنْجِليزِيٌّ	(pronounced ?ingiliiziyy) English (n. or adj.); Englishman
رَجَعَ	he returned
دَرَّسَ	he taught
مَدْرَسَةٌ	school
ثانَوِيٌّ	secondary
صَديقٌ	friend
دَرَسَتْ	she studied
سَنَةٌ	year
سَنَوِيٌّ	(nisba of سَنَةٌ) yearly, annual
اِنْتَقَلَتْ	she transferred, she moved
تِكساس	Texas
أوستِن	Austin
رَجَعَتْ	she returned
أَلشَّرْقُ الأَوْسَطُ	the Middle East (شَرْقٌ 'east')
دَرَّسَتْ	she taught
بَغْدادُ	Baghdad

Vocabulary note: الخ 'etc.' is an abbreviation of إِلى آخِرِهِ 'et cetera, and so forth' (lit., "to its end").

C. Grammar and drills ## القواعد والتمارين

1. The definite article: Generic use
2. Verbs: Perfect tense, 3 m.s. and 3 f.s.
3. Verbal sentences
4. Iḍāfa constructions (أَلْإِضافَةُ)

1. The definite article: Generic use

In English a singular noun with the definite article may refer to the whole class of beings or things indicated by the noun. Thus, in "The horse is a noble animal" reference is made not to some particular horse but to horses in general. Often, a plural noun without the article expresses the same idea: "Horses are noble animals." The use of the article to indicate a whole class is quite restricted in English: not only must the noun be singular; it must also refer to countable things rather than to substance in a mass, or to abstractions: the article can be used in "The wheel was their greatest invention" but not in "Sugar is expensive" or "Honesty is the best policy".

In Arabic the definite article is regularly used to express the whole class, but without the restrictions which apply to English. The Arabic article is used in this sense with both singular and plural nouns, and with countable or non-countable nouns. Three important categories where the article is used in Arabic are as follows:

a. General class of persons or things

"Students look forward to vacations."

"Watermelon is good for you."

"Prices are high there."

b. Abstractions

"Bravery was their most admirable quality."

"Truth is stranger than fiction."

c. Actions or states

"after obtaining a degree"	بَعْدَ الْحُصولِ عَلى شَهادَةٍ
"in studying here"	في الدِّراسَةِ هُنا
"after completing (one's) studies"	بَعْدَ الاِنْتِهاءِ مِنَ الدِّراسَةِ

2. Verbs: Perfect tense, 3 m.s. and 3 f.s.

The Arabic verb has two tenses, the perfect and the imperfect. Very briefly, the perfect tense is used to narrate completed events, e.g. "He arrived yesterday", while the imperfect basically describes situations or events which have not yet been completed, e.g. "He is studying for a test", "He is going to eat later". In this lesson the perfect tense is introduced.

The verbs

حَضَرَ الى	'he came to'	حَضَرَتْ الى	'she came to'
دَرَسَ	'he studied'	دَرَسَتْ	'she studied'
رَجَعَ	'he returned'	رَجَعَتْ	'she returned'
دَرَّسَ	'he taught'	دَرَّسَتْ	'she taught'

are in the perfect tense; they denote a completed action or event, corresponding in general to what in English is usually termed the past tense (as in "he went") or the present perfect (as in "he has gone"). Verbs in the perfect tense consist of a stem and a subject marker. The stem indicates the basic meaning and the tense of the verb; the subject marker indicates the person, gender, and number of the subject. The following chart shows the stems of the verbs shown above:

ḥaḍar-	'came'
daras-	'studied'
rajaʕ-	'returned'
darras-	'taught'

The two subject markers taken up in this lesson are:

-a	indicating that the subject is third person, masculine, singular (3 m.s.)
-at	indicating that the subject is third person, feminine, singular (3 f.s.)

Thus, in the verbs of this lesson, if the subject of the verb is masculine singular (for example كَرِيمٌ 'Karim'), the verb form ends in ـَ -a; if the subject is feminine singular (for example وِدادُ 'Widad') the verb form ends in ـَتْ -at. Examples:

حَضَرَ كَرِيمٌ.	'Karim came.'
حَضَرَتْ وِدادُ.	'Widad came.'

Since the verb form includes a subject-marker, it is not necessary in Arabic, as it is usually in English, to express a pronoun subject:

رَجَعَ	'he returned'
رَجَعَتْ	'she returned'

If a verb ending in the subject-marker ـَتْ -at is followed by waṣla, a helping vowel ـِ -i is added to it:

دَرَسَتِ الطّالِبَةُ	'the student (f.) studied'
دَرَسَتِ اللُّغَةَ	'she studied the language'

Now do Drills 1 and 2.

Drill 1. Recognition: Subject of verb.

Give the independent pronoun corresponding to the subject of each verb in the sentences read. Ex.

'He studied Arabic.' — درس اللغة العربية ـ هو

١ ـ درّست فى مدرسة ثانويّة.

٢ ـ رجع الى لبنان.

٣ ـ حضر الى الصفّ.

٤ ـ انتقلت الى جامعة تكساس.

٥ ـ درس اللغة الانكليزيّة.

٦ ـ رجعت من بيروت.

٧ ـ درّس في جامعة القاهرة

٨ ـ انتقل الى بغداد.

٩ ـ حضرت الى بيروت من دمشق.

١٠ ـ درست اللغة العربية في لبنان.

Drill 2. (Also on tape) Substitution: Verbal sentences.

Substitute the following words for the underlined item.

a. 'Karim came to America.' — حضر <u>كريم</u> الى امريكا.

سمير — المدير

الزائر الاجنبيّ — السيّد سليم

سامي

b. 'Widad studied French.' — درست <u>وداد</u> اللغة الفرنسيّة

الطالبة — السكرتيرة

سميرة — مريم

الآنسة هند

c. 'Farid transferred to the University of Baghdad.' — انتقل <u>فريد</u> الى جامعة بغداد

الطالبة	السيّد سامي
هند	الآنسة نانسي
الاستاذ	

3. Verbal sentences

In previous lessons we have described and illustrated equational sentences. Now we take up the second of the three main types of Arabic sentences, the verbal sentence. A *verbal sentence* contains a verb. In its simplest form a verbal sentence consists of only one word, the verb itself, the subject being indicated by the form of the verb:

رَجَعَ .	'He returned.'
رَجَعَتْ.	'She returned.'

A verbal sentence may also contain an expressed *subject*, for example a noun or a noun-adjective phrase. *The usual order is verb first, then subject. The subject is in the nominative case.* The verb agrees with the subject in gender: if the subject is masculine, the verb is in its masculine form; if the subject is feminine, the verb is in its feminine form. Examples:

Subject	Verb	
كَرِيمٌ.	رَجَعَ	'Karim returned.'
الطّالِبَةُ الْجَدِيدَةُ.	رَجَعَتْ	'The new student (f.) returned.'

If a feminine subject follows the verb, but is separated from it by another word or phrase, the verb may be either masculine or feminine:

{ حَضَرَ / حَضَرَتْ } إِلى الْجامِعَةِ زائِرَةٌ أَجْنَبِيَّةٌ.	'A foreign visitor (f.) came to the university.'

The verb agrees with the first member of a compound subject: رَجَعَتْ كَرِيمَةُ وَسَمِيرٌ .

A verbal sentence may contain an object of the verb. Here the usual order is verb - (subject) - object (the parentheses around the word "subject" mean that in such sentences there may or may not be an expressed subject). The object of a verb is in the accusative case. Examples:

Object	Subject	Verb	
اللُّغَةَ العَرَبِيَّةَ .	وِدادُ	دَرَسَتْ	'Widad studied the Arabic language.'
لُغَةً أَجْنَبِيَّةً .		دَرَسَتْ	'She studied a foreign language.'

Finally, a verbal sentence may contain one or more adverbs, or adverbial phrases, modifying the verb. These adverbial modifiers are typically words or phrases that answer such questions as "where?" (answer: in a secondary school, at Cairo University); "where to?" (to Egypt); "where from ?" (from Iraq); "when?" (yesterday), and so on. Adverbial modifiers may occur in various positions within the verbal sentence; they are underlined in the following examples:

بَعْدَ سَنَةٍ اِنْتَقَلَتْ إلى اوستِن .	'After a year she transferred to Austin.'
حَضَرَ كَرِيمٌ إلى أَمْرِيكا مِنْ لُبْنانَ .	'Karim came to America from Lebanon.'
دَرَّسَتْ في جامِعَةِ بَغْدادَ .	'She taught at the University of Baghdad.'

Sentences of any type may be introduced or joined by a conjunction, for example وَ 'and'. It is much more common for an Arabic sentence to begin with وَ than it is for an English sentence to begin with "and". Examples:

أَنا طالِبٌ وَأَنْتَ أُسْتاذٌ .	'I'm a student and you're a professor.'
حَضَرَ كَرِيمٌ مِنْ لُبْنانَ وَدَرَسَ في جامِعَةِ جورجتاون .	'Karim came from Lebanon and studied at Georgetown University.'
وَبَعْدَ سَنَةٍ رَجَعَ إلى بَيْروتَ .	'(And) after a year he returned to Beirut.'

Drill 3. Written. Recognition.

Copy the following sentences. If the subject is expressed, put it in (parentheses); if there is an object of the verb, underline it once; if there is an adverbial modifier, underline it twice. Ex.

'Karim studied Arabic in Baghdad.' درس (كريم) اللغة العربية في بغداد .

١ — رجعت وداد من القاهرة.

٢ — وبعد سنة انتقل الى جامعة الرياض.

٣ — درس فريد اللغة الفرنسية ودرست نانسي اللغة العربية.

٤ — رجع سليم وفريدة من المغرب.

٥ — هل حضر كريم الى الصفّ ؟

4. Iḍāfa constructions: أَلْإِضافَةُ

Note the examples shown below:

مَكْتَبُ ٱلْمُدِيرِ	'the office of the director'
بابُ ٱلْمَتْحَفِ	'the door of the museum'
لُغَةُ ٱلنَّصِّ	'the language of the text'

These are examples of a very common Arabic construction called an iḍāfa (a word meaning 'addition' or 'annexion'). An iḍāfa is a phrase consisting of two nouns, the second immediately following the first. These nouns are called the first term and the second term of the iḍāfa. The first term is the head of the phrase: in the examples above we are talking about some kind of office, or door, or language. The second term gives further information about the first: for example, it tells us whose office, which door, what language.

The iḍāfa is the usual way to express the relationship of possession--the first term being the possessed and the second term the possessor. But it serves also to express the various kinds of modifications expressed in the English translations outlined in the following paragraph.

An iḍāfa construction usually corresponds to one of three English constructions. The first is an "of" construction, as we have seen (in the following examples the Arabic first term and the corresponding English noun are underlined):

مَكْتَبُ الْمُدِيرِ 'the office of the director'

The second is a construction involving the possessive 's (or s'):

مَكْتَبُ الْمُدِيرِ 'the director's office

The third is a construction in which the two English nouns are directly juxtaposed, the first modifying the second:

مَكْتَبُ الْمَتْحَفِ 'the museum office'

From these three examples it can be seen that in Arabic the head noun (مَكْتَبٌ) is always the first, whereas in English the position of the head noun (office) varies. Which of the three types of English construction should be selected to translate an Arabic iḍāfa depends on English usage; as far as the Arabic is concerned, there is only one possible order of words.

Now let us examine more closely the function of the iḍāfa and its constituent elements. These are the important points to remember:

a. As a noun phrase, the whole iḍāfa functions as a single unit within a sentence, serving as subject, predicate, object of verb or preposition, and so on. The first term may be in any case, depending on the function of the iḍāfa within the sentence. The second term of an iḍāfa is always genitive. Examples:

First term nominative	
هٰذا مَكْتَبُ الْمُدِيرِ.	'This is the director's office.'

First term genitive

سَليمٌ في مَكْتَبِ المُديرِ.	'Salim is in the director's office.'

First term accusative

دَرَسَتْ نَصَّ الدَّرْسِ.	'She studied the text of the lesson.'

b. The first term never has the definite article or nunation. The second term may have either. All previous examples have shown the second term with the definite article. Here are examples in which it has nunation:

كِتابُ طالِبٍ	'a student's book'
مُوَظَّفُ جامِعَةٍ	'a university employee'
مُديرُ مَتْحَفٍ	'a museum director'

c. If the second term is definite, then the first term (and the whole iḍāfa) is definite. The second term, like any noun, is definite if it has the definite article or a pronoun suffix, or if it is a proper noun:

Second term definite

قَلَمُ المُدَرِّسِ	'the teacher's pencil'
قَلَمُ أُسْتاذِهِ	'his professor's pencil'
قَلَمُ مَرْيَمَ	'Maryam's pencil'
جامِعَةُ جورج تاون	'Georgetown University'

If the second term is indefinite, then the first term (and the whole iḍāfa) in indefinite.

Second term indefinite

قَلَمُ مُدَرِّسٍ	'a teacher's pencil'
مُدَرِّسُ لُغَةٍ	'a language teacher'

Now do Drills 4 and 5.

In 2.C.4 we learned that a noun after vocative يا is in the nominative case; if, however, that noun is the first term of an iḍāfa, it is put in the accusative case. Compare:

يا أُسْتاذُ 'O Professor!'
يا اسْتاذَ اللُّغَةِ الْعَرَبِيَةِ 'O Professor of Arabic!'

Now do Drills 4 and 5.

Drill 4. Written.

Underline the iḍāfa's in each of the following sentences: Ex.

'Karim studied at the University of Rabat.' درس كريم فى جامعة الرباط..

١ ـ مكتب المدير قريب من هنا.

completing ٢ ـ رجع بعد الإنْتِهاء من دراسة اللغة العربية.

٣ ـ انتقل بعد سنة الى جامعة بغداد.

٤ ـ صديقها مدير متحف وصديقتها مدرسة لغة.

٥ ـ كتاب الطالب جديد.

٦ ـ انتقل صديق وداد الى تونس.

Drill 5. Written.

Make the following into sentences by forming an iḍāfa from the words in parentheses. Vocalize each sentence and translate into English. Ex.

(الكتاب ـ الرجل) هنا ←

'The man's book is here.' كِتابُ الرَّجُلِ هُنا.

١ ـ صديقي في (المكتب ـ السكرتير).

٢ ـ هل درست (الكتاب ـ الاستاذ) أم (الكتاب ـ الاساتذة) ؟

٣ ـ (المتحف ـ الجامعة) مشهور.

٤ ـ (الشهادة ـ صديقه) في اللغة الانكليزية.

٥ ـ رجع من (المكتب ـ الموظف).

٦ ـ درّس (النص ـ الدرس) الجديد.

D. Comprehension passage — د ـ نُصوصٌ لِلْفَهْمِ

Read the following passages and then do Drills 6 and 7, which are based on them.

أ ـ حضر السيد فريد من السودان الى القاهرة • درس اللغة العربية في جامعة القاهرة • وبعد الدراسة رجع الى السودان وهو الآنَ موظف كبير في الخرطوم • (now)

Drill 6. Written. — أسئلة

١ ـ من أين السيد فريد ؟

٢ ـ اين درس ؟

٣ ـ هل حَصَلَ على شهادة جامعية في السودان؟ (he obtained)

٤ ـ هل هو طالب الان؟

ب ـ السيد الدكتور سمير سليم مدير المكتبة في جامعة القاهرة •مكتبة الجامعة بناء قديم قريب من المتحف • سكرتيرة الدكتور سمير آنسة مصرية وهي وداد نجيب • حَصَلَتِ الآنسة وداد على الوَظيفَةِ بعد سنة من اُنْتِهاءِ دراستها • (she obtained; position, job; end)

Drill 7. Written. — أسئلة

١ ـ من الدكتور سمير سليم ؟ ٤ ـ هل بناء المكتبة جديد ؟

٢ ـ من سكرتيرة الدكتور سليم ؟ ٥ ـ هل السكرتيرة لبنانية ؟

٣ ـ أين مكتبة الجامعة ؟

E. General drills — هـ ـ اَلتَّمارينُ الْعامَّةُ

Drill 8. Written.

Rewrite the Basic Text, changing masculine to feminine and feminine to masculine (substitute وداد for كريم and كريم for وداد) Ex.

حضرت وداد الى امريكا ....

Drill 9. Translation.

'The university library is a modern building.' — مكتبة الجامعة بناء حديث .

١ – درس نص الدرس .

٢ – صديق فريد طالب عراقي .

٣ – درّست هند في جامعة القاهرة .

٤ – انتقلت السكرتيرة الى مكتب المدير .

٥ – مدير المتحف رجل مشهور .

٦ – الاستاذ كريم مدرّس اللغة الانكليزية .

Drill 10. Give correct response: (Suggestions for teacher)

١ – مرحبا .

٢ – صباح الخير .

٣ – كيف الحال؟

٤ – من انت ؟

٥ – من اين انت ؟

٦ – هل انت لبناني ؟

٧ – ما هذا ؟ (كتاب ، لوح ، باب الخ) .

٨ – أهذا كتابك ؟

٩ – هل المكتبة قريبة من هنا ؟

١٠ – من استاذك ؟

١١ – من اين هو ؟

١٢ – شكرا .

Lesson Seven

ألدرس السابِعُ

أ ـ ألنصّ الاساسيّ

طالــــب وطالبـــة

سالي : ـ أين درست اللغة الانكليزيّة يا أحمد ؟

أحمد : ـ درست اللغة الانكليزيّة في مدرسة ثانويّة ·

سالي : ـ وأين درست بعد ذلك ؟

أحمد : ـ في جامعة اَلْأَزْهَرِ في القاهرة · Al-Azhar

سالي : ـ ماذا درست في تلك الجامعة ؟

أحمد : ـ ألتاريخ الاسلاميّ ·

سالي : ـ هل درست عن أمريكا ؟

أحمد : ـ ليس في الجامعة ، لكن قرأت شيئا عن تاريخ أمريكا. وأنــت يا سالي ، أين تعلّمت العربيّة ؟

سالي : ـ تعلّمت العربيّة في مدرسة خاصّة في مصر · وبعد ذلك بدأت الدراسة في جامعة القاهرة ·

أحمد : ـ هل أكملت الدراسة الجامعيّة هناك ؟

سالي : ـ لا · رجعت الى أمريكا وتابعت الدراسة في جامعة أمريكيّة ·

A. Basic text

A Pair of Students

Sally: Where did you study English, Ahmad?

Ahmad: I studied English in a secondary school.

Sally: And where did you study after that?

Ahmad: At Al-Azhar University in Cairo.

Sally: What did you study at that university?

Ahmad: Islamic history.

Sally: Did you study about America?

Ahmad: Not at the university, but I have read something on American history. And you, Sally--where did you learn Arabic?

Sally: I learned Arabic in a private school in Egypt. After that I began studying at the University of Cairo.

Ahmad: Did you finish your university studies there?

Sally: No, I returned to America and went on with my studies in an American university.

B. Vocabulary — ب ـ ألمفردات

أَلسَّابِعُ	the seventh
سالي	Sally
دَرَسْتَ	you (m.s.) studied
أَللُّغَةُ الْإِنْكِلِيزِيَّةُ ، أَلْإِنْكِلِيزِيَّةُ	(the) English (language)
أَحْمَدُ	Ahmad (m. name)
دَرَسْتُ	I studied
ماذا؟	what?
تِلْكَ	(f.) that
تاريخٌ	history
أَلْإِسْلامُ	Islam
عَنْ	about, concerning
لٰكِنْ	but, however
قَرَأْتُ	I read (past)
شَيْءٌ	thing, something
تَعَلَّمْتِ	you (f.s.) learned
أَللُّغَةُ الْعَرَبِيَّةُ ، أَلْعَرَبِيَّةُ	(the) Arabic (language)
تَعَلَّمْتُ	I learned
خاصٌّ	special; private
ذٰلِكَ	(m.) that

بَدَأْتُ	I began
أَكْمَلْتِ	you (f.s.) finished, completed
هُناكَ	there
رَجَعْتُ	I returned, went back, came back
تابَعْتُ	I continued, went on with

C. Grammar and drills — ج - القواعد والتمارين

1. Perfect tense: 2 m.s., 2 f.s., 1 s.
2. 'What?': ما and ماذا
3. Negation of word or phrase: لَيْسَ
4. Demonstratives: ذٰلِكَ and تِلْكَ
5. Numerals 11-19

1. Perfect tense: 2 m.s., 2 f.s., 1 s.

In perfect tense verbs, the subject marker ـتَ -ta indicates that the subject is 2 m.s. (that is, أَنْتَ 'you' when speaking to one male person), for example:

أَيْنَ دَرَسْتَ يا أَحْمَدُ ؟	'Where did you study, Ahmad?'

The subject-marker ـتِ -ti indicates that the subject is 2 f.s. (that is, أَنْتِ 'you' when speaking to one female person), for example:

أَيْنَ دَرَسْتِ يا سالي ؟	'Where did you study, Sally?'

The subject-marker ـتُ -tu indicates that the subject is 1 s. (أَنا 'I'), no matter whether the speaker is male or female, for example:

دَرَسْتُ في بَيْروتَ .	'I studied in Beirut.'

These subject-markers, like the 3 s. markers described in Lesson 6, are suffixed to the stem of the verb:

Stem		3 MS هو	3 FS هي	2 MS انتَ	2 FS انتِ	1 S انا
دَرَسْ -	'studied'	دَرَسَ	دَرَسَتْ	دَرَسْتَ	دَرَسْتِ	دَرَسْتُ
حَضَرْ - الى	'came'	حَضَرَ	حَضَرَتْ	حَضَرْتَ	حَضَرْتِ	حَضَرْتُ
رَجَعْ -	'returned'	رَجَعَ	رَجَعَتْ	رَجَعْتَ	رَجَعْتِ	رَجَعْتُ
قَرَأْ -	'read'	قَرَأَ	قَرَأَتْ	قَرَأْتَ	قَرَأْتِ	قَرَأْتُ
بَدَأْ -	'began'	بَدَأَ	بَدَأَتْ	بَدَأْتَ	بَدَأْتِ	بَدَأْتُ
دَرَّسْ -	'taught'	دَرَّسَ	دَرَّسَتْ	دَرَّسْتَ	دَرَّسْتِ	دَرَّسْتُ
تَعَلَّمْ -	'learned'	تَعَلَّمَ	تَعَلَّمَتْ	تَعَلَّمْتَ	تَعَلَّمْتِ	تَعَلَّمْتُ
تابَعْ -	'pursued'	تابَعَ	تابَعَتْ	تابَعْتَ	تابَعْتِ	تابَعْتُ
أَكْمَلْ -	'completed'	أَكْمَلَ	أَكْمَلَتْ	أَكْمَلْتَ	أَكْمَلْتِ	أَكْمَلْتُ
اِنْتَقَلْ -	'transfer'	اِنْتَقَلَ	اِنْتَقَلَتْ	اِنْتَقَلْتَ	اِنْتَقَلْتِ	اِنْتَقَلْتُ
Subject-markers:		ـَ	ـَتْ	تَ	تِ	تُ

Verb forms ending in the suffixes تَ -ta and تُ -tu have an identical pause form ending in -t:

دَرَسْتَ 'you (m.s.) studied'
دَرَسْتُ 'I studied'
} = darast

Verb forms ending in the feminine suffix تِ -ti remain unchanged in the pause form.

In dictionaries and vocabularies, Arabic verbs are customarily listed in the 3 m.s. form of the perfect tense, for example دَرَسَ , because this is the shortest of all the forms. This is literally 'he studied', but the English equivalent is usually listed as an infinitive, 'to study', and this practice will be observed in subsequent lessons.

Now do Drills 1, 2 and 3.

Drill 1. Written. Recognition: Singular verb endings.

Circle the subject-marker, i.e., the ending which shows the subject of the verb. Then give the independent pronoun corresponding to the verb form.

Ex. هو درسَ : دَرَسَ

'he' 'He studied'

دَرَسْتُ	أَكْمَلْتِ
دَرَسْتِ	بَدَأْتَ
قَرَأْتَ	رَجَعْتُ
تَعَلَّمَ	أَكْمَلَ
تابَعْتِ	تَعَلَّمْتُ

Drill 2. (Also on tape) Conjugation.

Change the verb in the model sentence, according to the items given below:

'I studied Arabic.' انا-درست اللغة العربية ٠

انتِ	سامي
هو	وداد
هي	انا

Repeat with:

١ ـ قرأتُ كتابا جديدا ٠

٢ ـ أكملتُ الدراسة هنا ٠

٣ ـ تعلّمتُ اللغة الانكليزية ٠

٤ ـ بدأتُ دراسة التاريخ الاسلامي ٠

Drill 3. Questions and answers.

Answer the following questions with the appropriate verb form. Ex.

'Did you study?' هل درستَ ؟

'Yes, I studied.' نعم درستُ .

١ ـ هل درستَ العربية ؟

درسَ

درستُ

درستِ

دَرَسْتُ

٢ ـ هل أكملتَ الدراسة هناك ؟

أكملَ

أكملتُ

أَكَمَلْتُ

أكملتَ

أكملتِ

2. 'What?': ما and ماذا

There are two Arabic words corresponding to the English interrogative 'what?', but they are used in different types of sentences. The interrogative ما occurs as the predicate of an equational sentence (and, as an interrogative, it comes first):

ما هٰذا ؟	'What's this?'
ما هٰذا البِناءُ الكَبيرُ ؟	'What's that big building?'

Only the interrogative ماذا , on the other hand, serves as the subject or object of the verb in a verbal sentence. In these examples it is the object:

ماذا دَرَسَتْ وِدادُ ؟	'What did Widad study?'
ماذا دَرَّسَ في جامِعَةِ جورجتاون ؟	'What did he teach at Georgetown University?'

When the interrogative ما 'what?' is the object of a preposition, it is written as one word with the preposition, and with a fatha rather than an ?alif:

مِنْ + ما = مِمَّ 'from what?' (with assimilation of n to m)

عَنْ + ما = عَمَّ 'about what?' (with assimilation of the n to m)

في + ما = فيمَ 'in what?'

الى + ما = إلامَ 'to what?'

ما 'what?' does not combine with بَعْدَ 'after' or أمامَ 'in front of', or any other preposition ending in fatha.

Now do Drill 4.

Drill 4. Written. Transformation: Statement → question with ما or ماذا .

Make questions based on the following sentences, using either ما or ماذا as appropriate. Ex.

'This is a big door.' هذا باب كبير.

'What's this?' ما هذا ؟

١ ـ تعلّمت العربيّة هنا .

٢ ـ هذه مدرسة ثانويّة .

٣ ـ درس اللغة الانكليزية .

٤ ـ هذا كرسيّ جديد .

٥ ـ هذا نصّ اساسيّ .

٦ ـ هذه طاولتي الجديدة .

٧ ـ درست تاريخ مصر .

٨ ـ هذه مكتبة المدير .

٩ ـ تعلّمت الآنسة هند الفرنسية .

١٠ ـ هذا متحف وطني .

3. Negation of word or phrase: لَيْسَ

In 4.C.1 we saw how the various forms of لَيْسَ are used to make an equational sentence negative. The third person masculine form لَيْسَ is also used to negate single words and phrases. This usage generally occurs in short replies--not complete sentences--to questions or suggestions:

هَلْ دَرَسْتَ عَنْ أَمْرِيكا ؟	'Did you study about America?'
لَيْسَ في الْجامِعَةِ .	'Not at the university.'

أَيْنَ دَرَّسَتِ الْعَرَبِيَّةَ ؟ هُنا ؟	'Where did she teach Arabic? Here?'
لا . لَيْسَ هُنا . دَرَّسَتِ الْعَرَبِيَّةَ في تِكساس .	'No, not here. She taught Arabic in Texas.'

Now do Drill 5.

Drill 5. (Also on tape) Negation of phrase.

Negate the second part of each of the following questions using لَيْسَ .

Ex.

'Where did you study Arabic? At the university?' ← أين درست العربية ؟ في الجامعة ؟

'No. Not at the university. لا . ليس في الجامعة .

١ – من اين انت ؟ من الخرطوم ؟

٢ – اين المدير ؟ في المكتبة ؟

٣ – أين تعلّم الانكليزية ؟ هنا ؟

٤ – من اين حضر كريم ؟ من سوريا ؟

٥ – أين جامعة الأَزْهَرِ ؟ في دمشق ؟

٦ – أين اكملت دراستك ؟ في جامعة ميشغان ؟

٧ – آين درّست بعد الحصول على الشهادة ؟ في الشرق الاوسط؟

4. Demonstratives: ذٰلِكَ and تِلْكَ

In addition to هٰذا (f. هٰذِهِ), there is another demonstrative ذٰلِكَ (f. تِلْكَ) 'that'. Like هٰذا , it may be used as a pronoun, functioning alone as subject, predicate, or object of verb or preposition; or it may occur with a noun (with definite article) in a demonstrative phrase:

بَعْدَ ذٰلِكَ	'after that'
فِي تِلْكَ السَّنَةِ	'in that year'

The difference between the two demonstratives is that هٰذا / هٰذِهِ may refer to something near the speaker or not so near, and thus may correspond to either 'this' or 'that' depending on the context; while ذٰلِكَ / تِلْكَ usually refers to something fairly distant, or remote in time, and is thus usually translated 'that'. Also, when two things are contrasted, هٰذا is often used for one and ذٰلِكَ for the other:

هٰذا حَديثٌ وذٰلِكَ قَديمٌ .	'This is modern and that is ancient.'

Now do Drill 6.

Drill 6. Written. Completion.

Fill in the correct form of the demonstrative pronoun.

١ ـ هذا الرجل اجنبيّ و ــــــ امريكيّ .

٢ ـ ــــــ بناء قديم وذلك حديث .

٣ ـ هذه الجامعة قريبة و ــــــ بعيدة .

٤ ـ ــــــ الآنسة هند و ــــــ وداد .

٥ ـ ــــــ المتحف حديث و ــــــ قديم .

5. Numerals 11 - 19 (Also on tape)

The following forms of these numerals are used in counting:

11	eleven	أَحَدَ عَشَرَ	١١
12	twelve	إِثْنا عَشَرَ	١٢
13	thirteen	ثَلاثَةَ عَشَرَ	١٣
14	fourteen	أَرْبَعَةَ عَشَرَ	١٤
15	fifteen	خَمْسَةَ عَشَرَ	١٥
16	sixteen	سِتَّةَ عَشَرَ	١٦
17	seventeen	سَبْعَةَ عَشَرَ	١٧
18	eighteen	ثَمانِيَةَ عَشَرَ	١٨
19	nineteen	تِسْعَةَ عَشَرَ	١٩

D. Comprehension passage — د • نُصوصٌ لِلْفَهْم

Read the following passage and then do Drill 7, which is based on it.

درس السيد احمد نجيب التاريخ الاسلامي في جامعة الازهر في القاهرة ودرس اللغة الفرنسية في مدرسة خاصة • انتقل بعد ذلك الى باريس وأكمل الدراسة الجامعية هناك •

رجع السيد احمد نجيب الى القاهرة ، وهو الآنَ مدير مدرسة ثانوية مشهورة في الإِسْكَنْدَرِيّة •

now — الآنَ

Alexandria — الإِسْكَنْدَرِيّة

Drill 7. True or false. — صَوابٌ أَمْ خَطَأٌ

١ ـ السيد احمد نجيب مدير متحف •

٢ ـ درس السيد احمد نجيب في امريكا •

٣ ـ درس السيد احمد نجيب اللغة الفرنسية •

٤ ـ درس السيد احمد نجيب في مدرسة خاصّة •

٥ ـ اكمل السيد احمد نجيب دراسته الجامعية في مصر •

٦ ـ الازهر مدرسة ثانوية في القاهرة •

E. General drills　　　　هـ ـ اَلتَّمارِينُ الْعامَّةُ

Drill 8. Transformation: Nisba.

'This student is from Beirut.'　　هذا الطالب من بيروت .

'This student is a Beiruti.'　　هذا الطالب بيروتيّ .

١ ـ هل أستاذك من أمريكا ؟

٢ ـ درست في جامعة في المغرب .

٣ ـ تعلّمت العربيّة من صديق من السعوديّة .

٤ ـ هذه الطالبة من العراق وتلك من الأردن .

٥ ـ هذا الرجل من السودان وذلك من مصر .

٦ ـ هل تعلّمت العربيّة في مدرسة في تونس ؟

Drill 9. (Also on tape) Substitution: Possessive pronouns.

Change the pronoun suffix in the model sentence, according to the cues given. Ex.

'My friend read an Arabic book.'　　قرأ صديقي كتابا عربيّا .

أنتَ	هي
هو	أنتِ
أنتِ	أنا

Repeat with:　　قرأت صديقتي كتابا عربيّا .

Drill 10. (On tape) Written. Recognition: Demonstrative.

Drill 11. Written. Completion. Fill in the blanks in the sentences below, based on the Basic Text for this lesson. (Try to do it without referring back to the text.)

درس أحمد الأنكليزيّة في ــــ ثانويّة وبعد ذلك درس ــــ

في جامعة الأزهر في ــــ . و ــــ شيئا عن تاريخ أمريكا .

تعلّمت سالي ــــ في مدرسة خاصّة وبعد ذلك ــــ الدراسة في

جامعة القاهرة . ــــ الى أمريكا و ــــ الدراسة هناك .

<u>Drill 12</u>. Translation.

1. Did you (f.s.) study Arabic in a secondary school?
2. No, not in (a) secondary school. I learned Arabic at the University of Michigan.
3. What did you study in (the) secondary school?
4. I studied English and the history of America.
5. Where is the University of Michigan?
6. It is in Ann Arbor.
7. Is it a big university?
8. Yes.

Lesson Eight

الدرس الثامِنُ

أ ـ النص الاساسي

اخبار من الجامعة

١ ـ رجع رئيس الجامعة الى الشرق الاوسط أمس بالطائرة .

٢ ـ اصدرت الجامعة كتابا جديدا بعنوان " نحن ولغتنا " .

٣ ـ استمع الطلاب الجدد لمحاضرة بعنوان " لستم الآن في مدرسة ثانوية ".

٤ ـ استقبل الرئيس الاساتذة الجدد وهم : استاذ اللغة الانكليزية ، واستاذ التاريخ الاسلامي ، واستاذة اللغة العربية .

٥ ـ عنوان محاضرة الاستاذ الزائر اليوم هو " انتم وجامعتكم ".

A. Basic text

News from the University

1. The president of the university returned to the Middle East yesterday by plane.

2. The university has published a new book by the title of We and Our Language.

3. The new students listened to a lecture with the title "You Are Not in Secondary School Now."

4. The president received the new professors. They are: the professor of English, the professor of Islamic history and the professor of Arabic.

5. The title of the visiting professor's lecture today is "You and Your University".

B. Vocabulary

ب ـ المفردات

أَلثّامِنُ	the eighth
أَخْبارٌ	(p.) news, news items
رَئيسٌ	president
أَمْسِ	yesterday
بِ	by, with, by means of
طائِرَةٌ	airplane
أَصْدَرَ	to publish

عُنْوانٌ	title
بِعُنْوانِ	by the title (of)
نَحْنُ	we
إِسْتَمَعَ لِـ / إِلى	to listen to
طُلّابٌ	students
جُدُدٌ	(p.) new
مُحاضَرَةٌ	lecture
لَسْتُمْ	you (m. p.) are not
أَلآنَ	now
إِسْتَقْبَلَ	to receive, welcome, meet
أَساتِذَةٌ	(p. of أُسْتاذٌ) professors
هُمْ	(m. p.) they
أَلْيَوْمَ	today
أَنْتُمْ	(m. p.) you

Additional vocabulary

لَيْسوا	they (m.) are not
لَسْنا	we are not
هُنَّ	they (f.p.)
أَنْتُنَّ	you (f.p.)
لَسْنَ	they (f.) are not
لَسْتُنَّ	you (f.p.) are not

C. Grammar and drills ج ـ القواعد والتمارين

1. Iḍāfa: Noun phrase as second term
2. Verb-subject agreement: Plural subject
3. Independent pronouns: Plural
4. Pronoun suffixes: Plural
5. Negative لَيْسَ : Plural forms
6. Helping vowels: Summary

1. Iḍāfa: Noun phrase as second term

The iḍāfa construction consists of two terms, each term being most commonly a single noun (see 6.C.4). Consider, however, the phrase بِعُنْوانِ «نَحْنُ وَلُغَتُنا» 'by the title (of) We and Our Language'. Here (as the object of the preposition بِ 'by') we have an iḍāfa whose first term is the single noun عُنْوان 'title' but whose second term is the whole phrase within the quotation marks. The first term, عُنْوان, follows the usual rules for the first term of an iḍāfa: appropriate case (here genitive after a preposition), no definite article, no nunation. The second term of an iḍāfa is genitive, but when it is a quoted item it has no genitive ending; rather it has whatever case endings may be required by its own internal structure. Other examples:

تَعَلَّمْنا كَلِمَةَ «إِضافَةٌ». 'We have learned the word "iḍāfa".'

في جُمْلَةِ «الطُّلّابُ هُنا» 'in the sentence "The students are here."'

These examples all illustrate the fact that the second term of an iḍāfa may be a phrase or clause which acts as a unit, as though it were a single noun.

Now consider the phrase:

عُنْوانُ مُحاضَرَةِ ٱلْأُسْتاذِ 'the title of the professor's lecture'

This is an iḍāfa in which the first term is a single noun (عُنْوانُ), and the second term is a noun phrase (مُحاضَرَةِ الْأُسْتاذِ) which is itself an iḍāfa, with a first term and a second term. This kind of construction is called a complex iḍāfa. The following statements apply to complex iḍāfas:

(1) The first word in the string may be any case, depending on its function in the sentence; the others are genitive.

(2) Only the last noun in the string may have the definite article or nunation.

The last term of any complex iḍāfa may be another iḍāfa, so that strings of four or even five nouns sometimes occur:

بابُ مَكْتَبِ رَئِيسِ جامِعَةِ ميشغان	'the door to the office of the president of the University of Michigan'

The last term of an idāfa may be a noun-adjective phrase (underlined in the following examples):

مُحاضَرَةُ الأُسْتاذِ الزّائِرِ	'the visiting professor's lecture
عُنْوانُ مُحاضَرَةِ الأسْتاذِ الزّائِرِ	'the title of the visiting professors's lecture'

Another kind of noun phrase is the demonstrative phrase, and this too may serve as the second term of an iḍāfa:

مُحاضَرَةُ هٰذا الأُسْتاذِ	'this professor's lecture
عُنْوانُ هٰذِهِ الْمُحاضَرَةِ	'the title of this lecture'

(For the demonstrative as the modifier of the first term of the iḍāfa, see 35.C.2.).

Now do Drills 1 and 2.

Drill 1. Written. Recognition.

Identify the iḍāfa's in the following sentences by enclosing the whole iḍāfa in parentheses; then translate each sentence into English: Ex.

'The lecture is entitled "You and the University".' المحاضرة ب(عنوان "انتم والجامعة")

'I read this famous professor's book.' قرأت(كتاب هذا الاستاذ المشهور).

١ _ استقبل الرئيس اساتذة جامعة الازهر .

٢ _ تابعت دراسة هذه اللغة الاجنبية .

٣ _ استمع احمد لمحاضرة بعنوان " التاريخ المصري القديم ".

٤ _ مدير متحف هذه الجامعة رجل بغدادي .

٥ _ اصدر كتاب " تاريخ الطائرة " .

٦ _ تعلّمت شيئا عن تاريخ المدرسة الخاصة في مصر .

Drill 2. Iḍāfa formation.

In the following sentences, combine the words in parentheses to form iḍāfas: Ex.

'The office of the director of this museum is in this building.' (المكتب ـ المدير ـ هذا ـ المتحف) في هذا البناء .

مكتب مدير هذا المتحف في هذا البناء.

١ ـ أكمل (الدراسة ـ اللغة الفرنسية)

٢ ـ قرأت (الكتاب ـ " تاريخ جامعة الازهر ")

٣ ـ استمع الطالب (المحاضرة ـ الرئيس ـ هذه ـ الجامعة)

٤ ـ (البناء ـ المتحف الاسلامي) حديث جدا .

٥ ـ رجع (الاساتذة ـ الجامعة ـ دمشق) من فرنسا .

٦ ـ هذا هو (لوح ـ صف ـ انا)

٧ ـ (شبّاك ـ مكتب ـ هذا ـ المدير) قديم جدا .

2. Verb-subject agreement: Plural subject (see also 6.C.2)

As we have seen in previous lessons, the verb normally precedes its subject. In such a case, the verb agrees in gender but is always singular, regardless of whether it is followed by a singular or a plural subject. Examples:

إِسْتَمَعَ الطّالِبُ الْجَديدُ لِمُحاضَرةٍ.	'The new student listened to a lecture.'
إِسْتَمَعَتِ الطّالِبَةُ الْجَديدَةُ لِمُحاضَرَةٍ.	'The new student listened to a lecture.'
إِسْتَمَعَ الطُّلّابُ الْجُدُدُ لِمُحاضَرَةٍ.	'The new students listened to a lecture.'
إِسْتَمَعَتْ فَريدَةُ وَوِدادُ وَهِنْدُ لِمُحاضَرَةٍ.	'Farida, Widad, and Hind listened to a lecture.'
رَجَعَ الْأُسْتاذُ الْيَوْمَ.	'The professor returned today.'
رَجَعَ الْأَساتِذَةُ الْيَوْمَ.	'The professors returned today.'

In the case of two or more subjects connected by وَ 'and', the verb takes the gender of the first:

رَجَعَ سَليمٌ وَوِدادُ مِنْ لُبْنانَ .	'Salim and Widad have returned from Lebanon.'
رَجَعَتِ الأُسْتاذَةُ وَطالِبُها مِنَ المُحاضَرَةِ .	'The professor (f.) and her student have returned from the lecture.'

Now do Drill 3.

Drill 3. Conjugation.

Give the correct form of the verb in parentheses in the following sentences:

Ex.

'The students studied the history of Egypt.'	(درس) الطلاب تاريخ مصر . ←
	درس الطلاب تاريخ مصر .

١ ـ (انتقل) الاساتذة الى جامعة دمشق .

٢ ـ (تعلم) وداد ونانسي وسالي اللغة الفرنسية .

٣ ـ (استقبل) فريد وسمير وهند المدير الجديد .

٤ ـ (بدأ) الطالبة دراسة العربية .

٥ ـ (قرأ) الطلاب نصّ الدرس .

3. Independent pronouns: Plural

Here is a table showing the five singular independent pronouns previously given, and the corresponding plural pronouns:

	Singular		Plural	
3 M	هُوَ	'he/it'	هُمْ	'they'
3 F	هِيَ	'she/it'	هُنَّ	'they'
2 M	أَنْتَ	'you'	أَنْتُمْ	'you'
2 F	أَنْتِ	'you'	أَنْتُنَّ	'you'
1	أَنا	'I'	نَحْنُ	'we'

The 3 m.p. pronoun هُمْ 'they' is used in referring to three or more human beings including at least one male; the 3 f.p. pronoun هُنَّ is used in referring to three or more female human beings. The 2 m.p. pronoun أَنْتُمْ 'you' is used in addressing three or more human beings including at least one male; the 2 f.p. pronoun أَنْتُنَّ is used in addressing three or more female human beings. (Masculine plural nouns are likewise used to include males and females.) Examples:

هُمْ فِي الْمَكْتَبَةِ.	'They (m.p.) are in the library.'
هَلْ أَنْتُنَّ مِنْ بَيْرُوتَ ؟	'Are you (f.p.) from Beirut?'

If followed immediately by wasla the two pronouns هُمْ and أَنْتُمْ add u as a helping vowel:

هُمُ الْأَسَاتِذَةُ .	'They are the professors.'
أَنْتُمُ الطُّلاَّبُ .	'You are the students.'

The 1 p. pronoun نَحْنُ is used by either a male or a female speaker in referring to himself/herself and one or more others, exactly like English 'we'.

There are special second and third person dual pronouns which are used in addressing or referring to two persons; these will be taken up later.

Now do Drill 4.

Drill 4. (Also on tape) Recognition.

In the following sentences, substitute the correct pronoun for the subjects. Ex.

'Farid and I are from Lebanon.' →	انا وفريد من لبنان. ←
'We are from Lebanon.'	نحن من لبنان.

١ـ فريد وسليم ونانسي طلاب.

٢ ـ نانسي مدرّسة هناك.

٣ ـ انتِ وهند ووداد في المكتبة.

٤ ـ انتَ وسامي وفريدة اساتذة.

٥ ـ انا وسالي من امريكا .

٦ ـ الاستاذ والطالبة والمديرة في مكتب المديرة .

٧ ـ انا وانتَ من لبنان .

٨ – فريد مدير المتحف .

٩ – انا وسليم ومريم طلاب من الرباط .

١٠ – الاساتذة في بناء الجامعة .

١١ – كريم سكرتير في المكتب .

١٢ – انتَ والطلاب جدد هنا.

١٣ – سامي ونانسي ومريم امام باب المتحف .

١٤ – انتِ وهند وسميرة فى القاهرة.

4. Pronoun suffixes: Plural

In 5.C.5 the singular pronoun suffixes were described, and illustrations were given of these suffixes attached to nouns to express possession. Shown below is a table of these suffixes, and the plural suffixes corresponding to the plural independent pronouns (see 3 above):

	Independent	Suffix	Example
Singular			
3 MS	هُوَ	ـهُ	لُغَتُهُ 'his language'
3 FS	هِيَ	ـها	لُغَتُها 'her language'
2 MS	أَنْتَ	ـكَ	لُغَتُكَ 'your language'
2 FS	أَنْتِ	ـكِ	لُغَتُكِ 'your language'
1 S	أَنا	ي	لُغَتِي 'my language'
Plural			
3 MP	هُمْ	ـهُمْ	لُغَتُهُمْ 'their language'
3 FP	هُنَّ	ـهُنَّ	لُغَتُهُنَّ 'their language'
2 MP	أَنْتُمْ	ـكُمْ	لُغَتُكُمْ 'your language'
2 FP	أَنْتُنَّ	ـكُنَّ	لُغَتُكُنَّ 'your
1 P	نَحْنُ	ـنا	لُغَتُنا 'our language'

Two points should be noted about the plural forms:

(1) The vowel of هُمْ and هُنَّ (like the vowel of ـهُ ; see 5.C.5) changes from u to i when the suffix is added to a word ending in ـِ -i, ي ii, or يْ ay. Thus the form is ـهِمْ in

هٰذِهِ لُغَتُهُمْ .	'This is their language.'
دَرَسْتُ لُغَتَهُمْ .	'I studied their language.'

but ـهِمْ in

تَعَلَّمْتُ شَيْئًا مِنْ لُغَتِهِمْ .	'I learned something of their language.'

(2) When words ending in the suffixes ـهُمْ or كُمْ are followed by waṣla, they add u as a helping vowel (see 3.C.2 and 6 below):

أُسْتاذُهُمُ ٱلْجَديدُ	'their new professor'
أُسْتاذُكُمُ ٱلْجَديدُ	'your new professor'

Now do Drills 5 and 6.

Drill 5. (Also on tape) Recognition.

Give the independent pronoun which corresponds to the pronoun suffix on each item below. Ex.

their study ⟶ they (f.p.) دراستهنّ ⟵ هنّ

درّسنا	صديقهم
كتابي	لغتكم
طلابهم	مدرّسكَ
مدرستكنّ	مكتبكِ
تاريخها	مديرهنّ
محاضرته	رئيسنا

Drill 6. Transformation.

In the following sentences, replace the noun and pronoun in parentheses with the noun and corresponding pronoun suffix and vocalize them. Ex.

'I read your book.' ← قرأت (كتاب ـ انتم)

قرأت كِتابَكُمْ.

١ ـ استمع الطلاب لـ (محاضرة ـ نحن) .

٢ ـ درّس الاساتذة (طلاب ـ هم) التاريخ الاسلامي .

٣ ـ (مكتب ـ هنّ) في هذا البناء القديم .

٤ ـ ما (اخبار ـ انتنّ) ؟

٥ ـ هل تابعت (دراسة ـ انت) في جامعة اجنبية ؟

٦ ـ في (كتاب ـ هم) شيء عن رئيس امريكا .

5. Negative لَيْسَ : Plural forms

The verb لَيْسَ is used to make equational sentences negative (see 4.C.1). Here are the singular forms previously given, and the five plural forms:

Singular			Plural	
3 M	لَيْسَ	'he is not'	لَيْسوا	'they are not'
F	لَيْسَتْ	'she is not'	لَسْنَ	'they are not'
2 M	لَسْتَ	'you are not'	لَسْتُمْ	'you are not'
F	لَسْتِ	'you are not'	لَسْتُنَّ	'you are not'
1	لَسْتُ	'I am not'	لَسْنا	'we are not'

This verb follows the usual rules of verb subject agreement outlined in 2 above: if the verb precedes the subject the verb agrees in gender but is always singular. Remember also that the predicate of لَيْسَ , if a noun or adjective, is in the accusative case.

لَيْسَ الطّالِبُ جَديدًا .	'The student is not new.'
لَيْسَتِ الطّالِبَةُ جَديدَةً .	'The student (f.) is not new.'
لَيْسَ الطُّلّابُ جُدُدًا .	'The students are not new.'
لَيْسوا جُدُدًا .	'They are not new.'
أَلَسْتُمْ طُلّابًا ؟	'Aren't you (m.p.) students?'
لَسْنا اْلآنَ في الْعِراقِ .	'We're not in Iraq now.'

Now do Drills 7, 8 and 9.

Drill 7. (Also on tape) Recognition.

Give the independent pronoun that corresponds to each of the following forms of لَيْسَ . Ex.

'We are not' ⟶ We   نحن ⟵ لَسنا

لستَ	لسن
لستم	لستُ
ليست	لستنّ
لسنا	ليس
لستِ	ليسوا

Drill 8. Negation.

Negate the following sentences with the proper form of ليس . Ex.

'They are from Saudi Arabia.' ⟶   ⟵ . هم من السعودية

'They are not from Saudi Arabia.'   ليسوا من السعودية .

١ ـ انتنّ في مدرسة خاصة .

٢ ـ انتم طلاب جدد .

٣ ـ نحن اساتذة في جامعة الازهر .

٤ ـ هنّ من مكتب الرئيس .

٥ ـ هم من فرنسا .

٦ ـ انا طالبة لبنانية .

٧ ـ انت السيدة فريدة .

٨ ـ هي مديرة المكتب .

٩ ـ هو استاذ زائر .

١٠ ـ انت سكرتير المتحف .

Drill 9. Written. Negation.

Negate the following sentences placing the proper form of ليس before the subject. Ex.

'The professors are new.' → ← الاساتذة جدد .

'The professors are not new.' ليس الاساتذة جددا .

١ – وداد وسميرة وسالي من لبنان .

٢ – الطلاب فى مدرسة خاصة في تونس .

٣ – الاساتذة الجدد من بغداد .

٤ – سمير وفريدة ونانسي طلاب من بيروت .

٥ – المدرّسة جديدة في هذه المدرسة .

6. Helping vowels: Summary

Within a sentence, when one word ends in a consonant and the following word begins with waṣla, a helping vowel is added to the end of the first word, since otherwise an impermissible sequence of three successive consonants would occur (see 3.C.2 and 4 above). The three vowels a, u, and i are all used as helping vowels, as follows:

The helping vowel َ a is used only with the preposition مِنْ 'from', and only if the following word begins with the definite article:

مِنَ ٱلْبِناءِ	'from the building'
مِنَ ٱلرَّئِيسِ	'from the president'

The helping vowel u is used after any pronoun, pronoun suffix, or verb form ending in -um, for example أَنْتُمْ 'you(m.p.)', جامِعَتُكُمْ 'your (m.p.) university', or لَسْتُمْ 'you (m.p.) are not':

أَنْتُمُ ٱلآنَ في جامِعَةٍ .	'You (m.p.) are now at a university.'
أَلَسْتُمُ ٱلطُّلابَ الجُدُدَ ؟	'Aren't you (m.p.) the new students?'

The helping vowel i is used in all other cases (including the case of مِنْ 'from' when not followed by the definite article). Examples:

هَلْ:	(interrogative particle)
هَلِ ٱلرَّئيسُ في مَكْتَبِهِ ؟	'Is the president in his office?'
مَنْ:	'who?'
مَنِ ٱسْتَمَعَ لِهٰذِهِ ٱلْمُحاضَرَةِ ؟	'Who listened to that lecture?'
رَجَعَتْ.	'she returned'
رَجَعَتِ ٱلآنِسَةُ سَميرَةُ الى ٱلْعِراقِ	'Miss Samira returned to Iraq.'

Now do Drill 10.

Drill 10. Written.

Supply the helping vowel on the underlined words. Ex.

'Our professor is from Cairo.' استاذنا مِنَ القاهرة .

١ - هم الطلاب الجدد .

٢ - قرأت كتابكم المشهور جدا .

٣ - استقبلت المدرّسة الآنسة مريم .

٤ - استَمَعَتَ اليوم لمحاضرتكَ الثانية عن تاريخ أمريكا .

٥ - تعلّمت لغتهم القديمة .

٦ - هل الزائر موجود هنا ؟

٧ - من المدرّس الاجنبي ؟

٨ - انتقلت المديرة الى مكتب جديد .

D. Comprehension passage د . نُصوصٌ لِلْفَهْمِ

Read the following passage; then do Drill 11, which is based on it.

استقبل رئيس الجامعة صَباحَ الْيَوْمِ الاستاذ الزائر الدكتور ولْيم فَلْتْشَر . (this morning)

الدكتور فلتشر درّس اللغة العربية والتاريخ الاسلامي فى جامعة هارفارد وجامعة برنستون ، وهو رجل مشهور في امريكا والشرق الاوسط. (Harvard; Princeton)

حضرتُ في الْمَساءِ الى الجامعة واستمعتُ لمحاضرة الدكتور فلتشر وعنوانها " دراسة اللغة العربية في امريكا " . (the evening)

Drill 11. Write five questions based on the comprehension passage above.

E. General drills　　　　　هـ ـ التَّمارينُ العامَّة

Drill 12. (On tape) Conjugation.

Drill 13. Written. Translation.

Translate the following sentences into Arabic.

1. I listened yesterday to the university president's lecture.
2. They are not new students.
3. Did you continue your studies at the University of Michigan?
4. She read a book entitled "Our New President."
5. Aren't you the new foreign student?
6. He came to America by airplane.
7. She returned to the Middle East after obtaining a degree.
8. Where did Ahmad study English?
9. He began studying in a private school in Egypt.
10. I learned a new English word today.

Lesson Nine

الدرس التاسِعُ

أ ـ النصّ الاساسيّ

في نيويورك

١ ـ سميرة : أين ذهبت يا روبرت ؟

٢ ـ روبرت : الى نيويورك .

٣ ـ سميرة : هل ذهبت بالسيّارة ؟

٤ ـ روبرت : لا ، ذهبت بالطائرة ورجعت بالاوتوبيس .

٥ ـ سميرة : لماذا ذهبت الى نيويورك ؟

٦ ـ روبرت : لزيارة بعض الاصدقاء والصديقات .

٧ ـ سميرة : ماذا فعلتم هناك ؟

٨ ـ روبرت : ذهبنا الى مطعم عربيّ .

٩ ـ سميرة : ماذا أكلتم ؟

١٠ ـ روبرت : أنا أكلت الكَباب وهم اكلوا الكُبّة ، وشربنا قهوة عربيّة . (kabob; kubba)

١١ ـ سميرة : أين ذهبتم بعد ذلك ؟

١٢ ـ روبرت : ذهبنا الى المسرح ، ولكن بعض الصديقات ذهبن الى السينما وشاهدن فيلم " رجل وامرأة " .

١٣ ـ سميرة : هل كلّ اصدقائك طلّاب في الجامعة ؟

١٤ ـ روبرت : بعضهم طلّاب وبعضهم موظّفون .

١٥ ـ روبرت : الى اللقاء .

١٦ ـ سميرة : مع السلامة .

اسئلـــة

١ ـ هل ذهب روبرت الى نيويورك للدراسة ؟

٢ ـ الى أين ذهب روبرت واصدقاؤه ؟

٣ ـ وماذا أكلوا هناك ؟

٤ ـ وأنت ؟ هل أكلت الكباب ؟ أين ؟

٥ ـ ماذا شربوا في المطعم ؟

٦ ـ ماذا فعل روبرت واصدقاؤه بعد ذلك ؟

٧ ـ من شاهد فيلم " رجل وامرأة " ؟

٨ ـ هل شاهدت هذا الفيلم ؟

٩ ـ هل كل اصدقاء روبرت موظفون ؟

A. Basic Text

In New York

1. Samira: Where did you go, Robert?
2. Robert: To New York.
3. Samira: Did you go by car?
4. Robert: No, I went by plane and returned by bus.
5. Samira: Why did you go to New York?
6. Robert: To visit some friends.
7. Samira: What did you do there?
8. Robert: We went to an Arab restaurant.
9. Samira: What did you eat?
10. Robert: I ate kabob and they ate kubba, and we drank Arabic coffee.
11. Samira: Where did you go after that?
12. Robert: We went to the theater, but some of my friends went to the movies and saw the film A Man and a Woman.

13. Samira: Are all of your friends students in the university?

14. Robert: Some of them are students and some are employees.

15. Samira: Good-bye.

16. Robert: Good-bye.

B. Vocabulary — ب ــ أَلْمُفْرَدات

أَلتّاسِعُ	the ninth
نيويورك	New York
ذَهَبَ	to go
سَيّارَةٌ	car
أُوتوبيس	bus
لِماذا ؟	why?
لِ (لِ + اَلْ = لِلْ)	in order to, for the purpose of
زِيارَةٌ	visiting; a visit
بَعْضٌ	some
أَصْدِقاءُ	friends (m.)
صَديقاتٌ	friends (f.)
فَعَلَ	to do; to make
مَطْعَمٌ	restaurant
أَكَلَ	to eat
شَرِبَ	to drink
قَهْوَةٌ	coffee
مَسْرَحٌ	theater
سينَما	(f.) cinema, movies
شاهَدَ	to see, watch, witness
فِلْمٌ ، فيلْمٌ	film; movie

إِمْرَأَةٌ	a woman
أَلْمَرْأَةُ	the woman
نِسائِيٌّ – ون	(nisba of نِساءٌ , p. of إِمْرَأَةٌ) female, womanly, women's
إِلى ٱللِّقاء	good-bye (said to person leaving or staying)
مَعَ السَّلامَةِ	good-bye (said to person leaving)
كُلٌّ	(followed by a definite plural form) all; (followed by an indefinite singular form) each; (followed by a singular definite form) all (of), the whole

C. <u>Grammar and Drills</u> ج – <u>القواعد والتمارين</u>

1. The nouns كُلٌّ 'each, all' and بَعْضٌ 'some'
2. Masculine and feminine sound plurals: Human nouns
3. Masculine sound plurals in iḍāfa and with pronoun suffix
4. Verb: Perfect tense plural
5. Verb-subject agreement: Verb following plural subject
6. Expressed pronoun subjects: Emphasis and contrast

1. <u>The nouns كُلٌّ 'each, all' and بَعْضٌ 'some'</u>

In Arabic the words كُلٌّ and بَعْضٌ are <u>nouns</u>, though their English equivalents are not. Like any noun, they have case endings and may have nunation. These two nouns occur most commonly as the first term of an iḍāfa, or with an attached pronoun suffix. Following are examples, with English equivalents:

(1) كُلٌّ with an <u>indefinite singular noun</u> corresponds to English 'each' or 'every':

كُلُّ طالِبٍ	'each student'
كُلُّ وَرَقَةٍ	'every sheet of paper'

With a <u>definite singular noun or singular pronoun suffix</u> it corresponds to English 'all of' or 'the whole':

كُلُّ الدَّرْسِ	'all of the lesson'
كُلُّ الجامِعَةِ	'the whole university'
كُلُّهُ / كُلُّها	'all of it'

With a <u>definite plural noun or plural pronoun suffix</u> it corresponds to English 'all of' or 'all':

مِنْ كُلِّ الطُّلّابِ	'from all the students'
كُلُّهُمْ	'all of them'

كُلّ with a noun can serve any function-subject, object, etc.:

حَضَرَ كُلُّ الطُّلّابِ .	'All of the students came.'	(= subject)
شَرِبْتُ كُلَّ الْقَهْوَةِ .	'I drank all of the coffee.'	(= object)

With a pronoun suffix it usually serves as a subject, or, for emphasis, after a plural verb or in apposition to a noun or pronoun:

كُلُّهُمْ هُنا	'They are all here.'	(= subject)
كُلُّهُمْ حَضَروا / حَضَرَ كُلُّهُمْ .	'All of them came.'	(= subject)
حَضَروا كُلُّهُمْ .	'<u>All</u> of them came.'	(= emphasis)
هَلْ شَرِبْتَ الْقَهْوَةَ كُلَّها ؟	'Did you drink <u>all</u> of the coffee?'	(= emphasis)

As an independent noun, (مِنْ) كُلّ when indefinite means "each, each one of". With the definite article, it means "everyone, everything, the whole thing."

ذَهَبَ لِزِيارَةِ كُلٍّ مِنْ أَصْدِقائِهِ .	'He went to visit each of his friends.'
تَحَدَّثْتُ إِلى الكُلِّ .	'I've talked to everyone.'
أَكَلَ الكُلَّ.	'He ate the whole thing.'

Now do Drill 1.

(2) بَعْضُ is usually followed by a definite noun in an iḍāfa or by a pronoun suffix. It corresponds to English 'some' or 'some of':

بَعْضُ الطُّلّابِ	'some students' or 'some of the students'
بَعْضُهُمْ	'some of them'

Now do Drill 2.

Drill 1. Written. Recognition: كُلّ

Each of the sentences below contains كُلّ with a noun. Choose the correct translation for each use of كُلّ from the choices given in parentheses.

(every student, all the students)	١ ـ كل الطلاب موجودون هنا الآن .
(every film, all the films, the whole film)	٢ ـ هل شاهدتم كل الفيلم ؟
(every employee, all the employees)	٣ ـ هل كل موظف في المكتب ؟
(every restaurant, all the restaurants, the whole restaurant)	٤ ـ أكلنا في كل مطعم هناك .
(every book, all the books, the whole book)	٥ ـ قرأ صديقي كل الكتاب امس .
(every friend, all the friends)	٦ ـ ذهب كل الاصدقاء الى المسرح .
(every woman, all the women)	٧ ـ هل شاهدت كل امرأة هذا الفيلم ؟
(every sentence, all the sentences, the whole sentence)	٨ ـ قرأت كل الجملة .
(every professor, all the professors)	٩ ـ كل الاساتذة في هذه الجامعة مصريون.
(every year, all the years, the whole year)	١٠ ـ ذهبنا الى فرنسا كل سنة .

Drill 2. Transformation: Noun ⟶ pronoun suffix after بعض ، كلّ

'Some of the friends are students.' ⟶ بعض الاصدقاء طلاب . ⟵

'Some of them are students.' بعضهم طلاب .

١ ـ كل الاساتذة من مصر .	٥ ـ كل الطلّاب في الصف .
٢ ـ كل الصديقات في الجامعة .	٦ ـ بعض الطلّاب موظفون .
٣ ـ بعض اصدقائي طلّاب .	٧ ـ بعض الصديقات طالبات .
٤ ـ بعض صديقاتنا من المغرب .	٨ ـ كل الاصدقاء طلّاب .

2. Masculine and feminine sound plurals: Human nouns

Arabic, like English, has various ways of making nouns plural. In English, for example, most nouns are made plural by the plural suffix spelled s or es, e.g. "cat-cats", "dog-dogs", and "lunch-lunches". Other devices are: special suffixes, as in "ox-oxen"; vowel change, as in "man-men"; a combination of vowel change and suffix, as in "child-children"; or none at all as in "sheep-sheep". Arabic plurals, whether nouns or adjectives, are formed by adding special suffixes, as in مُدَرِّس 'teacher', مُدَرِّسُونَ 'teachers' and مَشْهُورٌ 'famous', مَشْهُورُونَ; and by vowel change, as in طَالِبٌ 'student' and طُلَّابٌ 'students' (with doubling of the l also), جَدِيدٌ and جُدُدٌ 'new'; or a combination of vowel change and suffix, as in أُسْتَاذٌ 'professor' and أَسَاتِذَةٌ 'professors'. Arabic plurals formed by means of vowel change (with or without suffixes) are called "internal" or "broken" plurals, and those that are formed by means of certain suffixes are called "external" or "sound" plurals. This note will deal with sound plurals, and broken plurals will be treated later.

Sound plurals show distinctions in gender and case. The suffixes are:

	Masculine	Feminine
Nom.	‐ ونَ	‐ اتٌ
Gen.	‐ ينَ	‐ اتٍ
Acc.	‐ ينَ	‐ اتٍ

Note that the suffixes for the genitive and accusative cases are identical, and that only the feminine plurals may have nunation. The plurals of مُدَرِّس and مُدَرِّسة are given below to illustrate the forms:

'teachers'	Masculine	Feminine
Nom.	مُدَرِّسُونَ	مُدَرِّسَاتٌ
Gen.	مُدَرِّسِينَ	مُدَرِّسَاتٍ
Acc.	مُدَرِّسِينَ	مُدَرِّسَاتٍ

Masculine sound plurals are used only for words referring to male <u>human beings</u>, or to groups including at least one male. Of the nouns introduced so far, the following take masculine sound plurals:

<u>P.</u>	<u>S.</u>	
مُدَرِّسونَ	مُدَرِّسٌ	'teacher'
مُوَظَّفونَ	مُوَظَّفٌ	'employee'
سِكْرِتيرونَ	سِكْرِتيرٌ	'secretary'
مُديرونَ	مُديرٌ	'director'

Of the adjectives introduced up to now, the following take masculine sound plurals:

<u>P.</u>	<u>S.</u>	
مَوْجودونَ	مَوْجودٌ	'present'
مَشْهورونَ	مَشْهورٌ	'famous'
زائِرونَ	زائِرٌ	'visiting'
خاصّونَ	خاصٌّ	'special'
لُبْنانِيّونَ	لُبْنانِيٌّ	'Lebanese'

and all nisba adjectives (such as لُبْنانِيٌّ above) <u>except</u> عَرَبِيٌّ 'Arab, Arabic' and أَجْنَبِيٌّ 'foreign', which have broken plurals; and إِسْلامِيٌّ 'Islamic', which is not commonly used to refer to human beings. Examples:

مُدَرِّسونَ زائِرونَ	'visiting teachers'
الْمُوَظَّفونَ مَوْجودونَ.	'The employees are present.'
مِنَ السِّكْرِتيرينَ اللُّبْنانِيّينَ	'from the Lebanese secretaries'

As we noted above, masculine sound plurals can refer <u>only</u> to human beings (males or mixed groups). Feminine sound plurals, on the other hand, may refer either to human beings (female only) or to nonhuman things. In this lesson only human nouns will be dealt with; nonhuman nouns will be taken up in Lesson Eleven.

Following are the feminine human nouns introduced thus far:

	P.	S.	
1.	طالِباتٌ	طالِبَةٌ	'student'
2.	مُدَرِّساتٌ	مُدَرِّسَةٌ	'teacher'
3.	مُديراتٌ	مُديرَةٌ	'director'
4.	سِكْرِتيراتٌ	سِكْرِتيرَةٌ	'secretary'
5.	آنِساتٌ	آنِسَةٌ	'young lady'
6.	مُوَظَّفاتٌ	مُوَظَّفَةٌ	'employee'
7.	أُسْتاذاتٌ	أُسْتاذَةٌ	'professor'
8.	صَديقاتٌ	صَديقَةٌ	'friend'
9.	رَئيساتٌ	رَئيسَةٌ	'president'

In general, feminine singular human nouns ending in ـَةٌ form their plurals with اتٌ.

Most feminine adjectives take the feminine sound plural (rather than a broken plural). Examples:

مُدَرِّساتٌ جَديداتٌ	'new teachers'
الطّالِباتُ اللُّبْنانِيّاتُ	'the Lebanese students'
مِنْ صَديقاتٍ قَديماتٍ	'from old friends'

Henceforth you must learn each noun and adjective in its singular and plural forms. These will be listed in the vocabularies of subsequent lessons, first in the singular, and then in the plural: Sound m. and f. plurals will be given as ون ، ات respectively. Other plurals will be given in full. For example:

مُدَرِّسٌ — ون	'teacher' (m.)
طالِبَةٌ — ات	'student' (f.)
جَديدٌ — جُدُدٌ	'new'

Now do Drills 3 and 4.

Drill 3. Written. Recognition: Sound plurals.

Identify the gender of the following plural words and circle their plural suffixes: Ex.

M. مدرّسون

F. مدرّسات

١ ــ استاذات اجنبيّات

٢ ــ موجودون

٣ ــ من الموظّفين

٤ ــ صديقات جديدات

٥ ــ السكرتيرون المشهورون

٦ ــ مدرّسين فرنسيّين

٧ ــ من الزائرات

٨ ــ الطالبات الموجودات

Drill 4. (Also on tape) Substitution/transformation: Plurals.

Change each of the items given below to its plural form, and then substitute it for the underlined word in the model sentence.

a. 'The teachers saw a foreign movie.'

شاهد المدرّسون فيلما اجنبيّا .

١ ــ الموظّف

٢ ــ السكرتيرة اللبنانيّة

٣ ــ الطالبة الجديدة

٤ ــ الاستاذ المشهور

٥ ــ صديقتي

٦ ــ المدرّسة التونسيّة

٧ ــ الطالب الجامعيّ

٨ ــ الطالبة الجامعيّة

b. Repeat with:

'I saw the officials at the office.'

شاهدت الموظّفين في المكتب .

١ ــ المديرة الاجنبيّة

٢ ــ الاستاذة الجامعيّة

٣ ــ المدرّس الفرنسيّ

٤ ــ صديقه

٥ ــ السكرتير

٦ ــ الطالبة الجديدة

٧ ــ المدرّسة الامريكيّة

٨ ــ صديقتها

3. Masculine sound plurals in iḍāfa and with pronoun suffix

The masculine sound plural forms of the noun مُدَرِّس , (see 2 above) are given here again for reference:

Nom.	مُدَرِّسونَ
Gen.	مُدَرِّسينَ
Acc.	مُدَرِّسينَ

When a masculine sound plural noun like this occurs as the first term of an iḍāfa, or when it has an attached pronoun suffix, the final نَ– of the plural ending is dropped:

As first term of iḍāfa		
Nom.	رَجَعَ مُدَرِّسو التّاريخِ.	'The history teachers have returned.'
Gen.	ذَهَبْتُ الى مَكْتَبِ مُدَرِّسي التّاريخِ.	'I went to the history teachers' office.'
Acc.	اِسْتَقْبَلَ الرَّئيسُ مُدَرِّسي التّاريخِ.	'The president received the history teachers.'

With pronoun suffix		
Nom.	مُدَرِّسوهُ	'his teachers'
Gen./ Acc.	مُدَرِّسيهِ	

The first person singular pronoun suffix 'my' has the form يَ -ya (instead of يِ as in مَكْتَبي 'my office') when the stem to which it is attached ends in a long vowel. That is the case with these masculine plural forms after the dropping of the final نَ . In addition, when this suffix يَ -ya is attached to a nominative stem ending in وُ uu, the latter changes to ي ii (becoming identical to the genitive and accusative endings). The final ي ii of the stem and the suffix يَ ya are then written as a double ي with a shadda: يّ iyya. Here is the process:

Nom.	مُدَرِّسونَ	'teachers'
(drop نَ) :	مُدَرِّسو – ي	
(change و to ي) :	مُدَرِّسي – ي	
(write 2 ي's as 1) :	مُدَرِّسيَّ	'my teachers'
Gen./Acc.	مُدَرِّسينَ	'teachers'
(drop نَ –) :	مُدَرِّسي – ي	
(write 2 ي's as 1) :	مُدَرِّسيَّ	'my teachers'

Thus, with this suffix, all three cases are the same:

Nom. Gen. Acc.	مُدَرِّسيَّ	'my teachers'

Now do Drill 5.

Drill 5. Transformation.

Combine the two items in parentheses in each of the sentences below. If written, write only the resulting combination of noun + noun or noun + pronoun suffix, making any changes necessary. Ex.

'His students came to class.' حضر (طلاب ـ هو) الى الصف .

طلابه

١ ـ شاهد (مدرّسون ـ اللغة العربيّة) فيلما عربيّا .

٢ ـ هل أصدر (اساتذة ـ انتم) كتابا هذه السنة ؟

٣ ـ شاهدنا (طلاب ـ نحن) فى السينما .

٤ ـ هل استقبل الرئيس (موظفون ـ هو) الجدد ؟

٥ ـ (سكرتيرات ـ المدير) موجودات في المكتب .

٦ ـ كل (اصدقاء ـ انا) في هذا المطعم .

٧ ـ هل استمعت الى (مدرّسين ـ انت) ؟

٨ ـ ذهبت (صديقات ـ هنّ) الى المسرح .

٩ ـ رجع (مدرّسون ـ انا) الى المدرسة .

١٠ ـ درّست (استاذة ـ هي) في جامعة القاهرة .

4. <u>Verb: Perfect tense - plural</u>

The singular forms of the verb in the perfect tense were given in previous lessons (see 6.C.2 and 7.C.1). In this lesson we present the plural forms. Here is a table showing both singular and plural forms of the verb ذَهَبَ 'to go' (stem -ذَهَبْ <u>ðahab-</u>):

			Subject Marker		
3 MS	هو	ذَهَبَ	ـَ	-a	'he went'
3 FS	هي	ذَهَبَتْ	ـَتْ	-at	'she went'
2 MS	أنتَ	ذَهَبْتَ	تَ	-ta	'you (m.s.) went'
2 FS	أنتِ	ذَهَبْتِ	تِ	-ti	'you (f.s.) went'
1 S	أنا	ذَهَبْتُ	تُ	-tu	'I went'
3 MP	هم	ذَهَبوا	وا	-uu	'they (m.) went'
3 FP	هنّ	ذَهَبْنَ	نَ	-na	'they (f.) went'
2 MP	أنتم	ذَهَبْتُمْ	تُمْ	-tum	'you (m.p.) went'
2 FP	أنتنّ	ذَهَبْتُنَّ	تُنَّ	-tunna	'you (f.p.) went'
1 P	نحن	ذَهَبْنا	نا	-naa	'we went'

The following points may be noted about these plural forms:

(1) The 3 m.p. ending is written with a final <u>?alif</u>. This is a matter of spelling only, and does not affect the pronunciation of the ending, which is <u>-uu</u>. Cf. لَيْسوا 'they are not' which is also third person masculine plural

(2) The use of the masculine and feminine plural forms is like that of the corresponding pronouns (8.C.3): the 3 m.p. and 2 m.p. forms are used in referring to or addressing three or more <u>human beings</u> including at least one

male; while the 3 f.p. and 2 f.p. forms are used in referring to or addressing three or more female human beings. (But for the 3 m.p. and 3 f.p. forms see also 5 below.)

Now do Drills 6,7 and 8.

Drill 6. (On tape) Conjugation.

Drill 7. (On tape) Questions and answers.

Drill 8. Questions and answers.

Answer the following in the appropriate person:

١ ـ هل ذهبوا الى السينما ؟

٢ ـ هل اكلتِ الكبّة ؟

٣ ـ هل اصدرَتْ كتابا جديدا ؟

٤ ـ هل استقبلتم المدير ؟

٥ ـ هل درستْ الدرس الاوّل ؟

٦ ـ هل ذهبن الى المسرح ؟

٧ ـ هل قرأتِ الجملة ؟

٨ ـ هل استمعتِ الى محاضرة الاستاذ ؟

٩ ـ هل ذهبتنّ الى بيروت ؟

١٠ـ هل شربوا قهوة عربيّة ؟

١١ـ هل اكملن الدراسة في تلك الجامعة ؟

١٢ـ هل رجعتم الى الشرق الاوسط ؟

5. Verb-subject agreement: Verb following plural subject

In 8.C.2 it was seen that when a verb precedes a plural subject the verb is singular. It is masculine if the subject is masculine, and feminine if the subject is feminine, but it is always singular:

ذَهَبَ الطّلّابُ الى نيويورك.	'The students went to New York.'
ذَهَبَتْ صَديقاتِي الى نيويورك.	'My friends (f.) went to New York.'

This word order (verb first, then subject) is the usual order in an Arabic verbal sentence. The reverse order (subject first, then verb) is also possible, however, and that is when the plural verb forms are used. There is also agreement in gender. Examples:

الطُّلاّبُ ذَهَبُوا الى نيويورك .	'The students went to New York.'
صَديقاتي ذَهَبْنَ الى نيويورك .	'My friends (f.) went to New York.'

The choice of word order (verb first or subject first) is a matter of style in Arabic, depending on various matters such as length of the verb or the subject or focussing on the subject; the English translation is usually the same for both.

The plural verb forms are also used when a (human) plural subject has been mentioned in a previous sentence, or is clear from the context. In such cases the form of the verb indicates the subject:

رَجَعُوا أَمْسِ .	'They (m.) returned yesterday.'
رَجَعْنَ أَمْسِ .	'They (f.) returned yesterday.'

Now do Drill 9.

Drill 9. Written. Completion and translation.

Insert the correct form of the verb given in parentheses in each of the sentences below. Translate.

١ ـ أصدقائي ــــــ الى المطعم . (حضر)

٢ ـ ــــــ المدرّسات الى مدرستهن . (رجع)

٣ ـ ــــــ الطلّاب الى محاضرتي . (استمع)

٤ ـ الموظفون ــــــ مديرهم . (استقبل)

٥ ـ ــــــ استاذ التاريخ الاسلامي كتابا ثانيا . (اصدر)

٦ ـ صديقاتنا ــــــ الى بيروت . (انتقل)

٧ ـ الاساتذة ــــــ الى مكتب الرئيس . (ذهب)

٨ ـ ــــــ المدرّسات في مدرسة ثانويّة . (درّس)

٩ ـ الاساتذة ــــــ الى الجامعة . (رجع)

١٠ ـ ــــــ الطلاب الى المتحف . (ذهب)

6. <u>Expressed pronoun subjects: Emphasis and contrast</u>

Since the Arabic verb form alone indicates the person, gender, and number of the subject, it is normally not necessary to use an independent pronoun subject as in English. For example:

أَيْنَ كَريمَة ؟	'Where's Karima?'
ذَهَبَتْ إلى الْمَكْتَبَةِ .	'She went to the library.'

However, if some special emphasis is to be placed on the subject, or if a contrast is drawn between the actions of two different subjects, then the independent pronouns are used:

أنا أَكَلْتُ الكَباب وَهُمْ أَكَلوا الكُبّة.	'<u>I</u> ate kabob and <u>they</u> ate kubba.'

D. <u>Comprehension passage</u>   د ـ <u>نُصوصٌ لِلْفَهْمِ</u>

Read the following passage; then do Drill 10, which is based on it.

with — صديقي السيّد لُطْفي أَحْمَدُ موظّف في بنك مصر . حضر <u>مَعَ</u> بعض

اصدقائه الى امريكا للزيارة . استقبلنا السيّد لطفي أمس . وفي

evening; food — <u>المَساءِ</u> ذهبنا الى مطعم عربيّ وأكلنا <u>طَعامًا</u> عربيًّا وشربنا كلّنا القهوة.

ذهبنا بعد ذلك الى سينما قريبة من المطعم وشاهدنا عُمَر الشّريف في

فيلم " الدكتور جيفاكو " .

<u>Drill 10</u>. Complete the following sentences:

١ ـ بعض اصدقاء السيد لطفي ______ .

end — ٢ ـ بعد <u>اُنْتِهاءِ</u> الزيارة رجع السيد لطفي ______ .

٣ ـ في امريكا أكل السيد لطفي ______ وشرب ______ .

٤ ـ شاهد السيد لطفي فيلما فى سينما ______ .

٥ ـ " الدكتور جيفاكو " ______ .

E. General drills   هـ ـ التَّمارينُ الْعامَّةُ

Drill 11. Variable substitution.

'Some of the teachers went to the restaurant.'

١ ـ ذهب بعض المدرّسين الى المطعم ٠

٢ ـ ــــ ــــ الطلاب ــــ ــــ ٠

٣ ـ ــــ ــــ ــــ ــــ الجامعة ٠

٤ ـ رجع ــــ ــــ من ــــ ٠

٥ ـ ــــ كل ــــ ــــ ــــ ٠

٦ ـ ــــ ــــ هم ــــ ــــ ٠

Drill 12. Written. Transformation: 3 m.s. → 3 m.p. → 3 f.s. → 3 f.p.

In the sentences below, change the underlined items to: a) masculine plural, b) feminine singular, and c) feminine plural. Make any necessary changes in the rest of the sentence.

١ ـ الموظّف اللبنانيّ ذهب لزيارة صديقه ٠

٢ ـ شاهدت سكرتير الرئيس في المكتبة ٠

٣ ـ هل استمعت الى مدرّسك ؟

Drill 13. Question formation.

Use the question-words in parentheses to make questions based on the following statements:

١ ـ ذهب الى مصر لزيارة الاصدقاء ٠ (لماذا)

٢ ـ أكلوا الكباب في مطعم عربيّ ٠ (أين)

٣ ـ استقبلوا الرئيس امس ٠ (من)

٤ ـ ذهبوا الى الشرق الاوسط لدراسة العربيّة ٠ (لماذا)

٥ ـ أكملت الدراسة هناك ٠ (هل) ٠

٦ ـ سكرتير المدير موجود في مكتبه ٠ (أليس)

٧ ـ شربن قهوة عربيّة في مطعم ٠ (ماذا)

٨ ـ هذه كلمة فرنسية . (ما)

٩ ـ رجعت صديقتها الى بيروت . (الى اين)

١٠ ـ درست التاريخ الاسلامي في الجامعة . (ماذا)

١١ ـ هذه هي الاخبار الجامعية . (ما)

١٢ ـ أصدرت الجامعة كتابا جديدا بعنوان " الجامعة الامريكية اليوم " (ما)

١٣ ـ هذا كرسيّ جديد . (هل)

Lesson Ten

الدرس العاشر

أ ـ النصّ الاساسيّ

في المطار

١ ـ الآنسة لوسي : مرحبا يا سيّد حسين .

٢ ـ السيّد حسين : اهلا وسهلا يا آنسة لوسي . الى أين أنت ذاهبة ؟

٣ ـ الآنسة لوسي : الى نيويورك . وانت ؟

٤ ـ السيد حسين : الى الرياض .

٥ ـ الآنسة لوسي : متى موعد طائرتك ؟

٦ ـ السيد حسين : بعد وقت قصير .

٧ ـ الآنسة لوسي : على أيّ طائرة انت ذاهب ؟

٨ ـ السيد حسين : على طائرة شركة مصر .

٩ ـ الآنسة لوسي : هل عائلتك معك ؟

١٠ ـ السيد حسين : لا . تركتها في لندن .

١١ ـ الآنسة لوسي : كم ولدا لك ؟

١٢ ـ السيد حسين : لي ابن واسمه عادل ، وبنت واسمها سعاد .

١٣ ـ الآنسة لوسي : ما عملك ؟

١٤ ـ السيد حسين : انا مدير شركة . وانت ما عملك ؟

١٥ ـ الآنسة لوسي : انا موظفة في بنك .

١٦ ـ السيد حسين : حانَ موعد طائرتي . الى اللقاء .　　has come (time)

١٧ ـ الآنسة لوسي : مع السلامة .

A. Basic Text

At the Airport

1. Lucy: Hello, Mr. Hussein.

2. Hussein: Hello, Miss Lucy. Where are you going?

3. Lucy: To New York. And you?

4. Hussein: To Riyadh.

5. Lucy: When does your plane leave?

6. Hussein: In a short time.

7. Lucy: On what plane are you going?

8. Hussein: On Misr Air.

9. Lucy: Is your family with you?

10. Hussein: No, I left them in London.

11. Lucy: How many children do you have?

12. Hussein: I have a son--his name is ʻAdil--and a daughter--her name is Suʻad.

13. Lucy: What is your job?

14. Hussein: I am the director of a company. And you, what is your job?

15. Lucy: I am an employee in a bank.

16. Hussein: It's time for my plane. Good-bye.

17. Lucy: Good-bye.

B. Vocabulary ب ــ المفردات

مَطارٌ ــ ات	airport
لوسي	Lucy
حُسَيْنٌ	Hussein (m. name)
أَهْلاً وَسَهْلاً	welcome; hello

ذاهِبٌ ـ ون	going
مَتى	when?
مَوْعِدٌ ـ مَواعِدُ ، مَواعيدُ	appointed time; appointment
وَقْتٌ ـ أَوْقاتٌ	time
قَصيرٌ ـ قِصارٌ	short
عَلى ـ عَلَيْ	on
أَيٌّ	(foll. by gen. noun) which?, what?
شَرِكَةٌ ـ ات	company
عائِلَةٌ ـ ات	family
مَعَ	with
تَرَكَ	to leave
لَنْدَن	London
كَمْ	(foll. by s. acc.) how much?, how many?
وَلَدٌ ـ أَوْلادٌ	child; boy
لِـ	(prep.) belonging to; to, for; of
اِبْنٌ ـ أَبْناءٌ	(with waṣla) son
اِسْمٌ ـ أَسْماءٌ	(with waṣla) name
عادِلٌ	ʿAdil (m. name)
بِنْتٌ ـ بَناتٌ	girl; daughter
سُعادُ	Suʿad (f. name)
عَمَلٌ ـ أَعْمالٌ	work, job
بَنْكٌ ـ بُنوكٌ	bank

C. Grammar and notes — ج ـ القواعد والتمارين

> 1. Interrogative particle كَمْ 'how many?'
>
> 2. Preposition لِ 'belonging to'
>
> 3. Equational sentences: Predicate first with indefinite subject

4. Prepositions with pronoun suffixes
5. Verbs with pronoun suffixes
6. Interrogative noun أَيّ 'which?'

1. Interrogative particle كَمْ 'how many?'

The particle كَمْ is an interrogative corresponding to the English 'how many?'. Together with a noun it forms an interrogative phrase, and the noun is then always singular, indefinite, and in the accusative case:

كَمْ وَلَدًا لَكَ ؟	'How many children do you have?'
كَمْ طالِبًا ذَهَبَ إلى نيويورك ؟	'How many students went to New York?'

Now do Drills 1 and 2.

Drill 1. Recognition/translation.

Translate the underlined portion of the following sentences containing كَمْ:

١ - كم طائرة في المطار؟ ٥ - كم مدرّسة في تلك المدرسة ؟
٢ - كم طالبا درس العربية معكم ؟ ٦ - كم فيلما شاهدتم ؟
٣ - كم استاذا استقبل رئيس الجامعة ؟ ٧ - كم صديقا استقبل احمد في المطار ؟
٤ - كم مطعما عربيا في نيويورك ؟ ٨ - كم كتابا قرأت هذه السنة ؟

Drill 2. Question formation.

Form questions from the following sentences using كَمْ and a form of the underlined words. Ex.

T: 'Some of the employees drank coffee.' شرب بعض الموظفين قهوة .

S: 'How many employees drank coffee?' كم موظفا شرب قهوة ؟

١ ـ شاهد كل الاصدقاء الفلم .　　　　٥ ـ اصدر بعض الاساتذة كتابا .

٢ ـ استقبلوا بعض المدرسات في المطار ٦٠ ـ بعض المدرسين من فرنسا .

٣ ـ ذهب كل الطلاب الى المسرح .　　　٧ ـ شاهدتم بعض الموظفات فى السينما .

٤ ـ تركت كل الصديقات فى لندن .

٨ ـ حضرت كل الطالبات الى امريكا .

2. Preposition لِـ 'belonging to'

One of the meanings of the Arabic preposition لِـ is 'belonging to'. Thus one may say

أَلسَّيّارَةُ لِلْمَتْحَفِ .	'The car belongs to the museum.'

This is an equational sentence, with أَلسَّيّارَةُ as subject and the prepositional phrase لِلْمَتْحَفِ as predicate. Literally it means something like 'The car (is) of-the-museum.' Thus لِ is often used in this way to express possession. Other examples:

هٰذِهِ الطّائِرَةُ لِشَرِكَةٍ جَدِيدَةٍ .	'This plane belongs to a new company.'
هٰذا الْمَكْتَبُ لِلْمُدِيرِ .	'This office is the director's.'
لِمَنْ هٰذا الْقَلَمُ ؟	'Whose is this pencil?'

(In the last example the predicate is first because it is an interrogative phrase.)

When a pronoun suffix is serving as the object of the preposition لِـ , the vowel of the latter changes to لَـ except with the 1 s. suffix, where the combination is لي . The forms are as follows:

لَهُ	'belonging to him'	لَهُمْ	'belonging to them (m.)'
لَها	'belonging to her'	لَهُنَّ	'belonging to them (f.)'
لَكَ	'belonging to you (m.s.)'	لَكُمْ	'belonging to you (m.p.)'
لَكِ	'belonging to you (f.s.)'	لَكُنَّ	'belonging to you (f.p.)'
لي	'belonging to me'	لَنا	'belonging to us'

When this phrase follows a definite subject, it may be translated into English using the verb "to belong to" or a possessive pronoun; illustrations:

هٰذِهِ الْقَهْوَةُ لِسُعادَ .	'This coffee belongs to Su'ad.' 'This coffee is Su'ad's.'
هَلْ هٰذا الْقَلَمُ لَكَ ؟	'Does this pencil belong to you?' 'Is this pencil yours?'
هُوَ صَديقٌ لي .	'He is a friend of mine.'

See C.3 below for a لِ- phrase with an indefinite subject.

Now do Drills 3 and 4.

Drill 3. Question formation: لِمَنْ . Ex.

T : 'The bus belongs to the company.'	أ ـ الاوتوبيس للشركة .
S_1 : 'Whose is this bus?'	ط١ ـ لمن هذا الاوتوبيس ؟
S_2 : 'The company's.'	ط٢ ـ للشركة .

١ ـ الكتاب الجديد لك .

٢ ـ السيّارة الكبيرة لصديقنا .

٣ ـ هذا المتحف للجامعة .

٤ ـ هذا القلم لي .

٥ ـ هذا المكتب للمدير .

٦ ـ هذه الطاولة لها .

٧ ـ هذا الكرسيّ للمدرّسة .

٨ ـ كتاب التاريخ للطالب .

Drill 4. (Also on tape) Transformation: idāfa → لِ + noun. Ex.

a. 'This is the director's car.' → ← هذه سيّارة المدير .

'This car belongs to the director.' هذه السيّارة للمدير .

١ ـ هذا كتاب فريد .

٢ ـ هذه طائرة شركة مصر .

٣ ـ هذا قلم الاستاذ وليم .

٤ ـ هذا مكتب المدير .

٥ ـ هذا متحف الجامعة .

٦ ـ هذا كرسي السكرتير .

٧ ـ هذه طاولة الموظفة .

٨ ـ هذه سيّارة المرأة .

b. 'This is my car.' → ← هذه سيّارتي .

'This car is mine.' هذه السيّارة لي .

١ ـ هذه طاولتها.　　　　٥ ـ هذا كتابك.

٢ ـ هذا مطعمهم.　　　　٦ ـ هذا قلمنا.

٣ ـ هذه شهادتي.　　　　٧ ـ هذا مكتبه.

٤ ـ هذا مكتبكنّ.　　　　٨ ـ هذه سيّارتهنّ.

3. Equational sentences: Predicate first with indefinite subject

When the predicate of an equational sentence is an adverb (for example هُنا 'here') or a prepositional phrase (for example فِي ٱلْمَكْتَبِ 'in the office') and the subject is indefinite, then the usual order is predicate first, then subject. For many such sentences a good English translation begins 'There is a ...' or 'There are ...' Examples (predicate underlined):

فِي ٱلْمَكْتَبِ طاوِلَةٌ كَبِيرَةٌ.	'There's a big table in the office.'
عَلَى ٱلطّاوِلَةِ وَرَقَةٌ وَقَلَمٌ.	'On the table are a sheet of paper and a pencil.'
عَلَيْها كِتابٌ جَدِيدٌ كَذٰلِكَ.	'On it also is a new book.'

Such a construction is very commonly used to express possession, corresponding to English sentences using the verb 'to have'. In these cases the predicate is a prepositional phrase consisting of لِ with a noun or pronoun suffix object:

لِسَلِيمٍ سَيّارَةٌ جَدِيدَةٌ.	'Salim has a new car.'

Note that although the Arabic sentence and the English translation express the same idea, they do not have the same construction at all. In English the subject is Salim (the possessor), there is a verb has, and the object is a new car (the thing possessed). The Arabic sentence, on the other hand, is an equational sentence with no verb; the subject is سَيّارَةٌ جَدِيدَةٌ (the thing possessed), and the predicate is a prepositional phrase with سَلِيمٌ (the possessor) as the object of the preposition لِ ; the subject, being indefinite, follows the predicate. Thus the Arabic sentence is literally 'Belonging to

Salim (is) a new car.' Other examples (predicate underlined):

لَهُ سَيّارَةٌ جَدِيدَةٌ	'He has a new car.'
لِي ٱبْنٌ وَبِنْتٌ	'I have a son and a daughter.'
لِوِدادَ صَدِيقاتٌ عِراقِيّاتٌ	'Widad has Iraqi friends.'
لِلْأُسْتاذِ الْجَدِيدِ مَكْتَبٌ فِي هٰذا الْبِناءِ	'The new professor has an office in this building.'

Like any equational sentence, these constructions are made negative by the verb لَيْسَ , which agrees with the subject in the usual ways:

لَيْسَتْ لَهُ سَيّارَةٌ جَدِيدَةٌ	'He does not have a new car.'
لَيْسَ لِلْأُسْتاذِ مَكْتَبٌ هُنا	'The professor does not have an office here.'
لَيْسَ لَها صَدِيقاتٌ .	'She has no friends.'

The last sentence illustrates the fact that if a feminine subject is separated from its verb that verb may be masculine or feminine singular.

Drill 5. Transformation. Ex.

'The new book belongs to the student.' → ← الكتاب الجديد للطالب .

'The student has a new book.' للطالب كتاب جديد .

١ ـ المكتبة الحديثة للجامعة .
٢ ـ الطائرة الجديدة للشركة .
٣ ـ المطعم الكبير للسيد سليم .
٤ ـ المكتب الجديد للمدير .
٥ ـ البناء البعيد للمتحف .
٦ ـ السيّارة القديمة لسميرة .
٧ ـ الكرسيّ الجديد للسكرتيرة .
٨ ـ الطاولة الجديدة للمدرسة .

Drill 6. (On tape) Negation with لَيْسَ : Indefinite subject.

4. Prepositions with pronoun suffixes

Pronoun suffixes added to prepositions denote objects of prepositions. This will be illustrated with أَمامَ 'before, in front of':

أَمامَهُ	'in front of him/it'	أَمامَهُمْ	'in front of them (m.)'
أَمامَها	'in front of her/it'	أَمامَهُنَّ	'in front of them (f.)'
أَمامَكَ	'in front of you' (m.s.)	أَمامَكُمْ	'in front of you (m.p.)'
أَمامَكِ	'in front of you' (f.s.)	أَمامَكُنَّ	'in front of you (f.p.)'
أَمامي	'in front of me'	أَمامَنا	'in front of us'

When pronouns are suffixed to words ending in a long vowel or يْ y the suffix for أنا is يَ -ya. If the last letter of the stem is ي , that letter and the ي of the ending are written as one ي with a shadda: فِي fii 'in', فِيَّ fiyya 'in me'.

The preposition مِنْ 'from' has the special shape مِنّ before ي 'me': مِنّي 'from me'; likewise عَنْ 'about' + ي 'I' gives عَنّي 'about me'.

The pronoun suffixes with في and مِنْ are written out in full below:

في

فيهِ	'in him'	فيهِمْ	'in them (m.)'
فيها	'in her'	فيهِنَّ	'in them (f.)'
فيكَ	'in you' (m.s.)	فيكُمْ	'in you (m.p.)
فيكِ	'in you' (f.s.)	فيكُنَّ	'in you (f.p.)
فيَّ	'in me'	فينا	'in us'

من

مِنْهُ	'from him'	مِنْهُمْ	'from them (m.)'
مِنْها	'from her'	مِنْهُنَّ	'from them (f.)'

مِنْكَ	'from you' (m.s.)	مِنْكُمْ	'from you (m.p.)'
مِنْكِ	'from you' (f.s.)	مِنْكُنَّ	'from you (f.p.)'
مِنّي	'from me'	مِنّا	'from us'

The prepositions إِلى 'to' and عَلى 'on' have the stems إِلَيْ ?ilay- and عَلَيْ alay- when a pronoun suffix is attached. Here are complete tables:

الى

إِلَيْهِ	'to him'	إِلَيْهِمْ	'to them (m.)'
إِلَيْها	'to her'	إِلَيْهِنَّ	'to them (f.)'
إِلَيْكَ	'to you (m.s.)'	إِلَيْكُمْ	'to you (m.p.)'
إِلَيْكِ	'to you (f.s.)'	إِلَيْكُنَّ	'to you (f.p.)'
إِلَيَّ	'to me'	إِلَيْنا	'to us'

على

عَلَيْهِ	'on him'	عَلَيْهِمْ	'on them (m.)'
عَلَيْها	'on her'	عَلَيْهِنَّ	'on them (f.)
عَلَيْكَ	'on you (m.s.)'	عَلَيْكُمْ	'on you (m.p.)'
عَلَيْكِ	'on you (f.s.)'	عَلَيْكُنَّ	'on you (f.p.)'
عَلَيَّ	'on me'	عَلَيْنا	'on us'

Now do Drills 7 and 8.

Drill 7. Recognition.

Write the independent pronoun which corresponds to the pronoun suffix of the prepositions given. Ex. منه ← هو

فيكَ	اليْكم	معهنّ
منها	عنكِ	اما مكنّ
أمامنا	عليّ	عنّي
منّي	اليْه	معكَ
فيهم	بعدها	له

Drill 8. Production.

Replace the words in parentheses with a preposition + pronoun suffix. Ex.

'He went with her to the theater.' ← ذهب (مع + هند) الى المسرح .

ذهب معها الى المسرح .

١ – (في + المكتبة) كتاب جديد .

٢ – (امام + انت) بناء قديم .

٣ – كم بنتا (لـ + هي) .

٤ – رجعتم (من + المطار) .

٥ – ذهبن (الى + المدرسة) .

٦ – استمعوا (ل + المحاضرة) .

٧ – (على + الطاولة) قلم .

٨ – ذهب (مع + انا)الى العراق .

٩ – (لـ + انا) ولد في امريكا .

١٠ – اكلت (مع + هم) في مطعم عربي .

5. Verbs with pronoun suffixes

A pronoun suffix added to a verb denotes the object of the verb, for example:

تَرَكَهُ	'he left him'
تَرَكَتْنا	'she left us'

The forms of the pronoun suffixes added to verbs are the same as those added to nouns or prepositions, with one exception: with verbs the 1 s. suffix is not ي -ii or يَ -ya, but ني -nii 'me':

تَرَكَني	'he left me'

Remember that the vowel of the suffixes ـهُ and ـهُمْ changes from u to i when attached to a word ending in ـِ i, ي ii, or يْ y:

تَرَكْتَهُ	'you (m.) left him'
تَرَكْتِهِ	'you (f.) left him'

In addition there are two points applying to verbs with attached pronoun suffixes:

(1) When a suffix is attached to a 3 m.p. verb form ending in -uu and written with a final 'alif, the 'alif is dropped (this is a matter of spelling only):

تَرَكوا	'they left'
تَرَكوكَ	'they left you'

(2) When a suffix is attached to a 2 m.p. verb (ending in تُمْ -tum), that ending becomes تُمو -tumuu-:

تَرَكْتُمْ	'you (p.) left'
تَرَكْتُموني	'you (p.) left me'

The following table shows all the pronoun suffixes thus far given, attached to the verb تَرَكَ 'he left';

تَرَكَهُ	'he left him'	تَرَكَهُمْ	'he left them (m.)'
تَرَكَها	'he left her'	تَرَكَهُنَّ	'he left them (f.)'
تَرَكَكَ	'he left you (m.)'	تَرَكَكُمْ	'he left you (m.p.)'
تَرَكَكِ	'he left you (f.)'	تَرَكَكُنَّ	'he left you (f.p.)'
تَرَكَني	'he left me'	تَرَكَنا	'he left us'

Now do Drills 9 and 10.

Drill 9. Recognition.

Give in independent form both the pronoun subject and the pronoun object of the following verbs. Ex.

object	subject	
هي	أنا	← درستُها

١١ ـ استقبلَنا	٦ ـ تركوني	١ ـ تركناكِ
١٢ ـ تركتُه	٧ ـ تابعها	٢ ـ استقبلتموه
١٣ ـ قرأنها	٨ ـ تركتِه	٣ ـ تركتْه
١٤ ـ استقبلوكم	٩ ـ استقبلني	٤ ـ قرأتَها
١٥ ـ تركناها	١٠ ـ تركتَهم	٥ ـ أصدرنه

Drill 10. (Also on tape) Substitution.

Substitute the suffix form of the following for the pronoun object of the verb.

'He left them in London.' تركهم في لندن

هنّ	هي	انتَ
انتنّ	نحن	انتم
هم	انتِ	انا

Repeat with

١ ـ تركوهم في لندن.

٢ ـ استقبلَتْها في المطار.

6. <u>Interrogative noun أَيٌّ 'which?'</u>

The interrogative أَيٌّ 'which?' is a noun, and as such may, like other nouns, serve as subject or object of a verb or as object of a preposition, receiving the appropriate case inflection in each instance. It most commonly occurs as the first term of an iḍāfa, as in عَلى أَيِّ طائِرَةٍ 'on which plane?'.

أَيٌّ may be translated by 'which...?' or 'what...?', e.g. أَيُّ دَرْسٍ 'which lesson?' or 'what lesson?'. Notice that English "what" is equivalent to أَيٌّ only if it comes together with a noun, as "what boy?" (أَيُّ وَلَدٍ); otherwise "what?" is equivalent to ما ("What is this?" = ما هٰذا) or ماذا ("What did you drink?" = ماذا شَرِبْتَ).

Now do Drill 11.

<u>Drill 11</u>. (Also on tape) Substitution.

a. 'What lesson is this?' أيُّ <u>درسٍ</u> هذا ؟

كتاب	جامعة
صفّ	بناء
استاذ	متحف
مدرسة	درس

b. 'What language did you learn?' أيَّ لغةٍ تعلّمت ؟

درس	نصّ
جملة	كلمة

c. 'What university did you go to?' الى أيِّ جامعةٍ ذهبت ؟

مكتبة	بناء	مسرح
متحف	صفّ	جامعة
مطعم	مدرسة	

D. <u>Comprehension passage</u> د — نُصوصٌ لِلْفَهْمِ

Read the following passage; then do Drill 12, which is based on it.

ذهب كريم مع بعض اصدقائه الى المطار واستقبلوا صديقا لهم ٠ حضر هذا الصديق، واسمه مَحْمودٌ، من الشرق الاوسط الى امريكا لدراسة اللغة الانكليزية والتاريخ ٠

ذهب كل الاصدقاء الى السينما وشاهدوا فيلما اجنبيّا بعنوان " الخرطوم " ٠ بعد الفلم ذهبوا لزيارة كريم وعائلته ٠ أَعَدَّتْ بنت كريم القهوة العربية للزائرين ٠ شربوا القهوة العربية واستمعوا بعد ذلك للأخبار ٠

أَعَدَّتْ = prepared

Drill 12. Questions. أَسْئِلَةٌ

١ ــ من أين حضر محمود ؟

٢ ــ الى اين ذهب الاصدقاء؟

٣ ــ ماذا شاهدوا ؟

٤ ــ ماذا فعلوا بعد الفلم ؟

٥ ــ لماذا حضر محمود الى امريكا ؟

E. General drills هـ ــ اَلتَّمارينُ الْعامَّةُ

Drill 13. Written. Conjugation.

a. Fill in the blanks with the correct form of the verb تَرَكَ , using the pronouns on the vertical axis as the subject of the verb and the pronouns on the horizontal axis as the object.

Obj. / Subj.	نحن	انتم	انتنّ	هم	هنّ
نحن	X	تركناكم	____	____	____
أنتم	____	X	X	____	____
أنتنّ	____	X	X	____	____
هم	____	____	____	____	____
هنّ	____	____	____	____	____

b. Repeat using اِسْتَقْبَلَ .

Drill 14. Translation.

1. How many students went to Cairo on the Misr Air plane?

2. We have a daughter--her name is Widad.

3. I saw them in front of the window and went up (ذهب) to them.

4. Which man met (received) you (m.) in the airport?

5. Whose is this foreign car?

Lesson Eleven

الدرس الحادي عشر

أ ـ النص الاساسيّ

طلّاب جامعيّـــــون

١ ـ فريد : هل درس سامي في الجامعة اللبنانيّة ؟

٢ ـ مريم : لم يدرس في هذه الجامعة بل كان طالبا في الجامعة الامريكيّة في بيروت ٠

٣ ـ فريد : على أيّ شهادة حصل ؟

٤ ـ مريم : على شهادة الدكتوراه ٠

٥ ـ فريد : وزوجته ؟

٦ ـ مريم : لم تحصل على الدكتوراه ٠ حصلت على الماجستير فقط ، ثمّ عملت في مدرسة حكوميّة في لبنان ٠

٧ ـ فريد : هل رجع سامي بعد ذلك الى بلده ؟

٨ ـ مريم : لا ٠ لم يرجع الى بلده ، بل سافر مع زوجته الـــى الكويت للعمل هناك ٠

٩ ـ فريد : وأنت يا مريم ، ألم تدرسي في الجامعة الامريكيّة ؟

١٠ ـ مريم : لا ٠ لم ادرس هناك ، بل كنت طالبة في الجامعة اللبنانيّة ٠

A. Basic text

University Students

1. Farid: Did Sami study at the Lebanese University?

2. Maryam: He did not study at that university, but he was a student at the American University of Beirut.

3. Farid: What degree did he get?

4. Maryam: The doctorate.

5. Farid: And his wife?

6. Maryam: She didn't get the doctorate. She only got the master's; and then she worked in a public school in Lebanon.

7. Farid: Did Sami return to his country after that?

8. Maryam: No, he didn't return to his country; he went with his wife to Kuwait to work there.

9. Farid: And you, Maryam, didn't you study at the American University?

10. Maryam: No, I didn't study there. I was a student at the Lebanese University.

B. Vocabulary — ب ـ المفردات

الحادِيَ عَشَرَ	the eleventh
لَمْ	(neg. particle, foll. by jussive) did not, has/have not
لَمْ يَدْرُسْ	he did not study, he has not studied
بَلْ	but; rather; indeed
كانَ	he was
حَصَلَ عَلى	he obtained, got
الدُّكْتوراه	the doctorate, the Ph.D.
زَوْجٌ ـ أَزْواجٌ	husband
لَمْ تَحْصُلْ عَلى	she did not obtain
الماجِسْتير	the master's degree, the M.A.
فَقَطْ	only
ثُمَّ	then, thereupon, and then
عَمِلَ	he worked
حُكومَةٌ ـ ات	government
مَدْرَسَةٌ حُكومِيَّةٌ ـ مَدارِسُ حُكومِيَّةٌ	public school
بَلَدٌ ـ بِلادٌ	country
بَلَدِيٌّ ـ ون	(nisba of بَلَدٌ) native, indigenous, home (as opp. to foreign, alien)
لَمْ يَرْجِعْ	he did not return, he did not go back/come back

سَافَرَ	he travelled, departed, left went
لَمْ تَدْرُسِي	you (f.s.) didn't study
لَمْ أَدْرُسْ	I did not study
كُنْتُ	I was

Additional vocabulary

الْبَكَالُورِيُوس	the bachelor's degree, the B.A.
لَمْ يُسَافِرْ	he did not travel, depart, leave

C. Grammar and drills — ج ـ القواعد والتمارين

> 1. The root and pattern system
> 2. The forms of the Arabic verb
> 3. Negative of the perfect tense: لَمْ with jussive
> 4. Equational sentences: Past time
> 5. Feminine sound plural: Non-human nouns

1. The root and pattern system

Note the consonants in the following group of words:

دَرْسٌ	'lesson'
دِرَاسَةٌ	'studies, study'
مَدْرَسَةٌ	'school'
دَرَسَ	'he studied'
دَرَّسَ	'he taught'
مُدَرِّسٌ	'teacher (m.)
مُدَرِّسَةٌ	'teacher (f.)

All these words (and also some others not listed here) have three consonants in common: d r s. The words also have various vowels in various arrangements, and some of them have other consonants--but all have d r s. Such a set of consonants, in a certain order, common to a number of different words, is called a root, and the individual consonants of a root are called radicals. The great majority of roots consist of three radicals; a few contain one, two, four, or even five radicals. Roots will be written as capital letters, thus: D R S.

A given root generally has associated with it a basic meaning which is relatable to all words derived from it. For example, the root D R S means "study"; دَرْسٌ ('lesson') is a thing studied; دِراسَةٌ 'studies' is the activity of studying; مَدْرَسَةٌ 'school' is the place where studying goes on; دَرَسَ 'he studied' is the verb denoting this action; دَرَّسَ 'he instructed, taught' has the underlying meaning of 'he made (someone) study'; مُدَرِّسٌ and مُدَرِّسَةٌ 'teacher' have the underlying meaning of "one who teaches". These derived meanings are relatable to word patterns, which are discussed below.

Roots may be conveniently symbolized with the letters FML (F standing for the First radical of any root, M for the Middle radical, and L for the Last radical).

Now note the following groups of words:

(a)			(b)		
	حَضَرَ الى	'he came'		قَرِيبٌ	'near'
	دَرَسَ	'he studied'		جَدِيدٌ	'new'
	رَجَعَ	'he returned'		كَبِيرٌ	'big'
	تَرَكَ	'he left'		قَدِيمٌ	'old'
	أَكَلَ	'he ate'		حَدِيثٌ	'modern'

Group (a) are verbs, all in the perfect tense. They also have in common a similarity in pattern: FaMaL(-a). That is, they begin with a consonant (the first radical of the root), then the vowel a, then a second consonant, another vowel a, and then a third consonant. (The final vowel -a is the subject-marker suffix.) These verbs are accordingly said to be of the pattern FaMaL-, which represents the stem of perfect tense (see also 2 below). دَرَّسَ 'he taught' is a different verb pattern: FaMMaL-.

The words in group (b) are an example of a second pattern. They all fit the pattern FaMiiL (qariib, jadiid, etc.) and have the meaning "adjective". Two points must be made here. First, this is not to imply that all adjectives are of this pattern; this is one of many adjective patterns (some with specialized meanings) e.g. FaML (such as سَهْلٌ 'easy'), as well as the nisba adjectives (e.g. أساسِيٌّ 'basic'). Second, different patterns may look alike. For example, FaMiiL is an adjective pattern as described above; it may also be a noun pattern, as in صَديقٌ 'friend'. Thus, we have two patterns: FaMiiL (adj.) and FaMiil (n.). They are considered different patterns because, as you will see later, they have different plural patterns.

The great majority of words in Arabic can be analyzed into a root and a pattern (with a few exceptions, such as مِنْ 'from' or هُنا 'here'). This is extremely useful in mastering new vocabulary; that is, as you become familiar with more and more roots and patterns you will be able to analyze words on your own and to associate the meaning with the new word to be learned. For example, let us assume that you know that the pattern maFMaLa(t) (the combination a(t) represents the feminine suffix ـَةٌ) means "noun of place", on the basis of words like مَكْتَبَةٌ 'library' (lit., "place of books"), and also that you know the root D R S = "to study". When you come across the new word مَدْرَسَةٌ 'school', you can then analyze it as composed of the root D R S meaning "to study" and the pattern maFMaLa(t) meaning "noun of place", and deduce that its underlying meaning is "place of studying", or "school". In the pattern maFMaLa(t), the ma- at the beginning of the pattern is written with small letters to show that (1) m is not a radical and (2) m itself occurs in all nouns of place.

An understanding of roots and patterns is essential to the use of Arabic dictionaries: words therein are arranged alphabetically by root. To acquaint you with this system, the glossary at the end of this book is also arranged alphabetically by root; you will find it useful as a regular practice with every new lesson to look up in the glossary the words given in the vocabulary of the lesson.

One final remark: just as there are different patterns that look or sound the same, so there are different roots that look or sound the same. For example, جُمْلَةٌ 'sentence' has as its root J M L, and the adjective جَميلٌ 'handsome' also has a root J M L in the dictionary; both are listed under the same root, جمل . (The word جَمَلٌ 'camel', however, which also has a root J M L is listed under a second entry, جمل).

Now do Drills 1 and 2.

Drill 1. Written. Recognition.

Write the root and pattern of each of the following words. Ex.

دراسة   د • ر • س   FiMaaLa(t)

زوجة	شهادة
شرب	ذاهب
شركة	شيء
رجل	قصير
جامعة	سافر

Drill 2. Written.

Write the word which has the root and the pattern given, then look the word up in the dictionary to find the meaning. Ex.

ع • م • ل + maFMaL ← 'laboratory' مَعْمَلٌ

١ — س • ف • ر + FaMiiL ←

٢ — و • ج • ه + FaML ←

٣ — د • خ • ل + maFMaL ←

٤ — ب • و • ب + FaMMaaL ←

٥ — ت • ج • ر + FiMaaLa(t) ←

٦	–	ر • ك • ب	+	FaaMiL	⟵
٧	–	ك • ت • ب	+	FaMaL	⟵
٨	–	ق • ع • د	+	maFMaL	⟵

2. The Forms of the Arabic verb

An Arabic verb in the perfect tense consists of a perfect stem and a subject-marker; for example, in دَرَسْتُ 'I studied' the stem is دَرَسْ daras- (the root is D R S) and the subject-marker is تُ -tu, and in إِسْتَقْبَلْنا 'we received' the stem is إِسْتَقْبَل ?istaqbal- (the root is Q B L) and the subject-marker is نا -naa. Clearly the pattern of the stem daras- is shorter and simpler than the pattern of ?istaqbal-. It is in fact the simplest pattern of all verb stems. Arabic verbs are classified according to the pattern of their perfect stems. All verbs with stems of the same pattern as daras- (that is, consisting only of consonant-vowel-consonant-vowel-consonant) are labelled Form I verbs, since that is the simplest possible pattern. Other verbs fall into classes labelled Form II, Form III, and so on up to Form XV, each with its characteristic pattern. Form I verbs are also called simple verbs and all others derived verbs. Form XI through XV are extremely rare, so this book will deal only with Forms I to X.

Following is a list of all the Form I verbs which have so far occurred. Note (1) that in the perfect stems of Form I verbs the first vowel is always a, and (2) that the second vowel may vary: the list below has examples only of a and i, but there are other verbs which have u.

Form I verbs

Stem pattern FaMaL-

دَرَسْ -	daras-	'to study'
حَضَرْ-الى	haḍar-	'to come to'
رَجَعْ -	rajaʕ-	'to return'

بَدَأْ -	bada?-	'to begin'
قَرَأْ -	qara?-	'to read'
ذَهَبْ -	ðahab-	'to go'
فَعَلْ -	faʕal-	'to do'
أَكَلْ -	?akal-	'to eat'
تَرَكْ -	tarak-	'to leave'
حَصَلْ - على	ḥaṣal-	'to obtain'

Stem pattern FaMiL-

شَرِبْ -	šarib-	'to drink'
عَمِلْ -	ʕamil-	'to work'

Following also, for reference only, is a list of the derived verbs which have occurred thus far, with an indication of the form to which they belong:

Form II (FaMMaL)	
دَرَّسَ	'to teach'
Form III (FaaMaL)	
تابَعَ	'to continue with'
سافَرَ	'to travel'
شاهَدَ	' to see'
Form IV (?aFMaL)	
أَصْدَرَ	'to publish'
أَكْمَلَ	'to finish'
Form V (taFaMMaL)	
تَعَلَّمَ	'to learn'
Form VIII (?iFtaMaL)	
إِسْتَمَعَ لِ	'to listen to'
انْتَقَلَ	'to transfer, move'
Form X (?istaFMaL)	
اسْتَقْبَلَ	'to receive'

The vowel immediately before the last radical of any stem is referred to as the stem vowel. The stem vowels are underlined in the following perfect verb stems: dar<u>a</u>s-, šar<u>i</u>b-, darr<u>a</u>s-, saaf<u>a</u>r-, ?aṣd<u>a</u>r-, taʕall<u>a</u>m-, ?istam<u>a</u>ʕ-, and ?istaqb<u>a</u>l-.

Now do Drill 3.

Drill 3. Written.

a. Write the verb which has the root and pattern given, identify the form to which it belongs, then look it up in the dictionary or glossary to find its meaning. Ex.

III 'to meet' قابَلَ = FaaMaL- + ق • ب • ل

←	taFaMMaL-	+	١ – ل • خ • ص
←	?iFtaMaL-	+	٢ – ع • ب • ر
←	FaMMaL-	+	٣ – ق • د • م
←	?inFaMaL-	+	٤ – ص • ر • ف
←	?aFMaL-	+	٥ – خ • ب • ر
←	taFaaMaL-	+	٦ – ن • و • ل
←	FaMiL-	+	٧ – ش • م • ل
←	?istaFMaL-	+	٨ – ق • ب • ل
←	FaaMaL-	+	٩ – ص • د • ق
←	FaMaL-	+	١٠ – س • ك • ن

b. Look up the following unfamiliar verbs in the dictionary or glossary and give their meanings.

تَحَدَّثَ	اِعْتَمَدَ
صَدَّقَ	أَقْبَلَ
شارَكَ	اِسْتَخْدَمَ

3. Negative of the perfect tense: لَمْ with jussive

The Arabic perfect tense is used to refer to completed actions in the past--to say that someone did or has done something. The negation of actions in the past--saying that someone did not or has not done something--is most commonly expressed by the negative particle لَمْ and a verb form called the jussive:

لَمْ يَدْرُسْ	'he did not study/ has not studied'

The jussive indicates the same distinctions of person, gender, and number as does the perfect, but differs from the latter in two fundamental ways:

(1) Perfect verb forms consist of a stem and subject-marker suffixed to the stem (that is, attached to the end of the stem). Thus the form دَرَسْتُ 'I studied' consists of the stem دَرَسْ daras- and the subject-marker تُ -tu:

Subject-marker	+	Stem
تُ	+	-دَرَسْ-

Jussive forms, on the other hand, consist of a stem and subject-markers prefixed to the stem (that is, attached to the beginning of the stem) and, in some cases, suffixed to it as well. Thus the jussive forms in لَمْ يَدْرُسْ 'he did not study' and لَمْ تَدْرُسِي 'you (f.s.) did not study' both have stem دْرُسْ -drus-; the former has subject-marker يَـ ya- prefixed, and the latter has subject-marker تَـ ta- prefixed and ي -ii suffixed.

Subject-marker	+	Stem	+	Subject Marker
		-دْرُسْ-	+	يَـ
ي	+	-دْرُسْ-	+	تَـ

(2) The stem of jussive forms itself is (in most verbs) different from the perfect stem. Generally speaking, Arabic verbs have two stems: a perfect stem used only in perfect tense verbs, (see Note 2 above), and an imperfect

stem used in the jussive (and also in the imperfect indicative, subjunctive, and imperative, all of which will be treated later). The pattern of the imperfect stem of a verb usually differs from the perfect stem by having different vowels and/or a different number of vowels. Thus the perfect stem of دَرَسَ 'to study' is

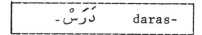

دَرَسْ- daras-

and the imperfect stem is

-دْرُسْ- -drus-

Now compare two actual perfect and jussive verb forms (stems underlined):

Jussive (with لَمْ)		
لَمْ يَدْرُسْ	lam ya-drus	'he did not study'
لَمْ تَدْرُسي	lam ta-drus-ii	'you (f.s.) did not study'
Perfect		
دَرَسَ	daras-a	'he studied'
دَرَسْتِ	daras-ti	'you (f.s.) studied'

Shown in the table below are the five singular forms of دَرَسَ 'to study' in the jussive:

	Jussive	Subject-marker	
3 MS	يَدْرُسْ	يَـ	ya-
3 FS	تَدْرُسْ	تَـ	ta-
2 MS	تَدْرُسْ	تَـ	ta-
2 FS	تَدْرُسي	تَـ ٠٠ ي	ta...ii
1 S	أَدْرُسْ	أَ	?a-

The following points may be noted:

(1) The 3 f.s. and 2 m.s. forms are identical. This is true of all imperfect verbs (those using the imperfect stem) in Arabic.

(2) The subject marker for the 2 f.s. form is a combination of prefix and suffix.

Form I verbs have perfect stems of the pattern FaMvL- (the v here stands for "any of the three short vowels"), as in دَرَسَ daras-(a) and imperfect stems of the pattern -FMvL-, as in يَدْرُسْ (ya)-drus. Therefore, if you know the perfect form of a Form I verb, you also know the jussive form--except for the stem vowel, which in general just has to be learned for each verb. There are, however, one or two hints which may help in the learning process:

(1) If the stem vowel of the perfect is a, the stem vowel of the imperfect may be u, i or a. It is very likely to be a if the second or third consonant of the stem is one of the throat sounds أ , ه , ح , or ع , as in the last four examples below. (These and the succeeding examples are all 3 m.s. forms.)

	Perfect	Stem	Jussive	Stem
'to study'	دَرَسَ	daras-	يَدْرُسْ	-drus
'to come'	حَضَرَ الى	ḥaḍar-	يَحْضُرْ	-ḥḍur-
'to eat'	أَكَلَ	ʔakal-	يَأْكُلْ	-ʔkul-
'to leave'	تَرَكَ	tarak-	يَتْرُكْ	-truk-
'to obtain'	حَصَلَ على	ḥaṣal-	يَحْصُلْ	-ḥṣul-
'to return'	رَجَعَ	rajaʕ-	يَرْجِعْ	-rjiʕ-
'to begin'	بَدَأَ	badaʔ-	يَبْدَأْ	-bdaʔ-
'to read'	قَرَأَ	qaraʔ-	يَقْرَأْ	-qraʔ-
'to go'	ذَهَبَ	ðahab-	يَذْهَبْ	-ðhab-
'to do'	فَعَلَ	faʕal-	يَفْعَلْ	-fʕal-

(2) If the vowel of the perfect stem is i, the vowel of the imperfect stem is almost always a.

'to drink'	شَرِبَ	šarib-	يَشْرَبُ	-šrab-
'to work'	عَمِلَ	ʕamil-	يَعْمَلُ	-ʕmal-

(3) If the vowel of the perfect stem is u, the vowel of the imperfect stem is always u (no examples yet).

Finally, verbs whose first radical is a hamza, for example أَكَلَ 'to eat' (root ? K L) have regular imperfect forms in all persons except the first person singular. Compare the following 3 m.s. forms:

lam ya-drus	لَمْ يَدْرُسْ	'He didn't study.'
lam ya-?kul	لَمْ يَأْكُلْ	'He didn't eat.'

If the 1 s. form were regular, it would be like the 1 s. form of 'to study' as follows:

lam ?a-drus	'I didn't study'
lam (?a-?kul)	'I didn't eat'

But this form ?a-?kul- does not actually occur, because it contains a sequence of sounds which is not permitted by the phonological rules of Arabic: the sequence ?a?- when the next sound is a consonant. Whenever this sequence is produced by the regular processes of word-formation (such as the conjugation of a verb) it is automatically changed to ?aa, which in Arabic is written آ . Thus the actual Arabic 1 s. form is لَمْ آكُلْ 'I didn't eat'. The following diagram illustrates the process (hypothetical regular form in parentheses, with the non-permitted sequence underlined):

lam ?a-drus	لَمْ أَدْرُسْ	'I didn't study'
lam (?a-?kul) → ?aakul	لَمْ آكُلْ	'I didn't eat'

This lesson deals only with Form I verbs. The jussive of derived verbs will be discussed later as each Form is discussed, beginning in Lesson 17. Now do Drills 4, 5 and 6.

<u>Drill 4</u>. (Also on tape) Recognition.

Give the independent pronoun which corresponds to each of the following jussive forms.

١ ـ لم يرجع الى بلده في ذلك الوقت .

٢ ـ لم تدرس الدرس الاساسيّ .

٣ ـ لم أذهب الى القاهرة .

٤ ـ ألم تتركي عائلتك في لندن ؟

٥ ـ لم تبدأ دراسة التاريخ هذه السنةَ .

٦ ـ لم يأكل كبة في المطعم العربي .

٧ ـ ألم تقرئي كتاب صديقك ؟

٨ ـ لم تحصل على شهادة في الانكليزيّة .

٩ ـ ألم تعملي في مكتب المدير ؟

١٠ ـ لم أشرب قهوة مع اصدقائي .

<u>Drill 5</u>. (Also on tape) Conjugation.

a. 'Didn't he work in the company office?' ألم يعمل في مكتب الشركة ؟

أنتِ	أنتَ
أنا	المديرة
السيد فريد	السكرتير
كريمة	الموظّف
ابنُكَ	بنته

b. Repeat with the following sentence.

'He didn't leave his family in Baghdad.' لم يترك عائلته في بغداد .

Drill 6. (Also on tape) Transformation: Affirmative ⟶ negative with لَمْ. Ex.

'He worked in a government office.' ⟶ ⟵ عمل في مكتب حكوميّ.

'He didn't work in a government office.' لم يعمل في مكتب حكوميّ .

١ ـ حصلتُ على شهادة في العربيّة .

٢ ـ فعلتِ ذلك في نيويورك .

newspaper ٣ ـ قرأ جَريدَةَ " أخبار اليوم " .

٤ ـ بدأتْ دراسة التاريخ المصريّ .

٥ ـ ذهبتَ الى الشركة لزيارة المدير .

٦ ـ أكلتِ في مطعم مع اصدقائك .

٧ ـ درس النصّ الاساسيّ .

٨ ـ رجعتُ الى الشرق الاوسط للعمل هناك .

4. Equational sentences: Past time

Equational sentences refer to present time:

سامي طالِبٌ . 'Sami is a student.'

The equivalent in past time is expressed by use of the verb كانَ 'to be':

كانَ سامي طالِبًا . 'Sami was a student.'

Notice that when كانَ is used, a predicate noun or adjective is in the accusative case.

The verb كانَ has the same distinctions of person, gender, and number, and follows the same rules of agreement with its subject as any verb. The perfect tense forms are as follows:

	Singular		Plural	
3 M	كَانَ	'he was'	كانوا	'they (m.) were'
3 F	كانَتْ	'she was'	كُنَّ	'they (f.) were'
2 M	كُنْتَ	'you (m.s.) were'	كُنْتُمْ	'you (m.p.) were'
2 F	كُنْتِ	'you (f.s.) were'	كُنْتُنَّ	'you (f.p.) were'
1	كُنْتُ	'I was'	كُنّا	'we were'

This verb, as the table shows, has two perfect stems, kaan- and kun-. The former is used with suffixes (subject-markers) beginning with a vowel: -a, -at, and -uu; while the latter is used with suffixes beginning with a consonant: -ta, -ti, etc. Thus we have

كَانَ kaan- + -a 'he was'

but كُنْتُ kun- + -tu 'I was'

Note also the spelling of كُنَّ 'they (f.) were' and كُنّا 'we were', in which the final نْ of the stem and the initial نَ of the suffixes are written as one نَّ with a shadda.

Additional examples, showing equational sentences (present) and their past time equivalents.

Present	وِداد السِكْرِتيرةُ هنا.	'Widad is the secretary here.'
Past	كانَتْ وِداد السِكْرِتيرَةَ هنا.	'Widad was the secretary here.'
Present	نَحْنُ طُلّابٌ جُدُدٌ.	'We are new students.'
Past	كُنّا طُلّابًا جُدُدًا.	'We were new students.'
Present	الدَّرْسُ قَصيرٌ.	'The lesson is short.'
Past	كانَ الدَّرْسُ قَصيرًا.	'The lesson was short.'
Present	الطاوِلَةُ في المَكْتَبِ.	'The table is in the office.'
Past	كانَتِ الطّاوِلَةُ في المَكْتَبِ.	'The table was in the office.'
Present	في المَكْتَبِ طاوِلَةٌ.	'There is a table in the office.'
Past	كانَ في المَكْتَبِ طاوِلَةٌ.	'There was a table in the office.'

For the agreement of كانَ in the last example, see 6.C.3.

Now do Drills 7 and 8.

Drill 7. (Also on tape) Transformation. Ex.

'He is a new student.' → هو طالب جديد. ←

'He was a new student.' كان طالبا جديدا .

١ ـ هي موظّفة في المتحف .

٢ ـ أنتم طلاب في مدرسة حكوميّة .

٣ ـ هم أصدقاء أحمد .

٤ ـ أنت مدرّسة في سوريا .

٥ ـ أنا ذاهب الى المسرح .

٦ ـ أنتنّ أستاذات في جامعة ألخرطوم .

٧ ـ أنتَ في مكتب الشركة .

٨ ـ هو رجل مشهور .

٩ ـ نحن أصدقاء الرئيس .

١٠ ـ هنّ موظّفات في مكتب حكوميّ .

Drill 8. Transformation. Present → Past. Ex.

'The woman is an employee in a bank.' → الاستاذ : المرأة موظّفة في بنك . ←

'The woman was an employee in a bank.' الطالب ١: كانت المرأة موظّفة في بنك

الطالب ٢: المرأة كانت موظّفة في بنك .

١ ـ عادل ذاهب الى الرياض . ٤ ـ المدرّسات الجديدات في دمشق .

٢ ـ الاساتذة في مكتبهم . ٥ ـ رئيس امريكا من ميشغان .

٣ ـ صديق وداد طالب في الأَزْهَرِ . ٦ ـ مريم زوجة استاذ مشهور .

5. Feminine sound plural: Non-human nouns

The feminine sound plural ending ـاتٌ -aat- is generally used to form the plural of feminine nouns referring to human beings, as was shown in 9.C.2 (p. 199). It is also used to form the plural of nouns not referring to human beings: a great many (not all) feminine nouns ending in ـَةٌ and a number of masculine nouns as well. The following list includes all such nouns which have occurred so far. The first two are masculine, the others feminine.

	Singular	Plural	
(m.)	مَطارٌ	مَطاراتٌ	'airports'
(m.)	أُوتوبيس	أوتوبيساتٌ	'buses'
	وَرَقَةٌ	وَرَقاتٌ	'sheets of paper'
	طاوِلَةٌ	طاوِلاتٌ	'tables'
	جامِعَةٌ	جامِعاتٌ	'universities'
	مَكْتَبَةٌ	مَكْتَباتٌ	'libraries'
	كَلِمَةٌ	كَلِماتٌ	'words'
	عائِلَةٌ	عائِلاتٌ	'families'
	دِراسَةٌ	دِراساتٌ	'studies'
	شَهادَةٌ	شَهاداتٌ	'diplomas, degrees'
	لُغَةٌ	لُغاتٌ	'languages'
	مُحاضَرَةٌ	مُحاضَراتٌ	'lectures'
	طائِرَةٌ	طائِراتٌ	'airplanes'
	زِيارَةٌ	زِياراتٌ	'visits'
	سَيّارَةٌ	سَيّاراتٌ	'cars'
	شَرِكَةٌ	شَرِكاتٌ	'companies'
	حُكومَةٌ	حُكوماتٌ	'governments'
	سَنَةٌ	سَنَواتٌ	'years'

Note the plural سَنَواتٌ 'years'. Like the nisba سَنَوِيٌّ 'yearly', it is based on a slightly different stem sanaw-.

It is worth noting that foreign words referring to non-humans, e.g. أوتوبيس 'bus', are generally made plural with ات .

Now do Drills 9 and 10.

Drill 9. Written. Recognition.

Give the singular of the following words.

لغات	اوتوبيسات
طائرات	سنوات
طلاب	كلمات
سيّارات	مطارات
اصدقاء	

Drill 10. (On tape) Transformation: Singular → plural.

D. Comprehension passage د — نُصوصٌ لِلْفَهْمِ

(1) Read the following passage; then do Drill 12, which is based on it.

السيّد مَحْمود فَريد رجل مشهور في المغرب • أكمل الدراسة الثانويّة في مدرسة حكوميّة في الرباط ، ثم سافر الى مصر لدراسة التاريخ في جامعة القاهرة •

حصل السيّد محمود على شهادة البكالوريوس من جامعة القاهرة ثم ذهب الى لندن للدراسة هناك • بعد الحصول على الدكتوراه ، رجع السيّد محمود الى بلده ، وعمل في الجامعة •

زوجة السيّد محمود مصريّة • اسمها فِرْيالُ • ذهبت معه الى لندن • لم تحصل السيّدة فريال على شهادة من لندن ، بل عملت في مكتبة الجامعة هناك • هي الآن مدرّسة في مدرسة خاصّة •

Drill 11. Written.

Fill in the blanks on the basis of the passage above.

١ ــ السّيّد فريد من ــــــ ، وزوجته من ــــــــ .

٢ ــ الرباط في ــــــــ .

٣ ــ درس السيّد فريد في ــــــ و ــــــــ و ــــــــ .

٤ ــ درس السيد فريد ــــــ في جامعة القاهرة .

٥ ــ السيدة فريال ــــــــ على شهادة من لندن .

٦ ــ السيد فريد الآن ــــــــ وزوجته ــــــــ .

(2) Listen to the passage on tape; then do Drill 12, which is based on it.

Drill 12. (Also on tape) Passage for Aural Comprehension.

اسئلـــــة

١ ــ هل درس كريم وحسين في مدرسة ثانويّة في مصر ؟

٢ ــ الى أيّ جامعة انتقل كريم وحسين ؟

٣ ــ هل حصل كريم على شهادة ؟

٤ ــ ماذا فعل بعد ذلك ؟

٥ ــ هل حصل حسين على شهادة ؟

٦ ــ لماذا رجع الى بلده ؟

E. General drills

هـ ــ التمارين العامة

Drill 13. Written.

Match the items in column (a) with those in column (b) to make meaningful sentences.

(b)	(a)
في ذلك المطـــــار	١ ــ حصلت زوجتي على
تعلّمتم في الجامعة	٢ ــ على أيّ اوتوبيس
عائلة	٣ ــ ألم تقرأ
هذا الكتاب	٤ ــ هل المتحف الوطني
بالسيّارة	٥ ــ طائرات شركة مصر

٦ ــ درس صديقي — شهادة جامعيّة

٧ ــ أليست لمدير الشركة — حديث أم قديم

٨ ــ رجعوا الى — في مدرسة حكوميّة

٩ ــ هل سافرتنّ — سافرت

١٠ ــ كم لغة — بلادهم أمس

Drill 14. Written. Sentence Formation-transformation.

Write complete sentences using the following groups of words in their appropriate forms. Translate your sentences. Ex.

ذهب ــ أي ــ أنتم ــ الى ــ عائلة ــ بلد ــ مع ــ أنتم ← 'What country did you go to with your family?'

الى أيّ بلد ذهبتم مع عائلتكم ؟

١ ــ استاذ ــ مع ــ ذهب ــ فريد ــ أنا ــ محاضرة ــ لم ــ الى .

٢ ــ بيروت ــ كان ــ في ــ طالب ــ زوجة ــ صديق ــ أنا .

٣ ــ جامعة ــ أنت ــ لغة ــ درس ــ كم ــ في .

٤ ــ بنك ــ مطار ــ في .

٥ ــ كريم ــ مكتب ــ اصدقاء ــ ليس ــ في .

Lesson Twelve

الدرس الثاني عشر

أ - النص الاساسيّ

زيارة الى لبنان

سافر عدد من طلّاب جامعة كاليفورنيا الى بيروت . واثناء اقامتهم في لبنان شاهدوا بعض الآثار التاريخيّة . وقبل عودتهم تحدّث اليهم مراسل جريدة " المساء " البيروتيّة وسألهم :-

- ماذا اعجبكم في بلدنا ؟

قالوا :

- اعجبنا جماله وآثاره القديمة في بعلبك .

ثمّ سألهم :

- ألم تذهبوا لزيارة الأرز ومتحف الكاتب اللبنانيّ الامريكيّ جبران خليل جبران ؟

قالوا :

- لا ، لم نذهب . وقتنا لم يسمح بهذا .

وسألهم :

- هل كنتم مع طلّاب لبنانيّين اثناء زيارتكم للآثار اللبنانيّة ؟

قالوا :

- لا . لم نكن .

أسئلة

١ - الى أيّ بلد سافر الطلّاب ؟

٢ - هل ذهبت الى لبنان؟

٣ - ماذا شاهد الطلّاب هناك ؟

٤ - هل ذهبوا لزيارة الارز؟ لماذا ؟

٥ - هل كانوا مع طلّاب لبنانيّين أثناء زيارتهم ؟

A. Basic text

A Visit to Lebanon

A number of students from the University of California travelled to Beirut, and during their stay in Lebanon they saw some of the historic ruins. Before their return, a reporter from the Beirut newspaper Al-Masā' talked with them and asked them:

"What did you like in our country?"

They said: "We liked the beauty of it, and the ancient ruins at Baalbek."

He then asked them, "Didn't you go to visit the Cedars, and the museum of the Lebanese-American writer Kahlil Gibran?"

They said, "No, we didn't. Our time didn't permit that."

Then he asked them, "Were you with Lebanese students during your visit to the Lebanese antiquities?"

They said, "No, we weren't."

B. Vocabulary — ب – المفردات

الثانيَ عَشَرَ	the twelfth
عَدَدٌ (مِنْ الـ)	a number (of)
كاليفورْنِيا	California
أَثْناءَ	during
إقامَةٌ	(verbal noun) stay (in a place); residence
آثارٌ، آثارٌ قَديمَةٌ	(pl.) ruins, antiquities
قَبْلَ	before (prep.)
عَوْدَةٌ	(verbal noun) return
تَحَدَّثَ (إلى) (عَنْ)	to speak (to) (about); to converse (with) (about) (indic.: يَتَحَدَّثُ عن)
مُراسِلٌ – ون	reporter, correspondent

جَرِيدَةٌ ـ جَرائِدُ	newspaper
" المَساءُ"	Al-Masā' (Beirut newspaper)
سَأَلَ	to ask (indic. يَسْأَلُ)
أَعْجَبَ	to please (s.o.) (see C.3 below) (indic. يُعْجِبُ)
قالوا	they said
جَمالٌ	beauty
بَعْلَبَكُّ	Baalbek
اَلأَرْزُ	The Cedars
كاتِبٌ ـ كُتّابٌ	writer, author
جُبْران خَليل جُبْران	Kahlil Gibran (full Arabic name is (Jubrān Khalīl Jubrān)
سَمَحَ (لِ) (بِ) ..	to allow, permit (s.o.) (to do...) (indic. يَسْمَحُ)
لَمْ نَكُنْ	we were not

Additional vocabulary

أَخْبَرَ بِ ..	to tell, inform of (indic. يُخْبِرُ)

C. Grammar and drills — ج ـ القواعد والتمارين

1. Plural of jussive: Form I
2. Equational sentences: Past negative with jussive of كانَ
3. The verb أَعْجَبَ 'to please'
4. Adjective modifying first term of iḍāfa
5. Adjective modifying noun with pronoun suffix

1. Plural of jussive: Form I

In the last lesson (11.C.3) we introduced the jussive and gave the singular jussive forms for Form I verbs. The table below gives these singular forms again for reference, and also gives the five plural forms for the verb دَرَسَ 'to study'.

Jussive							
Singular				Plural			
	Verb	Subject-marker			Verb	Subject-marker	
3 MS	يَدْرُسْ	يَـ	ya-	3 MP	يَدْرُسُوا	يَـ..وا	ya...uu
3 FS	تَدْرُسْ	تَـ	ta-	3 FP	يَدْرُسْنَ	يَـ..نَ	ya...na
2 MS	تَدْرُسْ	تَـ	ta-	2 MP	تَدْرُسُوا	تَـ..وا	ta...uu
2 FS	تَدْرُسِي	تَـ..ي	ta...ii	2 FP	تَدْرُسْنَ	تَـ..نَ	ta...na
1 S	أَدْرُسْ	أ	?a-	1 P	نَدْرُسْ	نَـ	na-

Note that in the plural all the forms except the 1 p. have both prefixed and suffixed subject-markers. Note also the following spelling convention: the 3 m.p. يَدْرُسُوا and the 2 m.p. تَدْرُسُوا , which end in <u>-uu</u>, are spelled with a final <u>?alif</u>. This does not affect the pronunciation. If a pronoun suffix is added to such a form, the <u>?alif</u> is dropped:

لَمْ يَدْرُسُوهُ.	'They didn't study it (m.).'

These remarks also apply to the 3 m.p. perfect form, for example دَرَسُوا 'they (m.) studied' (see 9.C.4), and we can now make this general statement: Any Arabic second or third person plural verb form ending in و is written with a final <u>?alif</u>, which is dropped before a pronoun suffix.

As we saw in the previous lesson, the jussive is used with لَمْ to express the negative of a past action. Here are some examples of the new plural forms:

لَمْ يَحْضُرُوا أَمْسِ.	'They (m.) didn't come yesterday.'
لَمْ يَقْرَأُوهَا.	'They (m.) haven't read it (f.)'
لَمْ يَحْصُلْنَ على عَمَلٍ هُناكَ.	'They (f.) didn't obtain a job there.'
لَمْ تَأْكُلُوا الكُبَّةَ.	'You (m.p.) haven't eaten the kubba.'

أَلَمْ تَشْرَبْنَ الْقَهْوَةَ ؟	'Didn't you (f.p.) drink the coffee?'
لَمْ نَقْرَأْ هذا الدَّرْسَ .	'We haven't read this lesson.'

Now do Drills 1 and 2.

Drill 1. (On tape) Conjugation.

Drill 2. Transformation. Affirmative → negative. Ex.

'Sami obtained a university degree.' → ← حصل سامي على شهادة جامعية .

'Sami didn't obtain a university degree.' . لم يحصل سامي على شهادة جامعية

١ ـ تركنا الولد في المطار .

٢ ـ الموظفون عملوا في مكتب حكومي .

٣ ـ أذهبتم مع عائلتكم الى المسرح ؟

٤ ـ الطالبات التونسيات درسن الفرنسية .

٥ ـ بدأت دراسة العربية فى الكويت .

٦ ـ أكلت زوجته معه في المطعم .

٧ ـ فعلوا ذلك امس .

٨ ـ رجعتنّ الى بلدكنّ بعد سنة .

٩ ـ حضر استاذنا الى الصف .

١٠ ـ أقرأت كتاب الكاتب المشهور ؟

2. Equational sentences: Negative past with jussive of كانَ

The verb كانَ 'to be' is used to place an equational sentence in past time. Like any verb, كانَ has jussive forms which, with لَمْ , expresses the past negative. (The present negative, as we have seen, is expressed by لَيْسَ .) Examples:

Present	
سَليمٌ طالِبٌ .	'Salim is a student.'
Present Negative	
لَيْسَ سَليمٌ طالِباً .	'Salim is not a student.'
Past	
كانَ سَليمٌ طالِباً .	'Salim was a student.'
Past negative	
لَمْ يَكُنْ سَليمٌ طالِباً .	'Salim was not a student.'

As the examples show, a predicate noun or adjective is in the accusative case after any form of لَيْسَ or كانَ .

The following table shows the singular and plural jussive forms of كانَ :

Jussive			
Singular		Plural	
3 MS	يَكُنْ	3 MP	يَكونوا
3 FS	تَكُنْ	3 FP	يَكُنَّ
2 MS	تَكُنْ	2 MP	تَكونوا
2 FS	تَكوني	2 FP	تَكُنَّ
1 S	أَكُنْ	1 P	نَكُنْ

This verb has two imperfect stems: one is كونْ -kuun-, used with a suffix beginning with a vowel; the other is كُنْ -kun-, used with a suffix beginning with a consonant, or when there is no suffix. Note also the two feminine plural forms, where the final نْ of the stem -kun- and the initial ن of the suffix -na are written as one نّ with a shadda.

Shown below are additional examples of the past negative of كانَ .

لَمْ يَكُنْ اِبْني هُنا في ذٰلِكَ ٱلْوَقْتِ.	'My son wasn't here at that time.'
لَمْ تَكُنْ سِكْرِتيرةً ـ كانَتْ أُسْتاذَةً.	'She wasn't a secretary--she was a professor.'
أَلَمْ تَكُنْ في الجامِعَةِ أَمْسِ ؟	'Weren't you (m.s.) at the university yesterday?'
لَمْ يَكُنْ في المَكْتَبِ كُرْسِيٌّ.	'There wasn't a chair in the office.'
لَمْ تَكونوا مُوَظَّفي حُكومَةٍ.	'You (m.p.) were not government employees.'

Now do Drills 3 and 4.

Drill 3. (On tape) Conjugation: كانَ + لَمْ .

Drill 4. Transformation: Negation of equational sentences.

'Adil is a bank employee.' → ← عادل موظف في بنك .

'Adil was a bank employee.' → ← كان عادل موظفا في بنك .

'Adil wasn't a bank employee.' لم يكن عادل موظفا في بنك .

١ ـ الدكتور فريد مشهور .

٢ ـ زوجتي استاذة جامعيّة .

٣ ـ بناء الجريدة حديث جدّا .

٤ ـ موعد طائرته قريب .

٥ ـ انا مدير الشركة .

٦ ـ صديقاتنا طالبات مغربيات .

٧ ـ أنتم موجودون هنا .

٨ ـ صديقتي سعاد من العراق .

3. The verb أَعْجَبَ 'to please'

The sentence أَعْجَبَنا جَمالُهُ is translated 'We liked its beauty' but the verb أَعْجَبَ literally means 'to please', and the word-for-word translation of the sentence above is 'Its beauty pleased us.' In the Arabic sentence the noun جَمالٌ 'beauty' is the subject, and the pronoun suffix نا 'us' is the object. Sentences with أَعْجَبَ are often best translated into English by sentences using the verb 'to like', 'to admire' but in that case the object in the Arabic sentence will be the subject in the English sentence and vice versa. Examples (with Arabic subject underlined):

ماذا أَعْجَبَكُمْ في بَلَدِنا ؟	'What pleased you in our country?' ('What did you like in our country?')
أَعْجَبَتْهُمُ الآثارُ القَديمَةُ .	'The ancient ruins pleased them.'* ('They liked the ancient ruins.')
أَعْجَبَ المُوَظَّفَةَ عَمَلُها الجَديدُ .	'Her new job pleased the employee.' ('The employee liked her new job.')

Now do Drills 5 and 6. *For this verb-subject agreement see bottom page 256.

Drill 5. (Also on tape) Substitution.

'I liked the beauty of this country.' أنا: اعجبني جمال هذا البلد .

الاستاذ سليم	الموظفون	أنتم
المرأة	وداد ومريم وهند	نحن
انا	أنتنّ	هي

Drill 6. (On tape) Substitution.

4. Adjective modifying first term of iḍāfa

There have already been many examples of noun-adjective phrases consisting of a simple noun followed by its adjective:

مَدْرَسَةٌ ثانَوِيَّةٌ	'a secondary school'
النَّصُّ الأَساسِيُّ	'the basic text'

There have also been examples where the last term of an iḍāfa is modified by an adjective (another way of describing this is to say that the last term is the whole noun-adjective phrase):

عُنْوانُ مُحاضَرَةِ الأُسْتاذِ الزائِرِ	'the title of the visiting professor's lecture'

Now here is an example in which a noun in an iḍāfa other than the last term is modified by an adjective:

جَريدَةُ " المَساءُ " البَيْروتِيَّةُ	'the Beiruti newspaper "Al-Masā'"'

The first noun in this iḍāfa (جَريدَةٌ) is modified by the adjective بَيْروتِيَّةٌ 'Beiruti'. The usual position for an adjective is immediately after the noun it modifies, but here that noun (جَريدَةٌ) is followed by another noun in an iḍāfa. Two nouns in an iḍāfa may not be separated by an adjective. Therefore, if the first noun (or any noun except the last) in an iḍāfa is to be modified by an adjective, that adjective must follow the whole iḍāfa; it agrees with the particular noun it modifies in the usual ways (definiteness, case, gender, number). Here is an example, with the noun and its modifying adjective underlined:

مُوَظَّفُ حُكومَةٍ جَديدٌ	'a <u>new</u> government <u>employee</u>'

In this example مُوَظَّفُ is <u>indefinite</u> (because the last noun in the iḍāfa, حُكومَةٍ , is indefinite) but it cannot have nunation since it is the <u>first</u> term of an iḍāfa. The adjective جَديدٌ is indefinite to agree with مُوَظَّفُ , and it <u>does</u> have nunation. It also of course agrees in case, gender, and number. Contrast this example with the following:

مُوَظَّفُ الحُكومَةِ الجَديدُ	'the <u>new</u> government <u>employee</u>'

Here مُوَظَّفُ is <u>definite</u> (because الحُكومَةِ is definite) but as the first term of an iḍāfa cannot have the definite article. The adjective الجَديدُ is definite to agree with مُوَظَّفُ, and, as a definite adjective, must have the definite article.

In the example above it is clear that الجَديدُ modifies مُوَظَّفُ and not الحُكومةِ , for if it modified the feminine noun الحُكومةِ it would have to agree with it in gender, as well as in case. That would then be:

مُوَظَّفُ الحُكومةِ الجَديدَةِ	'the employee of the <u>new government</u>'

Even if 'employee' also were feminine, the case ending of the adjective would indicate which noun it modified:

مُوَظَّفَةُ الحُكومةِ الجَديدةُ	'the <u>new employee</u> of the government'
مُوَظَّفَةُ الحُكومَةِ الجَديدةِ	'the employee of the <u>new government</u>'

There can be ambiguity only if the first noun also happens to be genitive, or if case endings are not written:

(مَعَ) مُوَظَّفَةِ الحُكومَةِ الجَديدَةِ	'(with) the new employee of the government' or...
(مَعَ) مُوَظَّفَةِ الحُكومَةِ الجَديدَةِ	'(with) the employee of the new government'

In practice, however, such ambiguity is rare, and where it does occur the general context will usually indicate the correct choice.

Occasionally more than one noun in an iḍāfa may be modified by an adjective. In that case the first adjective after the iḍāfa modifies the noun nearest it.

مُراسِلُ الجَريدَةِ البَيْروتِيَّةِ المِصْرِيُّ 1 2 2 1	'The Egyptian correspondent of the Beirut newspaper'
مُديرُ الشَّرِكَةِ الأَمْرِيكِيَّةِ الْجَديدُ 1 2 2 1	'The new director of the American company'
بِناءُ المَتْحَفِ الوَطَنِيِّ الحَديثُ 1 2 2 1	'The modern building of the National Museum'
بِناءُ المَتْحَفِ الوَطَنِيِّ الحَديثِ 1 2 2 2	'The building of the modern National Museum'

Now do Drills 7 and 8.

Drill 7. (On tape) Substitution.

Drill 8. Written. Recognition and translation: Adjective agreement in iḍāfas.

a. In each of the sentences below, underline all nouns of the iḍāfa construction, then number them, from right to left. Next underline the adjective(s) following the iḍāfa. Give each adjective the same number as the noun it modifies. Ex.

'He's the Egyptian correspondent of the Beirut newspaper.'	هو مراسل الجريدة البيروتية المصري . 1 2 2 1
'The director's new secretary is in his office.'	سكرتيرة المدير الجديدة في مكتبه . 1 2 1

١ ـ مدير الشركة الكبيرة صديقي .

٢ ـ استقبل الرئيس موظفي الحكومة المصريّة الجديدة .

٣ ـ قرأت كتاب الاستاذة الجامعيّة الجديد .

٤ ـ أين بناء المكتبة الوطنيّة ؟

٥ ـ هل أنت مراسل جريدة " اخبار اليوم " المصرية ؟

٦ ـ هل شاهدت طاولة الصفّ الجديدة ؟

٧ ـ هذا هو كرسيّ مدرّسة اللغة العربية الجديد.

٨ ـ قرأت جملة الدرس الثاني القصيرة .

b. Translate the sentences of (a) above.

5. Adjective modifying noun with pronoun suffix

A noun which has an attached pronoun suffix is definite, and therefore an adjective modifying that noun is also definite (i.e., always has the definite article). The adjective also agrees with the noun in case, gender, and number. Here are some examples, with the noun with pronoun suffix and its adjective underlined:

أُسْتاذُنا الجَديدُ مِنْ تونِس .	'Our new professor is from Tunis.'
ذَهَبوا الى بَغْدادَ مَعَ أَصْدِقائِهِم الجُدُدِ .	'They went to Baghdad with their new friends.'
لَمْ أَقْرَأْ كِتابَهُ المَشْهورَ .	'I haven't read his famous book.'
هَلْ صَديقَتُكَ اللُّبْنانِيَّةُ مِنْ بَيْروتَ ؟	'Is your Lebanese friend from Beirut?'

Note also the following example, which occurs in the text:

أَعْجَبَنا جَمالُهُ وآثارُهُ القَديمَةُ .	'Its beauty and its ancient ruins pleased us.'

This illustrates a new principle of agreement: If a singular noun does not refer to a single human being, its plural form takes a feminine singular adjective, verb or pronoun, regardless of the gender of the noun itself in the singular In this example the noun آثارٌ is plural and refers to things, not persons. Therefore, the adjective modifying it (القَديمَةُ) is in its feminine singular form. This point will be treated at greater length in later lessons.

Now do Drills 9 and 10.

Drill 9. Transformation: Adjective agreement.

Combine the following sentences into one sentence, as illustrated.

'The director's secretary is here.'	سكرتيرة المدير موجودة هنا .
'The director's secretary is new.'	سكرتيرة المدير جديدة .
'The director's new secretary is here.'	سكرتيرة المدير الجديدة موجودة هنا .

١ - استقبل استاذه . / استاذه مشهور .

٢ - لوح الصفّ هنا . / لوح الصف قديم .

٣ - ذهبنا مع اصدقائنا . / اصدقاؤنا مصريون .

٤ - تحدّثت الى موظفي الشركة . / موظفو الشركة جدد .

٥ - سيّارة المدير من فرنسا . / سيّارة المدير جديدة .

٦ - مراسل الجريدة هناك . / الجريدة مصرية .

٧ - عائلته في السيارة . / عائلته كبيرة .

٨ - استمعنا الى محاضرات اساتذتنا . / اساتذتنا مشهورون .

٩ - استقبل الرئيس استاذات الجامعة . / استاذات الجامعة جديدات .

١٠ - شاهد مدرسيه في المكتبة . / مدرّسوه لبنانيّون .

Drill 10. (Also on tape) Transformation: Plurals.

'The ruins' - 'ancient'	الآثار - قديم .
'Are the ruins ancient?'	هل الآثار قديمة ؟

١ ـ الاخبار ـ جامعي	٩ ـ الشركات ـ امريكي
٢ ـ الطائرات ـ حديث	١٠ ـ المحاضرات ـ قصير
٣ ـ الطلاب ـ جديد	١١ ـ الاصدقاء ـ موجود هنا
٤ ـ المطارات ـ كبير	١٢ ـ الجامعات ـ بعيد
٥ ـ الصديقات ـ لبنانيّ	١٣ ـ الطاولات ـ جديد
٦ ـ المكتبات ـ قديم	١٤ ـ الكلمات ـ قصير
٧ ـ السيّارات ـ اجنبي	١٥ ـ المراسلون ـ مصري
٨ ـ الاساتذة ـ مشهور	١٦ ـ الآثار ـ قديم

D. Comprehension passage — د ـ نُصوصٌ لِلْفَهْمِ

Read the following passage and then do Drill 11, which is based on it.

سافر عدد من مراسلي جريدة " النيويورك تايمز " ومراسلاتها الى مصر ، وفي مطار القاهرة استقبلهم بعض المراسلين المصريين . شاهد مراسلو "النيويورك تايمز" اثناء اقامتهم في مصر بعض الآثار التاريخية والجامعات وذهبوا لزيارة المتحف الوطني . ذهب المراسلون قبل عودتهم الى امريكا لزيارة بناء جريدة " الأَهْرام "القاهريّة . تحدّث اليهم مراسل لجريدة " الاهرام " وسألهم : (الأَهْرام = Al-Ahram)

ـ ماذا اعجبكم في مصر ؟

قالوا : اعجبتنا آثارها القديمة وجامعاتها الكبيرة وحِكْمَةُ رئيسها . (حِكْمَةُ = wisdom)

ثم سألهم :

ـ هل ذهبتم لزيارة الرئيس ؟

قالوا : لا . لم يسمح وقت الرئيس بهذا ، لكن بعض المراسلات ذهبن لزيارة زوجته . تحدّثت معهنّ هذه السيّدة الفاضِلَةُ عن المرأة في مصر . (الفاضِلَةُ = noble)

ثم سألهم :

ـ مـــــــاذا فعلتم بعد ذلك ؟

قالوا : ذهبنا لزيارة بعض الاصدقاء المصريين وأكلنا معهم الطَّعامَ المصريّ food

وشربنا القهوة العربيّة .

Drill 11. True or false. صَوابٌ أمْ خَطأٌ

١ ـ ذهب المراسلون لزيارة زوجة الرئيس .

٢ ـ تحدّث الرئيس مع المراسلين عن المرأة .

٣ ـ أكل المراسلون في مطعم عربيّ .

٤ ـ استقبل المراسلون الامريكيون المراسلين المصريين في مطار القاهرة .

٥ ـ أعجب الرئيس المصري مراسلي " النيويورك تايمز " .

٦ ـ ذهب المراسلون لزيارة مراسل لجريدة "الاهرام" بعد عودتهم الى امريكا .

E. General drills هـ ـ التمارين العامّة

Drill 12. Written. Conjugation.

Fill in the rest of the chart below, giving jussive + لَمْ .

	ذهب	قرأ	حصل على	رجع	كان
هو	لم يذهب				
هم		لم يقرؤوا			
أنت			لم تحصل على		
نحن				لم نرجع	
أنتنّ					لم تكنّ

Drill 13. Written. Transformation: m.p. → f.p.

Rewrite the Basic Text, changing all masculine plural forms (referring to people) to the corresponding feminine plural forms. Feminine plural of قالوا is قُلْنَ .

Lesson Thirteen

الدرس الثالث عشر

أ - النص الاساسيّ

رسـالة

واشنطن في ٧ نيسان (ابريل) ١٩٧٥ April

عزيزي سليم وعزيزتي فريدة :

أكتب هذه الرسالة بعد عودتي من عَمّان . أسكن الآن في مدينة واشنطن وأعمل في مكتبة الكونغرس . يعمل والدي في مصنع وتدرس أختي في جامعة جورج واشنطن .

تذكر يا سليم في رسالتك لي زيارتك القادمة لامريكا - ما موعد وصولك ؟ أنا مُشْتاقٌ الى لِقائِكَ . وأنت يا فريدة هل تدرسين الآن ام تبحثين عن عمل ؟

longing to, looking forward to; meeting

سلامنا الى العائلة والاصدقاء .

المخلص

هنري

٢٥ شارع فورد

واشنطن - امريكا

اسئلة :

١ - من كاتب هذه الرسالة ؟ والى من كتبها ؟

٢ - أين يسكن ؟

٣ - أين يعمل ؟

٤ - ماذا يفعل والده ؟

٥ - هل له أخت ؟

٦ - في أي جامعة تدرس أخته ؟

٧ - من ذكر زيارته لامريكا ؟

A. Basic text

A Letter

25 Ford Street

Washington, D.C., U.S.A.

April 7, 1975

Dear Salim and Farida,

I am writing this letter after my return from Amman. I am living in Washington now and working in the Library of Congress. My father works in a factory and my sister is studying at George Washington University.

Salim, you mention in your letter to me your coming visit to America. What is the date of your arrival? I am looking forward to seeing you. And you, Farida, are you studying now or looking for a job?

Our greetings to the family and friends.

Sincerely,

Henry

B. Vocabulary

أَلثّالِثَ عَشَرَ	the thirteenth
واشنطن	Washington
عَزِيزٌ – أَعِزّاءُ	dear
أَكْتُبُ	I write, I am writing
رِسالَةٌ – رَسائِلُ	letter
عَمّانُ	Amman (capital of Jordan)
أَسْكُنُ	I live, reside, I am living, residing (See note on page 165.)
مَدِينَةٌ – مُدُنٌ	city
مَدَنِيٌّ – ون	city-dwelling, urban; civilized
أَعْمَلُ	I work, I am working
الكونغرس	Congress
يَعْمَلُ	he works, he is working
والِدٌ	father

مَصْنَعٌ ـ مَصانِعُ	factory
تَدْرُسُ	she studies, she is studying
أُخْتٌ ـ أَخَواتٌ	sister
جامعة جورج واشنطن	George Washington University
تَذْكُرُ	you (m.s.) mention; you relate, tell
قادِمٌ ـ ون	coming (adj.); next (week, etc.)
وُصولٌ (الى)	(verbal noun) arrival (in, at)
تَدْرُسينَ	you (f.s.) study, you are studying
تَبْحَثينَ عَنْ	you (f.s.) look for, you are looking for
سَلامٌ ـ ات	peace; greeting
مُخْلِصٌ ـ ون	sincere
هنري	Henry

Additional vocabulary

شارِعٌ ـ شَوارِعُ	street
أَرْسَلَ	to send (Indic. يُرْسِلُ 'he sends'; neg.perf. لَمْ يُرْسِلْ 'he did not send')

C. Grammar and drills ج ـ القواعد والتمارين

1. Reading dates.
2. Imperfect indicative: Singular
3. Broken plurals
4. Diptotes

1. Reading dates

The heading at the beginning of this letter may be read in two ways:

(1) ١ ـ واشنطن في السابع من نيسان

(fissaabiʕi) min niisaan

or (2) ٢ ـ واشنطن في سبعة نيسان

(fii sabʕa niisaan)

The first is more formal.

How to read years will be explained later.

2. Imperfect indicative: Singular

To begin with, here is a very brief review of the components of the whole Arabic verb system: There are two tenses: perfect and imperfect. The perfect tense denotes completed actions; the imperfect tense denotes actions which have not taken place or have not been completed. The imperfect tense includes four moods: indicative, subjunctive, jussive, and imperative. So far we have introduced the perfect tense and the (imperfect) jussive, which as one of its functions expresses (with لَمْ) the negation of past actions. In this lesson we come to the imperfect indicative. (This is usually referred to as simply the "imperfect"; the other moods are also part of the imperfect tense, but they are referred to by their mood names "subjunctive", "jussive", and "imperative".)

The imperfect, denoting actions which have not been completed, may correspond to any of several English verbal constructions, depending on the context:

(1) A simple present-tense form or, in questions, a construction with "do" or "does":

يَعْمَلُ	'he works'
أَيْنَ يَعْمَلُ ؟	'Where does he work?'
أَكْتُبُ	'I write'

(2) A progressive construction with "is/are/am" and a verb in the -ing form:

يَعْمَلُ	'he is working'
هَلْ تَدْرُسِينَ الآنَ ؟	'Are you (f.s.) studying now?'
أَكْتُبُ	'I am writing.'

An Arabic verb in the imperfect indicative consists of a <u>subject-marker</u>, the <u>imperfect stem</u>, and a <u>mood-marker</u>. The subject-markers and the stems are the same as in the jussive. Example:

يَدْرُسُ 'he studies'

The subject-marker here is يَـ <u>ya-</u>, and the stem is دْرُسْ <u>-drus-</u>. The final vowel ـُ <u>-u</u> is the mood-marker, showing that this verb is in the indicative mood (as opposed, for example, to the jussive, which has no mood-markers. It is in fact the absence of mood-markers which distinguishes the jussive from other moods.)

Following is a chart showing the singular imperfect indicative forms of five verbs. If you compare these with the corresponding jussive forms (11.C.3) you will see that in forms where the jussive has no vowel ending (يَدْرُسْ)the indicative has the mood-marker <u>-u</u> (يَدْرُسُ), and where the jussive ends in a long vowel (تَدْرُسي) the indicative adds the mood-marker <u>-na</u> (تَدْرُسينَ).

	3 MS	3 FS	2 MS	2 FS	1 S
Stem	هو	هي	انتَ	انتِ	انا
-دْرُسْ- 'study'	يَدْرُسُ	تَدْرُسُ	تَدْرُسُ	تَدْرُسينَ	أَدْرُسُ
-كْتُبْ- 'write'	يَكْتُبُ	تَكْتُبُ	تَكْتُبُ	تَكْتُبينَ	أَكْتُبُ
-رْجِعْ- 'return'	يَرْجِعُ	تَرْجِعُ	تَرْجِعُ	تَرْجِعينَ	أَرْجِعُ
-ذْهَبْ- 'go'	يَذْهَبُ	تَذْهَبُ	تَذْهَبُ	تَذْهَبينَ	أَذْهَبُ
-عْمَلْ- 'work'	يَعْمَلُ	تَعْمَلُ	تَعْمَلُ	تَعْمَلينَ	أَعْمَلُ
Subject-markers	يَـ	تَـ	تَـ	تَـ ... يـ	أَ
Mood-markers	ـُ	ـُ	ـُ	ـنَ	ـُ

As in the jussive, the 3 f.s. and 2 m.s. forms are identical. Also note again the vowel variation in the imperfect stem: <u>u</u> in some verbs (first two examples above), <u>i</u> in others (third example). and <u>a</u> in others (last two examples).

Arabic verbs, as we have seen before, have two stems. The <u>perfect stem</u> is used for the perfect tense only. The <u>imperfect stem</u> is used for all four moods of the imperfect tense. To be able to use any Arabic verb, one must of course know both stems. This is particularly so in the case of Form I verbs, where the vowels of both stems vary from one verb to another. In learning a new verb, therefore, it is a good idea to learn the (3 m.s.) perfect and imperfect together as one item; for example, learn the Arabic for 'to study' not just as دَرَسَ , as that does not provide information about the imperfect stem, but as دَرَسَ يَدْرُسُ . Knowing this, you know that the perfect stem is <u>daras-</u> and the imperfect stem is <u>-drus-</u>, and you are then equipped to use the verb in all its forms.

Following is a list, for reference, of the perfect and imperfect (indicative) forms of all the Form I verbs which have appeared so far. Note the vowels of the stems, and the correspondences between the vowel of the perfect and that of the imperfect. The stem vowels are indicated below for each group.

<u>Imperfect</u>	<u>Perfect</u>	
(Stem vowel <u>u</u>)	(Stem vowel <u>a</u>)	
يَدْرُسُ	دَرَسَ	'to study'
يَكْتُبُ	كَتَبَ	'to write'
يَحْضُرُ الى	حَضَرَ الى	'to come'
يَأْكُلُ	أَكَلَ	'to eat'
يَتْرُكُ	تَرَكَ	'to leave'
يَحْصُلُ عَلى	حَصَلَ عَلى	'to obtain'
يَسْكُنُ	سَكَنَ	'to live'
يَذْكُرُ	ذَكَرَ	'to mention'
(stem vowel <u>a</u>)	(stem vowel <u>a</u>)	
يَذْهَبُ	ذَهَبَ	'to go'
يَبْدَأُ	بَدَأَ	'to begin'
يَسْمَحُ بِ	سَمَحَ	'to permit'

Note: The perfect means 'to take up residence, settle down' as well as 'to live, reside'

يَقْرَأُ	قَرَأَ	'to read'
يَسْأَلُ	سَأَلَ	'to ask'
يَفْعَلُ	فَعَلَ	'to do'
يَبْحَثُ عَنْ	بَحَثَ عَنْ	'to look for'
(stem vowel i)	(stem vowel a)	
يَرْجِعُ	رَجَعَ	'to return'
(stem vowel a)	(stem vowel i)	
يَشْرَبُ	شَرِبَ	'to drink'
يَعْمَلُ	عَمِلَ	'to work'

In the vocabulary listings of subsequent lessons (and in the glossaries) verbs will be given in the 3 m.s. form of the perfect, with the imperfect stem vowel. Example:

ـُ دَرَسَ 'to study'

ـِ رَجَعَ 'to return'

This indicates that the imperfect forms are يَدْرُسُ and يَرْجِعُ.
Now do Drills 1 and 2.

Drill 1. Written. Recognition.

Specify the mood (indicative or jussive) of each of the following verbs and give the pronoun subject of each. Ex.

Indicative - يَكْتُبُ ـ هو

تَدْرُسْ	تَعْمَلي	تَسْأَلُ
أَكْتُبُ	أَتْرُكْ	تَشْرَبي
يَسْكُنُ	يَفْعَلْ	تَقْرَأْ
تَذْكُرينَ	تَذْهَبْ	آكُلُ

Drill 2. (Also on tape) Transformation. Perfect → لَمْ + jussive → indicative. Ex.

'Henry wrote a letter to his friend.' → ← كتب هنري رسالة لصديقه .

'Henry didn't write a letter to his friend.' ← لم يكتب هنري رسالة لصديقه .

'Henry is writing a letter to his friend.' يكتب هنري رسالة لصديقه .

١ ـ ذكرت في رسالتك موعد وصولك .

٢ ـ بحثت عن عمل في الحكومة .

٣ ـ سكنت في عَمّان .

٤ ـ حصلت على شهادتها أثناء أقامتها هنا .

٥ ـ ترك عائلته في المطار اليوم .

٦ ـ شربت قهوة عربية في المطعم .

٧ ـ قرأت رسالة أختك .

٨ ـ كتبت عن آثار بعلبك في لبنان .

٩ ـ سمح وقتنا بزيارة بلدكم .

١٠ ـ سألت عن موعد عودته الى الشرق الاوسط .

3. Broken plurals

Broken plurals of nouns and adjectives are derived from their singular forms by internal vowel changes (like English foot-feet) and in some cases by the doubling of a consonant or the addition of a prefix or suffix as well. In other words, a broken plural has a different pattern from its singular. Broken plurals fall into a number of patterns; it is often possible to predict a plural from the pattern and meaning of the singular. Thus far we have had thirteen broken plural patterns, some with slight variations. These are listed below, with the plural forms under each pattern, and the corresponding singulars on the left. (For the symbolization of patterns with FML see 11.C.1; the letter C, standing for "any consonant", is used instead of F, M, or L when there are more than three consonants in the word and it does not matter which are radicals. DD stand for identical second and third radicals.)

Plural Patterns

1.a. ?aFMaaL

قَلَمٌ	أَقْلامٌ	'pencils'
خَبَرٌ	أَخْبارٌ	'news'
وَلَدٌ	أَوْلادٌ	'boys'
عَمَلٌ	أَعْمالٌ	'jobs'
عَدَدٌ	أَعْدادٌ	'numbers'
بابٌ	أَبْوابٌ	'doors'
وَقْتٌ	أَوْقاتٌ	'times'
لَوْحٌ	أَلْواحٌ	'boards'
شَيْءٌ	أَشْياءُ	'things'
فِلْمٌ	أَفْلامٌ	'films'
اِبْنٌ	أَبْناءٌ	'sons'
اِسْمٌ	أَسْماءٌ	'names'

b. ?aaMaaL (instead of ?a?MaaL)

أَثَرٌ	آثارٌ	'ruins, antiquities'
[أَمَلٌ	آمالٌ	'hopes']

2. FuMuuL

دَرْسٌ	دُروسٌ	'lessons'
بَنْكٌ	بُنوكٌ	'banks'
نَصٌّ	نُصوصٌ	'texts'

3. FiMaaL

رَجُلٌ	رِجالٌ	'men'
بَلَدٌ	بِلادٌ	'countries'
اِمْرَأَةٌ	نِساءٌ	'women'
كَبيرٌ	كِبارٌ	'big'
قَصيرٌ	قِصارٌ	'short'

4. <u>FuMaL</u>

جُمْلَةٌ	جُمَلٌ	'sentences'

5. <u>FuMuL</u>

كِتابٌ	كُتُبٌ	'books'
مَدِينَةٌ	مُدُنٌ	'cities'
جَدِيدٌ	جُدُدٌ	'new'

6. <u>FaaLa(t)</u>

سَيِّدٌ	سادَةٌ	'Mssrs., gentlemen'

7. <u>FuMMaaL</u>

طالِبٌ	طُلّابٌ	'students'
كاتِبٌ	كُتّابٌ	'authors'
زائِرٌ	زُوّارٌ	'visitors'

8. <u>?aFMiya(t)</u>

بِناءٌ	أَبْنِيَةٌ	'buildings'

9. <u>CaCaaCiCa(t)</u>

أُسْتاذٌ	أَساتِذَةٌ	'professors'
دَكْتورٌ	دَكاتِرَةٌ	'doctors'

10. <u>FuMaLaa?</u>

رَئِيسٌ	رُؤَساءُ	'chiefs, presidents'
قَدِيمٌ	قُدَماءُ	'old'

11.a. <u>?aFMiLaa?</u>

صَدِيقٌ	أَصْدِقاءُ	'friends'
قَرِيبٌ	أَقْرِباءُ	'relatives, relations'

b. <u>?aFiDDaa?</u>

عَزيزٌ	أَعِزّاءُ	'dear'

12.a. CaCaaCiC

مَكْتَبٌ	مَكاتِبُ	'offices'
مَتْحَفٌ	مَتاحِفُ	'museums'
مَطْعَمٌ	مَطاعِمُ	'restaurants'
مَسْرَحٌ	مَسارِحُ	'theaters'
مَصْنَعٌ	مَصانِعُ	'factories'
مَوْعِدٌ	مَواعِدُ	'appointments'
أَجْنَبِيٌّ	أَجانِبُ	'foreign; foreigners'
مَدْرَسَةٌ	مَدارِسُ	'schools'

b. CaCaaCin (instead of CaCaaCiyun)

كُرْسِيٌّ	كَراسٍ	'chairs'

c. CaCaa?iC

رِسالَةٌ	رَسائِلُ	'letters'
جَريدَةٌ	جَرائِدُ	'newspapers'

d. CawaaCiC

شارِعٌ	شَوارِعُ	'streets'

13.a. CaCaaCiiC

عُنْوانٌ	عَناوينُ	'titles'
شُبّاكٌ	شَبابيكُ	'windows'

b. CawaaCiiC

تاريخٌ	تَواريخُ	'dates'
ميعادٌ	مَواعيدُ	'appointments'

Notes:

1. In pattern 1.a, note the last two plurals, in which the place of the

last radical is filled by a hamza which is not present in the singular. Note the plural نِساء 'women' in pattern 3, which is completely different from its singular.

2. Pattern 1.b.?aaMaaL occurs instead of ?a?MaaL for reasons of pronunciation; see the rule explained in 11.C.3, p. 237.

3. In some words the singular or the plural may have a meaning not shared by the other; for example, under pattern 13.b. is تَوارِيخُ the plural of تارِيخٌ 'date'; تارِيخٌ in the meaning of "history" has no plural.

4. Some words have more than one possible plural with the same or different meanings. For example, كُرْسِيٌّ 'chair' has plural كَراسٍ (pattern 12.b. above) or كَراسِيُّ with no difference in meanings, whereas the word زائِرٌ 'visiting' as an adjective has the sound plural زائِرونَ , but as a noun 'visitor' it has the plural زُوّارٌ (pattern 7). جَدِيدٌ has two plurals: جُدُدٌ / جُدَدٌ

5. In plurals, the suffix ـَةٌ -a(t) does not indicate feminine gender. Note the words of patterns 6, 8, and 9, which refer to masculine nouns, including some denoting male human beings.

6. Predictability. In many cases, knowing the form and meaning of a singular makes it possible to predict what the broken plural will probably be--though not with complete certainty. It is wise always to learn the plural together with the singular, but the following general statements will help you to classify broken plurals and to remember them more easily.

(a) Patterns 1 and 2 very commonly serve as the plurals of singulars of the pattern FaMaL and FaML, FiML, FuML.

(b) Pattern 4 is common as the plural of feminines of the pattern FuMLa(t).

(c) Pattern 7 is typically the plural for singular nouns of the pattern FaaMiL which refer to human beings in a particular activity.

(d) Pattern 9 is the plural for various singular patterns--all referring to human beings.

(e) Pattern 10 is the usual plural for singular nouns of the pattern FaMiiL which refer to human beings. Some FaMiiL adjectives also have this plural.

(f) Pattern 11 is another possible plural for FaMiiL nouns referring to human beings (and some adjectives). 11.a. is for roots with three different radicals (i.e., FML), whereas 11.b. is for roots in which the second and third radicals are identical (i.e., FDD).

(g) Pattern 12.a. is the usual plural for singular nouns which have four consonants (whether three radicals and one other consonant, or four radicals) and no long vowels. (The plural كَراسٍ 'chairs' (pattern 12.b.) is a defective noun, a type which will be treated later.) Pattern 12.c. is the plural for feminine singular nouns with a short vowel in the first syllable and a long vowel in the second. Pattern 12.d. is for masculine or feminine singulars with a long vowel in the first syllable and a short vowel in the second.

(h) Pattern 13 is the usual plural for singulars containing four consonants (a double consonant counts as two) and at least one long vowel. If the long vowel is in the last syllable only, the plural is pattern 13.a.; if there is a long vowel in both syllables, the plural is pattern 13.b.

(7) <u>Diptotes</u>. In the table above you will see that أَشْياءُ in pattern 1.a. and the plural nouns of patterns 10 through 13 (except 12.b.; see (g) above) are written with final ـُ <u>-u</u> instead of the ـٌ <u>-un</u> with nunation. These plurals are all <u>diptotes</u>, a type of word which is described in the next note.

Now do Drills 3, 4 and 5.

<u>Drill 3</u>. (On tape) Repetition. Broken plurals. (s → p)

<u>Drill 4</u>. (On tape) Production. Broken plurals. (s → p)

Drill 5. (Also on tape) Recognition.

Give the singular forms of the following.

شبابيك	دكاترة	تواريخ
اجانب	اشياء	رسائل
اعزاء	كراس	زوّار
ابنية	جمل	قصار
سادة	شوارع	مدن
دروس	رؤساء	اصدقاء

4. Diptotes

We have seen that Arabic nouns (and adjectives) have three different case endings, and also have the n of nunation when indefinite as, for example:

	Indefinite		Definite	
Nom.	كِتابٌ	'a book'	أَلْكِتابُ	'the book'
Gen.	كِتابٍ		اَلْكِتابِ	
Acc.	كِتاباً		اَلْكِتابَ	

Certain types of nouns and adjectives, however, when indefinite and not serving as first term of an iḍāfa, have only two different case endings (ـُ u for the nominative, and ـَ a for both the genitive and the accusative), and never have the n of nunation. For example:

	Indefinite	
Nom.	مَكاتِبُ	
Gen.	مَكاتِبَ	'offices'
Acc.	مَكاتِبَ	

Such words are called diptotes; among them are some singular nouns and adjectives, and some plural nouns and adjectives. <u>When defined by the definite article ال or when they are the first term of any iḍāfa diptotes have all three case endings</u>:

Without or with definite article:

	<u>Indefinite</u> (2 endings)	<u>Definite</u> (3 endings)
Nom.	رُؤَساءُ 'presidents'	الرُّؤَساءُ 'the presidents'
Gen.	رُؤَساءَ	الرُّؤَساءِ
Acc.	رُؤَساءَ	الرُّؤَساءَ

Without or with pronoun suffix:

	<u>Indefinite</u>	<u>Definite</u>
Nom.	رَسائِلُ 'letters'	رَسائِلُنا 'our letters'
Gen.	رَسائِلَ	رَسائِلِنا
Acc.	رَسائِلَ	رَسائِلَنا

In an indefinite or definite iḍāfa (3 endings):

Nom.	شَوارِعُ مَدِينَةٍ 'city streets'	شَوارِعُ المَدِينَةِ 'the city streets'
Gen.	شَوارِعِ مَدِينَةٍ	شَوارِعِ المَدِينَةِ
Acc.	شَوارِعَ مَدِينَةٍ	شَوارِعَ المَدِينَةِ

In the lesson vocabularies, and in the various Glossaries in the book, diptotes are identified as such by the final vowel sign ـُ <u>u</u> instead of ـٌ <u>-un</u>, for example:

أَوَّلُ 'first'

أَصْدِقاءُ 'friends'

The following types of words which have occurred so far are diptotes:

a. Broken plurals of the following patterns:

(1) (a) CaCaaCiC

أَجانِبُ 'foreign, foreigners'

مَدارِسُ 'schools'

(b) CaCaa?iC

جَرائِدُ 'newspapers'

(c) CawaaCiC

شَوارِعُ 'streets'

(2) (a) CaCaaCiiC

شَبابيكُ 'windows'

(b) CawaaCiiC

تَواريخُ 'dates'

b. Singulars and plurals ending in the suffix ـاءُ -aa?u, where the final اء is not part of the root:

رُؤَساءُ 'presidents' (root R?S)

أَصْدِقاءُ 'friends' (root ṢDQ)

c. The adjective أَوَّلُ 'first' and the plural أَشْياءُ 'things' (pattern 1.a. in the preceding note).

d. All place names which end in a consonant and do not have the definite article (except those ending in اتٌ -aat, as عَرَفاتٌ '(Mount) Arafat'):

لُبْنانُ 'Lebanon'

مِصْرُ 'Egypt'

بَغْدادُ 'Baghdad'

مَكَّةُ 'Mecca'

e. All feminine personal names:

مَرْيَمُ 'Maryam'

وِدادُ 'Widad'

كَريمَةُ 'Karima'

(Feminine names with ـْ (no vowel) on the second of three letters are preferably diptotes, but are sometimes treated as regular:

هِنْدُ / هِنْدٌ 'Hind')

f. Masculine personal names, except those which are identical with (non-diptote) common nouns and adjectives, and those spelled with three letters and having ـْ (no vowel) on the second letter. Thus كَرِيمٌ 'Karim' (from adjective كَرِيمٌ 'noble, generous') and زَيْدٌ 'Zayd' (no vowel on second letter) are not diptotes. The following are examples of masculine names which are diptotes:

عُمَرُ 'Omar'

إِبْراهِيمُ 'Ibrahim (Abraham)'

يُوسُفُ 'Yusuf (Joseph)'

سُلَيْمانُ 'Sulaiman (Solomon)'

In future lessons, other classes of diptotes will be identified as such as they occur.

Now do Drills 6, 7 and 8.

Drill 6. (Also on tape) Transformation.

Make the underlined word plural, and make any other necessary changes. Ex.

'The man looked for work in New York.' ⟵ بحث الرجل عن عمل في نيويورك.

'The men looked for work in New York.' بحث الرجال عن عمل فى نيويورك .

١ – ذهبنا لزيارة المدينة .

٢ – أخبرني بعنوان الكتاب .

٣ – متى موعد عودة المرأة الى الشرق الاوسط ؟

٤ – كتب الكاتب عن جمال البلد .

٥ – سأل الزائر الاجنبى عن الاقامة فى لبنان .

٦ – ترك الولد امام باب المتحف .

٧ – استقبل الرئيس مدير الشركة .

٨ – درسنا جملة جديدة .

٩ _ قرأت الجريدة بعد وصولي الى المكتب .

١٠ _ صديق هنري يسكن فى بناء هناك .

١١ _ تحدّث الى مراسل الجريدة .

Drill 7. Written. Recognition.

Vowel the underlined words.

١ _ ذهب الطلاب الى المدارس الخاصّة .

٢ _ عمل كل الرجال في مصانع .

٣ _ قال الطالب : درسنا الدرس الاوّل .

٤ _ قرأت رسائل صديقي .

٥ _ قرأت الأخبار في الجرائد .

٦ _ يسكن رجال اجانب في هذا البناء .

٧ _ استقبل الرئيس المديرين في مكتبه .

٨ _ مكاتب الجامعة في بناء قريب .

Drill 8. Written. Transformation.

Make the underlined words plural and vowel them.

١ _ درّسوا في مدرسة الاولاد .

٢ _ سافرت مع رجل اجنبي .

٣ _ اعجبت الجامعة الاستاذ الجديد .

٤ _ مدير الشركة في المكتب .

٥ _ كتب كريم الى صديق عزيز .

٦ _ عمل المراسل في جريدة في لبنان .

٧ _ استقبل الرئيس مديرا مصريا .

٨ _ للشركة رئيس جديد .

٩ _ ما عنوان الكتاب ؟

١٠ _ كتبت رسالة لصديقي .

D. Comprehension passage — د – نُصوصٌ لِلْفَهْمِ

Read the following passage; then do Drill 9, which is based on it.

سمير طالب في جامعة تونس ، ووالده استاذ في جامعة القاهرة. هو السيد الدكتور فريد سرحان .

ذهب الدكتور فريد الى تونس لزيارة ابنه . استقبل سمير والده في المطار ، وبعد ذلك ذهب معه الى أوتيل هيلتون . — hotel (pron. 'uteel)

اثناء اقامة السيد فريد في تونس شاهد الآثار الرومانيّةَ — Roman

القديمة في قَرْطاجَنَّة. وفي مدينة تونس ذهب لزيارة الجامعة التونسية. — Carthage

كذلك ذهب لزيارة جامِعِ الزَّيْتونَةِ، وهو مَرْكَزٌ لدراسة التاريخ الاسلاميّ واللغة العربية . — Al-Zaitouna mosque; center

بعد اَنْتِهاءِ الزيارة ، رجع السيد فريد الى القاهرة وكتب — end

في جريدة اَلْأَهْرامُ عن زيارته لتونس . — Al-Ahram

Drill 9.

Fill in the blanks relying on your comprehension of the above passage:

١ – السيد فريد سرحان ـــــ سمير .

٢ – سمير طالب في بلد ـــــ .

٣ – سكن السيد فريد في ـــــ ـــــ اثناء زيارته لابنه .

٤ – شاهد السيد فريد ـــــ الرومانية القديمة .

٥ – ـــــ ـــــ مركز لدراسة التاريخ الاسلاميّ .

٦ – كتب السيد فريد فى جريدة الاهرام بعد عودته الى مصر عن ـــــ.

E. General drills — هـ – اَلتَّمارينُ الْعامَّةُ

Drill 10. Written. Translation.

My dear friends,

I am writing to you from Cairo after my arrival here yesterday. Before my arrival in Cairo I went to the city of Baalbek and I liked its ruins.

I study at the American University and I am reading Arabic in (في) books and newspapers.

My family did not come with me and I am anxious to see them (مُشْتاقَةٌ الى لِقائِهِمْ) during their coming visit. My father is a secretary to the president of a company in Washington.

My greetings to your (pl.) dear sister.

Your sincere friend,

Lucy

Drill 11.

Give the correct form of the word(s) in parentheses.

١ ـ (اعجب) هنري آثار المدينة القديمة .

٢ ـ ألم (سكن) في عمان يا سعاد ؟

٣ ـ (ليس) في المكتب مديرو شركات .

٤ ـ (بحث) كريمة عن عمل في بغداد الآن .

٥ ـ لم (كان) اختي طالبة في الجامعة .

٦ ـ (ذهب + انا) لزيارة صديقي امس .

٧ ـ لم (قرأ) فريد الجريدة امس .

٨ ـ لم (كان) مراسلين في جريدة "المساء"

٩ ـ (ليس) امام البناء سيارة كبيرة .

١٠ ـ (اعجب) والدتي جمال مدينة القاهرة .

Drill 12. Written.

Write the root of each of the following words and then look up each one in the dictionary and give its meaning and word pattern. Ex.

Pattern	Root	
FuMaLaa?	م · ل · ع علماء 'scholars'	
نجّار	سكّان	شاعر
حضارة	أعمال	صداقة
كثير	اعزّاء	مذهب
أصدقاء	فعل	وجود

Drill 13. Oral practice.

The following items are suggestions for "conversational" practice. They can be directed to individual students by the teacher, used in chain drills, used as conversation guidelines among small groups of students, etc.

١ ــ صَباحَ الْخَيْر .

٢ ــ كيف الحال؟

٣ ــ من أنت ؟

٤ ــ في أيّ مدينة تسكن ؟

٥ ــ أين تسكن عائلتك ؟

٦ ــ هل أنت طالب (ة) ؟

٧ ــ في أيّ جامعة تدرس (ين) ؟

٨ ــ أيّ لغة تدرس (ين) ؟

٩ ــ هل ذهبت الى الشرق الاوسط ؟

١٠ ــ الى أيّ بلد ذهبت ؟

١١ ــ هل لك سيّارة ؟

١٢ ــ الى اللقاء.

Lesson Fourteen

الدرس الرابع عشر

أ ـ النص الاساسيّ

مُوجَزُ الاخبار

summary

هنا دمشق.

ايّها السيّدات والسادة السلام عليكم.

ننقل اليكم مُوجَزَ الاخبار.

- رؤساء الدول العربية يبحثون الوضع السياسي الحاضر في العالم العربى اثناء اجتماعهم في الخرطوم .
- الرئيس التونسي لا يحضر هذا الاجتماع .
- المراسلون الامريكيون يرجعون الى واشنطن بعد زيارتهم لدمشق .
- وزير التَّرْبِيَةِ ينشر اسماء الاساتذة الجدد في الجامعة السورية . education
- بعض استاذات الجامعة يحضرن اجتماعا مع الرئيس السورى .
- كان هذا هو الموجز ، وتسمعون الآن تَفْصيلَ الاخبار . details

أسئلـــــــة

١ ـ ماذا يبحث الرؤساء أثناء اجتماعهم ؟

٢ ـ هل يحضر الرئيس التونسي الاجتماع ؟

٣ ـ من يرجع من دمشق ؟

٤ ـ ماذا ينشر وزير التربية السوري ؟

٥ ـ من حضر الاجتماع مع الرئيس السوري ؟

A. Basic text

The News Summary

This is Damascus.

Greetings ladies and gentlemen. We bring you the summary of the news.

-The presidents of the Arab states discuss the present political situation in the Arab world during their meeting in Khartoum.

-The Tunisian president is not attending this meeting.

-The American reporters return to Washington after their visit to Damascus.

-The Minister of Education announces the names of the new professors at the Syrian University.

-Some women professors at the university attend a meeting with the Syrian president.

This has been the summary. Now you will hear the details of the news.

B. Vocabulary

ب ـ المفردات

أَلرّابِعَ عَشَرَ	the fourteenth
أَيُّها	(fem. أَيَّتُها) (vocative particle: see C.3)
أَلسَّلامُ عَلَيْكُمْ	Greetings!
نَقَلَ ـُ	to transmit; to transfer, transport, move
نَنْقُلُ	we transmit
دَوْلَةٌ ـ دُوَلٌ	state, country, power
بَحَثَ ـَ	to discuss
يَبْحَثونَ	they discuss
وَضْعٌ ـ أَوْضاعٌ	situation, condition
سِياسِيٌّ ـ ون	political; politician
حاضِرٌ ـ ون	present; current (time)
عالَمٌ ـ عَوالِمُ	world

اِجْتِماعٌ ـ ات	meeting (noun)
حَضَرَ ـُ	to attend, be present at
يَرْجِعونَ	(m.p.) they return
وَزيرٌ ـ وُزَراءُ	(cabinet) minister
نَشَرَ ـُ	to publish; to announce
يَحْضُرْنَ	they (f.p.) attend
سَمِعَ ـَ (بـ)	to hear (about, of)
تَسْمَعونَ	you (m.p.) hear

Additional vocabulary

سِياسَةٌ	politics; policy
قابَلَ	to meet (with)

C. Grammar and drills ج ـ القواعد والتمارين

1. Imperfect indicative: Plural
2. Negative of imperfect indicative: لا
3. Vocative particle أَيُّها

1. Imperfect indicative: Plural

The chart in 13.C.2 showed the imperfect singular forms of five verbs. The following chart shows the imperfect plural forms of the same verbs:

	3 MP	3 FP	2 MP	2 FP	1 P
Stem	هم	هنّ	أنتم	أنتنّ	نحن
-دْرُس- 'study'	يَدْرُسونَ	يَدْرُسْنَ	تَدْرُسونَ	تَدْرُسْنَ	نَدْرُسُ
-كْتُب- 'write'	يَكْتُبونَ	يَكْتُبْنَ	تَكْتُبونَ	تَكْتُبْنَ	نَكْتُبُ
-رْجِع- 'return'	يَرْجِعونَ	يَرْجِعْنَ	تَرْجِعونَ	تَرْجِعْنَ	نَرْجِعُ

ذَهَبَ 'go'	يَذْهَبُونَ	يَذْهَبْنَ	تَذْهَبُونَ	تَذْهَبْنَ	نَذْهَبُ
عَمِلَ 'work'	يَعْمَلُونَ	يَعْمَلْنَ	تَعْمَلُونَ	تَعْمَلْنَ	نَعْمَلُ
Subject-marker	يَ...و ya-...-uu	يَ...نَ ya-...-na	تَ...و ta-...-uu	تَ...نَ ta-...-na	نَ -na
Mood-marker	نَ -na	(None)	نَ -na	(None)	ـُ -u

As the chart shows, all the plural forms except 1 p. have subject-markers consisting of both prefix and suffix. Where the subject-marker suffix ends in a long vowel (as in the 3 m.p. and 2 m.p. forms), the mood-marker is نَ -na. The mood-marker for the 1 p. form is ـُ -u, and the two feminine plural forms have no mood-marker.

Given below for reference is a chart showing all the singular and plural forms, imperfect indicative and jussive, for the verb دَرَسَ 'to study':

	Indicative	Jussive		Indicative	Jussive
3 MS	يَدْرُسُ	يَدْرُسْ	3 MP	يَدْرُسُونَ	يَدْرُسُوا
3 FS	تَدْرُسُ	تَدْرُسْ	3 FP	يَدْرُسْنَ	يَدْرُسْنَ
2 MS	تَدْرُسُ	تَدْرُسْ	2 MP	تَدْرُسُونَ	تَدْرُسُوا
2 FS	تَدْرُسِينَ	تَدْرُسِي	2 FP	تَدْرُسْنَ	تَدْرُسْنَ
1 S	أَدْرُسُ	أَدْرُسْ	1 P	نَدْرُسُ	نَدْرُسْ

Note the correspondences between the endings of the indicative and the jussive:

(1) In the 3 f.p. and 2 f.p., which never have mood-markers, the indicative and the jussive are identical.

(2) In the other forms, the indicative differs from the jussive only in having a mood-marker at the end, where the jussive has none.

(3) If the jussive form ends in a consonant, the corresponding indicative form ends in the mood-marker ـُ -u (jussive يَدْرُسْ , indicative يَدْرُسُ).

(4) If the jussive form ends in a long vowel, the indicative ends in the mood-marker نَ -na (jussive يَدْرُسوا , indicative يَدْرُسونَ).

(5) Or, to reverse the process, we can say: To change an indicative form to the jussive, cut off the mood-marker, if any. Thus تَدْرُسُ becomes تَدْرُسْ , تَدْرُسونَ becomes تَدْرُسوا , but تَدْرُسْنَ (which does not contain a mood-marker) remains تَدْرُسْنَ .

Now do Drills 1, 2, 3 and 4.

Drill 1. Written. Recognition.

Give the independent form of the pronoun subject of the following verbs and specify the mood (indicative or jussive) for each.

نـنقلُ	يـحملـنَ
يـسمحوا	يـتركون
تـنشرن	تـسألـوا
تـبحثـون	يـقرأنَ
نـسكنْ	تـكـتـبـون

Drill 2. (On tape) Conjugation.

Drill 3. (On tape) Conjugation: Question/answer.

Drill 4. (Also on tape) Transformation. Singular → Plural

Make the subject of the verb plural and make any other necessary changes. Ex.

'The president asks his ministers about the political situation.' ← الرئيس يسأل وزراءه عن الوضع السياسي

'The presidents ask their ministers about the political situation.' الرؤساء يسألون وزراءهم عن الوضع السياسى.

١ ـ المراسل يكتب لجريدة "المساء".

٢ ـ أسأل عن اخبار الاصدقاء.

٣ ـ تسكنُ فى بناء قريب. (أنتَ)

٤ ـ الطالبة تدرس في جامعة بغداد.

٥ ـ الرجل الاجنبي يسمع الاخبار .

٦ ـ تذكرين موعد الطائرة .

٧ ـ أبحث الوضع السياسي مع الوزير .

٨ ـ المرأة تعمل في الحكومة .

٩ ـ تكتب رسالة لزوجتك العزيزة .

١٠ ـ تحصلين على شهادة جامعية في السنة القادمة .

١١ ـ صديقي يبدأ دراسته في مصر .

2. <u>Negative of imperfect indicative: لا</u>

Verb forms in the imperfect indicative are made negative by the negative particle لا 'not' preceding the verb.

لا تَعْمَلُ أُخْتي في هٰذا الْمَكْتَبِ .	'My sister doesn't work in this office.'
أَلا تَكْتُبُ رَسائِلَ إِلى أَصْدِقائِكَ ؟	'Don't you write letters to your friends?'
فَريدٌ لا يَبْحَثُ عَنْ عَمَلٍ .	'Farid's not looking for work.'
كَريمَةُ لا تَدْرُسُ التّاريخَ .	'Karima is not studying history.'

Note (second example above) that the interrogative used before لا (as is usual before any negative) is أَ .

Now do Drills 5 and 6.

<u>Drill 5</u>. (Also on tape) Negation. <u>Ex.</u>

'Are you writing a letter to your friend now?' →	أتكتبين رسالة لصديقك الآن ؟ ←
'Aren't you writing a letter to your friend now?'	ألا تكتبين رسالة لصديقك الآن ؟

١ ـ تسكن في مدينة قريبة من بغداد .

٢ ـ أتقرأن جريدة " المساء " البيروتية ؟

٣ ـ ترجعون الى بلدكم بعد اجتماع اليوم .

٤ ـ أذهب لزيارة عائلتي كلَّ سنةٍ .

٥ ــ أيحضرون اجتماعا سياسيّا في القاهرة اليوم ؟

٦ ــ نبدأ اليوم دراسة الوضع السياسيّ في العالم العربي .

٧ ــ أيعمل في مطار بيروت ؟

٨ ــ أيكتبن كتبا عن المرأة العربية ؟

Drill 6. (Also on tape) Question-answer.

Answer the following questions in the negative. Ex.

'Does the author publish his books in Lebanon?' ⟶ هل ينشر الكاتب كتبه في لبنان ؟ ⟵

'No, he does not publish his books in Lebanon.' لا ، لا ينشر كتبه في لبنان .

١ ــ هل يبحث الوزراء الوضع السياسي ؟

٢ ــ هل تحضر المراسلات هذا الاجتماع ؟

٣ ــ هل تدرسون التاريخ الاسلامي ؟

٤ ــ هل تعمل سُعادُ في الحكومة المصرية ؟

٥ ــ هل يترك رئيس الشركة عائلته في لندن ؟

٦ ــ هل تذهب الى الشرق الاوسط هذه السنةَ ؟

٧ ــ هل يشرب الاساتذة قهوة في مكتب المدير ؟

٨ ــ هل تأكل الطالبات في المطعم ؟

٩ ــ هل تكتبين رسالة الى اختك الآن ؟

3. Vocative particle أَيُّها

In addition to يا there is another vocative particle أَيُّها (f. أَيَّتُها). While يا is usually followed by a proper name, a title, or an iḍāfa, أَيُّها is followed by a common noun with the definite article and in the nominative case. It is often used at the beginning of speeches and by radio and television announcers, and is often best left untranslated.

أَيُّها السَّيِّداتُ والسّادَةُ !	'Ladies and gentlemen!'
أَيُّها الطُّلابُ!	'Students!'

D. Comprehension passage — د - نُصوصٌ لِلْفَهْمِ

Read the following passage, then do Drill 7, which is based on it.

April — أنابوليس في ٩ نيسانَ ١٩٧٤

والدي العزيز :

one of our professors — ذهبت أمس مع استاذٍ مِنْ أساتذتِنا وبعض الطلاب لزيارة مدينة

morning — واشنطن . ذهبنا الى الكونغرس وحضرنا اجتماع الصَّباحِ ، واستمعنا

he said — للسناتور ريتشارد سميث . قالَ السناتور: "أيّها الاصدقاء: الوضع

bad — السياسي في العالم سَيِّءٌ" .

ذهبنا بعد ذلك الى مكتب جريدة " الواشنطن بوست " وهي جريدة مشهورة في امريكا . تنشر "الواشنطن بوست" بعض أخبار الشرق الاوسط. قابلنا رئيس المكتب وتحدثنا اليه .قالَ: " بعض الدول العربية لا تسمح للمراسلين الامريكيين بالاقامة فيها " .

ذهبنا كذلك الى المتحف الوطنيّ وشاهدنا بعض الآثار القديمة هناك ؛ أعجبنا المتحف ، وأعجبتنا آثاره .

بعد عودتي الى مدينة أنابوليس ، نشرت في جريدة الجامعة

details — تَفاصيلَ زيارتنا لواشنطن : تحدثت عن جمال المدينة ، وعن اجتماع

الكونغرس ، وعن جريدة "الواشنطن بوست".

سلامي الى والدتي وأختي .

ابنك المخلص

سليم

Drill 7.

Convert the above passage to a conversation between a student and his father, using the following outline as a guide:

١ - زيارة الكونغرس
٢ - زيارة مكتب " الواشنطن بوست " .
٣ - زيارة المتحف الوطنيّ في واشنطن .
٤ - العودة الى أنابوليس .
٥ - جريدة الجامعة .

E. General drills — هـ - التمارين العامّة

Drill 8. (Also on tape) Transformation. Perfect → Imperfect → Jussive

Ex.

'The president discussed this situation with the new ministers.' — بحث الرئيس هذا الوضع مع الوزراء الجدد . ←

'The president discusses this situation with the new ministers.' — يبحث الرئيس هذا الوضع مع الوزراء الجدد . ←

'The president did not discuss this situation with the new ministers.' — لم يبحث الرئيس هذا الوضع مع الوزراء الجدد .

١ - نشرت الجريدة أخبار المصانع والشركات .
٢ - الطلاب بحثوا الاخبار الجامعيّة .
٣ - المراسلات نقلن اخبار الحكومة العراقيّة .
٤ - سمح وقتنا بدراسة كل الدروس .
٥ - حضرتم اجتماع الوزراء الاجانب .

Drill 9. Written. Negation.

N Negate the following sentences, using لا , لم , or a form of ليس, as appropriate.

١ - أذلك الكاتب مشهور جدّا ؟

٢ ـ أكتب رسالة الى أختي .

٣ ـ عمل سامي في مصنع كبير .

٤ ـ هم مراسلو جريدة " المساء" .

٥ ـ أسمح الوقت بحضور الاجتماع الأوّل ؟

٦ ـ ألرؤساء يبحثون الوضع السياسيّ الحاضر .

٧ ـ أموعد طائرتك قريب ؟

٨ ـ كان لوح الصفّ قديما جدّا .

٩ ـ نسكن الآن في مدينة واشنطن .

١٠ ـ رجع حسين الى بلده بعد الحصول على شهادة .

١١ ـ السينما موجودة في شارع بعيد من هنا .

Drill 10. (On tape) Written. Dictation-translation.

Lesson Fifteen

الدرس الخامس عشر

أ – النصّ الاساسيّ

امتحان اللغة العربية

١ – وليم : هل أنت مستعدّة لامتحان اللغة العربية ؟

٢ – روث : أنا مستعدّة للامتحان في الدرس الاول والدرس الثاني والدرس الثالث وهي الدروس السهلة في الكتاب ٠

٣ – وليم : ماذا تدرسين اليوم ؟

٤ – روث : أدرس الجمل الاساسية من الدرس الرابع الى الدرس السابع ٠

٥ – وليم : وقواعد هذه الدروس كلها ؟

٦ – روث : أنا عادة أدرس القواعد بعد دراسة الجمل الاساسية ٠

٧ – وليم : هذه فكرة جميلة ٠ هل يشمل الامتحان محاضرة استاذنا الاخيرة ؟

٨ – روث : نعم ٠ هل أنت مستعد للامتحان يا وليم ؟

٩ – وليم : أنا مستعد للامتحان في معظم الدروس ٠

١٠ – روث : الى اللقاء في الساعة العاشرة والربع غدا صباحا ٠

١١ – وليم : الى اللقاء ٠

A. <u>Basic text</u>

The Arabic Exam

1. William: Are you ready for the exam in Arabic?
2. Ruth : I'm prepared for the exam in the first, second, and third lessons--they're the easy lessons in the book.
3. William: What are you studying today?
4. Ruth : I'm studying the basic sentences from the fourth lesson through the seventh.
5. William: And all the grammar of these lessons?
6. Ruth : I usually study the grammar after studying the basic sentences.
7. William: That's a good idea. Will the exam include our professor's last lecture?
8. Ruth : Yes. Are you ready for the exam, William?
9. William: I'm prepared for the exam on most of the lessons.
10. Ruth : So long--until a quarter past ten tomorrow morning.
11. William: So long.

B. <u>Vocabulary</u> ب ــ <u>المفردات</u>

أَلْخامِسَ عَشَرَ	the fifteenth
اِمْتِحانٌ ــ ات	examination
وِلْيم	William
روث	Ruth
مُسْتَعِدٌّ ــ ون (لِ)	ready, prepared (for)
أَلأَوَّلُ	the first
أَلثّاني	the second
أَلثّالِثُ	the third
سَهْلٌ	easy
أَلرّابِعُ	the fourth

أَلسّابِعُ	the seventh
قاعِدَةٌ – قَواعِدُ	rule (here: rule of grammar);(p.) grammar
عادَةً	usually
فِكْرَةٌ – فِكَرٌ	idea, thought; concept
فِكْرِيٌّ	(nisba of فِكْرَةٌ) mental, intellectual, speculative
جَميلٌ – ون	beautiful, handsome
شَمَلَ ، ـُ ، شَمِلَ ـَ	to include
أَخيرٌ	last, latest; final, recent; latter
مُعْظَمٌ	most; (in iḍāfa) most of
ساعَةٌ – ات	hour; watch
أَلْعاشِرُ	the tenth
رُبْعٌ – أَرْباعٌ	quarter
غَداً صَباحاً	tomorrow morning

Additional vocabulary

أَلْخامِسُ	the fifth	دَقيقَةٌ – دَقائِقُ	a minute
أَلسّادِسُ	the sixth	خَمْسُ دَقائِقَ	five minutes
أَلثّامِنُ	the eighth	نِصْفٌ – أَنْصافٌ	half
أَلتّاسِعُ	the ninth	ثُلْثٌ – أَثْلاثٌ	one-third
ظُهْرٌ	noon	إِلاَّ	but, except, less

C. Grammar and drills — ج – القواعد والتمارين

1. Ordinal numerals
2. Agreement: Non-human plurals
3. Noun with كُلٌّ and pronoun suffix
4. Telling time

1. Ordinal numerals

The ordinal numeral in Arabic is an adjective, and obeys the same rules of agreement as other adjectives. The ordinals will be presented here in order, according to their word patterns and patterns of combination.

a. "First". The form of this Arabic ordinal differs from all the rest: الأَوَّلُ is masculine singular and الأُولى is feminine singular, e.g., الدَّرْسُ الأَوَّلُ 'the first lesson', السَّاعَةُ الأُولى 'the first hour'.

b. "Second" through "tenth". These ordinals are illustrated below:

Masculine			Feminine		
الدَّرْسُ الثَّانِي		'the second lesson'	السَّاعَةُ الثَّانِيَةُ		'the second hour'
الثَّالِثُ	"	'the third lesson'	الثَّالِثَةُ	"	'the third hour'
الرَّابِعُ	"	'the fourth lesson'	الرَّابِعَةُ	"	'the fourth hour'
الْخامِسُ	"	'the fifth lesson'	الخامِسَةُ	"	'the fifth hour'
السَّادِسُ	"	'the sixth lesson'	السادِسَةُ	"	'the sixth hour'
السَّابِعُ	"	'the seventh lesson'	السابِعَةُ	"	'the seventh hour'
الثَّامِنُ	"	'the eighth lesson	الثامِنَةُ	"	'the eighth hour'
التَّاسِعُ	"	'the ninth lesson'	التاسِعَةُ	"	'the ninth hour'
العَاشِرُ	"	'the tenth lesson'	العاشِرَةُ	"	'the tenth hour'

The basic word pattern for this group of ordinals is FaaMiL, or perhaps al-FaaMiL, since the ordinals usually occur with definite nouns. The masculine singular ordinal الثَّانِي 'the second' differs in its inflection from the others in that الثاني is the form for both the nominative and genitive cases while the accusative is regular: الثانِيَ ; the f.s. الثانِيَةُ is regular in all three cases.

Now do Drill 1.

c. "Eleventh" through "nineteenth". These contain two elements, an ordinal plus عَشَرَ (f. عَشْرَةَ). Note the special form الْحادي in "eleventh", which is used instead of واحِدٌ in combinations of numbers:

أَلدَّرْسُ Masculine		السّاعَةُ	Feminine
الْحادِيَ عَشَرَ	'the eleventh lesson'	أَلسّاعَةُ الْحادِيَةَ عَشْرَةَ	'the eleventh hour'
" الثّانِيَ	'the twelfth lesson'	" الثّانِيَةَ "	'the twelfth hour'
" الثّالِثَ	'the thirteenth lesson'	" الثّالِثَةَ "	'the thirteenth hour'
" الرّابِعَ	'the fourteenth lesson'	" الرّابِعَةَ "	'the fourteenth hour'
" الخامِسَ	'the fifteenth lesson'	" الخامِسَةَ "	'the fifteenth hour'
" السّادِسَ	'the sixteenth lesson'	" السّادِسَةَ "	'the sixteenth hour'
" السّابِعَ	'the seventeenth lesson'	" السّابِعَةَ "	'the seventeenth hour'
" الثّامِنَ	'the eighteenth lesson'	" الثّامِنَةَ "	'the eighteenth hour'
" التّاسِعَ	'the nineteenth lesson'	" التّاسِعَةَ "	'the nineteenth hour'

These ordinals, "eleventh" through "nineteenth", are invariable in case: they are always in the accusative regardless of the case of the nouns they modify.

Now do Drill 2.

Drill 1. Chain drill.

'The first lesson is easy.'
'And the second?'

الدرس الاوّل سهل. والثاني ؟

'The second lesson is easy.'
'And the third?'

الدرس الثاني سهل • والثالث ؟

Repeat with: الجملة ، النصّ

Drill 2. Chain drill.

النص الحادي عشر قصير • هل النص الثاني عشر قصير كذلك ؟

نعم النص الثاني عشر قصير • هل النص الثالث عشر قصير كذلك ؟

Repeat with: الجملة

2. Agreement: Non-human plurals

Brief mention was made in 12.C.5 of the special rules of agreement applying to nouns which do not refer to human beings. Now we present these rules in more detail.

Certain classes of words in Arabic--adjectives, demonstratives, pronouns (and pronoun suffixes), verbs, and others--have both masculine and feminine singular forms, and masculine and feminine plural forms; in other words, they show distinctions of gender and number. Which of these forms is used in a given context depends on the particular noun to which the form refers or, in the case of a verb, which it has as its subject. It is the noun, then, which determines the form of the adjective, the pronoun, and so on; these words are said to agree with the noun. If the noun is singular, agreement is a simple matter: a masculine singular noun requires the masculine singular form of the agreeing words; a feminine singular noun, the feminine singular form (in all the following examples the words which must agree with their nouns--the agreeing words--are underlined):

أَلدَّرْسُ السَّهْلُ	(m.s.)	'the easy lesson'
أَلْجُمْلَةُ السَّهْلَةُ	(f.s.)	'the easy sentence'
أَلدَّرْسُ سَهْلٌ .	(m.s.)	'The lesson is easy.'
هُوَ سَهْلٌ .	(m.s.)	'It is easy.'
أَلْجُمْلَةُ سَهْلَةٌ .	(f.s.)	'The sentence is easy.'
هِيَ سَهْلَةٌ .	(f.s.)	'It is easy.'
رَجَعَ المُراسِلُ .	(m.s.)	'The reporter (m.) has returned.'
رَجَعَتِ الْمُراسِلَةُ .	(f.s.)	'The reporter (f.) has returned.'

If the noun is plural, however, a feature of meaning must be considered: Does its singular refer to one human being or not? If it does, then again a masculine

plural noun requires a <u>masculine plural</u> form of the agreeing words; a <u>feminine</u>
<u>plural</u> noun, the feminine plural form:

أَلْأَسَاتِذَةُ الْمَشْهُورُونَ	(m.p.)	'the famous professors'
أَلنِّسَاءُ اللُّبْنَانِيَّاتُ	(f.p.)	'the Lebanese women'
إِسْتَقْبَلَهُمُ الرَّئِيسُ.	(m.p.)	'The president received them.' (the professors)
إِسْتَقْبَلَهُنَّ الرَّئِيسُ.	(f.p.)	'The president received them.' (the women)
أَلْأَسَاتِذَةُ يَرْجِعُونَ غَدًا صَبَاحًا.	(m.p.)	'The professors are returning tomorrow morning.'
أَلنِّسَاءُ يَرْجِعْنَ غَدًا صَبَاحًا.	(f.p.)	'The women are returning tomorrow morning.'

But if the singular noun refers to anything other than a single human being--
an animal, group of people, inanimate object, abstraction, etc.--then any agreeing word is <u>feminine singular</u>, regardless of the gender of the noun in the sing.:

أَلْكُتُبُ الْجَدِيدَةُ	'the new books'
هٰذِهِ الدُّرُوسُ سَهْلَةٌ.	'These lessons are easy.'
أَلْمُدُنُ الْكَبِيرَةُ وَشَوَارِعُهَا	'the big cities and their streets'
لَيْسَتْ عَائِلَاتُهُمْ كَبِيرَةً.	'Their families are not big.'
أَلْإِمْتِحَانُ يَشْمَلُ الْجُمَلَ الْأَسَاسِيَّةَ.	'The exam includes the basic sentences.'
كَانَتِ الْأَقْلَامُ عَلَى الطَّاوِلَةِ.	'The pencils were on the table.'

(Remember also the special rule applying to verbs: if the verb precedes the
subject the verb is always singular. It agrees with its subject in gender,
however, according to the rules above.)

Shown below is a diagram summarizing the rules of agreement.

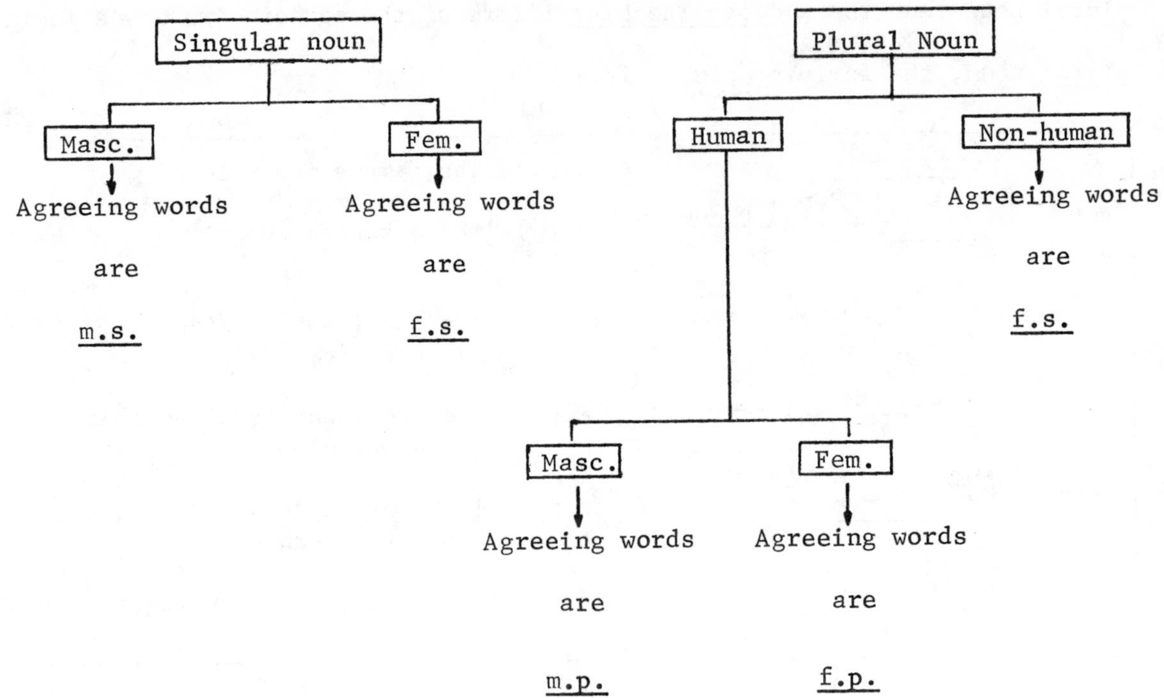

Whenever we say, then, that a certain form "agrees" with a noun in gender and number, the term should be understood to mean "agrees according to the rules" outlined above.

Now do Drills 3, 4, 5 and 6.

Drill 3. Written. Recognition.

Give the independent pronoun agreeing with each of the words below. Ex.

الطالبات ـ هنّ

الآثار ـ هي

الاساتذة	الامتحان	الاوّل
الدروس	القواعد	الوضع
الزوجات	المديرون	المصانع
المراسلون	المراسلات	الرؤساء
الساعات	الحكومة	الورقات

Drill 4. (On tape) Substitution/transformation.

Drill 5. Chain drill. Transformation: Singular ⟶ plural with كل .

'The lesson is easy.' ⟶ أ ـ الدرس سهل . ⟵

'Is the lesson easy? ⟶ ط١ ـ هل الدرس سهل ؟ ⟵

'All the lessons are easy.' ط٢ ـ كل الدروس سهلة .

١ ـ الطائرة جديدة .

٢ ـ الجملة قصيرة .

٣ ـ اللغة سهلة .

٤ ـ صديقه مخلص .

٥ ـ الرسالة بالعربيّة .

٦ ـ المدرسة ثانويّة .

٧ ـ الرجل ذاهب الى الاجتماع .

٨ ـ الاوتوبيس جديد .

Drill 6. (Also on tape) Transformation: Singular ⟶ plural.

Change the underlined word(s) in each of the sentences below to the plural, making all necessary changes in the rest of the sentence. Ex.

'Is this exam easy?' ⟶ أهذا الامتحان سهل ؟ ⟵

'Are these exams easy?' أهذه الامتحانات سهلة ؟

١ ـ اعجبني هذا الفيلم .

٢ ـ تسكن عائلتهم في مدينة لبنانية .

٣ ـ المدير ليس اجنبيا .

٤ ـ تابعت صديقتي دراستها فى مدرسة خاصّة .

٥ ـ مدير الشركة تحدث الى موظّفه الجديد .

٦ ـ يعمل صديقنا في متحف وطني .

٧ ـ الزائر الاجنبي سافر بالاوتوبيس .

3. Noun with كُلّ and pronoun suffix

There have previously been illustrations of an iḍāfa construction consisting of كُلّ plus a definite noun meaning 'the whole...' or 'all (of)...' (9.C.1), such as:

> كُلُّ الـدَّرْسِ 'the whole lesson, all of the lesson'
>
> كُلُّ الـمُوَظَّفِينَ 'all the employees'

There is another less usual construction, with the same meaning, in which the (definite) noun comes first, followed by كُلّ with an attached pronoun suffix referring to the noun and agreeing with it in gender and number. This construction is not an iḍāfa: here كُلّ is in apposition to the preceding noun, and is <u>in the same case</u>. Here are examples of both constructions:

> قَرَأْنَا كُلَّ الـدَّرْسِ.
>
> قَرَأْنَا الـدَّرْسَ كُلَّهُ.
>
> 'We read the whole lesson.'
>
> يَسْكُنُ كُلُّ الطُّلَّاب فِي بِنَاءٍ وَاحِدٍ.
>
> يَسْكُنُ الطُّلَّاب كُلُّهُمْ فِي بِنَاءٍ وَاحِدٍ.
>
> 'All the students live in one building.'
>
> لَمْ نَسْتَمِعْ لِكُلِّ الأَخْبَارِ.
>
> لَمْ نَسْتَمِعْ لِلأَخْبَارِ كُلِّهَا.
>
> 'We didn't listen to all the news.'
>
> كَتَبَ إِلَى كُلِّ أَصْدِقَائِهِ.
>
> كَتَبَ إِلَى أَصْدِقَائِهِ كُلِّهِمْ.
>
> 'He wrote to all his friends.'

If the noun is in an iḍāfa, كُلّ in the second kind of construction must follow the entire iḍāfa, as in the second sentence below:

> تَعَلَّمْنَا كُلَّ جُمَلِ الـدَّرْسِ.
>
> تَعَلَّمْنَا جُمَلَ الـدَّرْسِ كُلَّهَا.
>
> 'We learned all the sentences of the lesson.'

Now do Drill 7.

<u>Drill 7</u>. (Also on tape) كُلّ + pronoun. <u>Ex.</u>

'We studied the whole lesson.'

دَرَسْنَا كُلَّ الـدرس. ←

دَرَسْنَا الـدرس كله.

١ – يشمل الامتحان كل دروس الكتاب .

٢ – تحدث المدير الى كل موظفيه .

٣ – هل سافر الطلاب الى كل الدول العربية ؟

٤ – ذهبن لزيارة كل آثار لبنان .

٥ – قابل الرئيس كل الوزراء الجدد .

٦ – تسكن كل عائلتي في هذه المدينة .

٧ – كان كل المراسلين اجانب .

٨ – استمعنا الى كل المحاضرة .

٩ – نشرت الشركة كل الكتب .

١٠ – أعجبتني كل هذه الجمل .

١١ – ننقل اليكم كل الاخبار .

4. Telling time

The formulas used in referring to the time of day are illustrated below. Note that ordinal numbers are used in all cases except 'one o'clock,' which has the feminine form of the cardinal.

كَمِ السّاعَةُ ؟ ما السّاعَةُ ؟	'What time is it?'
السّاعَةُ الْواحِدَةُ .	'It's one o'clock.'
السّاعَةُ الثّانِيَةُ .	'It's two o'clock.'
السّاعَةُ الثالِثَةُ .	'It's three o'clock.'
السّاعَةُ الرّابِعَةُ وَالدَّقيقَةُ الْخامِسَةُ .	'It's 4:05.' 'It's five past four.'
السّاعَةُ الْخامِسَةُ وَالدَّقيقَةُ الْعاشِرَةُ .	'It's 5:10.' 'It's ten past five.'
السّاعَةُ السّادِسَةُ وَالرُّبْعُ .	'It's 6:15.' 'It's quarter past six.'

السّاعَةُ السّابِعَةُ وَالثُّلْثُ. — 'It's 7:20.' (lit., 'a third') / 'It's twenty past seven.'

السّاعَةُ الثّامِنَةُ وَالنِّصْفُ إلاّ خَمْسَ دَقائِقَ. — 'It's 8:25.'

السّاعَةُ التّاسِعَةُ وَالنِّصْفُ. — 'It's 9:30.'

السّاعَةُ العاشِرَةُ وَالنِّصْفُ وَخَمْسُ دَقائِقَ. — 'It's 10:35.'

الساعة الحادِيَةَ عَشْرَةَ إلاّ ثُلْثاً. — 'It's 10:40.' / 'It's twenty (lit., 'a third') to eleven.'

الساعة الثّانِيَةَ عَشْرَةَ إلاّ رُبْعاً. — 'It's 11:45.' / 'It's quarter to twelve.'

في أيِّ ساعَةٍ؟ ، مَتَى ؟ — 'At what time?'

في السّاعَةِ الرّابِعَةِ. — 'At four o'clock.'

في الساعَةِ الْخامِسَةِ وَالنِّصْفِ. — 'At 5:30.'

في السّاعَةِ الْحادِيَةَ عَشْرَةَ. — 'At eleven o'clock.'

In the first two sentences above, both meaning "What time is it?", السّاعَةُ is the subject of the sentence and therefore in the nominative case. كَمْ and ما function as predicates.

Now do Drills 8 and 9.

Drill 8. Telling time. الاستاذ: كم الساعة الآن ؟

a.	10:00	10:30
	10:05	10:40
	10:10	10:45
	10:15	11:00
	10:20	6:30
b.	8:15	12:20
	3:05	2:45
	7:40	1:00
	11:10	6:05

Drill 9. Written. Telling time.

Write the correct time for each of the clock-faces below.

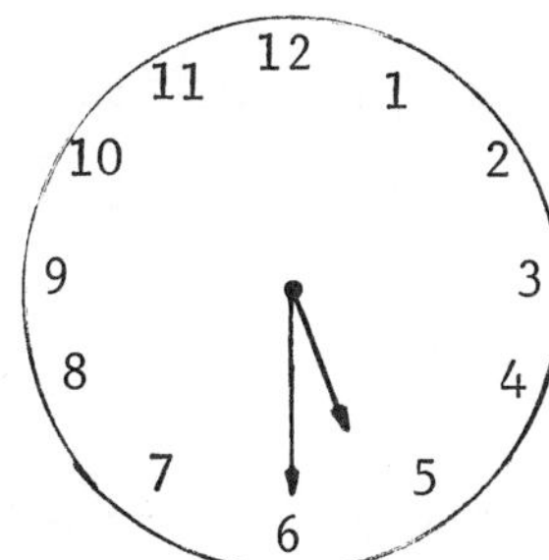

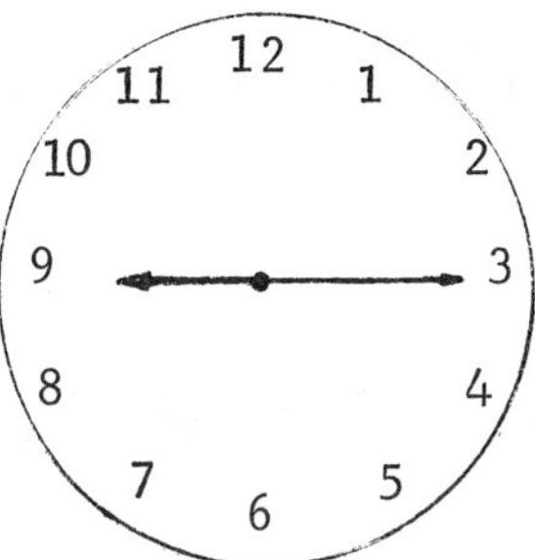

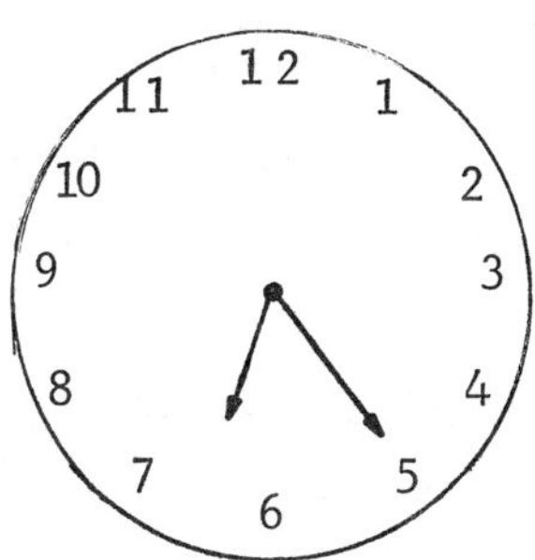

D. Comprehension passage   د - نصوص للفهم

Read the following passage; then do Drill 10.

شاهدت هذه السنةَ عددا من الافلام . بعض هذه الافلام عربية وبعضها امريكيـــــــة .

كان الفلم الاول فلما امريكيا عن استاذ جامعي . سافر هـــذا الرجل من بلده الى مصر لزيارة الآثار القديمة ودراسة شيء عن تاريخها .

وكان الفلم الثاني فلما مصريا بعنوان " المرأة المصرية فـي الجامعة " . تحدث هذا الفلم عن وضع المرأة في المدن المصرية .

الفلم الثالث تحدث عن عائلة امريكية . انتقلت هذه العائلـــة من مدينة الى مدينة فى امريكا وبحثت عن عمل .

الفلم الرابع فلم لبناني عن رجل من بيروت . اسم هذا الرجل سامي . ترك لبنان وسافر الى الْبَرازيلِ للعمل فى مصنع كبير هناك . (Brazil)
وفى البَرازيل قابل السيد سامي السيدة وداد وهي امرأة عراقية مـــن بغداد . اصدر سامي ووداد جريدة عربية هناك .

اعجبتني هذه الافلام كلها خاصّةً الفلم اللبناني . شاهدت هـــذا الفلم امس في الساعة التاسعة . (especially)

Drill 10. Written.   أسئلــــــــة

١ - عمّ كان الفلم الاوّل ؟

٢ - ما عنوان الفلم الثاني ؟

٣ - وما عنوان الفلم الثالث ؟ - هو فلم أمريكيّ معروف لستاينبيك .

٤ - عمّ تحدث الفلم الرابع ؟

٥ - متى شاهد الكاتب الفلم اللبنانيّ ؟

E. General drills　　　　هـ ـ التَّمارينُ الْعامَّةُ

Drill 11. (Also on tape) Transformation: Perfect → imperfect.

'He studied Islamic history.' → 　　درس التاريخ الاسلامي . ←

'He is studying Islamic history.' 　　يدرس التاريخ الاسلامي .

١ ـ الرؤساء بحثوا الوضع السياسي الحاضر .

٢ ـ ذهبنا الى الجامعة في الساعة العاشرة .

٣ ـ ماذا قرأتم هذه السنةَ ؟

٤ ـ عملت البنات في مصنع كبير .

٥ ـ ذكرت زيارتها القادمة في رسالتها .

٦ ـ حصل هذه السنة على البكالوريوس .

٧ ـ هل سكنتم في عمّان ؟

٨ ـ بدأ العمل في الساعة الثامنة .

٩ ـ شربت القهوة العربية في هذا المطعم مع بعض الاصدقاء .

١٠ ـ بحث حُسَيْنُ عن عمل في المدينة .

١١ ـ هل سمعتنّ الاخبار العالمية ؟

Drill 12. Written. Matching: Question-formation.

Form a question by combining one of the words in column (a) with the appropriate expression in column (b).

(a)	(b)
أين	فعلتنّ في دمشق ؟
من	ذهبوا الى تونس : للدراسة أم العمل ؟
لماذا	استقبلكم في المطار: صديقكم ؟

أ   جامعة الازهر : في بيروت أم في القاهرة ؟

متى   قابلتم الرئيس : أمس أم اليوم ؟

أيّ   هذه الكلمة اجنبية ؟

كم   استاذ أكل معكم فى المطعم : الاستاذ حسين ؟

هل   الجريدة مصريّة أم لبنانية ؟

ماذا   مراسلا لهذه الجريدة ؟

Drill 13. Translation.

1. Aren't you (m. pl.) prepared for the exam in the eighth lesson, the ninth lesson, and the tenth lesson?
2. No. Our exam doesn't include these lessons.
3. The time of the professor's lecture is (at) quarter past eleven tomorrow morning.

Lesson Sixteen

الدرس السادس عشر

أ - النصّ الاساسيّ

المرأة العربية الحديثة

للمرأة مكانة هامة في المجتمع العربي ، وللنساء في العالم العربي كثير من حقوق الرجال وواجباتهم : لهنّ حق الدراسة في الجامعات والحصول على الشهادات العالية وحضور الاجتماعات السياسية والعمل في الوظائف الحكومية • ومنهن المدرّسات والطبيبات والكاتبات• والنساء اليوم يقدّمن للمجتمع العربي الخدمات الكثيرة ويعملن على تقدّمه •

A. Basic Text

The Modern Arab Woman

Women have an important position in Arab society. Women in the Arab world have many of the rights and duties of men: they have the right to study in universities, to obtain advanced degrees, to attend political meetings, and to work in government positions; among them are teachers, doctors and writers. Women today render many services to Arab society and work for its advancement.

B. Vocabulary

ب - المفردات

أَلسّادِسَ عَشَرَ	the sixteenth
مَكانَةٌ - ات	position, status, prestige
هامٌّ	important
مُجْتَمَعٌ - ات	society
كَثيرٌ مِنْ	many of
حَقٌّ - حُقوقٌ	right (noun)

وَاجِبٌ ــ ات	duty
عَالِيَةٌ	(f.) high
حُضُورٌ	(verbal n.) attending, attendance (at)
وَظِيفَةٌ ــ وَظَائِفُ	position, post, job
مِنْ	(from) among
طَبِيبٌ ــ أَطِبَّاءُ	doctor, M.D.
يُقَدِّمْنَ لِ ، إِلَى	(f.p.) they present, offer, render (a service) (to)
خِدْمَةٌ ــ خَدَمَاتٌ	service
عَمِلَ ــَ ، عَمَلٌ على	to work for, toward (s.th.)
تَقَدُّمٌ	progress, advancement

Additional vocabulary

يُقَدِّمُونَ	(m.p.) they present, offer, render

C. __Grammar and notes__   ج ــ القواعد والتمارين

```
┌─────────────────────────────────────────────┐
│ 1.  Verbal nouns:  Meaning and function      │
│                                              │
│ 2.  Verbal nouns:  Form I                    │
│                                              │
│ 3.  Iḍāfa:  Expansion of first term          │
└─────────────────────────────────────────────┘
```

1. __Verbal nouns: Meaning and function__

A verbal noun is a noun which is (1) derived from a verb and (2) has the basic meaning "the act of doing" what the verb indicates. For example, دِرَاسَةٌ is derived from the verb دَرَسَ 'to study', and means "act of studying"; عَمَلٌ is derived from the verb عَمِلَ and means "act of working".

Verbal nouns correspond to English gerunds (nouns ending in _-ing_) such as 'studying', and to English infinitives such as 'to study.' Verbal nouns may also correspond to English nouns of a variety of other forms; for example all the nouns in the right-hand column below might serve as translations of an Arabic verbal noun in the appropriate context. The English nouns have various endings or are, in some cases, identical to the verb:

Verb	Noun
to arrive	arrival
to agree	agreement
to translate	translation
to rely	reliance
to work	work

Arabic verbal nouns function like other nouns: they serve as subjects or predicates of equational sentences, subjects or objects of verbs, objects of prepositions, either term of an iḍāfa, and so forth. Since the verbal noun is an abstraction--the naming of an action--it normally has the definite article unless it is the first term of an iḍāfa. The verbal noun as an abstraction has no plural. (On page 312 verbal nouns with concrete meaning are treated.)Examples:

a. As subject of equational sentence

اَلْعَمَلُ فِي هٰذا الْمَصْنَعِ سَهْلٌ.	'Working in this factory is easy.'

b. As subject of verb

بَدَأَ بَحْثُ الْمَوْضوعِ أَمْسِ.	'The discussion of the subject began yesterday.'

c. As object of verb

بَدَأُوا عَوْدَتَهُمْ الى الشَّرْقِ الأَوْسَطِ.	'They began their return to the Middle East.'

d. As object of preposition

رَجَعَتْ بَعْدَ الْحُصولِ عَلى شَهادةٍ.	'She returned after obtaining a degree.'

The preposition لِـ with a verbal noun takes on the meaning of "in order to, for the purpose of". The best translation is usually "in order to" or "to" plus an infinitive. Examples:

> سافَرَ الى هُناكَ لِلْحُصُولِ على شَهادَةٍ. 'He went there to get a degree.'
>
> رَجَعَتْ الى بَلَدِها لِلْعَمَلِ هُناكَ. 'She returned to her country in order to work there.'

e. <u>As second term of iḍāfa</u>

> لِلْمَرْأَةِ الْمِصْرِيَّةِ حَقُّ الْعَمَلِ فِـــي الْحُكُومةِ. 'The Egyptian woman has the right to work in the government.'

f. <u>As first term of iḍāfa</u>

When a verbal noun is the first term of an iḍāfa, the second term is, as usual, always genitive in case, but serves one of two functions:

(1) The second term may be the <u>actor</u>--the person or thing that in reality performs the action referred to by the verbal noun. Compare the following items. (The first has a subject and a verb. In the second there is a verbal noun corresponding to the verb of the first sentence, and serving as the first term of an iḍāfa. The second term of that iḍāfa corresponds to the subject of the first sentence, and is the actor.)

> وَصَلَ الرَّئِيسُ صَباحَ الْيَوْمِ. 'The president arrived this morning.'
>
> سَأَلُوني عَنْ وُصُولِ الرَّئِيسِ. 'They asked me about the arrival of the president.'

In the first sentence, الرَّئِيسُ is the subject of a verb (therefore nominative case) and <u>actor</u>. In the second, الرَّئِيسِ is the second term of an <u>iḍāfa</u> (therefore genitive case) and <u>actor</u>. In both sentences it was the <u>president</u> who did the arriving. If the verbal noun is from an intransitive verb (one that does not take an object), as above, the second term <u>must be</u> the actor.

(2) If the verbal noun is from a transitive verb, the second term may be either the actor or the <u>goal</u>--that is, the recipient, the person or thing

that <u>undergoes the action.</u> We will illustrate the goal function first:

حَضَرَتِ الاِجْتِماعَ.	'She attended the meeting.'
رَجَعَتْ إلى مَكْتَبِها بَعْدَ حُضورِ الاِجْتِماعِ.	'She returned to her office after attending the meeting.'

In the first sentence, أُلاِجْتِماعَ is the object of a verb (therefore accusative case) and <u>goal</u>. In the second, الاِجْتِماعِ is the second term of an iḍāfa (therefore genitive case) and <u>goal</u>. In both sentences the thing that someone attended was the <u>meeting</u>.

The second term may also be the actor:

دَرَّسَ الأُسْتاذُ سامي هُناكَ.	'Professor Sami taught there.'
أَعْجَبَني تَدْريسُ الأُسْتاذِ سامي.	'I liked Professor Sami's teaching.'

It is also possible to express both the actor and the goal of a verbal noun:

دَرَّسَ الأُسْتاذُ التّاريخَ.	'The professor taught history.'
أَعْجَبَني تَدْريسُ الأُستاذِ التّاريخَ.	'I liked the professor's teaching of history.'

In such cases the <u>actor</u> is expressed by the second term of the iḍāfa (genitive case), while the goal is expressed as a noun (not part of the iḍāfa) <u>in the accusative case</u>--here serving as the object of the verbal noun just as it is the object of the verb in the first sentence above.

A common variation of this last construction is one in which the goal is preceded by the preposition لِ (and is therefore in the genitive case):

أَعْجَبَني تَدْريسُ الأُستاذِ لِلتّاريخِ.	'I liked the professor's teaching of history.'

All these iḍāfa constructions of verbal noun plus second term are paralleled by constructions consisting of verbal noun plus attached pronoun suffix, the latter serving as actor or goal.

Actor	
سَأَلوني عَنْ وُصولِهِ .	'They asked me about his arrival.'
أَعْجَبَني تَدْريسُهُ .	'I liked his teaching.'
أَعْجَبَني تَدْريسُهُ التّاريخَ .	'I liked his teaching of history.'
Goal	
رَجَعَتْ بَعْدَ حُضورِهِ .	'She returned after attending it.' (e.g., the meeting).
أَعْجَبَني تَدْريسُهُ لَهُ .	'I liked his teaching of it.' (e.g., history).

Following are additional examples of all these constructions.

هَلْ قَرَأْتَ عَنْ عَوْدَةِ الرَّئيسِ إِلى أَمْريكا ؟	'Have you read about the president's returning to America?'
دَرَسْنا عَنْ بِنائِهِمْ مُدُنًا جَديدَةً .	'We studied about their building new cities.'
كَتَبْتُ رِسالَةً بَعْدَ زِيارَتي { الْمَتْحَفَ. / لِلْمَتْحَفِ. }	'I wrote a letter after my visiting the museum.'

If the verbal noun is followed only by a noun serving as goal it may be translated in either an active or a passive construction, e.g.

لَمْ يَسْمَحوا بِبِناءِ مَتْحَفٍ جَديدٍ .	'They did not allow the construction of a new museum.' or 'They did not allow a new museum to be built.'

In addition to their abstract meaning "act of doing something", many verbal nouns have developed concrete meanings. Thus بِناءٌ means not only 'building' (something) but also 'a building'. In their concrete meanings verbal nouns are like any noun; they can be indefinite, and they can be made plural. Other examples of verbal nouns which have become concretized (with plurals):

'study'	دِراسَةٌ	دِراساتٌ
'a visit'	زِيارَةٌ	زِياراتٌ
'a job'	عَمَلٌ	أَعْمالٌ

اِجْتِماعاتٌ	اِجْتِماعٌ	'a meeting'
تَفاصيلُ ، تَفْصيلاتٌ	تفصيل	'detail, details'
اِمْتِحاناتٌ	اِمْتِحانٌ	'an examination'
مَحاضَراتٌ	مُحاضَرَةٌ	'a lecture'

Now do Drills 1 and 2.

Drill 1. Written. Recognition.

Underline the verbal nouns in the following sentences and vocalize them:

١ – ليست الدراسة في الجامعة سهلة .

٢ – ذهبوا الى ديترويت للعمل في مصنع سيارات .

٣ – للمرأة العربية حق الحصول على الشهادات العالية .

٤ – كتب المراسل عن زيارة الرئيس لدمشق .

٥ – سافرت الى مصر لحضور الاجتماع .

٦ – بحث الوزراء بناء المصريين مصانع جديدة .

٧ – أعجبني عمله على تقدّم بلده .

٨ – بحثوا دراسة اللغات الاجنبية في المدارس الثانوية .

Drill 2. Written. Composition.

Use each of the following verbal nouns in a sentence.

الوصول – العمل – الحصول علي – الزيارة

2. Verbal nouns: Form I

The verbal nouns of derived verbs are almost entirely predictable in form; these will be introduced later. Verbal nouns of Form I, on the other hand, fall into a large number of different patterns. The most common of these are illustrated in the list which follows. This list includes the Form I verbal nouns that have occurred so far, along with the corresponding verbs (unfamiliar verbs are included in parentheses for your information only). Also listed are verbal nouns for all other Form I verbs that have occurred so far.

Verbal Noun

a. Pattern FaML

تَرْكٌ	'leaving'	تَرَكَ	'to leave'
بَحْثٌ	'discussion'	بَحَثَ	'to discuss
بَحْثٌ عَنْ	'looking for'	بَحَثَ عَنْ	'to look for'
نَقْلٌ	'transmitting'	نَقَلَ	'to transmit'
حَمْدٌ	'praising, praise'	(حَمِدَ	'to praise')
نَشْرٌ	'publication'	نَشَرَ	'to publish'
بَدْءٌ	'beginning'	بَدَأَ	'to begin'
أَكْلٌ	'eating'	أَكَلَ	'to eat'
شَمْلٌ	'inclusion'	شَمَلَ	'to include'

b. Pattern FiML

فِعْلٌ	'doing, action'	فَعَلَ	'to do'
ذِكْرٌ	'mentioning'	ذَكَرَ	'to mention'

c. Pattern FuML

شُرْبٌ	'drinking'	شَرِبَ	'to drink'
شُكْرٌ	'thanking'	(شَكَرَ	'to thank')

d. Patterns FaMLa(t), FiMLa(t), FuMLa(t)

عَوْدَةٌ	'returning'	(عادَ	'to return')
خِدْمَةٌ	'serving, service'	(خَدَمَ	'to serve')

e. Pattern FaMaL

عَمَلٌ	'work'	عَمِلَ	'to work'
سَكَنٌ	'living,residence'	سَكَنَ	'to live, reside'

f. Pattern FaMaaL

ذَهابٌ	'going'	ذَهَبَ	'to go'
سَماعٌ	'hearing'	سَمِعَ	'to hear'
سَماحٌ بِـ	'permitting'	سَمَحَ بِـ	'to permit'

g. Pattern FaMaaLa(t)

سَلامَةٌ	'safety'	(سَلِمَ	'to be safe')

شَهَادَة 'testifying; certificate'   (شَهِدَ 'to testify')

h. Pattern FiMaaL

بِنَاءٌ 'building'   (بَنَى 'to build')

لِقَاءٌ 'meeting'   (لَقِيَ 'to meet')

i. Pattern FiMaaLa(t)

دِرَاسَةٌ 'studying'   دَرَسَ 'to study'

زِيَارَةٌ 'visiting'   (زَارَ 'to visit')

كِتَابَةٌ 'writing'   كَتَبَ 'to write'

قِرَاءَةٌ 'reading'   قَرَأَ 'to read'

j. Pattern FuMaaL

سُؤَالٌ 'asking; question'   سَأَلَ 'to ask'

k. Pattern FuMuuL (these are generally from intransitive verbs of motion)

وُصُولٌ 'arrival'   (وَصَلَ 'to arrive')

حُضُورٌ 'attending'   حَضَرَ 'to attend'

حُضُورٌ إِلَى 'coming (to)'   حَضَرَ إِلَى 'to come (to)'

رُجُوعٌ 'returning'   رَجَعَ 'to return'

حُصُولٌ عَلَى 'obtaining'   حَصَلَ عَلَى 'to obtain'

شُمُولٌ 'inclusion'   شَمَلَ 'to include'

There are other, less common, verbal noun patterns. Some verbs, like شَمَلَ above, have more than one verbal noun, in many cases associated with different meanings of the verb. It is necessary to learn the verbal noun together with its verb. You are now expected to know the verbal nouns given above; and from now on this information will be given in the vocabularies for all Form I verbs. Now do Drills 3, 4, 5 and 6.

Drill 3. (On tape) Repetition: Verbal nouns.

Drill 4. (On tape) Production: Verbal nouns.

Drill 5. (Also on tape) Substitution. Ex.

a. 'She went to New York to attend the meeting.' — سافرت الى نيويورك لحضور الاجتماع .

١ ــ نشرت الكتاب .

٢ ــ عملت في مصنع .

٣ ــ سكنت هناك .

٤ ــ حصلت على شهادة .

٥ ــ درست في جامعة نيويورك .

b. 'I returned after drinking coffee.' — رجعت بعد شرب القهوة .

١ ــ ابحث الوضع السياسي .

٢ ــ اعمل في مصنع الطائرات .

٣ ــ اذهب الى المسرح .

٤ ــ اقرأ جرائد عربية .

٥ ــ اكتب رسائل لمعظم اصدقائي .

٦ ــ احضر اجتماعات هامة .

Drill 6. Transformation.

Combine the following sentences into one, using the verbal noun. Ex.

'He studied history.' — درس التاريخ . +

'He returned to Egypt after that.' → رجع الى مصر بعد ذلك .

'He returned to Egypt after studying history.' — رجع الى مصر بعد دراسة التاريخ .

١ ــ حضر الاجتماع . رجع الى بلده بعد ذلك .

٢ ــ كتب كتابا عن السعوديّة . ذهب الى الرياض قبل ذلك .

٣ ــ بحث الوزراء الوضع السياسيّ . سافر الوزراء بعد ذلك .

٤ ــ حصل كريم على شهادة في التاريخ . درس كريم في جامعة بغداد بعد ذلك .

٥ ــ ذهب الى المتحف الوطني . قرأ كتابا عن الآثار التاريخية قبل ذلك .

3. Idāfa: Expansion of the first term

Note the following Arabic construction taken from the Basic Text:

حُقوقُ الرِّجالِ وَواجِباتُهُمْ	'the rights and duties of men'

This illustrates the way in which the first term of an iḍāfa (here حُقوق) may be expanded: the additional item (here واجِبات) follows the entire iḍāfa, and has attached to it a pronoun suffix referring to the second term (here الرِجال). The literal translation of this example is: 'the rights of men and their duties'.

Another way of looking at a construction of this type is to consider it as a combination of two simple iḍāfas.

حُقوقُ الرِجالِ	'The rights of men'
وَواجِباتُ الرِّجالِ	'(and) the duties of men'

When the two are combined, the second occurrence of the noun is replaced by the appropriate pronoun suffix:

حُقوقُ الرِجالِ وَواجِباتُهُمْ	'the rights and duties of men'

Further examples:

حُقوقُ النِساءِ وَواجِباتُهُنَّ	'the rights and duties of women'
والِدُ سامي وَأُخْتُهُ	'Sami's father and sister'
مَدارِسُ بَيْروتَ وَجامِعاتُها	'the schools and universities of Beirut'

Drill 7. (Also on tape) Transformation. Ex.

'Women have some of the rights of men and (some of) the duties of men.' ⟶ للنساء بعض حقوق الرجال وواجبات الرجال . ⟵

'Women have some of the rights and duties of men.' للنساء بعض حقوق الرجال وواجباتهم .

١ ـ قابل الرئيس طلاب الجامعة + اساتذة الجامعة في الساعة العاشرة والنصف .

٢ ـ اعجبني جمال بلدكم + آثار بلدكم .

٣ ـ درست جمل الدرس + قواعد الدرس .

٤ ـ تعمل النساء في مصانع البلد + شركات البلد .

٥ ـ استقبلوا وزراء العراق + رئيس العراق .

٦ ـ طاولات الصف + كراسي الصف جديدة .

D. Comprehension passage　　　　د ـ نصوص للفهم

Read the following passage; then do Drill 8.

تحدثت جريدة قاهرية مَعْروفَةٌ عن الاجتماع الثاني لِمُؤْتَمَرِ الاطباء المصريين . قالت الجريدة : ـ

well-known; conference

حضر الاجتماع عدد كبير من الأطباء المصريين ، وحضره كذلك مراسلون مصريون وأجانب . وبحث الأطباء في اجتماعهم الثاني حقوق الأطباء وواجباتهم . تحدث في الاجتماع عدد من الأطباء المشهورين في مصر منهم الدكتور عَلِيّ حَسَنٌ ، وهو استاذ في جامعة القاهرة . ذكر الدكتور علي زيارته لامريكا ودراسته لوضع الأطباء فيها ، وذكر كذلك حضوره اجتماعا للأطباء في فرنسا هذه السنةَ .

وقالت الجريدة : " الأطباء يقدمون للمجتمع خدمات هامة ولُكنْ لهم كذلك حقوقٌ ، وبحث هذه الحقوق من واجبات المُؤْتَمَرِ " .

Drill 8. Written. Questions/answers.　　　　أَسْئِلَةٌ

١ ـ هل الجريدة لبنانية ؟

٢ ـ عن أيّ اجتماع تحدثت الجريدة ؟

٣ ـ كم طبيبا حضر الاجتماع؟

٤ ـ ماذا بحث الأطباء في اجتماعهم الثاني ؟

٥ ـ من هو الدكتور علي حسن ؟ عن أيّ شيء تحدث في الاجتماع ؟

E. General drills   هـ ـ التمارين العامة

Drill 9. Negation. Negate the following sentences.

١ ـ صديقي مستعدّ للامتحان.
٢ ـ تعمل اخته في مكتبة الجامعة
٣ ـ هذه فكرة جميلة .
٤ ـ سكنت في تلك المدينة .
٥ ـ كانوا موظفين في مكتب حكومي.
٦ ـ الزوّار من الشرق الاوسط.
٧ ـ هذه الدروس هامّة جدا .
٨ ـ حصلت على الماجستير.
٩ ـ يكتب رسالة الآن .
١٠ ـ معظم هذه الكلمات قصيرة .

Drill 10. Chain drill. Review:

'I talked to some of the students.' →   ← تحدّثت الى بعض الطلاب .

'I talked to all the students.' →   ← تحدّثت الى كل الطلاب.

'I talked to all the students.'   تحدّثت الى الطلاب كلهم.

١ ـ بعض الاصدقاء
٢ ـ بعض المراسلات
٣ ـ بعض الاطباء
٤ ـ بعض الكاتبات
٥ ـ بعض النساء
٦ ـ بعض الرجال
٧ ـ بعض السكرتيرات
٨ ـ بعض المراسلين

Drill 11. Written. Substitution - translation.

'I spoke to them about publishing the new book.'   تحدّثت اليهم عن نشر الكتاب الجديد .

the president's return from the Middle East

the building of the national airport

the ministers' discussion of the political situation

women's working for the progress of Arab society

the foreign directors' visiting the Egyptian company

Drill 12. Written. Transformation: Singular → plural.

Make the underlined words plural and make any other necessary changes.

١ ـ عملت الشركة على بناء المدرسة الجديدة .

٢ ـ درست قواعد الدرس الجديد .

٣ ـ المرأة العربية تعمل على تقدم المجتمع العربي .

٤ ـ مطعم المطار كبير جدّاً .

٥ ـ كان المصنع حديثا .

٦ ـ الطبيبة تقدم الخدمات الكثيرة للمجتمع اللبنانيّ.

٧ ـ اعجبني الامتحان الاخير .

٨ ـ الدرس يشمل عادة قراءات كثيرة .

Drill 13. Written. Dictionary.

Write the root and pattern of each of the following words, then look each one up in the dictionary to find the meaning.

مَحْكَمَةٌ   هَنْدَسَةٌ   نِعْمَةٌ

سَفَرٌ   مَجْلِسٌ   وَداعٌ

جانِبٌ   خُروجٌ   مَناعَةٌ

عَريضٌ   وِزارَةٌ   مَنْحٌ

Lesson Seventeen

الدرس السابع عشر

أ - النص الاساسيّ

مَراحِلُ التعليم في العالم العربي

stages

primary; preparatory

مَراحِلُ التعليم في العالم العربيّ هي الاِبْتِدائِيَّةُ والإِعْدادِيَّةُ والثانويّة والجامعيّة . تقرّر وزارات التربية والتعليم مناهج التعليم وتحدّد مواعيد الامتحانات وتعيّن المعلّمين والمعلّمات في المدارس الحكوميّة . تدرّس المدارس والجامعات في العالم العربيّ الفرنسيّة والانجليزيّة والعربيّة الى جانب المواضيع الاخرى .

ومعظم المدارس والجامعات في العالم العربيّ حكوميّة ،لكنْ هناك عدد من المدارس والجامعات الخاصّة : بعضها اجنبيّة وبعضها عربيّة .

Europe

تخرّج الجامعات العربيّة عددا كبيرا من الطلّاب والطالبات كلّ سنة ، وبعض هؤلاء يذهبون الى اوروبّا أو امريكا للحصول على الشهادات العالية ، ثم يرجعون للتدريس في الجامعات العربيّة أو للعمل في الشركات أو الحكومة .

أسئلة

١ - ماهي مراحل التعليم في البلاد العربيّة ؟

٢ - وماهي مراحل التعليم في بلدك ؟

٣ - ماهي واجبات وزارات التربية والتعليم في العالم العربيّ ؟

٤ - أيّ اللغات تدرّس المدارس والجامعات العربيّة ؟

٥ - وأنت ؟ أيّ مواضيع تدرس الآن ؟

٦ - هل كل المدارس والجامعات في العالم العربيّ حكوميّة ؟

٧ - هل درست في مدرسة حكوميّة ؟

A. Basic text

Stages of Education in the Arab World

The stages of education in the Arab world are: primary, preparatory (roughly, junior high), secondary, (roughly, high school) and university. The ministries of education determine the programs of instruction, set the examination times, and appoint the teachers (m. and f.) in the public schools. Schools and universities in the Arab world teach French, English, and Arabic, along with other subjects. Most of the schools and universities in the Arab world are government-run but there are a number of private schools and universities, some foreign and some Arab.

Arab universities graduate a large number of students (m. and f.) each year. Some of these go to Europe or America to obtain advanced degrees, then return to teach in Arab universities or to work in companies or in the government.

B. Vocabulary ب – المفردات

تَعْلِيمٌ	education; teaching
تُقَرِّرُ	she, it decides, determines (something) (+ verbal noun) decides to (do something)
وِزارَةٌ – ات	ministry
تَرْبِيَةٌ	education; upbringing (nisba = تَرْبَوِيٌّ)
مَنْهَجٌ – مَناهِجُ	program
مَنْهَجُ التَّعْلِيمِ	program of study, curriculum
تُحَدِّدُ	she, it defines, sets (a date, time, etc.)
تُعَيِّنُ	she, it appoints (s.o. as s.th.)

مُعَلِّمٌ – ون	teacher
إِلى جانِبِ	in addition to, besides, along with
مَوْضوعٌ – مَواضيعُ	subject, topic
آخَرُ – ون	other; another
أُخْرى – أُخْرَياتٌ	(f.) other; another
هُناكَ	there is, there are
تُخَرِّجُ	she, it graduates (s.o.)
هٰؤُلاءِ	(m.p., f.p.) these, those
أُورُوبّا ، أُورُبّا ، أُرُوبّا	Europe
تَدْريسٌ	teaching, instruction
أَوْ	or

Additional vocabulary

أُولٰئِكَ	(m. or f.p.) those
أَلْجَزائِرُ	Algeria; Algiers
صَباحٌ	morning
مَساءٌ – أَمْساءٌ ، أَمْسِيّاتٌ	evening
يَوْمٌ – أَيّامٌ	day
غَدٌ ، أَلْغَدُ	the morrow, the next day
عَلَّمَ	to teach, instruct

C. Grammar and notes — ج – القواعد والتمارين

1. "There is/there are": هُناكَ
2. Agreement of بَعْضٌ 'some'
3. Demonstratives: The plurals هٰؤُلاءِ and أُولٰئِكَ
4. Accusative case: Adverbials of time
5. Form II verbs and verbal nouns

1. "There is/there are":   هُنَاكَ

The English phrase "there is" or "there are", in the sense not of pointing to the location of something but of expressing general existence ("there exist(s)") is rendered in Arabic by the adverb   هُنَاكَ   'there' at the beginning of an equational sentence. In such sentences, هُنَاكَ is the predicate; the following noun, which must be indefinite, is the subject:

هُنَاكَ عَدَدٌ مِنَ الْمَدَارِسِ الْخَاصَّةِ .	'There are a number of private schools.'
هَلْ هُنَاكَ جَامِعَةٌ إِسْلَامِيَّةٌ أَمْرِيكِيَّةٌ ؟	'Is there an American Islamic University?'

2. Agreement of   بَعْضٌ   'some'

The word   بَعْضٌ   'some' is a masculine singular noun. It occurs most frequently as the first term of an iḍāfa or with a pronoun suffix. Verb agreement may then also be masculine singular, especially when the verb precedes and the term following بَعْضٌ refers to human beings:

يَحْضُرُ بَعْضُ الرِّجَالِ الْاجْتِمَاعَ كُلَّ يَوْمٍ .	'Some of the men attend the meeting every day.'
يَحْضُرُ بَعْضُ النِّسَاءِ الْاجْتِمَاعَ كُلَّ يَوْمٍ .	'Some of the women attend the meeting every day.'

In other cases, however, it is very common for verb or adjective agreement to be based on the gender and number of the term following بَعْضٌ --that is, on the "logical subject"--rather than on the word بَعْضٌ , which is the "grammatical subject", (that is, the word that has the nominative case ending).

Examples:

بَعْضُ الْمُوَظَّفِينَ يَعْمَلُونَ فِي هَذَا الْمَكْتَبِ .	'Some of the employees work in this office.'
بَعْضُ الطَّبِيبَاتِ يُدَرِّسْنَ هُنَا .	'Some of the doctors (f.) teach here.'

بَعْضُهُنَّ لُبْنانِيّاتٌ .	'Some of them (the female doctors) are Lebanese.'
بَعْضُ هٰؤُلاءِ يَذْهَبُونَ إِلى أُورُوبّا .	'Some of these (the students) go to Europe.'
تَشْمَلُ بَعْضُ الدُّرُوسِ جُمَلاً قَصِيرَةً .	'Some of the lessons include short sentences.'
بَعْضُها أَجْنَبِيَّةٌ .	'Some of them (the schools) are foreign.'

Now do Drill 1.

Drill 1. Completion. Agreement with بَعْضٌ .

Supply the correct form of the word in parentheses.

١ ـ (ذهب) بعض الوزراء الى الاجتماع السياسي امس .

٢ ـ بعض هذه المواضيع (سهل) .

٣ ـ (قدّم) بعض النساء خدمات هامة .

٤ ـ بعض الرجال (يبحث) الوضع السياسي .

٥ ـ (اعجبني) بعض الدروس (الاخير) .

٦ ـ (حضر) بعض الطبيبات (المصري) المحاضرة .

٧ ـ بعض الكتب (يشمل) فِكَرا جميلة .

٨ ـ (ينقل) بعض المراسلين اخبار اليوم .

٩ ـ بعض الموظفات (يعمل) في وظائف حكومية .

١٠ ـ بعض قواعد اللغة (هام) جدّا .

3. Demonstratives: The Plurals هٰؤُلاءِ and أُولٰئِكَ

The plural demonstrative هٰؤُلاءِ 'these,those' refers only to human beings, whether male or female; it is the plural of هٰذا 'this' (m.s.) and of هٰذِهِ 'this'(f.s.). It is invariable in form. Examples:

Singular		Plural	
هٰذا الطّالِبُ	'this student'	هٰؤُلاءِ الطُّلاّبُ	'these students'
هٰذِهِ الطّالِبَةُ	'this student'	هٰؤُلاءِ الطّالِباتُ	'these students'

أُولٰئِكَ 'those', similarly, is the plural of ذٰلِكَ 'that' (m.s.) and of تِلْكَ 'that' (f.s.), and refers only to human beings, as in أُولٰئِكَ الطُّلاّبُ 'those students'.

The following chart lists these forms:

	Singular	Plural
M	هٰذا	هٰؤُلاءِ
F	هٰذِهِ	
M	ذٰلِكَ	أُولٰئِكَ
F	تِلْكَ	

هٰؤُلاءِ and أُولٰئِكَ are invariable in form, although the following noun is inflected for case. Examples:

Nom.	مَتى رَجَعَ هٰؤُلاءِ الْمُدَرِّسونَ إِلى بَلَدِهِمْ ؟	'When did these teachers return to their country?'
Gen.	لَيْسَتْ مُحاضَراتُ هٰؤُلاءِ الأَساتِذَةِ هامَّةً جِدًّا .	'These professors' lectures are not very important.'
Acc.	سَأَلْتُ أُولٰئِكَ الْمُراسِلينَ عَنِ الْعَمَلِ في جَريدَتِهِمْ .	'I asked those reporters about working on their newspaper.'

Now do Drills 2 and 3.

Drill 2. Written. Completion.

Provide the correct form of the demonstrative in the sentences below.

١ ـ (هذا) الاساتذة مغربيّون و (ذلك) جزائريون .

٢ ـ هل شاهدت كل (هذا) الافلام يا سميرة ؟

٣ ـ (هذا) المرأة صديقتي و (ذلك) ليست صديقتي .

٤ _ استقبل الرئيس (هذا) الوزراء في الساعة التاسعة والدقيقة العاشرة .

٥ _ أكُلّ (ذلك) النساء استاذات جامعيّات ؟

٦ _ (هذا) الجمل الاساسية سهلة جدّا .

٧ _ تعيّن الوزارة (ذلك) الموظفين .

٨ _ هل شمل الامتحان قواعد (هذا) الدروس كلها ؟

٩ _ هل أخبرك باسماء (هذا) الاساتذة الجدد ؟

Drill 3. (On tape) Substitution-transformation: Demonstrative-singular → plural.

4. Accusative case: Adverbials of time

In both English and Arabic, prepositional phrases may function as adverbial modifiers in a sentence, very commonly expressing the time of an action--that is, answering the question "When?". Examples:

في الصَّباحِ	'in the morning'
في الْمَساءِ	'in the evening'
في السّاعَةِ الْعاشِرَةِ	'at ten o'clock'
في هٰذا الْيَوْمِ	'on this day'
في الْغَدِ	'on the morrow, tomorrow'

In Arabic, the same kind of adverbial function may also be served by <u>a noun in the accusative case</u>, without any preposition:

صَباحًا	'mornings, in the morning'
مَساءً	'evenings, in the evenings'
ساعَةَ الْاِمْتِحانِ	'at the hour/time of the examination'

$$\text{أَلْـيَوْمَ} \quad \text{'today'}$$

$$\text{أَلْـمَسَاءَ} \quad \text{'this evening'}$$

$$\text{غَدًا} \quad \text{'tomorrow'}$$

With صَبَاحٌ 'morning' and مَسَاءٌ 'evening' various combinations of these

constructions may occur, for example:

$$\left.\begin{array}{r}\text{أَلْـيَوْمَ فِي الصَّبَاحِ}\\ \text{أَلْـيَوْمَ صَبَاحًا}\\ \text{صَبَاحَ الْـيَوْمِ}\end{array}\right\} \quad \text{'this morning'}$$

$$\left.\begin{array}{r}\text{أَلْـيَوْمَ فِي الْـمَسَاءِ}\\ \text{أَلْـيَوْمَ مَسَاءً}\\ \text{مَسَاءَ الْـيَوْمِ}\end{array}\right\} \quad \text{'this evening'}$$

$$\left.\begin{array}{r}\text{غَدًا فِي الصَّبَاحِ}\\ \text{غَدًا صَبَاحًا}\\ \text{صَبَاحَ غَدٍ}\end{array}\right\} \quad \text{'tomorrow morning'}$$

$$\left.\begin{array}{r}\text{أَمْسِ فِي الْـمَسَاءِ}\\ \text{أَمْسِ مَسَاءً}\\ \text{مَسَاءَ أَمْسِ}\end{array}\right\} \quad \text{'yesterday evening'}$$

Note that أَمْسِ 'yesterday' is invariable, always ending in -i. The accu-

sative form أَلْـيَوْمَ means 'today'; يَوْمٌ 'day' is a regular noun which may

have any case ending, and the same is true of صَبَاحٌ "morning", مَسَاءٌ 'even-

ing', and غَدٌ 'morrow, next day.' الآن is an adverb and ends only in a.

Iḍāfas with كُلّ as the first term are very common as adverbials of time.

One of these occurs in the Basic Text:

$$\boxed{\text{كُلَّ سَنَةٍ} \quad \text{'every year'}}$$

Other examples follow. Note that as we have seen before (see Lesson 9.1), with an indefinite noun كُلّ is translated 'every'; with a definite noun 'all' or 'the whole';

كُلَّ السَّنَةِ	'all year, all year long'
كُلَّ سَنَةٍ	'every year'
كُلَّ السّاعَةِ	'the whole hour'
كُلَّ ساعَةٍ	'every hour'
كُلَّ اليَوْمِ	'the whole day long'
كُلَّ يَوْمٍ	'every day'

Now do Drills 4, 5 and 6.

Drill 4. (on tape) Repetition: Time expressions.

Drill 5. (Also on tape) Transformation: Time expressions. Ex.

'The reporters left this morning.'

سافر المراسلون اليوم في الصباح. ←

سافر المراسلون اليوم صباحاً. ←

سافر المراسلون صباح اليوم.

١ – يحضر الوزراء الاجتماع اليوم في المساء.

٢ – يرجع المديرون غدا في المساء.

٣ – بحثت عن كتابي امس في الصباح .

٤ – عينوا موظفي البنك امس في المساء.

٥ – اصدقائي ذاهبون غدا في الصباح .

٦ – أرسل رسالة الى زوجته اليوم في الصباح .

Drill 6. Translation.

١ – هل تذهب الى المسرح كل يوم ؟

٢ – درسوا العربية كل السنة .

٣ – استمعت الى المحاضرة كل الساعة .

٤ – تعمل فريدة في المكتب كل الصباح .

٥ ــ بحث الوزراء الوضع كل اليوم .

٦ ــ نذهب لزيارة اصدقائنا كل سنة .

٧ ــ شربوا القهوة العربية كل مساء .

٨ ــ يقرأ الجريدة كل مساء في المكتبة .

5. Form II verbs and verbal nouns

a. Form

Form II verbs are characterized by having stems with a double middle radical, for example:

Perfect	Imperfect	
دَرَّسَ	يُدَرِّسُ	'to teach'

The perfect stem has the pattern FaMMaL- (both vowels being invariably a) as in دَرَّسَ above: stem darras-. The imperfect stem has the pattern -FaMMiL- (the first vowel always a, the second always i) as in يُدَرِّسُ above: stem -darris-. The vowel in all subject-marker prefixes is u, but in all other respects the subject-markers and mood-markers are the same as in Form I verbs.

Following is a chart giving the perfect and the imperfect indicative and jussive forms of a typical Form II verb:

دَرَّسَ 'to teach'

	PERFECT	IMPERFECT	
		Indicative	Jussive
3 MS	دَرَّسَ 'he taught'	يُدَرِّسُ 'he teaches'	يُدَرِّسْ
FS	دَرَّسَتْ 'she " '	تُدَرِّسُ 'she " '	تُدَرِّسْ
2 MS	دَرَّسْتَ 'you " '	تُدَرِّسُ 'you " '	تُدَرِّسْ
FS	دَرَّسْتِ 'you " '	تُدَرِّسِينَ 'you " '	تُدَرِّسي
1	دَرَّسْتُ 'I " '	أُدَرِّسُ 'I " '	أُدَرِّسْ

3 MP	دَرَّسُوا	'they taught'	يُدَرِّسُونَ	'they teach'	يُدَرِّسُوا
FP	دَرَّسْنَ	'they " '	يُدَرِّسْنَ	'they " '	يُدَرِّسْنَ
2 MP	دَرَّسْتُمْ	'you " '	تُدَرِّسُونَ	'you " '	تُدَرِّسُوا
FP	دَرَّسْتُنَّ	'you " '	تُدَرِّسْنَ	'you " '	تُدَرِّسْنَ
1 P	دَرَّسْنَا	'we " '	نُدَرِّسُ	'we " '	نُدَرِّسْ

The verbal noun of most Form II verbs has the pattern taFMiil; for example the verbal noun of دَرَّسَ 'to teach' is تَدْرِيسٌ 'teaching, instruction'. Following is a list of all the Form II verbs which have occurred so far (3 MS imperfect in parentheses) with their verbal nouns:

Form II verb		Verbal Noun	
حَدَّدَ (يُحَدِّدُ)	'to set, define'	تَحْدِيدٌ	'setting, defining'
خَرَّجَ (يُخَرِّجُ)	'to graduate, (trans.)	تَخْرِيجٌ	'graduating'
دَرَّسَ (يُدَرِّسُ)	'to teach'	تَدْرِيسٌ	'teaching'
عَيَّنَ (يُعَيِّنُ)	'to appoint'	تَعْيِينٌ	'appointment'
قَدَّمَ (يُقَدِّمُ)	'to present'	تَقْدِيمٌ	'presenting'
قَرَّرَ (يُقَرِّرُ)	'to decide' (on)	تَقْرِيرٌ	'decision'
عَلَّمَ (يُعَلِّمُ)	'to teach'	تَعْلِيمٌ	'teaching; education'

Now do Drills 7, 8 and 9.

b. Meaning

Most derived verbs are based on a Form I verb or another derived verb, the remainder being based on nouns, adjectives, prepositions, or other words. Thus, if you know the base form, you can predict with great accuracy the form of a verb derived from it; for example, if you know the Form I verb دَرَسَ 'to study', you can predict that a Form II verb derived from it will have the form دَرَّسَ (with a double middle radical). It is also possible, in a much more general and less precise way, to predict the meaning of a derived verb with relation to the meaning of the base form. For example, the great majority of Form II verbs have <u>causative</u> meaning: they mean "to cause or make someone do (the action designated by the corresponding Form I verb)". Thus, if the Form I verb دَرَسَ means 'to study', the Form II verb derived from it, دَرَّسَ , expresses the general notion to "cause someone to study"--that is, specifically, 'to teach'. To a considerable extent it is possible to ascribe one or more such meanings to each of the derived Forms. There is not complete predictability in each case, but there are sufficiently discernible trends to make generalizations worthwhile. In this note we treat Form II verbs; in subsequent lessons we take up the other derived verbs. It should be noted that not all the derived Forms occur with any one root; for example, the root DRS (with the general meaning of "studying") occurs in verbs of Forms I, II, III, and VI only; another root might occur in Forms I, IV, and X only; and so on. Thus one cannot make up new verbs at will. It is very useful, however, to know something about the general meaning of the various Forms and their semantic relationships with other Forms, as these associations will help in recognizing new words and will make it easy to learn whole sets of related words at a time instead of memorizing each one separately.

Following are additional illustrations of the <u>causative</u> meaning of Form II verbs. (Some of the words in these and subsequent examples have not occurred in the book. They are used here for illustrative purposes only and need not be learned.)

Form I		Form II	
ذَكَرَ	'to mention'	ذَكَّرَ	'to cause someone to mention = 'to remind'
شَرِبَ	'to drink'	شَرَّبَ	'to give (someone)(something) to drink'
سَمِعَ	'to hear'	سَمَّعَ	'to let (someone) hear (something)'

Closely associated with this causative meaning is the transitivizing function of Form II: if a Form I verb is intransitive (i.e. cannot take an object) the corresponding Form II verb is transitive (can take an object):

Form I	Form II
رَجَعَ 'to return' (intr.)	رَجَّعَ 'to return (something)'

and if the Form I verb is transitive, the Form II verb is doubly transitive (can take two objects):

Form I	Form II
دَرَسَ 'to study' (something)	دَرَّسَ 'to teach' (somebody) (something)

as in

دَرَسَ الْعَرَبِيَّةَ .	'He studied Arabic.'
دَرَّسَنِي الْعَرَبِيَّةَ .	'He taught me Arabic.'

Some Form II verbs have intensive or frequentative (to do again and again) meaning:

Form I		Form II	
كَسَرَ	'to break'	كَسَّرَ	'to smash'
قَتَلَ	'to kill'	قَتَّلَ	'to massacre'

Another possible meaning is estimative: to consider (someone or something) to be (such-and-such):

Form I		Form II	
صَدَقَ	'to speak the truth, be truthful'	صَدَّقَ	'to consider someone truthful, to believe'
كَذَبَ	'to lie'	كَذَّبَ	'to call someone a liar; to disbelieve'

Finally, some Form II verbs are applicative: to apply (something to someone), to give, make, deal with, utter (an expression) and so on. Here the base form is often a word other than a verb.

Base Form		Form II	
إِسْمٌ	'name'	سَمَّى	'to name'
مَرِيضٌ	'sick'	مَرَّضَ	'to nurse (a patient)'
خَيْمَةٌ	'tent'	خَيَّمَ	'to pitch one's tent'
عِيدٌ	'feast-day'	عَيَّدَ	'to celebrate a feast'
أَلسَّلامُ عَلَيْكُمْ	'Peace be with you'	سَلَّمَ عَلى	'to say أَلسَّلامُ عَلَيْكُمْ to (s.o.), greet (s.o.)'

Drill 7. Written. Recognition drill: Pattern of Form II verb.

Write the Form II verb for each of the following roots, along with its verbal noun. Ex.

taFMiiL	FaMMaLa	←	FML
تَدْرِيسٌ	دَرَّسَ	←	درس

قدم	لقب
فكر	صدق
علم	فسر
فصل	قدر
وحد	فرق

Drill 8. (on tape) Conjugation: Form II.

Drill 9. Transformation: Perfect → imperfect → jussive. Ex.

'The ministers decided on the programs of instruction.' → — الوزراء قرروا مناهج التعليم . ←

'The ministers decide on the programs of instruction.' → — الوزراء يقررون مناهج التعليم . ←

'The ministers did not decide on the programs of instruction.' — الوزراء لم يقرروا مناهج التعليم .

١ ـ وزارة التربية والتعليم حدّدت مواعيد الامتحانات .

٢ ـ خرّجت هذه الجامعة كثيرا من الطلاب .

٣ ـ عيّن رئيس الجامعة الاساتذة .

٤ ـ درّسته اللغة الانكليزية .

٥ ـ قررت الوزارة مناهج التعليم في المدارس الثانوية .

٦ ـ قدّمن خدمات كثيرة للمجتمع .

D. Comprehension passages — د ـ نصوص للفهم

(1) Read the following passage; then do Drill 10.

المرأة ألامريكيّة

للنساء في امريكا حقوق الرجال وواجباتهم : لهن حق الدراسة والتدريس في المدارس والجامعات الخاصة والحكومية ، وحق الحصول على وظائف عالية في الحكومات والشركات . والمرأة الامريكية تحضر الاجتماعات الهامة وتبحث مع الرجال اوضاع السياسة . وَالدُّسْتورُ الامريكي يسمح للمرأة بالحصول على كل الوظائف الحكومية .

constitution — وَالدُّسْتورُ

تخرّج الجامعات الامريكية عددا كبيرا من الطالبات كل سنة . وبعضهن يحصلن على الماجستير او الدكتوراه . تقدم النساء الامريكيات اليوم خدمات كثيرة للمجتمع ، فَمنهن المراسلات والاستاذات والمديرات والطبيبات والكاتبات . من نساء امريكا المشهورات مارغريت ميد ، واليانور روزفلت ، واملي ديكنسون ، وماريان اندرسون .

for, and — فَـ

Drill 10. Multiple choice completion

١ ـ التدريس في جامعات امريكا حق لـ ______________

(الرجال فقط ، النساء فقط ،

الرجال والنساء) .

٢ ـ تحصل النساء الامريكيات على ______________

(الماجستير ، كل الشهادات ،

البكالوريوس) .

٣ ـ للمرأة الامريكية الحق في الحصول على ________ في الحكومة .

(بعض الوظائف ، معظم الوظائف ،

كل الوظائف) .

٤ ـ في امريكا مدارس ________ (خاصة ، حكومية ، خاصة وحكومية)

٥ ـ ________ السياسيين في امريكا رجال . (بعض ، كل) .

(2) Listen to the passage on tape then do Drill 11.

Drill 11. (On tape) Written. Questions on aural comprehension passage.

أسئلة

١ ـ هل كريمة سورية ؟

٢ ـ أين أكملت كريمة دراستها الثانوية ؟

٣ ـ الى أيّ دولة ذهبت كريمة بعد حصولها على البكالوريوس ؟

٤ ـ من أيّ جامعة حصلت كريمة على الماجستير ؟

٥ ـ أين تدرّس كريمة الآن ؟

E. General drills — هـ ــ التمارين العامة

Drill 12. Substitute the appropriate pronouns for the underlined items below.

'There's a new secretary in the president's office.' → في مكتب الرئيس سكرتيرة جديدة . ←

'There's a new secretary in his office.' — في مكتبه سكرتيرة جديدة .

١ ــ في الدروس الاخيرة قواعد هامة .

٢ ــ المعلّم يدرّس الطلاب التاريخ الاسلامي .

٣ ــ سيارة اختي امام الباب .

٤ ــ تحدّث المدير الى موظفيه .

٥ ــ هل قرأتم عن تاريخ المغرب ؟

٦ ــ الوزارة تعين المدرسين والمدرسات .

٧ ــ ذهبت مع هؤلاء النساء الى الاجتماع .

٨ ــ متى موعد طائرة الوزراء ؟

Drill 13. Translation.

1. The professor went to the office of the secretary of the university in order to set the examination time.

2. Do some of those doctors work in Algeria?

3. Among the duties of the minister of education is appointing the new teachers.

4. Who determines the programs of instruction in government schools?

5. What is the position of women in Arab society today? Does the society permit them to work for their advancement?

Lesson Eighteen

الدرس الثامن عشر

أ ـ النصّ الاساسيّ

نهر النيل

النيل نهر طويل جدّا ، بل هو من أطول أنهار العالم وأكبرها .

فَهْوَ أطول من الامازون وأكبر من المسيسبي . (and, thus)

تَقَعُ على النيل مدن مصريّة هامّة . منها القاهرة وأسوان . (are located)

ومدينة الأقصر مشهورة بآثارها الْفِرْعَوْنِيَّةِ . (Pharaonic;)

السَّدُّ الْعالِي سدّ كبير قريب من أسوان . بذل المصريّون جهودا (The High Dam)

عظيمة في بنائه ، وشاركتهم في ذلك بعض الدول الاجنبيّة . ويساعد هذا

السد مساعدة عظيمة على تقدّم الاقتصاد المصريّ .

ومصر تعتمد على مياه النيل الى أبعد حدّ . وقديماً قالَ هيرودُتُس: (Hero- dotus;)

" مصر هِبَةُ النيل " . (gift)

أسئلـة

١ ـ هل نهر الامازون أطول من النيل ؟

٢ ـ أيّ مدن مصريّة تقع على النيل ؟

٣ ـ بِمَ مدينة الأقصر مشهورة ؟

٤ ـ ما هو السدّ العالى ؟ أين هو ؟

٥ ـ من عمل على بناء السد العالي ؟

٦ ـ هل نهر النيل هامّ في مصر ؟ لماذا ؟

A. Basic text

The River Nile

The Nile is a very long river; indeed it is one of the longest and biggest rivers in the world. It is longer than the Amazon, and bigger than the Mississippi.

Important Egyptian cities are situated on the Nile. Among them are Cairo and Aswan. The city of Luxor is famous for its Pharaonic ruins.

The High Dam is a big dam near Aswan. The Egyptians expended great efforts in building it and some foreign countries joined them in this. This dam assists a great deal in the advancement of the Egyptian economy.

Egypt relies on the waters of the Nile to the utmost extent. Long ago, Herodotus said: "Egypt is the gift of the Nile."

B. Vocabulary

نَهْرٌ ـ أَنْهارٌ	river
أَلنِّيلُ	the Nile
طَوِيلٌ ـ طِوالٌ	long; tall (person)
أَطْوَلُ (مِن)	longer (than); longest
كَبِيرٌ ـ كِبارٌ ، كُبَراءُ	big; old (person)
أَكْبَرُ	bigger, biggest; older, oldest (person)
اَلأَمازون	the Amazon
اَلْمِسِيسِبِّي	the Mississippi
أَسْوانُ	Aswan
اَلأُقْصُرُ	Luxor
سَدٌّ ـ سُدُودٌ	dam
بَذَلَ ـُـ ، بَذْلٌ	to exert
جَهْدٌ ـ جُهودٌ	effort
شارَكَ (في)	he participated with (s.o.) (in), joined (s.o.) (in)
يُساعِدُ (على)	he helps, assists (s.o.) (in)

مُساعَدَةٌ	assistance
عَظيمٌ – عِظامٌ ، عُظَماءُ، عَظائِمُ	great, huge, grand; enormous
اِقْتِصادٌ	economy
تَعْتَمِدُ على	she depends on, relies on
ماءٌ – مِياهٌ	water
أَبْعَدُ	furthest; utmost
حَدٌّ – حُدودٌ	extent; border, limit
قَديمًا	in ancient times, long ago

Additional vocabulary

صَغيرٌ – صِغارٌ	little, small; young (person)
كَثيرٌ – ون ، كِثارٌ	much; many
كَثيرًا	a lot; often
اَلإِسْكَنْدَرِيَّةُ	Alexandria

C. Grammar and drills ج – القواعد والتمارين

1. The elative: Comparative and superlative
2. Cognate accusative
3. Form III verbs and verbal nouns
4. Verb-preposition idioms
5. Use of the dictionary: Verbal nouns

1. The Elative: Comparative and superlative

English adjectives have three degrees of comparison: positive (e.g. "big"), comparative ("bigger") and superlative ("biggest"). Arabic has two forms to express these meanings: the positive (e.g. كَبيرٌ 'big') and the elative (e.g. أَكْبَرُ 'bigger; biggest'). The English and Arabic positives correspond to each other, e.g. نَهْرٌ كَبيرٌ 'a big river' and مَدينَةٌ كَبيرَةٌ 'a big city'. The Arabic elative, on the other hand, expresses both the comparative and the superlative of English.

The elative has two forms which will concern us in this book: the masculine singular, e.g. أَكْبَرُ , and the feminine singular, e.g. كُبْرى . أَكْبَرُ is a diptote and كُبْرى is invariable--it has no inflections whatsoever.

The Elative Pattern. The masculine elative is of the pattern أَفْعَلُ ?aFMaLu and the feminine elative is فُعْلى FuMLaa. Following is the elative of all adjectives studied so far which can be put in the elative:

Positive

a. ?aFMaL

سَهْلٌ	'easy'	أَسْهَلُ	'easier/easiest'
قَرِيبٌ	'near'	أَقْرَبُ	'nearer/nearest'
جَمِيلٌ	'beautiful'	أَجْمَلُ	'more/most beautiful'
كَبِيرٌ	'big'	أَكْبَرُ	'bigger/biggest'
مَشْهُورٌ	'famous'	أَشْهَرُ	'more/most famous'
قَدِيمٌ	'old'	أَقْدَمُ	'older/oldest'
حَدِيثٌ	'new'	أَحْدَثُ	'newer/newest'
بَعِيدٌ	'distant'	أَبْعَدُ	'more/most distant'
قَصِيرٌ	'short'	أَقْصَرُ	'shorter/shortest'
كَثِيرٌ	'much,many'	أَكْثَرُ	'more/most'
طَوِيلٌ	'long, tall'	أَطْوَلُ	'longer/longest'; taller/tallest'
عَظِيمٌ	'great, mighty'	أَعْظَمُ	'greater/greatest'
صَغِيرٌ	'small'	أَصْغَرُ	'smaller/smallest'

b. ?aFaDD

جَدِيدٌ	'new'	أَجَدُّ	'newer/newest'
هامٌّ	'important'	أَهَمُّ	'more/most important'
عَزِيزٌ	'dear'	أَعَزُّ	'dearer/dearest'

c. ?aFMaa

اَلْعالي	'the high'	أَعْلى	'higher/highest'

The adjectives under (a) above conform to the basic pattern; group (b) adjectives have the pattern ?aFaDD (where DD represents two identical radicals), and group (c) have the invariable pattern ?aFMaa (where the third radical of the positive form is W or Y).

مَشْهُورٌ 'famous' has no elative; the elative of شَهِيرٌ 'famous' is used for it: أَشْهَرُ 'more/most famous'.

The masculine may take a plural of the pattern ?aFaaMiL (a diptote pattern), e.g. أَكَابِرُ or, most rarely, a sound plural أَكْبَرُونَ .

The plural of the feminine FuMLaa is FuMLayaat, e.g. كُبْرَيَاتٌ، كُبْرَى ; the plural FuMaL, i.e. كُبَرٌ , is rare.

<u>Expression of comparative degree</u>. In comparing two items—"A is better than B"—only the masculine singular elative is used; it is always indefinite and does not show agreement in gender or number. Examples:

أَيُّ مَدِينَةٍ أَكْبَرُ ؟	'Which city is bigger?'
أَلرِّبَاطُ أَكْبَرُ .	'Rabat is bigger.'

The object to be compared is introduced by مِنْ , which is translated "than".

أَلنِّيلُ أَكْبَرُ مِنَ الدَّانُوبِ .	'The Nile is bigger than the Danube.'
أَلَيْسَتْ مَرْيَمُ أَطْوَلَ مِنْكَ ؟	'Isn't Mary taller than you?'
تَعَلَّمْنَا أَكْثَرَ مِنْكُمْ .	'We learned more than you.'

The elative may follow an indefinite noun, forming a noun-adjective phrase; the elative agrees with the noun in case, but not in gender or number. Examples:

هٰذَا بِنَاءٌ كَبِيرٌ ، لٰكِنْ ذٰلِكَ بِنَاءٌ أَكْبَرُ .	'That is a big building, but that one (over there) is a bigger one.'
قَرَأْنَا عَنْ مَدِينَةٍ أَكْبَرَ .	'We read about a bigger city.'
لَمْ نَدْرُسْ عَنْ بَلَدٍ أَكْبَرَ مِنْ ذٰلِكَ .	'We have not studied about a country bigger than that.'

Now do Drills 1, 2 (on tape), and 3.

Expression of Superlative Degree. When the elative is definite--that is, having the definite article or a pronoun suffix, or serving as the first member of any iḍāfa--it has superlative meaning: it singles out the highest degree of three or more. Examples with the article:

هٰذا هُوَ الأَكْبَرُ .	'This is the biggest one (m.).'
عَلى الأَكْثَرِ	'at the most, at most'

When the elative has the definite article, it then agrees in gender; the feminine elative is used to refer to a feminine noun or pronoun:

هٰذِهِ هِيَ الكُبْرى .	'This is the biggest one (fem.).'
هِيَ المَدينَةُ الكُبْرى .	'It is the biggest city.'

As the first term of an iḍāfa, only the masculine elative is used. If the second term does not have the article the meaning is "the (__est) (__)". Examples:

أَكْبَرُ مَدينَةٍ	'the largest city'
أَطْوَلُ نَهْرٍ	'the longest river'
أَجْمَلُ مُدُنٍ	'the prettiest cities'
أَجْمَلُ بِناءٍ تونِسِيٍّ	'the most beautiful Tunisian building'

(There exists an alternative but rare way of saying "the (__est)(__)"; this involves making a noun-adjective phrase of the noun plus elative, e.g. أَلنَّهْرُ الأَكْبَرُ 'the biggest river'; أَلْمَدينَةُ الكُبْرى 'the biggest city.' Note that there is gender agreement here, since the elative has received the definite article.)

If the second term of the iḍāfa has the definite article, then the elative may refer to one or to several, and it is usually best translated with "(one) of", "(some) of", into English:

هُوَ مِنْ أَطْوَلِ أَنْهارِ الْعالَمِ.	'It is one of the longest rivers in the world.'
وَهْيَ مِنْ أَطْوَلِ أَنْهارِ الْعالَمِ.	'They are some of the longest rivers in the world.
أَقْدَمُ الْمُدُنِ	'the oldest (one) of the cities' 'the oldest (ones) of the cities'
أَكْثَرُ الْوَقْتِ	'most of the time'

Now do Drill 4.

<u>The Elative with Positive Meaning</u>. For some words the elative has only positive meaning, e.g. أَوْسَطُ (fem. وُسْطى) 'middle, central' and آخَرُ (fem. أُخْرى) 'other; another'. These words form a noun-adjective phrase with the noun modified, and are in full agreement with them. Illustrations:

اَلشَّرْقُ الأَوْسَطُ	'The Middle East'
أُورُوبّا الْوُسْطى	'Central Europe'
سُؤالٌ آخَرُ	'another question
وِزاراتٌ أُخْرى	'other ministries'

This usage is extended to include feminine elatives that do have comparative or superlative meaning, but correspond to English positives, such as:

أَلدُّوَلُ الْكَبِيرَةُ الدُّوَلُ الْكُبْرى	'the major powers, the Great Powers'
بَرِيطانِيا الْعُظْمى	'Great Britain'

This usage is particularly common in certain set phrases.

Finally, كَبِيرٌ 'big; old' and صَغِيرٌ 'little, small; young', when referring to humans, often have superlative meaning as the first term of an iḍāfa:

كَبِيرُ الْمُوَظَّفِينَ	'the head employee'
كِبارُ الْمُوَظَّفِينَ	'the senior employees'
صَغِيرُهُمْ	'the youngest of them'

The ordinal adjective أَوَّلُ 'first' is also of the elative pattern, and has the various forms of the elative:

	Singular	Plural	
m.	أَوَّلُ	أَوَائِلُ ، أَوَّلُونَ ، أُوَلُ	'first'
f.	أُولَى		

It is normally used in noun-adjective phrases rather than in iḍāfas, as in أَلدَّرْسُ الأَوَّلُ 'the first lesson'.

Summary chart with كَبِيرٌ :

	Singular		Plural		
	Masculine	Feminine	Masculine	Feminine	
Positive	كَبِيرٌ	كَبِيرَةٌ كُبْرَى	كِبَارٌ	كَبِيرَاتٌ كُبْرَيَاتٌ	'big'
Comparative	أَكْبَرُ مِنْ				'bigger than'
Superlative	أَلأَكْبَرُ				'the biggest (m.)'
	أَلكُبْرَى				'the biggest (f.)'
	أَكْبَرُ نَهْرٍ (أَلنَّهْرُ الأَكْبَرُ)				'the biggest river'
	أَكْبَرُ مَدِينَةٍ (أَلْمَدِينَةُ الْكُبْرَى)				'the biggest city'

Now do Drill 5.

<u>Drill 1</u>. Written. Recognition: Elative pattern.

Write the elative form of the following adjectives; <u>ex</u>.

جَمِيل ← أجمل

?aFMaL ← {FaMiiL / FaML

سهل ← أسهل

غريب	عجيب
سعيد	فقير
صعب	قبيح
حسن	سهل
بعيد	عميق

b. Ex.

عزيز ← أعز

FaDiiD / FaaDD ← ?aFaDD

هامّ ← أهمّ

صحيح

جديد

عامّ

عزيز

لذيذ

Drill 2. (On tape) Repetition: Elative.

Drill 3. (Also on tape) Transformation: Positive → comparative.

'The office is near--the school.' → المكتب قريب ـ المدرسة →

'The office is nearer than the school.' المكتب أقرب من المدرسة

١ ـ الكرسي قديم ـ الطاولة

٢ ـ المتحف بعيد ـ المصنع

٣ ـ السيارة جديدة - الاوتوبيس

٤ ـ النيل طويل ـ المسيسبي

٥ ـ الوالد عزيز ـ الصديق

٦ ـ الطبيبة مشهورة ـ الكاتبة

٧ ـ اختي طويلة ـ زوجتي

٨ ـ الصف كبير ـ المكتب

٩ ـ هذا البناء حديث ـ ذلك البناء

١٠ ـ دراستك هامة ـ الذهاب الى السينما .

Drill 4. Substitution-translation: Superlative.

Substitute the following phrases for the underlined phrase making any necessary changes.

'This is the longest river in the world.' هذا هو أطول نهر فى العالم .

1. the most famous doctors (f.)
2. the most modern airplane
3. the shortest street
4. the biggest factory
5. the newest airport
6. the largest restaurant
7. the highest building
8. the most beautiful language
9. the tallest man
10. the greatest country
11. the oldest ruins

Drill 5. (Also on tape) Transformation: Positive → superlative.

'This is a beautiful country.' → هذا بلد جميل . ←

'Indeed it is one of the most beautiful countries.' بل هو من اجمل البلاد .

١ – هذه جملة قصيرة .

٢ – هذه آثار قديمة .

٣ – هذه طبيبة مشهورة .

٤ – هذا موضوع هامّ .

٥ – هذا رجل طويل .

٦ – هؤلاء مراسلون مشهورون .

٧ – هؤلاء اصدقاء اعزاء .

٨ – هذا لوح قديم .

2. Cognate accusative

This sentence from the basic text

يُساعِدُ هذا السَّدُّ مُساعَدَةً عَظيمَةً .	'This dam helps greatly...'

illustrates an important use of verbal nouns, the cognate accusative. In such constructions the verb is followed by its own verbal noun (the verbal noun which is derived from--is "cognate" with--that verb). The verbal noun then serves as an adverbial modifier of the verb, and is in the accusative case; it is indefinite unless it is in an iḍāfa. The verbal noun may occur alone, or may itself be modified by an adjective (as above), by another noun in an iḍāfa, and so on. A common construction is with a noun of quantity, like كُلّ or بَعْض , or an elative as the first term of the iḍāfa, in which case the verbal noun usually has the definite article. When it is modified by an adjective, the whole phrase (verbal noun plus adjective) is often best translated by an English adverb, as above. The cognate accusative expresses intensity, emphasis, or manner. Additional examples:

تَقَدَّمَتْ مِصْرُ تَقَدُّمًا كَبِيرًا.	'Egypt has advanced greatly.'
إِحْتَرَمَهُ احْتِرامَ الِابْنِ لِوالِدِهِ.	'He respected him as a son respects his father.' ("He respected him the respect of a son for his father")
ساعَدَها كُلَّ المُساعَدَةِ.	'He helped her in every way.'
إِسْتَقْبَلَهُمْ أَعْظَمَ اسْتِقْبالٍ.	'He gave them a great welcome.'

3. Form III verbs and verbal nouns

a. Form

Form III verbs are characterized by having stems with a long vowel after the first radical, for example:

Perfect	Imperfect	
ساعَدَ	يُساعِدُ	'to help'

The perfect stem has the pattern FaaMaL- (always long vowel aa after the first radical, short vowel a after the second), as in ساعَدَ above: stem saaʕad-. The imperfect stem has the pattern -FaaMiL- (always long vowel aa after the first radical, short vowel i after the second) as in يُساعِدُ above: stem -saaʕid-. As in Form II verbs, the vowel in all subject-marker prefixes is u. In all other respects the subject-markers and mood-markers are the same as in Form I verbs (this statement is true of all derived verbs and hereafter may be taken for granted).

The chart below gives the perfect, imperfect, and jussive forms of a typical Form III verb:

سَاعَدَ 'to help'

	PERFECT		IMPERFECT		
			Indicative		Jussive
3 MS	سَاعَدَ	'he helped'	يُسَاعِدُ	'he helps'	يُسَاعِدْ
FS	سَاعَدَتْ	'she " '	تُسَاعِدُ	'she " '	تُسَاعِدْ
2 MS	سَاعَدْتَ	'you " '	تُسَاعِدُ	'you help'	تُسَاعِدْ
FS	سَاعَدْتِ	'you " '	تُسَاعِدِينَ	'you " '	تُسَاعِدِي
1 S	سَاعَدْتُ	'I " '	أُسَاعِدُ	'I " '	أُسَاعِدْ
3 MP	سَاعَدُوا	'they " '	يُسَاعِدُونَ	'they " '	يُسَاعِدُوا
FP	سَاعَدْنَ	'they " '	يُسَاعِدْنَ	'they " '	يُسَاعِدْنَ
2 MP	سَاعَدْتُمْ	'you " '	تُسَاعِدُونَ	'you " '	تُسَاعِدُوا
FP	سَاعَدْتُنَّ	'you " '	تُسَاعِدْنَ	'you " '	تُسَاعِدْنَ
1 P	سَاعَدْنَا	'we " '	نُسَاعِدُ	'we " '	نُسَاعِدْ

The <u>verbal noun</u> of most Form III verbs has the pattern <u>muFaaMaLa(t)</u>; for example, the verbal noun of سَاعَدَ 'to help' is مُسَاعَدَةٌ 'helping, help, assistance'. The following list shows all the Form III verbs which have occurred so far (imperfect in parentheses) and their verbal nouns:

<u>Form III verb</u>			<u>Verbal noun</u>	
(يُحَاضِرُ)	حَاضَرَ	'to lecture'	مُحَاضَرَةٌ	'lecturing, a lecture'
(يُتَابِعُ)	تَابَعَ	'to pursue, continue'	مُتَابَعَةٌ	'pursuing'
(يُسَاعِدُ)	سَاعَدَ	'to help'	مُسَاعَدَةٌ	'assistance'

	Verbal noun	
(يُشارِكُ) شارَكَ 'to participate'	مُشارَكَةٌ	'participation'
(يُشاهِدُ) شاهَدَ 'to see'	مُشاهَدَةٌ	'seeing'
(يُقابِلُ) قابَلَ 'to have a meeting with'	مُقابَلَةٌ	'meeting with, interviewing'
(يُسافِرُ) سافَرَ 'to travel'	سَفَرٌ	'travelling' (see below)

The verb سافَرَ 'to travel' is unusual in that its verbal noun is a Form I pattern.

Some Form III verbs have verbal nouns of the pattern FiMaaL instead of, or in addition to, muFaaMaLa(t). An example, which has not occurred in the book so far, is

Form III verb		Verbal noun	
قاتَلَ	'to fight with, combat'	مُقاتَلَةٌ / قِتالٌ	'fighting, combat'

Now do Drills 6 and 7.

b. Meaning

Form III verbs typically have attemptive meaning ("to try to do something to someone" or associative meaning ("to involve someone in something"). Almost all are transitive, and many of these have the same meaning as the corresponding Form I verb plus a preposition. (Unfamiliar verbs are for illustration only.)

Form I		Form III	
قَتَلَ	'to kill'	قاتَلَ	'to fight with, try to kill'
قَبِلَ	'to receive'	قابَلَ	'to confront, meet with'
قامَ (عَلى)	'to stand up (against)'	قاوَمَ	'to stand up against, resist, oppose'
جَلَسَ (إلى)	'to sit down (with)'	جالَسَ	'to sit down with'

Drill 6. Written. Recognition: Form III pattern.

Fill in the blanks in the chart below.

	Verbal noun	Form III verb	Root
Example:	(MuFaaMaLaT) مُشارَكَةٌ	(FaaMaLa) شارَكَ	(FML) شرك
			طلب
			صدق
			رسل
			عصر
			كفح
			حفظ

Drill 7. (On tape) Conjugation: Form III.

Drill 8. (Also on tape) Transformation: Perfect ⟶ لم +Jussive. Ex.

'The director met with the employee in his office.' ⟶ قابل المدير الموظف في مكتبه . ⟵

'The director did not meet with the employee in his office.' لم يقابل المدير الموظف فى مكتبه •

١ ـ ذكرت في رسالتك لي اقامتك هناك •

٢ ـ ساعد المنهج على تقدّم البلد •

٣ ـ شاركت الدول الكبرى فى بناء المصنع الجديد •

٤ ـ الوزراء قابلوا الرئيس اثناء زيارته لمصر •

٥ ـ شاهدنا فيلما عربيا مساء امس •

٦ ـ سافرن الى فرنسا لحضور الاجتماع •

٧ ـ شاركت هذه السنة في تقرير منهج التعليم •

٨ ـ عيّن الوزير المعلمين الجدد •

٩ ـ أكلت وشربت بعد عودتها من المدرسة •

4. Verb-preposition idioms

In English there are some verbs which mean one thing when followed directly by an object and another when combined with a preposition; for example, 'He deals the cards' versus 'He deals with the problems'. Some verbs, also, have differing meanings when combined with different prepositions: 'He looks for the book' versus 'He looks at the book'. Still other verbs occur only in combination with prepositions: 'He relies on his friends.' In Arabic there are also verbs of exactly the same types, although of course not necessarily the same particular verbs as in English. In previous lessons, for example, we have seen the verb بَحَثَ meaning 'to discuss' and the combination بَحَثَ عَنْ meaning 'to look for'. In this lesson we see the combination إِعْتَمَدَ عَلى meaning 'to depend on' (the verb إِعْتَمَدَ without a preposition means 'to authorize, to sanction').

Such a combination of a verb and a preposition is called a verb-preposition idiom. From the point of view of meaning, a verb-preposition idiom constitutes a single unit distinct from the verb alone or from other verb-preposition idioms. From the point of view of grammar, the verb in such an idiom has the same forms (of person, tense, and so on) as any verb; and the preposition, as usual, takes as its object a noun in the genitive case, or a pronoun suffix:

بَحَثوا مَواضيعَ كَثيرَةً وَمِنْها السَّلامُ في الشَّرْقِ الأَوْسَطِ .	'They discussed many topics, among them peace in the Middle East.'
بَحَثوا عَنْ قَلَمِكَ في كُلِّ صَفٍّ .	'They looked for your pencil in every classroom.'

These verb-preposition idioms have occurred so far:

حَضَرَ إِلى	'to come to'	(cf. حَضَرَ 'to attend')
بَحَثَ عَنْ	'to look for'	(cf. بَحَثَ 'to discuss')
حَصَلَ عَلى	'to acquire, obtain, get'	

سَمَحَ بِ	'to permit'
اِعْتَمَدَ عَلَى	'to depend on'

There are also quite a few Arabic verbs which are not parts of idioms like those above, but may be associated with particular prepositions without a change in their basic meaning. For example, the verb سَاعَدَ means "to help" (someone) and سَاعَدَ عَلَى means "to help" (someone) "in" (doing something):

هَلْ سَاعَدَكَ الْكِتَابُ ؟	'Did the book help you?'
نَعَمْ، سَاعَدَنِي عَلَى التَّعْلِيمِ.	'Yes, it helped me in teaching.'

While the distinction must be kept clear between verb-preposition idioms like اِعْتَمَدَ عَلَى and verbs like سَاعَدَ , they must all be learned together with their associated prepositions. Parentheses identify such prepositions, as in

اِسْتَمَعَ (لِ)	'to listen (to)'
أَخْبَرَ (بِ)	'to inform (of)'
شَارَكَ (فِي)	'to participate (in)'
سَاعَدَ (عَلَى)	'to help (in)'
عَمِلَ (عَلَى)	'to work (for, towards)'

Now do Drill 9.

Drill 9. Written. Completion.

Write the correct preposition in the blank.

١ ـ بحث المراسل ــــــ عمل في جريدة "الاهرام" المصرية .

٢ ـ ساعدت الدول الكبرى ــــــ بناء السد العالي .

٣ ـ يحصل عدد كبير من الطلاب ــــــ شهادات عالية كل سنة .

٤ ـ أخبرني ــــــ وصول الرئيس الامريكي .

٥ ـ يعمل الرجال والنساء ــــــ تقدم المجتمع العربي .

٦ ـ شارك المدرّس ــــــ تدريس التاريخ الاسلامي .

٧ - لم يسمح وقتنا ـــــ زيارة آثار بعلبك .

٨ - استمعنا ـــــ محاضرة الاستاذ الزائر بعنوان " جمال مصر".

٩ - حصلت الطالبة ـــــ البكالوريوس وبدأت عملا جديدا .

5. Use of the dictionary: Verbal nouns

Various formats are used by different Arabic dictionaries in arranging, within the entry for a particular root, all the words which share that root. Verbal nouns for Form I verbs are often given directly after the verb itself at the beginning of the entry for that root. An example of such an entry would be as follows:

verb	verb transliterated	stem vowel	verbal noun transliterated	definition of verb
شَغَلَ	šaḡala	a	(šaḡl, šuḡl)	to occupy, busy...

If more than one verbal noun is given, then the first one given is usually the more common, or they may have slightly different meanings. The verbal nouns so listed are usually dealt with again in more detail later on in the entry.

If your dictionary does not use this format then it is necessary to consult the introduction to the dictionary, where the format used will be described.

Drill 10. Written. Dictionary drill.

Look up the following verbs and write their meanings as well as their verbal nouns.

رَحَّبَ بـ	صادَقَ
راسَلَ	أَثَّرَ على
أَجَّلَ	نَظَرَ في
رَحَلَ	طالَبَ

D. Comprehension passage

د – نصوص للفهم

Read the following passage; then do Drill 11.

السد العالي سد كبير جدّا على نهر النيل، بل هو أكبر سد في الشرق الاوسط. بذل المصريون اعظم الجهود في بنائه وشاركتهم في ذلك روسيا. ساعد بناء هذا السد المدن الواقِعَة عَلى نهر النيل مساعدة كبيرة ونقلت الحكومة المصريّة بعض الآثار التاريخية القديمة من مِنْطَقَة السد الى مَكانٍ جديد. والسّدّ العالي اليوم اشهر سَدّ في العالم ، فَهو يساعد على تقدم الاوضاع الاقتصادية في مصر ، بل يعتمد الاقتصاد المصري عليه الى ابعد حدّ .

Russia; located on; region; place; thus

وفي مصر سدّ كبير آخر على النيل واسمه سدّ أسوان . وهذا السدّ اقدم من السدّ العالي لكن السدّ العالي اكبر منه . وعلى النيل سُدودٌ صغيرة اخرى .

Drill 11.

الاسئلة

١ – من شارك المصريين في بناء السدّ العالي ؟

٢ – ماذا نقلت الحكومة المصرية من منطقة السدّ العالي ؟

٣ – علامَ ساعد بناء السدّ العالي ؟

٤ – هل على النيل سُدودٌ اخرى ؟

٥ – هل سد اسوان اكبر من السد العالي ؟

E. General drills   هـ – التمارين العامة

Drill 12. Substitution: Telling time. Ex.

'What time is it now?' →   ما الساعة الآن ؟ ←

'It's eleven o'clock.'   الساعة الحادية عشرة .

10:20	3:15
7:55	5:45
8:40	12:10
6:30	2:30

Drill 13. Variable substitution.

'Ahmad is the first student in the class.'   أَحْمَدُ هو الطالب الاول في الصف.

فَريدةُ	٦	سَليمٌ
٢	هِنْدُ	١١
حُسَيْنُ	١٠	سُعادُ
١٩	عادِلٌ	٥
وِدادُ	٤	فَريدٌ

Drill 14. Written. Translation.

1. The minister of education met with the senior employees of the ministry to appoint the new teachers and to decide on the programs of instruction in the secondary schools.

2. The government assisted the companies a great deal (use cognate accus.). The companies depended upon this assistance to the utmost extent.

3. The great powers are participating in the building of the largest factory in the world.

Lesson Nineteen

الدرس التاسع عشر

أ - النصّ الاساسيّ

البدو

يسكن البدو في الخِيامِ ويرحلون في الصحراء من مكان الى مكان للبحث عن الماء، وهم مشهورون بِحُسْنِ الضِّيافَةِ : يقبل عليهم الزائر فيظهرون له الترحيب ويسرعون الى اكرامه فيقدّمون له الطعام والشَّرابَ .

tents; hospitality; drink

والمدينة لا تعجب البدويّ لأنّ الحياة فيها تختلف عن الحياة في الصحراء : فالبدويّ يُفَضِّلُ حرّيّة الصحراء على قُيودِ المدينة ، لكنّ بعض البدو يذهبون الى المدينة أحيانا للتجارة .

prefers...to; fetters

أسئلة

١ - أين يسكن البدو عادة ؟

٢ - لِمَ يرحلون من مكان الى مكان ؟

٣ - هل في الصحراء كثير من الماء ؟

٤ - كيف تختلف الحياة في الصحراء عن الحياة في المدينة ؟

٥ - هل تعجب البدو حياة المدينة ؟

٦ - هل تعجبك حياة المدينة ؟

A. Basic text

The Bedouins

The Bedouins live in tents and move about the desert from place to place to look for water. They are famous for their hospitality: if a visitor comes up to them they welcome him and hasten to honor him, and they offer him food and drink.

The Bedouin does not like the city because life there differs from life in the desert: the Bedouin prefers the freedom of the desert to the fetters of the city, but some Bedouins do go to the city at times to trade.

B. Vocabulary

بَدَوِيٌّ – بَدْوٌ	Bedouin
رَحَلَ – َ ، رَحِيلٌ	to move about, travel
صَحْرَاءُ – صَحَارَى	(f.) desert
صَحْرَاوِيٌّ	(nisba of صَحْرَاءُ) desert, desolate
مَكَانٌ – أَمَاكِنُ ، أَمْكِنَةٌ	place
يُقْبِلُ عَلَى	he approaches
فَـ	and, and then, and so
يُظْهِرُونَ (لِ)	they demonstrate, show (to)
رَحَّبَ ، تَرْحِيبٌ بِـ	II to welcome
يُسْرِعُونَ (إِلَى)	they hasten (to)
إِكْرَامٌ	(verbal noun) to honor
طَعَامٌ	food
تُعْجِبُ	she, it pleases
لِأَنَّ	because (See Note C.2, pages 263-5.)
حَيَاةٌ – حَيَوَاتٌ	life; life-blood
حَيَوِيٌّ – ون	(nisba of حَيَاةٌ) lively, vital
تَخْتَلِفُ (عَن)	she, it differs (from), varies
حُرِّيَّةٌ	freedom

لٰكِنَّ but, however (conjunction; see note C.2)

أَحْيانًا sometimes, at times

تِجارَة commerce, business, trade

Additional vocabulary

أَنَّ that (conjunction; see C.2)

إِنَّ that (conjunction; see C.2)

يَخْتَلِف (عن) he differs (from), varies

C. Grammar and drills — ج - القواعد والتمارين

1. Form IV verbs and verbal nouns
2. Particles لِأَنَّ 'because', لٰكِنَّ 'but', إِنَّ 'that' and أَنَّ 'that'
3. Human collective nouns
4. Particle فَ 'and, and then'

1. Form IV verbs and verbal nouns

a. Form

Form IV verbs are characterized by having a perfect stem beginning with the prefix - أَ ?a-. This prefix, however, is not present in the imperfect stem. Example:

Perfect	Imperfect	
أَكْمَلَ	يُكْمِلُ	'to complete'

The perfect stem has the pattern ?aFMaL- (prefix - أَ ?a-, stem vowel a), as in أَكْمَلَ above: stem ?akmal-. The imperfect stem has the pattern -FMiL- (stem vowel i in all verbs), as in يُكْمِلُ above: stem: -kmil-. (Thus the imperfect stem of Form IV verbs is like the imperfect stem of those Form I verbs which have i as the vowel, as in يَرْجِعُ 'he returns': stem -rjiʕ-. The perfect stems are of course different.) As in Form II and Form III verbs, the vowel of Form IV subject-marker prefixes is u. Of Forms I to X, only these three Forms have the prefix u; in Form I and Forms V through X, this vowel is a.

The following chart shows the perfect, imperfect, and jussive forms of a typical Form IV verb:

أَكْمَلَ 'to complete'

	PERFECT		IMPERFECT		
			Indicative		Jussive
3 MS	أَكْمَلَ	'he completed'	يُكْمِلُ	'he completes'	يُكْمِلْ
FS	أَكْمَلَتْ	'she completed'	تُكْمِلُ	'she completes'	تُكْمِلْ
2 MS	أَكْمَلْتَ	'you completed'	تُكْمِلُ	'you complete'	تُكْمِلْ
FS	أَكْمَلْتِ	'you completed'	تُكْمِلِينَ	'you complete'	تُكْمِلِي
1 S	أَكْمَلْتُ	'I completed'	أُكْمِلُ	'I complete'	أُكْمِلْ
3 MP	أَكْمَلُوا	'they completed'	يُكْمِلُونَ	'they complete'	يُكْمِلُوا
FP	أَكْمَلْنَ	'they completed'	يُكْمِلْنَ	'they complete'	يُكْمِلْنَ
2 MP	أَكْمَلْتُمْ	'you completed'	تُكْمِلُونَ	'you complete'	تُكْمِلُوا
FP	أَكْمَلْتُنَّ	'you completed'	تُكْمِلْنَ	'you complete'	تُكْمِلْنَ
1 P	أَكْمَلْنَا	'we completed'	نُكْمِلُ	'we complete'	نُكْمِلْ

The verbal noun of Form IV verbs has the pattern ?iFMaaL; for example, the verbal noun of أَكْمَلَ 'to complete' is إِكْمَالٌ 'completing, completion'. The following list shows the Form IV verbs which have occurred so far (imperfect in parentheses) and their verbal nouns.

Form IV verb		Verbal noun	
أَسْرَعَ (يُسْرِعُ) إلى	'to hasten (to)'	إِسْراعٌ	'hastening'
أَظْهَرَ (يُظْهِرُ)	'to demonstrate, show'	إِظْهارٌ	'demonstrating'
أَعْجَبَ (يُعْجِبُ)	'to please'	إِعْجابٌ	'pleasing'
أَخْبَرَ (يُخْبِرُ)	'to inform, tell'	إِخْبارٌ	'informing'
أَقْبَلَ (يُقْبِلُ) على	'to approach'	إِقْبالٌ على	'approaching'
أَكْمَلَ (يُكْمِلُ)	'to complete'	إِكْمالٌ	'completion'
أَكْرَمَ (يُكْرِمُ)	'to honor'	إِكْرامٌ	'honoring'
أَصْدَرَ (يُصْدِرُ)	'to publish'	إِصْدارٌ	'publication'
أَرْسَلَ (يُرْسِلُ)	'to send'	إِرْسالٌ	'sending'

Now do Drills 1 and 2.

b. Meaning

As in the case of Form II verbs, a great many verbs of Form IV are causative in meaning, and have a transitivizing function (making an intransitive Form I verb transitive, and a transitive Form I verb doubly transitive):

Form I		Form IV	
ظَهَرَ	'to appear'	أَظْهَرَ	'to cause (something) to appear, to show'
كَمُلَ	'to become complete'	أَكْمَلَ	'to make (something) complete, to complete'
سَكَنَ	'to live, reside'	أَسْكَنَ	'to lodge (someone), put (someone) up'
سَمِعَ	'to hear'	أَسْمَعَ	'to have (someone) listen to (something), to tell (someone)(something)'

Some Form IV verbs have the meaning of going to or toward a place, or getting into a state or condition:

Base Form		Form IV	
قُبْلٌ	'front, face'	أَقْبَلَ على	'to approach'
سَرُعَ	'to be fast'	أَسْرَعَ	'to hasten'

Now do Drill 3.

Drill 1. Written. Recognition: Patterns of Forms I-IV.

a. Provide the root and the verb for the Form IV verbal nouns given below:

Verbal Noun (?iFMaaL)	Form IV Verb (?aFMaLa)	Imperfect (yuFMiLu)	Root (FML)
إِكْمالٌ	أَكْمَلَ	يُكْمِلُ	كمل
انتاج			
اخراج			
اجلاس			
اشراف			
اعجاب			

b. Identify each of the verbs below as Form I, II, III, or IV. Provide verbal noun for Form II, III and IV verbs. Ex. (تَعْيينٌ) II — عيّن

أشرف　　　أنتج

اثّر　　　علم

خرج　　　حافظ

فسّر　　　وحّد

راسل　　　أخرج

Drill 2. (On tape) Conjugation: Form IV (perfect, imperfect, jussive).

Drill 3. Transformation: Perfect → negative → negative imperfect.

'I liked working in the company.' → ← أعجبني العمل فى الشركة .

'I didn't like working in the company.' → ← لم يعجبني العمل في الشركة .

'I don't like working in the company.' لا يعجبني العمل في الشركة .

١ ـ أسرعنا لاكرامه .

٢ ـ أقبلوا على الزوّار .

٣ ـ أظهرت لهم الترحيب .

٤ ـ هل أكملت عملك ؟

٥ ـ البنات اسرعن لاكرامنا .

٦ ـ أكرمني أولئك الرجال .

٧ ـ أعجبته محاضرة الاستاذ عن الوضع الحاضر .

٨ ـ هل أكملتم دراستكم ؟

2. Particles لِأَنَّ 'because', لٰكِنَّ 'but', إِنَّ and أَنَّ 'that'

These words belong to a small group of particles which share the following characteristics:

(1) They introduce clauses. (A clause is an independent sentence or a sentence which forms part of a larger sentence.)

(2) They may not be followed immediately by a verb. They are most commonly followed by a noun or a pronoun suffix, which functions as the subject of the clause.

(3) When the subject is a noun, it is in the accusative case (but a predicate noun or adjective, if present, remains nominative), for example:

لٰكِنَّ الرَّجُلَ مَشْهُورٌ. 'But the man is famous.'

Following are examples of these particles in equational and verbal sentences (clauses). The examples are in pairs, the first without the particle and the second with it. Subjects are underlined.

Equational

هٰذَا الْمَصْنَعُ جَدِيدٌ.	'This factory is new.'
لٰكِنَّ هٰذَا الْمَصْنَعَ جَدِيدٌ.	'But this factory is new.'
هِيَ ذَاهِبَةٌ اِلَى بَيْروتَ.	'She is going to Beirut.'
لِأَنَّهَا ذَاهِبَةٌ إِلَى بَيْروتَ.	'... because she is going to Beirut.'
فِي الْمَكْتَبِ رَجُلٌ.	'There's a man in the office.'
لٰكِنَّ فِي الْمَكْتَبِ رَجُلاً.	'But there's a man in the office.'

(This last example illustrates the context in which لٰكِنَّ or one of the other particles may be followed immediately by something other than the subject noun or pronoun suffix: In an equational sentence, when the subject is an indefinite noun and the predicate is an adverbial word or phrase such as هُنَاكَ 'there' or فِي الْمَكْتَبِ 'in the office', then the predicate follows the particle immediately, and the subject (in the accusative) comes after the predicate.)

Verbal

أَلْمُوَظَّفونَ يَعْمَلونَ كُلَّ الْيَوْمِ.	'The employees work all day.'
لٰكِنَّ الْمُوَظَّفينَ يَعْمَلونَ كُلَّ الْيَوْمِ.	'But the employees work all day.'
دَرَسْتَ التَّارِيخَ فِي الْأَزْهَرِ.	'You (m.) studied history at Al-Azhar.'
لِأَنَّكَ دَرَسْتَ التَّارِيخَ فِي الْأَزْهَرِ.	'...because you (m.) studied history at Al-Azhar'
بَعْضُ الْبَدْوِ يَذْهَبونَ إِلَى الْمَدِينَةِ.	'Some Bedouins go to the city.'
لٰكِنَّ بَعْضَ الْبَدْوِ يَذْهَبونَ إِلَى الْمَدِينَةِ.	'But some Bedouins go to the city.'

In previous lessons the word لٰكِنْ has occurred. Although this also means 'but', it differs from لٰكِنَّ in usage: لٰكِنْ never has a pronoun suffix, and may be followed by a verb or any other word. If it is followed by a noun, that noun is nominative.

The particles إِنَّ and أَنَّ both correspond to the English conjunction "that", in such constructions as "He said <u>that</u> he was a student" and "The minister reported that the assignment had been completed". (Do not confuse this with the demonstrative "that", as in "<u>That</u> is a good idea" or "Hand me <u>that</u> pencil", which corresponds to Arabic هٰذَا or هٰذِهِ.) The difference between إِنَّ and أَنَّ is that إِنَّ is used after the verb قَالَ 'to say' (or any of its forms), and أَنَّ is used elsewhere. Examples:

قَالَ الزَّائِرُ إِنَّهُ مِنْ بَغْدَادَ.	'The visitor said that he was from Baghdad.'
فِي هٰذَا الدَّرْسِ تَعَلَّمْتُ أَنَّ الْحَيَاةَ فِي الصَّحْرَاءِ تَخْتَلِفُ عَنِ الْحَيَاةِ فِي الْمَدِينَةِ.	'I have learned in this lesson that life in the desert is different from life in the city.'

In English, "that" may sometimes be omitted: "The visitor said he was from Baghdad"; but in Arabic إِنَّ or أَنَّ may not be omitted in this way.

When a first person pronoun suffix (singular or plural) is attached to one of these particles, there are two possible forms for each, for example:

لِأَنِّي طَالِبٌ لِأَنَّنِي طَالِبٌ	'because I am a student'
سَمِعُوا أَنَّا نَدْرُسُ الْعَرَبِيَّةَ. سَمِعُوا أَنَّنَا نَدْرُسُ الْعَرَبِيَّةَ.	'They heard that we are studying Arabic.'

These four particles, and a few others which you will meet later, are traditionally referred to as إِنَّ وَأَخَوَاتُهَا '<u>inna</u> and its sisters'. Now do Drills 4, 5 and 6.

<u>Drill 4</u>. Written. Recognition: إِنَّ وَأَخَوَاتُهَا

Vowel the words underlined below.

١ ـ هو مصريّ لكنّ زوجته من لبنان •

٢ ـ قالوا انّ الرئيس سافر الى فرنسا.

٣ ـ هل سمعتم أنّ الامتحان قصير جدا ؟

٤ ـ انتقلت الى سوريا لانّ عائلتها تسكن هناك •

٥ ـ قال انّ المرأة هامة جدا في مجتمعنا •

٦ ـ لم يدرس الفرنسية لكن درستها اخته •

٧ ـ هل ذكرت أنّ القهوة العربية لا تعجبك ؟

٨ ـ ذهبنا الى المطار لانّ موعد الطائرة قريب •

٩ ـ قرأنا انّ اقتصاد مصر يعتمد على مياه النيل الى ابعد حدّ •

Drill 5. (Also on tape) Transformation: Sentence → clause after قال انّ

'His country is beautiful.' → ← بَلَدُه جميلٌ.

'He said that his country was beautiful.' قال إنّ بلدَه جميلٌ •

١ ـ الحياة في المدينة تختلف عن الحياة فى الصحراء•

٢ ـ السدّ العالي يساعد على تقدّم الاقتصاد •

٣ ـ الموظفون يعملون كل اليوم •

٤ ـ وزارة التربية والتعليم تقرر مناهج التعليم •

٥ ـ الاساتذة الجزائريون رجعوا الى بلدهم •

٦ ـ هذه الطبيبة مشهورة جدا •

٧ ـ بذلوا جهودا كبيرة في بناء السد الاوّل •

٨ ـ هو مستعدّ للامتحان في التاريخ الاسلامي •

Drill 6. Written. Combination: Sentences joined with لِأَنَّ or لٰكِنَّ

a. With subject pronoun

'The Nile River is very important.' ← نهر النيل هامّ جدّا •

'The Egyptian economy depends upon it.' الاقتصاد المصري يعتمد عليه.

'The Nile River is very important because the Egyptian economy depends upon it.' — نهر النيل هامّ جدّا لأنّ الاقتصاد المصريّ يعتمد عليه .

١ ـ درسنا كل اليوم . الامتحان يشمل دروس الكتاب كلّه .

٢ ـ لا يعجبني هذا الصف . شبابيكه صغيرة .

٣ ـ قرأت هذا النص في ربع ساعة . ذلك النص طويل جدّا .

٤ ـ حرية الصحراء شيء جميل . الحياة فيها ليست سهلة .

b. With pronoun suffix

'They honored the old man.' — أكرموا الرجل الكبير .

'He is their father.' — هو والدهم .

'They honored the old man because he is their father.' — أكرموا الرجل الكبير لأنّه والدهم .

١ ـ أظهروا لي الترحيب . أنا زائر في مدينتهم .

٢ ـ البدو يرحلون من مكان الى آخر في الصحراء . هم يبحثون عن الماء .

٣ ـ أعجبني هذا الفيلم العراقي . هو طويل جدا .

3. Human collective nouns

The nouns عَرَبٌ 'Arabs' and بَدْوٌ 'Bedouins' illustrate a small group of nouns referring to humans that have plural meaning and that form a singular noun by means of the nisba suffix. Thus:

	Singular 'an Arab'	Plural 'Arabs'
Masculine	عَرَبِيٌّ	عَرَبٌ
Feminine	عَرَبِيَّةٌ	عَرَبِيّاتٌ

The corresponding four forms of بَدْوٌ are بَدَوِيٌّ and بَدَوِيَّةٌ 'a Bedouin', and بَدْوٌ and بَدَوِيّاتٌ 'Bedouins'.

Another word of this type that has already occurred is إِنْكِلِيزِيَّةٌ which is based on أَلْإِنْكِلِيزُ 'the English' (also spelled الإِنْجِلِيزُ); its masculine

singular form إِنْكِلِيزِيّ 'English' may of course be either a noun or an adjective.
The noun for "Americans" is أَمْرِيكَان ; its nisba 'American' may be either

أَمْرِيكَانِيّ or أَمْرِيكِيّ , which is based on أَمْرِيكَا 'America'. These two

nisba adjectives may have not only the usual feminine singular and plural, but
a masculine sound plural as well, أَمْرِيكِيّونَ , which is equivalent to أَمْرِيكَان

in meaning.

These nouns, called <u>human collectives</u>, will henceforth be listed in the vocabularies as plural nouns, with the nisba singular after a dash:

بَدْوٌ ــ بَدَوِيّ   'Bedouins'

4. <u>Particle فَ 'and, and then, and so'</u>

Both وَ and فَ may mean "and", but differ in the way they are used. وَ
is a simple connector:

أَلْأُسْتَاذُ وَالطّالِبُ	'the professor and the student'
أَلْقَلَمُ وَالْوَرَقَةُ	'the pen and the paper'
أَكَلُوا وَشَرِبُوا.	'They ate and drank.'

On the other hand فَ in such contexts implies a certain sequence or order of
events: that one thing follows another. Thus it most commonly connects clauses,
and can often be translated by "then", "and then", "and so":

رَحّبُوا بِهِم فَقَدّمُوا لَهُمُ الْقَهْوَةَ.	'They welcomed them and (then) served them coffee.'

D. <u>Comprehension passage</u>   د ــ نصوص للفهم

Read the following passage and then do Drill 7.

orienta-list — ادوارد لين مُسْتَشْرِقٌ انكليزيّ مشهور. أقبل لين على مصر في

century — القَرْنِ التاسِعَ عَشَرَ فدرس حياة المصريّين ولغتهم ، وكتب عنهم كتابا مشهورا .

قال لين فى كتابه ان الحياة في مصر تختلف عن الحياة في اوربا ، قال كذلك ان المصري يرحب بالزوار ويكرمهم ويقدم اليهم الطعام . سكن فى القاهرة ، وكان له فيها عدد كبير من الاصدقاء . تحدّث في كتابه عن حياته في مصر وعن اصدقائه المصريين فقال : أخبرني صديق

marriage; is my duty — مصري بأن الزَّواجَ واجِبٌ عَلَيَّ لانه واجِبُ كل مصريّ .

Drill 7. Oral composition.

Prepare a brief conversation (to be presented in class) based on the passage above, using words from the list provided below, or other words you have had.

أين	انّ	هنا	درس	مشهور	ادوارد لين	مستشرق
هل	بعض	هناك	كتب	انكليزي	مصر	حياة
ماذا	ل	جدّا	قال	مصريّ	أوربا	لغة
ما	لم	فقط	اختلف		القاهرة	زائر
من	بل	أثناء	رحّب ب			طعام
متى	كل		أكرم			صديق
	لكن		قدّم الى			زوجة
	ذلك		سكن			واجب على
	هو					
	هم		تحدّث عن			
	ليس		كان			
	هؤلاء					
	معظم					
	لانّ					

E. General drills

Drill 8. Written. Fill in the blanks in the chart below. Please vowel verb forms fully.

Verbal Noun	Verb		Translation
	Imperfect	Perfect	
كِتابَةٌ	يَكْتُبُ	كَتَبَ	'to write'
	يقدّم		
اسراع			
			'to please'
		أظهر	
سفر			
	يشارك		
ذهاب			
			'to appoint'
	يكرم		
			'to read'
		شاهد	

Drill 9. (Also on tape) Transformation: Singular → plural.

'The Bedouin moves from place to place.' البدويّ يرحل من مكان الى مكان.

'The Bedouins move from place to place.' البدو يرحلون من مكان الى مكان.

١ ـ هذا الكتاب الامريكي مشهور جدّا .

٢ ـ المرأة تقدّم الخدمات للمجتمع .

٣ ـ أرسلت رسالة طويلة الى عائلته .

٤ ـ ذلك الرجل الانكليزيّ موظّف في الحكومة .

٥ ـ هل لوح هذا الصف قديم ؟

٦ ـ موظّف الشركة استقبل مديره .

٧ ـ ذهب لزيارة ذلك البلد .

Drill 10. (Also on tape) Transformation: Positive → elative.

'The chair is new' -- 'the table' → الكرسيّ جديد . ـ الطاولة

"The chair is newer than the table.' الكرسيّ أجدّ من الطاولة .

١ ـ القراءة هامّة ـ الكتابة
٢ ـ السدّ العالي كبير ـ سدّ اسوان
٣ ـ هذه الكلمة طويلة ـ تلك الكلمة
٤ ـ عدد الاطبّاء كثير ـ عدد الطبيبات
٥ ـ هذا الشارع قصير ـ ذلك الشارع
٦ ـ المكتبة بعيدة ـ المتحف
٧ ـ المكتب صغير ـ الصفّ
٨ ـ الكاتب مشهور ـ الاستاذ
٩ ـ جهودي عظيمة ـ جهودك
١٠ ـ مكتبي قريب ـ مكتبك

Drill 11. Written. Completion/Translation.

Complete the following sentences, and then translate them.

١ ـ ذكر فريد أنّه ______ .

٢ ـ قُلْتُ انّي ______ . I said

٣ ـ سافرت الى الشرق الاوسط لـ ______ .

٤ ـ رجعوا الى بلدهم بعد ______ .

٥ ـ كانت صديقتي مريم ______ .

٦ ـ بعض الطلاب ______ .

٧ ـ ذهبنا الى نيويورك فـ ______ .

٨ ـ هذا البناء أعلى ______ .

٩ ـ مراسلو الجريدة كلّهم ______ .

١٠ ـ موعد الامتحان في الساعة ______ .

Drill 12. (On tape) Written. Dictation.

Lesson Twenty

الدرس العشرون

أ ـ النصّ الاساسيّ

مراسل اجنبيّ في تونس

تقدّم مراسل امريكيّ بطلب ليعمل في جريدة " العمل " التونسيّة وقابل المدير . وهذا مُوجَزُ المقابلة : summary

المدير : شكرا على تقدّمك بهذا الطلب . كيف عرفت أنّ جريدتنا بحاجة الى مراسل أجنبيّ ؟

المراسل : عرفت ذلك من صديق .

المدير : أيّ اللغات تتكلّم ؟

المراسل : أتكلّم العربيّة والفرنسيّة الى جانب الانكليزية .

المدير : وأين تعمل الآن ؟

المراسل : أعمل في جريدة" التايمز" . أتناول في مقالاتي العالم العربيّ.

المدير : هل ستتمكّن من الاقامة في تونس ؟

المراسل : لن أتمكّن من ذلك حتى أحصل على عمل في جريدتكم .

المدير : حسنًا . الحكومة عادة تتعاون معنا في مثل هذه الامور . سوف ننظر في طلبك .

المراسل : شكرا . سأكون في الانتظار .

A. Basic text

A Foreign Reporter in Tunis

An American reporter submitted an application to work on the Tunisian newspaper *Al-ʻAmal*, and he had an interview with the director. This is a summary of the interview:

Director: Thank you for submitting this application. How did you learn that our newspaper was in need of a foreign reporter?

Reporter: I found out from a friend.

Director: What languages do you speak?

Reporter: I speak Arabic and French, in addition to English.

Director: Where do you work now?

Reporter: I work on the *Times*. In my articles I deal with the Arab world.

Director: Will you be able to stay in Tunis?

Reporter: I won't be able to until I get a job on your newspaper.

Director: Fine. The government usually cooperates with us in matters such as these. We will consider your application.

Reporter: Thank you. I will be waiting.

B. Vocabulary ب ـ المفردات

تَقَدَّمَ بِ	he submitted; he presented, offered, served
طَلَبَ ـُ ، طَلَبٌ	to request, ask for; to apply for
شُكْرًا (على)	thanks (for)
تَقَدُّمٌ بِ	submission, presenting
كَيْفَ	how?
عَرَفَ ـِ ، مَعْرِفَةٌ	(perfect tense) to find out, learn, come to know; (imperfect tense) to know
حاجَةٌ ـ ات	need
بِحاجَةٍ الى ، فى حاجَةٍ الى	in need of

تَتَكَلَّمُ	you (m.s.) speak
أَتَكَلَّمُ	I speak
ألتّايْمْز	The Times
أَتَناوَلُ	I deal with, treat
مَقالٌ ، مَقالَةٌ ـ ات	article; essay
سَـ	(foll. by indic.) will, going to
تَتَمَكَّنُ مِنْ	(foll. by verbal noun) you are able to, can
لَنْ	(foll. by subjunctive) will not
أَتَمَكَّنَ من	(subjunctive) I can
حَتّى	(foll. by subjunctive) until; in order that; (foll. by perfect) until
حَسَنًا	fine! that will be fine!
تَتَعاوَنُ (مع)	she cooperates (with)
مِثْلٌ	the likes of, such...as...
أَمْرٌ ـ أُمورٌ	matter, affair, concern
سَوْفَ	(foll. by indic.) will, going to...
نَظَرَ ـُـ ، نَظَرٌ في	to look into, consider, study
سَأَكونُ	I will be
اِنْتِظارٌ	waiting (n.), wait; expectation
سَأَكونُ في الاِنْتِظارِ	I will be waiting, expecting

C. Grammar and drills ج ـ القواعد والتمارين

1. Form V verbs and verbal nouns
2. Form VI verbs and verbal nouns
3. Future: سَوْفَ or سَ with imperfect
4. The subjunctive mood
5. Cardinal and ordinal numbers: 20 to 99

1. Form V verbs and verbal nouns

a. Form

Form V verbs are characterized by having stems with a prefix تَـ ta- and a double middle radical, for example:

Perfect	Imperfect	
تَكَلَّمَ	يَتَكَلَّمُ	'to speak'

The perfect stem has the pattern taFaMMaL- (prefix تَـ ta-, middle radical double, stem vowel and preceding vowel both always a), as in تَكَلَّمَ above: stem takallam-. The imperfect stem also has the pattern taFaMMaL- as in يَتَكَلَّمُ above: stem -takallam-. The vowel of Form V subject-marker prefixes is a, as it is in Form I and Forms VI through X.

The following chart shows the perfect, imperfect, and jussive forms of a typical Form V verb.

تَكَلَّمَ 'to speak'

	PERFECT		IMPERFECT		
			Indicative		Jussive
3 MS	تَكَلَّمَ	'he spoke'	يَتَكَلَّمُ	'he speaks'	يَتَكَلَّمْ
FS	تَكَلَّمَتْ	'she spoke'	تَتَكَلَّمُ	'she speaks'	تَتَكَلَّمْ
2 MS	تَكَلَّمْتَ	'you spoke'	تَتَكَلَّمُ	'you speak'	تَتَكَلَّمْ
FS	تَكَلَّمْتِ	'you spoke'	تَتَكَلَّمِينَ	'you speak'	تَتَكَلَّمِي
1 S	تَكَلَّمْتُ	'I spoke'	أَتَكَلَّمُ	'I speak'	أَتَكَلَّمْ
3 MP	تَكَلَّمُوا	'they spoke'	يَتَكَلَّمُونَ	'they speak'	يَتَكَلَّمُوا
FP	تَكَلَّمْنَ	'they spoke'	يَتَكَلَّمْنَ	'they speak'	يَتَكَلَّمْنَ
2 MP	تَكَلَّمْتُمْ	'you spoke'	تَتَكَلَّمُونَ	'you speak'	تَتَكَلَّمُوا
FP	تَكَلَّمْتُنَّ	'you spoke'	تَتَكَلَّمْنَ	'you speak'	تَتَكَلَّمْنَ
1 P	تَكَلَّمْنا	'we spoke'	نَتَكَلَّمُ	'we speak'	نَتَكَلَّمْ

The verbal noun of Form V verbs has the pattern taFaMMuL; for example, the verbal noun of تَكَلَّمَ 'to speak' is تَكَلُّمٌ 'speaking, speech'. The following list shows the Form V verbs which have occurred so far (imperfect in parentheses) and their verbal nouns:

Form V verb		Verbal noun	
تَحَدَّثَ (يَتَحَدَّثُ)	'to talk'	تَحَدُّثٌ	'talking, talk'
تَعَلَّمَ (يَتَعَلَّمُ)	'to learn'	تَعَلُّمٌ	'learning'
تَقَدَّمَ (يَتَقَدَّمُ)	'to advance'	تَقَدُّمٌ	'advancement, progress'
تَقَدَّمَ (يَتَقَدَّمُ) بِـ	'to submit (something)'	تَقَدُّمٌ بِـ	'submitting'
تَكَلَّمَ (يَتَكَلَّمُ)	'to speak'	تَكَلُّمٌ	'speaking'
تَمَكَّنَ (يَتَمَكَّنُ) مِنْ	'to be able to'	تَمَكُّنٌ مِنْ	'ability to'

Some Form V verbs have not only their regular verbal nouns but also employ a common noun as an alternate verbal noun. Thus, in addition to تَكَلُّمٌ 'talking' the noun كَلامٌ 'talk, speech' is often used as the verbal noun of تَكَلَّمَ 'to talk, speak'. For example, in the sentence

تَكَلَّمَ كَثيراً ، وَكانَ كَلامُهُ جَميلاً .	'He spoke a lot, and his speech was beautiful.'

it is less usual to use تَكَلُّمٌ in place of كَلامٌ .

Such nouns which may replace verbal nouns will be listed in the vocabularies after a slash, e.g.

تكلّم ، تكلّم / كلام	'to talk, speak'
تحدّث ، تحدّث / حديث	'to talk, converse'
تعلّم ، تعلّم / علم	'to learn, be educated'
تزوّج ، تزوّج / زواج	'to marry'

b. Meaning

Form V verbs are typically related in meaning to Form II verbs rather than Form I. Their meaning is often reflexive--the action indicated by the Form II verb (for example عَلَّمَ 'to teach') is viewed as being undergone by the subject of the Form V verb, whether as a result of that subject's own action or that of another agency (تَعَلَّمَ to teach oneself', or 'to be taught'; that is, 'to learn'). In many cases a Form V verb is best translated as an English passive. Following are examples of these various meanings.

Form II		Form V	
قَدَّمَ	'to present (something)'	تَقَدَّمَ	'to present oneself; to come forward; progress'
قَرَّرَ	'to decide (something)	تَقَرَّرَ	'to be decided'
مَكَّنَ مِنْ	'to enable (someone) to (do something)'	تَمَكَّنَ مِنْ	'to become able to (do something)'
كَلَّمَ	'to speak to, address (someone)'	تَكَلَّمَ	'to speak'

Some Form V verbs are based on nouns, and have imitative meaning: "to be, become, or pretend to be like that noun or those associated with it", for example:

Base form		Form V	
مِصْرُ	'Egypt'	تَمَصَّرَ	'to become an Egyptian, adopt Egyptian ways'

Now do Drills 1 and 2.

Drill 1. Written. Recognition: Pattern of Forms II and V.

Fill in the blanks in the chart below. Write in the vowels.

Imperfect yataFaMMaLu	Form V Verb (taFaMMaLa)	Form II Verb (FaMMaLa)	Root (FML)
يَتَقَدَّمُ	تَقَدَّمَ	قَدَّمَ	قدم
			صرف
			وفر
			زوج
			غير
			أثر

Drill 2. (On tape) Conjugation: Form V .

2. Form VI verbs and verbal nouns

a. Form

Form VI verbs are characterized by having stems with a prefix تَ ta- and a long vowel after the first radical, for example:

Perfect	Imperfect	
تَراسَلَ	يَتَراسَلُ	'to correspond' (exchange letters)

The perfect stem has the pattern taFaaMaL- (prefix تَ ta-, long vowel aa after the first radical, stem vowel a), as in تَراسَلَ above: stem taraasal-. The imperfect stem also has the pattern -taFaaMaL-, as in يَتَراسَلُ above; stem -taraasal-. The vowel of Form VI subject-marker prefixes is a, as it is in all the ten Forms except II, III, and IV.

The following chart shows the perfect, imperfect, and jussive forms of a typical Form VI verb.

تَراسَلَ 'to correspond'

	PERFECT		IMPERFECT			
			Indicative			Jussive
3 MS	تَراسَلَ	'he corresponded'	يَتَراسَلُ	'he corresponds'		يَتَراسَلْ
FS	تَراسَلَتْ	'she corresponded'	تَتَراسَلُ	'she corresponds'		تَتَراسَلْ
2 MS	تَراسَلْتَ	'you corresponded'	تَتَراسَلُ	'you correspond'		تَتَراسَلْ
FS	تَراسَلْتِ	'you corresponded'	تَتَراسَلِينَ	'you correspond'		تَتَراسَلي
1 S	تَراسَلْتُ	'I corresponded'	أَتَراسَلُ	'I correspond'		أَتَراسَلْ
3 MP	تَراسَلوا	'they corresponded'	يَتَراسَلونَ	'they correspond'		يَتَراسَلوا
FP	تَراسَلْنَ	'they corresponded'	يَتَراسَلْنَ	'they correspond'		يَتَراسَلْنَ
2 MP	تَراسَلْتُمْ	'you corresponded'	تَتَراسَلونَ	'you correspond'		تَتَراسَلوا
FP	تَراسَلْتُنَّ	'you corresponded'	تَتَراسَلْنَ	'you correspond'		تَتَراسَلْنَ
1 P	تَراسَلْنا	'we corresponded'	نَتَراسَلُ	'we correspond'		نَتَراسَلْ

The verbal noun of Form VI verbs has the pattern taFaaMuL; for example, the verbal noun of تَراسَلَ 'to correspond' is تَراسُلٌ 'correspondence'. (Note that both Form V and Form VI verbal nouns have u as their stem vowel: تَقَدُّمٌ 'progress' and تَراسُلٌ 'correspondence'.) In addition to تَراسَلَ, used as a model above, two Form VI verbs have occurred so far. These three verbs are listed below (imperfect in parentheses) with their verbal nouns:

	Form VI verb		Verbal noun	
(يَتَراسَلُ)	تَراسَلَ	'to correspond'	تَراسُلٌ	'correspondence'
(يَتَعاوَنُ)	تَعاوَنَ	'to cooperate'	تَعاوُنٌ	'cooperation'
(يَتَناوَلُ)	تَناوَلَ	'to deal with'	تَناوُلٌ	'dealing with'

b. Meaning

Form VI verbs are typically related in meaning to Form III verbs. In some cases the relationship is similar to that of Form V with Form II: the Form VI verb is the <u>reflexive</u> of the Form III. In particular, Form VI verbs typically (not always) express <u>reciprocity</u>: two or more subjects perform on each other the action denoted by the Form III verb, for example

Form III		Form VI	
عاوَنَ	'to help'	تَعاوَنَ	'to help one another, to cooperate'
قابَلَ	'to meet (someone)'	تَقابَلَ	'to meet, meet together'
راسَلَ	'to write to (someone)'	تَراسَلَ	'to write to one another, to correspond'

In this meaning, of course, the subject is often dual or plural:

تَعاوَنوا في بِناءِ السَّدِّ .	'They cooperated in the building of the dam.'

When the subject of a reciprocal Form VI verb is singular, a preposition is generally required. Contrast this with the corresponding Form III verb, which usually takes a direct object:

<u>Form III</u>	
قابَلَ فَريدٌ مَرْيَمَ .	'Farid met Maryam.'
عاوَنَهُمْ في عَمَلِهِمْ .	'He helped them in their work.'
<u>Form VI</u>	
تَقابَلَ فَريدٌ وَمَرْيَمُ	'Farid and Maryam met.'
تَعاوَنَ مَعَهُمْ في عَمَلِهِمْ .	'He cooperated with them in their work.'

Now do Drills 3, 4, and 5.

<u>Drill 3</u>. Written. Recognition: Pattern of Forms III and VI.

Provide the Form III and Form VI verb and verbal noun for each of the roots below:

Verbal Noun VI taFaaMuL	Form VI (taFaaMaLa)	Form III (FaaMaLa)	Root (FML)
تَعاوُنٌ	تَعاوَنَ	عاوَنَ	عون
			رسل
			بدل
			قبل
			شرك
			صدق

Drill 4. (On tape) Conjugation: Form VI.

Drill 5. Substitution.

Substitute the following phrases for the underlined phrase, using the verbal noun that corresponds to the verb in the phrase. Ex.

'You were able to stay in Egypt.' تمكنت من الاقامة في مصر.

'You went to the meeting.' ذهبت الى الاجتماع .

'You were able to go to the meeting.' تمكنت من الذهاب الى الاجتماع.

١ ـ نظرت في طلبه .

٢ ـ درّست العربية .

٣ ـ شاركت في بناء المصنع .

٤ ـ عيّنت الوزير الجديد .

٥ ـ تعاونت معه .

٦ ـ نشرت كتابا جديدا .

٧ ـ تناولت موضوع الحرية السياسية في مقالتك .

٨ ـ حصلت على شهادة الدكتوراه .

٩ ـ بذلت جهودا عظيمة .

١٠ ـ تابعت دراستك .

١١ ـ اظهرت الترحيب له .

3. Future: سَوْفَ or سَ with imperfect

Future time in Arabic is expressed by the particle سَوْفَ 'will, shall, going to' (invariable in form) followed by an imperfect indicative verb form:

سَوْفَ نَنْظُرُ في طَلَبِكَ .	'We will look into your request.'
سَوْفَ يَتَقَدَّمُ مُعْظَمُ الطُّلاّبِ بِطَلَباتٍ أُخْرى لِلْعَمَلِ .	'Most of the students are going to submit other job applications.'

سَوْفَ, which is more formal, is usually shortened to سَـ , which is prefixed to the indicative form of the verb:

سَنَنْظُرُ في طَلَبِكَ .	'We will look into your request.'
سَأَدْرُسُ الْعَرَبِيَّةَ في جامِعَةِ جورجتاون	'I'm going to study Arabic at Georgetown University.'

The imperfect indicative forms of كانَ 'to be', used with سَوْفَ or سَـ to mean "he will be", "she will be", etc. are as follows.

3 MS	يَكونُ	3 MP	يَكونونَ
FS	تَكونُ	FP	يَكُنَّ
2 MS	تَكونُ	2 MP	تَكونونَ
FS	تَكونينَ	FP	تَكُنَّ
1 S	أَكونُ	1 P	نَكونُ

Examples:

سَأَكونُ هُنا غَدًا .	'I'll be here tomorrow.'
سَيَكونُ الْمُديرُ في مَكْتَبِهِ غَدًا مِنَ السّاعَةِ الثّامِنَةِ حَتّى السّاعَةِ الرّابِعَةِ .	'The director will be in his office tomorrow from eight to four.'

A سَوْفَ construction may be made negative by use of the negative particle لا 'not' immediately before the imperfect verb, particularly in journalistic Arabic:

سَوْفَ لا أَتَمَكَّنُ مِنَ الإِقامَةِ هُنا .	'I will not be able to stay here.'

If the prefix سَـ is used, no negative is possible. For the usual way to express future negative, see C.4 below.

Now do Drill 6.

Drill 6. (Also on tape) Transformation: ـسَ and سَوْفَ .

Make the following sentences future using first ـسَ and then سَوْفَ . Ex.

'I can (am able to) stay here.'→ ←أتمكنُ من الاقامة هنا.

'I will be able to stay here.'→ ←سأتمكنُ من الاقامة هنا.

'I will be able to stay here.' سوف أتمكنُ من الاقامة هنا.

١ ـ يتناول هذا الموضوع في مقالته.

٢ ـ تتكلّم العربية في محاضراتها.

٣ ـ يرحلون من مكان الى مكان في الصحراء.

٤ ـ المراسلات يقابلن الرئيس غدا.

٥ ـ أبحث عن عمل في هذه المدينة.

٦ ـ يسرعون الى الترحيب بالزائر الاجنبي.

٧ ـ تقدّم لهم الطعام والشراب.

٨ ـ يساعد على تقدّم الاقتصاد.

٩ ـ يقبل الزائر على البدو فيكرمونه.

١٠ ـ افعل ذلك كل يوم.

١١ ـ نترك الكتب في الصف كل يوم.

4. The Subjunctive Mood

a. Form

The subjunctive differs from the indicative in two ways: (1) final ـُ u mood marker is changed to ـَ a, e.g. يَدْرُسُ and يَدْرُسَ ; and (2) ـنَ after a long vowel is dropped e.g. يَدْرُسونَ and يَدْرُسوا . (Note that, as with any plural verb ending in و an ا is added here.) The feminine plural ـنَ remains the same for indicative, jussive and subjunctive. The following chart compares the three moods of دَرَسَ :

	Singular				
	انا	انتِ	انتَ	هي	هو
Indicative	أَدْرُسُ	تَدْرُسِينَ	تَدْرُسُ	تَدْرُسُ	يَدْرُسُ
Subjunctive	أَدْرُسَ	تَدْرُسي	تَدْرُسَ	تَدْرُسَ	يَدْرُسَ
Jussive	أَدْرُسْ	تَدْرُسي	تَدْرُسْ	تَدْرُسْ	يَدْرُسْ
	Plural				
	نحن	انتن	انتم	هن	هم
Indicative	نَدْرُسُ	تَدْرُسْنَ	تَدْرُسونَ	يَدْرُسْنَ	يَدْرُسونَ
Subjunctive	نَدْرُسَ	تَدْرُسْنَ	تَدْرُسوا	يَدْرُسْنَ	يَدْرُسوا
Jussive	نَدْرُسْ	تَدْرُسْنَ	تَدْرُسوا	يَدْرُسْنَ	يَدْرُسوا

b. Uses.

The subjunctive is used only when required by a word or expression in the sentence. Three such words are لَنْ 'will not', حَتّى 'until, up to the point that' and لِ 'in order that'. No word may separate them and their verb.

(1) لَنْ 'will not', 'will not at all' negates the future; it directly precedes the subjunctive without سَـ or سَوْفَ and is stronger than سَوْفَ لا :

لَنْ نُشارِكَ في تَعْيينِ وُزَراءَ جُدُدٍ .	'We will not participate in the appointment of new ministers.'
لَنْ يُسافِروا غَدًا .	'They will not leave tomorrow.'
أَلَنْ تَتَكَلَّمي عَنْ تاريخِهِمْ ؟	'Won't you talk about their history?'
لَنْ يَكونَ الْمُديرُ في مَكْتَبِهِ غَدًا .	'The director will not be in his office tomorrow.'

(2) حَتّى 'in order that' is illustrated in the following:

حَضَروا إِلى أَمْريكا حَتّى يَحْصُلوا عَلى الشَّهادَةِ .	'They came to America in order to get their degree.'

حَتَّى 'until' may also occur with the perfect tense if the action has been completed:

دَرَسُوا حَتَّى حَصَلُوا عَلَى الدُّكْتُوراه .	'They studied until they got the Ph.D.'
سَاعَدْتُهُ حَتَّى حَصَلَ عَلَى الشهادَةِ .	'I helped him until he got his degree.'

(3) لِ 'in order that, so that' denotes purpose; it is generally best translated into English with "to" plus an infinitive:

قَدَّموا طَلَبًا لِيَعْمَلوا فِي جَريدَةِ "الْحَياةُ" .	'They submitted a request to work (in order that they work) on the Hayat.'

There are several common particles that mean the same as لِ and function the same way: لِكَيْ , كَيْ , and حَتَّى , all meaning "in order that". The negatives of purpose are كَيْلا or لِكَيْلا , or لِئَلّا , 'in order that... not, so that...not', 'lest'. Further examples:

بَحَثَ عَنْ كِتابِ تاريخِ لِيَقْرَأَ عَنْ اوروبا الْقَديمةِ .	'He looked for a history book to read about ancient Europe.'
سَنَتَكَلَّمُ مع الْمُديرِ لِكَيْ نَعْمَلَ فِي الشركةِ .	'We're going to talk with the director so that we can work in the company.'
شارَكوا فِي بِناءِ السَّدِّ حَتَّى يُساعِدوا عَلَى تَقَدُّمِ الْبَلَدِ .	'They participated in the building of the dam in order to help in the country's progress.'
بَذَلْنا جُهودًا كَيْلا يُسافِروا .	'We did our best so they would not leave.'

If an equational sentence follows a word requiring the subjunctive, the appropriate form of the subjunctive of كانَ is inserted; compare:

هُوَ مُعَلِّمٌ .	'He is a teacher.'
يَدْرُسُ لِيَكونَ مُعَلِّمًا .	'He is studying to be a teacher.'

Another major use of the subjunctive will be dealt with in Lesson 22.
Now do Drills 7 (on tape), 8, and 9.

Drill 7. (On tape) Conjugation: Subjunctive.

Drill 8. Transformation/Translation.

Combine the two sentences into one using the word indicated in parentheses. Translate each sentence. Ex.

'He travelled to Lebanon.'	سافر الى لبنان .
'He looked for work there.'	بحث عن عمل هناك . (لِ)
'He travelled to Lebanon to look for work there.'	سافر الى لبنان ليبحث عن عمل هناك .

١ ــ ذهبت الى مصر . شاهدت الآثار القديمة هناك . (كي)

٢ ــ سكن هنا . حضرت عائلته . (حتى)

٣ ــ أسرعنا . رحّبنا بالزائر . (لِ)

٤ ــ يقدمون الخدمات الكثيرة . تقدّم المجتمع . (حتى)

٥ ــ يسافر احيانا الى نيويورك . حضر اجتماعات هامة . (لكي)

Drill 9. (Also on tape) Transformation: Verbal noun → ل + Subjunctive.

'He travelled to Lebanon to look for work.' ← . سافر الى لبنان للبحث عن عمل

سافر الى لبنان ليبحث عن عمل .

١ ــ يبذلون جهودا كبيرة للحصول على شهادة الماجستير .

٢ ــ سافرت الى فرنسا للمشاركة في بناء المصنع الجديد .

٣ ــ يرحلون من مكان الى مكان للبحث عن الماء .

٤ ــ رجعت الى بلدها للدراسة هناك .

٥ ــ ذهبن الى السينما لمشاهدة الفيلم الجديد .

5. Cardinal and ordinal numbers: 20 to 99

a. Cardinals

The multiples of ten from 'twenty' to 'ninety' have the masculine sound plural endings ـونَ -uuna (nominative) and ـينَ -iina (genitive and accusative). They are as follows:

٢٠	عِشْرونَ	'twenty'
٣٠	ثَلاثونَ	'thirty'
٤٠	أَرْبَعونَ	'forty'
٥٠	خَمْسونَ	'fifty'
٦٠	سِتّونَ	'sixty'
٧٠	سَبْعونَ	'seventy'
٨٠	ثَمانونَ	'eighty'
٩٠	تِسْعونَ	'ninety'

Numbers between the multiples of ten are phrases consisting of (first) the units number and (second) the tens number preceded by وَ, for example, خَمْسَةٌ وَعِشْرونَ 'twenty-five' (literally "five and twenty"). For "one" in such phrases, both واحِدٌ and أَحَدٌ are used. Examples:

٢١	واحِدٌ وَعِشْرونَ	'twenty-one'
٢١	أَحَدٌ وَعِشْرونَ	'twenty-one'
٢٢	اِثْنانِ وَعِشْرونَ	'twenty-two'
٢٣	ثَلاثَةٌ وَعِشْرونَ	'twenty-three'
٣٤	أَرْبَعَةٌ وَثَلاثونَ	'thirty-four'
٦٧	سَبْعَةٌ وَسِتّونَ	'sixty-seven'

b. Ordinals

The ordinals corresponding to the multiples of ten are simply the cardinals themselves with the definite article. They agree in case with the noun they modify but are invariable as to gender.

أَلْيَوْمُ الْعِشْرونَ	'the twentieth day'
بَعْدَ الْيَوْمِ الْعِشْرينَ	'after the twentieth day'
أَلسَّنَةُ الْأَرْبَعونَ	'the fortieth year'
في السَّنَةِ الْأَرْبَعينَ	'in the fortieth year'

Ordinals between the multiples of ten are phrases consisting of (first) one of the ordinals "first" to "ninth" with the definite article and (second) one of the ordinals "twenty" to "ninety" also with the definite article. The unit ordinal agrees with the noun in case and gender; the tens ordinal agrees in case. For "first" in these phrases, أَلْحادي (f. أَلْحادِيَةٌ) is used instead of أَلأَوَّلُ (f. أَلأُولى). Examples:

أَلدَّرْسُ الْحادي وَٱلْعِشْرونَ	'the twenty-first lesson'
في الدَّرْسِ الْحادي والْعِشْرينَ	'in the twenty-first lesson'
هٰذِهِ هي الْجُمْلَةُ الْحادِيَةُ وٱلْعِشْرونَ.	'This is the twenty-first sentence.'
قَرَأْتُ الْجُمْلَةَ الْحادِيَةَ والْعِشْرينَ.	'I have read the twenty-first sentence.'
أَلْيَوْمُ الثّاني والثّلاثونَ	'the thirty-second day'
في السَّنَةِ الْخامِسَةِ والثّمانينَ	'in the eighty-fifth year'

Now do Drills 10, 11, and 12.

Drill 10. Written: Cardinal numbers.

Ex. '23' → ← ٢٣

'twenty-three' ثلاثة وعشرون

٧٠ ٣٤

٥٨ ٦٥

٩٢ ٤٩

٨٠ ٢٧

Drill 11. (Also on tape) Substitution: Ordinal numerals.

a. 'The twenty-seventh letter is long.' الرسالة السابعة والعشرون طويلة .

١ — ثلاثة وثلاثون ٤ — خمسة وعشرون

٢ — ستة وتسعون ٥ — ثمانية وسبعون

٣ — اربعون ٦ — واحد وخمسون

b. 'There are important rules in the twenty-seventh lesson.'

في الدرس السابع والعشرين قواعد هامة .

١ - واحد وعشرون

٢ - ستة وستون

٣ - خمسة وثمانون

٤ - اثنان وثلاثون

٥ - اربعة وسبعون

٦ - تسعون

Drill 12. Variable Substitution: Ordinals.

'I read the twenty-first lesson.'

قرأت الدرس الحادي والعشرين .

الرسالة	المقالة
ستة وخمسون	اربعون
النص	الكتاب
اثنان وثمانون	واحد وستون

D. Comprehension passage

د - نصوص للفهم

(1) Read the following passage; then do Drill 13.

قابل عدد من مديري المصانع الجزائرية وزير الصِناعَةِ في الساعة العاشرة من صباح امس . تحدّث الوزير معهم وقتًا طويلاً. قال : " في الجزائر الآن عدد كبير من المصانع ، ولكن دولتنا بحاجة الى عدد اكبر . سوف تقدّم بعض الدول الأوربّيةِ لنا المساعدة في بناء هذه المصانع ، وسوف تتعاون معنا بعض الجامعات الاجنبية في تَدْريبِ الموظفين . وقدمت الى رَئيسِ الْوُزَراءِ طلبًا يَتَعَلَّقُ بهذا الامر ، وسوف ينظر في الطلب قَريبًا " .

industry; European; training; a request which is related to; prime minister; soon

نشرت جريدة "المُجاهِدُ" الجزائرية صباح اليوم مقالة عن

مقابلة المديرين للوزير . قال كاتب المقالة :

"حكومتنا اليوم تعمل على تقدّم الاقتصاد الجزائري ، والصناعة تساعد على التقدّم " .

Drill 13. Questions.

أسئلة

١ – الى من تحدّث الوزير صباح امس ؟

٢ – أيّ دول ستساعد الجزائر في بناء المصانع الجديدة ؟

٣ – من سيساعد على تعليم الموظفين الجزائريّين ؟

٤ – أيّ جريدة نشرت مقالة عن المقابلة ؟

٥ – ماذا قالت المقالة عن الصناعة ؟

(2) Listen to the passage on tape and then do Drill 14.

Drill 14. (On tape) Passage for aural comprehension.

أسئلة

١ – هل ميخائيل نعيمة كاتب مشهور ؟

٢ – أين درس ميخائيل نعيمة ؟

٣ – الى أين رحل نعيمة بعد دراسته في أوربا ؟

٤ – من أين ميخائيل نعيمة ؟

٥ – أين سكن ميخائيل نعيمة بعد رجوعه من أمريكا ؟

E. General drills

هـ – التمارين العامّة

Drill 15. Negation.

'I found that out from my friend.' → ← عرفت ذلك من صديقي .

'I didn't find that out from my friend.' لم اعرف ذلك من صديقي .

١ – سأتمكن من مساعدتك .

٢ ـ الحياة في الصحراء سهلة ٠

٣ ـ تعجبني زيارة المتاحف ٠

٤ ـ يتعاون عادة مع المصريين في جهودهم ٠

٥ ـ احمد اطول طالب في الصف ٠

٦ ـ سافر الى الجزائر لحضور الاجتماع ٠

٧ ـ قواعد هذا الدرس هامّة ٠

٨ ـ تختلف الحياة في بلدنا عن الحياة في بلدكم ٠

٩ ـ سافر صديقي الى الشرق الاوسط للتجارة فقط ٠

١٠ ـ قرأت شيئا عن تاريخ مصر ٠

Drill 16. Written: Cognate accusative.

Fill in the blank with the noun or verbal noun which corresponds to the verb of the sentence.

١ ـ تقدّم اقتصاد مصر ـــــ عظيما بعد بناء السد العالي ٠

٢ ـ رحّبنا بالزائر ـــــ جميلا ٠

٣ ـ تساعد النساء ـــــ كبيرة على تقدّم المجتمع الامريكي ٠

٤ ـ بحث الوزراء الوضع ـــــ طويلا ٠

٥ ـ تعاونت الدول ـــــ عظيما في بناء السد ٠

Drill 17. Written. Translation.

Farid met with Professor Hussein at 10:00 to discuss studying in America next year. The professor welcomed Farid and served (presented) him Arabic coffee. During the visit Farid said, "I will not return until I get the masters degree."

And Professor Hussein said, "After your return you will be able to render many services to Arab society and to work for its advancement."

Drill 18. Completion. Vocabulary.

Fill in the blanks choosing from the following list of words. Make any necessary changes.

جريدة ، وظائف ، جهود ، ليس ، ساعة ، منهج ، مستعد

امرأة ، ذلك ، جمل ، قابل ، بناء ، صف ، نهر ، واجب

عنوان ، عودة ، عدد ، طعام ، امام .

١ ـ بذل المصريون ــــ كبيرة في بناء السد العالي .

٢ ـ النيل اطول ــــ في العالم .

٣ ـ تقرر وزارة التربية والتعليم ــــ التعليم في المدارس .

٤ ـ للنساء في بعض البلاد العربية حق الحصول على ــــ حكومية عالية .

٥ ـ ما ــــ محاضرة استاذنا اليوم ؟

٦ ـ سَأَسْتَقْبِلُ صديقي في ــــ العاشرة في المطار . I will meet

٧ ـ ــــ المدير المراسل في مكتبه .

٨ ـ هل انت ــــ للامتحان في اللغة العربية يا وليم ؟

٩ ـ اكتب لك هذه الرسالة بعد ــــ من الشرق الاوسط .

١٠ ـ هل تعرف هذا ــــ الجديد ؟

١١ ـ بعد ــــ شربنا قهوة عربية في المطعم .

١٢ ـ رحب البدوي بالزائر وقدّم له ــــ .

١٣ ـ قرأ فريد ــــ النص الاساسي .

١٤ ـ شاهدنا فيلما بعنوان رجل و ــــ .

١٥ ـ قرأت عن ذلك في ــــ المساء البيروتية .

Lesson Twenty-one

الدرس الحادي والعشرون

أ _ النص الاساسيّ

الانتخابات

في الولايات المتّحدة الامريكيّة

١ _ شريف : كيف تنتخبون رئيس الجمهوريّة في امريكا ؟

٢ _ جولي : يجتمع الحزبان الرئيسيّان لينتخبا مرشّحيهما ، ثم ينتخب الشعب أحد هذين المرشّحين .

٣ _ شريف : متى تَجْري الانتخابات في امريكا ؟ take place

٤ _ جولي : كلّ اربعة اعوام .

٥ _ شريف : أين يعقد الحزبان مؤتمريهما ؟

٦ _ جولي : في مدينتين كبيرتين .

٧ _ شريف : متى ينعقد هذان المؤتمران ؟

٨ _ جولي : في الصيف .

٩ _ شريف : هل تعتبرون انتخاب الرئيس أمرا هامّا ؟

١٠ _ جولي : نعم ، لانّ له تأثيرا كبيرا على الحياة في امريكا وفي كلّ دول العالم .

A. Basic text

Elections in the United States of America

Sharif: How do you elect the president in America?

Julie: The two main parties meet to elect their (two) candidates, then the people elect one of these two candidates.

Sharif: When do the elections take place in America?

Julie: Every four years.

Sharif: Where do the two parties hold their conventions?

Julie: In two large cities.

Sharif: When are these two conventions held?

Julie: In the summer.

Sharif: Do you (pl.) consider the election of the president an important matter?

Julie: Yes, because it has a great effect on life in America and in all the countries of the world.

B. Vocabulary — ب ـ المفردات

إِنْتِخابٌ ـ ات	election
وِلايَةٌ ـ ات	province; state
اَلْوِلاياتُ الْمُتَّحِدَةُ (الأَمْرِيكِيَّةُ)	the United States (of America)
شَرِيفٌ	Sharif (m. name)
تَنْتَخِبُونَ	you (m.p.) elect
جُمْهُورِيَّةٌ ـ ات	republic
رَئِيسُ جُمْهُورِيَّةٍ ـ رُؤَساءُ جُمْهُورِيّاتٍ	president
رَئِيسِيٌّ ـ ون	(nisba of رَئِيسٌ) main, chief, principal, leading
يَجْتَمِعُ ، إِجْتِماعٌ (ب ، مع)	he meets (with)
حِزْبانِ	(nom.) two (political) parties
حِزْبٌ ـ أَحْزابٌ	(political) party
رَئِيسِيّانِ	(du., nom.) principal, main
يَنْتَخِبا	(subjunctive) they (du.) elect
مُرَشَّحَيْنِ	(gen./acc.) two candidates
مُرَشَّحٌ ـ ون	candidate, nominee
شَعْبٌ ـ شُعُوبٌ	a people
أَحَدٌ (إِحْدى)	one, someone; (in iḍāfa) one of
هٰذَيْنِ	(du., gen./acc.) these, those

عامٌ ـ أَعْوامٌ	year
عَقَدَ ـِ ، عَقْدٌ	to hold (a meeting)
مُؤْتَمَرَيْن	(gen./acc.) two conferences, conventions
يَنْعَقِدُ	it is held (a meeting)
هٰذان	(du., nom.) these, those
مُؤْتَمَران	(nom.) two conferences, conventions
صَيْفٌ ـ أَصْياف	summer
تَعْتَبِرونَ	you (m.p.) consider (s.th.) as (s.th.)
أَثَّرَ ، تَأْثيرٌ على ، في	II to influence, affect

Additional vocabulary

اِخْتَلَفَ ، اِخْتِلافٌ (مَعَ) ... (في)	VIII to disagree (with)...(about)
اِنْصَرَفَ ، اِنْصِرافٌ	VII to go away, leave
اِنْتَظَرَ ، اِنْتِظارٌ	VIII to wait (for), to await (s.o.)

C. Grammar and drills   ج ـ القواعد والتمارين

1. Form VII verbs and verbal nouns
2. Form VIII verbs and verbal nouns
3. The dual of nouns, adjectives, and pronouns
4. The dual of verbs
5. The noun أَحَدٌ 'someone'
6. Numerals with nouns

1. Form VII verbs and verbal nouns

a. Form

The characteristic feature of Form VII verbs is a prefixed n-. The perfect stem is -nFaMaL- and the imperfect stem is -nFaMiL-, the difference in tense being indicated by the stem vowel a for perfect and i for imperfect. The perfect forms are written with <u>waṣla</u>, since they would otherwise begin with two consonants. The two tenses are illustrated below.

<u>Root</u>	<u>Perfect</u>	<u>Imperfect</u>	
ṢRF	إِنْصَرَفَ	يَنْصَرِفُ	'to go away'

The following chart shows the perfect and the imperfect indicative, subjunctive and jussive of a typical VII verb. (Duals are treated on pages 307-8.)

إِنْصَرَفَ 'to go away'

PERFECT		IMPERFECT		
Singular		Indicative	Subjunctive	Jussive
3 M	إِنْصَرَفَ	يَنْصَرِفُ	يَنْصَرِفَ	يَنْصَرِفْ
F	إِنْصَرَفَتْ	تَنْصَرِفُ	تَنْصَرِفَ	تَنْصَرِفْ
2 M	إِنْصَرَفْتَ	تَنْصَرِفُ	تَنْصَرِفَ	تَنْصَرِفْ
F	إِنْصَرَفْتِ	تَنْصَرِفِينَ	تَنْصَرِفِي	تَنْصَرِفِي
1	إِنْصَرَفْتُ	أَنْصَرِفُ	أَنْصَرِفَ	أَنْصَرِفْ
Dual				
3 M	إِنْصَرَفَا	يَنْصَرِفَانِ	يَنْصَرِفَا	يَنْصَرِفَا
F	إِنْصَرَفَتَا	تَنْصَرِفَانِ	تَنْصَرِفَا	تَنْصَرِفَا
2	إِنْصَرَفْتُمَا	تَنْصَرِفَانِ	تَنْصَرِفَا	تَنْصَرِفَا
Plural				
3 M	إِنْصَرَفُوا	يَنْصَرِفُونَ	يَنْصَرِفُوا	يَنْصَرِفُوا
F	إِنْصَرَفْنَ	يَنْصَرِفْنَ	يَنْصَرِفْنَ	يَنْصَرِفْنَ
2 M	إِنْصَرَفْتُمْ	تَنْصَرِفُونَ	تَنْصَرِفُوا	تَنْصَرِفُوا
F	إِنْصَرَفْتُنَّ	تَنْصَرِفْنَ	تَنْصَرِفْنَ	تَنْصَرِفْنَ
1	إِنْصَرَفْنَا	نَنْصَرِفُ	نَنْصَرِفَ	نَنْصَرِفْ

Roots with first radical W or N are exceedingly rare in Form VII in MSA.

<u>The verbal noun of Form VII verbs</u> has the pattern <u>-nFiMaaL-</u>, written with a <u>waṣla</u> in Arabic script, e.g. إِنْصِرافٌ 'going away'.

Compare the perfect stem and the verbal noun stem:

Perfect	-nṣaraf-
Verbal Noun	-nṣiraaf-

For the verbal noun the stem vowel is lengthened and the other vowel(s) becomes i. The following chart gives the verbal nouns of some representative VII verbs for purposes of illustration:

Form VII Verb	Verbal Noun
(يَنْعَقِدُ) إِنْعَقَدَ 'to be held'	إِنْعِقادٌ
(يَنْقَطِعُ) إِنْقَطَعَ 'to be cut'	إِنْقِطاعٌ
(يَنْكَسِرُ) إِنْكَسَرَ 'to be broken'	إِنْكِسارٌ

b. Meaning.

Form VII verbs combine the meanings of reflexive of Form I and passive of Form I. For example the Form I verb صَرَفَ may mean (a) "to send away" (someone) or (b) "to spend" (money). The Form VII إِنْصَرَفَ may be reflexive of (a), i.e. "to send oneself away" = "to go away, départ" if the subject is a person, or it may be the equivalent of a passive of (b), "to be spent", if speaking of money. The Form VII إِنْعَقَدَ 'to be held' may be considered as a passive of عَقَدَ (I) 'to hold' (a meeting) and إِنْقَطَعَ 'to be cut' (and so 'to come to an end, to end') as the passive of قَطَعَ (I) 'to cut'. Thus VII is the intransitive counterpart of a transitive I verb, e.g.

I	سَحَبَ 'to withdraw (s.th.)'
VII	إِنْسَحَبَ 'to withdraw, retreat' (intransitive)
I	فَتَحَ 'to open (s.th.)'
VII	إِنْفَتَحَ 'to open up, unfold (intransitive)
I	كَسَرَ 'to break (s.th.)'
VII	إِنْكَسَرَ 'to break, get broken'

Drill 1. (On tape) Conjugation: Form VII.

2. Form VIII verbs and verbal nouns

a. Form.

The characteristic feature of Form VIII is the reflexive affix -t- inserted after the first radical of the root.

	'to meet'	Pattern	Root
Perfect	إِجْتَمَعَ	-FtaMaL-	
Imperfect	يَجْتَمِعُ	-FtaMiL-	JMʕ
Verbal Noun	إِجْتِمَاعٌ	-FtiMaaL-	

As in Form VII, the difference between the two tenses is the stem vowel a for the perfect tense and the stem vowel i for the imperfect. The following chart illustrates the conjugation of the tenses in Form VIII:

إِجْتَمَعَ 'to assemble, get together'

	PERFECT	IMPERFECT		
		Indicative	Subjunctive	Jussive
Singular				
3 M	إِجْتَمَعَ	يَجْتَمِعُ	يَجْتَمِعَ	يَجْتَمِعْ
F	إِجْتَمَعَتْ	تَجْتَمِعُ	تَجْتَمِعَ	تَجْتَمِعْ
2 M	إِجْتَمَعْتَ	تَجْتَمِعُ	تَجْتَمِعَ	تَجْتَمِعْ
F	إِجْتَمَعْتِ	تَجْتَمِعِينَ	تَجْتَمِعِي	تَجْتَمِعِي
1	إِجْتَمَعْتُ	أَجْتَمِعُ	أَجْتَمِعَ	أَجْتَمِعْ
Dual				
3 M	إِجْتَمَعَا	يَجْتَمِعَانِ	يَجْتَمِعَا	يَجْتَمِعَا
F	إِجْتَمَعَتَا	تَجْتَمِعَانِ	تَجْتَمِعَا	تَجْتَمِعَا
2	إِجْتَمَعْتُمَا	تَجْتَمِعَانِ	تَجْتَمِعَا	تَجْتَمِعَا

	PERFECT	IMPERFECT		
		Indicative	Subjunctive	Jussive
Plural				
3 M	اِجْتَمَعوا	يَجْتَمِعونَ	يَجْتَمِعوا	يَجْتَمِعوا
F	اِجْتَمَعْنَ	يَجْتَمِعْنَ	يَجْتَمِعْنَ	يَجْتَمِعْنَ
2 M	اِجْتَمَعْتُمْ	تَجْتَمِعونَ	تَجْتَمِعوا	تَجْتَمِعوا
F	اِجْتَمَعْتُنَّ	تَجْتَمِعْنَ	تَجْتَمِعْنَ	تَجْتَمِعْنَ
1	اِجْتَمَعْنا	نَجْتَمِعُ	نَجْتَمِعَ	نَجْتَمِعْ

In the following, unfamiliar verbs will be given to illustrate the discussion.

Assimilation of t:

If the first radical is a dental stop, fricative or sibilant, the inserted -t- is assimilated to it. Involved here are the following consonants:

ت ث د ذ ز ص ض ط ظ

(a) After the voiced consonants ز and د , the inserted ت becomes voiced and is written د . For example, compare the following:

ز			
	I	زادَ	'to add, make additions to'
	VIII	اِزْدادَ	'to increase, grow larger'

د			
	I	دَعا	'to call; to invite'
	VIII	اِدَّعى	'to claim, allege, maintain'

(b) After ذ , ت becomes د but ذ itself also becomes د , and both د 's are written دّ :

ذ			
	I	ذَكَرَ	'to mention'
	VIII	اِدَّكَرَ	'to remember'

(c) After first radical ت there is no question of assimilation, but both letters are combined with shadda:

ت	I	تَبِعَ	'to follow, succeed, come after'
	VIII	اِتَّبَعَ	'to follow, succeed, come after'

(d) After the emphatic consonants ص ض ط , ت becomes emphatic: ط . Examples:

ص	I	صَدَمَ	'to bump, knock'
	VIII	اِصْطَدَمَ	'to collide'

ض	I	ضَرَّ	'to harm, hurt'
	VIII	اِضْطَرَّ	'to force, compel'

ط	I	طَلَعَ	'to rise, come into view'
	VIII	اِطَّلَعَ	'to look; to be well informed about' عَلَى

(e) After the fricatives ث ظ there is complete assimilation and the resultant double consonant is written with shadda:

ث	I	ثَأَرَ	'to avenge'
	VIII	اِثَّأَرَ	'to get one's revenge, be avenged'

ظ	I	ظَلَمَ	'to oppress'
	VIII	اِظَّلَمَ	'to suffer injustice'

Assimilation of first radical W. A special feature of verbs whose first radical is W is that this W itself assimilates to the inserted t. Compare:

I	وَصَلَ	'to arrive'	وَحَدَ	'to be unique'
VIII	اِتَّصَلَ	'to get in touch'	اِتَّحَدَ	'to unite, form a union'

The verbal noun of Form VIII has the pattern -FtiMaaL-. Following is a listing of the verbal nouns of all Form VIII verbs occurring so far, as well as two new Form VIII verbs whose verbal nouns have already occurred:

Form VIII Verb		Verbal Noun	Root
اِنْتَقَلَ (يَنْتَقِلُ)	'to move'	اِنْتِقالٌ	NQL
اِسْتَمَعَ (يَسْتَمِعُ)	'to listen'	اِسْتِماعٌ	SMʕ
اِعْتَمَدَ (يَعْتَمِدُ) على	'to rely on'	اِعْتِمادٌ	ʕMD
اِخْتَلَفَ (يَخْتَلِفُ)	'to differ'	اِخْتِلافٌ	XLF
اِنْتَخَبَ (يَنْتَخِبُ)	'to elect'	اِنْتِخابٌ	NXB
اِعْتَبَرَ (يَعْتَبِرُ)	'to consider'	اِعْتِبارٌ	ʕBR
اِجْتَمَعَ (يَجْتَمِعُ)	'to assemble'	اِجْتِماعٌ	JMʕ
اِنْتَظَرَ (يَنْتَظِرُ)	'to wait for'	اِنْتِظارٌ	NẒR

Now do Drills 2 (on tape) and 3.

b. Meaning

The basic meaning of the inserted -t- is reflexive; thus Form VIII verbs are often reflexive of I, with the subject acting on itself. Illustrations:

I	جَمَعَ	'to gather, collect' (s.th.)
VIII	اِجْتَمَعَ	'to gather together, assemble, meet'

I	عَمَدَ	'to support, prop up' (s.th.)
VIII	اِعْتَمَدَ على	'to lean against; to rely, depend on'
I	نَقَلَ	'to transport' (s.th.)
VIII	اِنْتَقَلَ	'to move, transfer' (intransitive)

Form VIII may also have <u>middle</u> meaning, that is, to do something <u>for oneself</u>, for example:

I	سَمِعَ	'to hear'
VIII	اِسْتَمَعَ	'to listen' ("to hear for oneself")
I	أَخَذَ	'to take'
VIII	اِتَّخَذَ	'to take for oneself' = 'to adopt' (with ? assimilated to <u>t</u>)

Some middle VIII verbs take on an <u>abstract</u> or <u>figurative</u> sense, as in

I	فَتَحَ	'to open'
VIII	اِفْتَتَحَ	'to inaugurate'
I	عَرَفَ	'to know'
VIII	اِعْتَرَفَ	'to acknowledge, recognize' (e.g. a country); 'to confess'
I	خَتَمَ	'to seal' (s.th.)
VIII	اِخْتَتَمَ	'to conclude' (an agreement)

Some VIII verbs have <u>reciprocal</u> meaning: to interact with each other.

Examples are:

I	لَقِيَ	'to find, meet'
VIII	اِلْتَقَى	'to encounter one another'
I	أَمَرَ	'to order; to entrust, charge'
VIII	اِئْتَمَرَ	'to deliberate, conspire, plot with each other'

Finally, some VIII verbs with reflexive meaning may be translated as passive if the subject is inanimate:

I قَصُرَ	'to become short, limited, inadequate'
VIII إِقْتَصَرَ على	'to limit, restrict oneself to' (s.th.);
	'to be limited, restricted, confined to' (s.th.)

Now do Drills 4 and 5.

Drill 2. (On tape) Conjugation: Form VIII

Drill 3. Written. Recognition.

Write the Form VII and VIII verbs and verbal nouns for the following roots. Then look up the verbs to see what they mean. An X marks forms which do not exist.

VIII		VII		
VN	Verb	VN	Verb	Root
				عقد
		X	X	تبع
		X	X	حرم
				فعل
				كتب
		X	X	صبر
				قسم
		X	X	ضرب
				ظلم

Drill 4. (Also on tape) Transformation: Perfect → imperfect.

'The party elected its candidate.' → ← انتخب الحزب مرشحه.

'The party elects its candidate.' • ينتخب الحزب مرشحه

١ ـ الطلاب انصرفوا من الصف في المساء .

٢ ـ انعقدت المؤتمرات في الصيف .

٣ ـ انتظرناه في المطعم الجديد .

٤ ـ اعتمد المصنع على مساعدة الحكومة .

٥ ـ هل استمعتم الى المحاضرات كلّها ؟

٦ ـ اعتبرت انتخاب الرئيس امرا هامّا .

٧ ـ انتقلت الى لبنان هذا الصيف .

٨ ـ الاستاذات اجتمعن احيانا مع رئيس الجامعة .

Drill 5. Written. Completion.

Supply the correct form of the verb in the sentences below.

١ ـ سيجتمعون غدا لكي ــــــ مرشحهم (انتخب) .

٢ ـ ذهبت الى البنك لـ ــــــ مع المدير (اجتمع) .

٣ ـ لم ــــــ والدي ذلك امرا هاما (اعتبر) .

٤ ـ لن ــــــ مؤتمر الحزب في مدينتنا (انعقد) .

٥ ـ المصانع ــــــ على مساعدة الحكومة الى ابعد حدّ (اعتمد) .

٦ ـ ألم ــــــ الى المحاضرة ، يا مريم (استمع) ؟

٧ ـ ــــــ الحزبان مرشحيهما فى الصيف (انتخب) .

٨ ـ المراسلات ــــــ عادة العالم العربي فى مقالاتهن (تناول) .

3. The dual of nouns, adjectives and pronouns

As you know, Arabic has three numbers: singular, dual and plural. Singular denotes one referent, dual denotes two (exactly), and plural refers to three or more. Since singular and dual nouns are so explicit in specifying number, the noun alone may be translated into English with numerals, e.g.

لي وَلَدٌ وَبِنْتانِ . 'I have one boy and two girls.'

The inflections for the dual are ـانِ -aani for the nominative and ـيْنِ -ayni for the genitive or accusative, as illustrated below:

DUAL NOUNS	(masc.)	(fem.)
Singular:	وَلَدٌ 'one son'	سَنَةٌ 'one year'
Dual:		
Nom.	وَلَدانِ 'two sons'	سَنَتانِ 'two years'
Gen./Acc.	وَلَدَيْنِ 'two sons'	سَنَتَيْنِ 'two years'

	DUAL ADJECTIVES		DUAL DEMONSTRATIVE	
	Masculine	Feminine	Masculine	Feminine
Nom.	قَديمانِ	قَديمَتانِ 'old'	هٰذانِ	هاتانِ 'these'
Gen./Acc.	قَديمَيْنِ	قَديمَتَيْنِ 'old'	هٰذَيْنِ	هاتَيْنِ 'these'

The نِ -ni of the dual is dropped on the first member of an iḍāfa, or if the noun has a pronoun suffix, as in the following examples:

أَيْنَ وَلَدايَ وَأَيْنَ وَلَدا أَحْمَدَ ؟	'Where are my (two) sons and where are Ahmad's (two) sons?'

The second and third person independent pronouns are made dual by the addition of ـا -aa to the masculine plural forms:

أَنْتُما	'you' (dual, m. or f.)
هُما	'they' (dual, m. or f.)

There are no first person dual forms. The dual pronouns show no distinction in gender or case.

The corresponding pronoun suffixes are:

أَنْتُما -	كُما	:	كِتابُكُما 'your (d.) book'
هُما -	ـهُما	:	كِتابُهُما 'their (d.) book'

Illustrations of the dual forms:

هٰذان هُما الْكاتِبان الْجَديدان.	'These are the two new writers.'
تَعَلَّمْتُ لُغَتَيْنِ أَجْنَبِيَّتَيْنِ جَديدَتَيْنِ في سَنَتَيْنِ .	'I learned two more foreign languages in two years.'
أَيْنَ مَدْرَسَتُكُما يا فَريدُ وَفَريدَةُ ؟	'Where is your school, Farid and Farida?'
السّاعَةُ الْعاشِرَةُ وَدَقيقَتانِ .	'10:02'

Now do Drills 6 and 7.

Drill 6. Written. Recognition: Dual.

Examine the underlined items in the sentences below and give the corresponding pronoun: هو , هي , هما (m.), هما (f.), هم , هنّ

١ ـ سينتخب الحزبان المرشحين .

٢ ـ شاهدت الورقتين على الطاولة .

٣ ـ انعقد المؤتمر في هذه السنة .

٤ ـ سنكرم الزوّار اثناء اقامتهم .

٥ ـ في مكتبي كرسيّان كبيران .

٦ ـ تناول الوضع السياسى الحاضر فى مقالتين طويلتين .

٧ ـ هذه فكرة جميلة جدا .

٨ ـ هل تحدّثت الى الموظفين الجدد بعد وصولك ؟

٩ ـ تقدمت بطلب للعمل في هذه الوظيفة الحكومية .

١٠ ـ فى بلدنا نهران عظيمان.

١١ ـ هل ستتمكّن من حضور المحاضرة عن جمال دمشق ؟

Drill 7. Transformation: Singular → dual → plural

'The man is in the bus.' →	الرجل فى الأوتوبيس. ←
'The two men are in the bus.' →	الرجلان في الأوتوبيس . ←
'The men (p.) are in the bus.'	الرجال فى الأوتوبيس .

١ ـ في صفّنا لوح جديد ٠

٢ ـ هذا الاستاذ مشهور جدّا ٠

٣ ـ درست درسا طويلا جدّا ٠

٤ ـ الجريدة بحاجة الى مراسل اجنبيّ ٠

٥ ـ سينظر مدير الشركة في الطلبات ٠

٦ ـ هل بلدك جميل ؟

٧ ـ اكلنا في المطعم مع هذه الصديقة العربيّة ٠

4. Dual of verbs.

The sign of the dual in verbs is ا -aa. There are only three duals in verbs: third person masculine, third person feminine and second person common gender (masculine or feminine).

a. Perfect tense.

In the perfect tense the dual suffix ا -aa is added to the singular of the third person forms, e.g.

Third person:	Masculine	Feminine
Singular	دَرَسَ 'he studied'	دَرَسَتْ 'she studied'
Dual	دَرَسَا 'they (d.) studied'	دَرَسَتَا 'they (d.) studied'

but it is added to the masculine plural of the second person, for both genders:

Plural	دَرَسْتُمْ	'you studied' (m.p.)
Dual	دَرَسْتُمَا	'you studied' (m. or f. dual)

Summary chart for the perfect dual:

	Verb	Pronoun	
3 M	دَرَسا	هُما	'they (two) studied'
F	دَرَسَتا	هُما	'they (two) studied'
2	دَرَسْتُما	أَنْتُما	'you (two) studied'

b. Imperfect Tense.

In this tense the three dual forms are added to the singular verb, the second masculine singular serving as the base for the second person dual. The suffix is ا -aa for the subjunctive and the jussive and انِ -aani for the indicative; نِ -ni is of course the marker of the indicative mood. The forms are given in the following chart:

Dual	Indicative	Subjunctive	Jussive	Pronoun
3 M	يَدْرُسانِ	يَدْرُسا	يَدْرُسا	هُما
F	تَدْرُسانِ	تَدْرُسا	تَدْرُسا	هُما
2	تَدْرُسانِ	تَدْرُسا	تَدْرُسا	أَنْتُما

Note that the second person dual is identical with the third person feminine dual.

c. Use

In accordance with the general rule, the verb preceding an expressed subject is singular. Thus, the dual verb is used only when a dual subject (human or non-human) has already been mentioned or referred to.

إِجْتَمَعَ الْحِزْبانِ أَمْسِ وَانْتَخَبا مُرَشَّحِيهِما .	'The two parties met yesterday and selected their candidates.'

Now do Drills 8 (on tape) and 9.

Drill 8. (On tape) Conjugation: Dual of verb

Drill 9. (Also on tape) Transformation: Singular → dual.

Change the underlined items to the dual, making any other necessary changes. Ex.

'The party elected its candidate' → ← الحزب انتخب مرشحه .

'The two parties elected their two candidates.' الحزبان انتخبا مرشحيهما.

١ – الدولة شاركت فى بناء هذا السد .

٢ – الوزير يعيّن الموظفين فى وزارته .

٣ – الطالب استمع لمحاضرة استاذه .

٤ – المراسل الاجنبي سيتقدّم بطلب للعمل .

٥ – هذه الجامعة تصدر كتبا هامة كثيرة كل سنة .

٦ – ينعقد المؤتمر في مدينة كبيرة

5. The noun أَحَدٌ 'someone'

The noun أَحَدٌ (fem. إِحْدى) means 'one; someone, somebody'; in negative sentences or in questions, it may often be translated as 'anyone' or 'anybody' (or, including the negative, 'no one' or 'nobody'). أَحَدٌ and واحِدٌ both mean "one"; only أَحَدٌ , however, may be used as a pronoun. As a pronoun, أَحَدٌ normally occurs either as the first term of an iḍāfa or independently in negative and interrogative sentences.

رَجَعَ أَحَدُ الْمُراسِلينَ بَعْدَ الاِجْتِماعِ .	'One of the reporters came back after the meeting.'
تَكَلَّمْتُ مَعَ أَحَدِ الطُّلّابِ .	'I spoke with one of the students.'
يَعْمَلُ في إِحْدى الْمَدارِسِ الأَجْنَبِيَّةِ .	'He works in one of the foreign schools.'
أَلا تَعْرِفُ أَحَدًا في هٰذِهِ الْمَدينَةِ ؟	'Don't you know anyone in this city?'
لَيْسَ في الْمَدْرَسَةِ أَحَدٌ .	'There's nobody in the schoolhouse.'

Now do Drill 10.

Drill 10. (Also on tape) أَحَدٌ in iḍāfa.

Repeat the sentence given, inserting احد before the underlined noun.

'The men came.' → ← حضر الرجال.

'One of the men came.' حضر احد الرجال.

١ – تحدّث الى الموظفين.

٢ – ينتخبون المرشحين.

٣ – يعملون في المصانع.

٤ – سيجتمع مع الوزراء.

٥ – يدرّس في المدارس الخاصّة.

٦ – سيعقدان مؤتمريهما في هاتين المدينتين.

٧ – ذهبت لزيارة اصدقائي.

٨ – تعجبني هاتان المدينتان.

٩ – ذهبوا الى المسارح الجديدة.

6. Numerals with nouns: Summary

This note describes the use of numerals together with the counted noun in such phrases as "four books" or "twenty-four hours". As the various numerals behave somewhat differently in these phrases, the groups will be described separately below.

a. One

A singular noun alone specifies singular number and may be translated with "one" in English:

كِتابٌ	'a book; one book'
إِمْرَأَةٌ	'a woman; one woman'

The numeral also may be used, however, especially when some emphasis is intended. The numeral واحِدٌ (f. واحِدَةٌ) is an adjective; it follows the noun and agrees in gender and case:

كِتابٌ واحِدٌ	'one book'
إِمْرَأَةٌ واحِدَةٌ	'one woman'

b. Two

A dual noun alone indicates "two" of that noun:

حِزْبانِ	'two parties'
سَنَتانِ	'two years'

For special emphasis, however, the numeral اِثْنانِ (f اِثْنَتانِ) may also be used. It follows the noun and agrees in gender and case:

لي قَلَمانِ اِثْنانِ.	'I have two pens.'
دَرَسْتُ دَرْسَيْنِ اِثْنَيْنِ.	'I studied two lessons.'
في الْمَدِينَةِ جامِعَتانِ اِثْنَتانِ.	'There are two universities in the city.'
عَمِلْنا ساعَتَيْنِ اِثْنَتَيْنِ.	'We worked for two hours.'

c. Three to ten

The Arabic equivalent of phrases like "three books" or "five men", where the numeral is one of those from "three" to "ten" inclusive, is an iḍāfa construction. The numeral serves as the first term of the iḍāfa and thus has no nunation, and takes whatever case its function in the sentence requires; the noun serves as the second term of the iḍāfa and is always genitive, plural and indefinite:

Nom.	ثَلاثَةُ رِجالٍ	'three men'
Gen.	ثَلاثَةِ رِجالٍ	
Acc.	ثَلاثَةَ رِجالٍ	

In constructions of this type, each numeral has two forms: one with a final ـَةٌ -a(t) (the feminine form) and one without (the masculine form).

These are as follows:

Masculine	Feminine	
ثَلاثٌ	ثَلاثَةٌ	'three'
أَرْبَعٌ	أَرْبَعَةٌ	'four'
خَمْسٌ	خَمْسَةٌ	'five'
سِتٌّ	سِتَّةٌ	'six'
سَبْعٌ	سَبْعَةٌ	'seven'
ثَمانٍ	ثَمانِيَةٌ	'eight'
تِسْعٌ	تِسْعَةٌ	'nine'
عَشْرٌ	عَشَرَةٌ	'ten'

The <u>masculine</u> form is used when the <u>singular</u> of the following noun is <u>feminine</u>, and vice versa:

خَمْسُ نِساءٍ	'five women'
خَمْسَةُ رِجالٍ	'five men'
عَشْرُ سَيّاراتٍ	'ten cars'
عَشَرَةُ كُتُبٍ	'ten books'

This rule of reverse agreement also applies when the numeral is used alone to refer to a previously mentioned noun:

كَمْ طالِبًا حَضَرَ الْيَوْمَ ؟	'How many students (m.) came today?'
سَبْعَةٌ .	'Seven.'
وَكَمْ طالِبَةً ؟	'And how many students (f.)?'
سِتٌّ .	'Six.'

The masculine form ثَمانٍ 'eight' belongs to a group of nouns called defective, which are discussed in a later lesson. When followed by a noun, ثَمانٍ has the following forms:

Nom./Gen.	ثَماني ساعاتٍ	'eight hours'
Acc.	ثماني ساعاتٍ	

d. Eleven to nineteen.

The table below shows the forms of these numerals used with masculine and feminine nouns.

	With masculine noun	With feminine noun	
	أَحَدَ عَشَرَ	إِحْدى عَشْرَةَ	'eleven'
(Nom.)	اِثْنا عَشَرَ	اِثْنَتا عَشْرَةَ	'twelve'
(Gen./Acc.	اِثْنَيْ عَشَرَ	اِثْنَتَيْ عَشْرَةَ	
	ثَلاثَةَ عَشَرَ	ثَلاثَ عَشْرَةَ	'thirteen'
	أَرْبَعَةَ عَشَرَ	أَرْبَعَ عَشْرَةَ	'fourteen'
	خَمْسَةَ عَشَرَ	خَمْسَ عَشْرَةَ	'fifteen'
	سِتَّةَ عَشَرَ	سِتَّ عَشْرَةَ	'sixteen'
	سَبْعَةَ عَشَرَ	سَبْعَ عَشْرَةَ	'seventeen'
	ثَمانِيَةَ عَشَرَ	ثَمانيَ عَشْرَةَ	'eighteen'
	تِسْعَةَ عَشَرَ	تِسْعَ عَشْرَةَ	'nineteen'

Note:

(1) Except for the first element in the forms for "twelve", all these forms are invariable as to case, always ending in َ -a (or, in one case, ى -aa).

(2) In "eleven" and "twelve" both elements agree in gender with the following noun.

(3) In "thirteen" through "nineteen", the second element (عَشَرَ or عَشْرَةَ) agrees in gender with the following noun, but the first element shows the reverse agreement typical of these numerals. The counted noun follows the numeral; it is accusative in case, singular, and indefinite. (A counted noun is plural only after a numeral from "three" to "ten"; see (c) above.) Examples:

أَحَدَ عَشَرَ كِتابًا	'eleven books'
إِحْدى عَشْرَةَ وِزارَةً	'eleven ministries'
عَلى الطّاوِلَةِ اِثْنا عَشَرَ قَلَمًا .	'There are twelve pencils on the table.' (masc., nom.)
أَنا بِحاجَةٍ الى اثْنَيْ عَشَرَ قَلَمًا .	'I need twelve pencils.' (masc., gen.)
في الْمَكْتَبِ اثْنَتا عَشْرَةَ مُوَظَّفَةً جَديدَةً .	'There are twelve employees (f.) in the office.' (fem., nom.)
عَيَّنوا اثْنَتَيْ عَشْرَةَ مَوَظَّفَةً جَديدَةً .	'They appointed twelve new employees (f.).' (fem., acc.)
خَمْسَةَ عَشَرَ وَلَدًا	'fifteen boys'
خَمْسَ عَشْرَةَ بِنْتًا	'fifteen girls'

e. Twenty to ninety-nine.

The table below gives examples of these forms:

With masculine noun	With feminine noun	
عِشْرونَ	عِشْرونَ	'twenty'
وَاحِدٌ وَعِشْرونَ أَحَدٌ وَعِشْرونَ	إِحْدى وَعِشْرونَ	'twenty-one'
اِثْنانِ وَعِشْرونَ	اِثْنَتانِ وَعِشْرونَ	'twenty-two'
ثَلاثَةٌ وَعِشْرونَ	ثَلاثٌ وَعِشْرونَ	'twenty-three'
سَبْعَةٌ وَأَرْبَعونَ	سَبْعٌ وَأَرْبَعونَ	'forty-seven'
ثَمانِيَةٌ وَسِتّونَ	ثَمانٍ وَسِتّونَ	'sixty-eight'

Note (1) Except for the first element إِحْدى in "twenty-one", both elements in each of these forms are inflected for case.

(2) In "twenty", "thirty" and so on, whether alone or in combination with a unit number, the same form is used with a masculine and a feminine noun.

(3) The first element (the unit number) in each combination agrees in gender with the following noun according to the rules applicable to that element: agreement for "one" and "two", reverse agreement for "three" to "nine".

(4) The first element in each combination is indefinite, and those which can take nunation do so (all except إِحْدى and اِثْنَتانِ، اِثْنانِ).

The counted noun follows the numeral; it is accusative, singular, and indefinite. Examples:

عِشْرون يَوْمًا	'twenty days'
بَعْدَ عِشْرينَ يَوْمًا	'after twenty days'
إِحْدى وَعِشْرونَ ساعَةً	'twenty-one hours'
بَعْدَ إِحْدى وَعِشْرينَ ساعَةً	'after twenty-one hours'
خَمْسَةٌ وأَرْبَعونَ دَرْسًا	'forty-five lessons'
دَرَسْنا خَمْسَةً وَأَرْبَعينَ دَرْسًا .	'We have studied forty-five lessons.'
اِثْنَتانِ وَسَبْعونَ كَلِمَةً	'seventy-two words'
تَعَلَّمْنا أَكْثَرَ مِن اِثْنَتَيْنِ وَسَبْعينَ كَلِمَةً .	'We have learned more than seventy-two words.'

f. The hundreds.

The word meaning "hundred" is a feminine noun مِئَةٌ , with a dual form مِئَتانِ "two hundred". (These forms are also commonly spelled مائَةٌ and مائَتانِ, but this ?alif does not affect the pronunciation.) The phrases "three hundred", "four hundred", and so on, are iḍāfa constructions in which the units numeral (masculine form, since مِئَةٌ is feminine) is the first term and the word مِئَةٌ (in the singular) is the second:

ثَلاثُ مِئَةٍ 'three hundred'

Such combinations are also commonly written as one word, for example, ثَلاثُمِئَةٍ or ثَلاثُمائَةٍ . Note, however, that the first element is inflected for case even when written together with مِئَة :

Nom.	ثَلاثُمِئَةٍ	ثَلاثُ مِئَةٍ
Gen.	ثَلاثِمِئَةٍ	ثَلاثِ مِئَةٍ
Acc.	ثَلاثَمِئَةٍ	ثَلاثَ مِئَةٍ

Following is the complete list of the even hundreds:

مِئَةٌ	'one hundred'	سِتُّ مِئَةٍ	'six hundred'
مِئَتانِ	'two hundred'	سَبْعُ مِئَةٍ	'seven hundred'
ثَلاثُ مِئَةٍ	'three hundred'	ثماني مئة	'eight hundred'
أَرْبَعُ مِئَةٍ	'four hundred'	تِسْعُ مِئَةٍ	'nine hundred'
خَمْسُ مِئَةٍ	'five hundred'		

The counted noun follows; it is <u>genitive</u>, <u>singular</u>, and <u>indefinite</u>.

This noun, with the preceding element, forms an iḍāfa. Examples:

مِئَةُ يَوْمٍ	'a hundred days'
مِئَةُ سَنَةٍ	'a hundred years'
مِئَتا رَجُلٍ	'two hundred men'
مَعَ مِئَتَيْ رَجُلٍ	'with two hundred men'
رَجَعَ خَمْسُ مِئَةِ زائِرٍ إلى بَلَدِهِمْ.	'Five hundred visitors returned to their country.'
إِسْتَقْبَلَ الرَّئيسُ خَمْسَ مِئَةِ زائِرٍ.	'The president received five hundred visitors.'

Numbers between the even hundreds are expressed by phrases in which the components are connected by وَ :

مِئَةٌ وَوَاحِدٌ	'101'
مِئَةٌ وَاثْنَانِ	'102'
مِئَةٌ وَثَلَاثَةٌ	'103'
مِئَتَانِ وَأَرْبَعَةَ عَشَرَ	'214'
ثَلَاثُ مِئَةٍ وَعِشْرُونَ	'320'
أَرْبَعُ مِئَةٍ وَخَمْسَةٌ وَثَلَاثُونَ	'435'

The counted noun follows the phrase. It is <u>indefinite</u>. If the number involved is an even hundred plus "one" or "two", the construction is as folllows:

مِئَةُ كِتَابٍ وَكِتَابٌ	'101 books'
مِئَتَا بِنْتٍ وَبِنْتَانِ	'202 girls'

In other cases, the case and number of the counted noun are determined by the <u>last</u> component of the numeral:

أَرْبَعُ مِئَةٍ كِتَابٍ	'400 books'
أَرْبَعُ مِئَةٍ وَخَمْسَةُ كُتُبٍ	'405 books'
أَرْبَعُ مِئَةٍ وَخَمْسَةَ عَشَرَ كِتَابًا	'415 books'
أَرْبَعُ مِئَةٍ وَخَمْسَةٌ وَعِشْرُونَ كِتَابًا	'425 books'

There is a **plural** form مِئَاتٌ 'hundreds'. This is not used in counting, but only in expressing a large but indefinite number. It is commonly followed by مِنْ 'of' and a definite noun.

مِئَاتٌ مِنَ الرِّجَالِ	'hundreds of men'

g. <u>The thousands</u>.

The word for "thousand" is a masculine noun أَلْفٌ , dual أَلْفَانِ , plural آلَافٌ . In counting, it follows the rules applicable to any masculine noun. For example:

أَلْفٌ	'1,000'
أَلْفانِ	'2,000'
ثَلاثَةُ آلافٍ	'3,000'
خَمْسَةَ عَشَرَ أَلْفًا	'15,000'
ثَلاثونَ أَلْفا	'30,000'
مِئَةُ أَلْفٍ	'100,000'

With any even multiple of a thousand, the counted noun is genitive, singular, and indefinite. It forms an iḍāfa with the preceding word أَلْفٌ or آلافٌ :

ثَلاثَةُ آلافِ سَنَةٍ	'3,000 years'
ثَلاثونَ أَلْفَ سَنَةٍ	'30,000 years'
ثَلاثُمِئَةِ أَلْفِ سَنَةٍ	'300,000 years'

Numbers between the even thousands are compounds, with components connected by وَ .

أَلْفٌ وَأَرْبَعُ مِئَةٍ وَسَبْعَةٌ وَخَمْسونَ	'1457'
ثَلاثَةٌ وَتِسْعونَ أَلْفًا وثَمانيمِئَةٍ وَسِتَّةٌ وَسَبْعونَ	'93,876'

As with the hundreds, there are special constructions for an even thousand plus "one" or "two":

أَلْفُ لَيْلَةٍ وَلَيْلَةٌ	'1001 nights'
أَلْفُ لَيْلَةٍ وَلَيْلَتانِ	'1002 nights'

In the other cases, the case and number of the counted noun are determined by the last component of the numeral:

ثَلاثَةُ آلافٍ وَخَمْسَةُ كُتُبٍ	'3005 books'
ثَلاثَةُ آلافٍ وَخَمْسُ سَنَواتٍ	'3005 years'
سِتَّةُ آلافٍ وَعِشْرونَ سَنَةً	'6020 years'

There is also an indefinite plural أُلوفٌ 'thousands', not used in specific counting:

أُلوفٌ مِنَ الْكَلِماتِ	'thousands of words'

h. Summary.

Following is a brief summary of the various numeral-noun constructions described above.

One: The singular noun alone, or followed by the numeral. The numeral agrees in gender and case.

كِتابٌ كِتابٌ واحِدٌ	'one book'
لُغَةٌ لُغَةٌ واحِدَةٌ	'one language'

Two: The dual noun alone or, for special emphasis, followed by the numeral. The numeral agrees in gender and case.

كِتابانِ	'two books'
كِتابانِ اثْنانِ	'two books'
لُغَتانِ	'two languages'
لُغَتانِ اثْنَتانِ	'two languages'

Three to ten: An iḍāfa construction, with the numeral as first term and the noun as second term. The numeral has its masculine form with a feminine noun and vice versa. The numeral has whatever case ending is required by its function in the sentence. The noun is indefinite, genitive, plural.

ثَلاثَةُ كُتُبٍ	'three books'
ثَلاثُ لُغاتٍ	'three languages'

Eleven to nineteen: A compound numeral followed by the noun. For case and gender of the numerals see d above. The noun is indefinite, accusative, singular.

ثَلاثَةَ عَشَرَ كِتاباً 'thirteen books'
ثَلاثَ عَشْرَةَ لُغَةً 'thirteen languages'

Twenty to ninety-nine: A numeral followed by the noun. For case and gender of the numerals see e above. The noun is indefinite, accusative, singular.

ثَلاثونَ يَوْماً 'thirty days'
ثَلاثونَ سَنَةً 'thirty years'

Even multiples of a hundred or a thousand: A numeral followed by the noun. For details see f and g above. The noun is indefinite, genitive, singular.

سِتُّمِئَةِ كِتابٍ '600 books'
أَرْبَعَةُ آلافِ سَنَةٍ '4000 years'

i. Definite nouns with numerals.

In all the constructions illustrated above the noun is indefinite. Sometimes, however, it is necessary to use a definite noun with a numeral, for example in such phrases as "the four books", "those ten universities", "his twenty students". In Arabic, in such phrases, the definite noun (with the article or a pronoun suffix) comes first, and has whatever case or number it would have without the numeral. The numeral agrees in case with the noun (except for the invariable elements in "eleven" to "nineteen") and in gender follows the rules of agreement given above. The numeral has the definite article.

أَلْكُتُبُ الأَرْبَعَةُ	'the four books'
فِي هٰذِهِ اللُّغاتِ الأَرْبَعِ	'in these four languages'
طُلّابُهُ الْعِشْرونَ	'his twenty students'

If the numeral is one from "eleven" to "nineteen", the article is attached only to the first element:

مَعَ طُلّابِنا الْخَمْسَةَ عَشَرَ	'with our fifteen students'

In higher compound numerals with components connected by وَ 'and', the article is attached to the first element and to every element following a وَ :

فِي السّاعاتِ الأَرْبَعِ وَالْعِشْرينَ الْقادِمَةِ	'in the next twenty-four hours'

Now do Drills 11 and 12.

Drill 11. Written. Recognition: Numerals.

a. Translate the underlined items in each of the sentences below.

١ – شاهدنا اربعة افلام .

٢ – حضر ستمئة زائر الى المدينة .

٣ – في مكتبه باب وشبّاكان .

٤ – في هذه المدينة مئات من الابنية .

٥ – عيّنوا سبعة عشر معلما جديدا .

٦ – سأقرأ كتابا واحدا فقط .

٧ – حصلت المرأة اللبنانية على اكثر حقوقها في الاعوام العشرين الاخيرة .

٨ – في المكتبة ثماني مئة وخمسة واربعون كتابا .

٩ – يعمل الف وخمسمئة موظف في ذلك المصنع .

١٠ – خرّجت هذه المدرسة الثانوية الوفا من الطلاب .

b. Write the following in Arabic numerals (١، ٢، ٣ ...):

ثلاثة　　　　　خمسة وثمانون

احد عشر

مئتان واثنان وخمسون

الف وتسعمئة وخمسة وسبعون

Drill 12. Oral translation: Numerals: 1-10

1. She has two boys and a girl.
2. He is learning two languages.
3. I saw three foreign films.
4. He mentioned four new names.
5. They elected five candidates.
6. We attended six political meetings.
7. You (m.s.) have lived in seven large cities.
8. I know eight doctors (f.)
9. He is meeting with nine ministers.
10. Ten airplanes are in the national airport.

D. Comprehension passage.　　　　　　د — نصوص للفهم

Read the following passage; then do drill 13.

انتخاب رئيس الجمهورية في لبنان

تَجْري في لبنان كل اربعة اعوام انتخابات لِلْبَرْلَمان، كذلك يَجْري　　takes place; Parliament
كل ستة اعوام انتخاب لرئيس الجمهورية. ينتخب الشعب البرلمان وينتخب
البرلمان رئيس الجمهورية .

في لبنان احزاب وَكُتَلٌ سياسية كثيرة ، ولكل حزب منها الحق في　　blocs
تقديم مرشح ، ولكن هذه الاحزاب والكتل تقدم عادة مرشحين فقط، وينتخب
البرلمان احد المرشحين .

يعتبر الشعب انتخاب الرئيس امرا هاما ، يتحدث عنه اللبنانيون ويعقدون المؤتمرات السياسية لبحثه ، وتنشر الجرائد مقالات طويلة عنه .

وواجبات الرئيس اللبناني تختلف عن واجبات الرئيس الامريكي ، فله الحق في تعيين رئيس الوزراء ، وله الحق في حَلِّ البَرْلَمان . to dissolve

Drill 13. أسئلة

١ — من ينتخب رئيس الجمهورية في لبنان ؟

٢ — متى يجري انتخاب رئيس الجمهورية فى لبنان ؟

٣ — هل ينتخب الشعب رئيس الوزراء ؟

٤ — متى يجري انتخاب البرلمان اللبناني ؟

٥ — كم حزبا فى لبنان ؟

E. General Drills. هـ — التمارين العامة

Drill 14. Written. Matching: iḍāfas.

Fill in the numbered blanks below with an appropriate item from the corresponding column.

١ — رجعت الى بلدهنّ ______ (1) ______ (2) .

٢ — درست في ______ (1) ______ (2) .

٣ — انعقد اجتماع في ______ (1) ______ (2) ______ (3) .

٤ — ______ (1) ______ (2) " التجارة الحديثة " .

٥ ــ نشرت الجامعة ________ ________ ________ .
1 2 3

٦ ــ من ________ ________ ________ ؟
1 2 3

1	2	3
جامعة	المقالة	الجامعة
احدى	رئيس	الجدد
اسماء	هذا	الحزب
عنوان	النساء	
مكتب	القاهرة	
مرشح	الاساتذة	

Drill 15. Question-formation.

Make questions for each of the following sentences, based on the underlined portion of the sentence.

١ ــ درّست عشرين طالبا .

٢ ــ انتظروه في مطعم قريب من هنا .

٣ ــ سيجتمع مع رئيس الجامعة .

٤ ــ قابل المدير في الساعة الحادية عشرة والربع .

٥ ــ يرحلون في الصحراء للبحث عن الماء.

٦ ــ عنوان مقالته " نحن والتاريخ " .

٧ ــ شرب معظم الطلاب القهوة العربية .

٨ ــ عقدوا اجتماعا لكي ينتخبوا مرشحا .

٩ ــ تعاونت بعض الدول الاجنبية فى بناء السد .

١٠ ــ قال انّ الاقتصاد سيتقدّم تقدّما عظيما .

١١ ــ للمرأة مكانة هامّة فى مجتمعنا .

Drill 16. Written.

Fill in the blanks in the chart below. Vowel the verb forms.

Verbal noun	Imperfect	Perfect
إِعْجابٌ	تُعْجِبُ	أَعْجَبَتْ
________	________	قَرَأْتِ
________	تَعْتَمِدُ على	________
________	________	أَظْهَرْتُ
________	يَخْتَلِفُ	________
________	يَعْمَلْنَ على	________
________	________	رَحَّبوا بِـ
________	________	اِنْصَرَفْتُمْ
________	يَنْتَخِبانِ	________
________	________	شارَكْنا
________	تُكْرِمْنَ	________
________	يَعْقِدونَ	________
________	________	حَدَّدْتَ
________	يَتَناوَلُ	________
________	________	تَحَدَّثْتُ
________	________	اِجْتَمَعَتْ

Lesson Twenty-two الدرس الثاني والعشرون

أ ـ النص الاساسيّ

رأي في وضع المرأة

الدكتورة نَوالُ السَّعْداوي كاتبة مصريّة مشهورة • تحدّثت في كتبها ومقالاتها عن وضع المرأة في المجتمع العربيّ •

في احد كتبها ذكرت انّ المرأة العربيّة حقّقت بعض التقدّم في الاعوام الاخيرة ، ولكنّ حقوقها لا تزال غير مساوية لحقوق الرجل • وقالت: يجب ان تتوفّر للمرأة العربيّة كلّ حقوق الرجل : يجب مثلاً ان تتوفّر لها حرّيّة الرأي والتصرّف ، وان يسمح لها المجتمع بالحصول على الوظائف العالية •

وكثير من المفكّرين العرب اليوم لا يختلفون في الرأي مع الدكتورة نوال السعداوي ، فهم يطالبون بأن يمنح المجتمع المرأة كلّ حقوقها. لكنّ البعض منهم لا يزالون يعتقدون أنّ الجمع بين البيت والعمل أمر صعب جدّا وأن وظيفة المرأة في بيتها من اهمّ الوظائف الاجتماعيّة •

A. Basic text

An Opinion on the Status of Women

Dr. Nawāl Al-Sa'dāwi is a famous Egyptian writer. In her books and articles she speaks about the status of women in Arab society.

In one of her books she points out that the Arab woman has realized some progress in recent years, but her rights are still unequal to those of men. She says, "All the rights of men must be provided to Arab women in full measure. They must be given, for example, complete freedom of opinion and behavior, and society must permit them to obtain high offices."

Many Arab thinkers today do not differ in opinion with Dr. Nawāl Al-Saʿdāwi, for they demand that society grant women all their rights. Some of them, however, still believe that combining home and work is a very difficult matter, and that woman's function in her home is one of the most important functions of society.

B. Vocabulary — ب ـ المفردات

رَأْيٌ ـ آراءٌ (في)	opinion, view (on)
نَوالُ السَّعْداويّ	Nawāl Al-Saʿdāwī (f. name)
حَقَّقَ ، تَحْقيقٌ	II to realize, accomplish
تَقَدَّمَ ، تَقَدُّمٌ	V to advance, progress
لا تَزالُ	she is still
غَيْرُ	other than; (before adj.) not, non-, un-
مُساوِيَةٌ (لِ)	(f.s.) equal (to)
يَجِبُ (على) أَنْ	it is necessary (for s.o.) that
أَنْ	that (conjunction)
تَوَفَّرَ ، تَوَفُّرٌ (لِ)	V to be given abundantly (to), provided in full measure (to)
مَثَلاً	for example
تَصَرَّفَ ، تَصَرُّفٌ	V to behave, conduct oneself
مُفَكِّرٌ ـ ون	thinker
طالَبَ ، مُطالَبَةٌ بـ	III to demand
مَنَحَ ـَ ، مَنْحٌ	to grant (s.o.) (s.th.)
اِعْتَقَدَ ، اِعْتِقادٌ (بِ)	VIII to believe (in)

بَيْنَ	between
جَمَعَ ـَ ، جَمَعَ بَيْنَ الـ...وَالـ...	to combine...and...
بَيْتٌ ـ بُيوتٌ	house; home
صَعْبٌ ـ صِعابٌ	difficult
اِجْتِماعِيٌّ	sociological, societal, social

Additional Vocabulary

أَصْبَحَ	IV to become; to come to (be, do)
ما زالَ ـَ	he is still
ظَلَّ ـَ	he remained; he continued to (be, do)
غَيْرُهُمْ ؛ غَيْرُ (هُمْ) مِنَ الْ(كُتّابِ)	others (pronoun, m. pl.); other (writers)

C. Grammar and drills

ج ـ القواعد والتمارين

1. Nominalizers: أَنَّ , إِنَّ , أَنْ 'that'
2. The sisters of كانَ: ظَلَّ ، ما زالَ ، أَصْبَحَ
3. The noun غَيْرٌ 'other than'
4. Verbs with two accusatives: Verbs of giving
5. Use of the tenses in English and Arabic

1. Nominalizers: أَنَّ , إِنَّ , أَنْ 'that'

The particles أَنَّ and إِنَّ were discussed in 19.C.2. To recapitulate briefly:

(1) Both mean "that", but إِنَّ is used only after the verb قالَ 'to say', and أَنَّ elsewhere:

قالوا إِنَّ الدَّرْسَ سَهْلٌ.	'They said that the lesson was easy.'
ذَكَروا أَنَّ الدَّرْسَ سَهْلٌ.	'They mentioned that the lesson was easy.'

(2) As members of the group called " إِنَّ and its sisters", <u>they may not be followed by a verb</u>. They are most commonly followed by a noun (in the <u>accusative</u>) or by a pronoun suffix; this following noun or pronoun serves as the <u>subject</u> of the clause:

قالَتْ إِنَّ حُقوقَها غَيْرُ مُساوِيَةٍ لِحُقوقِ الرِّجالِ .	'She said that her rights were unequal to those of men.'
ذَكَرَ أَنَّهُ سافَرَ إِلى تونِسَ .	'He mentioned that he had travelled to Tunisia.'

The particle أَنْ may also be translated "that", but it is not a sister of إِنَّ , and it differs from إِنَّ and أَنَّ in that <u>it must be followed by a verb</u>. The verb following أَنْ is <u>in the subjunctive</u>. For example:

يَجِبُ أَنْ يَذْهَبَ .	'It is necessary <u>that he go</u>.'

The basic difference in meaning between إِنَّ / أَنَّ on the one hand and أَنْ on the other is the difference between <u>fact</u> and <u>possibility</u>. A clause introduced by أَنَّ or إِنَّ describes a fact, or something which has actually occurred or is occurring, or something which it is assumed will occur, and may often be translated "the fact that...". Examples:

نَعْرِفُ أَنَّ دِمَشْقَ مَدينَةٌ في سوريا .	'We know that Damascus is a city in Syria.'
قالَ إِنَّهُ سَيَسْتَمِعُ الى مُحاضَرَةٍ عَنِ السَّلامِ العالَمِيِّ .	'He said he would listen to a lecture on world peace.'

A clause introduced by أَنْ , however, generally refers to a possible event, one which is perhaps desired, or feared, but one which may or may not be realized. Such clauses commonly are found in expressions such as "It is necessary (proper, desirable, etc.) that...", or "I want..." or "He ordered that...". The Arabic verbs we have had so far which are commonly followed by an أَنْ clause are illustrated below.

يَجِبُ أَنْ نَنْظُرَ في هٰذا الطَّلَبِ .	'It is necessary (for us) to look into this request.'
هَلْ سَمَحوا بِأَنْ يُسافِرَ ؟	'Did they allow him to leave?'
لِماذا طَلَبْتُمْ مِنّا أَنْ نَسْتَقْبِلَهُ ؟	'Why did you ask us to meet him?'
طالَبوهُ بِأَنْ يَتَعَلَّمَ الْعَرَبِيَّةَ .	'They required him to learn Arabic.'
لَمْ أَتَمَكَّنْ مِنْ أَنْ أُكْمِلَ هٰذا التَّمْرينَ .	'I was not able to finish this drill.'

Now do Drills 1, 2, and 3.

The particles أَنْ , أَنَّ , and إِنَّ at the beginning of a clause have the effect of nominalizing the clause--that is, of turning the clause into a single unit which functions in a sentence like a noun. These particles are therefore called <u>nominalizers</u>. Just as a noun may function as subject or object of a verb, or object of a preposition, etc., so may a clause beginning with أَنْ , أَنَّ , or إِنَّ function in the same ways. The examples given below illustrate these functions. The examples are given in pairs for comparison; the first of each pair shows a noun (or noun phrase) in a given function; the second shows a clause in the same function:

(1) <u>Object of verb</u>

ذَكَرَتْ تَقَدُّمَ الْمَرْأَةِ.	'She mentioned the progress of women.'
ذَكَرَتْ أَنَّ الْمَرْأَةَ الْعَرَبِيَّةَ حَقَّقَتْ بَعْضَ التَّقَدُّمِ.	'She mentioned that Arab women have realized some progress.'
قالوا هٰذِهِ الْأَشْياءَ.	'They said these things.'
قالوا إِنَّ الِانْتِخاباتِ هامَّةٌ جِدًّا.	'They said that the elections are very important.'

(2) <u>Object of preposition</u>

يُطالِبونَ بِحُقوقِهِمْ.	'They demand their rights.'
يُطالِبونَ بِأَنْ يَمْنَحَ الْمُجْتَمَعُ الْمَرْأَةَ كُلَّ حُقوقِها.	'They demand that society grant women all their rights.'
أَخْبَرَني بِحُضورِهِمْ.	'He informed me of their coming.'
أَخْبَرَني بِأَنَّهُمْ حَضَروا. أَخْبَرَني أَنَّهُمْ حَضَروا.	'He informed me (of the fact) that they had come.'

In some cases, when the preposition is part of a verb-preposition idiom, it may be omitted before أَنَّ or أَنْ , as in the last example above. The prepositions قَبْلَ 'before' and بَعْدَ 'after' often have أَنْ - clauses as objects. After قَبْلَ أَنْ the verb must be subjunctive even if the action referred to has been completed. After بَعْدَ أَنْ , however, the subjunctive is used for future action and the perfect tense is used for completed actions. Examples:

رَجَعَ إِلى لِيبيا قَبْلَ الْحُصولِ عَلى شَهادةٍ.	'He returned to Libya before obtaining a degree.'
رَجَعَ إِلى لِيبيا قَبْلَ أَنْ يَحْصُلَ عَلى شَهادةٍ.	'He returned to Libya before he obtained a degree.'

رَجَعَ إلى ليبيا بَعْدَ الحُصولِ على شهادةٍ .	'He returned to Libya after obtaining a degree.'
سَيَرْجِعُ الى ليبيا بَعْدَ أَنْ يَحْصُلَ على شهادةٍ .	'He will return to Libya after he obtains a degree.'
رَجَعَ الى ليبيا بَعْدَ أَنْ حَصَلَ على شهادةٍ .	'He returned to Libya after he obtained a degree.'

(3) Subject of verb

أَعْجَبَهُ الْعَمَلُ .	'The work pleased him.'
أَعْجَبَهُ أَنَّ ابْنَهُ حَصَلَ على شَهادَةٍ .	'That his son got a degree pleased him' or 'It pleased him that his son got a degree.'

One verb which very often has a clause as its subject is يَجِبُ 'is necessary'. This is an impersonal verb, i.e., invariably 3 m.s. The subject clause begins with أَنْ :

يَجِبُ أَنْ تَذْهَبَ .	'That you go is necessary.' or 'It is necessary that you go.'

Such sentences may often be translated by English "must": 'You must go.'

To specify the person on whom the obligation falls, the preposition عَلى is used, corresponding in this context to "for":

يَجِبُ عَلَيْكَ أَنْ تَذْهَبَ .	'It is necessary for you to go' = 'You must go.'

There are two ways to make يَجِبُ constructions negative, with no difference in meaning. Compare:

لا يَجِبُ أَنْ تَذْهَبَ . 'It is not necessary that you go' = 'You mustn't go.'
يَجِبُ أَلّا تَذْهَبَ . 'It is necessary that you not go' = 'You mustn't go.'

(In the last example, أَلّا is a contraction of أَنْ لا 'that not'.)

To express past time يَجِبُ may be used after كانَ , but normally عَلى or مِنَ الْواجِبِ is used:

كانَ يَجِبُ (عَلَيْكَ) أَنْ تَذْهَبَ . كانَ عَلَيْكَ أَنْ تَذْهَبَ . كانَ مِنَ الْواجِبِ أَنْ تَذْهَبَ .	'It was necessary that you go.' = 'You had to go.' or 'You should have gone.'

Note the different meanings that obtain depending on which verb is negated:

لَمْ يَكُنْ مِنَ الْواجِبِ أَنْ تَذْهَبَ.	'It was not necessary that you go.' = 'You didn't have to go.'
كانَ مِنَ الْواجِبِ أَلّا تَذْهَبَ .	'It was necessary that you not go.' = 'You should not have gone.'

A clause introduced by أَنَّ or أَنْ is often equivalent to a verbal noun, and can replace it or be replaced by it:

يَجِبُ أَنْ يَنْتَخِبوا رَئيسًا جَديدًا.	'They must elect a new president.'
يَجِبُ انْتِخابُ رَئيسٍ جَديدٍ .	'The election of a new president is necessary.' = 'A new president must be elected.'
أَعْجَبَهُ أَنَّ ابْنَهُ حَصَلَ عَلى شَهادةٍ.	'It pleased him that his son got a degree.'
أَعْجَبَهُ حُصولُ ابْنِهِ على شَهادةٍ.	'His son's getting a degree pleased him.'

Now do Drill 4.

Drill 1. Written. Completion: Nominalizers

Fill in the blank with the appropriate nominalizer.(إِنَّ ، أَنَّ ، أَنْ)

١ ــ قال ــــ الشعب الامريكي ينتخب الرئيس كل اربعة اعوام .

٢ ــ يسمح المجتمع (بـ + ــــ) تحصل النساء على وظائف عالية .

٣ ــ ذكرت لي (ــــ + هي) تنظر في طلبي .

٤ ــ يتمكّن الحزب (من ــــ) يعقد المؤتمر في نيويورك هذا الصيفَ.

٥ ــ قرأنا ــــ الزائر يقبل على البدو فيظهرون له الترحيب .

٦ ــ قال رئيس الجامعة (ــــ + هو) يعتبر التعاون أمرا هامّا جدّا .

٧ ــ يطالب الطلاب (بـ + ــــ) يشاركوا في تعيين الاساتذة .

٨ ــ يجب ــــ يذهبوا الى المدينة للتجارة .

Drill 2. (On tape) Substitution: يَجِبُ أَنْ

Drill 3. Transformation: يجب أن Negative.

أ ــ يجب أن تذهب. ← 'You must go.' →

ط١ ــ لا يجب أن تذهب . ← 'You do not have to go.' →

ط٢ ــ يجب ألّا تذهب . 'You must not go.'

١ ــ يجب أن يعقد الاجتماع .

٢ ــ يجب أن ننظر في الطلب .

٣ ــ يجب أن يرحلوا من مكان الى مكان .

٤ ــ يجب أن تعتمدي عليه .

٥ ــ يجب أن تبذل جهودا كبيرة .

٦ ــ يجب أن يشمل الامتحان الدروس الاخيرة .

٧ ــ يجب أن تسمح الحكومة بذلك.

٨ ــ يجب أن تتركوا البيت.

Drill 4. Transformation: أن clause → verbal noun

'They demand that the meeting be held tomorrow.' → ← يطالبون بأن ينعقد الاجتماع غداً.

'They demand the holding of the meeting tomorrow.' يطالبون بانعقاد الاجتماع غداً .

١ ـ يجب أن ينتخبوا رئيس الجمهورية .

٢ ـ ذكرتم أنّ البدو رحّبوا بكم .

٣ ـ سمعت بأنّه تعاون مع الشركة بعد عودته .

٤ ـ يجب أن تقدم قهوة للزائر .

٥ ـ أخبرني بأنك تتناول الوضع الاجتماعي الحاضر في مقالاتك .

٦ ـ قررت أن تدرّس في مدرسة ثانويّة .

2. The Sisters of كانَ : ما زالَ ـ أَصْبَحَ ـ ظَلَّ

The "sisters of كانَ" are a small group of linking verbs that, like كانَ, take their subjects in the nominative case and their predicates, if inflected, in the accusative. These include verbs of becoming, like أَصْبَحَ 'to become'; of remaining, like بَقِيَ 'to remain' and ما زالَ and ظَلَّ 'to continue, to...still, keep on'; or negation, like لَيْسَ 'is not'. In more formal prose لَيْسَ is also used to negate a verb in the imperfect indicative, equivalent in meaning to the imperfect negated with لا . (This is a representative and not an exhaustive listing of these verbs.) Illustrations:

أَصْبَحَ دُكْتورًا بَعْدَ عِشْرينَ سَنَةً مِنَ الدِّراسَةِ .	'He became a doctor after twenty years of study.'
هَلْ بَقِيَ فَريدٌ صَديقًا لَكَ حَتّى الآنَ يا مُنيرُ ؟	'Has Farid remained your friend up until now, Munir?'
لا تَزالُ الطّاوِلَةُ أَمامَ الْبابِ.	'The table is still in front of the door.'

ظَلَّتْ في بَيْتِ والِدِها حَتّى تَزَوَّجَتْ.	'She remained in her father's house until she got married.'
لَسْنا بِحاجَةٍ الى مُحاضَرَةٍ يا فرانك .	'We aren't in need of a lecture, Frank.'

A characteristic of كانَ and its sisters is that they may be followed by a verb in the imperfect indicative instead of an accusative predicate, in which case the latter verb is usually translated as an infinitive or active participle. The subject comes between the two verbs. In this construction أَصْبَحَ means "to develop to the point of, to come to (do or be)", and ما زالَ means "still" or "still be...". Illustrations:

أَصْبَحَ السِّياسِيّونَ يَعْتَبِرونَهُ صَديقًا لَهُمْ .	'The politicians came to consider him their friend.'
هَلْ بَقِيَتْ تَتَكَلَّمُ عَنْ عائِلَتِها ؟	'Has she continued talking about her family?'
لا يَزالُ الْمُدَرِّسُ يَشْرَبُ الْقَهْوَةَ في الصَّفِّ .	'The teacher still drinks coffee in class.'
ظَلَّ صَديقي يَنْتَقِلُ مِنْ بَلَدٍ عَرَبِيٍّ الى آخَرَ .	'My friend kept on moving from one Arab country to another.'
لا يَزال فَريدٌ يَعْمَلُ فيالْمَصْنَعِ.	'Farid is still working in the factory.'
لَسْتُ أَعْتَمِدُ عَلى أَحَدٍ.	'I don't depend on anybody.'

The expression ما زالَ requires further comment. زالَ (imperfect يَزالُ) means 'to cease to be'; it normally appears in the negative in the meaning 'to continue, to continue to be, still...,' etc. Its conjugation for the third person, perfect and imperfect, is given below for the two tenses.

	Negative of the Perfect		Negative of the Imperfect	
3 MS	ما زالَ	'he still...'	لا يَزالُ	'he still...'
FS	ما زالَتْ	'she still...'	لا تَزالُ	'she still...'
3 MD	ما زالا	'they still...'	لا يَزالانِ	'they still...'

FD	ما زالَتا	'they still...'	لا تَزالانِ	'they still...'
3 MP	ما زالوا	'they still...'	لا يَزالونَ	'they still...'
FP	ما زِلْنَ	'they still...'	لا يَزَلْنَ	'they still...'

Note:

(1) The perfect tense of زالَ is usually negated with the negative particle ما 'not'; the imperfect is, as usual, negated with لا 'not'. The perfect tense of كانَ 'to be' may also be negated with ما as well as with لَمْ plus jussive: لَمْ يَكُنْ ،ما كانَ 'he was not'.

(2) The two tenses of زالَ are, in effect, synonymous in the negative, the imperfect being the one more commonly used.

(3) Both forms have present meaning: 'he still...'. To indicate past time, كانَ is usually used with the negative imperfect:

لا يَزالُ طالِبًا.	'He is still a student.'
كانَ لا يَزالُ طالِبًا.	'He was still a student.'
كانَتْ لا تَزالُ تَدْرُسُ تاريخَ أوربا في الجامعَةِ.	'She was still studying European history in the university.'

The conjugation of زالَ parallels that of كانَ that was introduced in Lesson 11.C.4. The full conjugation of this class of verbs will be given in Lesson 31, and that of ظَلَّ in lesson 34.

Now do Drills 5 and 6.

Drill 5. (Also on tape) Substitution/transformation with أَصْبَحَ

a. 'Farid is a famous doctor.' → ← فريد طبيب مشهور.

'Farid became a famous doctor.' أصبح فريد طبيبا مشهورا.

١ ــ الجمع بين البيت والعمل أمر صعب •

٢ ــ نحن بحاجة الى مساعدتك •

٣ ــ أنتم اصدقائي •

٤ ــ هذا من أهمّ المواضيع •

٥ ــ هى أعظم دولة فى العالم •

b. 'The government participated in the construction of the factories.'

شاركت الحكومة فى بناء المصانع • ←

'The government has come to participate in the construction of the factories.'

أصبحت الحكومة تشارك فى بناء المصانع •

١ ــ اعتمدت مصر على السد العالي الى ابعد حدّ •

٢ ــ اعتقد المفكرّون أنّ انتخاب الرئيس أمر هامّ •

٣ ــ توفّر للمرأة حقوق الرجل كلها •

٤ ــ أثرت القراءة على آرائه تأثيرا عظيما •

٥ ــ رحل من مكان الى مكان بعد ذهاب زوجته •

Drill 6. (Also on tape). Substitution: لا يَزالُ

'Ahmad is still the tallest boy in the class.'

لا يزال أحمد أطول ولد في الصف •

١ ــ حقوق المرأة غير مساوية لحقوق الرجل•

٢ ــ هما تطالبان بحرية التصرف •

٣ ــ فريدة طالبة في جامعة بغداد •

٤ ــ يعتبرونك صديقا مخلصا وعزيزا •

٥ ــ القاهرة أكبر مدينة في العالم العربي •

٦ ــ البدو يرحلون من مكان الى مكان للبحث عن الماء •

3. <u>The noun غَيْرٌ 'other than'</u>

The word غَيْرٌ is a noun. It occurs mainly as the first term of an iḍāfa or with a pronoun suffix. One meaning is "other (than)"; it also serves to negate nouns and adjectives and may be translated "non-", "un-" and so on. Examples:

حَضَرَ اجْتِماعَنا الطّلابُ وَغَيْرُ الطلابِ	'Students and non-students (other than students) attended our meeting.'
دَرَسْتُ الْعَرَبِيَّةَ وَغَيْرَها مِنَ اللُّغاتِ.	'I studied Arabic and other languages.'
مِنْهُنَّ الطَّبيباتُ والْكاتِباتُ وَغَيْرُهُنَّ.	'Among them are doctors, writers, and others.'

When a noun is modified by an iḍāfa consisting of غَيْرٌ with an adjective, غَيْرٌ agrees with the noun in case, while the adjective is always genitive but agrees with the noun in number, gender and definiteness:

مُوَظَّفونَ غَيْرُ لُبْنانِيّينَ	'non-Lebanese employees'
في هٰذِهِ الْمَواضيعِ غَيْرِ الْهامَّةِ	'in these unimportant subjects'

Now do Drills 7 and 8.

<u>Drill 7</u>. Written. Recognition: غَيْرٌ

Vocalize and translate the underlined words.

١ _ لا تزال حقوق المرأة <u>غير مساوية</u> لحقوق الرجل .

٢ _ نعتبر هذا أمرا <u>غير هام</u> .

٣ _ سافرنا الى مصر والعراق <u>وغيرها</u> من الدول العربية .

٤ _ اجتمع الاساتذة والاستاذات <u>وغيرهم</u> من موظفي الجامعة .

٥ _ اصبح الجمع بين العمل والدراسة <u>غير سهل</u> .

٦ _ يعتقد الاستاذ فريد <u>وغيره</u> من المفكرين ان هذا الحقّ حقّ اساسيّ .

٧ – لم ينتخب هذا الشعب غير العربي رئيس الجمهورية .

٨ – سوف يجتمعون في هذه الدولة غير الاسلامية .

Drill 8. Written. Translation: غَيْرٌ

1. New York ("the state of New York") and other American states depend on government assistance.

2. Studying Arabic is not difficult.

3. The Arabs and the non-Arabs are cooperating to realize great economic progress.

4. This employee is insincere.

5. Among them are ministers and teachers and others.

4. Verbs with two accusatives: Verbs of giving

Among verbs that take two accusatives is a group that mean "to give" or "to grant"; these are illustrated by مَنَحَ 'to grant' in the sentence below:

مَتى سَيَمْنَحُ الْمُجْتَمَعُ الْمَرْأَةَ كُلَّ حُقوقِها ؟	'When will society grant women all their rights?

The first of two accusatives after a verb of giving--in this instance الْمَرْأَةَ --is the indirect object, and the second accusative--كُلَّ حُقوقِها-- is the direct object. It is worth noting that this is exactly parallel to the English construction. A pronoun may also serve as either object. It is suffixed to the verb or verbal noun if it is an indirect object, but a special construction (44.C.3) is used if the pronoun is the second accusative. Additional examples:

عَرَفْتُ أَنَّ جامِعَتَكُمْ تَمْنَحُ الطُّلابَ مُساعداتٍ كثيرةً .	'I have learned that your university grants students a lot of assistance.'
مَنَحوني حقَّ الْعَمَلِ في الْمَتْحَفِ .	'They granted me the right to work in the museum.'

5. <u>Use of the tenses in English and Arabic</u>

In dealing with the real world, English--like Arabic and no doubt most other languages--can deal with an act or deed as a completed event or it can deal with the situation resulting from that act. For example, if I had breakfast at seven o'clock this morning I can say "I had breakfast at seven this morning"--a completed event--or I can say "I've had breakfast today"--my present condition. If my guest arrived on the 4:30 train I can say "John arrived at 4:30 this afternoon"--a completed event--or I can say "John is here now"--the resultant present situation. Or if you told me yesterday that you are leaving for Europe next week I can say "I learned that yesterday" or "I found that out yesterday"--a completed event--or I can say "I know that"--the result of my having learned that fact. We can also say, to take another example, that Shakespeare <u>depicted</u> Hamlet as indecisive--a historical fact--or that he <u>depicts</u> Hamlet as indecisive--a present truth.

Arabic has these same choices, and also makes this distinction between completed events, as in a narrative, and the existing situation. The important point is that English and Arabic do not always make the same choices. For example, in the Basic Text of this lesson, the references to Dr. Saʿdawi's observations are all reported in Arabic in the perfect tense: تَحَدَّثَتْ 'she spoke', ذَكَرَتْ 'she pointed out', قالَتْ 'she said', while they are translated into English in the present tense. Arabic often views things as completed events where English presents them in terms of the present state of affairs. Thus, if we see our guest pulling up in the driveway, the Arab will say وَصَلَ 'he arrived' while the American will say "He's here now." When the teacher's explanation of a point has penetrated, the Arabic speaker says فَهِمْتُ 'I understood, I caught on' while the English speaker says "I understand." This is not to say that وَصَلَ means "he is here" or فَهِمْتُ means "I understand", but that Arabic tends to prefer to deal with events while English, by comparison, tends to prefer to present the resultant situation. That is, you must not only know what the verb tenses mean, you must know how they are used and how Arabic and English usage of the tenses agree and disagree.

D. <u>Comprehension passage</u>   د - <u>نصوص للفهم</u>

Read the following passage and then do Drill 9.

مقالة في جريدة الجامعة

نشرت جريدة الجامعة أمس مقالة طويلة بعنوان " وضع الطلاب في الجامعة " . كتب المقالة احدى الطالبات واسمها سوزان ولیامز . تطالب كاتبة المقالة بمنح الطلاب عددا من الحقوق واهمها المشاركة في تقرير المناهج الدراسية . وتقول : "حقوق الطلاب في هذه الجامعة لا تزال غير مساوية لحقوق الطلاب في كثير من الجامعات الاخرى ، ويجب ان تعمل الجامعة على تحقيق هذه <u>الْمُساواةِ</u> . يجب أن نتقدم بطلب الى رئيس الجامعة للنظر في هذا الامر".

equality

ونشرت الجريدة صباح اليوم رأي رئيس الجامعة في هذا الموضوع . قال الرئيس : " نحن نعتقد أنّ المشاركة في تقرير المناهج حق للطلاب وسوف نعمل علي منحهم هذا الحق . نحن نرحب بالتعاون مع الطلاب ، لان <u>هَدَفَنا واحِدٌ</u> وهو تقدّم الجامعة ".

our goal is one and the same

Drill 9. Written. Completion.

Complete the following sentences in light of the above text.

١ ــ طالبت سوزان في مقالتها ببعض الحقوق واهم هذه الحقوق ———— .

٢ ــ قالت سوزان ان حقوق الطلاب فى جامعتها ———— .

٣ ــ نشرت سوزان مقالتها في ———— .

٤ ــ قال رئيس الجامعة فى مقالته انه يرحّب ———— .

٥ ــ قال رئيس الجامعة انّ الطلاب والاساتذة يعملون علي تحقيق شئ واحد هو ———— .

E. General Drills. هـ ــ التمارين العامّة

Drill 10. (On tape) Perfect → Imperfect

Drill 11. Written. Singular ↔ plural

Fill in the blanks in the chart:

Plural	Singular
Ex. يعتقد المفكّرون	يعتقد المفكّر
________	١ ــ عام دراسيّ
ولايات اخري	٢ ــ ________
________	٣ ــ انعقد الاجتماع
توفرت الحقوق	٤ ــ ________
________	٥ ــ للمراسل
________	٦ ــ الطبيب المشهور
عين الموظفين	٧ ــ ________
________	٨ ــ المرشحة تنصرف
________	٩ ــ بدأ الفلم
________	١٠ ــ سألت البنت
________	١١ ــ نقلنا اليكم خبرا هامّا

Drill 12. (On tape) Written. Dictation.

Drill 13. Written. Recognition: اخوات انّ

Vowel the underlined words and then translate the sentences below.

١ ــ أتمكّن صديقى من ان يصبح طبيبا ؟

٢ ــ تعجبني مدينة بيروت لانها جميلة جدّا ٠

٣ ــ هل تعرف ان نهر النيل يؤثّر على اقتصاد مصر تأثيرا عظيما ؟

٤ ــ قال انّ أمر انتخاب الرئيس هامّ جدّا ٠

٥ ــ يجب ان نسرع الى الترحيب بالزائر الاجنبيّ ٠

٦ ــ تقدمت بطلب للعمل لكنّ المدير لم ينظر في طلبي ٠

٧ ــ ذكرنا أنّ حرية الرأي حقّ أساسيّ ٠

Lesson Twenty-three

الدرس الثالث والعشرون

أ - النص الاساسيّ

مذكّرات طالب امريكيّ

١ - القائد المسلم الذي فتح الأَنْدَلُسَ هو طارِقُ بْنُ زِيادٍ .

٢ - هيرودِتُس هو الكاتب الذي قال قديماً : مصر هِبَةُ النيل . قال ذلك لأنّ النيل حياة مصر . — gift

٣ - يحترم العرب المستشرق الذي يبذل جهودا كبيرة لخدمة الادب العربيّ.

٤ - من المدن التي تَقَعُ على نهر النيل : القاهرة والإسْكَنْدَرِيّة وأسْوان ، وهي من أكبر المدن المصريّة وأجملها . — are located

٥ - "تاريخ الادب العربيّ" من أهم الكتب التي كتبها كارْل بْروكِلْمان.

٦ - " الهِلالُ " هي المجلّة التي أنشأها جُورْجي زَيْدان ، ولا تزال من أشهر المجلّات المصريّة .

٧ - مَيّ زِيادة هي المرأة العربيّة التي تأثّرت بها النهضة الادبية النسائية تأثّرا كبيرا .

٨ - يَقولُ بعض المفكّرين انّ القوميّة العربيّة هي الفكرة التي تجمع العرب معا . — says

٩ - " الأَهْرامُ " جريدة تتحدّث باسم الحكومة المصريّة ، وهي اليوم أشهر جريدة في العالم العربيّ .

١٠ - جُبْران خَليل جُبْران أديب لبنانيّ رحل الى امريكا ، وهناك كتب عددا من الكتب أشهرها " النَبِيّ " . — The Prophet

١١ - إبْراهيم طوقان أديب فلسطينيّ كتب شعرا قوميّا كثيرا .

١٢ - مُحَمَّدٌ عَلِيّ رجل حَكَمَ مصر عندما كانت ولاية عُثْمانِيَّةً . — governed; Ottoman

١٣ - نازِكُ المَلائِكة أديبة عراقيّة ساعدت على تطوّر الشعر العربيّ الحديث .

١٤ ـ إِبْنُ خَلْدون عربيّ كتب كتابا عن فَلْسَفَةِ التاريخ ، وله في الكتاب philosophy
آراءهامّة يدرسها اليوم طلاب التاريخ في كلّ بلاد العالم .

١٥ ـ لنَجيب مَحْفوظ كتب يقرأها عدد كبير من العرب ، وهو يتحدّث في
كتبه عن الحياة الاجتماعيّة المصريّة .

A. Basic text

An American Student's Notes

1. The Muslim leader who conquered Spain was Ṭāriq Ibn Ziyād.

2. Herodotus is the writer who said, long ago; "Egypt is the gift of the Nile." He said that because the Nile is Egypt's life-blood.

3. The Arabs respect the orientalist who exerts great efforts in the service of Arabic literature.

4. Among the cities which are located on the Nile are Cairo, Alexandria, and Aswan; these are among the biggest and most beautiful of Egyptian cities.

5. The History of Arabic Literature is one of the most important books which Carl Brockelmann wrote.

6. Al-Hilāl is the magazine which Jurjī Zaydān founded; it is still one of the most famous Egyptian magazines.

7. Mayy Ziyādah is the Arab woman by whom the women's literary movement was greatly influenced.

8. Some thinkers say that Arab nationalism is the concept which joins the Arabs together.

9. Al-Ahrām is a newspaper which speaks in the name of the Egyptian government; today it is the most famous newspaper in the Arab world.

10. Kahlil Gibran was a Lebanese writer who went to America and there wrote a number of books, the most famous of which is The Prophet.

11. Ibrahīm Ṭūqān was a Palestinian literary figure who wrote much na-

tionalist poetry.

12. Mohammad ʿAlī was a man who ruled Egypt when it was an Ottoman province.

13. Nāzik Al-Malāʾika is an Iraqi author who helped in the development of modern Arabic poetry.

14. Ibn Khaldūn was an Arab who wrote a book on the philosophy of history; he has in the book important views which students of history study today in all countries of the world.

15. Naguib Maḥfouẓ has books which a large number of Arabs read; in his books he speaks about life in Egyptian society.

B. Vocabulary — ب ـ المفردات

مُذَكِّرَةٌ ـ ات	note, reminder; (p.)notes; memoires
قائِدٌ ـ قُوّادٌ ، قادَةٌ	leader, commander, general
مُسْلِمٌ ـ ون	Muslim
أَلَّذي	(m.s.) who, that, which
فَتَحَ ـَ ، فَتْحٌ	to open; to conquer
أَلأَنْدَلُسُ	Andalusia; Spain
طارِقُ بْنُ زِيادٍ	Ṭāriq Ibn Ziyād
اِحْتَرَمَ ، اِحْتِرامٌ	VIII to respect
مُسْتَشْرِقٌ ـ ون	orientalist (western scholar specializing in oriental studies)
أَدَبٌ ـ آدابٌ	literature, letters
أَلَّتي	(f.s.) who, that, which
كارل بروكلمان	Carl Brockelmann
"أَلْهِلالُ"	Al-Hilāl (Egyptian literary magazine; lit. "The Crescent")
مَجَلَّةٌ ـ ات	magazine
أَنْشَأَ ، إِنْشاءٌ	IV to create, establish, found
جورجي زَيْدان	Jūrjī Zaydān (m. writer)

مَيّ زِيادَة	Mayy Ziyādah (f. writer)
تَأَثَّرَ ، تَأَثُّرٌ بِـ ، في	V to be influenced, affected by
نَهْضَةٌ ـ نَهَضاتٌ	awakening, rebirth, renaissance; upswing, boom
قَوْمِيَّةٌ ـ ات	nationalism
قَوْمِيٌّ ـ ون	national(ist), nationalistic
جَمَعَ ـَـ ، جَمْعٌ	to gather, collect, assemble; to unite
مَعًا	(adv.) together
أَلْأَهْرامُ	Al-Ahrām (Cairo newspaper; lit."The Pyramids")
أَديبٌ ـ أُدَباءُ	man of letters, author, writer, littérateur
إِبْراهيمُ طوقان	Ibrahīm Ṭūqān (m. writer)
فِلَسْطينُ	Palestine
شِعْرٌ ـ أَشْعارٌ	poetry; poem
مُحَمَّدٌ عَلِيّ	Muhammad 'Alī
عِنْدَ	(prep.) at the place of, at the time of, at; (after verbal noun) upon, on (doing s.th.)
عِنْدَما	(conj.) at the time when, when
نازِكُ الْمَلائِكَة	Nāzik al-Malā'ikah (f. writer)
تَطَوَّرَ ، تَطَوُّرٌ	V to develop, evolve (intransitive)
إِبْنُ خَلْدون	Ibn Khaldūn
نَجيب مَحْفوظ	Najīb Maḥfūð (in Egypt Nagīb Maḥfūẓ)

C. Grammar and drills   ج ـ القواعد والتمارين

1. Relative clauses
2. Gender of names and titles
3. The nominalizer ما
4. Adverbial use of the accusative

1. Relative clauses

a. Definite relative clauses.

In the sentence

مَنِ الْقائِدُ الْمُسْلِمُ الَّذي فَتَحَ الْأَنْدَلُسَ؟	'Who is the Muslim general who conquered Andalusia?'

الَّذي 'who' is a relative pronoun introducing the relative clause فَتَحَ الْأَنْدَلُسَ 'he conquered Andalusia'.

The special features of the Arabic relative clause are as follows:

(1) the relative pronoun agrees with the antecedent in gender, number and case. أَلَّذي in the sentence above is masculine singular nominative like its antecedent أَلْقائِدُ. The antecedent of الَّذي must be definite.

(2) the relative clause is a complete sentence in itself--that is, it can stand alone as an independent sentence: فَتَحَ اْلأَنْدَلُسَ 'He conquered Andalusia' is a viable sentence.

If, however, the relative clause is an equational sentence, and the subject is a pronoun, that pronoun is usually omitted. Thus,

أَلرَّجُلُ الَّذي هُوَ مِنْ مِصْرَ	'The man who is from Egypt'

becomes

أَلرَّجُلُ الَّذي مِنْ مِصْرَ	'The man who is from Egypt' or 'The man from Egypt'

Accordingly, the phrase

أَلرَّجُلُ الَّذى في الْبَيْتِ	'The man who is in the house' or 'The man in the house'

implies the existence of a pronoun subject--here هُوَ --which has been omitted.

The last two examples illustrate the important point that a definite noun modified by a prepositional phrase in English must be translated into Arabic with the proper form of أَلَّذي . The phrase "the woman from Beirut", for example, is rendered in Arabic أَلْمَرْأَةُ الَّتي مِنْ بَيْروتَ and is equivalent to "the woman who is from Beirut."

(3) There must be a word in the relative clause itself which refers to the antecedent and agrees with it; in the sentence at the beginning of this section, the subject of the verb فَتَحَ is the same as the antecedent and so this verb agrees with it. <u>The word in the relative clause which refers back to the antecedent and agrees with it is called the relator</u>.

The illustrative sentence above can be diagrammed as below:

relative clause		antecedent clause
فَتَحَ الْأَنْدَلُسَ .	الذي	مَنِ الْقائِدُ الْمُسْلِمُ؟
'He conquered Andalusia.'		'Who is the Muslim general?'

The antecedent clause and the relative clause are both complete sentences and the relative pronoun الذي is a part of neither. The relative pronoun's role is to link the relative clause to the antecedent, in this case أَلْقائِدُ الْمُسْلِمُ .

If the relator is not the verb of the relative clause it will be a pronoun suffix, whether object of the verb or the object of a preposition or suffixed to a noun. Note well that <u>the relator as pronoun suffix is not translated into English</u>. When translating <u>into</u> Arabic, do not forget to insert this pronoun in the Arabic relative clause. The various types of relator are illustrated below:

<u>Relator = object of verb:</u>

ما اسْمُ الْكِتابِ الَّذي كَتَبَهُ كارل بروكلمان؟	'What is the name of the book that Carl Brockelmann wrote?'

Literally, the Arabic says "What is the name of the book which Carl Brockelmann wrote _it_?"

Relator = object of preposition

هٰذَا هُوَ الْكُرْسِيُّ الَّذِي بَحَثْتَ عَنْهُ .	'This is the chair that you searched for.' [Lit.:'...that you searched for _it_.']

Relator = suffixed to a noun

هٰذَا هُوَ الْكَاتِبُ الَّذِي قَرَأْتَ كُتُبَهُ .	'This is the author whose books you read.' [Lit.:'...who you read his books']
هٰذَا هُوَ الْكَاتِبُ الَّذِي مَاتَتِ امْرَأَتُهُ .	'This is the author whose wife died.' [Lit.:'...who his wife died']
هٰذَا هُوَ الْكَاتِبُ الَّذِي أَوْلادُهُ طُلّابٌ فِي الْقُدْسِ .	'This is the author whose children are students in Jerusalem.' [Lit.:'...who his children are students in Jerusalem.']

b. **The forms of** الَّذِي are given in the box below:

الَّذِي 'who'

		Masculine	Feminine
Singular		أَلَّذِي	أَلَّتِي
Dual	nom.	أَللَّذَانِ	اللَّتَانِ
	gen./acc.	اللَّذَيْنِ	أَللَّتَيْنِ
Plural		الَّذِينَ	أَللَّوَاتِي

Note that case is distinguished only in the dual. The الـ of الَّذِي is the definite article, and therefore is subject to _wasla_.

Remember that the relative pronoun must agree in _case_ with the _antecedent_; this agreement affects the dual only, as in

أَيْنَ الْقَلَمَانِ اللَّذَانِ كَانَا عَلَى هٰذَا الْكُرْسِيِّ ؟	'Where are the two pencils that were on this chair?'
هَلِ اجْتَمَعْتُمْ بِالْمَرْأَتَيْنِ اللَّتَيْنِ قَرَّرَتَا الذَّهَابَ مَعَكُمْ ؟	'Have you met with the two women who decided to go with you?'

Now do Drills 1 and 2.

  b. <u>Indefinite relative clauses.</u>

  The relative pronoun أَلَّذِي is definite, since it begins with the definite

article, (see <u>b</u>. above). Accordingly, it can only refer back to a definite

antecedent as in all the illustrations in part <u>a</u> above, and in sentences 1-8

in the Basic Text. <u>If the antecedent is indefinite, no relative pronoun at all</u>

<u>is used</u> (see sentences 9-15 in the Basic Text). Features (2) and (3) of part <u>a</u>

above must still be met, however, so that if the antecedent is indefinite a

modifying relative clause will immediately follow it without أَلَّذِي . Thus:

هُوَ قَائِدٌ مُسْلِمٌ فَتَحَ الْأَنْدَلُسَ .	'He is a Muslim general who conquered Andalusia.'
لِنَجِيب مَحْفُوظ كُتُبٌ يَقْرَأُها عَدَدٌ كَبِيرٌ مِنَ الْعَرَبِ .	'Najīb Maḥfūẓ has books which a great number of Arabs read.'
هَلْ هُنَاكَ كَاتِبٌ لُبْنَانِيٌّ قَرَأْتَ كُلَّ كُتُبِهِ ؟	'Is there a Lebanese writer all of whose books you have read?'

  The indefinite relative clause comes immediately after the antecedent. If

there is a pause in reading, or if there is written punctuation, the result is

two independent sentences.

جُبْران خَلِيل جُبْران أَدِيبٌ لُبْنَانِيٌّ رَحَلَ إِلَى أَمْرِيكا وَسَكَنَ فِي نِيويورك.	'Gibran Kahlil Gibran was a Lebanese writer who travelled to the States and lived in New York.'
جُبْران خَلِيل جُبْران أَدِيبٌ لُبْنَانِيٌّ. رَحَلَ إِلَى أَمْرِيكا وَسَكَنَ فِي نِيويورك.	'Gibran Kahlil Gibran was a Lebanese writer. He travelled to the States and lived in New York.'

Now do Drills 3 and 4.

<u>Drill 1.</u> (Class exercise) Recognition: Relative pronoun.

  Underline each occurrence of the relative pronoun (الذي in any of its

forms) in the basic text of this lesson. Give the antecedent (i.e. the noun it

refers back to) for each occurrence. <u>Ex.</u>

الْقَائِدُ الذِي فتح الاندلس .... القائد

Drill 2. (Also on tape) Embedding: Relative clause with الذى .

a. Each of the following pairs of sentences contains identical subjects (underlined). Incorporate the second sentence into the first, using the appropriate form of الذى as shown in the example. Ex.

'The instructor is (a) Muslim.' 'The instructor teaches Islamic history.'	←	المعلّمة مسلمة . المعلّمة تدرس التاريخ الاسلامي .
'The instructor who teaches Islamic history is (a) Muslim.'		المعلّمة التي تدرس التاريخ الاسلامي مسلمة .

١ – الاديب المشهور من امريكا . الاديب كتب هذه المقالة القصيرة .

٢ – الجرائد مصريّة . الجرائد نشرت اخبارا هامّة .

٣ – المراسلون اجانب . المراسلون ذهبوا لزيارة آثار بعلبك .

٤ – هاتان المرأتان امريكيّتان . هاتان المرأتان عملتا على تقدّم النهضة النسائيّة .

٥ – العائلة عربيّة . العائلة تسكن فى ذلك البيت الصغير .

٦ – الطالبات صديقاتي . الطالبات قابلن رئيس الجمهوريّة .

b. Each of the following pairs of sentences also contains identical nouns or noun phrases, though no longer the subject of both sentences. As before, incorporate the second sentence into the first, using a form of الذى and providing pronoun suffixes where necessary. Ex.

'The book is very famous.' 'My professor wrote the book.'	←	ألكتاب مشهور جدّا . كتب أستاذى الكتاب .
'The book which my professor wrote is very famous.'		الكتاب الذي كتبه استاذي مشهور جدّا .

١ ـ البنك بعيد من هنا .
عملت في البنك اربع سنوات .

٢ ـ المرشح رجل كبير .
انتخب الحزب المرشح في الصيف .

٣ ـ المجلة هي " الهلال : .
أنشأ جورْجي زَيْدان المجلّة .

٤ ـ الدرسان طويلان وصعبان .
درست الدرسين مساء امس .

٥ ـ يحترم العرب المستشرقين المعاصرين.
المستشرقون يبذلون جهودا كبيرة في تقدّم الادب العربيّ .

٦ ـ اجتمعنا مع الرجلين .
الرجلان يتعاونان معنا في العمل .

٧ ـ كتبت الاديبة هذا الشعر القوميّ .
قرأت هذا الشعر القوميّ امس .

٨ ـ يسرع البدو الى اكرام الزوّار .
يقبل الزوّار عليهم .

Drill 3. (Also on tape) Transformation: Definite → indefinite relative clauses

'They elected the candidate who attended the convention.' → انتخبوا المرشح الذي حضر المؤتمر.

'They elected a candidate who attended the convention.' انتخبوا مرشحا حضر المؤتمر .

١ ـ قرأت الكتاب الذي كتبه صديقي .

٢ ـ اكملنا المناهج الدراسية التي قرّرتها وزارة التربية .

٣ ـ اعرف النساء اللواتي ساعدن على تقدّم النهضة الادبية في مصر .

٤ ـ قابل الرجلين اللذين يتكلّمان العربيّة .

٥ _ درست في المدرسة الثانويّة التي خرّجت بعض القوّاد القوميّين ٠

٦ _ هاتان هما المذكّرتان اللتان كتبهما اثناء المحاضرة ٠

٧ _ ذكرت الموضوع الذي تناولته في مقالتي ٠

Drill 4. Written. Completion: Relative pronoun.

Fill in the appropriate form of the relative pronoun, if necessary, in each of the following sentences:

١ _ هذه هي المجلّة ـــــ أنشأها والدي ٠

٢ _ ذهبوا الى مطعم ـــــ أكلنا فيه امس ٠

٣ _ تقدّمت بطلب للعمل ـــــ سينظر فيه المدير ٠

٤ _ سيتحدّث الوزير الى الموظفين ـــــ يعملون في وزارته ٠

٥ _ قابلت مفكرا ـــــ كتب مقالة بعنوان " يجب أن تحقّق المرأة حقوقها " ٠

٦ _ بحث الاساتذة الدول العربية ـــــ يسافرون اليها هذا الصيف ٠

٧ _ ذهبنا لزيارة مصنعين حديثين ـــــ شاركت في بنائهما الحكومة ٠

٨ _ درست مع أولئك النساء ـــــ اصبحن كاتبات مشهورات ٠

٩ _ قرأت في الجريدة عن حكومة جديدة ـــــ منحت حق الانتخابات لكل الشعب ٠

١٠ _ متى موعد الطائرة ـــــ ستسافر الى الاردن ؟

2. Gender of names and titles

It has been noted previously that names of cities are feminine; this is perhaps because the word مَدينَةٌ 'city', which is feminine, can be understood as preceding every name, for example مَدينَةُ بَيْروتَ '(the city of) Beirut'. For similar reasons, the names of magazines and newspapers are treated as feminine because the words مَجَلَّةٌ 'magazine' and جَريدَةٌ 'newspaper' are feminine, while book titles are masculine because كِتابٌ 'book' is masculine.

Thus one says

اَلْهِلالُ هِيَ الْمَجَلَّةُ الَّتي	'Al-Hilāl is the magazine which...'
"اَلأَهْرامُ" هِيَ الْجَريدَةُ الَّتي ...	'Al-Ahrām is the newspaper which...'
هَلْ قَرَأْتَ الأَهْرامَ أَمْسِ؟ نَعَمْ، أَقْرَأُها كُلَّ يَوْمٍ .	'Did you read Al-Ahrām yesterday? Yes I read it every day.'
" سِتَّةُ أَيّامٍ " هُوَ الْكِتابُ الَّذي ...	'Sitta Ayyām is the book that...'

3. The nominalizer ما

The particle ما has a number of different meanings and functions. In previous lessons we have seen the interrogative ما 'what?' and the negative ما 'not' (in ما زالَ, see 22.C.2). This particle also has a nominalizing function like that of أَنْ or أَنَّ, namely to introduce a clause functioning like a noun. Unlike أَنْ or أَنَّ, however, clauses introduced by this ما serve only as the object of certain prepositions. One of these occurs in this lesson: the preposition عِنْدَ. When the object of عِنْدَ is a verbal noun, it may be translated into English as "upon, on"("at the time of"), for example:

عِنْدَ رُجوعِهِمْ كَتَبوا مَقالَةً .	'Upon their return they wrote an article.'

When, on the other hand, the object of عِنْدَ is a clause introduced by ما, the combination عِنْدَما is equivalent to the English conjunction "when" ("at the time when"):

عِنْدَما رَجَعوا كَتَبوا مَقالَةً .	'When they returned they wrote an article.'

Now do Drill 5.

Drill 5. Written. Recognition: Use of ما .

In the sentences below, underline each occurrence of ما and describe its usage in the sentence, i.e., interrogative, negative or nominalizer.

١ _ سألني : ما عنوان محاضرة الاستاذ ؟

٢ _ بنته ما زالت تسكن في مدينة اخرى .

٣ _ ما اسماء الادباء الذين قابلتهم في الاجتماع ؟

٤ _ استقبلنا الرئيس عندما رجع من سفره .

٥ _ أما زال المدير في مكتبه ؟

٦ _ تحدّث اليّ بالعربيّة عندما قابلته .

٧ _ ما اسم الشارع الذي تسكن فيه ؟

٨ _ ما زالوا يرحلون من مكان الى مكان في الصحراء للبحث عن الماء .

4. Adverbial use of the accusative

Arabic has few true adverbs, such as هُنا 'here', اَلآنَ 'now', فَقَطْ 'only' and أَمْسِ 'yesterday'. Adverbs are invariable in form. The function of adverbs is to a great extent performed by nouns and adjectives in the accusative case and with nunation. The following "adverbs" that we have had, for example, are nouns or adjectives in the accusative indefinite used adverbially:

Adverb		- based on -	Noun	
عادَةً	'usually'		عادَةٌ	'custom, habit
أَحْيانًا	'sometimes'		حينٌ ـ أَحْيانٌ	'time (times)'
مَثَلاً	'for example'		مَثَلٌ	'example, model'
جِدًّا	'very'		جِدٌّ	'earnestness'
قَديمًا	'in ancient times, in former times'		قَديمٌ	'old, ancient'
كَثيرًا	'a lot; often'		كَثيرٌ	'much; many'

In like manner, the following nouns and adjectives are used adverbially:

Noun/adjective		- is the base for -	Adverb	
أَوَّلُ	'first		أَوَّلاً	'first, firstly'
أَلثّاني	'the second'		ثانِيًا	'secondly'
ثالِثٌ	'third'		ثالِثًا	'thirdly'
رابِعٌ	'fourth'		رابِعًا	'fourthly'
قَريبٌ	'nearby'		قَريبًا	'soon, before long'
طَويلٌ	'long; tall'		طَويلاً	'at length, a long time'
كَثيرٌ	'much, many'		كَثيرًا	'very, very much; often'
حَديثٌ	'new, recent, modern'		حَديثًا	'recently'
أَخيرٌ	'last; latest'		أَخيرًا	'finally, at last; recently, lately'
حَقٌّ	'right' (noun)		حَقًّا	'really, indeed, truly'

Henceforth the nouns and adjectives in the list above may occur in this adverbial function. Beginning with the vocabulary list of the next lesson, we will list the adverbial form of any noun or adjective so used; for example:

قَديمٌ ـ قُدَماءُ old, ancient

قَديمًا in ancient times, in former times, once

Definite nouns of time are also used adverbially in the accusative case; the definite article has the force of a demonstrative 'this':

اَلْيَوْمَ	'today'
اَللَّيْلَةَ	'tonight'
اَلسَّاعَةَ	'at this time, now'
تِلْكَ اللَّيْلَةَ	'on that night'
هٰذِهِ السَّنَةَ	'this year'
كُلَّ يَوْمٍ	'every day'

D. Comprehension passage

د • نصوص للفهم

(1) Read the following passage and then do Drills 6 and 7.

محمد عبده

Muhammad Abdu — كان مُحَمَّد عَبْدُهُ من اهمّ قواد النهضة الاسلاميّة فى العالم العربي • أكمل دراسته في مدينة طَنْطا في مصر ، ثمّ انتقل الي القاهرة ودرس في الازهر ثمانية اعوام ، ثم درّس في الازهر وكتب مقالات كثيرة في جريدة الاهرام •

Jamal Al-Din Al-Afghani — وفي القاهرة قابل جَمالَ الدّينِ الأَفْغاني الذي كان من اشهر المفكّرين في العالم الاسلاميّ • تأثّر محمد عبده بالافغاني تأثّرا كبيرا

he considered himself; disciple — وكانَ يَعْتَبِرُ نَفْسَهُ تِلْميذَ الافغاني : لكن بعض الكُتّاب يعتبرون محمد عبده اعظم من الافغاني •

اختلف محمد عبده في الرأي مع الحكومة فرحل الي بيروت ومنها الى فرنسا • وفي باريس تعاون مع صديقه الافغاني في اصدار جريدة عربيّة ثم رجع الى مصر ، وهناك درّس في الازهر ونشر عددا من الكتب والمقالات

served — التي خَدَمَتِ العالم الاسلاميّ خدمة عظيمة • كانت في العالم العربي حياتان:

حياة اسلامية تأثّرت بأوربا واخرى لم تتأثّر بها • وكان محمد عبده يحترم الحياتين ويعمل على التَوْفيقِ بَيْنَهُما • — to reconcile them

(2) Listen to the passage on tape and then do Drill 8.

Drill 6. Written and oral. Composition. Questions and answers.

Make up five questions based on the reading passage above to bring to class for an oral exercise and/or to hand in.

Drill 7. Translation.

Translate the last paragraph of the reading passage into English.

Drill 8. Written. Questions.

أسئلة

١ – من أيّ جامعة حصل نجيب محفوظ على البكالوريوس ؟

٢ – هل عمل نجيب محفوظ في وظائف حكوميّة ؟

٣ – عمّ تحدّث نجيب محفوظ في كتبه ؟

٤ – ما رأي طه حسين في كتب نَجيب مَحْفوظ ؟

٥ – بم تأثّر أدب نجيب محفوظ ؟

E. General drills — هـ – التمارين العامّة

Drill 9. (Also on tape) Transformation: Affirmative → negative.

Negate the following sentences, using غَيْرٌ ، لَيْسَ ، لَنْ ، ألاّ ، لا or لَمْ as appropriate.

١ – سأحضر الاجتماع • ٢ – انا مستعدّ للامتحان •

٣ – ينتخب الحزب مرشحا كل صيف• ٤ – ارسلت الرسالة امس •

٥ – يجب ان تذهب معي • ٦ – سأقرأ الجريدة هذا المساء•

٧ ـ أهذا مكتبك الجديد يا أحمد؟

٨ ـ نعرف أنكم بحاجة الى مساعدتنا ٠

٩ ـ مكانة المرأة في معظم بلاد العالم مساوية لمكانة الرجل ٠

١٠ ـ قواعد هذا الدرس سهلة ٠

Drill 10. (Also on tape) Review: Ordinals.

'I have read this writer's first book.' (4) ⟶	⟵ قرأت الكتاب الاول لهذا الكاتب ٠ (٤)
'I have read this writer's fourth book.'	قرأت الكتاب الرابع لهذا الكاتب ٠

٥	٦
١٠	٨
٣	٢
٧	٤
٩	١

Drill 11. Review: Time-telling.

'He met him at the airport at 11 o'clock.'	استقبله فى المطار فى الساعة الحادية عشرة ٠

3:20	10:30
2:40	6:15
12:00	4:45
	1:00

Drill 12. Written. Completion: Cognate accusative.

Provide the correct verbal noun in the blanks below. Ex.

'It influenced him greatly.'	أثّر عليه تأثيرا عظيما ٠

١ – اعتمدنا عليكم ـــــ عظيما .

٢ – رحّبوا بنا ـــــ جميلا .

٣ – بحثوا الوضع السياسيّ ـــــ طويلا .

٤ – تحدّث رئيس الجمهوريّة ـــــ طويلا .

٥ – تختلف آرائي عن آراء والدي ـــــ عظيما .

٦ – يحترم الشعب رئيسه ـــــ خاصّا .

٧ – تطوّر الادب العربيّ ـــــ عظيما في الاعوام الخمسين الاخيرة .

٨ – تقدّم الاقتصاد المصريّ ـــــ عظيما بعد بناء السد العالي .

Lesson Twenty-four

الدرس الرابع والعشرون

أ ـ النصّ الاساسيّ

قناة السويس

لقناة السويس اهمّيّة دوليّة عظيمة ، فهي تُقَصِّرُ المسافة بين الشرق والغرب ، وتؤثّر بذلك على التجارة العالميّة . وليس في العالم قناة لها اهمّيّتها سوى قناة بَناما .

shortens — thereby

والمدينتان اللّتان تربط بينهما قناة السويس هما بور سَعيد والسويس . وقد اصبحت هاتان المدينتان بعد حفر القناة من أهمّ المدن المصريّة .

تمّ حفر القناة في سنة ١٨٦٩ ، وكان الذين اشرفوا على حفرها مهندسين مصريّين وفرنسيّين .

كانت شركة قناة السويس في البداية شركة مصريّة فرنسيّة لكنّ الدولتين اللّتين نجحتا في السيطرة عليها بعد ذلك هما فرنسا وبريطانيا وقد انْتَهَتْ هذه السيطرة في عام ١٩٥٦ عندما اصبحت الشركة وطنيّة .

ended

وقد تأثّرت حياة مصر السياسيّة والاقتصاديّة تأثّرا كبيرا بقناة السويس ، خاصّةً في زمن الرئيسين اللّذين حكما مصر بعد الثورة ، وهما جَمال عَبْد الناصر وأَنْوَر السادات.

أسئلة

١ ـ أين قناة السويس ؟

٢ ـ أي قناة أخرى لها أهمّيّة قناة السويس ؟

٣ ـ ما المدينتان اللّتان تربط بينهما قناة السويس ؟

٤ ـ من أشرف على حفر قناة السويس ؟

٥ ـ هل شركة قناة السويس شركة فرنسيّة الآن ؟

٦ ـ هل تأثّرت حياة مصر بالقناة ؟

٧ ـ من الرئيسان اللذان حكما مصر بعد الثورة ؟

A. Basic text

The Suez Canal

The Suez Canal has great international importance, for it shortens the distance between East and West, and thereby affects world trade. There is no (other) canal in the world which is of equal importance ("which has its importance") except the Panama Canal.

The two cities that the Suez Canal links are Port Said and Suez; these two cities have become, after the digging of the canal, two of the most important cities of Egypt.

The digging of the canal was completed in 1869; those who supervised the digging of it were Egyptian and French engineers.

The Suez Canal Company was at first a Franco-Egyptian company, but the two nations that succeeded in gaining control of it after that were France and Britain. This control ended in 1956 when the company became state-owned.

The political and economic life of Egypt has been greatly influenced by the Suez Canal, especially in the time of the two presidents who governed Egypt after the revolution, Jamal Abd Al-Nasir and Anwar Al-Sadat.

B. Vocabulary — ب ـ المفردات

قَناةٌ ـ قَنَواتٌ	canal
أَلسُّوَيْسُ	Suez (pronounced 'as-suwees)
أَهَمِّيَّةٌ	importance
دُوَلِيٌّ	international

مَسافَةٌ ـ ات	distance
شَرْقٌ	east
غَرْبٌ	west
سِوى	(prep.) except
بَناما	Panama
رَبَطَ ـِ ، رَبْطٌ (بين)	to connect, bind, tie; to combine, unite
بور سَعيد	Port Said
حَفَرَ ـِ ، حَفْرٌ	to dig
تَمَّ	(fem. تَمَّتْ) it was completed
أَشْرَفَ ، إِشْرافٌ على	IV to supervise
مُهَنْدِسٌ ـ ون	engineer
بِدايَةٌ	beginning
نَجَحَ ـَ ، نَجاحٌ (في)	to succeed (in)
سَيْطَرَةٌ (على)	control (of, over)
بَريطانِيا	Britain
قَدْ	(verbal particle: see C.1 below)
خاصَّةً	especially
زَمَنٌ ـ أَزْمانٌ	time; period, stretch of time
حَكَمَ ـُ ، حُكْمٌ	to govern, rule
ثَوْرَةٌ ـ ات (على)	revolution, revolt, rebellion (against)
ثَوْرِيٌّ ـ ون	(nisba of ثَوْرَةٌ) revolutionary
جَمال عَبْدُ الناصِر	Jamal Abd Al-Nasir
أَنْوَر السّادات	Anwar Al-Sadat

Additional Vocabulary

بِلادٌ	(f.s.) country; homeland

C. Grammar and drills — ج – القواعد والتمارين

1. The relative pronoun أَلَّذي without antecedent
2. Particle قَدْ
3. Form IX verbs and verbal nouns
4. Form X verbs and verbal nouns
5. Form I to X verbs and verbal nouns: Summary
6. How to read years in dates

1. The relative pronoun أَلَّذي without antecedent

The relative pronoun الَّذي in its various forms may be used without an antecedent, in which case it may be translated 'he who ('she who', 'those who', etc.), 'the one who', 'the person who', etc. Illustrations:

أَلَّذي قالَ ذٰلِكَ يوسُفُ .	'The one who said that was Yusuf.'
كانَ الَّذينَ أَشْرَفوا عَلى حَفْرِ الْقَناةِ مُهَنْدِسينَ مِصْرِيّينَ وَفَرَنْسِيّينَ .	'Those who supervised the digging of the canal were Egyptian and French engineers.'

2. Particle قَدْ

The primary function of the perfect tense is to narrate events. When preceded by قَدْ , however, it often does not have this function, but instead denotes an action as background against which other events may be depicted. The perfect with قَدْ may be translated into English as a simple past tense (e.g., "he studied"), a present perfect ("he has studied"), or a past perfect ("he had studied"), depending on the context. In the following pair of sentences, the sentence without قَدْ tells what took place, without reference to the present, while the sentence with قَدْ refers to the present situation (that is, that the effect of the event is still being felt):

تَأَثَّرَتْ حَيَاةُ مِصْرَ الْاِقْتِصَادِيَّةِ تَأَثُّرًا كَبِيرًا بِقَنَاةِ السُّوَيْسِ .	'The economic life of Egypt <u>was</u> affected greatly by the Suez Canal.'
قَدْ تَأَثَّرَتْ حَيَاةُ مِصْرَ الْاِقْتِصَادِيَّةِ تَأَثُّرًا كَبِيرًا بِقَنَاةِ السُّوَيْسِ .	'The economic life of Egypt <u>has been affected</u> greatly by the Suez Canal.'

Occasionally قَدْ simply reinforces the meaning of the verb and is best left untranslated.

When the perfect tense is preceded by كَانَ قَدْ , the resultant meaning is <u>past perfect</u>, where a sense of "already" may be implied, as in

عِنْدَمَا قَابَلْتُهُ كَانَ قَدْ كَتَبَ الرِّسَالَةَ .	'When I met him, he had written the letter.'
كَانَتِ الْبِنْتُ قَدْ أَخْبَرَتْنِي بِوُصُولِهِمْ .	'The girl had informed me of their arrival.'
عِنْدَمَا وَصَلْتُ كَانَ الزُّوَّارُ قَدْ شَرِبُوا الْقَهْوَةَ .	'When I arrived the visitors had drunk their coffee.'

(<u>Future perfect</u> results from the combination سَيَكُونُ قَدْ and perfect tense, e.g. سَتَكُونُ قَدْ وَصَلَتْ 'she will have arrived.')

In this construction both كَانَ and the following verb agree with <u>the subject</u> according to the usual rules; <u>the subject</u>, if expressed, goes between كَانَ and قَدْ .

In a relative clause a perfect tense verb may have past perfect meaning without قَدْ if the main verb is also perfect:

عَرَفْتُ الرَّجُلَ الَّذِي كَتَبَ الْمَقَالَةَ .	'I recognized the man who had written the article.'

For the meaning of قَدْ with the imperfect see Lesson 37. C. 2.

3. <u>Form IX verbs</u>

Form IX verbs are the least common of the ten Forms, and no examples have occurred so far. For the sake of completeness, however, a brief comment is presented here.

Form IX verbs are characterized by having stems with the last radical doubled, for example

Perfect	Imperfect	
اِحْمَرَّ	يَحْمَرُّ	'to turn red; to blush'

The initial hamza of the perfect tense is elidable.

Most Form IX verbs are based on adjectives which denote colors or physical and mental defects, and have the meaning "to become (what the adjective denotes)". Examples:

Adjective		Form IX verb	
أَحْمَرُ	'red'	اِحْمَرَّ	'to become red; to blush'
أَسْوَدُ	'black'	اِسْوَدَّ	'to turn black'
أَحْوَلُ	'crosseyed'	اِحْوَلَّ	'to become crosseyed'

Form IX verbs have the patterns -FMaLL- (perfect tense) and -FMaLiL- (imperfect tense); the verbal noun has the pattern (?i)FMiLaaL, for example اِحْمِرارٌ 'turning red; blushing'. The initial hamza is elidable. Further examples and complete conjugations are given in Lesson 35. C.1.

4. Form X verbs and verbal nouns

a. Form

Form X verbs are characterized by having stems beginning with sta- for example

Perfect	Imperfect	
اِسْتَقْبَلَ	يَسْتَقْبِلُ	'to meet'

The perfect stem has the pattern (?i)staFMaL-, as in اِسْتَقْبَلَ 'he met', stem (?i)staqbal-. The initial hamza is elidable, and the form is written with a waṣla when not first in the sentence: وَٱسْتَقْبَلَ 'and he met', pronounced wastaqbala. Both the stem vowel and the preceding vowel are always a. The imperfect stem has the pattern -staFMiL-, as in يَسْتَقْبِلُ 'he meets', stem -staqbil-. The first vowel is always a, the stem vowel always i.

Following is a chart showing the perfect and the imperfect indicative, subjunctive, and jussive forms of استقبل .

	Perfect	Imperfect		
		Indicative	Subjunctive	Jussive
Singular				
3 M	اِسْتَقْبَلَ	يَسْتَقْبِلُ	يَسْتَقْبِلَ	يَسْتَقْبِلْ
F	اِسْتَقْبَلَتْ	تَسْتَقْبِلُ	تَسْتَقْبِلَ	تَسْتَقْبِلْ
2 M	اِسْتَقْبَلْتَ	تَسْتَقْبِلُ	تَسْتَقْبِلَ	تَسْتَقْبِلْ
F	اِسْتَقْبَلْتِ	تَسْتَقْبِلِينَ	تَسْتَقْبِلِي	تَسْتَقْبِلِي
1	اِسْتَقْبَلْتُ	أَسْتَقْبِلُ	أَسْتَقْبِلَ	أَسْتَقْبِلْ
Dual				
3 M	اِسْتَقْبَلا	يَسْتَقْبِلانِ	يَسْتَقْبِلا	يَسْتَقْبِلا
F	اِسْتَقْبَلَتا	تَسْتَقْبِلانِ	تَسْتَقْبِلا	تَسْتَقْبِلا
2	اِسْتَقْبَلْتُما	تَسْتَقْبِلانِ	تَسْتَقْبِلا	تَسْتَقْبِلا
Plural				
3 M	اِسْتَقْبَلُوا	يَسْتَقْبِلُونَ	يَسْتَقْبِلُوا	يَسْتَقْبِلُوا
F	اِسْتَقْبَلْنَ	يَسْتَقْبِلْنَ	يَسْتَقْبِلْنَ	يَسْتَقْبِلْنَ
2 M	اِسْتَقْبَلْتُمْ	تَسْتَقْبِلُونَ	تَسْتَقْبِلُوا	تَسْتَقْبِلُوا
F	اِسْتَقْبَلْتُنَّ	تَسْتَقْبِلْنَ	تَسْتَقْبِلْنَ	تَسْتَقْبِلْنَ
1	اِسْتَقْبَلْنا	نَسْتَقْبِلُ	نَسْتَقْبِلَ	نَسْتَقْبِلْ

The verbal noun of Form X verbs has the pattern (?i)stiFMaaL, for example اِسْتِقْبالٌ 'meeting, receiving'. Again here the initial hamza is elidable: بَعْدَ ٱسْتِقْبالِ الزُّوّارِ 'after meeting the visitors'.

Now do Drills 1, 2, and 3 (on tape).

b. Meaning

The characteristic prefix of Form X st- is composed of s and t. The s has causative meaning, and is equivalent to the causative ? of Form IV; t is the reflexive affix found in Forms V, VI and VIII. Form X then is, basically, causative-reflexive of I or reflexive of IV. In the following discussion, verbs are given for illustrative purposes only and will not necessarily be used for drill in this book.

(1) Causative-reflexive of Form I.

I (بِـ)	وَطَنَ	'to dwell, reside (in)'
X	اِسْتَوْطَنَ	'to settle down permanently in'

The Form X verb can be analyzed as meaning to "cause oneself to dwell in"; the main difference between this and Form I is an element of volition or deliberate intent. (This feature of volition also characterizes some Form V verbs, e.g. مَشَى 'to walk' and تَمَشَّى 'to go for a walk, stroll'.)

(2) Reflexive of IV

IV	أَعَدَّ	'to prepare' (s.th.)
X	اِسْتَعَدَّ	'to ready' (o.s.), 'get ready

As in Form VIII, the reflexive t in some X verbs has middle meaning--doing something for one's own benefit. X in this middle meaning may be related to I and/or IV; for example:

I	عَمِلَ	'to do, act, work'	I	عادَ	'to come, go back'
IV	أَعْمَلَ	'to put to work, operate'	IV	أَعادَ	'to send back'
X	اِسْتَعْمَلَ	'to put to work for oneself, use'	X	اِسْتَعادَ	'to cause to come back to oneself = to regain, recapture' (s.th.)

IV	أَفادَ	'to benefit, be of use to' (s.o.)
X	إِسْتَفادَ (مِن)	'to benefit (from), take advantage (of)' (s.th.)

(3) Estimative of I: to consider s.o. or s.th. to be such-and-such.

I	غَرُبَ	'to be strange'
X	إِسْتَغْرَبَ	'to find (s.th.) strange'
I	حَسُنَ	'to be good, nice, proper'
X	إِسْتَحْسَنَ	'to deem (s.th.) nice, approve of, come to like'

(4) Requestative of I or IV

I	نَجَدَ	'to help, assist'
X	إِسْتَنْجَدَ	'to ask for help'
IV	آجَرَ	'to rent out to' (lessor)
X	إِسْتَأْجَرَ	'to hire from' (lessee)
IV	أَعارَ	'to lend'
X	إِسْتَعارَ	'to borrow'
I	فَهِمَ	'to understand'
IV	أَفْهَمَ	'to make (s.o.) understand'
X	(عن) إِسْتَفْهَمَ	'to inquire (about)'

(5) Appointive: to appoint someone as (s.th.), based on Form I or nouns, e.g.

I	خَلَفَ	'to be the successor of'
X	إِسْتَخْلَفَ	'to appoint (s.o.) as successor'
Noun	وَزِيرٌ	'(cabinet) minister'
X	إِسْتَوْزَرَ	'to appoint (s.o.) as (cabinet) minister'

(6) Denominative: verbs based directly on nouns, e.g.

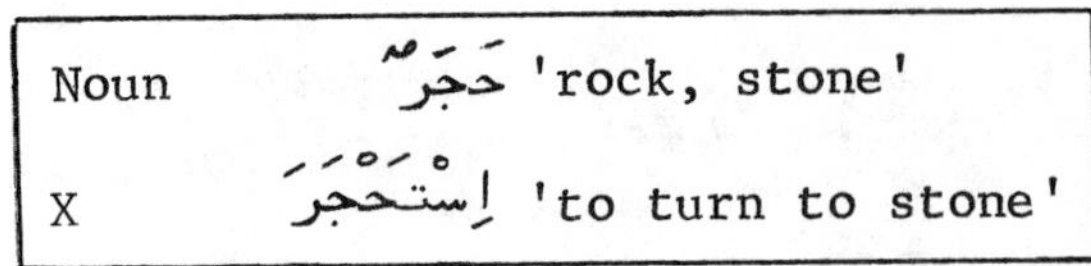

Noun	حَجَرٌ 'rock, stone'
X	إِسْتَحْجَرَ 'to turn to stone'

Now do Drills 1, 2 and 3.

Drill 1. Written. Recognition.

Give the Form X verb and verbal noun for the following roots and look up the meaning of the verb in the dictionary.

Meaning	Verbal Noun	Verb	Root
			عجب
			عمل
			خرج
			خدم
			فهم
			ضحك
			سلم
			صحب
			شرك
			قبل

Drill 2. (On tape) Conjugation: Form X

Drill 3. (On tape) Substitution: Form X

5. Form I to X verbs: Summary

Presented below is a brief summary of the patterns of verbs of Form I to Form X. These verbs fall into four groups, those of each group having certain features in common.

a. Form I

(1) Perfect stem vowel: u, a, or i

(2) Imperfect stem vowel: u, a, or i

(3) Vowel of imperfect subject marker: a

(4) Verbal noun: various patterns

The main perfect-imperfect stem vowel combinations are:

	Perfect	Imperfect	
a - u	FaMaL- كَتَبَ	-FMuL- يَكْتُبُ	'to write'
a - a	 ذَهَبَ	-FMaL- يَذْهَبُ	'to go'
a - i	 عَرَفَ	-FMiL- يَعْرِفُ	'to know'
i - a	FaMiL- شَرِبَ	-FMaL- يَشْرَبُ	'to drink'
u - u	FaMuL- كَبُرَ	-FMuL- يَكْبُرُ	'to grow big'

b. Forms II, III, IV

(1) Perfect stem vowel: a

(2) Imperfect stem vowel: i

(3) Vowel of imperfect subject marker: u

(4) Verbal noun: See each Form below

Form II: Doubled middle radical

Perfect	Imperfect	Verbal noun	
FaMMaL-	-FaMMiL-	taFMiiL	
دَرَّسَ	يُدَرِّسُ	تَدْرِيسٌ	'to teach'

Form III: Long vowel after first radical

FaaMaL-	-FaaMiL-	muFaaMaLa(t)	
ساعَدَ	يُساعِدُ	مُساعَدَةٌ	'to help'

(Verbal noun in some cases may also be FiMaaL, as in دِفاعٌ 'defense')

Form IV: Prefix ?a- in perfect

?aFMaL-	-FMiL-	?iFMaaL	
أَكْمَلَ	يُكْمِلُ	إِكْمالٌ	'to complete'

The initial hamzas are not elidable.

c. Forms V and VI

(1) Perfect stem vowel: a

(2) Imperfect stem vowel: a
(perfect and imperfect stems are same)

(3) Vowel of imperfect subject marker: a

(4) Verbal noun: see each Form below (stem vowel: u)

Form V: Prefix ta- and doubled middle radical

Perfect	Imperfect	Verbal noun	
taFaMMaL-	-taFaMMaL-	taFaMMuL	
تَعَلَّمَ	يَتَعَلَّمُ	تَعَلُّمٌ	'to learn'

Form VI: Prefix ta- and long vowel after first radical

taFaaMaL-	-taFaaMaL-	taFaaMuL	
تَعاوَنَ	يَتَعاوَنُ	تَعاوُنٌ	'to cooperate'

d. Forms VII, VIII, IX, X

(1) Perfect stem vowel: a

(2) Perfect forms begin with elidable hamza.

(3) Imperfect stem vowel: i (for Form IX see 35.C.1)

(4) Vowel of imperfect subject marker: a

(5) Verbal nouns: All begin with elidable hamza; all have i as next to last vowel and aa as last vowel.

Form VII: Prefix -n-

Perfect	Imperfect	Verbal noun	
-nFaMaL-	-nFaMiL-	-nFiMaaL	
اِنْصَرَفَ	يَنْصَرِفُ	اِنْصِرافٌ	'to go away'

Form VIII: Infix -t- after first radical

-FtaMaL-	-FtaMiL-	-FtiMaaL	
اِجْتَمَعَ	يَجْتَمِعُ	اِجْتِماعٌ	'to meet, gather together'

Form IX: Doubled last radical

-FMaLL-	-FMaLiL-	-FMiLaaL	
اِحْمَرَّ	يَحْمَرُّ	اِحْمِرارٌ	'to blush'

Form X: Prefix -st-

-staFMaL-	-staFMiL-	-stiFMaaL	
اِسْتَقْبَلَ	يَسْتَقْبِلُ	اِسْتِقْبالٌ	'to meet, receive'

Now do Drill 4.

Drill 4. (Also on tape) Transformation: Negation with لَمْ + jussive

Ex. 'The revolutionaries succeeded in realizing their demands.' → The revolutionaries did not succeed in realizing their demands.'

نجح الثوريون في تحقيق طلباتهم. ←
لم ينجح الثوريون في تحقيق طلباتهم .

١ _ المهندسون الاجانب اشرفوا على بناء القناة الجديدة .

٢ _ تطوّر اقتصاد ذلك البلد اثناء السنوات الخمس الاخيرة .

٣ ـ تناولنا موضوع النهضة العربية في المجلة التي انشأناها .

٤ ـ استقبلت الاديب المشهور صباح اليوم في بيتي .

٥ ـ تابعا قراءة مذكرات القائد الذي ساعد على تحقيق النهضة القوميّة .

٦ ـ حدّدت الوزارة مناهج للتقدم الاقتصادي .

٧ ـ الحزبان عقدا مؤتمريهما في هذه المدينة .

٨ ـ استمع الطلاب لمحاضرة الاديب الكبير .

6. How to read years in dates

The year in a date is normally read in one of the following ways:

(1) Preceded by the phrase ... فِي سَنَةِ 'in the year of ...', for example:

فِي سَنَةِ ١٩٧٥ 'in 1975'

فِي سَنَةِ أَلْفٍ وَتِسْعِمِئَةٍ وَخَمْسٍ وَسَبْعِينَ

The noun سَنَةٌ in such phrases is the first term of an iḍāfa; this iḍāfa has several second terms (connected by وَ). The second terms are: أَلْفٍ , تِسْعٍ , خَمْسٍ , and سَبْعِينَ , and these are consequently all genitive (مِئَةٍ is genitive because it is the second term of an iḍāfa with تِسْعٍ). Further, خَمْسٍ has its masculine form in reverse agreement with سَنَةٍ , as do all numbers from "three" to "ten" (see 21. C. 6).

(2) Preceded by the word سَنَةَ in the accusative case (adverbial of time). All other details are exactly as above:

سَنَةَ ١٩٧٥ 'in 1975'

سَنَةَ أَلْفٍ وَتِسْعِمِئَةٍ وَخَمْسٍ وَسَبْعِينَ

(3) Preceded by the phrase فِي عامٍ 'in the year of...' All other

details are as above, except that, since عامٌ is a masculine noun, خَمْسَة now has its feminine form:

١٩٧٥ في عامٍ 'in 1975'

في عامِ أَلْفٍ وَتِسْعِمِئَةٍ وَخَمْسَةٍ وَسَبْعينَ

(4) Preceded by عامَ in the accusative case. Other details are as in (3) above.

١٩٧٥ عامَ 'in 1975

عامَ أَلْفٍ وَتِسْعِمِئَةٍ وَخَمْسَةٍ وَسَبْعينَ

Additional examples:

في عام ١٠١٢ = (في عامِ أَلْفٍ وَاثْنَيْ عَشَرَ)

سنة ١٨١٥ = (سَنَةَ أَلْفٍ وَثَمانِي مِئَةٍ وَخَمْسَ عَشْرَةَ)

Now do Drill 5.

Drill 5. Written: Years

Vowel the following phrases; then write the years in Arabic numerals.

Ex. في سَنَةِ أَلْفٍ وَثَماني مِئَةٍ وَتِسْعٍ وَسِتّينَ = ١٨٦٩

١ ـ سنة سبع مئة واحدى عشرة

٢ ـ في عام الف وستة وستين

٣ ـ في سنة ست مئة واثنتين وعشرين

٤ ـ عام الف وسبع مئة وثمانية وتسعين

٥ ـ سنة الف واثنتين .

٦ ـ في عام الف ومئة وستة وخمسين

D. Comprehension passage — د ـ نصوص للفهم :

Read the following passage and then do Drill 6.

نابليون ومحمد علي

كان نابُليون قائد الْحَمْلَةِ الفرنسية التي فتحت مصر. وقد ارسلت — Napoleon; campaign, military expedition

Lord Nelson; to expel — بريطانيا الى الاسكندرية حَمْلَةً اخرى قائدها اللورد نلسون لِإِخْرَاجِ الفرنسيين من مصر . لكن نلسون لم ينجح في ذلك .

from — رحل نابليون عن مصر بعد وقت قصير ، واصبح "كليبر" قائدا للحملة الفرنسيـــة .

حكم الفرنسيون مصر ثلاثة اعوام ونصف عام ، ثم رحلوا عنها فحكمها محمد علي الذي عمل على نشر التعليم بين المصريين ، فارسل عددا من

ordinary people — أَبْنَاءِ الشَّعْبِ الى اوربا للحصول على شهادات جامعية . رجع هؤلاء الرجال الى مصر بعد ان أكملوا دراستهم ، وساعدوا على تقدم البلاد . وقد أثّرت

civilization — الْحَضَارَةُ الاوربية على مصر تأثيرا كبيرا في زمن محمد علي ، ولا يـــزال تأثيرها عظيما .

Drill 6. Written.

أسئلـــة :

١ ـ من القائد الفرنسي الذي فتح مصر؟ من أصبح قائدا بعده ؟

٢ ـ ماذا فعلت بريطانيا بعد ان فتحت فرنسا مصر ؟

٣ ـ كم عاما حكم الفرنسيّون مصر ؟

٤ ـ من حكم مصر بعد رحيل الفرنسيّين ؟

٥ ـ الى اين ذهب المصريّون للدراسة ؟

٦ ـ هل تأثّر العرب بأوربا في زمن محمد علي؟

E. General Drills

هـ ـ تمارين عامـــة :

Drill 7. Transformation: Noun → pronoun.

Substitute the correct pronoun for the underlined item and make any other necessary changes. Ex.

'He offered him food' → قدّم له الطعام .

'He offered it to him.' قدّمه له .

١ – يشرف هذا الاديب الكبير على كتابة المقالات .

٢ – تمّ حفر القناة في سنة ١٨٦٩ .

٣ – تطورت مصر وغير مصر من البلاد العربية تطورا كبيرا .

٤ – المستشرقون يحترمون العرب احتراما عظيما .

٥ – اعجبني جمال بلدك وآثار بلدك .

٦ – يعتبر المفكرون القومية نهضة هامة .

٧ – شعر نازك الملائكة جميل جدّا .

٨ – حضر الطلاب وغير الطلاب الى الاجتماع الذي انعقد أمس .

٩ – ذهبنا الى السينما بالسيّارة لمشاهدة الفلمين الاجنبيين .

١٠ – قدّم له القهوة .

١١ – كلام الاستاذ في هذا الموضوع هام جدّا .

Drill 8. Written. Completion: Positive → elative

Fill in the blanks below, as in the example.

'This student is younger than that one.'	هذا الطالب اصغر من ذلك الطالب . (اصغر = comp.)
'Indeed, he is the youngest student in the class.'	بل هو اصغر طالب في الصف . (صغير) (اصغر = super., طالب = noun)

١ – نهر النيل ــــ من الامازون . بل هو ــــ ــــ في العالم.(طويل)

٢ – السد العالي ــــ من سد اسوان. بل هو ــــ ــــ على النيل. (كبير)

٣ – هذه الابنية ــــ من تلك الابنية . بل هي ــــ ــــ في المدينة.(عالية)

٤ – اللغة العربية ــــ من اللغة الفرنسية . بل هي ــــ ــــ درستها.(صعب)

٥ – هذه الجملة ــــ من تلك . بل هي ــــ ــــ في الدرس.(قصير)

Drill 9. Embedding: Nominalizers

Combine the two sentences or phrases using the correct nominalizer and making all necessary changes: أن , أنّ , or إنّ . Ex.

'All rights are provided to the people.' (must) → | تتوفر كل الحقوق للشعب (يجب) →

'All rights must be provided to the people.' | يجب أن تتوفر كل الحقوق للشعب •

'The Orientalists respect the Arabs.' (We know) → | يحترم المستشرقون العرب (نعرف) →

'We know that the Orientalists respect the Arabs.' | نعرف أن المستشرقين يحترمون العرب •

١ ـ التعاون بين الغرب والشرق الاوسط أمر هام.(يعتقد المفكرون)

٢ ـ سيشرف المهندس على بناء المدرسة الجديدة • (قال المهندس)

٣ ـ يحدد الحزب منهج تطوره • (يجب)

٤ ـ يتأثر الشعر العربي تأثرا كبيرا بالنهضة القومية . (اعرف)

٥ ـ الحكومة تمنح الشعب حق انتخاب الرئيس . (طالبوا بـ)

٦ ـ يعتمدون على مساعدة اصدقائهم • (قالوا)

٧ ـ هذه المجلة تنشر مقالات تتناول هذا الموضوع • (اخبرني بـ)

٨ ـ اعمل على اكمال دراستي الجامعية • (طلب استاذي)

٩ ـ خدم ذلك القائد المشهور بلده وقتا طويلا • (قرأت)

Drill 10. Transformation and translation: عند + verbal noun

Change the construction عند + verbal noun to عندما + verb. Translate the sentences.

'Muhammad Ali governed Egypt when the French left.' | حكم محمد علي مصر عند رحيل الفرنسيين عنها •

حكم محمد علي مصر عندما رحـــــــل الفرنسيون عنها •

١ ـ أنشأ مجلة ادبية عند حصوله على شهادة الماجستير •

٢ ـ يسرع البدو الى الترحيب بالزائر عند اقباله عليهم •

٣ ـ قابلتهم عند حضوري الاجتماع في القاهرة •

٤ ـ استقبل الرئيس النساء عند نجاحهن في تحقيق طلباتهن •

٥ ـ كتب لي رسالة عند انتقاله الى مدينة اخرى.

Drill 11. (On tape) Dictation/translation.

Drill 12. Written. Translation.

1. That author (m.) is one of the leaders of the modern literary movement.

2. Do you know the woman who started this women's magazine?

3. Al-Ahram is the newspaper that my friend (m.) works for ("in") sometimes.

4. Upon our arrival we met two orientalists who spoke Arabic.

5. I believe that the right to work is among the most important rights which Arab women are demanding.

6. What is the most important concept that this writer discusses in his book?

7. The company manager met with all the employees whose families were leaving the country.

8. You must respect your parents, Hind. They are ready to help you at any time

9. The economy of the U.S. has been greatly affected by the development of international commerce.

10. Sixteen students in the class passed the exam and three did not. Those who passed the exam will be able to graduate next month.

Lesson Twenty-five

الدرس الخامس والعشرون

أ ـ النص الاساسيّ

حكـــــــم

١ ـ اجعل لكلّ شيء وقتا ٠

Plato ٢ ـ قال أَفْلاطونُ : اعرف نفسك !

٣ ـ احكم على نفسك قبل أن يحكم عليها غيرك ٠

look for ٤ ـ فَتِّشْ عَنِ الجار قبل الدار ٠

٥ ـ أكرم والديك ٠

٦ ـ لا تمنع الخير عن أهله ٠

٧ ـ لا تؤجّل عمل اليوم الى الغد ٠

٨ ـ لا تقاوموا الشر بالشر بل قاوموه بالخير ٠

discipline ٩ ـ ليسمع الابناء تَأْديبَ الوالد ٠

praise ١٠ ـ قال سُلَيْمانُ الحَكيم قديما : لِيَمْدَحْكَ الغريب لا فمك ٠

A. Basic text

Words of Wisdom

1. Make time for everything.
2. Plato said, "Know thyself."
3. Judge yourself before someone else judges you.
4. Look for the neighbor before (you look for) the house.
5. Honor your parents.
6. Don't forbid good things to those who deserve them.
7. Don't put off today's work until tomorrow.
8. Don't fight evil with evil but rather (fight it) with good.

9. Let the sons heed the chastisement of the father.

10. Solomon the Wise said of old, "Let the stranger praise you, not your own mouth.

B. Vocabulary ب ـ المفردات

حِكْمَةٌ ـ حِكَمٌ	saying, word of wisdom
اِجْعَلْ	make! (imperative)
جَعَلَ ـَـ ، جَعْلٌ	to make, render, create
اِعْرِفْ	know! (imperative)
نَفْسٌ ـ أَنْفُسٌ	(f.) soul; self
أُحْكُمْ على ..	judge...! (imperative)
حَكَمَ ـُـ ، حُكْمٌ (على)	to judge, pass judgment (on)
جارٌ ـ جيرانٌ	neighbor
دارٌ ـ دورٌ	(f.) house
أَكْرِمْ	honor! (imperative)
والِدانِ	(d.) parents
والِدٌ	father (f. = 'mother')
لا تَمْنَعْ .. عَنْ	don't deny (s.th.) to (s.o.)
مَنَعَ ـَـ ، مَنْعٌ (عن ، من)	to deny, prevent, forbid (s.th.) (to s.o.)
خَيْرٌ ـ خُيورٌ	good thing; property; welfare
أَهْلٌ ـ ون ، أَهالٍ	people, family; owners; deserving
لا تُؤَجِّلْ	don't postpone
أَجَّلَ ، تَأْجيلٌ	II to postpone, delay,
لا تُقاوِموا	don't fight, oppose!
قاوَمَ ، مُقاوَمَةٌ (بـ)	III to resist, oppose; to fight (with)
شَرٌّ ـ شُرورٌ	evil, wickedness
لِـ	(imperative particle; see C.3 below)

سُلَيْمانُ الْحَكيمُ	Solomon the Wise
غَريبٌ ـ غُرَباءُ	stranger (n.); strange (adj.)
فَمٌ ـ أَفْواهٌ	mouth

Additional Vocabulary

أَخَذَ ـُـ ، أَخْذٌ	to take
رَأْسٌ ـ رُؤُوسٌ	(m. or f.) head
قَلْبٌ ـ قُلوبٌ	heart
أُذْنٌ ـ آذانٌ	(f.) ear
عَيْنٌ ـ عُيونٌ	(f.) eye
يَدٌ ـ أَيْدٍ ، أَيادٍ	(f.) hand (nisba: يَدَوِيٌّ 'manual')
رِجْلٌ ـ أَرْجُلٌ	(f.) leg, foot

Note:
Most parts of the body that occur in pairs are feminine, such as عَيْنٌ 'eye', أُذْنٌ 'ear', يَدٌ 'hand' and رِجْلٌ 'foot' above.

C. Grammar and drills ج ـ القواعد والتمارين

1. The imperative mood: Positive commands
2. The jussive mood: Negative commands
3. The jussive mood: Indirect commands

1. The imperative mood: Positive commands

The imperative mood of the verb is used in giving someone a positive command or request, for example أُكْتُبْ هٰذِهِ الْجُمْلَةَ ! 'Write this sentence!' (For negative commands, see the following note.) The imperative is formed from the second person jussive forms by the following steps:

(1) Remove the subject marker prefix.

(2) If the resultant form begins with a single consonant, then that form is the imperative with no further modification. For example, the second

person masculine singular jussive of دَرَّسَ 'to teach' is تُدَرِّسْ . Remove the subject-marker tu-, and you have دَرِّسْ . This begins with one consonant; thus it is the (2 m.s.) imperative form "teach!" The chart below shows the five second-person jussive and imperative forms of this verb:

	Jussive	Imperative	
2 MS	تُدَرِّسْ	دَرِّسْ	
2 FS	تُدَرِّسي	دَرِّسي	
2 D	تُدَرِّسا	دَرِّسا	'teach!'
2 MP	تُدَرِّسوا	دَرِّسوا	
2 FP	تُدَرِّسْنَ	دَرِّسْنَ	

Other examples of imperatives similarly formed from the second person jussive are as follows (all m.s. forms)

Jussive	Imperative	
تُقَرِّرْ	قَرِّرْ	'decide!'
تُساعِدْ	ساعِدْ	'help!'
تَتَكَلَّمْ	تَكَلَّمْ	'speak!'
تَتَعاوَنْ	تَعاوَنْ	'cooperate!'

(3) In many verbs, however, the removal of the subject-marker prefix leaves a form beginning with two consonants. (For example: the 2 m.s. jussive of كَتَبَ 'to write' is تَكْتُبْ . Remove the subject-marker ta-, and you have كْتُبْ -ktub.) In such cases, hamza with a vowel must be prefixed (Arabic does not permit initial CC sequences), as follows:

(a) In the case of Form IV verbs only, prefix أَ ʔa-. This hamza is never elided (i.e. dropped). Examples:

Jussive	Imperative	
تُكْمِلْ	أَكْمِلْ	'complete!'
تُكْرِمْ	أَكْرِمْ	'honor!'

(b) In the case of other stems beginning with two consonants, prefix أُ ?u- if the following stem vowel is u (this occurs only in some Form I verbs) and إِ ?i- in all other cases. These hamzas are elidable. Examples:

Jussive	Imperative	
تَكْتُبْ	أُكْتُبْ	'write!'
تَدْرُسْ	أُدْرُسْ	'study!'
تَرْجِعْ	إِرْجِعْ	'return!'
تَذْهَبْ	إِذْهَبْ	'go!'
تَنْصَرِفْ	إِنْصَرِفْ	'go away!'
تَسْتَمِعْ	إِسْتَمِعْ	'listen!'
تَسْتَعْمِلْ	إِسْتَعْمِلْ	'use!'

The verbs أَكَلَ 'to eat' and أَخَذَ 'to take' have irregular imperatives, as follows:

2 MS	خُذْ	'take!'	كُلْ	'eat!'
2 FS	خُذِي		كُلِي	
2 D	خُذَا		كُلَا	
2 MP	خُذُوا		كُلُوا	
2 FP	خُذْنَ		كُلْنَ	

Shown below are examples of imperative forms in sentences:

إِذْهَبْ إِلى اللَّوْحِ وَٱكْتُبْ هٰذِهِ الْكَلِماتِ .	'Go to the board and write these words.'
أُدْرُسِ ٱلدُّروسَ كُلَّها يا سامي .	'Study all the lessons, Sami.'
كُلي الْكُبَّةَ وَٱشْرَبي الْقَهْوَةَ يا كَريمَةُ .	'Eat the kubba and drink the coffee, Karima.'
أَكْمِلا عَمَلَكُما !	'Finish your work!'
خُذوا فَريدَةَ مَعَكُمْ .	'Take Farida with you!'
إِبْحَثوا عَنِ الْكُتُبِ .	'Look for the books!'
إِسْتَمِعْنَ إِلى الْمُحاضَرَةِ وَاكْتُبْنَ مَقالَةً عَنْها .	'Listen to the lecture and write an article about it.'

Imperatives, like any verb form, may have pronoun suffixes as objects:

2 MS	ساعِدْني	'Help me.'
2 FS	أَكْرِميهِمْ	'Honor them.'
2 D	دَرِّساهُ	'Teach him.'
2 MP	خُذونا	'Take us.'
2 FP	إِسْتَقْبِلْنَها	'Meet her.'

Now do drills 1, 2, and 3.

Drill 1. Recognition: Commands.

The teacher addresses the following commands to one or more members of the class, who carry them out. Note that alternate imperatives are given where appropriate.

١ ــ اذهب الى اللوح . (اذهبي ، اذهبا ، اذهبوا ، اذهبن)

٢ ــ اكتبِ اسمك على اللوح . (اكتبي ، اكتبا ، اكتبوا ، اكتبن)

٣ ــ خذ هذا القلم . (خذي)

٤ ــ اسأل جارك عن عائلته . (اسألي)

٥ ــ اقرأ الجملة الاولى من النص الاساسيّ . (اقرئي)

٦ ـ انصرف من الصف ۰ (انصرفى ، انصرفا ، انصرفوا ، انصرفن ، (ثمّ ارجع) ٠

٧ ـ انظر من الشبّاك ٠ (انظرى ، انظرا ، انظروا ، انظرن)

٨ ـ خذ ورقة واكتب كلمة عربية عليها ٠ (خذي ٠٠٠٠ أكتبى)

Drill 2. Written. Transformation: Jussive → imperative.

Provide the appropriate imperative form for each of the jussives given below, and then use each in a short command. Ex:

'You (m.p.) study' (jussive) → تدرسوا :

'Study your lessons!' ادرسوا دروسكم !

تقدّمي	تبحث	تستمعوا
تتعاونوا	تمنحوا	تشرب
تتناولي	تعملي على	تحترم
ترحبا بـ	تستمع	تنتظري
تساعدن	تسألن	تستقبل
تشرفوا على	تسرعي الى	تكرم
تنشئوا	تخبري بـ	

Drill 3. (Also on tape) Transformation: Perfect → imperative

'You considered this application.' → نظرت فى هذا الطلب

'Consider this application.' أنظر في هذا الطلب ٠

١ ـ بحثت عن عمل جديد ٥   ٢ ـ قرأتِ هذه الجملة ٠

٣ ـ أظهرتم له الترحيب ٠   ٤ ـ استمعتَ الى المحاضرة ٠

٥ ـ درست درسك قبل وصوله .

٦ ـ حضرت الاجتماع .

٧ ـ ذهبتم الى المسرح .

٨ ـ أكرمت الزائر .

٩ ـ حكمت على نفسك .

١٠ ـ طالبتم بهذه الحقوق .

2. The jussive mood: Negative commands

The jussive mood of the verb, preceded by لا 'not' is used in giving a negative command or request (telling someone not to do something). The examples below show the contrast between positive commands (for which imperative forms are used) and negative commands (لا plus jussive forms):

	Positive		Negative	
2 MS	دَرِّسْ	'teach!'	لا تُدَرِّسْ	'don't teach!'
2 FS	تَكَلَّمي	'speak!'	لا تَتَكَلَّمي	'don't speak!'
2 D	اُكْتُبا	'write!'	لا تَكْتُبا	'don't write!'
2 MP	اِذْهَبوا	'go!'	لا تَذْهَبوا	'don't go!'
2 FP	خُذْنَ	'take!'	لا تَأْخُذْنَ	'don't take!'

Some illustrative sentences containing negative imperatives are shown below:

لا تَتَكَلَّموا ٱلْإِنْكِليزِيَّةَ هُنا .	'Don't speak English here.'
لا تَشْرَبِ ٱلْقَهْوَةَ بَعْدَ ٱلسّاعَةِ ٱلْعاشِرَةِ مَساءً .	'Don't drink coffee after ten o'clock in the evening.'
لا تَتْرُكينا يا سَميرَةُ .	'Don't leave us, Samira!'
لا تُعَيِّنْهُمْ مُدَرِّسينَ .	'Don't appoint them (as) teachers.'

Drill 4. (Also on tape) Transformation: Positive → negative imperative.

'Go with him!' → ← اذهب معه!

'Don't go with him!' لا تذهب معه!

١ – اشرب الماء!

٢ – احكم على نفسك!

٣ – سافروا بالاوتوبيس!

٤ – ابحث الوضع السياسي!

٥ – اسألها عن دراستها!

٦ – اعملوا على تقدم الوضع الاقتصادي فقط.

٧ – اعقدوا الاجتماع هنا مساء غد!

Drill 5. Transformation: Statement → imperative → negative imperative.

'You (m.s.) returned to your country.' → ← رجعتَ الى بلدك.

'Return to your country.' → ← إرْجِعْ الى بلدك.

'Don't return to your country.' لا تَرْجِعْ الى بلدك.

١ – جعلتم وقتا لذلك.

٢ – سافرتَ بالطائرة.

٣ – اعتمدتِ عليه.

٤ – ذكرتَ ذلك الامر.

٥ – انصرفتم من البيت.

٦ – تركتِ عملك.

٧ – رحّبتَ به.

٨ – نظرتم في هذا الامر.

٩ – اخذتِها.

١٠ – ربطتموهم.

3. The jussive mood: Indirect commands

As the preceding note showed, the jussive mood is used in giving direct negative commands. The jussive, usually preceded by the particle لِ is also used in giving indirect commands or suggestions. With a first person plural form, this corresponds to an English "let's" construction:

لِنَذْهَبْ .	'Let's go.'
لِنَأْكُلْ هُنا .	'Let's eat here.'

It is rarely used with the second person, in which case it becomes a polite command. With a third person form, it corresponds to English "have, let, make (s.o. do s.th.)":

لِيَنْصَرِفْ .	'Have him go away.'
لِيَسْتَمِعا لِلْمُحاضَراتِ .	'Let them (d.) listen to the lectures.'
لِيَدْرُسوا أَكْثَرَ .	'Make them (m.p.) study more.'

All these constructions are very commonly preceded by فَ 'and, so'; the vowel of لِ is then dropped. This فَ is often better left untranslated.

فَلْنَذْهَبْ .	'Let's go.'
فَلْيَكْتُبِ الْجُمْلَةَ بِالْعَرَبِيَّةِ .	'Have him write the sentence in Arabic.'

Drill 6. (Also on tape) Transformation: سَ + imperfect → لِ + jussive

a. 'We're going to go to the movies.' → سَنَذْهَبُ الى السينما . ←
'Let's go to the movies.' فَلْنَذْهَبْ الى السينما .

١ – سنشرب قهوة عربية هناك .
٢ – سنستقبل الرئيس في المطار .
٣ – سنجتمع مع السياسيّين اثناء اقامتهم هنا .
٤ – سننتخب رئيس المؤتمر .
٥ – سنكتب رسالة الى والدينا .
٦ – سنحدّد مواعيد الامتحان .

b. 'He will attend the meeting.' → سيحضر الاجتماع . ←
'Let him attend the meeting.' فليحضر الاجتماع .

١ – سيشارك في حفر القناة .
٢ – سيشرفون على العمل .
٣ – سينصرفون قبل بداية المحاضرة .
٤ – سيقاوم الشر بالخير .
٥ – سيتكلّم مع المهندس بعد عشر دقائق .
٦ – سيؤجل ذلك الى الغد .

D. Comprehension passage د – نصوص للفهم :

Read the following passage; then do Drill 7, which is based on it.

speech; dean

خِطــــابُ الْعَميـــــدِ

ايها السيدات والسادة :

حضرتم من بلاد كثيرة لتدرسوا وتحصلوا على شهادات جامعية .

والطلاب الاجانب يحضرون الى هذه الجامعة عاما بعد عام وكلّهم يسألون:

كيف ننجح في دراستنا وفي حياتنا هنا ؟

سيداتي وسادتي :

احكموا افواهكم وليكن تَفْكيرُكُمْ اكثر من كلامكم .فالمفكر ينجح — your thinking

ويحترم النّاسُ آراءه . — people

اجعلوا لكل أمر وقتا : للدرس وقتا ولاصدقائكم وقتا ، ولانفسكم

وقتا . لا تؤجلوا الدراسة ولا تسمحوا للاصدقاء بأن يأخذوا من وقتها .

ايها السيدات والسادة : لكم حقوق وعليكم واجبات ، وليست

حقوقكم أكثر من واجباتكم .لاتطالبوا بحقوقكم حتى تُؤَدّوا واجباتكم . — carry out; perform

أكرموا جيرانكم وأصدقاءكم ، فالجيران والاصدقاء أهل للغريب

والحَكيمُ يحترم أهله ويكرمهم . — the wise person

لا تَمْدَحوا أنفسكم امام غيركم . فالغريب يرحب بالاحترام بل يطلبه — praise

لكن آراءكم في انفسكم لا تَفْرِضُ عَلى غيركم ان يحترموكم . — oblige, force

أَرْجو لكم يا أَبْنائي كل نجاح . — I wish, hope; my children

Drill 7. Written. Paraphrasing.

Write briefly in English and then in Arabic what the dean said about:

(a) thinking vs. speaking
(b) rights vs. privileges
(c) neighbors

E. General Drills — هـ ـ التمارين العامّة

Drill 8. (Also on tape) Transformation: Singular ⟶ plural

In each of the sentences below, replace the underlined word(s) or phrase(s) with the plural, making any necessary changes.

١ ـ هذا المهندس سيشارك في بناء السد •

٢ ـ سأشاهد فيلما جميلا في الصيف القادم •

٣ ـ البدوي اكرم الزائر •

٤ ـ البنت عملت في ذلك المصنع •

٥ ـ ساعد هذا النهر على تقدّم اقتصاد البلد •

٦ ـ قرّر منهج التعليم في المدرسة القومية •

٧ ـ الطالب مستعد للامتحان •

٨ ـ تعلّم الاديب لغة اجنبية •

٩ ـ في مقالتك فكرة هامّة •

١٠ ـ النص يشمل جملة صعبة •

Drill 9. Written. Transformation: Singular ⟶ dual ⟶ plural

Replace the underlined word with the dual, then the plural, making any necessary changes.

١ ـ هذا هو قائد النهضة الادبية الذي قرأت مقالاته في الجريدة اليومية •

٢ ـ الدولة ستساعد الشركة على بناء مصنع حديث •

٣ ـ الحزب الرئيسي انتخب مرشحا اثناء مؤتمره الصيفي •

٤ ـ هذه هي الرسالة التي كتبها الطالب •

٥ ـ الطالب الامريكي ذاهب لزيارة ذلك البلد العربي •

Drill 10. (Also on tape) Transformation: Perfect ⟶ subjunctive with يجب أن

١ ـ تكلمتَ العربية كل يوم •

٢ ـ شاركتموه في عمله •

٣ ـ أصدر كتابا كل سنتين •

٤ ـ استقبلنا رئيس الجمهورية عند وصوله •

٥ ـ انتظرت اختها بعد الانصراف من الصفّ •

٦ ــ تناول هذا الموضوع في مقالته .

٧ ــ حدّدوا مواعيد الامتحانات هذا الصباح .

٨ ــ عقدنا اجتماعنا في مدينة قريبة من هنا .

٩ ــ انصرفتنّ في الساعة التاسعة والربع .

١٠ ــ منعتَهم من حضور الاجتماع .

Drill 11. (Oral) Translation

1. Go (m.s.) with them to their house!

2. Help (m.s.) your father in his work!

3. Let's co-operate with our neighbors!

4. Finish (f.s.) your letter after the lecture!

5. Don't eat in that restaurant!

6. Don't read this sentence!

Drill 12. Written. Dictionary drill.

Look up each of the following verbal nouns in the dictionary. Give: 1) the verb it is derived from, 2) the meaning of the verb and 3) the imperative (2 m.s.) of the verb. Ex.

ذهاب : ذَهَبَ / 'to go' / اِذْهَبْ !

تزوّج

مصادقة

تراسل

تفكير

اتّباع

رسم

Drill 13. Completion. Vocabulary.

Make any necessary changes.

صحراء، ترحيب ، حدّ ، مناهج ، السيطرة على ، انتخب ، مذكرات ، الاعتماد على ، مكانة ، مفكّر ، جمهورية ، إنَّ ، اشرف ، منح ، رحل ، شعر ، أَنَّ ، نهضة ، مجلة ، واجب ، حرّية .

١ ـ نجحت فرنسا وبريطانيا في ـــــ شركة قناة السويس .

٢ ـ يعتبرون هذا الرجل من أعظم ـــــ في العالم .

٣ ـ كان جمال عبد الناصر رئيس ـــــ مصر .

٤ ـ استمعت لمحاضرة الاستاذ وكتبت ـــــ كثيرة .

٥ ـ ـــــ المهندس على بناء السد الجديد على الامازون .

٦ ـ تقرر الوزارة ـــــ التعليم كل سنة .

٧ ـ ـــــ الحكومة الطلاب مساعدات كثيرة .

٨ ـ ستتمكن من ـــــ اصدقائك المخلصين .

٩ ـ يعجبني كثيرا ـــــ نازِك المَلائكة .

١٠ ـ تعتقد نوال السعداوي انه من ـــ ان تتوفر للنساء الحقوق المساوية لحقوق الرجال .

١١ ـ حقّق المفكرون العرب ـــــ ادبية قومية في العالم العربي .

١٢ ـ شعب مصر يعتمد على مياه النيل الى ابعد ـــــ .

١٣ ـ ـــــ الشعب مرشح هذا الحزب رئيسا للجمهورية .

١٤ ـ يعتقدون ـــــ للثورة المصرية اهمية كبيرة جدّا في التاريخ الحديث للشرق الاوسط .

١٥ ـ يسرع البدو الى ـــــ بالزائر وتقديم القهوة له .

Lesson Twenty-six

الدرس السادس والعشرون

أ ـ النص الاساسيّ

سوزان وعلـــــــي

كان اسمه علي . واسمها هي سوزان . الخرطوم . لندن . درست الفنّ في مَعْهَدِ سْليد . درس العلوم السياسيّة في مَعْهَدِ الاقتصاد بجامعة لندن . institute

قالت : " تزوّجني "

قال : " لا . صعب "

قالت : " لكنّي أحبّك "

قال : " وأنا ايضا احبّك . لكن ...

ومن ثمّ عادَ الى بلده . وأخذا يتراسلان . he returned

" لكنّي أحبّك يا علي "

" وأنا أحبّك يا سوزان . لكن ...

ستّة اشهر .

كتبت تقول : " قابلت رجلا . سأتزوّجه " .

كتب يقول : " لكنّي أحبّك يا سوزان " .

انقطعت الرسائل .

يفكّر بها في غالب الاحيان .

وتفكّر به من حين لآخر .

لكن ...

ل : الطيّب صالح
من: مُقَدّمات مجلة حِوار
السنة الرابعة ، العدد الثالث
آذار ـ نيسان ١٩٦٦ ، صَفْحة ٤٠

A. Basic text

Suzanne and Ali

His name was Ali. And her name was Suzanne. Khartoum. London. She studied art at Slade Institute. He studied political science at the Institute of Economics at the University of London.

She said, "Marry me."

He said, "No. It's difficult."

She said, "But I love you."

He said, "And I love you, too. But..."

Then he returned to his country.

And they began to correspond.

"But I love you, Ali."

"And I love you, Suzanne. But..."

Six months.

She wrote saying, "I have met a man. I am going to marry him."

He wrote saying, "But I love you, Suzanne."

The letters stopped.

He thinks about her most of the time.

And she thinks about him from time to time.

But...

By: Al-Tayyib Ṣāliḥ

From: "Muqaddimāt"

Ḥiwār magazine, Vol. IV, No. 3 (March-April, 1966), p. 40.

B. Vocabulary ب – المفردات :

سوزان Suzanne

عَلِيّ Ali

فَنٌّ ـ فُنونٌ	art (nisba: فَنِّيٌّ 'artistic; technical; professional')
عِلْمٌ (بِ) ـ عُلومٌ	knowledge (of); science (nisba: عِلْمِيٌّ 'scientific, learned')
عَلِمَ ـَ ، عِلْمٌ	to know, have knowledge of
بِ	in
قالَتْ	she said
تَزَوَّجَ ، تَزَوُّجٌ / زَواجٌ	V to marry
أُحِبُّ	I love; I like
حُبٌّ	love
أَيْضًا	also
مِنْ ثَمَّ	hence; then
أَخَذَ ـُ ، أَخْذٌ	to take; (with foll. indicative) to begin to (do s. th.) (imperative: خُذْ ،خُذي ، خُذوا)
تَراسَلَ ، تَراسُلٌ	VI to correspond (with each other)
شَهْرٌ ـ أَشْهُرٌ	month
تَقولُ	she says
يَقولُ	he says
اِنْقَطَعَ ، اِنْقِطاعٌ	VII to be cut off; to stop, come to an end
فَكَّرَ ، تَفْكيرٌ (بِ)	II to think (of, about)
غالِبٌ	(with foll. gen.) most, majority of
حينٌ ـ أَحْيانٌ	time; occasion

Additional Vocabulary

حَبيبٌ ـ أَحِبّاءُ	beloved, sweetheart; dear
ناسٌ ، أُناسٌ	(p.) people
رَغِبَ ـَ ، رَغْبَةٌ في	to desire, wish for
أَحَبَّ	IV he fell in love with, he loved; he took a liking to, he liked (f.s.= أَحَبَّتْ)

C. Grammar and Drills

ج - القواعد والتمارين

1. Independent pronouns used for contrast and emphasis
2. Verbs of beginning
3. The tenses: Past imperfect

1. Independent pronouns used for contrast and emphasis

Compare these two sentences:

كانَ اسْمُهُ عَلي.	'His name was Ali.'
كانَ اسْمُها هِيَ سوزان.	'<u>Her</u> name was Suzanne.'

There is an opposition here between two pronouns:

اِسْمُهُ	'his name'
اِسْمُها	'her name'

English can emphasize this contrast by pronouncing the words in question louder--"<u>his</u> name and <u>her</u> name". (This is achieved in writing by underlining or italicizing.) In Arabic this emphasis is expressed by repeating the independent form of the pronoun after the pronoun suffix:

اِسْمُهُ هُوَ	'<u>his</u> name	عُنْوانُكَ أَنْتَ	'<u>your</u> address'
اِسْمُها هِيَ	'<u>her</u> name	بَيْتُنا نَحْنُ	'<u>our</u> house'
سافَرَ هُوَ وَرَجَعَتْ هِيَ.		'<u>He</u> left and <u>she</u> came back.'	

Now do Drill 1.

<u>Drill 1</u>. (Also on tape) Transformation: Pronouns for contrast and emphasis

<u>Ex</u>. 'His name is Aḥmad and her name is Suʿad.' → اسمه احمد و<u>اسمها</u> سعاد. ←

'His name is Aḥmad and <u>her</u> name is Suʿad.' اسمه احمد واسمها هي سعاد.

١ - اعرفكم ولكن لا <u>اعرفهم</u>.

٢ - سافر عندما <u>رجعت</u>.

٣ - هذا القلم لي وليس لك .

٤ - سيّارتي امام المتحف وسيارتكم امام بيتكم .

٥ - هذا رأينا .

٦ - نعتبره اعظم اديب في العالم .

٧ - لا تذهبن معها بل اذهبن معه .

٨ - تعجبنا المجلة ولكنها لا تعجبكم .

٩ - يعتقدون انها المرأة التي تحدثت الى المدير .

2. Verbs of beginning

The verb أَخَذَ means 'to take', as in هَلْ أَخَذَتِ ٱلْقَلَمَ مَعَها ؟ 'Did she take the pencil with her?' The perfect tense of this verb, however, may be used with a following verb in the imperfect indicative, in which case it means "to begin..."; the second verb may be translated as an infinitive or as a participle. Both verbs agree with the subject, which is placed between them if expressed:

فَأَخَذَ النّاسُ يَتَحَدَّثونَ .	'Then the people began to talk to each other.'
أَخَذا يَتَراسَلانِ .	'They began to correspond (corresponding) with each other.'

There is a small group of verbs that, like أَخَذَ , take on the meaning of 'to begin' when followed by an imperfect indicative. Another common one is جَعَلَ 'to make', e.g.

جَعَلَ يَرْحَلُ في الصَّحْراءِ .	'He began to travel about in the desert.'

These verbs of beginning are synonymous with بَدَأَ 'to begin', but differ from it in that بَدَأَ always has the meaning 'to begin' whether in the perfect or imperfect tense; further, بَدَأَ may be followed by a verbal noun instead of the indicative:

مَتى سَيَبْدَأونَ يَدْرُسونَ ؟ مَتى سَيَبْدَأونَ الدِّراسَةَ ؟	'When are they going to start studying?'

بَدَأَ بِ means 'to start with', as in

فَلْنَبْدَأْ بِالدَّرْسِ الرّابِعِ ٠	'Let's start with the fourth lesson.'

Now do Drills 2 (on tape), 3, and 4.

<u>Drill 2</u>. (On tape) Conjugation: Verbs of beginning

<u>Drill 3</u>. Written. Transformation: Verbs of beginning

<u>Ex</u>. 'The two friends corresponded.' ⟶ تراسل الصديقان ٠ (أخذ) ⟵

'The two friends began to correspond.' أخذ الصديقان يتراسلان ٠

١ ـ فكر فريد بها ٠ (جعل)

٢ ـ تحدّث الناس عن الوضع الاقتصادي وعن السلام ٠ (أخذ)

٣ ـ فعل كريم ذلك كل يوم ٠ (بدأ)

٤ ـ درس الطلاب العربية في جامعة لندن ٠ (أخذ)

٥ ـ بحثت المرأة عن عمل في هذه المدينة ٠ (بدأ)

٦ ـ كتب المراسل مقالات في هذه المجلة ٠ (جعل)

٧ ـ بذل الاطبّاء جهودا كبيرة في خدمة المجتمع ٠ (أخذ)

٨ ـ تعاونت الدولتان في هذا الامر الهام ٠ (جعل)

٩ ـ بحثت الشركة عن الماء في الصحراء ٠ (بدأ)

<u>Drill 4</u>. Transformation: Verb ⟶ Verbal Noun

<u>Ex</u>. 'When are you going to start studying?' متى ستبدأ تدرس ؟ ⟵

متى ستبدأ الدراسة ؟

١ ـ بدأ يعمل هذه السنة ٠

٢ ـ بدأ يدرس الأدب الفرنسيّ ٠

٣ ـ هل سيبدأون يحفرون القناة الجديدة قريبا ؟

٤ ـ بدأت ادرس في مدرسة ثانويّة سنة ١٩٦٩ ٠

٥ ـ بدأوا يبحثون الوضع السياسيّ في ولاية ميشغان ٠

٦ ـ بدأن يجمعن الكتب القديمة ٠

3. The tenses: Past imperfect

We have pointed out that the imperfect tense may denote various kinds of action:

a. habitual action, e.g.

يَدْرُسُ في بَيْتِهِ عادَةً ٠ 'He usually studies at home.'

b. progressive action, e.g.

ماذا يَدْرُسُ الآنَ ؟ 'What is he studying now?'

c. future action, e.g.

سَيَدْرُسُ غَداً ٠ 'He's going to study tomorrow.'

d. state (no action at all), e.g.

هَلْ يَعْرِفُ ذٰلِكَ ؟ 'Does he know that?'

You must study the context in which the imperfect verb occurs in order to determine which of these translations is most appropriate. In these sentences, the verbs refer to present time--the time of the sentence itself. In order to denote such actions or states in past time, the past tense of كانَ is used with the imperfect verb:

a. Past habitual:

كانَ يَدْرُسُ في بَيْتِهِ عادَةً .	'He used to study at home usually' (or 'He would usually study at home' or 'He usually studied at home.')

b. Past progressive:

ماذا كانَ يَدْرُسُ في ذٰلِكَ الْحينِ؟	'What was he studying at that time?'

c. Past future:

كانَ سَيَدْرُسُ أَمْسِ .	'He was going to study yesterday.'

d. Past state:

هَلْ كانَ يَعْرِفُ ذٰلِكَ ؟	'Did he know that?'

These constructions are all negated by لا before the imperfect verb:

كانَ لا يَدْرُسُ أَحْياناً .	'Sometimes he didn't study.'

This construction with its various meanings is referred to as the past imperfect.

A comment about state verbs in particular: these are verbs that denote a condition or quality, but no action or activity, like know, want, love, like, understand, to matter, etc. These verbs as a class do not occur in the progressive form in English. In English, the past tense of state verbs expresses a past state: I know and I knew. In Arabic, however, the perfect tense, which always denotes a completed event, signifies, for a state verb, the entering of that state or condition. For example, يَعْرِفُ means "he knows"; the perfect عَرَفَ means "he entered upon a state of knowing" = "he came to know"= "he learned, found out." ("he knew" is كانَ يَعْرِفُ). Similarly, all state verbs in the perfect tense may be translated with the idea of "to come to..., to begin to..." which will often be a totally different expression in English. Examples:

Imperfect		Perfect	
يَعْرِفُ	'he knows'	عَرَفَ	'he found out, learned'
يُحِبُّ	'he loves; he likes'	أَحَبَّ	'he fell in love with; he took a liking to'

It is essential to distinguish between the various possible meanings of the English and Arabic tenses. Past habitual, past progressive, past future and past state cannot be expressed by the Arabic perfect tense; the perfect tense can only denote a completed event, e.g.

> دَرَسَ ذٰلِكَ أَمْسِ . 'He studied that yesterday.'

or a series of events, e.g.

> دَرَسَ الدَّرْسَ الثالِثَ كَثيرًا . 'He studied Lesson Three many times.'

The following chart contrasts expressions of present and past time in Arabic:

	Present Time	Past Time
a. Habitual action	يَدْرُسُ 'he studies'	كانَ يَدْرُسُ 'he studied' <u>or</u> 'he used to study'
b. Progressive action	يَدْرُسُ 'he is studying'	كانَ يَدْرُسُ 'he was studying'
c. Future	سَيَدْرُسُ 'he is going to study'	كانَ سَيَدْرُسُ 'he was going to study'
d. State	يَعْرِفُ 'he knows'	كانَ يَعْرِفُ 'he knew'
e. Completed event	دَرَسَ 'he studied; he has studied'	دَرَسَ 'he studied; he had studied'

Notice that the perfect دَرَسَ and the past habitual كانَ يَدْرُسُ can both be translated 'he studied'. This means that the English past tense, unlike the Arabic perfect, may mean either a completed event ("he studied it yesterday") or past habitual ("he always studied at home"). It is important to distinguish between these two meanings, since they correspond to two different constructions in Arabic:

'he studied' < دَرَسَ (one event) / كانَ يَدْرُسُ (past habitual)

A simple test for an English past tense is to substitute for it "used to...", which means past habitual action. If the meaning does not change, then Arabic كانَ plus imperfect is indicated; if, on the other hand, substituting "used to ______" changes the meaning, then it is equivalent to the Arabic perfect. For example, for "I saw him yesterday" it does not make sense to say "I used to see him yesterday"; therefore "I saw" = Arabic perfect شاهَدْتُ . In "I usually saw him in school" it does not change the meaning to say "I used to see him in school"; this is equivalent to the Arabic past imperfect كُنْتُ أُشاهِدُ

An imperfect indicative verb after past tense كانَ refers to past time. It also refers to past time after any perfect tense verb in the main clause; this imperfect may follow immediately after another verb, e.g.

كَتَبَ يَقولُ :	'he wrote and said' = 'he wrote saying'
كانَتْ تَكْتُبُ إِلَيْهِ كُلَّ يَوْمٍ ، تَتَحَدَّثُ إِلَيْهِ عَنْ حُبِّها .	'She would write him every day and speak (or "speaking") to him of her love.'

It may also be in a subordinate clause, e.g.

عَرَفَتْ أَيْضًا أَنَّهُ يُحِبُّها .	'She also found out that he loved her.'
كُنْتُ أَعْرِفُ أَنَّهُ سَيَتَزَوَّجُ فَرَنْسِيَّةً .	'I knew that he was going to marry a French woman.'

The equational sentence, if it is a subordinate clause, likewise assumes the same time as the main verb; illustrations:

كُنْتُ أَعْرِفُ أَنَّهُ في الْمَكْتَبِ .	'I knew that he was in the office.'
أَعْتَقَدْتُ أَنَّهُمْ هُناكَ .	'I thought they were there.'

Now do Drills 5-9.

Drill 5. Question-answer: Meanings of imperfect.

١ – هل تدرس عادة في بيتك ام في المكتبة ؟

٢ – هل تفكر بصديقك كثيرا ؟

٣ – هل تقرأ الجريدة كل يوم ؟

٤ – هل تعرف اسم المهندس الذي اشرف على حفر قناة السويس ؟

٥ – هل ستذهب مع صديقك غدا لتأكلا في المطعم العربيّ ؟

٦ – هل تتكلم العربية الآن ؟

٧ – هل يعقد الحزب الجمهوري الامريكي مؤتمرا كل اربع سنوات ؟

٨ – هل ترغب في الذهاب الى السينما غدا مساء ؟

٩ – هل ستبذل جهودا كبيرة في دراستك هذه السنة ؟

١٠ – هل تعين وزارة التعليم كل الاساتذة الجامعيّين في هذا البلد ؟

١١ – هل يسمح الوقت بذلك ؟

١٢ – هل يشمل الامتحان محاضرة استاذنا الاخيرة ؟

Drill 6. (On tape) Transformation. Perfect ⟶ كانَ + imperfect

Drill 7. Written. Translation: Tenses.

Translate the following sentences using the best English equivalent.

١ – كان علي وسوزان يتراسلان .

٢ – فتحنا الشباك ونظرنا منه .

٣ – هل تعرف اسم القائد المسلم الذي فتح مصر ؟

٤ _ ماذا تفعلون في الوقت الحاضر ؟

٥ _ هل كان يعرف ذلك عندما تحدثت اليه ؟

٦ _ شاهدت فلما جميلا جدا امس .

٧ _ ترغب النساء في الحصول على مكانة عالية في المجتمع .

٨ _ كنت ادرس عندما انصرفت .

٩ _ كنا نشاهد افلاما كثيرة معا .

١٠ _ كانوا سيذهبون لزيارة اصدقائهم في البلاد العربية .

١١ _ يدرس الفن في جامعة لندن .

١٢ _ كنّا نذهب الى مؤتمر الحزب كل اربع سنوات .

Drill 8. (On tape) Conjugation: كتب يسأل .....

Drill 9. Written. Sentence formation: Tenses.

Use the following verbs in sentences, and then translate the sentences. (Hint: use adverbs of time, e.g. عادة ، احيانا ، كل يوم ، الآن etc., when necessary to prevent ambiguity.)

	كان يرغب	سألت	عرفت
(use in progressive meaning)	ندرس	تقدّم	فكّر بـ
(use in habitual meaning)	يدرسون	تقرّر	أجّلنا
		كنت سأسافر	بذلوا

D. Comprehension passage — د . نصوص للفهم

(1) Read the following passage and then do Drill 10.

*

أين الحبيب

كانت طالبة في الجامعة الامريكية في بيروت ، وكان طالبا في نَفْسِ الجامعة . تقابلا . فأحبّها بعد اللِّقاءِ الاول ، واخبرها بحبه ، فقالت:

meeting / the same

*Adapted from a short story; author and publication date unavailable.

انا ايضا احبّك . تقابلا بعد ذلك كثيرا ، وتحدثا طويلا ، فعرفت عن حياته كل شيء ، وعرفت ايضا انه يرغب في السفر الى فرنسا للحصول على الدكتوراه في العلوم السياسية ، لكن الْفَقْرَ يمنعه من تحقيق رغبته . poverty وحصل على البكالوريوس قبل ان تحصل عليها ، فقالت له : قرّرت الاّ اكمل الدراسة الجامعية . سوف اعمل حتى تتمكن من السفر الى اوربا وتحصل على الدكتوراه . لم تعجبه الفكرة ، لكنها قالت سترجع وسنصبح بعد ذلك زوجين . الا تساعد الزوجة المخلصة زوجها ؟

وذهب الى فرنسا ، واخذا يتراسلان . كانت تكتب اليه كل يوم تتحدّث اليه عن حبها وتخبره بانها في انتظاره . وكان لا يكتب احيانا فتقول: ان الدراسة لا تسمح له بأن يكتب .

وبعد عامين انقطعت رسائله . سألتني عنه كثيرا فقد كنت صديقه . وكنت اقول : لست اعرف عن اخباره شيئا ، لكني كنت اعرف . كنت اعرف انه تزوج فرنسية وانه قرر الا يرجع . وكنت اسأل نفسي : هل تؤثّر المسافات في الحب ، وهل تُغَيِّرُ القلب ؟ . it changes

(2) Listen to the passage on tape and then do Drill 11, which is based on it.

Drill 10. Written

Paraphrase the reading passage in five or more sentences.

Drill 11. (On tape) Aural comprehension

أسئلة

١ ـ هل كان قيس بدويّا ؟ وليلى ؟

٢ ـ هل احب قيس ليلى ؟ هل احبته ؟

٣ ـ لماذا لم يتزوّج قيس ليلى ؟

٤ ـ هل يقرأ العرب الآن عن حبّ قيس لليلى ؟

٥ ـ عمّ تحدّث قيس في شعره ؟

E. General Drills — هـ ـ التمارين العامّة

Drill 12. (Also on tape) Negation

Negate the underlined expressions.

١ ـ فكّروا بهذا الموضوع ٠

٢ ـ هذه بلاد اسلاميّة ٠

٣ ـ دراسة العلوم السياسيّة سهلة ٠

٤ ـ ستمنع الحكومة عقد الاجتماع في هذا البناء٠

٥ ـ كان يرغب في انشاء مجلة ادبيّة ٠

٦ ـ يجب ان ينصرف الطلاب بعد الصف ٠

٧ ـ انقطعت الرسائل بين الحبيبين ٠

٨ ـ يعتقد بعض الناس ان وظيفة رئيس الجمهوريّة لها اهميّة كبيرة ٠

٩ ـ قال والد احمد : تزوّجها ٠

١٠ ـ المسافة بين هاتين المدينتين بعيدة ٠

١١ ـ تشرف الحكومة على الانتخابات ٠

Drill 13. Substitution/transformation: أَنْ-clause → verbal noun

'He collected these old books.' → جمع هذه الكتب القديمة ٠

'He wants to collect these old books.' → يرغب في ان يجمع هذه الكتب القديمة ٠

'He wants to collect these old books.' يرغب في جمع هذه الكتب القديمة ٠

١ ـ تراسل مع صديق اجنبيّ ٠

٢ ـ أجّل دراسة الموضوع الى وقت آخر ٠

٣ ـ يذهب الى الاسكندريّة في الصّيف ٠

٤ ـ اشرف على حفر القناة الجديدة ٠

٥ ـ توفّرت حرّية الرأي للشّعب الى ابعد حدّ ٠

٦ ـ حصل على الدكتوراه في الاقتصاد السياسيّ ٠

٧ ـ رحل من مكان الى آخر ٠

Drill 14. Embedding: Relative clauses

Incorporate the second sentence into the first by making it a relative clause. Ex.

'The letters between the lovers stopped.'	انقطعت الرسائل بين الحبيبين ٠
'The lovers were going to marry.'	كان الحبيبان سيتزوّجان ٠
'The letters of the lovers who were going to marry stopped.'	انقطعت الرسائل بين الحبيبين اللذين كانا سيتزوّجان ٠

١ ـ المفكرون يساعدون على تقدم المجتمع ٠
المفكرون يدرسون الاوضاع الاجتماعية ٠

٢ ـ قرأت كتابا عن القائد ٠
فتح القائد العراق ٠

٣ ـ تأثّر الشعر بالنهضة القوميّة ٠
حقق المفكرون العرب النهضة القوميّة ٠

٤ ـ تمّ حفر قناة كبيرة ٠
ستساعد القناة على تقدّم اقتصاد البلد ٠

٥ ـ سكنت في مدينة صغيرة ٠
انعقد مؤتمر هام في المدينة الصغيرة ٠

٦ ـ حضرت في القاهرة مؤتمرا هاما ٠
انعقد المؤتمر لدراسة الوضع الاقتصادي في الشرق الاوسط ٠

٧ ـ احترم هذه المرأة ٠
ساعدت هذه المرأة على تقدم النهضة النسائيّة ٠

استقبلتني في المطار احدى البنات ٠

٨ — درست مع البنات في الجامعة ٠

Drill 15. Written. Translation

1. Suzanne and Ali began to correspond after (بعد أن) Ali travelled to Europe.

2. Was he drinking coffee when you met him in the restaurant?

3. Don't broadcast ("transmit") this news!

4. That's your opinion, not my opinion.

5. I know that because my friend who studies political science mentioned it to me.

الدرس السابع والعشرون

Lesson Twenty-seven

أ ـ النص الاساسي

رسالة

عزيزي فرانك :

ترغب في أن تراسل عربيّا وتصادقه ، وأنا سعيد بأن أراسلك وأصادقك . اسمي مُحَمّد بَغْدادي ، وأنا مهندس في أحد المصانع المنتشرة خارج الظَهْران ، (وأخي عامل في نفس المصنع) .

أنا حاصل على البكالوريوس من جامعة القاهرة وقد درست عاما في لندن . لي عائلة صغيرة تشمل ابنا وابنة . أنا ساكن مع عائلتي في بيت قريب من المصنع . ابني طالب في مدرسة ثانويّة وابنتي صغيرة فهي لا تدرس . زوجتي لبنانيّة انتقلت مع والديها الى الظهران في الخامسة من عمرها ، وكانت عندما قابلتها موظّفة في شركة أرامْكو .

أنا وزوجتي نعرف شيئا كثيرا عن سياسة بلادك وعن الوضع الاقتصاديّ فيها ، لاننا نقرأ الصحف الامريكية . لعلّك في رسالتك القادمة تذكر رأيك في ذلك الوضع .

نحن في السعوديّة مقبلون على نهضة صناعيّة عظيمة وحياتنا اليوم مختلفة عن الحياة التي كانت كتب الغرب تتحدّث عنها الى زمن قريب .

سوف اكتب اليك عن هذا الامر في رسالتي القادمة .

المخلص

محمد بغدادي

A. <u>Basic text</u>

A Letter

Dear Frank,

You wish to correspond with an Arab and be friends with him; I am happy to correspond with you and be your friend. My name is Muhammad Baghdadi and I am an engineer in one of the many factories found outside Dhahran. (My brother is a worker in the same factory.)

I obtained my B.A. from the University of Cairo and studied for one year in London. I have a small family which includes a son and a daughter. I live with my family in a house near the factory. My son is a student in secondary school; my daughter is small, and so she does not go to school. My wife is a Lebanese who moved to Dhahran with her parents at the age of five, and was when I met her an employee at Aramco.

My wife and I know quite a lot about the (foreign) policy of your country and the economic conditions there, because we read American newspapers. Perhaps in your next letter you could mention your opinion about the situation there.

We in Saudi Arabia are embarking upon a great industrial boom, and our life today is different from the life which Western books have talked about up to recent times. I will write to you about this matter in my next letter.

Sincerely,

Muhammad Baghdadi

B. Vocabulary

ب ــ المفردات

رَاسَلَ ، مُرَاسَلَةٌ	III to correspond with (s.o.)
صَادَقَ ، مُصَادَقَةٌ	III to be friends with, to befriend (s.o.)
سَعِيدٌ ــ سُعَدَاءُ (ب)	happy (about, at, with)
مُنْتَشِرٌ	scattered, spread out, widespread, prevailing
خَارِجَ	outside (prep.), outside of
الظَّهْرَانُ	Dhahran (town in Saudi Arabia)
أَخٌ (أَخُو) ــ إِخْوَةٌ	brother
أَخَوِيٌّ	(nisba of أَخٌ) brotherly, fraternal
عَامِلٌ ــ عُمَّالٌ	worker, laborer
نَفْسٌ ــ أَنْفُسٌ	(f.) soul; self; (as 1st term of iḍāfa) the same
حَاصِلٌ ــ ون عَلى	having obtained
اِبْنَةٌ ــ بَنَاتٌ	daughter
سَاكِنٌ ــ ون	living (in a place), dwelling, residing
عُمْرٌ ــ أَعْمَارٌ	age (of a person), life span, life-time
في الْخَمْسينَ مِنَ الْعُمْرِ	at the age of fifty
أرامكو	Aramco (= The Arabian-American Oil Company)
سِيَاسَةٌ ــ ات	policy; politics
صَحِيفَةٌ ــ صُحُفٌ	newspaper
صُحُفِيٌّ	(nisba of صَحِيفَةٌ) journalistic; journalist
لَعَلَّ	perhaps, maybe
مُقْبِلٌ ــ ون على	approaching; embarking upon; devoting (o.s.) to
صِنَاعَةٌ ــ ات	industry
مُخْتَلِفٌ ــ ون (عَنْ ، مِنْ)	differing, different (from)

Additional Vocabulary

خَرَجَ ـُ ، خُرُوجٌ (من)	to go out, leave, emerge (from)
الخَارِجُ	the outside world, abroad

خارِجِيٌّ	external, outer
أَخْرَجَ ، إِخْراجٌ	IV to take out, remove; to expel, dismiss
أَبٌ (أَبو) ـ آباءٌ	father
أَبَوِيٌّ	(nisba of أَبٌ) fatherly, paternal

C. Grammar and drills ج ـ القواعد والتمارين:

> 1. Active participles: Form I
> 2. Sister of إِنَّ: لَعَلَّ 'perhaps'
> 3. The noun نَفْسٌ 'self; same'
> 4. Case forms of أَبٌ 'father' and أَخٌ 'brother'

1. Active participles: Form I

A participle in Arabic is an adjective derived in specific ways from a verb, and having a meaning closely associated with that of the verb. (It is sometimes called a "verbal adjective", a term which parallels "verbal noun".) A participle may be active or passive. Passive participles will be treated later; in this lesson we deal with active participles: general meaning and Form I forms.

The basic meaning of an active participle (AP) is "performing (or having performed) the action indicated by the verb". The English equivalent is commonly an adjective ending in -ing, for example:

هَلْ أَنْتَ ذاهِبٌ ؟	'Are you going?'
أَلأُسْتاذُ الزّائِرُ	'the visiting professor'

Form I APs have the pattern FaaMil, regardless of the stem vowel of the underlying verb. Examples:

Verb		AP	
كَتَبَ	'to write'	كاتِبٌ	'writing'
ذَهَبَ	'to go'	ذاهِبٌ	'going'
رَجَعَ	'to return	راجِعٌ	'returning'
عَمِلَ	'to work'	عامِلٌ	'working'

Since they are adjectives, APs are inflected for *case*, *gender*, *number*, and *definiteness*, and agree with the noun they modify in the usual ways. They take sound plurals, éither masculine or feminine. Examples:

أَلرَّجُلُ السّاكِنُ في ذٰلِكَ الْبَيْتِ	'the man living in that house'
أَلْمَرْأَةُ السّاكِنَةُ في ذٰلِكَ الْبَيْتِ	'the woman living in that house'
أَلرِّجالُ السّاكِنونَ في ذٰلِكَ الْبَيْتِ	'the men living in that house'
أَلنِّساءُ السّاكِناتُ في ذٰلِكَ الْبَيْتِ	'the women living in that house'

APs may have several specific meanings, but these differ from verb to verb and must generally be learned in each case. For some verbs, the AP has *progressive meaning*. These include verbs indicating a change of location such as "going", "coming", "walking", "travelling" and the like; and verbs indicating absence of change, such as "staying", "stopping", "standing" and so on.

أَنا ساكِنٌ في بَيْتٍ قَريبٍ مِنَ الْمَصْنَعِ .	'I am living in a house near the factory.'
هِيَ ذاهِبَةٌ إِلى دِمَشْقَ .	'She's going to Damascus.'

The participles may also have future meaning, according to the context:

نَحْنُ مُسافِرونَ غَدًا .	'We are leaving (or 'going to leave') tomorrow.'

The participles of stative verbs are usually best translated by the English simple present tense, e.g. أنا عارِفٌ 'I know', أنا سامِعٌ 'I hear', etc. or a simple adjective, e.g. حاضِرٌ 'present; ready'.

For other verbs, the AP may have present perfect meaning:

أَنا حاصِلٌ عَلى الْبَكالوريوس .	'I have obtained the bachelor's degree.'
هُنَّ ناجِحاتٌ في ٱلإمْتِحان .	'They (f.) have succeeded in the examination.'

In many cases, a noun modified by an AP is equivalent in meaning to a noun modified by a relative clause containing the corresponding verb, where the subject of the verb is the same as the modified noun:

أَعْرِفُ الرَّجُلَ الَّذي يَسْكُنُ هُناكَ .	'I know the man who lives there.'
أَعْرِفُ الرَّجُلَ السّاكِنَ هُناك .	'I know the man living there.'
أَعْرِفُ رَجُلاً يَسْكُنُ هُناكَ .	'I know a man who lives there.'
أَعْرِفُ رَجُلاً ساكِنًا هُناكَ .	'I know a man living there.'

Both Arabic constructions may be translated with a relative clause in English, which often makes a smoother translation: 'I know the man who lives there.'

Where the AP has present perfect meaning, it is often equivalent in meaning to a relative clause containing a verb in the perfect:

أَلطّالِبُ الّذي دَرَسَ دُروسَهُ	'the student who studied (or 'has studied) his lessons'
أَلطّالِبُ الدّارِسُ دُروسَهُ	'the student who has studied his lessons'

As the last example shows, an AP may take a direct object in the accusative case, just like its verb.

A great many AP forms have taken on specific concrete meanings and are used as ordinary nouns, often with the meaning "one who performs the activity indicated by the verb". As nouns, the AP forms may have broken plurals. Examples:

كاتِبٌ ـ كُتّابٌ	'writer, author'
عامِلٌ ـ عُمّالٌ	'worker'
ساكِنٌ ـ سُكّانٌ	'inhabitant'
طالِبٌ ـ طُلّابٌ	'student' ("seeker")
حاكِمٌ ـ حُكّامٌ	'governor; judge'
عالِمٌ ـ عُلَماءُ	'scholar'
باحِثٌ ـ باحِثونَ	'researcher'
جامِعٌ ـ جَوامِعُ	'mosque'
شارِعٌ ـ شَوارِعُ	'street'

Now do Drills 1 and 2.

Drill 1. Written. Recognition: Active participle.

In each of the sentences below, underline the active participle; then write it down, along with the verb it is derived from. Ex.

هي ساكنة في ذلك البيت .

'She's living in that house.'

ساكنة ـ سَكَنَ

living-to live

١ ــ المستشرقون ذاهبون الى مصر قريبا ٠

٢ ــ والدي عامل في مصنع سيّارات ٠

٣ ــ قابلت كاتبة هذا المقال ٠

٤ ــ راسلت طالبا ساكنا في تونس ٠

٥ ــ أخي ناجح في الامتحانات كلها ٠

٦ ــ هما راغبان في العمل هنا ٠

٧ ــ صديقي حاصل على شهادة الدكتوراه ٠

٨ ــ من حاكم بلدكم ؟

٩ ــ هل هنّ ناجحات في الامتحان ؟

<u>Drill 2</u>. Written. Use of active participle.

For each of the Form I verbs given below, write a sentence using the appropriate active participle; the English meaning of the participle is given. Translate your sentences into English.

ترك	'having left'	حضر	'present, ready'	سمع	'hear'
درس	'having studied'	رحل	'traveling'	عرف	'know'

2. <u>Sister of إِنَّ : لَعَلَّ 'perhaps'</u>

لَعَلَّ 'perhaps, maybe', is a particle that introduces clauses; it often has the implication of hopeful expectation. As with أَنَّ it may introduce an equational sentence, with the subject in the accusative and the predicate (if inflected) in the nominative;

لَعَلَّ جَميعَ الْوُزَراءِ يَحْضُرونَ الاِجْتِماعَ.	'Perhaps all the ministers will attend the conference.'
لَعَلَّ في الْبَيْتِ أَصْدِقاءَ.	'Perhaps there are friends in the house.'

The subject of لَعَلَّ may also be a pronoun, as in لَعَلَّهُ طالِبٌ 'Perhaps he is a student.'

If لَعَلَّ introduces a verbal sentence, it cannot be followed immediately by a verb; it must therefore receive a pronoun suffix agreeing with a verb that would otherwise come immediately after it:

لَعَلَّهُ لا يَعْرِفُ ذٰلِكَ. 'Maybe he does not know that.'
لَعَلّي أَنْجَحُ. 'Maybe (I hope) I will succeed.'

Now do Drill 3.

Drill 3. (Also on tape) Transformation: Statement → statement with لعلّ

'He speaks English.' → يتكلّم الانكليزية . ←

'Maybe he speaks English.' لعلّه يتكلّم الانكليزيّة .

١ - يعتبرونه امرا هاما.

٢ - سيسافر أخي بالطائرة.

٣ - ستنشر المجلة شعري .

٤ - سينجح المرشح في الانتخابات هذه السنة .

٥ - كانت عائلته معه .

٦ - جمل النص الاساسي سهلة .

٧ - تمكنوا من الاقامة هنا .

٨ - ينعقد المؤتمر في مدينتنا هذا الصيف .

٩ - هي استاذة جامعية .

١٠ - أنت بخير .

١١ - انتم مستعدون للامتحان .

١٢ - هم بحاجة الى معلمين واطبّاء .

3. The noun نَفْسٌ 'self; same'

The word نَفْسٌ (plural أَنْفُسٌ) is a feminine noun meaning "soul". In certain constructions it may also correspond to English "same" or "self", as follows:

a) Followed by a definite noun in an iḍāfa: "the same":

فِي نَفْسِ الْمَصْنَعِ	'in the same factory'
هٰؤُلاءِ نَفْسُ الْكُتّابِ .	'These are the same writers.'

b) Following a noun (and agreeing with it in case and number), and with an attached pronoun suffix referring to that noun: "the same" or "himself, herself," etc.:

فِي الْمَصْنَعِ نَفْسِهِ .	'in the same factory'
حَضَرَ الرَّئِيسُ نَفْسُهُ .	'The president himself came.'
تَحَدَّثْنا مَعَ الْوُزَراءِ أَنْفُسِهِمْ .	'We spoke with the ministers themselves.'

c) With an attached pronoun suffix: "himself, herself," etc. in the reflexive sense:

أُحْكُمْ عَلى نَفْسِكَ قَبْلَ أَنْ تَحْكُمَ عَلى غَيْرِكَ .	'Judge yourself before you judge someone else.'
عَيَّنَ نَفْسَهُ وَزِيرًا .	'He appointed himself minister.'

Now do Drills 4 and 5.

Drill 4. Written. Recognition: Uses of نَفْسٌ .

Translate the underlined words in each of the sentences below, showing the different uses of نَفْسٌ .

١ _ يعمل في نفس الشركة التي كنت اعمل فيها .

٢ _ احبّ هذان الرجلان نفس البنت .

٣ _ درستِ الفن في نفس الجامعة التي درستُ فيها .

٤ _ اجتمعنا مع رئيس الجمهورية نفسه .

٥ _ كانا يفكران بنفس الشيء .

٦ _ لا اعتمد على احد غير نفسي .

٧ ـ اسألوا انفسكم هذا السؤال •

٨ ـ يعتبر نفسه زوجا مخلصا •

٩ ـ ننقل اليكم هذا الخبر من وزارة التربية نفسها •

Drill 5. Oral translation.

1. We work in the same bank.

2. She considers herself very beautiful.

3. They studied political science in the same university.

4. I spoke to him myself.

5. They (m. dual) will receive their degrees on the same day.

4. Case forms of أَبٌ 'father' and أَخٌ 'brother'

There is a small group of nouns which have special forms (ending in long vowels) when followed by another noun in an iḍāfa or by a pronoun suffix other than ي 'my'. The two most common of these are أَبٌ 'father' and أَخٌ 'brother'. Examples:

Nom. أَبو الْوَلَدِ Gen. أَبي الْوَلَدِ Acc. أَبا الْوَلَدِ	'the boy's father'
Nom. أَخوها Gen. أَخيها Acc. أَخاها	'her brother'

With the pronoun suffix ي 'my', the forms are as follows, with no case distinctions:

Nom./Gen./Acc.	أَبي	'my father'	أَخي	'my brother'

Now do Drill 6.

Drill 6. Production: Cases of أَبٌ and أَخٌ

a. Fill in the blanks with the correct form of أَبو صَديقي 'my friend's father'.

١ ـ حضر ______ .

٢ ـ قابلت ______ .

٣ ـ ذهبت لزيارة ______ .

٤ ـ عيّن ______ وزيرا .

٥ ـ استقبلن ______ .

٦ ـ تحدّثنا الى ______ .

٧ ـ تقدّم ______ بطلب لعمل جديد .

b. Repeat with أَخوهُ 'his brother.'

c. Repeat with أَخي 'my brother.'

D. Comprehension passage — د ـ نصوص للفهم :

Read the following passage and then do Drill 7.

الثورة المصرية

كان جمال عبد الناصر قائدا للثورة التي طالبت المَلِكَ فاروقًا بترك مصر . وبعد ان رحل فاروق الى "نابولي" واصبحت مصر جمهورية ، انتخب الشعب المصري جمال عبد الناصر رئيسا .

(king)

تحدث عبد الناصر في خِطاباتِهِ ومؤتمراته عن الاوضاع السياسية والاقتصادية والاجتماعية في مصر قبل الثورة فقال :

(speeches)

ـ لم تكن السياسة الخارجية ناجحة ، ولم تكن السياسة الداخِلِيَّةُ أَكْثَرَ نَجاحًا .

(internal, domestic; more successful)

ـ لم تكن الصحف تتأثر بآراء الشعب ولم يكن لها حرّية الرأي .

ـ لم تكن الصناعة تتقدم ،لم تكن في مصر مصانع كثيرة ولم يكن عدد العمال كبيرا .

ـ كان الفَقْرُ منتشرا بين أَبْناءِ الشَّعْبِ . لم يكن الشعب سعيدا ولم يكن بين ابنائه شيء من التعاون .

(poverty; ordinary people)

- لم تكن المدارس كثيرة ، ولم يكن التعليم منتشرا بين المصريين .

كتب عبد الناصر كتابا هو " فَلْسَفَةُ الثورة " ، تحدث فيه عن الثورة فقال ان مصر مقبلة على عَهْدٍ جديد ، وقال ان مصر دولة عربية ولِذٰلِكَ يجب ان تتعاون مع كل بلد عربي ، وهي دولة اسلامية ولِذٰلِكَ يجب ان تتعاون مع كل بلد اسلامي . وهي دولة إِفْريقيَّةٌ ولذلك يجب ان تتعاون مع كل بلد افريقي .

philosophy
age , era
therefore
African

أسئلة :

Drill 7. Question/answer

١ - من كان جمال عبد الناصر ؟

٢ - من الرجل الذي حكم مصر قبل الثورة ؟ الى اين رحل بعد الثورة ؟

٣ - كيف كانت سياسة مصر الخارجية في زمن فاروق ؟

٤ - هل كانت للصحف المصرية حرية في زمن فاروق ؟

٥ - لماذا لم يكن عدد العمال في مصر كبيرا قبل الثورة ؟

٦ - أكان التعاون منتشرا بين المصريين في زمن الملك فاروق ؟

٧ - هل كانت المدارس تخرّج عددا كبيرا من المصريين قبل الثورة ؟ لماذا ؟

٨ - هل كل الدول الاسلامية عربية ؟ هل كل الدول الافريقية عربية ؟ هل كل الدول الافريقيّة اسلاميّة ؟

ج - التمارين العامة :

E. General Drills

Drill 8. Written. Iḍāfas.

Fill in the blanks in the sentences below with the appropriate form of the Arabic word. Ex.

شاركوا في حفر ______ القناة ______.

the canal   digging

١ ـ ــــــــ ــــــــ مهندس مشهور .
the brother my friend

٢ ـ عرفت من استاذ التاريخ ــــــــ ــــــــ المصرية .
the importance the revolution

٣ ـ أخذ ــــــــ ــــــــ يتحدث الى الناس في المؤتمر السياسي.
the president the republic

٤ ـ بدأ حسين و ــــــــ ــــــــ يتراسلان .
the father Sami

٥ ـ لم يبدأ ــــــــ ــــــــ الاقتصادي حتى الساعة الحادية عشرة .
the discussion the situation

٦ ـ اعتبر ــــــــ ــــــــ اجمل عينين في العالم .
the (two) eyes his beloved (girl)

٧ ـ سأتمكن من الاقامة في القاهرة ــــــــ ــــــــ .
four months

٨ ـ تفكر به في ــــــــ ــــــــ .
most the times

٩ ـ كنّا نرغب في ــــــــ ــــــــ الدولي في الصيف .
attending the conference

١٠ ـ للابنة عادة مكانة خاصة في ــــــــ ــــــــ .
the heart her mother

Drill 9. Review: Nominalizers.

Fill in the blanks below with إِنَّ ، أَنَّ ، أَنْ ، ما as appropriate:

١ ـ قال ــــ الوزير سينظر في طلبات الموظفين .

٢ ـ استقبلها اهلها عند ــــ رجعت من فرنسا .

٣ ـ قرأت ــــ الصناعة تقدّمت تقدّما عظيما في الشرق الاوسط .

٤ ـ يجب ــــ تصادقوا الجيران .

٥ ـ منعتني من ــــ اخرج من الصفّ .

٦ ـ اصبح رجلا سعيدا عند ــــــ تزوّج حبيبته •

٧ ـ سمعنا ــــــ حفر القناة تمّ في خمسة اعوام •

٨ ـ هل ستتمكّن من ــــــ تذهب الى المسرح ؟

Drill 10. Written. Translation.

1. Leave (go out) and take your brother with you!

2. He wanted to visit the historic ruins scattered outside the city.

3. The director said that his company is embarking upon a new industrial program.

4. He began to publish a small newspaper when he was thirty (=in the thirtieth year from his age).

5. I wrote saying "I have met a man. I am going to marry him."

6. Is there freedom of action for women in the East?

Lesson Twenty-eight

الدرس الثامن والعشرون

أ ـ النص الاساسي

زيارة وزير الخارجيّة الامريكيّ لمصر

كتب مراسل اوروبي مقالة عن الشرق الاوسط متناولا فيها زيارة وزير الخارجيّة الامريكيّ لمصر . قال كاتب المقالة :

وصل وزير الخارجيّة الى القاهرة ليلة أمس حاملا رسالة هامة الى الرئيس المصريّ من الرئيس الامريكيّ . وفي تلك الرسالة تحدّث الرئيس الامريكي عن الوضع في الشرق الاوسط ، مظهرا اهتماما خاصا بموضوع السلام في المنطقة .

وجاء في الرسالة التى ارسلها الرئيس الامريكي : the letter included

" لقد درسنا مشكلة الشرق الاوسط دراسة شاملة ، وطلبنا من وزير خارجيّتنا ان ينقل اليكم رأينا فيها ويبحث معكم سياستنا بشأنها . نعلم ان الوصول الى حلّ لهذه المشكلة ليس سهلا ، وأنه سوف يتطلّب تعاون جميع الحكومات في المنطقة . نحن متأكّدون انّكم من الراغبين في السلام ، الباذلين اعظم الجهود لتحقيقه والمحافظة عليه ، العاملين على ان ينتشر بين شعوب الشرق الاوسط " .

وسوف يترك الوزير الامريكي مصر غدا لزيارة سوريا. والمعروف انه سيقابل اثناء زيارته للشرق الاوسط كل الرؤساء الذين لهم علاقة بموضوع السلام فى المنطقة ، وانه سيحمل الى كل منهم رسالة مثل الرسالة التى حملها الى الرئيس المصريّ .

A. Basic text.

The Visit of the American Secretary of State to Egypt

A European reporter wrote an article on the Middle East dealing with the visit of the American Secretary of State to Egypt. The writer of the article said:

"The Secretary of State arrived in Cairo last night bearing an important letter to the Egyptian president from the American president. In this letter the American president spoke of the situation in the Middle East, displaying particular concern about the subject of peace in the area.

"The letter which the American president sent said:

'I have studied the Middle East problem thoroughly, and I have requested my Secretary of State to transmit to you my opinion on it and to discuss with you our policy concerning it. I know that arriving at a solution to this problem is not easy, and that it will necessitate the cooperation of all the governments in the area. I am certain that you are among those desiring peace and exerting the greatest of efforts to realize and preserve it, and working for its spread among the peoples of the Middle East.'

"The American Secretary of State will leave Egypt tomorrow to visit Syria. It is known that during his visit to the Middle East he will meet with all the heads of state who are involved in the matter of peace in the area, and that he will carry to each of them a letter like the one which he carried to the Egyptian president."

B. Vocabulary — ب ـ المفردات :

اَلْخارِجيَّةُ (= الشُّؤونُ الْخارِجيَّةُ) foreign affairs

وَزِيرُ الْخَارِجِيَّةِ	foreign minister; secretary of state
وَصَلَ	he arrived
مُتَنَاوِلٌ – ون	dealing with, treating
لَيْلَةٌ – لَيَالٍ	evening, night
حَمَلَ ــِ ، حَمْلٌ	to carry, bear
مُظْهِرٌ – ون	showing, demonstrating; revealing
اِهْتِمَامٌ – ات (بِ)	interest, concern, care (concerning, in)
مِنْطَقَةٌ – مَنَاطِقُ	area, region
لَ	(intensifying particle: see C.3 below)
مُشْكِلَةٌ – ات ، مَشَاكِلُ	problem
شَأْنٌ – شُؤُونٌ	matter, affair, concern; situation, condition
بِشَأْنِ	in regard to, regarding
وُصُولٌ (الى)	(verbal noun) arriving (at), arrival (in)
حَلٌّ – حُلُولٌ	solution, resolution
تَطَلَّبَ ، تَطَلُّبٌ	V to require, necessitate
جَمِيعٌ	whole, entire; all
مُتَأَكِّدٌ – ون (مِن)	certain, convinced (of)
حَافَظَ ، مُحَافَظَةٌ على	III to preserve, to maintain; to protect, defend
اِنْتَشَرَ ، اِنْتِشَارٌ	VIII to spread, become widespread; be scattered; to prevail (peace)
بَيْنَ	between, among (بَيْنَ must be repeated before each pronoun object)
مَعْرُوفٌ (بِ)	known; well-known, famous (for)
الْمَعْرُوفُ أَنَّ ، مِنَ الْمَعْرُوفِ أَنَّ	it is known that
عَلَاقَةٌ – ات (بِ)	relationship (to), connection (with)
مِثْلَ	(prep.) like

Additional Vocabulary

تَأَكَّدَ ، تَأَكُّدٌ (مِن)	V to be, become certain, convinced (of)
كَمْ عُمْرُهُ ؟	how old is he?
مِن	from; among, one of

C. Grammar and drills. ج – القواعد والتمارين

1. Active participles: Derived Forms
2. The ḥāl construction
3. The intensifying particle لَ
4. The noun جَميعٌ 'all'
5. The "royal we" and the use of the plural for respect

1. Active participles: Derived Forms

All active participles of verbs other than Form I begin with the prefix مُـ mu-, and all except Form IX show stem vowel i. For example, the AP of دَرَّسَ 'to teach' is مُدَرِّسٌ. The AP of any derived verb is easily formed from the imperfect in two steps, as follows:

(1) Remove subject marker and mood marker, leaving the imperfect stem:

يُدَرِّسُ	←	-دَرِّسْ-
يَتَكَلَّمُ	←	-تَكَلَّمْ-

(2) Prefix مُـ mu-; and, in Forms V and VI, change stem vowel to i.

-دَرِّسْ-	←	مُدَرِّسٌ
-تَكَلَّمْ-	←	مُتَكَلِّمٌ

This process gives the AP stem, which then takes the usual adjective endings for case, gender, and number.

The following chart shows the perfect, imperfect and AP of Forms II to X.

Active Participle	Imperfect	Perfect	Form	
مُدَرِّسٌ	يُدَرِّسُ	دَرَّسَ	II	'to teach'
مُساعِدٌ	يُساعِدُ	ساعَدَ	III	'to help'
مُكْمِلٌ	يُكْمِلُ	أَكْمَلَ	IV	'to complete'
مُتَكَلِّمٌ	يَتَكَلَّمُ	تَكَلَّمَ	V	'to speak'
مُتَراسِلٌ	يَتَراسَلُ	تَراسَلَ	VI	'to correspond'
مُنْصَرِفٌ	يَنْصَرِفُ	اِنْصَرَفَ	VII	'to go away'
مُسْتَمِعٌ	يَسْتَمِعُ	اِسْتَمَعَ	VIII	'to listen'
مُحْمَرٌّ	يَحْمَرُّ	اِحْمَرَّ	IX	'to blush'
مُسْتَقْبِلٌ	يَسْتَقْبِلُ	اِسْتَقْبَلَ	X	'to receive'

Derived APs which have recently occurred are shown below with their verbs:

Active Participle	Imperfect	Perfect	Form	
مُقْبِلٌ على	يُقْبِلُ على	أَقْبَلَ على	IV	'to approach'
مُخْلِصٌ (لِ)	يُخْلِصُ (لِ)	أَخْلَصَ (لِ)	IV	'to be sincere, devoted to'
مُسْلِمٌ	يُسْلِمُ	أَسْلَمَ	IV	'to surrender; to embrace Islam'
مُتَأَكِّدٌ	يَتَأَكَّدُ	تَأَكَّدَ	V	'to be convinced'
مُنْتَشِرٌ	يَنْتَشِرُ	اِنْتَشَرَ	VIII	'to spread'
مُخْتَلِفٌ	يَخْتَلِفُ	اِخْتَلَفَ	VIII	'to differ'

Examples:

نَحْنُ مُقْبِلُونَ عَلي نَهْضَةٍ صِناعيَّةٍ عَظيمَةٍ. 'We are approaching a great industrial boom.'

في أَحَدِ الْمَصانِعِ الْمُنْتَشِرَةِ خارِجَ الظَّهْرانِ. 'in one of the many factories which are outside Dhahran'

وَحَياتُنا الْيَوْمَ مُخْتَلِفَةٌ عَنِ الْحَياةِ الَّتي ... 'And our life today is different from the life which...'

As in the case of Form I APs, the AP of a derived verb denotes the same types of action as the verb from which it is derived. The AP can replace a relative pronoun and a verb, as for example:

الرَّجُلُ الَّذي يَنْتَظِرُ في الْمَكْتَبِ. 'the man who is waiting in the office'

الرَّجُلُ الْمُنْتَظِرُ في الْمَكْتَبِ. 'the man waiting in the office'

If the AP replaces an imperfect tense verb it may have progressive, future or habitual meaning; if it replaces a perfect tense verb it may have present perfect (including state) meaning. An AP from a transitive verb may take a direct object (in the accusative case if inflected). Illustrations:

Progressive (= imperfect tense)

الرَّجُلُ الَّذي يَنْتَظِرُ أَخاكَ. 'the man who is waiting for your brother'

الرَّجُلُ الْمُنْتَظِرُ أَخاكَ. 'the man waiting for your brother'

Future (= imperfect tense)

الرَّجُلُ الَّذي سَيُسافِرُ غَدًا. 'the man who will leave tomorrow'

الرَّجُلُ الْمُسافِرُ غَدًا. 'the man leaving tomorrow'

Habitual (= imperfect tense)

الرَّجُلُ الَّذي يَتَناوَلُ هٰذا الْمَوْضوعَ عادَةً. 'the man who usually deals with this topic'

الرَّجُلُ الْمُتَناوِلُ هٰذا الْمَوْضوعَ عادَةً. 'the man who usually deals with this topic'

Present perfect (= perfect tense)

الرَّجُلُ الذي تَزَوَّجَ .	'the man who got married'
الرَّجُلُ الْمُتَزَوِّجُ .	'the married man'

State (= perfect tense)

الرَّجُلُ الذي حَضَرَ صَفَّنا .	'the man who attended our class'
الرَّجُلُ الحاضِرُ صفّنا .	'the man attending our class'

Some participles, like مُسافِرٌ may have progressive or future meaning: "traveling (now)" or "traveling (later)." The student must learn the specific meaning or meanings that each AP has.

Transitive APs may, as has been stated earlier, take an accusative object. With some APs, for stylistic reasons, an alternative construction is used in which the direct object is made the object of the preposition لِ instead of being placed in the accusative case, as in

مَنْ هذا الأُسْتاذُ الْمُقاوِمُ لِفِكْرَةِ الْحُرِّيَّةِ في التَّعْليمِ ؟	'Who is this professor (who is) opposing the idea of freedom of instruction?'

Again as in the case of Form I APs, many derived APs have taken on concrete meaning and are used as nouns; these derived APs normally have sound plurals. Ex.

مُدَرِّسٌ ـ مُدَرِّسونَ	'teacher'
مُساعِدٌ ـ مُساعِدونَ	'assistant'
مُتَكَلِّمٌ ـ مُتَكَلِّمونَ	'speaker, spokesman'

Since the rules for the formation of all APs are completely regular, you will after this lesson be expected to form and to recognize them with ease. They will be listed in the vocabulary only if they have developed concrete or other specialized meaning.

Now do Drills 1, 2 (on tape) and 3.

Drill 1. Written. Recognition: Active participles

Underline and vocalize all the active participle forms in the following sentences. Then translate the sentences. Note: Not all sentences have APs.

١ – نحن متأكّدون انّهم من الراغبين في التقدم الصناعيّ .

٢ – صادقت المراسل المتناول في مقالاته مشاكل هذه المنطقة .

٣ – أنا منتظرة رسالتكم القادمة .

٤ – قابل رئيس الجمهوريّة المتكلّم باسم الحكومة الاجنبيّة .

٥ – يجب ان تتوفّر للعمّال في البلاد كل الحقوق .

٦ – جيراني مسافرون الى اوربا غدا .

٧ – اجتمع مساعد المدير مع موظفي الشركة .

٨ – بلادنا من البلاد المقبلة على نهضة صناعية .

٩ – تحدّث الصحفيّ الى الرجل المقاوم لسياسة الحكومة .

Drill 2. On tape. Active participles.

Drill 3. Transformation: Relative clause → Active participle

Ex. 'Who is the woman who is waiting for your brother in his office?'

من هي المرأة التي تنتظر اخاك في مكتبه ؟

'Who is the woman waiting for your brother in his office?'

من هي المرأة المنتظرة اخاك في مكتبه ؟

١ – اعرف الرجل الذي تزوّج .

٢ – قرأت كتابا عن المفكرين الذين يقاومون سياسة الحكومة .

٣ – من هم الوزراء الذين سيسافرون الى بلاد الشرق الاوسط ؟

٤ – من هم الرجال الذين يتعاونون في حل هذه المشاكل الصعبة ؟

٥ – من هما المستشرقان اللذان يتحدّثان فى كتبهما عن العالم العربيّ؟

٦ – عيّن الرئيس مهندسا تعلّم خارج البلد .

٧ – من هم المفكّرون المسلمون الذين حققوا النهضة الاسلاميّة ؟

٨ – هذا من الرجال الذين تأثّروا بالأدب الفرنسيّ .

2. The ḥāl construction.

In addition to the coordinating conjunction وَ 'and' there is also a subordinating conjunction وَ 'while, as' that introduces what is called a circumstantial, or ḥāl clause. In the sentence

وَصَلَ الْوَزِيرُ وَهُوَ يَحْمِلُ رِسالَةً هامَّةً مِنَ الرَّئِيسِ.	'The minister arrived while carrying an important letter from the president.'

the clause وَهُوَ يَحْمِلُ رِسالَةً مِنَ الرَّئِيسِ 'while he carries an important letter from the president' modifies الْوَزِيرُ and describes the condition or attendant circumstances surrounding the وَزِير at the time of the event in question, his arrival. It is therefore called a circumstantial clause, or, more commonly, a ḥāl clause (from حالٌ - أَحْوالٌ 'condition, circumstance'). The features of the ḥāl clause are as follows:

(1) The structure of the ḥāl clause is (reading from right to left):

(a.)	Equational Sentence		وَ 'while'
(b.)	Verbal Sentence	+ Independent Pronoun	

The independent pronoun agrees with the noun modified by the ḥāl clause. Illustrations of the two types of clauses (ḥāl clauses are underlined):

(a)	وَصَلَ وَبَيْنَ كُتُبِهِ رِسالَةُ الرَّئِيسِ.	'He arrived with the president's letter among his books.'
	حَضَرَ إلى أمْريكا وَهُوَ صَغِيرٌ.	'He came to America while he was young.'
(b)	وَصَلَ الْوَزِيرُ وَهُوَ يَحْمِلُ رَسائِلَ هامَّةً.	'The minister arrived carrying ("as he carried") important letters.'

Note that verbs in these ḥāl clauses are in the imperfect tense, and that the imperfect tense is translated in the same tense as the main verb.

(2) There is in the ḥāl clause a pronoun referring to the modified noun. These are ـهِ (on كُتُبِهِ) in the first sentence and هُوَ in the second and third sentences.

Variation a: The particle وَ 'while' and the independent pronoun are often omitted as in:

حَضَرَ إلى أمْريكا أسْتاذًا .	'He came to America as (while he was) a professor.'
وَصَلَ الْوَزيرُ يَحْمِلُ رَسائِلَ هامَّةً .	'The minister arrived carrying important letters.'
كَتَبَتْ تَسْأَلُ عَنِ الْوَضْعِ السِّياسيِّ في بَلَدِهِ .	'She wrote asking about the political situation in his country.'

وَ 'while' plus independent pronoun may be omitted from an equational sentence if its predicate is an unmodified indefinite noun, like أُسْتاذٌ in وَهُوَ أُسْتاذٌ 'while he was a professor'; once وَهُوَ is omitted this predicate noun must then be put in the accusative case, as in the example above.

The omission of وَ plus pronoun does not otherwise change the word order of the clause, whether it is an equational or a verbal sentence.

Variation b: If the ḥāl clause in variation a above is a verbal sentence, then a further change is possible. The imperfect tense verb of the ḥāl may be replaced by an active participle:

وَصَلَ الْوَزيرُ حامِلاً رَسائِلَ هامَّةً .	'The minister arrived carrying important letters.'
كَتَبَتْ سائِلَةً عَنِ الْوَضْعِ السِّياسيِّ في بَلَدِهِ .	'She wrote asking about the political situation in his country.'

The participle must be accusative and indefinite, but it agrees with the modified noun in gender and number. If it is a transitive AP it may take an accusative object.

Thus there are three possible ḥāl constructions involving verbal sentences:

وَصَلَ { وَهُوَ يَحْمِلُ رِسالَةً . / يَحْمِلُ رِسالَةً . / حامِلاً رِسالَةً . } 'He arrived carrying a letter.'

Ḥāl with perfect tense. The verbs in the ḥāl clauses cited above are all imperfect indicative; they denote actions that are taking place at the same time as the main verb. The perfect tense verb also occurs in the ḥāl clause, preceded by وَقَدْ . This construction indicates a completed action whose results are still in effect; the verb is often best translated as "having (done something)", "who had (done something)", "now that...", etc. Examples:

رَجَعَ الْمُرَاسِلُ الى بَلَدِهِ وَقَدْ تَحَدَّثَ طَوِيلاً مع الرَّئِيسِ وَبَعْضِ وُزَرائِهِ .	'The reporter returned to his country, having talked at length with the president and some of his ministers.'
نَشَرَتِ الْكاتِبَةُ وَقَدْ سَكَنَتْ سَنَواتٍ طَوِيلَةً في الشَّرْقِ الأَوْسَطِ مَقالاتٍ طَوِيلَةً عَـنِ الأَوْضاعِ السِّياسِيَّةِ في الْمِنْطَقَةِ .	'The writer, after having resided many years in the Near East, published long articles about the political conditions in the area.'

Imperfect verbs in the ḥāl are negated by لا (or وَما) and perfect verbs, by وَلَمْ plus the jussive. Examples:

وَصَلَ لا يَعْرِفُ (وَما يَعْرِفُ) مَنْ أَنا .	'He arrived not knowing who I was.'
رَجَعَ وَلَمْ يَحْصُلْ على شَيْءٍ .	'He returned without having obtained anything.'

Now do Drills 4, 5 (on tape), 6 and 7.

<u>Drill 4</u>. Written. Recognition: Ḥāl clauses.

Underline the ḥāl clauses in the following sentences. Then translate the sentences.

١ ‐ كتب المراسل مقالة طويلة متناولا فيها مشاكل بعض البلاد .

٢ ‐ وصل الوزير الى الرياض وهو يحمل رسالة من رئيس مصر .

٣ ‐ تحدّثت التي تسألني رأيي في هذا الموضوع .

٤ ‐ حمل الرسالة وهو لا يعرف ما فيها .

٥ ‐ كنت ارغب وانا صغيرة في السفر الى بلاد بعيدة .

٦ ‐ شاهدنا آثار بعلبك ونحن في لبنان .

٧ ‐ خرج من مكتب الشركة ولم يحصل على عمل .

٨ ـ تحدّث اليّ سعيدا .

٩ ـ رجع من امريكا وقد درس سياستها الخارجيّة دراسة شاملة .

١٠ ـ خرج من داره مسرعا .

Drill 5. (Also on tape) Transformation: Ḥāl clause equational sentences.

Translate the transformed sentences. Ex.

'Nancy studied Arabic.' — درست نانسي اللغة العربية .

'Nancy is a student at the University.' — نانسي طالبة في الجامعة .

→

'Nancy studied Arabic when she was a student at the university.' — درست نانسي اللغة العربية وهي طالبة في الجامعة .

١ ـ وصل الوزير الى القاهرة . مع الوزير عائلته .

٢ ـ خرجت من المكتب . بيدها جريدة .

٣ ـ صادق احمد طلابا كثيرين . احمد استاذ في الجامعة .

٤ ـ فكر بحبيبته كثيرا . حبيبته بعيدة عنه .

٥ ـ اشرف المهندس على حفر القناة . المهندس في الخمسين من عمره .

٦ ـ شارك في تعيين الاساتذة . هو مساعد لوزير التربية والتعليم .

٧ ـ درست في جامعة جورجتاون . انا ساكن في مدينة واشنطن .

٨ ـ كان يكتب شعرا جميلا . هو طالب في الجامعة .

Drill 6. Transformation: Perfect → ḥāl perfect

Translate the transformed sentences. Ex.

'The girl travelled to her country.' — سافرت البنت الى بلدها.

'The girl finished her university studies.' — أكملت البنت دراستها الجامعية.

→

'The girl returned to her country having completed her university studies.' — سافرت البنت الى بلدها وقد أكملت دراستها الجامعية .

١ ـ قابل الرئيس الوزير . تأكد الرئيس من اهمية المشكلة .

٢ ـ تقدم المراسل بطلب للعمل في الجريدة • عرف انها بحاجة الى مراسل اجنبي •

٣ ـ رجع وزير الخارجية من فرنسا • حمل الوزير رسالة الى الرئيس الفرنسي •

٤ ـ تحدث عن الوضع السياسيّ • درس الوضع دراسة شاملة •

٥ ـ ترك السيد احمد المؤتمر • انتخب الحزب السيد احمد مرشحا •

Drill 7. Transformation: Imperfect → active participle

كتب اليّ رسالة يسأل عن الوضع السياسيّ •	→	'He wrote me a letter asking about the political situation.'
كتب اليّ رسالة سائلا عن الوضع السياسيّ •		

١ ـ ارسلوا يطلبون عملا في شركة السيارات •

٢ ـ وصلت تحمل كتبها •

٣ ـ كتب رسالة يتناول الوضع الحاضر في الشرق الاوسط •

٤ ـ خرجا يتحدثان معا عن حب قيس لليلى •

٥ ـ ترك المكتبة وَهْوَ يقرأ جريدة عربية •

٦ ـ أرسل اليه يطالب بحقه •

3. The Intensifying particle لَ

The particle لَ intensifies or emphasizes the truth value of a statement. It usually occurs before قَدْ and the perfect tense, as in

لَقَدْ دَرَسْنا مُشْكِلَةَ الشَّرْقِ الْأَوْسَطِ دِراسَةً شامِلَةً •	'We have indeed made a comprehensive study of the Middle East.'

English does not have an exact equivalent; it means "it is certainly true that ...; assuredly, indeed." It is often best left untranslated.

4. The noun جَميعٌ 'all'

The word جَميعٌ is a noun, like كُلٌّ, and has the same general meaning:

"all". Like كُلٌّ , also, it may

(1) precede a definite noun, usually in the plural, in an iḍāfa:

حَضَرَ جَميعُ الْمُهَنْدِسينَ .	'All the engineers came.'

or (2) follow a noun, agreeing with it in case, and having a pronoun suffix referring to the noun:

حَضَرَ الْمُهَنْدِسونَ جَميعُهُمْ .	'All the engineers came.'

Unlike كُلٌّ , the noun جَميعٌ may occur in the accusative indefinite, functioning as an adverb, after the noun:

حَضَرَ الْمُهَنْدِسونَ جَميعًا .	'All the engineers came.'
تَحَدَّثَ الْمُديرُ إِلى الْمُهَنْدِسينَ جَميعًا .	'The director talked to all the engineers' or '... to the engineers all together.'

Finally, أَلْجَميعُ as an independent noun corresponds generally to English "everyone", whereas أَلْكُلُّ can mean "everything".

حَضَرَ الْجَميعُ .	'Everyone came.'

When جَميعٌ is in an iḍāfa, agreement is with the gender and number of the second term; otherwise أَلْجَميعُ takes plural agreement.

جَميعُ الدُّروسِ صَعْبَةٌ .	'All the lessons are hard.'
أَلْجَميعُ يَعْرِفونَ ذٰلِكَ .	'Everyone knows that.'

Now do Drills 8, 9 (on tape) and 10 (on tape).

Drill 8. Transformation: Noun ⟶ جميع + noun ⟶ جميع + pronoun

Ex.

'The students studied political science.' ⟶ درس الطلاب العلوم السياسية . ⟵

'All the students studied political science.' ⟶ درس جميع الطلاب العلوم السياسية. ⟵

'All the students studied political science.' درس الطلاب جميعهم العلوم السياسية .

١ – تأكد المفكرون من اهمية هذه السياسة .

٢ – صادق المدير العمال .

٣ – اراسل اصدقائي الاجانب .

٤ – الطلاب حاصلون على شهادات عالية .

٥ – درست الحِكَمَ في النص الاساسيّ .

٦ – للقنوات اهمية كبيرة في الاقتصاد العالمي .

٧ – اخرجوا المراسلين من المؤتمر .

Drill 9. (On tape) Transformation: جميع in iḍāfa ⟶ جميع + pronoun ⟶ adverb

Drill 10. (On tape) Transformation: جميع in iḍāfa ⟶ الجميع

5. The "royal we" and the use of the plural for respect

In Arabic, as in English and other European languages, the "royal we" is often used instead of "I" by persons in high office. Indeed, it is probably even more common in Arabic; it is illustrated by the following sentence taken from an imaginary letter sent by the president of one country to another:

'I have asked my Minister of Foreign Affairs to convey to you my view on that matter.'	طَلَبْنا مِنْ وَزيرِ خارِجيَّتِنا أَنْ يَنْقُلَ إِلَيْكُمْ رَأْيَنا في ذٰلِكَ الأَمْرِ .

In this sentence the plural pronoun in إِلَيْكُمْ is used instead of the singular to convey <u>respect</u>. It is not at all unusual in Arabic to use a plural form (pronoun, adjective, verb) in this way as a sign of respect for the person addressed.

C. <u>Comprehension passage</u> د — <u>نصوص للفهم</u>

Read the following passage, then do Drill 11.

فلـــــــــــم

ذهبت ليلة امس مع صديق الى السينما لمشاهدة فلم امريكـــي
جديد موضوعه مشكلة <u>اَلْبَطَالَةِ</u> وعلاقتها بالمشكلات الاجتماعية الاخرى . unemployment

في <u>قِصَّةِ</u> الفلم تطلّب الوضع الاقتصادي في منطقة قريبة من نيويورك story
ان <u>يَفْقِدَ</u> كثيرٌ من الناس وظائفهم ، ومن هؤلاء رجل في الخمسين من عمـره lose
اسمه رِتْشارد فِلَتْشَر ، له ابن يدرس التجارة في الجامعة وثلاث بنـــات
اصغرهن في الثامنة من عمرها .

قدم السيد فلتشر عددا كبيرا من طلبات العمل الى الشركات المنتشرة
في المنطقة ، ولكنه لم ينجح في الحصول على وظيفة .

حصلت زوجته على عمل في بنك معروف ، فأصبحت العائلة تعتمد علـى
الزوجة ، وأخذ الرجل <u>يَقومُ بِـ</u>الاعمال البيتية التي تقوم بها المرأة عادة . under-take
كان لهذا الوضع تأثير <u>سَيِّئٌ</u> على السيد فلتشر . وبعد وقت قصير <u>فَقَـدَتِ</u> bad / lost
الزوجة وظيفتها فكان لذلك تأثير <u>سَيِّئٌ</u> على العائلة كلها .

والفلم يظهر المشكلات <u>النَاتِجَةَ عَنِ</u> البَطالَةِ ويحدّدها ويربط بينها resulting from
<u>وَبَيْنَ</u> ثورة العائلة ، خاصّةً الزوج ، على المجتمع . -and-

Drill 11. Written. Question/answer

أسئلـــة :

١ ـ أيـن يـسكن الـسيّد فلـتشر ؟ كم عمره ؟

٢ ـ كم ابـنا تشمل عائلة فلـتشر ؟ وكم بـنـتا ؟ ماذا يـدرس الابـن ؟

٣ ـ أيـن عملـت زوجة فلـتشر ؟

٤ ـ لماذا أخذ فلـتشر يـعمل في الـبيت ؟

٥ ـ كيف أثّر هذا الـوضع على فلـتشر ؟

٦ ـ هل موضوع الـفلـم اجتماعي أم سياسيّ ؟

٧ ـ ما رأيك في موضوع الـفلـم ؟

E. General Drills

هـ ـ تمارين عامة :

Drill 12. Written. Transformation: Plural nouns.

Add the words in parentheses to the sentences as indicated by the underlining. Make any necessary changes. Ex.

'The student studied at the University of London.' (All) →

درس الـطالـب في جامعة لـندن. (كل) ←

'All the students studied at the University of London.'

درس كل الـطلاب في جامعة لـندن .

١ ـ يـبحثون عن حل لـمشكلة الـشرق الاوسط . (جميع)

٢ ـ لا تـعجبـنا سياسة الـحكومة. (بـعض)

٣ ـ لـيس الـعامل حاصلا على شهادة عالـية . (معظم)

٤ ـ يـتـناول في مقالـته الاخيرة الـثورة الـشعبية في هذا الـبلد . (نصف)

٥ ـ اخي ساكن في مدينة بـغداد . (جميع)

٦ ـ سيـنعقد الـمؤتمر في بـناء كبـير في نـيويورك . (كل)

٧ ـ يـعتقد الـمستشرق ان لـهذا الاديب اهمية كبـيرة في الادب الـعربـي الـحديث . (جميع)

٨ ـ شاهد صديقي الفيلم مساء امس . (بعض)

٩ ـ منحته الدولة حقّه . (جميع)

١٠ ـ تحدّد الوزارة منهج التعليم في المدارس.(كل)

Drill 13. (Also on tape) Question formation.

Form questions from the following statements, questioning the underlined items.

١ ـ تم حفر قناة السويس عام ١٨٦٩ .

٢ ـ ليس حل مشكلة الشرق الاوسط سهلا .

٣ ـ اسم القائد المسلم الذي فتح الاندلس طارق بن زياد .

٤ ـ الصناعة منتشرة في البلاد العربية .

٥ ـ تعلّمت ثلاث لغات اوربية اثناء اقامتها في فرنسا .

٦ ـ ذلك الرجل هو المهندس الذي اشرف على بناء المصنع الجديد.

٧ ـ والدها يسكن في بيت خارج مدينة واشنطن .

٨ ـ لا يعتقد ان هذا البلد مقبل على نهضة صناعية .

٩ ـ حكمت هاتان الدولتان ـ بريطانيا وفرنسا ـ منطقة القناة .

١٠ ـ كتب الطالب مذكرات طويلة .

Drill 14. Oral translation.

1. Perhaps he returned to his country, having received his university degree.
2. The reporter writes in his article about the books of the Egyptian writer (litterateur) Naguib Maḥfouẓ.
3. I was waiting for him when he arrived at Beirut airport.
4. It is necessary that the ministers search for a solution to this difficult problem.
5. Do you want to correspond with her?
6. I have a small family which includes a son and two daughters.
7. This government continues to establish (أَنْشَأَ) new dams on the river.

Drill 15. Written: Verb Forms I-X.

Fill in the blanks in the chart below. Vocalize each word fully.

	Jussive with لِـ	Active Participle	Verbal Noun	Verb	Form
Ex.	لِيَفْتَحْ	فاتِحٌ	فَتْحٌ	فَتَحَ	I
			انتشار		
		مدرّس			
				علم	
			تصرّف		
				انقطع	
			متابعة		
		متعاون			
				اشرف على	
			استقبال		
					IV
				حكم	
			تراسل		
				حمل	
	ليبحث				
					I

Lesson Twenty-nine

الدرس التاسع والعشرون

الجاحظ

الجاحظ من كبار ادباء القرن التاسع الميلاديّ . لسنا نعرف شيئاً كثيرا عن حياته وهو صغير ، لكنّنا نعرف أنه وُلِدَ في البَصْرَةِ وانه احبّ العلم حبّا عظيما ، كما نعرف انه درس كثيرا من الكتب العربية والكتب الاجنبية التى ترجمت الى العربيّة .

عُرِفَ الجاحظ بانتاجه الادبيّ العظيم ، فقد كتب عددا كبيرا من الكتب ، لكنّ كتبه التى وصلتنا ليست اكثر من ثلاثين . وقد تُرْجِمَتْ بعض كتبه في هذا القرن الى اللغات الاجنبيّة .

عمل الجاحظ في وظائف كثيرة منها التدريس ، وكان ابناء الخَلِيفَةِ (Caliph) المُتَوَكِّلِ من طلّابه مدّة قصيرة .

ذُكِرَ ان الجاحظ اصبح كاتِبًا (scribe) لرجل من رجال السياسة هو ابْراهيمُ بْنُ عَبّاس الصّولِيِ ، لكن الصّولِي طَرَدَهُ (dismissed) بعد ثلاثة ايّام لانه كان قبيح الوجه . وذُكِرَ ايضا ان الجاحظ شوهد يَتَجَوَّلُ (wandering about) في بغداد ، فأقبلت عليه امرأة وأخذته من يده وذهبت به الى صائِغ (goldsmith) دون ان تتكلم . فلمّا وَصَلا (they arrived) قالت المرأة للصائغ : ارسم لي صورة مثل صورة هذا الرجل ، وانصرفت . فسأل الجاحظ الصائغ : ما قصّة هذه المرأة ؟ فقال : لقد طلبت مني ان ارسم لها صورة الشَيْطانِ (Satan, Devil) على خاتِمِها (ring) ، فأخبرتها بأنني لم اشاهد الشَيْطانَ حتى ارسم لها صورة كصورته . فتركتني دون ان تتكلّم . وبعد ساعة رجعت وانت معها . فانصرف الجاحظ وهو يضحك .

أسئلة

١ – ماذا تعرف عن حياة الجاحظ وهو صغير ؟

٢ – اذكر شيئين عرف بهما الجاحظ ؟

٣ ـ كم وصلتنا من كتب الجاحظ ؟ هل يعرف الغرب شيئا عنها ؟

٤ ـ هل كان الجاحظ يعرف أحدا من كبار رجال السياسة ؟

٥ ـ كيف تعرف ان الجاحظ كان قبيح الوجه جدّا ؟

٦ ـ ماذا طلبت المرأة من الصائغ ؟

٧ ـ ماذا قال لها الصائغ ؟

٨ ـ لماذا اخذت المرأة الجاحظ الى الصائغ ؟

Vocabulary note: In a sentence like

كَمْ كِتابًا وَصَلَتْنا مِنْ كُتُبِ الْجاحِظِ؟ 'How many books from among the books by Al-Jāḥiẓ have come down to us?'

The noun after كَمْ is usually omitted, giving كَمْ وَصَلَتْنا مِنْ كُتُبِ الجاحِظِ ؟ as in question 3 above, or alternatively كَمْ وَصَلَنا مِنْ كُتُبِ الْجاحِظِ ؟

A. Basic text

Al-Jāḥiẓ was one of the great literary figures of the ninth century A.D. We do not know a great deal about his life as a boy, but we do know that he was born in Basra, and that he developed a great love for knowledge; we also know that he studied many Arabic books and foreign books that had been translated into Arabic.

Al-Jāḥiẓ became known for his prodigious literary output, for he wrote a great number of books, but no more than thirty of his books have come down to us. Some of his books have been translated in this century into foreign languages.

Al-Jāḥiẓ worked in many positions, including teaching; the sons of the Caliph Al-Mutawakkil were among his students for a short while.

It has been reported that Al-Jāḥiẓ became a scribe to a certain political figure, Ibrāhīm Ibn 'Abbās Al-Ṣūlī, but Al-Sūlī dismissed him after three days because he was ugly ("ugly of face").

It has also been reported that Al-Jāḥiẓ was seen walking around in Baghdad when a woman approached him, took him by the hand and led him to a goldsmith without speaking. When they arrived, the woman said to the goldsmith, "Draw me a picture like the image of this man," and went away. Thereupon Al-Jāḥiẓ asked the goldsmith, "What is this woman's story?" He said, "She asked me to engrave a picture of the Devil on her ring for her, and I informed her that I had not seen the Devil (to be able) to draw for her a picture like his image. Then she left me without saying a word. After an hour she returned with you." Then Al-Jāḥiẓ went away laughing.

B. Vocabulary — ب ــ المفردات

اَلْجاحِظُ	Al-Jāḥiẓ
قَرْنٌ ــ قُرونٌ	century
ميلاديّ	A.D., of the Christian era
وُلِدَ	(passive) he was born
اَلْبَصْرَةُ	Basra
كَما	as, and in addition, and also (followed by sentence)
تُرْجِمَتْ	(passive) it (f.) was translated
عُرِفَ بِ	(passive) he became known for
أَنْتَجَ ، إِنْتاجٌ	IV to produce, put out
وَصَلَ	(foll. by acc. obj.) to come to
اَلْمُتَوَكِّلُ	Al-Mutawakkil
مُدَّةٌ ــ مُدَدٌ	period (of time), while
قَبيحٌ ــ قِباحٌ	ugly
وَجْهٌ ــ وُجوهٌ	face
ذُكِرَ	(passive) it was mentioned, reported, related
شوهِدَ	(passive) he was seen
ذَهَبَ ـَـ ، ذَهابٌ بِ	to take, conduct (s.o.)
دونَ	without

لَمّا	when, at the time that (conj.)
رَسَمَ ـُ رَسْمٌ	to draw, engrave
صورَةٌ ـ صُوَرٌ	image, form; picture
قِصَّةٌ ـ قِصَصٌ	story
كَـ	like, as (prep.)
ضَحِكَ ـَ ، ضَحِكٌ	to laugh

Additional vocabulary

سَيْطَرَ ، سَيْطَرَةٌ على	to control, dominate

C. Grammar and drills   ج ـ القواعد والتمارين :

1. Quadriliteral verbs
2. Passive voice: Perfect tense
3. Adjective iḍāfas
4. The noun مِثْلٌ and the preposition كَـ .
5. Verbs of arriving with accusative object
6. Iḍāfas with both members modified

1. Quadriliteral verbs

The great majority of Arabic verbs have roots consisting of three radicals, for example كَتَبَ 'to write' (root KTB) or إِسْتَقْبَلَ 'to receive' (root QBL). These are termed triliteral verbs. There are some verbs, however, whose roots have four radicals, for example تَرْجَمَ 'to translate' (root TRJM) and سَيْطَرَ عَلى 'to control, gain control (of)', (root SYṬR); these are called quadriliteral verbs. There are no verbs with fewer than three or more than four radicals.

Quadriliteral verbs have a simple Form (QI) and three derived Forms (QII, III, and IV). Forms QIII and IV are quite rare and will not be dealt with here.

Form QI is conjugated like Form II of triliteral verbs, the only difference being that the former has two different radicals in the place of the doubled middle radical of Form II. Thus the perfect stem pattern for QI verbs is *FaSTaL-* (the capital letters representing respectively the *F*irst, *S*econd, *T*hird, and *L*ast radical), and the imperfect stem pattern is *-FaSTiL-*. The following chart shows the conjugation of تَرْجَمَ 'to translate.'

	PERFECT	IMPERFECT			
		Indicative	Subjunctive	Jussive	Imperative
3 MS	تَرْجَمَ	يُتَرْجِمُ	يُتَرْجِمَ	يُتَرْجِمْ	
FS	تَرْجَمَتْ	تُتَرْجِمُ	تُتَرْجِمَ	تُتَرْجِمْ	
2 MS	تَرْجَمْتَ	تُتَرْجِمُ	تُتَرْجِمَ	تُتَرْجِمْ	تَرْجِمْ
FS	تَرْجَمْتِ	تُتَرْجِمِينَ	تُتَرْجِمِي	تُتَرْجِمِي	تَرْجِمِي
1	تَرْجَمْتُ	أُتَرْجِمُ	أُتَرْجِمَ	أُتَرْجِمْ	
3 MD	تَرْجَمَا	يُتَرْجِمَانِ	يُتَرْجِمَا	يُتَرْجِمَا	
FD	تَرْجَمَتَا	تُتَرْجِمَانِ	تُتَرْجِمَا	تُتَرْجِمَا	
2 D	تَرْجَمْتُمَا	تُتَرْجِمَانِ	تُتَرْجِمَا	تُتَرْجِمَا	تَرْجِمَا
3 MP	تَرْجَمُوا	يُتَرْجِمُونَ	يُتَرْجِمُوا	يُتَرْجِمُوا	
FP	تَرْجَمْنَ	يُتَرْجِمْنَ	يُتَرْجِمْنَ	يُتَرْجِمْنَ	
2 MP	تَرْجَمْتُمْ	تُتَرْجِمُونَ	تُتَرْجِمُوا	تُتَرْجِمُوا	تَرْجِمُوا
FP	تَرْجَمْتُنَّ	تُتَرْجِمْنَ	تُتَرْجِمْنَ	تُتَرْجِمْنَ	تَرْجِمْنَ
1 P	تَرْجَمْنَا	نُتَرْجِمُ	نُتَرْجِمَ	نُتَرْجِمْ	

The active participle is also like that of Form II triliteral verbs, having the pattern muFaSTiL:

مُتَرْجِمٌ	'translating; translator'
مُسَيْطِرٌ	'controlling; sovereign'

but the verbal noun has the pattern FaSTaLa(t):

تَرْجَمَةٌ	'translating, translation'
سَيْطَرَةٌ	'control, rule'

Now do Drill 1. (On tape) Conjugation: Quadriliterals

Form QII is characterized by a prefix ta-, and is conjugated like Form V of triliteral verbs. The perfect stem is taFaSTaL-; the imperfect stem is also -taFaSTaL-. Shown below as examples are the third person masculine singular forms of تَأَمْرَكَ 'to become Americanized, act or behave like an American':

PERFECT	IMPERFECT		
	Indicative	Subjunctive	Jussive
تَأَمْرَكَ	يَتَأَمْرَكُ	يَتَأَمْرَكَ	يَتَأَمْرَكْ

The AP has the pattern mutaFaSTiL-:

مُتَأَمْرِكٌ	'behaving like an American'

The verbal noun is taFaSTuL-:

تَأَمْرُكٌ	'act of behaving like an American'

In general, QII verbs bear the same relation of meaning to QI verbs as do triliteral Form V verbs to Form II. In particular, QII verbs are commonly derived from nouns with four or more radicals, and have the meaning "to behave like, pretend to be, assume the characteristics of (the noun)":

Noun		QII	
أَمْرِيكا	'America'	تَأَمْرَكَ	'to behave like an American'
شَيْطانٌ	'devil'	تَشَيْطَنَ	'to be devilish'
فَيْلَسوفٌ	'philosopher'	تَفَلْسَفَ	'to pretend to be a philospher, talk pompously'

2. Passive voice: Perfect tense

a. Form

All the verbs that we have encountered before this lesson have been in the active voice; in this lesson we take up the passive voice. The principal difference between active and passive voice is, in brief, that the subject of the passive verb is acted upon by some other agent, while this is not the case with the subject of an active verb. Compare:

Active	Passive
John saw some friends at the fair.	John was seen at the fair.
They robbed the bank.	The bank was robbed by professionals.
I mentioned your name at the party.	Your name was mentioned at the party.

The subjects of the active verbs performed the acts, while the subjects of the passive verbs underwent the action.

The passive voice in Arabic is indicated by special <u>vowel patterns</u> in the <u>stem of the verb</u>. In the perfect tense, the active-passive contrast is illustrated below:

Form I	Active Voice	Passive Voice
Pattern	FaM$^{a}_{i}$L-	FuMil-
	دَرَسَ 'he studied'	دُرِسَ 'it was studied'
	شَرِبَ 'he drank'	شُرِبَ 'it was drunk'

All verbs that have the stem vowel <u>u</u> in the perfect tense are intransitive and therefore do not form a passive.

The rule for the formation of the passive of the perfect tense in all verb Forms is: (a) change the stem vowel (the vowel before the last radical L) to <u>i</u>; then (b) change all preceding vowels to <u>u</u> if short or <u>uu</u> if long. This is illustrated below for the various verb Forms (there is no passive in Forms VII and IX, and the passive is rare in V and VI):

Form	Active	Passive	Passive Pattern
I	دَرَسَ 'to study'	دُرِسَ 'to be studied'	FuMiL-
II	قَدَّمَ 'to offer'	قُدِّمَ 'to be offered'	FuMMiL-
III	شاهَدَ 'to see'	شوهِدَ 'to be seen'	FuuMiL-
IV	أَرْسَلَ 'to send'	أُرْسِلَ 'to be sent'	?uFMiL-
V		rare	tuFuMMiL-
VI		rare	tuFuuMiL-
VII		none	
VIII	إِنْتَخَبَ 'to elect'	أُنْتُخِبَ 'to be elected'	?uFtuMiL-

cont.

IX		none	
X	اِسْتَقْبَلَ 'to receive'	أُسْتُقْبِلَ 'to be received'	?ustuFMiL-
QI	تَرْجَمَ 'to translate'	تُرْجِمَ 'to be translated'	FuSTiL-
QII		rare	tuFuSTiL-

The conjugation of the passive is exactly like that of the active, since only an internal vowel change is involved. The conjugation of all perfect passive verbs is illustrated below with the passive verb وُلِدَ 'to be born' (from وَلَدَ 'to bear, give birth to').

وُلِدَ 'to be born'			
	Singular	Dual	Plural
3 M	وُلِدَ 'he was born'	وُلِدا 'they were born'	وُلِدوا 'they were born'
F	وُلِدَتْ 'she was born'	وُلِدَتا 'they were born'	وُلِدْنَ 'they were born'
2 M	وُلِدْتَ 'you were born'	وُلِدْتُما 'you were born'	وُلِدْتُم 'you were born'
F	وُلِدْتِ 'you were born'		وُلِدْتُنَّ 'you were born'
1	وُلِدْتُ 'I was born'		وُلِدْنا 'we were born'

Now do Drills 2 (on tape) and 3.

b. Usage

The Arabic passive construction is like the English passive construction in that the object of an active transitive verb may be made the subject of the passive form of that verb. In the following, the preposition بِ 'by means of, by, with' is used to indicate the instrument or thing used:

Active:

كَتَبْتُ الرِّسالَةَ بِهٰذا الْقَلَمِ. 'I wrote the letter with this pencil.'

Passive:

كُتِبَتِ الرِّسالَةُ بِهٰذا الْقَلَمِ. 'The letter was written with this pencil.'

In both sentences, الرِّسالَة 'the letter' is the thing acted upon (the undergoer of the action, or goal), قَلَم 'pencil' is the instrument, and أنا (in the active sentence only) 'I' is the agent (the performer of the action).

The big difference between Arabic and English is that Arabic cannot express the agent in the passive construction. Thus, Arabic has no construction parallel to

'The letter was written by me.'

The only way to express the agent in Arabic is as the subject of an active verb. To rephrase this, if the agent is to be expressed in Arabic, only the active verb can be used. We can accordingly set up the following equation:

Agent expressed:

Arabic	English
كَتَبْتُ الرِّسالَةَ.	'I wrote the letter.' 'The letter was written by me.'

<u>Agent not expressed</u>:

Arabic	English
كُتِبَتِ الرِّسالَةُ بِهٰذا الْقَلَمِ.	'The letter was written with this pen.'

a. Notes: <u>Active voice</u>. When the agent is mentioned, the verb must be in the active voice, and the agent is the subject of the verb. The noun الرَّئِيسُ is agent and subject of the verb in the following sentence.

عَقَدَ الرَّئِيسُ الْيَوْمَ مُؤْتَمَرًا صُحُفِيًّا بِشَأْنِ الْإِنْتِخابـاتِ الْـقادِمَةِ.	'The president held a press conference today regarding the coming elections.'

b. <u>Passive voice</u>. If the agent is not mentioned, the noun referring to the undergoer of an action becomes the subject of the passive verb, like مُؤْتَمَر صُحُفِي in the following sentence:

عُقِدَ الْيَوْمَ مُؤْتَمَرٌ صُحُفِيٌّ بِشَأْنِ الْإِنْتِخابـاتِ الْـقادِمَةِ.	'A press conference was held today regarding the coming elections.'

c. In the two cases above, the agent is directly involved in the act, whether mentioned or not. There are other cases where the agent's involvement is not of immediate concern. With the verb "to break", for example, we can say

(a) "I broke the dish." (active voice)

(b) "The dish was broken by the waiter." (passive voice)

(c) "The dish got broken" or "The dish broke." (active voice, but agent not a matter of concern)

In the case of (c) above, the dish may have gotten broken from any cause, including normal wear and tear; or the identity of the agent may be logically deduced from the circumstances, as when the mother sees her child all alone in the kitchen with a broken dish on the floor beside him. These three usages can be contrasted in Arabic with the Form I verb كَسَرَ 'to break' (transitive) and the Form VII verb اِنْكَسَرَ 'to be broken, to break' (intransitive).

(a) Form I, active:

كَسَرَ وَلَدُكَ الْفِنْجانَ .	'Your child broke the cup.' (agent known and mentioned)

(b) Form I, passive:

كُسِرَ الْفِنْجانُ .	'The cup was broken.' (agent unknown or deliberately concealed)

(c) Form VII:

اِنْكَسَرَ الْفِنْجانُ .	'The cup broke.' (agent not necessarily involved)

Verbs of type (c) are mostly Form V, VI, and VII verbs; they typically occur as a substitute for the passive of Form II, III and I verbs respectively. Some illustrations follow; verbs that do not occur in this textbook are included here merely for purposes of illustration:

Form	Active meaning		Passive meaning		
I	قَطَعَ	'to cut'	I	قُطِعَ	'to be cut off'
			VII	اِنْقَطَعَ	'to be cut; to come to an end, to end'
I	عَقَدَ	'to hold' (a meeting)	I	عُقِدَ	'to be held'
			VII	اِنْعَقَدَ	'to be held, take place'
II	طَوَّرَ	'to develop' (s. th.)	V	تَطَوَّرَ	'to be developed, to evolve'
II	أَثَّرَ	'to influence'	V	تَأَثَّرَ	'to be influenced'
II	زَوَّجَ	'to marry off, give in marriage'	V	تَزَوَّجَ	'to be married, get married; to marry (s.o.)'
II	غَيَّرَ	'to change' (s.th.)	V	تَغَيَّرَ	'to be changed, to change' (intransitive)
III	بارَكَ	'to bless'	VI	تَبارَكَ	'to be blessed'

Remark: As a matter of translating from Arabic to English, it often makes for a smoother translation to translate an Arabic active as an English passive, especially when the Arabic subject is much longer than the object.

Example:

اِسْتَقْبَلَنِي فِي الْمَطَارِ أَحَدُ الأَصْدِقاءِ الذين دَرَسْتُ مَعَهُمْ في أمريكا .	'I was met at the airport by one of my friends with whom I had studied in the States.'

Verbs with two accusatives form their passive construction by making the first accusative the subject of the passive verb and leaving the second accusative unchanged. Thus:

Active:

مَنَحوا الطّالِبَ أَلْفَ دولارٍ .	'They granted the student a thousand dollars.'

Passive:

مُنِحَ الطّالِبُ أَلْفَ دولارٍ .	'The student was granted a thousand dollars.'

Active:

إِنْتَخَبْنا مُحَمَّدًا رَئِيسًا .	'We elected Muhammad president.'

Passive:

أُنْتُخِبَ مُحَمَّدٌ رَئِيسًا .	'Muhammad was elected president.'

Verb-preposition idioms form their passives as illustrated below:

Active:

بَحَثوا عَنِ الْقَلَمِ .	'They searched for the pencil.'

Passive:

بُحِثَ عَنِ ٱلْقَلَمِ . 'The pencil was searched for.'

In a verb-preposition idiom the goal of the action is the object of the preposition; it remains the object of the preposition in the passive construction, the verb being placed in the third masculine singular regardless of the number and gender of the goal. (A verb used thus, exclusively in the third person masculine singular, is called an impersonal verb.) Further illustrations:

رُحِّبَ بِرَئيسِ ٱلْجُمْهورِيَّةِ تَرْحيبًا كَبيرًا	'The president was welcomed warmly.'
هَلْ نُظِرَ في هٰذِهِ ٱلْأُمورِ ؟	'Have these matters been looked into?'
لَقَدْ سُمِحَ لَكَ بِٱلذَّهابِ .	'You have been permitted (=granted permission) to go.'

Now do Drill 4.

Drill 2. (On tape) Conjugation: Perfect passive

Drill 3. (Also on tape) Conjugation: Perfect passive

a. 'He was met with a tremendous reception.' أُسْتُقْبِلَ اسْتقبالاً عظيماً .

انا	انتما	الرجل
نحن	انتنّ	المراسلون
انتم	هم	النساء
انتَ	هو	المرأتان

b. 'He was thrown out of the office.' أُخْرِجَ من المكتب .

انا	نحن	الاولاد
انتم	هو	الرجال
هما	هم	

Drill 4. (Also on tape) Transformation: Active → passive

a. 'They met the president with a tremendous reception.' → ← إِسْتقبلوا الرئيسَ استقبالا عظيما.

'The president was met with a tremendous reception.' أُسْتقبِل الرئيسُ استقبالا عظيما.

١ – اخبرني سليم بان نانسي تدرس العربية.

٢ – تركها في الدار.

٣ – شاهدكم في الشارع مساءأمس.

٤ – نشرت الجامعة كثيرا من الكتب.

٥ – انشأ الاديب هذه المجلة في النصف الاول من هذا القرن.

٦ – منعني من حضور الاجتماع.

٧ – رسموا صورة جميلة.

٨ – منحوا الاديب الفي دولار.

b. 'The Bedouin welcomed the visitor.' → ← رَحّب البدويُّ بالزائر.

'The visitor was welcomed.' رُحّب بالزائر.

١ – بحثنا عن السلام في الشرق الاوسط.

٢ – نظرت في هذه المشكلة الصعبة.

٣ – اعتمدوا على مساعدته.

٤ – سمحتم لها بالذهاب.

3. Adjective iḍāfas

The phrase قَبيحُ ٱلْوَجْهِ means "ugly of face". This is a fairly common construction in both Arabic and English, as in "sound of limb", "fleet of foot" and so on. In the Arabic construction the adjective and the following noun form an iḍāfa. The adjective, as first term, never has nunation; and the following noun, as second term, is always genitive. This noun always takes the definite article. The noun defines the applicability of the adjective: "ugly as far as the face is concerned". The adjective agrees with whatever noun it modifies in the sentence, not with the noun in the iḍāfa:

اَلرَّجُلُ قَبِيحُ الْوَجْهِ.	'The man is ugly of face.'
اَلْمَرْأَةُ قَبِيحَةُ الْوَجْهِ.	'The woman is ugly of face.'

In the examples above, the adjective iḍāfa is functioning as a predicate adjective in an equational sentence. It may also function as the adjective in a noun-adjective phrase. If the noun in that phrase is indefinite, the adjective in the iḍāfa of course has no definite article:

قابَلْتُ رَجُلاً قَبِيحَ الْوَجْهِ.	'I met a man (who was) ugly of face.'

But--and here is where an adjective iḍāfa differs from an ordinary iḍāfa--if the preceding noun is definite, the adjective has the definite article even though it is the first term of an iḍāfa:

قابَلْتُ الرَّجُلَ الْقَبِيحَ الْوَجْهِ.	'I met the man (who was) ugly of face.'

Other examples of adjective iḍāfas are

تَحَدَّثْتُ أَمْسِ إِلى بِنْتٍ جَمِيلَةِ الْوَجْهِ.	'Yesterday I talked to a girl with a beautiful face.'
رَشِيدٌ كَثِيرُ الْكَلامِ.	'Rashid is garrulous (copious of speech).'

Now do Drill 5.

Drill 5. Written. Transformation: Predicate adjective → adjective iḍāfa

'The face of the man is ugly.' →	وجهُ الرجلِ قبيحٌ. ←
'The man is ugly of face.' (= The man has an ugly face.) →	الرجلُ قبيحُ الوجهِ. ←
'The man ugly of face came.' (= The man with the ugly face came.)	حضر الرجلُ القبيحُ الوجهِ .

١ ــ عينا المرأة جميلتان .

٢ ــ رأس الولدِ كبير .

٣ ــ اذنا البنت صغيرة .

٤ ــ قلب الحبيب مخلص .

٥ ــ نفس صديقي جميلة .

٦ ــ أسئلة ابني كثيرة .

4. The noun مِثْلٌ 'like' and the preposition كَ 'like, as'

These two forms can both often be translated into English as "like" or "as" but their usage in Arabic is slightly different:

(a) مِثْلٌ is a noun, and can serve independently as the first term of an iḍāfa, or take a pronoun suffix. Several possible translations are illustrated below.

لا يَنْجَحُ مِثْلُ هٰذا الرَّجُلِ.	'Such a man as that (or A man like that) does not succeed.'
لَمْ أَقْرَأْ مِثْلَ هٰذِهِ الْقِصَصِ.	'I haven't read such stories as these.'
أَنْتُمْ مِثْلُهُمْ.	'You are like them.'

The مِثْلٌ constructions described above may follow another noun, in which case مِثْلٌ is in apposition with that noun (agrees with it in case) and is usually translated "like".

أُرْسُمْ لِي صورَةً مثلَ صورَةٍ هٰذا الرَّجُلِ.	'Draw me a picture like the image of this man.'
حَصَلَتْ عَلَى صورَةٍ مثلِ صورَةٍ هٰذا الرَّجُلِ.	'She obtained a picture like the image of this man.'

Finally, the accusative form مِثْلَ may introduce an adverbial phrase modifying a verb (used this way it acts like a preposition):

يَتَكَلَّمُ الْعَرَبِيَّةَ مِثْلَ أَجْنَبِيٍّ.	'He speaks Arabic like a foreigner.'

(b) The particle كَـ is a preposition, followed by a noun in the genitive case. Unlike most prepositions, it does not take pronoun suffixes. In some contexts it is interchangeable with مِثْلَ and may be translated similarly:

هَلِ الْحَيَاةُ فِي الشَّرْقِ الْأَوْسَطِ كَالْحَيَاةِ فِي أُمْرِيكا ؟ = هَلِ الْحَيَاةُ فِي الشَّرْقِ الْأَوْسَطِ مِثْلَ الْحَيَاةِ فِي أُمْرِيكا ؟	'Is life in the Middle East like life in America?'
تَحَدَّثَ إِلَيَّ كَالْوَالِدِ. = تَحَدَّثَ إِلَيَّ مِثْلَ الْوَالِدِ.	'He talked to me like a father.'

In addition, كَـ has the special meaning "as" in the sense of "in the capacity of", for example:

مَا رَأْيُكَ كَمُسْتَشْرِقٍ فِي هٰذا الْمَوْضُوعِ؟	'What is your opinion as an orientalist on this subject?'

(c) Both مِثْلَ and كَـ may have as their object a clause introduced by مَا (see 23.C.3). The combinations مِثْلَمَا and كَمَا are equivalent to the English conjuction "as":

أُنْتُخِبَ الرَّئيسُ هُنا مِثْلَما انْتُخِبَ هُناكَ .	'The president was elected here as (the way that) he was elected there.'
إِفْعَلْ كَما تُحِبُّ .	'Do as you like.'

In addition, كَما may be translated "and also":

تَحَدَّثَ عَنْ حَياةِ الْجاحِظِ كَما ذَكَرَ إِنْتاجَهُ الْعَظيمَ .	'He spoke about the life of Al-Jāḥiẓ, and also mentioned his prodigious (literary) output.'

كَ may also be followed by an أَنَّ -clause (see 19.C.2); the combination كَأَنَّ has the meanings "as if, as though, it is as if...":

يَتَكَلَّمُ الْعَرَبِيَّةَ كَأَنَّهُ أَجْنَبِيٌّ .	'He speaks Arabic as though he were a foreigner.'
يَتَصَرَّفُ كَأَنَّهُ مُديرُ الْبَنْكِ .	'He behaves as though he were the bank director.'
نَظَرَ إِلَيَّ كَأَنَّهُ يَعْرِفُني .	'He looked at me as though he knew me.'

5. Verbs of arriving with accusative object

The verb وَصَلَ الى 'to arrive' is normally used with the preposition إلى before a noun of place, e.g.

وَصَلوا أَمْسِ إِلى بَغْدادَ .	'They arrived yesterday in Baghdad.'

In the following sentence, however, وَصَلَ is used with an accusative object and is translated differently into English:

وَصَلَتْني رِسالَةٌ هامَّةٌ الْيَوْمَ .	'I received an important letter today.' (Lit.. "An important letter reached me today.")

In this construction, the verb is translated as "to receive", but the subject of the Arabic sentence becomes the object of the English sentence, and the Arabic object becomes the English subject. This construction is true of a few other verbs meaning "to arrive" or "to come", such as جاءَ 'to come' which will be introduced in Lesson 31. Further illustrations:

هَلْ وَصَلَكَ الْكِتابُ الْجَديدُ ؟	'Have you received the new book?'
كُتُبُهُ الَّتي وَصَلَتْنا لَيْسَتْ أَكْثَرَ مِنْ ثَلاثينَ .	'His books which have come down to us (or 'which we have received') are no more than thirty.'

6. Idāfas with both members modified

In lesson 12.C.4. idāfas with both members modified are described; an example from that discussion is:

مُراسِلُ الْجَريدَةِ الْبَيْروتيَّةِ الْمِصْريُّ A_1 A_2 N_2 N_1	'The Egyptian correspondent of the Beirut newspaper'

In such a construction, the adjective A_2 modifies the noun N_2, and A_1 modifies N_1. Since the lines of modification are awkward in such an idāfa, the idāfa is often replaced by two noun-adjective phrases joined by لِ 'of'.

اَلْمُراسِلُ الْمَصْريُّ لِلْجَريدَةِ الْبَيْروتيَّةِ	'the Egyptian correspondent of the Beirut newspaper'
اَلْبِناءُ الْجَديدُ لِلْمَتْحَفِ الْوَطَنيِّ	'the new building of the national museum'
اَلْمُؤْتَمَرُ الْقادِمُ لِلْحِزْبِ الْجُمْهوريِّ	'the next convention of the Republican Party'

D. Comprehension passage — د – نصوص للفهم

1. Read the following passage and then do Drill 6 which is based on it.

البصرة مدينة بناها قائد عربيّ في النصف الاول من القرن السابع الميلادي ، واصبحت مدينة تجارية هامّة . he built

وفي القُرونِ الْوُسْطى عرفت في العراق مدرستان لغويّتان كانت احداهما في البصرة . ومن اللغويين الذين انتجتهم مدرسة البصرة ، الْخَليلُ بْنُ أَحْمَدَ الذي كتب " كِتابُ الْعَيْنِ " وَاسْتَنْبَطَ قواعد الشعر العربيّ ومنهم كذلك سِيبَوَيْهِ الذي كتب عن قواعد اللغة العربية كتابا طويلا عرف باسم "الكتاب" ولا يزال العرب يعتبرون هذين الرجلين من اعظم اللغويين . وكانت المدرسة اللغوية الاخرى في الكوفَةِ .

Middle Ages; extracted, discovered; the letter ع; Kufa

عَرفت البصرة في القرون الوسطى نهضة فكرية عظيمة من اهمّ رجالها واصِلُ بْنُ عَطاءٍ والنَّظّامُ، وعرفت نهضة ادبية من اهم رجالها أَبو نُوّاس والجاحِظ .

والبصرة اليوم ثالثة المدن العراقية في الاهمية ، فقد اصبحت منطقة تجاريّة وصناعية مشهورة .

Drill 6. Written. Question/Answer

أسئلة

١ ــ أين مدينة البصرة ؟

٢ ــ ما المدرستان اللغويتان المشهورتان في العراق ؟

٣ ــ هل سمعت عن سيبويه قبل اليوم ؟ والخليل بن احمد؟ ماذا تعرف عنهما الآن ؟

٤ ــ هل البصرة اليوم اهم المدن العراقية ؟

٥ ــ ما اهمية البصرة اليوم ؟

2. Listen to the passage on tape and then do Drill 7. (Note: the word جَلَسَ means "to sit")

Drill 7. Written. Question/Answer

١ ـ لماذا كان السيد فرانك وليامز يذهب الى القاهرة كل عام ؟

٢ ـ ما هي الصور المصرية التي كانت في بيت السيد وليامز ؟

٣ ـ لماذا منع السيّد وليامز من اخذ صور في متحف القاهرة ؟

٤ ـ كيف حصل السيّد وليامز على الصور ؟

٥ ـ ماذا فعل مدير المتحف لمّا شاهد الصور التي رسمها السيدوليامز ؟

E. General drills — هـ ـ التمارين العامة

Drill 8. Transformation: Affirmative ⟶ negative

١ ـ النساء ذهبن الى السينما ليلة امس .

٢ ـ له علاقة بالموضوع الذي سنتحدث عنه في الاجتماع .

٣ ـ بعلبك في منطقة شرق لبنان .

٤ ـ يرغب فرانك في ان يراسل سليم .

٥ ـ سأشاركه في عمله .

٦ ـ الصناعة في السعودية مختلفة عن الصناعة في الكويت .

٧ ـ سيذهبون مساء الغد في الساعة الثامنة .

٨ ـ انقطعت الرسائل بعد عام واحد .

٩ ـ الحلول التي قدمها بشأن هذه المشكلة سهلة .

Drill 9. Written. Combination: Elative

Combine each pair of sentences below, as shown:

'The man is ugly. His son is ugly.' ⟶ ⟵ الرجل قبيح . ابنه قبيح .

'The man is ugly, but his son is (even) uglier than he is.' الرجل قبيح ولكن ابنه اقبح منه .

١ ـ حل هذه المشكلة صعب . حل تلك المشكلة صعب .

٢ ـ اخوك صغير . اخي صغير .

٣ ـ قناة بناما طويلة • قناة السويس طويلة •

٤ ـ قصتي غريبة • قصتها غريبة •

٥ ـ مدة اقامتهم قصيرة • مدة اقامتنا قصيرة •

٦ ـ شعره جميل • شعرها جميل •

٧ ـ اهتمامك بهذا الامر كبير • اهتمامي به كبير •

٨ ـ المرأة سعيدة • ابنتها سعيدة •

Drill 10. Written. Review: Verb Forms

Fill in the blanks in the chart below, vowelling all words completely.

	Active Participle	Verbal N.	(Perfect) Passive	(Perfect) Active	Meaning
Ex.	دارِسٌ	دِراسَةٌ	دُرِسَ	دَرَسَ	to study
	حاكم على				
		المحافظة على			
				منح	
		اكرام			
			حمل		
	مستقبل				
		تخريج			
				تناول	
					to translate

Drill 11. Written. Translation: English → Arabic

1. The American Secretary of State arrived last night bearing important

letters.

2. He took his beloved by the hand, laughing.

3. That ruler was known for being (بِأَنَّهُ) ugly ("ugly of face").

4. What's the name of the boy with the beautiful eyes ("the handsome of eyes")?

5. Are you certain he will be able to translate such a difficult article?

Drill 12. Oral practice: Sentence completion.

The first student completes one of the sentences below, addressing it to a fellow student, who must answer it.

١ ـ هل انت ______ ؟

٢ ـ لماذا ذهبت ______ ؟

٣ ـ من الرجل الذي ______ ؟

٤ ـ اين ______ ؟

٥ ـ اهذا ______ ؟

٦ ـ ماذا ______ ؟

٧ ـ ما اسم ______ ؟

٨ ـ كم ______ ؟

٩ ـ اليس ______ ؟

١٠ ـ هل لك ______ ؟

١١ ـ هل جميع ______ ؟

١٢ ـ هل يتطلّب ______ ؟

Drill 13. Written. Vocabulary

Fill in the blanks choosing from among the words listed, making any necessary changes.

ولاية ، مصنع ، سنوي ، تحقيق ، صباحا ، المؤتمر ، يبذل ، حفر ،
يترك ، القومية ، المحافظة على ، شر ، فم ، حقوق ، مدة ، يتمكن من،
تم ، مسافة ، يفكر ، تأثر ، سمح ، حكم ، انقطعت ، خدم

١ ـ ______ المهندس بلاده عندما ساعد على ______ القناة .

٢ ـ سينعقد ______ ______ للحزب في ______ كالفورنيا .

٣ ـ ______ عمال هذا ______ الكبير جهودا عظيمة للحصول على حقوقهم .

٤ ـ ــــ جيراننا المدينة غدا ــــ .

٥ ـ تربط هذه الحكومة بين ــــ والمحافظة على حقوق الشعب .

٦ ـ انتشرت هذه المجلة الاسلامية ــــ طويلة .

٧ ـ سافر " السندباد " ــــ بعيدة قبل ان ــــ الاقامة في مكان واحد .

٨ ـ لن ــــ له الحكومة بان يعمل كطبيب قبل ان يحصل على الشهادة .

٩ ـ ــــ القائد البلد سنوات و ــــ بالحياة الشعبية تأثرا عظيما .

١٠ ـ اخذ يفكر كثيرا بـ ــــ السلام في داخل البلاد وخارجها .

١٢ ـ تراسلا مدة طويلة ثم ــــ الرسائل بينهما .

١٣ ـ هل ــــ بناء السد العالي في مدة قصيرة ؟

١٤ ـ قاوموا ــــ بالخير .

Lesson Thirty

الدرس الثلاثون

أ - النص الاساسيّ

الفصحى والعامّيّة

العربيّة المستخدمة اليوم في العالم العربيّ تشمل اللغة الفصحى واللهجات العامّيّة . الفصحى هي لغة القرآن وانتاج الادباء العرب من بداية تاريخهم الادبيّ . وهي لا تزال الى اليوم اللغة المستخدمة في المجلّات والجرائد والكتب والمحاضرات ونشرات الاخبار وفي المُناسَباتِ (occasions) الرسميّة وغيرها . أما اللهجات العامّيّة فتستخدم للتّخاطُبِ (conversation) في الحياة اليوميّة ، فهي تستخدم مثلا في البيت والشارع .

لقد تطوّرت الفصحى والعامّيّة خلال تاريخهما الطويل تطوّرا كبيرا . فالفصحى قد تطوّرت في مفرداتها وأساليبها واصبحت ما يعرف عند البعض بالعربيّة المعاصرة ، ولكنّ قواعدها لا تختلف عن القواعد المتّبعة في القرآن والادب العربي القديم عامّة . أما العامّيّة فقد تغيّرت لهجاتها وَأَشْكالُها (its forms) القديمة واصبحت تختلف من بلد الى آخر اختلافا كبيرا : فاللهجة المصريّة مثلا تختلف عن اللهجة العراقيّة ، واللهجة اللبنانيّة تختلف عن اللهجة التونسيّة ، بل ان اللهجات تختلف في الدولة الواحدة فلهجة القاهرة تختلف عن لهجة الاسْكَنْدَرِيَّةِ ، وهما تختلفان عن لهجة أَسْوَانَ .

وكثير من الادباء العرب المعاصرين يكتبون القصّة بالفصحى ، لكنّ البعض يفضّلون كتابة الحِوارِ (dialogue) بالعامّيّة .

ومن المتّفق عليه ان اللغة العربية هي الرابطة اللغوية التي تربط بلاد العالم العربيّ المعاصر .

أسئلـــــــة

١ ـ ماذا تشمل العربية المستخدمة اليوم في العالم العربي ؟

٢ ـ ماهي الفصحى ؟

٣ ـ كيف تستخدم اللغة الفصحى اليوم ؟

٤ ـ كيف تستخدم اللهجات العامية ؟

٥ ـ بأيّ اسم اصبحت الفصحى تعرف عند البعض ؟

٦ ـ هل تطوّرت الفصحى ؟ والعامية ؟

٧ ـ هل تختلف العامية من بلد الى آخر ؟

٨ ـ هل للغة العربية اهمّيّة سياسية ؟

٩ ـ كيف تكتب القصّة العربية اليوم ؟

A. Basic text

Classical and Colloquial Arabic

The Arabic used today in the Arab world includes Classical Arabic and the colloquial dialects. Classical Arabic is the language of the Qur'an and of the production of Arab authors since the beginning of their literary history. And up until today it is still the language used in magazines, newspapers, books, lectures, news bulletins, on official occasions, and so on. As for the colloquial dialects, they are used for conversation in daily life; they are used, for example, at home and on the street.

Classical and colloquial Arabic have developed considerably during their long history. Classical has developed in its vocabulary and style, and has become what is known among some as contemporary Arabic. But its rules of grammar do not differ in general from the rules followed in the Qur'an and ancient Arabic literature. As for colloquial, its ancient dialects and forms have changed, and they have come to differ greatly from one country to another. Thus, the Egyptian colloquial, for example, differs from the Iraqi, and the Lebanese from the Tunisian. Indeed, the colloquials vary within the same country; thus, the Cairo dialect differs from the Alexandria dialect, and both differ from the Aswan dialect.

Many modern Arab writers write short stories in Standard Arabic, but some prefer to write the dialogue in the colloquial.

It is agreed that the Arabic language is the linguistic tie which binds together the countries of the contemporary Arab world.

B. Vocabulary — ب ـ المفردات

اَلْفُصْحى	Classical ("Literary" or "Standard") Arabic
اَلْعامِّيَّةُ	colloquial Arabic
عامِّيٌّ	common, popular; colloquial
مُسْتَخْدَمٌ ـ ون	used
لَهْجَةٌ ـ لَهَجاتٌ	dialect
اَلْقُرْآنُ	the Qur`ān
نَشْرَةٌ ـ نَشَراتٌ	report, bulletin, broadcast
رَسْمِيٌّ	official; formal
أَمّا ... فَ	as for...
تُسْتَخْدَمُ	(f.s. passive) it is used
مَثَلاً	for example
خِلالَ	during
مُفْرَداتٌ	(p.) vocabulary items, vocabulary
أُسْلوبٌ ـ أَساليبُ	style
ما	that which, what (relative pronoun)
عِنْدَ	in the opinion of, in the view of
عاصَرَ ، مُعاصَرَةٌ	III to be contemporary (to)
مُتَّبَعٌ ـ ون	followed, observed, adhered to
عامَّةً	generally
تَغَيَّرَ ، تَغَيُّرٌ	V to change (intrans.), evolve, develop
فَضَّلَ ، تَفْضيلٌ على	II to prefer (s.th.) to

مِنَ ٱلْمُتَّفَقِ عَلَيْهِ أَنَّ it is agreed upon that...

رابِطَةٌ ـ رَوابِطُ bond, link; league, society

C. Grammar and drills   ج ـ القواعد والتمارين

1. Topic and comment: ... فَـ ... أَمّا
2. Passive voice: Imperfect tense
3. Passive participles
4. The indefinite relative pronouns مَنْ and ما

1. Topic and comment: ... فَـ ... أَمّا

أَمّا 'as for' is used to focus attention on a given item; in the sentence

أَمّا اللَّهَجاتُ الْعامِّيَّةُ فَهِيَ لُغَةُ التَّخاطُبِ .	'As for the colloquial dialects, they are the language of conversation.'

أَمّا introduces the central topic of discussion: the colloquial dialects (as opposed to the literary language, which was the subject of discussion up to this point). فَـ then introduces a statement, or comment, about that topic, namely that the dialects are used in conversation; this فَـ is not translated into English. The topic-comment construction is very common in Arabic.

In general, any noun in a sentence (subject, object of verb, object of preposition) can have special attention focused on it by means of the ... أَمّا فَـ topic-comment construction. The noun to be highlighted as topic is placed (in the nominative case) after أَمّا and <u>is replaced in its original position in the sentence by a pronoun agreeing with it.</u> فَـ is then put before the comment (the sentence itself). Thus:

(1) <u>Original sentence</u>:

اَلْجامِعَةُ تَعْتَمِدُ عَلى الْمُدَرِّسينَ كُلَّ الِاعْتِمادِ .	'The university is completely dependent upon the teachers.'

(2) <u>Topic</u>:

> أَمَّا الْمُدَرِّسُونَ 'as for the teachers'

(3) <u>Topic replaced by pronoun</u>:

> اَلْجَامِعَةُ تَعْتَمِدُ عَلَيْهِمْ كُلَّ الِاعْتِمَادِ. 'The university is completely dependent upon them.'

(4) <u>فَ introduced before comment sentence</u>:

> فَالْجَامِعَةُ تَعْتَمِدُ عَلَيْهِمْ كُلَّ الِاعْتِمَادِ. 'The university is completely dependent upon them.'

(5) <u>Topic-comment sentence</u>:

> أَمَّا الْمُدَرِّسُونَ ، فَالْجَامِعَةُ تَعْتَمِدُ عَلَيْهِمْ كُلَّ الِاعْتِمَادِ . 'As for the teachers, the university is completely dependent upon them.'

If the substitute pronoun is the subject in a verbal sentence, it is usually omitted. The subject of the verbal sentence

> لَمْ تَتَغَيَّرْ أَشْكَالُ الْفُصْحَى تَغَيُّرًا كَبِيرًا. 'The forms of the <u>fuṣḥā</u> have not changed greatly.

is made a topic as follows:

> أَمَّا أَشْكَالُ الْفُصْحَى فَلَمْ تَتَغَيَّرْ تَغَيُّرًا كَبِيرًا . 'As for the forms of the <u>fuṣḥā</u>, they have not changed greatly.'

In this sentence the substitute pronoun هِيَ 'they' has been omitted, since the verb لَمْ تَتَغَيَّرْ means 'they have not changed.' Finally, if the verb following فَ in the comment is the perfect tense, قَدْ is inserted before it:

> أَمَّا اللَّهَجَاتُ فَقَدْ أَصْبَحَتْ تَخْتَلِفُ مِنْ بَلَدٍ إِلَى آخَرَ . 'As for the dialects, they came to differ from one country to another.'

Other examples:

يوسُفُ كاتِبٌ مَشْهورٌ . أَمّا لُطْفي فَلا أعْرِفُهُ .	'Yusuf is a famous writer. As for Lutfi, I do not know him.'
أَمّا الْمَدينَةُ فَالحَياةُ فيها لا تُعْجِبُ الْعامِلَ .	'As for the city, life in it is not to the workingman's liking.'
والِدي مِنَ الْعِراقِ . أَمّا والِدَتي فَهِيَ مِنْ عُمانَ .	'My father is from Iraq. As for my mother, she is from Oman.'

The independent pronoun following فَ may also be omitted in an equational sentence if it is followed by an indefinite predicate:

أَمّا والِدَتُهُ فَسورِيَّةٌ .	'As for his mother, she is Syrian.'

<u>Omission of أَمّا and فَ</u>. Once a topic-comment sentence has been formed, it is a very common practice to omit the words أمّا and فَ , with no other changes. Thus:

أَمّا هٰذا الأُسْلوبُ فَنَعْتَبِرُهُ جَميلاً جِدّاً.	'As for this style, we consider it most beautiful.'
هٰذا الأُسْلوبُ نَعْتَبِرُهُ جَميلاً جِدّاً.	'This style we consider most beautiful.'

In case of a topic-comment sentence after أَنَّ , the omission of the words أَمّا and فَ is obligatory; illustration:

أَمّا هٰذِهِ الْفِكْرَةُ فَلا يَعْرِفُها الْعَرَبُ .	'As for this concept, the Arabs do not know it.'
وَمِنَ الْمَعْروفِ أَنَّ هٰذِهِ الْفِكْرَةَ لا يَعْرِفُها الْعَرَبُ .	'And it is known that this concept is not known to the Arabs.'

Now do Drills 1, 2, and 3.

<u>Drill 1</u>. Written. Recognition and composition: Topic-comment construction

In the following sentences underline the topic once and the comment twice; then write a meaningful sentence in regular (non-topic comment) word order which can precede أمّا. Ex.

'As for city life, the Bedouin does not like it.' ← أمّا حياة المدينة فلا تعجب البدويّ.

'The Bedouin likes desert life. As for life in the city, the Bedouin does not like it.' ← حياة الصحراء تعجب البدويّ. أمّا حياة المدينة فلا تعجب البدويّ.

١ _ أمّا الجمع بين البيت والعمل فأمر صعب جدّا .

٢ _ أمّا البصرة فهي المدينة التي ولد فيها الجاحظ .

٣ _ أمّا الفصحى فيستخدمها العرب في الصحف والكتب ونشرات الاخبار .

٤ _ أمّا الشعب المصري فيعتمد على مياه النيل .

٥ _ أمّا صديقي التونسي فقد ارسل اليّ هذه الرسالة .

٦ _ أمّا هذه المشكلة فتتطلب التعاون بين الحكومات العربية .

٧ _ أمّا الحكومات العربية فسوف تتعاون .

٨ _ امّا الجاحظ فولد في البصرة .

٩ _ امّا هذه الرسالة فقد ارسلها الى صديق تونسيّ .

Drill 2. (Also on tape) Transformation: Topic-comment

a. Ex.

'Colloquial is the language of speech. Classical is the language of writing.' → ← العامية هى لغة التكلم . الفصحى لغة الكتابة .

'Colloquial is the language of speech; as for classical, it is the language of writing.' العامية هى لغة التكلم ، أمّا الفصحى فهي لغة الكتابة .

١ _ اسلوبك جميل . اسلوبه ليس جميلا .

٢ _ هذه القصة طويلة . تلك قصيرة .

٣ _ انا ساكن في هذه المدينة . صديقي ساكن في مدينة اخرى .

٤ _ اخى طالب في الجامعة . والدى عامل في مصنع .

٥ _ السيد فريد مهندس . السيدة كريمة استاذة .

b. Ex.

'The writer wrote many books.
'The reporter wrote only articles.' → ← كتب الاديب كتبا كثيرة . كتب المراسل مقالات فقط .

'The writer wrote many books; as for the reporter, he wrote only articles.'

كتب الاديب كتبا كثيرة . أمّا المراسل فقد كتب مقالات فقط .

١ – تغيرت قواعد اللهجات العامية . لم تتغير قواعد الفصحى تغيراكبيرا .

٢ – ولد نجيب في القاهرة . ولد أحمد في الرياض .

٣ – عرف طارِقُ بْنُ زِياد بفتحه الأَنْدَلُس . عرف عَمْرُو بْنُ الْعاص بفتح مصر .

٤ – قرر علي الرجوع الى الخرطوم . قررت سوزان الاقامة في لندن .

٥ – أدرس العلوم السياسية . يدرس صديقي التجارة .

Drill 3. Transformation: Topic-comment

'In this library there are Arabic books. In the other library there are European books.' ← في هذه المكتبة كتب عربية . في المكتبة الاخرى كتب اوربية .

'In this library there are Arabic books; as for the other library, there are European books in it.'

في هذه المكتبة كتب عربية
أما المكتبة الاخرى ففيها كتب اوربية .

١ – في السويس مصانع كثيرة . ليس في الاسكندرية مصانع كثيرة .

٢ – لي سيارة . ليس لصديقي سيارة .

٣ – استمعت الى نشرة الاخبار . لم استمع الى المحاضرة .

٤ – اخبرني بحصوله على البكالوريوس . لم يخبرني بحصوله على شهادة الماجستير .

٥ – احمد صديقي المخلص . لا اعتمد على نجيب .

٦ – تأثّر الشعر العربي بالحياة البدوية . تأثّر بالادب الاوربي كذلك .

2. Passive Voice: Imperfect tense

a. Forms

The essence of the vowel pattern for passive voice in the perfect tense is *u* - *i* (see Lesson 29. C.2). The vowel pattern for the imperfect is basically *u* - *a*: the vowel of the subject-marker prefix is *u* in all verb Forms, and all the following vowels of the stem are *a* (or *aa*). The active-passive contrast in the imperfect indicative is illustrated below using اِسْتَقْبَلَ 'to receive, meet' (a visitor or guest):

Form X	Active Voice	Passive Voice
Pattern	yastaFMiL- يَسْتَقْبِلُ 'he meets'	yustaFMaL- يُسْتَقْبَلُ 'he is met'

There are passive forms of the indicative, subjunctive and the jussive, but not of the imperative. The passive conjugation of imperfect verbs is illustrated in the table below.

أُسْتُقْبِلَ 'to be received, welcomed'

	Indicative	Subjunctive	Jussive
3 MS	يُسْتَقْبَلُ	يُسْتَقْبَلَ	يُسْتَقْبَلْ
FS	تُسْتَقْبَلُ	تُسْتَقْبَلَ	تُسْتَقْبَلْ
2 MS	تُسْتَقْبَلُ	تُسْتَقْبَلَ	تُسْتَقْبَلْ
FS	تُسْتَقْبَلِينَ	تُسْتَقْبَلِي	تُسْتَقْبَلِي
1 S	أُسْتَقْبَلُ	أُسْتَقْبَلَ	أُسْتَقْبَلْ
3 MD	يُسْتَقْبَلَانِ	يُسْتَقْبَلَا	يُسْتَقْبَلَا
FD	تُسْتَقْبَلَانِ	تُسْتَقْبَلَا	تُسْتَقْبَلَا
2 D	تُسْتَقْبَلَانِ	تُسْتَقْبَلَا	تُسْتَقْبَلَا
3 MP	يُسْتَقْبَلُونَ	يُسْتَقْبَلُوا	يُسْتَقْبَلُوا
FP	يُسْتَقْبَلْنَ	يُسْتَقْبَلْنَ	يُسْتَقْبَلْنَ
2 MP	تُسْتَقْبَلُونَ	تُسْتَقْبَلُوا	تُسْتَقْبَلُوا
FP	تُسْتَقْبَلْنَ	تُسْتَقْبَلْنَ	تُسْتَقْبَلْنَ
1 P	نُسْتَقْبَلُ	نُسْتَقْبَلَ	نُسْتَقْبَلْ

The passive imperfect of the derived verb Forms is illustrated below:

Form	Active	Passive	Passive Pattern
I	يَمْنَحُ 'he grants	يُمْنَحُ 'he is granted'	yuFMaL-
II	يُعَيِّنُ 'he appoints'	يُعَيَّنُ 'he is appointed'	yuFaMMaL-
III	يُشاهِدُ 'he sees'	يُشاهَدُ 'he is seen'	yuFaaMaL-
IV	يُرْسِلُ 'he sends'	يُرْسَلُ 'he is sent'	yuFMaL-
V		rare	yutaFaMMaL-
VI		rare	yutaFaaMaL-
VII		none	
VIII	يَعْتَبِرُ 'he considers'	يُعْتَبَرُ 'he is considered	yuFtaMaL-
IX		none	
X	يَسْتَقْبِلُ 'he meets'	يُسْتَقْبَلُ 'he is met'	yustaFMaL-
QI	يُتَرْجِمُ 'he translates'	يُتَرْجَمُ 'it is translated	yuFaSTaL-
QII		rare	yutaFaStaL-

Now do Drill 4. (On tape) Conjugation: Imperfect passive.

b. Usage. The imperfect passive is subject to the same rules of usage as the perfect passive. Examples:

سَيُدْرَسُ ذٰلِكَ الْمَوْضوعُ قَريباً .	'That subject will be studied soon.'
أَمّا السَّيِّدُ نَجيبٌ فَيُعْتَبَرُ مُعَلِّماً عَظيماً .	'As for Mr. Najib, he is considered a great teacher.'
لَمْ يُسْمَحْ لَكَ بِالذَّهابِ يا سَليمُ .	'You have not been permitted (granted permission) to go, Salim.'

c. Potential meaning of the passive. The imperfect passive of the verb sometimes has potential meaning--that is, that a given act is possible. Consider the sentence:

لَمْ نَعْلَمْ شَيْئاً يُذْكَرُ .	'We did not learn anything worth mentioning.'

The noun شَيْئًا and its indefinite relative clause يُذْكَرُ can be translated literally as "a thing that will be mentioned," which means "a thing to be mentioned" or, more idiomatically, "mentionable, remarkable, worth mentioning". Now do Drills 5, 6 and 7.

Drill 5. (Also on tape) Transformation: Active → passive imperfect

'The ministers expend great efforts in solving the problems.' →	يبذل الوزراء جهودا كبيرة في حل المشكلات . ←
'Great efforts are expended to solve the problems.'	تبذل جهود كبيرة في حل المشكلات .

١ ـ ستنتج المصانع سيارات كثيرة كل سنة .

٢ ـ يعتبره اصدقاؤه مفكرا عظيما .

٣ ـ سيحمل الوزير رسالة الى الرئيس الامريكي .

٤ ـ سيرسل اليّ رسالة هامّة .

٥ ـ سنؤجل الاجتماع الى الشهر القادم .

٦ ـ سيستقبلنا الوزير في مطار القاهرة .

٧ ـ جميع المصريين يحترمون نجيب محفوظ احتراما كبيرا .

٨ ـ سيكرم البدويّ الزوّار اكراما عظيما .

٩ ـ ستنشر الاديبة الكتاب الجديد في بيروت .

١٠ ـ سيجعل الفصحى لغة الكلام في كل كتبه .

<u>Drill 6</u>. Transformation: Passive perfect → passive imperfect (jussive)

Translate the transformed sentences. <u>Ex</u>.

'The government forbade him to leave the country.' →	أ : منعته الحكومة من ترك البلد. ←
'Was he forbidden to leave the country?'	ط١ : هل مُنع من ترك البلد ؟
'No, he was not forbidden to leave the country.'	ط٢ : لا،لم يُمْنَعْ من ترك البلد .

١ ـ عقد الوزراء الاجتماع اليوم .

٢ ـ طلب الاستاذ منه ان يقرأ الكتاب .

٣ ـ ذكر الكاتب ان الجاحظ كان قبيح الوجه .

٤ – أخذت البنت الصغيرة الصورة .

٥ – ترجم المستشرقون كتب الاديب الى لغات اوربية كثيرة .

٦ – اخرجهم المدير من مكتبه .

٧ – عرف المراسل ان المشكلة صعبة .

٨ – قاوم الشعب سياسة الحكومة .

٩ – سمحت الحكومة بعقد المؤتمر في مدينة واشنطن .

١٠ – اصدرت الجامعة كتابين جديدين عن الفنّ .

Drill 7. (Also on tape) Transformation: Active → passive imperfect (subjunctive)

'The professor will permit you to leave.' → سوف يسمح لك الاستاذ بالانصراف . ←

'You will not be permitted to leave.' لن يسمح لك بالانصراف .

١ – سوف يحفرون القناة هذا العام .

٢ – سوف يفتح القائد بلادا اخرى .

٣ – سوف ينتخب الشعب هذين المرشحين .

٤ – سوف يترك عائلته فى تونس .

٥ – سوف تعينه الوزارة استاذا جامعيا .

3. Passive participles

a. Form

There is one rule for the formation of Form I passive participles and another rule for all derived Form passive participles.

(1) Form I passive participles. The pattern is maFMuul-. Some examples are:

Verb	Active Participle	Passive Participle
دَرَسَ 'to study'	دارِسٌ 'having studied'	مَدْروسٌ 'having been studied, studied'
قَرَأَ 'to read'	قارِئٌ 'having read'	مَقْروءٌ '(having been)read'
فَعَلَ 'to do, make'	فاعِلٌ 'having made'	مَفْعولٌ '(having been)made'

سَكَنَ 'to live, dwell'	ساكِنٌ 'living'	مَسْكونٌ 'dwelled in, inhabited'
سَمِعَ 'to hear'	سامِعٌ 'hearing'	مَسْموعٌ 'heard'
حَكَمَ 'to govern'	حاكِمٌ 'ruling'	مَحْكومٌ 'governed'

(2) Derived Form Passive Participles

The passive participles of derived Forms are formed by changing the stem vowel i of the active participle to a. The chart below shows both the active and the passive participles of Form I and of the derived Forms.

Form	Active Participle	Passive Participle	Pass. Part. Pattern
I	دارِسٌ 'having studied'	مَدْروسٌ '(having been) studied'	maFMuuL-
II	مُقَدِّمٌ 'presenting'	مُقَدَّمٌ 'presented'	muFaMMaL-
III	مُطالِبٌ 'demanding'	مُطالَبٌ 'required' (to do s.th.)	muFaaMaL-
IV	مُرْسِلٌ 'sending'	مُرْسَلٌ 'sent'	muFMaL-
V	rare		mutaFaMMaL-
VI	rare		mutaFaaMaL-
VII	none		
VIII	مُعْتَبِرٌ 'considering'	مُعْتَبَرٌ '(is) considered'	muFtaMaL-
IX	none		
X	مُسْتَخْدِمٌ 'using'	مُسْتَخْدَمٌ 'used'	mustaFMaL-
QI	مُتَرْجِمٌ 'translating'	مُتَرْجَمٌ 'translated'	muFaSTaL-
QII	rare		mutaFaSTaL-

Now do Drill 8. (On tape) Active and passive participles.

b. Meaning and usage

The basic meaning of the passive participle is "undergoing or having undergone (the action denoted by the verb)"; the English equivalent is the past participle of a transitive verb, e.g.

اَلْمَقالَةُ اَلْمَنْشورَةُ	'the published article'

The passive participle is equivalent in meaning to a relative clause with a passive verb; the equivalent of the preceding sentence is

اَلْمَقالَةُ الَّتي نُشِرَتْ	'the article which was (has been) published'

Indeed, it is often preferable to translate a passive participle as a relative clause:

اَلْمَقالَةُ اَلْمَنْشورَةُ في مَجَلَّةِ "اَلْهِلال" قَبْلَ ثَلاثَةِ أَشْهُرٍ	'the article that was published in Al-Hilal magazine three months back '

The impersonal passive participle is a passive participle used only in its masculine singular form. It occurs in verb-preposition idioms, as well as for other verbs whose object is introduced by a preposition; thus:

Passive Verb:

ما أَسْماءُ كُتُبِ التّاريخِ الَّتي بُحِثَ عَنْها ؟	'What are the names of the history books that were searched for?'

Passive Participle:

ما أَسْماءُ كُتُبِ التّاريخِ الْمَبْحوثِ عَنْها ؟	'What are the names of the history books that were searched for?'

Note, as in this sentence, the impersonal participle in a noun-adjective phrase agrees in case with its noun.

تَعْتَبِرُهُ الْحُكومَةُ رَجُلاً غَيْرَ مَرْغوبٍ فيهِ	'The government considers him an undesirable man.'

Another common use of the impersonal participle is in the construction

مِنَ الـ (participle) أَنْ ...

which means "one of the things which (participle) is that...", or "it is (participle) that..."; the predicate is a prepositional phrase with مِنْ and a definite participle or adjective and the subject is an أَنْ- or أَنَّ- clause. Example:

مِنَ الْمَعْرُوفِ أَنَّ الْجاحِظَ كانَ قَبِيحَ الْوَجْهِ إِلى أَبْعَدِ حَدٍّ .	'It is known that Al-Jāḥiẓ was extremely ugly.'
مِنَ الْمُتَّفَقِ عَلَيْهِ أَنَّ الْعَرَبِيَّةَ هِيَ مِنَ اللُّغاتِ الْهامَّةِ فِي الْعالَمِ .	'It is agreed that Arabic is one of the important languages of the world.'
مِنَ الْواجِبِ أَنْ تَحْضُرَ الْمُحاضَرَةَ .	'It is necessary for you to attend the lecture.'

Notice that the pronoun object of the preposition in such an impersonal verb-preposition idiom is always masculine singular.

Potential meaning of the passive participle. Like the imperfect passive of the verb, some Form I participles may have potential meaning, in which case they can often be rendered by an adjective ending in -able or -ible. Thus:

مَقْرُوءٌ	'read; readable'
مَأْكُولٌ	'eaten; edible'
مَسْمُوحٌ	'permitted; permissible'
مَسْمُوعٌ	'heard; audible, perceptible'
مَحْمُولٌ	'carried; bearable'
مَسْؤُولٌ	'asked; responsible' ('for' عَنْ)
مَرْغُوبٌ فِيهِ	'desired; desirable'

Now do Drills 9 (on tape), 10 and 11.

Drill 9. (On tape) Passive verb ⟶ passive participle

Drill 10. Transformation: Verb ⟶ passive participle

Replace the verb in parentheses by the corresponding passive participle.

'It has been decided that a new canal be dug.' ⟵ من الـ (يقرّر) ان تحفر قناة جديدة .

من المُقرَّر ان تحفر قناة جديدة .

١ - قرأت المقالة الـ (تنشر) في مجلة "الرسالة" المصرية .

٢ - هذا الكتاب (يترجم) الى أكثر اللغات الاوربية .

٣ - من الـ (يعرف) ان الوزير سيرجع اليوم .

٤ - الخروج من هذه المنطقة (يمنع) الآن .

٥ - العامية هي اللغة الـ (تستخدم) في الحياة اليومية .

٦ - المحاضرة (تؤجّل) الى الشهر القادم .

٧ - من الـ (يفضّل) ألاّ يؤجّل بحث المشكلة .

Drill 11. Written. Transformation: Verb ⟶ passive participle

Replace the underlined phrase with one containing a passive participle. Ex.

'The government does not permit foreigners to stay there long.'	لا تسمح الحكومة للاجانب بالاقامة هناك طويلا . ⟵
'Foreigners are not permitted to stay there long.'	ليس مسموحا للاجانب بالاقامة هناك طويلا .

١ - من الامور التي يعرفها الناس ان حرية الرأي من اهم الحقوق .

٢ - ما هي اللغة التي يستخدمها العرب في الكتابة ونشرات الاخبار ؟

٣ - نجيب محفوظ اديب يحترمه ناس كثيرون في مصر .

٤ - هذه الفكرة لا يذكرها الكاتب في هذا الكتاب .

٥ - عَقْدُ الاجتماعات السياسية في هذا المكان أمر تمنعه الحكومة .

4. The indefinite relative pronouns مَنْ and ما .

In previous lessons we have seen مَنْ and ما used as interrogatives meaning "who?' and "what?" respectively. These forms have another important function: as indefinite relative pronouns, مَنْ meaning "whoever, he who, those who, the one(s) who", and ما meaning "whatever, that which, the one(s) which". They differ from the relative pronoun اَلَّذي اَلَّتي , etc. in that they never have a specified antecedent (and that is why they are called "indefinite"). That is, with الذى there is usually some noun preceding:

اَلْكِتابُ الَّذي قَرَأْتُهُ	'the book that I read'

With مَنْ or ما , there is no preceding noun; the forms ما and مَن in effect serve simultaneously as both antecedent and relative pronoun.

ما قَرَأْتُهُ	'that which I read' 'the one that I read' 'what I read'

Clauses beginning with مَنْ or ما parallel relative clauses with specified antecedents in all functions: subject same as antecedent, object of preposition same as antecedent, or object of verb same as antecedent. The following examples illustrate these functions, showing the contrasts between constructions with specified antecedents and those with مَنْ or ما. Note that verb and pronoun forms referring to مَنْ may be singular or plural, while those referring to ما are masculine singular. Remember also that relative clauses with specified antecedents are preceded by الذي when the antecedent is definite, but are without الذي when the antecedent is indefinite.

Subject same as antecedent

كانَ بَيْنَهُمْ طالِبٌ أَجْنَبِيٌّ لا يَعْرِفُ شَيْئاً عَنِ الحَياةِ في امْريكا .	'Among them was a foreign student who knows nothing about life in America.'
كانَ بَيْنَهُمْ مَنْ لا يَعْرِفُ شَيْئاً عَنِ الحَياةِ في امْريكا .	'Among them was one who (or someone who) knows nothing about life in America.'
مِنْهُمْ رِجالٌ يَدْرُسونَ الْعَرَبِيَّةَ .	'Among them are men who are studying Arabic.'
مِنْهُمْ مَنْ يَدْرُسونَ الْعَرَبِيَّةَ .	'Among them are those who are studying Arabic.'
لا تُعْجِبُني الْآراءُ الَّتي ذُكِرَتْ في المَقالَةِ .	'I don't like the opinions which were mentioned in the article.'
لا يُعْجِبُني ما ذُكِرَ في المَقالَةِ .	'I don't like what was mentioned in the article.'

Object of preposition same as antecedent (in all these the preposition must

have a pronoun suffix referring to the antecedent):

هٰذِهِ هِيَ الْكُتُبُ الَّتِي كُنْتُ أَبْحَثُ عَنْهَا .	'These are the books I was looking for.'
هٰذَا مَا كُنْتُ أَبْحَثُ عَنْهُ .	'This is what/the one(s) that I was looking for.'

Object of verb same as antecedent (in clauses with specified antecedents the

verb must have a pronoun suffix referring to the antecedent, but in مَنْ or

مَا clauses this suffix is optional):

أَكْرِمِ الزَّائِرَ الَّذِي أَكْرَمَهُ أَبُوكَ .	'Honor the visitor whom your father honored.'
أَكْرِمْ مَنْ أَكْرَمَهُ أَبُوكَ [أَكْرَمَ أَبُوكَ]	'Honor the one whom your father honored.'
أُنْشُرِ الْمَقَالَةَ الَّتِي كَتَبْتَهَا عَنْ هٰذَا الْمَوْضُوعِ .	'Publish the article you wrote on this subject.'
أُنْشُرْ مَا كَتَبْتَهُ [كَتَبْتَ] عَنْ هٰذَا الْمَوْضُوعِ .	'Publish what you wrote on this subject.'

كُلّ with the indefinite relative pronouns

The relatives مَنْ and مَا are particularly common in the phrases

كُلّ مَنْ 'everyone who' and كُلّ مَا 'everything that'. In these phrases كُلّ has

no nunation because it is the first term of an iḍāfa (the second term being

the entire مَا / مَنْ clause). Examples:

سَأَلْتُ كُلَّ مَنْ أَعْرِفُهُ .	'I asked everyone I know.'
تَحَدَّثَتْ عَنْ كُلِّ مَا شَاهَدَتْ .	'She talked about everything she saw.'

Now do Drills 12, 13 and 14 (on tape).

Drill 12. Completion: مَا and مَنْ

Fill in the blanks with مَا or من .

١ ـ كان ــــ قرأته سهل الاسلوب. ٥ ـ هذا ــــ كنت اتحدث عنه .

٢ ـ يؤثّر ــــ يقرأه على آرائه . ٦ ـ أعجبنا كلّ ــــ أكلناه .

٣ ـ أرغب في ــــ ترغب فيه . ٧ ـ صادقوا ــــ يصادقونكم .

٤ ـ ساعد ــــ يساعدك .

Drill 13. (Also on tape) Transformation: Relative clause with antecedent → relative clause without antecedent. Ex.

'I know the men who did that.' → ← اعرف الرجال الذين فعلوا ذلك .

'I know the ones who did that.' اعرف من فعلوا ذلك .

١ ـ ليس هذا هو الرأي الذي تحدثت عنه المقالة .

٢ ـ خذ الشيء الذي يعجبك .

٣ ـ الناس الذين نرحب بهم يرحبون بنا .

٤ ـ الشيء الذي يعجبني في كتبه هو اسلوبه .

٥ ـ احترم الاستاذ الذي درّسني العربية .

٦ ـ كان معنا ناس لا يتكلّمون الانكليزية .

٧ ـ ليست هذه هي المقالات التي جمعتها .

٨ ـ هل هذا هو الرجل الذي عاد من بيروت أمس ؟

Drill 14. (On tape) Transformation: كلّ + {ما / من}

D. Reading Comprehension د ـ نصوص للفهم

Read the following passage and then do Drill 15

جريــــدة النهـــــار

جريدة "النهار" من اهم الصحف اليومية في لبنان، وهي ايضا من اشهر الصحف في العالم العربي. يعمل فيها عدد من كبار الصحفيين

اللبنانيين ، ولها مراسلون في كثير من الدول العربيّة والاجنبية .

وجريدة "النهار" كغيرها من الجرائد العربية تستخدم اللغة الفصحى المعاصرة ، وهي لغة تختلف في بعض الامور عن لغة القرآن والادب لانها متأثرة باللهجات العامية واللغات الاجنبية .

ومن المتفق عليه ان جريدة "النهار" تطورت تطورا كبيرا خلال السنوات الاخيرة نَتيجَةً لِتطوّر السياسة العربية وتغيّر الاوضاع الاجتماعية والاقتصادية في الشرق الاوسط وانتشار الثَّقافَةِ العربية بين العرب .

as a result of — culture

" والنهار " متأثرة الى حد بعيد بالاساليب الصحفية المتبعة في الغرب . فالصحفيون الذين يكتبون في "النهار" يقولون ما يُحِبّونَ عن حكومتهم وعن الاوضاع الاجتماعية في بلادهم ، اما الصحف العربية الاخرى ، خاصة غير اللبنانية ، فانها تُعَبِّرُ عادة عَنْ رأي الحكومة او رأي حزب من الاحزاب عندما تتحدث عن المواضيع السياسية .

they like — express

Drill 15. Written. صَوابٌ أَمْ خَطَأٌ

In the light of the preceding passage, indicate which of the following statements are true (T) and which are false (F):

١ ـ جريدة "النهار" مصرية .

٢ ـ جريدة "النهار" مشهورة في العالم العربي .

٣ ـ لجريدة "النهار" مراسلون في العالم العربي .

٤ ـ تختلف لغة "النهار" عن لغة القرآن .

٥ ـ لغة "النهار" هي اللغة العربية المعاصرة .

٦ ـ ليس للعامية تأثير على لغة "النهار" .

٧ ـ تطورت "النهار" في السنوات الاخيرة .

٨ ـ تكتب جريدة "النهار" بحرية عن الاوضاع السياسية .

٩ ـ جميع الجرائد العربية تكتب بحرّية عن الاوضاع السياسية .

E. General drills

هـ ـ تمارين عامة

Drill 16. (Also on tape) Variable substitution: Ordinals.

اعجبني الدرس الثالث

الكتاب

٨

١١

١٠

قصّة

المقالة

١٥

١

فلم

٢٥

٩

Drill 17. Written. Completion: Verbs and participles

Complete the following chart, vocalizing each form.

	Negative Imperative	PP	AP	Imperfect	Perfect	Form
Ex.	لا تُشاهِدْ	مُشاهَدٌ	مُشاهِدٌ	يُشاهِدُ	شاهَدَ	III
				يختلف		
			ناتج			
					تناول	
				يحترم		
			مترجم			
		مستخدم				
					أنتج	
		(none)	متأثر			
		مترجم				
				يفضّل		
		(none)			انصرف	

Drill 18. Written. Combination: Ḥāl

Combine the following pairs of sentences into one sentence using the ḥāl construction. Translate the sentences. Ex.

'He wrote a long article. In the article he dealt with the world economy.' →	كتب مقالة طويلة • تناول في المقالة الاقتصاد العالمي • ←
'He wrote a long article, dealing in it with the world economy.'	كتب مقالة طويلة متناولا فيها الاقتصاد العالمي •

١ ـ ارسل رسالة الى المدير • طلب ان يعمل في الشركة •

٢ ـ كتب الاديب كتابا هاما • كان في الخامسة والثلاثين من عمره •

٣ ـ رجع الوزير الى بلده • كان يحمل رسالة هامة الى رئيس الجمهورية •

٤ ـ بدأت دراسة العلوم السياسية • كنت طالبا في جامعة القاهرة •

٥ ـ تحدّث اليها طويلا • لا يعرف من هي •

ARABIC-ENGLISH GLOSSARY

This glossary lists all words used in Part 1 of this book. Words are arranged alphabetically by root; the symbol # indicates the first entry under a new root. Under a given root the order of entry is as follows: verbs, in order of Form (I to X); participles (in order of Form number); and m-derivatives.

Nouns and adjectives are listed in the nominative masculine singular form; feminines, where given, are in parentheses ( ). The plural is indicated by a dash –. Alternate forms are separated by an Arabic comma, ، . Verbs are cited in the 3 m.s. perfect tense; the imperfect vowel is written over a line ___ immediately following the perfect, and the verbal noun, if given, is separated by an Arabic comma, ، . Any preposition identified with a particular verb comes after the verbal noun.

The following have not been included: feminines of nouns and adjectives derivable from the masculine by the addition of ة ; nisba adjectives; and participles. Exceptions to this rule were made only when either the form or the meaning was not mechanically predictable from the base of form.

The first and last roots found on a given page are indicated at the top of the page.

For abbreviations used in this glossary, see page xiii.

ARABIC-ENGLISH GLOSSARY

أ

أ # (interrogative particle)

أَبٌ ، أَبو – آباءٌ # father (nisba = أَبَوِيٌّ)

أَثَّرَ، تَأْثيرٌ على، في # II to influence, affect

تَأَثَّرَ، تَأَثُّرٌ (ب) V to be influenced (by)

أَثَرٌ – آثارٌ trace, mark, sign; (p.) ruins, antiquities

أَجَّلَ ، تَأْجيلٌ # II to put off, postpone

أَحَدٌ # one, someone; (with neg.) no one

أَحَدَ عَشَرَ eleven

حادي عَشَرَ eleventh

أَخَذَ ـُ ، أَخْذٌ # to take; (with foll. indic.) to begin to

آخَرُ – ون # other, another
(أُخْرى – أُخْرَياتٌ)

أَخيرٌ last, final; recent; latter

أَخيرًا # finally; recently, lately

أَخٌ ، أَخو – إِخْوَةٌ # brother (nisba = أَخَوِيٌّ)

أُخْتٌ – أَخَواتٌ sister

أَدَبٌ – آدابٌ # literature, belles-lettres

أَديبٌ – أُدَباءُ man of letters, writer, author

تَأْديبٌ discipline; punishment; education

أَدَّى ، تَأْدِيَةٌ # II to carry out, perform

أُذُنٌ – آذانٌ # (f.) ear

أرامكو # ARAMCO (The Arabian American Oil Co.)

ام

تاريخٌ – تَواريخُ # history; date

أَلْأُرْدُنُّ # Jordan

أَرْزٌ # (coll.) cedars, cedar

أُوروبّا # Europe

أَساسِيٌّ # basic

أُسْتاذٌ – أَساتِذَةٌ # professor

أَلْإِسْكَنْدَرِيَّةُ # Alexandria

أَسْوانُ # Aswan

أَفْلاطونُ # Plato

الأَقْصُرُ # see under قصر

تَأَكَّدَ، تَأَكُّدٌ (مِن) # V to become certain, convinced (of)

أَكَلَ ـُ ، أَكْلٌ # to eat

أَكْلٌ eating; food

إِلّا # except; (with neg.) only

اَلَّذي – اَللَّذانِ، اللَّذَيْنِ – الَّذينَ
(اَلَّتي – اَللَّتانِ
اللَّتَيْنِ – اللَّواتي) # (relative pronoun) who, that, which

أَلْفٌ – آلافٌ # (one) thousand

أُلوفٌ مِنْ thousands of

أَللهُ # God

لِلّهِ belonging to God

إِلى # to, up to

إِلى جانِبِ in addition to; besides; apart from

أَمْ # or

أم

أَمامَ # in front of

أَلأَمازون # the Amazon

أَمّا ... فَ # as for...

أَمْرٌ ـ أُمورٌ # matter, affair, concern

مُؤْتَمَرٌ ـ ات conference; convention

أَمْريكا # America

أَمريكي ـ أمريكان American (n. or adj.)

أَمْسِ # yesterday

آن آربر # Ann Arbor

أَنْ # (foll. by subjunctive) that (conj.)

أَنَّ # the fact that, that (conj.)

إِنَّ (after قالَ) that (conj.)

إِنَّ (intensifying particle) verily, indeed

أَنا # I

أَنْتَ ـ أَنْتُما ـ أَنْتُمْ # you

(أَنْتِ ـ أَنْتُما ـ أَنْتُنَّ)

أَلأَنْدَلُس # Andalusia, Spain

ناسٌ # people

آنِسَةٌ ـ ات young lady; Miss

إِنْكِليزِيٌّ، إِنْجِليزِيّ ـ إِنْكِليزٌ، إِنْجِليزٌ # English (n. or adj.)

أَلأنكليزية ، الأنكليزية the English language, English

أَهْلٌ ـ أَهالٍ # people; family; owners

أَهْلاً وَسَهْلاً welcome! hello!

أَوْ # or

بدو

أُوتوبيس ـ ات # bus

أُورُبّا ، أوروبّا ، أروبّا # Europe

أوستن # Austin

أَوَّلُ ـ أَوائِلُ (أُولي) # first

أَوَّلاً first, firstly

أَلآنَ # now

أَيْ # that is to say, that is

أَيٌّ # (interrogative particle) what?, which?; (in a statement) any; (with a neg.) not any, no

أَيْضاً # also

أَيْنَ # where?

أَيُّها (أَيَّتُها) # o (vocative)

ب

بِـ # in; by means of, by, with

بَحَثَ ـَ ، بَحْثٌ # to discuss

بَحَثَ ـَ ، بَحْثٌ عَنْ to look, search for

بَحْثٌ ـ بُحوثٌ، أَبْحاثٌ (عن) discussion (about); research on; study (about)

باحِثٌ ـ ون researcher

بَدَأَ ـَ ، بَدْءٌ (ب) # to begin, start (with)

بِدايَةٌ beginning

إِبْتِدائيٌّ primary

بَدَوِيٌّ ـ بَدْوٌ # bedouin

بَذَلَ ـُـ ، بَذْلٌ # to exert

بَرْلَمان # parliament

إِبْراهيمُ طوقان # Ibrāhīm Ṭūqān (poet)

إِبْراهيمُ بْنُ عَبّاس الصّولي . Ibrāhīm b. Abbās al-Ṣūlī

بَريطانيا (العُظْمى) # (Great) Britain

بَسْكِنْتا # Baskinta (town in Lebanon)

أَلْبَصْرَةُ # Basra (city in Iraq)

بَطالَةٌ # unemployment

بَعْدَ # after (prep.)

بَعْدَ أَنْ after (conj.)

بَعيدٌ ـ بُعَداءُ (عن ، من) far, distant (from)

بَعْضٌ # some, some of

بَعْلَبَكُّ # Baalbek

بَغْدادُ # Baghdad

بكالوريوس # B.A., bachelor's degree

بَلْ # but, rather

بَلَدٌ ـ بِلادٌ ، بلدان # country

بَلَدِيٌّ native, indigenous, home

بِلادٌ (f.) country; homeland

اِبْنٌ ـ أَبْناءٌ # son

اِبْنُ خَلْدون Ibn Khaldoun (medieval historian and sociologist)

اِبْنَةٌ ـ بَناتٌ daughter

بِنْتٌ ـ بَناتٌ girl; daughter

بَنْكٌ ـ بُنوكٌ # bank

بَناما # Panama

بِناءٌ # (verbal noun) building, constructing

بِناءٌ ـ أَبْنِيَةٌ a building

بابٌ ـ أَبْوابٌ # door; gate

بور سَعيد # Port Said

بَيْتٌ ـ بُيوتٌ # house; home

بَيْروتُ # Beirut

بَيْنَ # between

ت

تابَعَ ، مُتابَعَةٌ # III to continue; pursue, follow up

اِتَّبَعَ ، اِتِّباعٌ VIII to follow, adhere to, observe

تِجارَةٌ # commerce, trade

تحد ، مُتَّحِدَةٌ # see under وحد

مَتْحَفٌ ـ مَتاحِفُ # museum

تَرْجَمَ ، تَرْجَمَةٌ # (quad.) to translate

تَرَكَ ـُـ ، تَرْكٌ # to leave, leave behind

تِسْعَةٌ # nine

تِسْعونَ (nom.) ninety; (foll. definite sing. n.) ninetieth

تاسِعٌ ninth

تكساس # Texas

تِلْميذٌ ـ ، تَلاميذُ # disciple, student

تَمَّ ـِـ # to be completed; to take place

تونِسُ # Tunis; Tunisia

ثَقافَةٌ – ات # culture, refinement

ثُلْثٌ – أَثْلاثٌ # one-third

ثَلاثَةٌ three

ثالِثٌ third

ثالِثاً thirdly

ثَلاثونَ (nom.) thirty; (foll. definite n.) thirtieth

مِنْ ثَمَّ # hence, therefore

ثُمَّ then, there upon

ثَمانِيَةٌ # eight

ثَمانونَ (nom.) eighty; (foll. definite n.) eightieth

ثامِنٌ eighth

أَثْناءَ # during

اِثْنانِ two

ثانٍ second

ثانِياً secondly

ثانَوِيٌّ secondary

ثَوْرَةٌ – ات (على) # revolution, rebellion (against)

ثَوْرِيٌّ – ون revolutionary (n. or adj.)

ج

جِبْران خَليل جِبْران # Kahlil Gibran

الجاحِظُ # Al-Jāḥiz (medieval writer)

جِدًّا # very

جَديدٌ – جُدُدٌ new

جَريدَةٌ – جَرائِدُ # newspaper

اَلْجَزائِرُ # Algiers; Algeria

جَعَلَ ـَـ ، جَعْلٌ # to create, make (s.th. into s.th.), render; (with foll. indic.) to begin to

مَجَلَّةٌ # magazine

جَمَعَ ـَـ ، جَمْعٌ # to gather, collect, combine

جَمَعَ بَيْنَ ... وَ to combine...and

اِجْتَمَعَ ، اِجْتِماعٌ (مع ، بـ) VIII to meet (with)

جَميعٌ all

اَلْجَميعُ everyone, everybody

جَميعاً all together, one and all

اِجْتِماعٌ – ات meeting

اِجْتِماعِيٌّ social; sociological

جامِعٌ – جَوامِعُ mosque

جامِعَةٌ – ات university

مُجْتَمَعٌ – ات society, community

جُمْلَةٌ – جُمَلٌ # sentence, clause

جَمالٌ beauty

جَمال عَبْدُ النّاصِر Gamal Abd Al-Nasser

جَميلٌ – ون beautiful, handsome

جمهر	
جُمْهورِيَّةٌ ـ ات	# republic
رَئِيسُ الْجُمْهورِيَّةِ	president
إِلى جانِبِ	# in addition to; besides; apart from
أَجْنَبِيٌّ ـ أَجانِبُ	foreign; foreigner
جَهْدٌ ـ جُهودٌ	# effort, exertion
جارٌ ـ جيرانٌ	# neighbor
جورج واشنطن	# George Washington
جورجتاون	# Georgetown
جورجي زَيْدان	# Jūrjī Zaydān (writer)
تَجَوَّلَ ، تَجَوُّلٌ	# V to walk, roam, wander around
جاءَ ـِ (في)	# to be included (in a written document)

ح

أَحَبَّ ، حُبٌّ	# IV to love, like, take a liking to, to fall in love with,
حُبٌّ	love
حَبيبٌ ـ أَحِبّاءُ	beloved, sweetheart, dear
حَتَّى	# (foll. by perfect) until; (foll. by subjunctive) in order that, so that; until; (adverb) even
حَدَّدَ ، تَحْديدٌ	# II to define, limit, set bounds (to)
حَدٌّ ـ حُدودٌ	extent, limit; boundary
تَحَدَّثَ ، تَحَدُّثٌ (الى) (عن)	# V to speak (to) (about); to converse (with) (about)

حفر	
حَديثٌ ـ حِداثٌ	new, modern
حَديثاً	recently, lately
حُرِّيَّةٌ ـ ات	# freedom
تَحْريرٌ	liberation, freeing
اِحْتَرَمَ ، اِحْتِرامٌ	# VIII to respect, honor, revere
حِزْبٌ ـ أَحْزابٌ	# (political) party
حُسْنُ الضِّيافَةِ	# hospitality
لِحُسْنِ الْحَظِّ	fortunately
حَسَناً	fine!
حُسَيْنٌ	Hussein (m. name)
حَصَلَ ـُ ، حُصولٌ على	# to obtain, get
حُصولٌ على	obtaining
حاصِلٌ ـ ون على	having obtained
حَضَرَ ـُ ، حُضورٌ	# to attend, be present (at)
حَضَرَ ـُ ، حُضورٌ الى، لِ	to come to
حاضَرَ ، مُحاضَرَةٌ	III to give a lecture; to lecture
حُضورٌ	attendance, presence (at)
حُضورٌ الى	coming to
حَضارَةٌ	civilization; culture
مُحاضَرَةٌ ـ ات	lecture
حاضِرٌ ـ ون	present, attending; current (time)
لِحُسْنِ الْحَظِّ	# fortunately
حَفَرَ ـِ ، حَفْرٌ	# to dig, excavate

حافَظَ ، مُحافَظَةٌ على	# III to preserve, maintain; to protect, defend
حَقَّقَ ، تَحْقيقٌ	# II to realize, accomplish
حَقٌّ ـ حُقوقٌ	right; truth
حَقًّا	really, indeed, truly
حَكَمَ ـُـ ، حُكْمٌ	# to govern, rule
حَكَمَ ـُـ ، حُكْمٌ على	to pass judgment on, to judge
حِكْمَةٌ ـ حِكَمٌ	saying, maxim, word of wisdom
حَكيمٌ ـ حُكَماءُ	wise
حُكومَةٌ ـ ات	government
حاكِمٌ ـ ون ، حكّام	ruler, governor
حَلٌّ ـ حُلولٌ	# solving, solution; dissolution, breaking-up
اَلْحَمْدُ لِلّٰهِ	# praise be to God
أَحْمَدُ	Ahmad (m. name)
مُحَمَّدٌ	Muhammad
مُحَمَّد عَليّ	Muhammad Ali
حَمَلَ ـِـ ، حَمْلٌ	# to carry, bear
حَمْلَةٌ ـ حَمَلاتٌ (على)	(military) campaign (against)
حاجَةٌ ـ ات (الى)	# need (for)
بِحاجَةٍ الى	in need of
حِوارٌ	# dialogue, conversation
حالٌ ـ أَحْوالٌ	# condition, state, circumstance

كَيْفَ الْحالُ	How are you?
حَياةٌ ـ حَيَواتٌ	# life, life blood
حَيَوِيّ	lively, vital
حانَ ـِـ	# to be time, to draw near, come, approach (time)
حينٌ ـ أَحْيانٌ	time; occasion
حينَ	at the time that, when (conj.)
أَحْيانًا	sometimes

خ

أَخْبَرَ ، إِخْبارٌ (ب)	# IV to inform s.o. (of s.th.); to tell
خَبَرٌ ـ أَخْبارٌ	news item; (p.) news
خاتِمٌ ـ خَواتِمُ	# ring
خَدَمَ ـُـ ، خِدْمَةٌ	# to serve, render a service to
اِسْتَخْدَمَ ، اِسْتِخْدامٌ	X to use
خِدْمَةٌ ـ خَدَماتٌ	service
خَرَجَ ـُـ ، خُروجٌ (من)	# to go out (of)
خَرَّجَ ، تَخْريجٌ	II to graduate (transitive); to educate
أَخْرَجَ ، إِخْراجٌ	IV to take out, remove, expel
خارِجٌ	exterior
في الْخارِجِ	abroad
خارِجَ	outside of
خارِجيٌّ	external
الْخارِجِيَّةُ	foreign affairs
اَلْخَرْطومُ	# Khartoum

خصّ

خاصٌّ # special; private

خاصَّةً especially

خِطابٌ ــ ات # speech

تَخاطُبٌ conversation

خِلالَ # during

الْخَليلُ بْنُ أَحْمَد Al-Khalīl b. Ahmad (Arab grammarian)

مُخْلِصٌ ــ ون # sincere

اِخْتَلَفَ ، اِخْتِلافٌ (عن ، مع) # VIII to differ (from); to differ, disagree (with)

خَليفَةٌ ــ خُلَفاءُ (m.) Caliph

خَمْسَةٌ # five

خَمْسونَ (nom.) fifty; (foll. definite n.) fiftieth

خامِسٌ fifth

خَيْرٌ ــ خُيورٌ # good (things), blessing, benefit; welfare;

بِخَيْر fine, (I'm) fine

خَيْمَةٌ ــ خِيامٌ # tent

د

داخِليٌّ # inner, internal; domestic

دَرَسَ ـُـ ، دِراسَةٌ دَرْسٌ # to study

دَرَّسَ ، تَدْريسٌ II to teach

دَرْسٌ ــ دُروسٌ lesson

دِراسَةٌ ــ ات study; studying

مَدْرَسَةٌ ــ مَدارِسُ school

مَدْرَسَةٌ حُكوميَّةٌ public school

ذهب

مَدْرَسَةٌ لُغَويَّةٌ linguistic school

تَدْريسٌ teaching, instruction

مُدَرِّسٌ ــ ون teacher, instructor

دُسْتورٌ ــ دَساتيرُ # constitution

دَقيقَةٌ ــ دَقائِقُ # (a) minute

دُكْتورٌ ــ دَكاتِرَةٌ # doctor; Ph. D.

دُكْتوراه doctorate, Ph. D.

دِمَشْقُ # Damascus

دارٌ ــ دورٌ ، دِيارٌ # (f.) house

مُديرٌ ــ ون director

دَوْلَةٌ ــ دُوَلٌ # state, country, power

اَلدُّوَلُ الْكُبْرى the major powers

دُوَلِيٌّ international

دولارٌ ــ ات # dollar

دونَ # without (prep.)

دونَ أَنْ without (conj.)

ذ

ذٰلِكَ ــ أُولٰئِكَ (تلك) # that

كَذٰلِكَ thus, so, likewise, also

أَلَيْسَ كَذٰلِكَ ؟ isn't that so?

ذَكَرَ ـُـ ، ذِكْرٌ # to mention, relate, tell

مُذَكِّرَةٌ ــ ات note; reminder

ذَهَبَ ـَـ ، ذَهابٌ (الى) # to go (to)

ذَهَبَ ـَـ ، ذَهابٌ بـ (الى) — to take, conduct (s.o. or s.th.) (to)

ذاهِبٌ ـ ون — going

رَأْسٌ ـ رُؤُوسٌ # (m. and f.) head

رَئِيسٌ ـ رُؤَساءُ — president, head, chief

رَئِيسُ الْوُزَراءُ — prime minister

رَئِيسُ الْجُمْهُورِيَّةِ — president

رَأْيٌ ـ آراءٌ (فى) # opinion, view (on)

رَبَطَ ـِـ ، رَبْطٌ (الى ، بَيْنَ ٠ وبَيْنَ) # to bind, tie (to); to connect (with); to combine (s.th. with)

أَلرِّباطُ — Rabat

رابِطَةٌ ـ رَوابِطُ — bond, tie; connection, link; league, society

أَلرّابِطَةُ الْقَلَمِيَّةُ — The Literary Club

رُبْعٌ ـ أَرْباعٌ # one fourth, quarter

أَرْبَعَةٌ — four

أَرْبَعونَ — (nom.) forty; (foll. definite n.) fortieth

رابِعٌ — fourth

تَرْبِيَةٌ ـ ات # education· upbringing (nisba: تَرْبَوِيٌّ)

رَجَعَ ـِـ ، رُجوعٌ # to return, come *or* go back

رَجُلٌ ـ رِجالٌ # man

رَجاءٌ # wish, hope

رَحَّبَ ، تَرْحِيبٌ ب # II to welcome

مَرْحَبًا — hello!

رَحَلَ ـَـ ، رَحِيلٌ # to move about, travel, leave

مَرْحَلَةٌ ـ مَراحِلُ — stage, phase

راسَلَ ، مُراسَلَةٌ # III to correspond with

أَرْسَلَ ، إِرْسالٌ — IV to send

تَراسَلَ ، تَراسُلٌ — VI to correspond with one another

رِسالَةٌ ـ رَسائِلُ — letter

مُراسِلٌ ـ ون — reporter, correspondent

رَسَمَ ـُـ ، رَسْمٌ # to draw

رَسْمِيٌّ — official, formal, ceremonial

مُرَشَّحٌ ـ ون # candidate, nominee

رَغِبَ ـَـ ، رَغْبَةٌ فى # to desire, wish for

رُوسِيا # Russia

أَلرِّياضُ # Riyadh

ز

زَمَنٌ ـ أَزْمانٌ # time; period; stretch of time

أَلْأَزْهَرُ # Al-Azhar (university)

تَزَوَّجَ ، تَزَوُّجٌ ، زَواجٌ (من) # V to get married (to); to marry (with)

زَوْجٌ ـ أَزْواجٌ — husband

زَوْجَةٌ ـ ات — wife

زَواجٌ — marriage

زِيارَةٌ ـ ات # visit

زائِرٌ ـ ون — visiting

زائِرٌ ـ زُوّارٌ — visitor, guest

ما زالَ # is still

زول

لا يَزالُ is still

س

سَ # (future particle) will, going to

سَأَلَ ـَـ ، سُؤالٌ # to ask

سُؤالٌ ـ أَسْئِلَةٌ question

سَبْعَةٌ # seven

سَبْعونَ (nom.) seventy; (foll. definite n.) seventieth

سابِعٌ seventh

سِتَّةٌ # six

سِتّونَ (nom.) sixty; (foll. definite n.) sixtieth

سَدٌّ ـ سُدودٌ # dam

أَلسَّدُّ ٱلْعالي the High Dam

سادِسٌ # sixth

مَسْرَحٌ ـ مَسارِحُ # theater; stage

أَسْرَعَ ، إِسْراعٌ # IV to hasten, hurry

ساعَدَ ، مُساعَدَةٌ # III to help, assist (in)
(على ، فى)

سَعيدٌ ـ سُعَداءُ (ب) happy (over, at, with)

أَلسَّعودِيَّةُ Saudi Arabia

سُعادُ Su'ad (f. name)

سافَرَ ، سَفَرٌ # III to travel, go on a trip; to leave, depart

سَفَرٌ ـ أَسْفارٌ departure; travel, trip

سَكَتَ ـُـ ، سُكوتٌ # to fall silent, say nothing

سم

سِكْرِتيرٌ ـ ون # secretary

سَكَنَ ـُـ ، سَكَنٌ # to live, dwell, reside; take up residence

ساكِنٌ ـ ون living, residing

ساكِنٌ ـ سُكّانٌ inhabitant, resident, occupant

أُسْلوبٌ ـ أَساليبُ # style

سَلامٌ # peace; greeting

أَلسَّلامُ عَلَيْكُمْ greetings! (lit. "peace be upon you")

وَعَلَيْكُمُ السَّلامُ greetings! (lit. "and upon you be peace" (reply to السَّلامُ عَلَيْكُمْ)

سَلامَةٌ well-being

مَعَ السَّلامَةِ goodbye

سَليمٌ Salim (m. name)

سُلَيْمانُ ٱلْحَكيمُ Solomon the Wise

إِسْلامٌ Islam

مُسْلِمٌ ـ ون Muslim

سَمَحَ ـَـ ، سَماحٌ # to permit (s.o) (s.th.)
(لِ) (ب)

سَميرٌ # Samir (m. name)

سَمِعَ ـَـ ، سَماعٌ # to hear

اِسْتَمَعَ ، اِسْتِماعٌ VIII to listen (to)
(لِ ، الى)

سامي # Sami (m. name)

اِسْمٌ ـ أَسْماءٌ # name

سَنَةٌ ـ سَنَواتٌ # year

سَنَوِيٌّ annual, yearly

سَهْلٌ # easy

سَيِّئٌ # bad, evil

أَلسُّودانُ # The Sudan

سَيِّدٌ # mister, Mr.

سوريا # Syria

سِياسَةٌ ـ ات # policy; politics

أَلسُّوَيْسُ # Suez

ساعَةٌ ـ ات # hour; clock, watch

سَوْفَ # (future particle) will, going to

مَسافَةٌ ـ ات distance

سِوى # (with foll. gen. or suffix) other than, except

مُساوٍ (لِ) equal, equivalent (to)

سِيبَوَيْهِ # Sibawayhi (medieval grammarian)

سَيّارَةٌ ـ ات # car, automobile

سَيْطَرَ ، سَيْطَرَةٌ على # (quad.) to control, dominate

سينَما # (f.) cinema, movies

ش

شَأْنٌ ـ شُؤُونٌ # matter, affair; situation

بِشَأْنِ in regards to, regarding (s.th.)

شُبّاكٌ ـ شَبابيكُ # window

شَرٌّ ـ شُرُورٌ # evil, harm

شَرِبَ ـَـ ، شُرْبٌ # to drink

شَرابٌ ، أَشْرِبَةٌ drink, beverage

شارِعٌ ـ شَوارِعُ # street

أَشْرَفَ ، إِشْرافٌ على # IV to supervise

شَرِيفٌ Sharīf (m. name)

شَرْقٌ # East

أَلشَّرْقُ ٱلْأَوْسَطُ The Middle East

مُسْتَشْرِقٌ ـ ون orientalist

شارَكَ ، مُشارَكَةٌ في # III to participate, join in

شَرِكَةٌ ـ ات company

شَعْبٌ ـ شُعُوبٌ # a people; nation

شِعْرٌ ـ أَشْعارٌ # poetry; poem

شُكْرٌ ـ شُكُورٌ # thanks; gratefulness, gratitude

شُكْرًا thank you!

شَكْلٌ ـ أَشْكالٌ # form, shape, type

مُشْكِلَةٌ ـ مَشاكِلُ problem

شَمِلَ ـَـ ، شَمَلَ ـُـ ، شَمْلٌ ، شُمُولٌ # to include, comprise

شاهَدَ ، مُشاهَدَةٌ # III to see, watch, witness

شَهادَةٌ ـ ات degree, diploma, certificate

شَهْرٌ ـ أَشْهُرٌ # month

مَشْهُورٌ ـ ون (ب) famous (for)

مُشْتاقٌ ـ ون الى # eager for, longing to

شَيْءٌ ـ أَشْياءُ # thing, something

شَيْطانٌ ـ شَياطينُ # Satan, devil

ص

أَصْبَحَ # IV to become

صَباحٌ morning

صَباحَ ٱلْخَيْرِ good morning!

صَباحَ ٱلنّورِ good morning! (response)

صَحْراءُ ـ صَحارى # (f.) desert (صَحْراوِيٌّ)

صَحيفَةٌ ـ صُحُفٌ # newspaper (صُحُفِيٌّ)

أَصْدَرَ ، إِصْدارٌ # IV to export; to publish

صادَقَ ، مُصادَقَةٌ # III to become friends with

صَديقٌ ـ أَصْدِقاءُ friend

تَصَرَّفَ ، تَصَرُّفٌ # V to behave, conduct oneself

اِنْصَرَفَ، اِنْصِرافٌ VII to go away, leave

صَعْبٌ ـ صِعابٌ (على) # hard, difficult (for s.o.)

صَغيرٌ ـ صِغارٌ # little, small; young (person)

صَفٌّ ـ صُفوفٌ # class; classroom

صِناعَةٌ ـ ات # industry

مَصْنَعٌ ـ مَصانِعُ factory

صورَةٌ ـ صُوَرٌ # image, form; picture

صائِغٌ ـ صاغَةٌ # goldsmith; jeweler

صَيْفٌ ـ أَصْيافٌ # summer

ض

ضَحِكَ ـَـ ، ضِحْكٌ # to laugh

حسن الضيافة # hospitality

ط

طاوِلَةٌ ـ ات # table

طَبيبٌ ـ أَطِبّاءُ # doctor, M.D.

طَرَدَ ـُـ ، طَرْدٌ (من) # to reject, dismiss expel (from)

طارِقُ بْنُ زِيادٍ # Tariq b. Ziyad

طَعامٌ ـ أَطْعِمَةٌ # food

مَطْعَمٌ ـ مَطاعِمُ restaurant

طَلَبَ ـُـ ، طَلَبٌ # to request

طالَبَ ، مُطالَبَةٌ بـ III to demand (of s.o.) (s.th)

تَطَلَّبَ ، تَطَلُّبٌ V to require, necessitate

طَلَبٌ ـ ات request; application; demand

طالِبٌ ـ طُلّابٌ student

تَطَوَّرَ ، تَطَوُّرٌ # V to develop, evolve

طَويلٌ ـ طِوالٌ # long; tall

طَويلاً at length, a long time

مَطارٌ ـ ات # airport

طائِرَةٌ ـ ات airplane

ظ

ظَلَّ ـَـ # to remain; to continue to do

أَظْهَرَ ، إِظْهارٌ # IV to show, demonstrate

أَلظَّهْرانُ Dhahran (city in Saudi Arabia)

ع

عَبَّرَ ، تَعْبيرٌ عن # II to express

إِعْتَبَرَ ، إِعْتِبارٌ VIII to consider (s.o.) as (s.th.)

عَبّاس مَحْمود العَقّاد # Abbās Mahmūd Al-'Aqqād

عُثْمانِيٌّ # Ottoman

أَعْجَبَ ، إِعْجابٌ # IV to please, delight

عَدَدٌ ـ أَعْدادٌ # number

إِعْدادِيٌّ preparatory; elementary (school)

مُسْتَعِدٌّ ـ ون (لِ) ready, prepared (for)

عَرَبِيٌّ ـ عَرَبٌ # Arab, Arabic, Arabian

أَلْعَرَبِيَّةُ the Arabic language, Arabic

عَرَفَ ـِ ، مَعْرِفَةٌ # (perfect) to find out (about), learn, know; (imperfect) to know

عُرِفَ بِـ to be known for

مَعْرِفَةٌ ـ مَعارِفُ knowing; knowledge

مَعْرُوفٌ known, well-known

أَلْمَعْرُوفُ أَنَّ it is known that...

أَلْعِراقُ # Iraq

عَزِيزٌ ـ أَعِزّاءُ # dear, beloved

عَشَرَةٌ # ten

عِشْرُونَ (nom.) twenty; (foll. definite n.) twentieth

عاشِرٌ tenth

عاصَرَ ، مُعاصَرَةٌ # III to be contemporary to

مُعاصِرٌ contemporary

عَظِيمٌ ـ عُظَماءُ # great, big, grand, vast, enormous

مُعْظَمُ most of

عَفْوًا # you're welcome!

عَقَدَ ـِ ، عَقْدٌ # to hold (a meeting)

إِنْعَقَدَ ، إِنْعِقادٌ VII to be held (meeting)

إِعْتَقَدَ ، إِعْتِقادٌ (بِـ) VIII to believe (in)

إِعْتِقادٌ belief

عَلاقَةٌ ـ ات (بِ) # relationship (to), connection (with)

لَعَلَّ # perhaps, maybe

عَلِمَ ـَ ، عِلْمٌ # to know, have knowledge of, be familiar with

عَلَّمَ ، تَعْلِيمٌ II to teach (s.o. or s.th.); to educate (s.o.)

تَعَلَّمَ ، تَعَلُّمٌ V to learn; to become educated

عِلْمٌ learning; knowledge; science

عالَمٌ ـ عَوالِمُ world

تَعْلِيمٌ education

مُعَلِّمٌ ـ ون teacher

عَلَى # on; over; to the debt of

عالٍ (عالِيَةٌ) high

عَلِيٌّ Ali (m. name)

عامَّةً # generally, in general

أَلْعامِّيَّةُ colloquial Arabic

إِعْتَمَدَ ، إِعْتِمادٌ عَلَى # VIII to depend on, rely on

عَمِيدٌ ـ عُمَداءُ dean

عُمْرٌ ـ أَعْمارٌ # age (of a person), lifetime

عَمِلَ ـَ ، عَمَلٌ # to work

عَمِلَ ـَ ، عَمَلٌ عَلَى to work for, be active in service of

عَمَلٌ ـ أَعْمالٌ work, job

عمل

- عامِلٌ ـ عُمّالٌ worker
- عَمّانُ # Amman
- عَنْ # about, concerning
- عِنْدَ # at, with (time or place); (with verbal noun) on, upon; in the view, opinion of; among
- عِنْدَما when, whenever
- عُنْوانٌ ـ عَناوِينُ # title; address
- مَعْنًى ـ مَعانٍ # meaning, sense
- مَعْهَدٌ ـ مَعاهِدُ # institute
- عَوْدَةٌ # return
- عادَةً usually
- عائِلَةٌ ـ ات # family
- عامٌ ـ أَعْوامٌ # year
- تَعاوَنَ ، تَعاوُنٌ # VI to cooperate
- عَيَّنَ ، تَعْيِينٌ # II to appoint (s.o.) as (s.th.)
- عَيْنٌ ـ عُيونٌ (f.) eye

غ

- غَدٌ # the morrow, the following day
- غَدًا tomorrow
- غَرْبٌ # west
- غَرِيبٌ ـ غُرَباءُ stranger (n); strange (adj.)
- اَلْمَغْرِبُ Morocco
- غالِبٌ # (with foll. genitive) most, majority of
- غَيَّرَ ، تَغْيِيرٌ # II to change (s.th.)
- تَغَيَّرَ ، تَغَيُّرٌ V to be changed, change

فكر

- غَيْرٌ other than

ف

- فَ # and; and then; and so
- فَتَحَ ـَـ ، فَتْحٌ # to open; to conquer
- فَتَّشَ ، تَفْتِيشٌ عن # II to search, look for
- تَفَحَّصَ ، تَفَحُّصٌ # V to examine
- فَدْوى طوقان # Fadwa Tūqān (woman poet)
- فَرِيدٌ # Farid (m. name)
- مُفْرَداتٌ vocabulary items
- فَرَضَ ـِـ ، فَرْضٌ على # to impose (s.th.) upon
- فِرْعَوْنِيٌّ # pharaonic
- فَرَنْسا # France
- اَلْفُصْحى # classical (literary) Arabic
- تَفْصِيلٌ ـ تَفاصِيلُ # detail
- فَضَّلَ ، تَفْضِيلٌ على # II to prefer (s.o. or s.th.) to
- فَعَلَ ـَـ ، فِعْلٌ # to do, act; to make
- فِعْلٌ ـ أَفْعالٌ doing, action, deed
- فَقَدَ ـِـ ، فَقْدٌ ، فِقْدانٌ # to lose, miss, be bereft of
- فَقْرٌ # poverty
- فَقَطْ # only
- فَكَّرَ ، تَفْكِيرٌ (ب) # II to think (of, about)

فِكْرَةٌ – فِكَرٌ	idea, thought, concept
فِكْرِيٌّ	intellectual, mental
مُفَكِّرٌ – ون	thinker
# فِلَسْطِينُ	Palestine
# فَلْسَفَةٌ	philosophy
# فِلْمٌ، فيلْمٌ – أَفْلامٌ	film, movie
# فَمٌ – أَفْواهٌ	mouth
# فَنٌّ – فُنونٌ	art
# فِي	in; on the subject of

ق

# قَبِيحٌ – قِباحٌ	ugly
# قابَلَ، مُقابَلَةٌ III	to meet (with)
أَقْبَلَ، إِقْبالٌ على IV	to approach, go to; to devote o.s. to, begin to do s.th.
اِسْتَقْبَلَ، اِسْتِقْبالٌ X	to receive, welcome, meet
قَبْلَ	before
مُقابَلَةٌ – ات	an interview
# قَدْ	(particle) (with perfect: denotes completion of act) has, had; already
# قَدَّمَ، تَقْديمٌ II	to present, offer; to render (services)
تَقَدَّمَ، تَقَدُّمٌ V	to advance, progress
تَقَدَّمَ، تَقَدُّمٌ بِ V	to submit, present
قَديمٌ – قُدَماءُ	old, ancient
قَديمًا	in ancient times, long ago
إلى قُدّامِ	forward

تَقَدُّمٌ	progress, advancement
قادِمٌ – ون	coming; next
# قَرَّرَ، تَقْريرٌ II	to decide
# قَرَأَ – ، قِراءَةٌ	to read
أَلْقُرْآنُ	The Qur'an, Koran
# قَريبٌ – ون (من)	near (to), close (by)
قَريبًا	soon, before long
# قَرْنٌ – قُرونٌ	century
أَلْقُرونُ الْوُسْطى	the Middle Ages
# قاسِم أَمين	Qāsim Amīn
# قِصَّةٌ – قِصَصٌ	story
اِقْتِصادٌ	economy
اِقْتِصاديٌّ	economic
# أَقْصَرَ، إِقْصارٌ IV	to shorten (s.th.)
قَصيرٌ – قِصارٌ	short
أَلْأَقْصُرُ	Luxor
# اِنْقَطَعَ، اِنْقِطاعٌ VII	to be cut off, stop, come to an end
# قاعِدَةٌ – قَواعِدُ	grammar rule; (p.) grammar
# قَلْبٌ – قُلوبٌ	heart
# قَلَمٌ، أَقْلامٌ	pen; pencil
# قَناةٌ – قَنَواتٌ	canal
# أَلْقاهِرَةُ	Cairo
# قَهْوَةٌ – قَهَواتٌ	coffee
# قائِدٌ – قُوّادٌ، قادَةٌ	leader, commander, general

قالَ ـُـ ، قَوْلٌ # to say

مَقالَةٌ ، مَقالٌ ـات — article, essay

قامَ ـُـ ، قِيامٌ ب # to undertake

قاوَمَ ، مُقاوَمَةٌ — III to oppose, resist, fight

قَوْمِيٌّ — national, nationalist(ic)

قَوْمِيَّةٌ — nationalism

إِقامَةٌ — stay, sojourn, residing

قَيْدٌ ـ قُيودٌ # bond, chain, fetter

ك

كَ # like, as

كَذٰلِكَ — see under ذٰلِكَ

أَلَيْسَ كَذٰلِكَ — see under ذٰلِكَ

كَما — (foll. by a sentence) as, and also, and in addition

كارل بروكلمان # Karl Brockelmann

كاليفورنيا # California

كُبَّةٌ # kubba

كَبابٌ — kabob

كَبيرٌ ـ كِبارٌ # large, big; old (person) senior, eminent

كَتَبَ ـُـ ، كِتابَةٌ # to write

كِتابٌ ـ كُتُبٌ — book

كاتِبٌ ـ كُتّابٌ — writer, author; scribe

مَكْتَبٌ ـ مَكاتِبُ — office

مَكْتَبَةٌ ـ ات — library; bookstore

كُتْلَةٌ ـ كُتَلٌ # bloc

كَثيرٌ ـ كِثارٌ # much; many

كَثيرًا — very, very much; often

كَثيرٌ من — many of

كُرْسِيٌّ ـ كَراسٍ # chair

أَكْرَمَ ، إِكْرامٌ # IV to honor

كَريمٌ — Karim (m. name)

كُلٌّ # all

أَلْكُلُّ — everything

تَكَلَّمَ ، تَكَلُّمٌ # V to speak, talk

كَلِمَةٌ ـ ات — word

كَلامٌ — speech, speaking, conversation

كَمْ # how many? how much?

أَكْمَلَ ، إِكْمالٌ # IV to finish, complete, perfect

كونجرس # Congress

أَلْكُوَيْتُ # Kuwait

كانَ ـُـ ، كَوْنٌ # to be

مَكانٌ ـ أَماكِنُ — place

مَكانَةٌ ـ ات — position, status, rank

كَيْ ، لِكَيْ # see لِ

كَيْلا ، لِكَيْلا — see لِ

كَيْفَ # how?

كَيْفَ ٱلْحالُ ؟ — how are you?

ل

لِ # (prep.) to, for; belonging to, of; (conj.) in order that, so that...; (with jussive) let, have...

لِكَيْ ، كَيْ ، لِأَنْ (with subjunctive) in order that, so that...

لِكَيْلا ، كَيْلا، لِئَلّا (with subjunctive) in order that...not

لِماذا ، لِمَ why?

لَـ (emphasis particle) indeed

لا no

لٰكِنْ ، لٰكِنَّ but, however

لُبْنانُ Lebanon

لَعَلَّ see عَلَّ

لُغَةٌ — ات language

لُغَوِيٌّ language-related, linguistic; linguist, grammarian

لِقاءٌ meeting, encounter

لَمْ (with jussive) did not

لَمّا when, at the time that

لَنْ (with subjunctive) will not

لَنْدَن London

لَهْجَةٌ — لَهَجاتٌ dialect

لَوْحٌ — أَلْواحٌ blackboard

لَيْسَ not to be, he (it) is not

لَيْلَةٌ — لَيالٍ night; evening

م

ما (interrog. pron.) what? (spelled مَ as object of prep.)

ماذا (object of verb) what?

لماذا ، لِمَ why?

ما (relative pron.) that which, what, whatever

ماجِسْتير masters degree, M.A.

مِئَةٌ ، مائَةٌ (one) hundred

مِئاتٌ من hundreds of

مَتى when?

مِثْلٌ (with foll. gen.) the likes of, something like

مِثْلَ (prep.) like

مَثَلاً for example

اِمْتِحانٌ — ات examination

مُدَّةٌ — مُدَدٌ period (of time)

مَدَحَ — َ ، مَدْحٌ to praise

مَدينَةٌ — مُدُنٌ city (nisba = مَدَنِيٌّ)

اِمْرَأَةٌ، اَلْمَرْأَةُ — نِساءٌ ، نِسْوَةٌ woman (nisba = نِسائِيٌّ)

مَرْيَمُ Maryam, Miriam, Mary (f. name)

اَلْمِسيسيبي the Mississippi

مَساءٌ evening

مَساءً in the evening

ميشِجان Michigan

مِصْرُ Egypt

مَعَ with, together with

مَعاً together

V تَمَكَّنَ ، تَمَكُّنٌ من to be able to, capable of

مَلِكٌ — مُلوكٌ king

مَنْ # who? whoever, the one who

مِنْ # from, (from) among, of; out of, because of; one of, some of

مَنَحَ ـَـ ، مَنْحٌ # to grant (s.o.) (s.th.)

مَنَعَ ـَـ ، مَنْعٌ # deny, prevent, forbid, (s.th.) (to s.o.)
(من ، عن)

ماءٌ ـ مِياهٌ # water

مَيّ زِيادَة # Mayy Ziyada (woman writer)

ن

نابُلِيون # Napoleon

اِسْتَنْبَطَ ، اِسْتِنْباط # X to induce

نَبِيٌّ ـ أَنْبِياءُ # prophet

أَنْتَجَ ، إِنْتاجٌ # IV to produce, put out

نَتِيجَةً لِـ as a result of

إِنْتاجٌ production, output; literary output

ناتِجًا عن resulting from

نَجِيب مَحْفوظ # Nagib Mahfouz (writer)

نَجَحَ ـَـ ، نَجاحٌ # to succeed

نَحْنُ # we

اِنْتَخَبَ ـ اِنْتِخابٌ # VIII to elect

اِنْتِخابٌ ـ ات election

نازِك المَلائِكة # Nāzik Al-Malā'ika (woman writer)

مُناسَبَةٌ ـ ات # occasion, opportunity

نِساء ، نِسْوَة # see اِمْرَأَة

نيسان # April

أَنْشَأَ ، إِنْشاءٌ # IV to establish, found, start

نَشَرَ ـُـ ، نَشْرٌ # to publish; to announce

اِنْتَشَرَ ، اِنْتِشارٌ VIII to be scattered, spread out, wide-spread; to prevail (peace)

نَشْرٌ publication

نَشْرَةٌ ـ نَشَرات report, bulletin

مُنْتَشِرٌ scattered, spread out, wide-spread; prevailing (peace)

نَصٌّ ـ نُصوصٌ # text, passage

نِصْفٌ ـ أَنْصافٌ # half

مِنْطَقَةٌ ـ مَناطِقُ # region, area, zone

نَظَرَ ـُـ ، نَظَرٌ # to look, consider, view

نَظَرَ ـُـ ، نَظَرٌ في to look into, study, examine

اِنْتَظَرَ ، اِنْتِظارٌ VIII to wait (for), await

نَظَرٌ ـ أَنْظارٌ gaze, look; view, opinion

كانَ في الاِنْتِظارِ to be waiting (for)

أَلنَّظّامُ # Al-Nazzām (m. name)

نَعَمْ # yes

نَفْسٌ ـ أَنْفُسٌ # (f.) soul, self; same

نَقَلَ ـُـ ، نَقْلٌ # to transmit, transport, transfer, move

اِنْتَقَلَ ، اِنْتِقالٌ VIII to move, transfer (to) (intrans.), change residence (to)
(الى)

مَنْهَجٌ ـ مَناهِجُ # program

مَنْهَجُ التَّعْلِيمِ program of instruction, curriculum

نَهْرٌ ـ أَنْهارٌ ، أَنْهُر # river

نهض

نَهْضَة – ات # rebirth, renaissance; movement; boom

انتهى، اِنْتِهاء (من) # VIII to end, come to an end; to be finished (with) (s.th.)

اِنْتِهاء من completing, finishing with (s.th.)

أَنْوَر السّادات # Anwar Al-Sādāt

أبو نُواس # Abū Nuwās (medieval poet)

تَناوَلَ ، تَناوُل # VI to deal with, take up, treat

نَوال السَّعْداوي Nawāl Al-Sa'dawī (woman writer)

اَلنّيل # the Nile

نيويورك # New York

ه

هٰذا – هٰذانِ ، هٰذَيْنِ – هٰؤُلاءِ (هٰذِهِ – هاتانِ هاتَيْنِ – هٰؤُلاءِ) # this, that

أَلأَهْرام # Al-Ahram (Egyptian newspaper; lit., "The Pyramids")

هَلْ # (interrogative particle)

أَلْهِلال # Al-Hilal (Egyptian literary periodical; lit., "The Crescent")

هُمْ # they (m.p.)

أَهَمِّيَّة # importance

اِهْتِمام – ات interest, concern, care

هامّ important

هُنَّ # they (f.p.)

هُنا # here

وزر

هُناكَ there

هِنْدُ # Hind (f. name)

مُهَنْدِس – ون # engineer

هُوَ # he

هِيَ # she

و

وَ # and; (in ḥāl construction) while, as

واشنطن # Washington

وَجَبَ يَجِبُ ،وُجوب # to be incumbant, (على) (أَنْ) necessary (on or for s.o.) (that he do..)

واجِب – ات duty

واجِب على incumbent upon, necessary for (s.o.)

مَوْجود # present; existing

مُوجَز # summary

وَجْه – وُجوه # face

واحِد # one

الأُمَم المُتَّحِدَة The United Nations

الوِلاياتُ المُتَّحِدَةُ (الأمْريكيّة) The United States (of America)

وِداد # Widad (f. name)

وَرَقَة – ات # sheet, piece of paper

وَزير – وُزَراء # (cabinet) minister

وَزيرُ الخارِجِيَّة foreign minister, Secretary of State

رَئيسُ الوُزَراء prime minister

وِزارة – ات (cabinet) ministry

وسط

أَلشَّرْقُ ٱلْأَوْسَطُ # the Middle East

وَصَلَ يَصِلُ ، وُصُولٌ # to arrive; (with object pronoun) to reach

وُصُولٌ arrival

واصِلُ بْنُ عَطاء Wāsil b. 'Aṭā'

وَضْعٌ ـ أَوْضاعٌ # situation, condition

مَوْضُوعٌ ـ مَواضِيعُ subject, topic

وَطَنِيٌّ # national; nationalist(ic)

وَظِيفَةٌ ـ وَظائِفُ # office, position, job; function, task

مُوَظَّفٌ ـ ون employee; official

مَوْعِدٌ ـ مَواعِدُ ، مَواعِيدُ # time, appointment (مَواعِيدُ p. of ميعادٌ is commonly used as p. of مَوْعِدٌ)

تَوَفَّرَ ، تَوَفُّرٌ # V to be given abundantly, provided in full measure

تَوْفِيقٌ بَيْنَ # reconciliation

مِنَ ٱلْمُتَّفِقِ عَلَيْهِ (أَنَّ) it is agreed upon (that)

وَفاةٌ # death

وَقْتٌ ـ أَوْقاتٌ # time

وَقَعَ يَقَعُ ، وَقْعٌ # to be located

واقِعٌ located, situated

وَلَدَ ، يَلِدُ ، وِلادَةٌ # to give birth to

وَلَدٌ ـ أَوْلادٌ child, boy

مِيلادِيٌّ A.D.

والِدٌ father

والِدانِ (nom.) parents

وِلايَةٌ ـ ات # state, province

يوم

أَلْوِلاياتُ ٱلْمُتَّحِدَةُ (ٱلْأَمْرِيكِيَّةُ) The United States (of America)

هِبَةٌ ـ ات # gift

ي

يا # (vocative particle)

يَدٌ ـ أَيْدٍ ، أَيادٍ # (f.) hand

يَدَوِيٌّ (nisba of يَدٌ) manual

يَوْمٌ ـ أَيّامٌ # day

أَلْيَوْمَ today

يَوْمِيٌّ daily

SUBJECT INDEX